Research Methods for Public Administrators

Fourth Edition

Elizabethann O'Sullivan
North Carolina State University

Gary R. Rassel
University of North Carolina at Charlotte

Maureen Berner
University of North Carolina at Chapel Hill

Longman

New York San Francisco Boston
London Toronto Sydney Tokyo Singapore Madrid
Mexico City Munich Paris Cape Town Hong Kong Montreal

For Doug, Merry, and Andy—with much love

Vice President/Publisher:	Priscilla McGeehon
Associate Editor:	Anita Castro
Senior Marketing Manager:	Megan Galvin-Fak
Production Manager:	Denise Phillip
Project Coordination, Text Design, and Electronic Page Makeup:	WestWords, Inc.
Cover Design Manager:	John Callahan
Cover Designer:	Laura Shaw
Cover Image:	Bob Commander, Courtesy of SIS
Manufacturing Buyer:	Roy Pickering
Printer and Binder:	Courier Corporation
Cover Printer:	Phoenix Color Corporation

Library of Congress Cataloging-in-Publication Data
O'Sullivan, Elizabethann.
    Research methods for public administrators/Elizabethann O'Sullivan, Gary R.
Rassel.—4th ed.
        p. cm.
    Includes index.
    ISBN 0-321-08558-2
    1. Public administration—Research—Methodology. I. Rassel, Gary Raymond, 1944–II.
Title.

JF1338.A2 O78 2002
351'.07'2—dc21

2001050438

Copyright © 2003 by Addison Wesley Longman, Inc.

Please visit our website at http://www.ablongman.com

ISBN 0-321-08558-2

1 2 3 4 5 6 7 8 9 10—CRW—05 04 03 02

Brief Contents

Detailed Contents   v

Preface   xii

Chapter 1   Beginning a Research Project: The Preliminary Steps   1

Chapter 2   Designs for Description   24

Chapter 3   Designs for Explanation   55

Chapter 4   Measuring Variables   98

Chapter 5   Sampling   133

Chapter 6   Contacting and Talking to Subjects   171

Chapter 7   Data Collection: Questions and Questionnaires   207

Chapter 8   Protection of Human Research Subjects and
Other Ethical Issues   243

Chapter 9   Secondary Data Analysis: Finding and
Analyzing Existing Data   264

Chapter 10   Combining Indicators: Index Construction   291

Chapter 11   Univariate Analysis   315

Chapter 12   Examining Relationships among Variables: Tests
of Statistical Significance   359

Chapter 13   Examining Relationships among Variables: Contigency Tables
with Measures of Association, Analysis of Variance   388

Chapter 14   Regression Analysis and Correlation   427

Chapter 15   Communicating Findings and Completing the Project   463

Glossary   483

Index   494

Detailed Contents

Preface   xii

Chapter 1   **Beginning a Research Project: The Preliminary Steps**   **1**

Starting a Research Project: Defining the Research Question   2
Organizing the Research Study: The Use of Models   3
Identifying the Elements to Study: Model Building   6
Presenting the Model: Types of Models   11
Limitations of Models and Model Building for Specific Users   12
The Components of Models: An Introduction to the Terminology   13
Selecting a Research Question   18
Summary   19
   Notes   *20*
   Terms for Review   *20*
   Questions for Review   *21*
   Problems for Homework and Discussion   *21*
   Disk Work   *23*
   Recommended for Further Reading   *23*

Chapter 2   **Designs for Description**   **24**

Designs to Find Relationships and Show Trends   26
Qualitative Research and Designs to Fill in the Details   37
Case Studies   39
Meta-Analysis   44
Summary   47
   Notes   *49*
   Terms for Review   *50*
   Questions for Review   *51*

Problems for Homework and Discussion   *51*
Disk Work   *53*
Recommended for Further Reading   *54*

Chapter 3   **Designs for Explanation**   **55**

Internal and External Validity   57
Threats to Internal Validity   58
External Validity   62
Experimental Designs   66
Quasi-Experimental Designs   74
Nonexperimental Designs   84
Observational Studies   88
Causality and Cross-Sectional Studies   89
Summary   90
   Notes   *92*
   Terms for Review   *93*
   Questions for Review   *94*
   Problems for Homework and Discussion   *95*
   Disk Work   *97*
   Recommended for Further Reading   *97*

Chapter 4   **Measuring Variables**   **98**

Measurement and Measurement Scales   102
Reliability   107
Operational Validity   116
Sensitivity   126
Summary   127
   Notes   *128*
   Terms for Review   *129*
   Questions for Review   *129*
   Problems for Homework and Discussion   *130*
   Disk Work   *132*
   Recommended for Further Reading   *132*

Chapter 5 **Sampling** **133**

Sampling Terminology   134
Sampling Designs   136
Nonprofitability Sampling Designs   146
Sample Size   149
Summary   161
   Notes   162
   Terms for Review   163
   Questions for Review   163
   Problems for Homework and Discussion   163
   Disk Work   165
   Recommended for Further Reading   165
   Appendix 5.1 *Calculation of Standard Error   167*
   Appendix 5.2 *Calculation of Sample Size for Means   169*
   Appendix 5.3 *Sample Size for Small Populations   169*

Chapter 6 **Contacting and Talking to Subjects** **171**

Mailed Questionnaires   173
Telephone Surveys   179
Internet Surveys   186
In-person Interviewing   187
Selecting a Method of Data Collecting   196
Summary   199
   Notes   202
   Terms for Review   203
   Questions for Review   204
   Problems for Homework and Discussion   204
   A Class Project   205
   Recommended for Further Reading   205

Chapter 7 **Data Collection: Questions and Questionnaires** **207**

Questionnaire and Question Content   208
Questionnaire Structure   211
Question and Response Wording   218

Question Sequencing and Questionnaire Design   227
Summary   236
   Notes   238
   Terms for Review   239
   Questions for Review   239
   Problems for Homework and Discussion   239
   Disk Work   241
   Recommended for Further Reading   241

Chapter 8   **Protection of Human Research: Subjects and Other Ethical Issues   243**

Illustrative Cases   244
Principles of Ethical Treatment of Human Subjects   247
Protecting Privacy and Confidentiality   251
Federal Policy of Protection of Human Subjects and Institutional
   Review Boards   254
Beyond Informed Consent and Confidentiality: Issues of Interest to
   Administration   256
Summary   258
   Notes   260
   Terms for Review   262
   Questions for Review   262
   Problems for Homework and Discussion   262
   Recommended for Further Reading   263

Chapter 9   **Secondary Data Analysis: Finding and Analyzing Existing Data   264**

Working with Secondary Data   265
U.S. Census Data   272
Using Census Data   280
Vital Statistics   284
Summary   286
   Notes   287
   Terms for Review   288
   Questions for Review   288
   Problems for Homework and Discussion   289

Disk Work   289

Recommended for Further Reading   290

Chapter 10   Combining Indicators: Index Construction   291

Defining the Concept   293

Selecting the Items   293

Combining the Items in an Index   295

Weighting the Separate Items   295

Examples of Creating Indices   299

Factor Analysis   303

Index Numbers   307

Summary   307

Notes   308

Terms for Review   309

Questions for Review   309

Problems for Homework and Discussion   310

Disk Work   310

Recommended for Further Reading   311

***Appendix 10.1** Calculating Factor Scale Scores   313*

***Appendix 10.2** Using z-Scores to Standardize Measures for Indices   314*

Chapter 11   Univariate Analysis   315

Computer Software for Data and Management and Analysis   316

Analyzing and Presenting the Data   319

Visual Presentation of Data   322

Quantitative Measures   329

Characteristics of a Distribution   333

Exploratory Data Analysis   345

Summary   347

Notes   348

Terms for Review   350

Questions for Review   350

Problems for Homework and Discussion   350

Disk Work   353

Recommended for Further Reading   353

Appendix 11.1 *Statistical Calculations*   *355*
Appendix 11.2 *Data Preparation*   *357*

Chapter 12   **Examining Relationships among Variables: Tests of Statistical Significance   359**

Stating the Null Hypothesis   361
Selecting an Alpha Level   365
Selecting and Computing a Test Statistic   367
Making a Decision   372
Reporting Tests of Statistical Significance   374
Modifications and Alternatives to Tests of Statistical Significance   376
Summary   378
  Notes   *379*
  Terms for Review   *380*
  Questions for Review   *380*
  Problems for Homework and Discussion   *380*
  Disk Work   *383*
  Recommended for Further Reading   *383*
  Appendix 12.1 *Calculating Chi-Square and Two-Sample t-Tests*   *384*

Chapter 13   **Examining Relationships among Variables: Contigency Tables with Measures of Association, Analysis of Variance   388**

An Overview of Contingency Tables and Related Measures of Association   389
Constructing and Interpreting Contingency Tables   389
Selecting and Using Measures of Association   392
Measures of Association with Control Variables   404
Tests of Statistical Significance and Measures of Association   409
Comparison of Means and Analysis of Variance   410
Summary   414
  Notes   *416*
  Terms for Review   *417*
  Questions for Review   *417*
  Problems for Homework and Discussion   *419*
  Disk Work   *421*

Recommended for Further Reading   423

Appendix 13.1 Same Measure for Association for Nominal and Ordered Data   424

Chapter 14   Regression Analysis and Correlation   427

Analyzing Two Interval Variables   428

Regression Analysis: The Multivariate Case   435

Statistical Signigicance and Linear Regression   442

Multicollinearity   442

Regression and Non-Interval Variables   445

Regression Models to Analyze Time-Series Data   447

Regression and Causality   451

Summary   451

Notes   453

Terms for Review   454

Questions for Review   454

Problems for Homework and Discussion   456

Disk Work   459

Recommended for Further Reading   460

Appendix 14.1 Calculating Regression Statistics for Bivariate Relationships   461

Chapter 15   Communicating Findings and Completing the Project   463

Variations in Audiences and Their Needs   464

Components of the Quantitative Report   465

Ethical Issues   474

Summary   478

Notes   480

Terms for Review   480

Questions for Review   480

Problems for Homework and Discussion   481

Recommended for Further Reading   481

Glossary   483

Index   494

Preface

With this edition of *Research Methods for Public Administrators* we are pleased to welcome a third author, Maureen Berner. Maureen is closer to her graduate school experience and has dealt with this material as a student more recently than have the two senior authors. She is a serious researcher who also teaches research methods to MPA students—those who are or will soon be practitioners—and works regularly with practitioners. Her careful reading of the manuscript has uncovered several new ways to word the material and introduced other improvements.

As with the earlier editions, the fourth edition of this book is designed for advanced undergraduate and introductory graduate courses in research methods. The intended audiences are those who are or soon will be administrators and those who teach them. We have been pleased with the response to the first three editions of this text and are grateful that teachers and students found them to be useful. We have continued to emphasize methods, analysis, and application rather than the calculation of statistics. In the fourth edition we attempted to update information and exercises, making changes in current material where we thought it would be helpful.

We have incorporated material from the 2000 Census and increased the number of references using the Internet. Perhaps the biggest and most rapid technological change related to research methods that has taken place in recent years is the Internet. It has greatly expanded the access to data sources and made this access much more convenient than ever before. We have included examples and have provided useful Internet addresses in several chapters. Homework problems using the Internet are included as well.

The graphical user interface (GUI) or window continues to make software packages easier to use. With this in mind we moved more of the material in Chapter 11 dealing with preparing data for computer analysis to a chapter appendix. The process of preparing data for computer entry and analysis is more constant than are the specifics of computer hardware and software.

An innovation with edition three of the text was the inclusion of a data disk and homework problems keyed to the data files on the disk. The disk includes information for using the files, information about the data, and data saved in ASCII, spreadsheet, and SPSS formats. The homework problems at the end of the chapters include computer problems using the data files on the disk to illustrate concepts and techniques discussed in the chapter. Some of these problems have been revised to overcome difficulties that users may have encountered with the disk files. We have also revised other problems at the end of the chapters and included some new ones. A revised instructor's manual with solutions to the end of chapter problems has been prepared for this edition.

Although this text includes basic as well as more advanced material, we have attempted to present information in a way that is useful to administrators with a wide range of experiences. We intend for instructors to be able to select from the material, adapt it to their needs, and have more than enough for a one-semester course. Chapters can be omitted or used in different order depending on the instructor's needs and approach.

In writing and revising this book, we hope to help administrators collaborate more effectively with researchers. We observe administrators regularly asking for specific pieces of research from subordinates, colleagues, and consultants. They frequently question investigators about studies to decide whether a particular finding justifies further administrative action. They often read research reports to decide whether the findings can be used in their professions. We hope that administrators and students will find this book to be useful as a reference when they want to find out more about a topic or technique.

We intended to write a text for applied research that administrators would find realistic. In this endeavor we wanted to present a systematic approach to empirical investigation and to discuss the logic of research design and scientific method so that it did not seem arbitrary or the result of unnecessary abstraction. Research is a problem-solving process and we wanted to present it as such. We have drawn on our experience and that of students, teachers, colleagues, researchers, and administrators. The process of translating teaching materials, ideas, lecture notes, examples, and exercises into a textbook has been difficult and time-consuming but very rewarding. As a field of study, research methods can be surprisingly dynamic. Keeping up with changes and new applications is interesting and challenging. Presenting them effectively to an audience of instructors and students is also interesting and challenging.

This edition has also benefited from the suggestions, reactions, and encouragement of many people. Colleagues and faculty at various universities who have used or read the earlier editions have been especially helpful with comments and suggestions. Some have helped us to correct errors in the text or Instructor's Manual. Others have suggested material to add, delete, or revise. Student suggestions and questions are always useful and often humbling. Many times we have heard a version of the following question: "What did they mean when they said . . . ?" These questions go to the heart of what we do as teachers and we appreciate them.

We appreciate the many reviewers of this text who over the years have provided useful comments. Their suggestions have led to many changes and improvements for which we are grateful. Reviews of earlier editions were encouraging and also addressed areas for revisions. We thank the authors of these reviews and hope that our response has had the intended effect and improved the book. We appreciate hearing from all who read or use the book.

We are grateful to our publisher for supporting a fourth edition and in embracing our request to include a third author. The editorial staff of Longman, Inc.

has provided much critical help and support. Our association with Longman, Inc. has been lengthy and has provided us the opportunity to work with many helpful individuals. Anita Castro has been the editorial contact for this fourth edition. We thank her for all of her work and patience. We acknowledge the support and encouragement of our respective universities, North Carolina State University, the University of North Carolina at Charlotte, and the University of North Carolina at Chapel Hill. The index and glossary, originally prepared by Robin Goodpasture for the second edition, were up-dated for the third edition by Dina Smith. Dina also prepared the index for the fourth edition, while Jennifer Snow made changes in the glossary. Robin, Dina and Jennifer are to be commended for their fine work. Many others read, commented, copied, retrieved books from the library, and listened during the process of revision. We are grateful to all of you.

And finally we recognize the participation and support of our families, Doug Hale, Merry Chambers, Brendan and Colin O'Sullivan-Hale, and Andy, Will, and Yvette Berner in this endeavor. Doug helped produce the data disk for the computer problems; Merry provided valuable editorial and other advice. Families and family members have grown and matured along the way. We appreciate their encouragement and their understanding of the times devoted to "revising the textbook."

ELIZABETHANN O'SULLIVAN
GARY R. RASSEL
MAUREEN BERNER

Chapter 1

Beginning a Research Project: The Preliminary Steps

In this chapter you will learn

1. why knowledge of research methods is valuable for public administrators.
2. when, why, and how to go about building a model, the framework of social science research.
3. strategies for presenting models.
4. definitions of some common research terms, including variables and hypotheses.
5. what to consider in selecting a research question.

Public administrators often ask questions that begin "how many," "how much," "how efficient," "how effective," "how adequate," and "why." They may want to learn something about a group of people, how much a program will cost, or what it can accomplish for each dollar spent. They need to decide how serious a problem is, whether a policy solved a problem, what distinguishes more effective programs from less effective ones, and whether clients are satisfied with program performance. They are accountable to politicians, parents, citizens, program clients and the courts for public services.

Administrators rely on data to make better decisions, to monitor them, and to examine their effects. Data are another way to refer to information. Understanding research methods is key to gathering, using, and evaluating information. And as a current or future public administrator, you know that adequate information is key to making effective decisions.

As an administrator you may need to collect and summarize data and act on your findings or supervise others who do so. You may conduct studies to answer questions about programs under your jurisdiction, or you may contract with others to perform studies for you. You may receive regular reports to monitor the performance of your organization and employees. You may read research and get ideas you wish to implement. Even if you never initiate a study, your knowledge of the research process should leave you better able to determine the adequacy of data, interpret reports, question investigators, and judge the value of published research.

This book will provide you with the ability to produce valuable information using a variety of research tools. More importantly, we hope it will provide you with better judgment as you *use* information to make decisions. Our goal is to help you make better decisions, and in doing so, make you better public administrators.

STARTING A RESEARCH PROJECT: DEFINING THE RESEARCH QUESTION

Research should begin with careful planning. Even though determining the purposes of a study and whether or not it will produce the desired information is tedious, experience has convinced us that administrators who take the time to define clearly the purpose of a study and critique carefully the research plan spend their time well. They will have a better understanding of the problem being studied and be able to reduce the incidence of poorly conceived research strategies and useless data collection. In this chapter we present guidelines for better research planning. No matter who is actually carrying out a study, administrators who spend time defining the problem, planning the study, debating it with others, and reviewing related research markedly improve research and experience fewer disappointments and wasted efforts.

A study should begin by stating the research question and the purpose of the study. A research question is a question with more than one possible answer. Otherwise, why spend the time and money needed to produce the answer? The research question requires empirical or observable information in order to be answered. By definition, research involves the study of observable information, so without observable information no research takes place. This text stresses numerical or quantitative information; however, qualitative information also is empirical and may appropriately be used to answer a research question.

Let's consider the research question: "Do electronic communications improve the performance of office staff?" Note that the question has more than one answer. Furthermore, the answer requires empirical information. Still, this simple question masks the amount of work that lies ahead. What is meant by electronic communication and performance? Which office staff? All staff members, or just people holding certain positions? Staff in all offices, or just particular types of offices? What type and how much impact is expected? To help limit the study's focus, the administrator indicates the purpose of a study. A study to determine whether to install a communications system will be different from a study evaluating an existing system.

Establishing a study's purpose goes beyond stating exactly why it is being done. An investigator must know who wants the study done, how she plans to use its findings, when she plans to use them, what resources she has to invest in the study, and what has been done before. After an investigator answers these questions, she can list the research questions and decide what evidence will provide adequate answers. Thus she avoids "shooting ants with an elephant gun." She also avoids planning a study that exceeds the available resources or yields information after it is needed. A study's purpose evolves; it becomes more focused and better understood as investigators and decision makers begin their work together.

ORGANIZING THE RESEARCH STUDY: THE USE OF MODELS

After the research question and study's purpose are stated, a preliminary research model should be built. A model could be thought of as a simple explanation of relationships. A model includes selected elements, e.g., characteristics or events, and links them to each other. The elements included in any model depend on its purpose. Investigators use models to simplify reality by eliminating irrelevant details.

Models consist of *elements* and *relationships*. A single element does not constitute a model until the element is linked with another. Elements that have no relationship with other elements should be eliminated from a model. Elements that have only weak links also may be eliminated.

How does an investigator know which elements to include and how to link them? Even if the purpose of the study is to identify relevant elements and their linkages, she has to have a way to decide what to include. She draws on her own ideas and experiences and the ideas and experiences of colleagues. She may review previous research, manipulate existing datasets, and conduct a preliminary study. To find out how the elements are linked, an examination of previous research studies and exploratory data analysis is particularly helpful.

Before we study *model building,* let's look at a preliminary model designed to guide a research project. Example 1.1 presents a model developed as part of a study to identify how to slow down the rate of increase in Medicare costs. Investigators identified the elements representing the general strategies available to reduce costs. The central element was the rate of increase of Medicare costs. The other elements were the number of beneficiaries, the number of services covered, and the payment for each service; these elements were linked to Medicare costs. If the number of beneficiaries, the number of covered services, or the amount paid for each service were reduced, the rate of increase in Medicare costs would decrease. In Example 1.1 the model is presented as a schematic. The arrows link the elements and show which variables are thought to act on other variables. A model also may be presented as a statement. The sentence, "If the number of beneficiaries, the number of covered services, or the amount paid for each service were reduced, the rate of increase in Medicare costs would decrease," is another way to present the model. A model also may be presented as an equation.

The investigators assumed that reducing the number of beneficiaries, the number of covered services, or the amount paid for each service would reduce the rate of increase in Medicare costs. The major relationships are between reducing the rate of increase and the other elements; however, relations may exist among the other elements. For example, reducing the number of services covered probably will reduce the number of beneficiaries.

EXAMPLE 1.1

Applying a Model

Research question: How may the rapid increase in Medicare costs (Medicare: federally funded health care for the elderly) be reduced?

Purpose: To recommend change(s) in Medicare coverage that will contain the costs of the Medicare program.

Procedure: An initial model is sketched out with the major elements representing general strategies to reduce costs. Its purpose is to identify the basic types of strategies available.

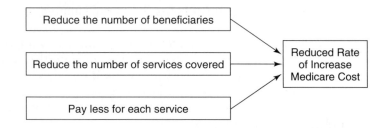

Discussion: The sketch places each element in a separate "box." The strategies, which also may be identified as "inputs," are placed on the left. Lines indicate the links between elements and arrows indicate the direction of the links. Here, each strategy was linked to the outcome of reducing the rate of increased costs. The arrows suggest that each strategy should reduce the rate of increase in Medicare costs. A sketch keeps track of the model's elements and relationships, helps communicate the model to others, and facilitates discussion about the model and the research plan.

With the elements identified, the investigators may:

1. Identify feasible strategies associated with each element. Should the number of beneficiaries be reduced by changing income requirements or age limits? What services should be reduced? How might less be paid for services?
2. Incorporate the specific strategies into the model.
3. Develop a research plan: What elements and relations will be studied first? Exactly how will they be studied?

A model requires its creators to organize their thoughts and helps the creators and the users to communicate more effectively. The model in Example 1.1 should center policy makers' attention on possible solutions and facilitate their communications with each other and others concerned with Medicare costs. With the basic model, investigators can define what they mean by each element. They may include other elements and alter the linkages among elements. They can decide which strategies to investigate further and set priorities for examining strategies.

A model may be altered and refined often during the early stages of designing a study. Many elements may be listed and linked or only the essential components may be included. A common question among public administration students is how detailed a model must be. The answer is, "It depends." Investigators may brainstorm to identify all possible elements, and they may build a very detailed model. To confirm points of agreement, they may develop a simplified version with just a few elements included. The model in Example 1.1 was limited to the basic components of a study. Other models may elaborate on the basic model. For example, a model can spell out how strategies for reducing the number of beneficiaries would affect Medicare rates. Another model can focus on ways of reducing services and the effects of alternate strategies on Medicare rates. A model may be created to monitor the progress of the research. Regardless of the purpose or level of detail, a research model should be based on theory. That is, there should be reasonable theoretical linkages between the elements.

Maps provide a homey illustration of how models vary according to their purpose. For a mountain hike, you need a topographical map with details about the terrain. Such a detailed map, if you could find one and fit it into a car, would be virtually useless on a drive from New York to California. On the other hand, imagine using an ordinary road map to hike through the Grand Canyon! Elements important for one purpose may be useless for another purpose. And just as developing a research model is based on good theory, choosing a map is based on understanding where you want to go and how you think you might get there.

By the time they are ready to collect data, the investigators should be satisfied that they have included the relevant elements in the model. The included elements and their relationships become important components of decisions about which data to collect and how to analyze them. The model should be considered preliminary. It may change during the course of a study.

Even though models rarely stay the same throughout a study, a researcher should not begin working without an explicit model. Writing down the purpose of the research and creating a model to achieve it are first steps in ensuring that the research effort accomplishes its purposes. An explicit model serves as a vehicle to allow people directly or indirectly involved in a study to agree on its purposes and the value of the resulting information. The investigators also use the model to communicate the purposes of a study to others and to present its findings later.

Model building starts the researcher on an iterative process to collect, analyze, and present data that are consistent with the study's purpose. Starting with a model is especially important for quantitative studies. Without a proper road map, researchers can wander in the wilderness of data—gathering numbers and facts without a clear direction. Models allow us to go beyond simply looking at data. Precise-looking data can be wrong and apparent relationships among elements may be due to statistical errors. By the end of a study, models enable a user to reach reasonable conclusions about the importance of elements and their relationships to one another.

Occasionally, an investigator "falls in love with his model." This happens when a person has labored over a research plan and then becomes trapped by his own inflexibility. Instead of considering the model as preliminary and rejecting it or adjusting it as appropriate, the researcher goes through all sorts of data manipulations to demonstrate that his preliminary model is correct.

IDENTIFYING THE ELEMENTS TO STUDY: MODEL BUILDING

To identify the elements, defend their relevance, and postulate the nature of their relationships, investigators integrate their ideas, the observations of others, the research literature, and their own research. The process is seldom as systematic and logical as research reports or public presentations make it appear. Nor does each investigator follow the same strategy for identifying elements and their relationships. Designing a study requires creativity and insight. Furthermore, understanding the problem at hand is a prerequisite to good model-building skills.

The order associated with research presentations springs from a desire to communicate effectively. An audience can more easily follow a presentation that proceeds from a statement of the problem to a description of the model, its elements, and their relation to each other. Normally, a researcher does not dwell on false starts, mistakes, and backtracking.

Ideas

Ideas refer to the knowledge, beliefs, or impressions one has about a research question. We rarely approach a situation with no knowledge or insight. Most of us retain a wealth of information to help us solve problems. Do not downplay the value or importance of this information. If you do not make use of your experience, knowledge, or opinions when faced with problems, you will be an inefficient administrator.

Building a model requires you to make your ideas explicit. Through words, drawings, or equations, you identify the elements you consider important and how you believe they are related to each other. Thus you clarify fuzzy ideas and expose them to critical examination. You will find that some of your beliefs will not make sense. Some of your ideas suddenly may seem naive or incomplete. Nevertheless, unless you are willing to take the risk of having your ideas challenged, you may miss elements and relationships critical to problem solving.

Peer Interaction

Peer interaction refers to the discussions and debates among colleagues about the research question and possible answers. To understand model building, we recommend strongly that you read about how scientists go about their work.[1] This should dispel the myth of the isolated scientist working alone. Research is much more dynamic than you might imagine. Administrators can learn much from scientists. A major lesson is the value of criticism and debate. Without it errors may go uncorrected and oversights may abound. However, few people find criticism easy to accept or arguments easy to verbalize.

Another notable aspect of peer interaction is the influence of our backgrounds. For example, our disciplines shape the questions we ask, the data we use, and how we use them. Imagine, as a city administrator, you are interested in studying ways to address homelessness in your city. As a first step, you want to gather data on the causes of homelessness in your area. One analyst with an economics background may want to focus on quantitative data from city employment and support programs. Another analyst with a background in social work may turn first to interviews with clients of local shelters. An analyst with a public safety background may wish to test a possible relationship between homelessness and paroles from the new federal prison in the area. If they had to work together, we suspect they might experience frustration and tension. Yet, ideally, the conflict of ideas and the resulting compromises should yield a research plan superior to that developed by any one of the individuals working alone. The concept of drawing from other disciplines has been called "borrowing strength."

An example of peer interaction in public administration is performance measurement. Local and state governments and non-profits turn to each other for ideas and strategies on how to assess their own performance. In building a model, understanding what your peers have encountered in the same or similar process will save valuable time.

Review of Existing Knowledge

Research often is an iterative process in which investigators build on the work of others. Shortly after identifying the purpose of a study, investigators go to the library and look for information on similar studies. Some people assume that quantitative researchers have little need for library information. Applied researchers may not see their studies as part of a larger body of knowledge. Nevertheless, a few hours in the reference or documents section of a university library should convince you of the value of library materials.

Too often researchers studying an unfamiliar problem may start by "reinventing the wheel." In other words, they may begin to build a model that has already been developed and refined many times. The objective of library research is not to ensure the originality of ideas. Rather, it provides a wealth of information and ideas that we may incorporate into our research. As we conduct a *literature review,* we think about the planned study and better understand its purpose and what we can expect to accomplish. An examination of existing research identifies

elements included in studies with a similar purpose.

definitions currently used for the elements.

techniques for measuring the elements.

sources of data.

strategies for collecting data.

methods of linking the elements.

strength of the relationships between elements.

suggestions for further research.

With this information, investigators avoid wasting time. They may find that their research question has already been answered. They may learn that others failed to confirm relationships that at first seemed important or obvious. The investigators may find appropriate models, definitions, data, and the analytic techniques of others to incorporate into a study. Of course, the source of the ideas, data, or method must be acknowledged properly.

"State of the art" articles that summarize the nature of existing research especially are helpful. They cite the major research work in the field and the major research themes. You will find that such articles quickly bring you up to date. They may help you avoid the temptation to go too far afield in your investigation.

You will find that a reference librarian is an invaluable resource in uncovering appropriate literature. This is especially true given the rapid changes taking place in information technology. A reference librarian can direct you to abstracts and indices that describe research articles and their findings. He can introduce you to useful online resources and suggest efficient search strategies for locating relevant research.

Example 1.2 suggests how an investigator brings together ideas, peer interaction, and the existing literature to build a model. The example applies model building to the process of conducting citizen surveys. Surveys often start with a sample questionnaire that investigators plan to adapt. The survey may be designed and conducted with no thought of explicit model building. Yet model building helps ensure that the survey includes needed information. The study planners may find that an existing questionnaire focuses their discussion on the information they want and whether it will be gathered in the survey. Nevertheless, one should not assume that a questionnaire or questions developed for one study are appropriate for another.

Manipulating a Dataset

Investigators who have access to datasets, including data from a pilot test, may examine and manipulate the data as they focus and develop their ideas.[2] In this way investigators may get a better idea of the importance of elements and the strength of their relationships. If a dataset does not contain the specific elements desired, the investigator may study similar elements. The similar elements may be considered as stand-ins or proxies. For example, a neighborhood or postal ZIP code may act as a proxy measure for racial or ethnic groups, social class, or even family composition.

Investigators manipulating a dataset may simultaneously rethink the study's purpose and the model's adequacy. Through the process they may gain greater insight into the study and revise their original ideas.

Pilot Testing the Model

Before collecting data on a large scale, the research plan should be piloted or rehearsed. A small study, called a *pilot study*, is launched to test the adequacy of the proposed data-collection strategy. During the pilot study, investigators discover the feasibility of their research plans and how much time and effort will be needed to collect, compile, and analyze the data. Investigators should carry out the entire plan, including the data analysis and interpretation. Often investigators fail to analyze and interpret the pilot test data, which is unfortunate. From these data the investigators can infer the model's appropriateness. They may identify elements left out of the original model and find that other elements are unneeded.

Collecting data without a preliminary model is not a sound research practice. Too often research projects begin prematurely. After identifying the research question, some investigators begin collecting data eagerly. They cut off further

---

EXAMPLE 1.2

Building a Model

Research question: What do residents think about their town? Are they satisfied with available services? What changes do they want?

Purpose: To consider citizen perceptions in preparing the town's comprehensive plan.

Procedure: The planning director planned to survey residents to learn how they judge the town and its services.

To identify variables of interest she

1. solicited existing surveys from local planners (peer interaction).
2. examined handbooks published by the American Planning Association and the International City/County Management Association to find sample surveys (literature review).
3. drew on what she learned during her professional training, from her career experience (ideas), and from shop talk (peer interaction).

Several variables seem linked to perceptions of public services. She selected the following variables as relevant:

1. where residents live; if they are homeowners or renters (based on the town council's interest)
2. the gender and age of residents; whether they work in town or in the nearest city (based on the planning staff's interest)

She met with the Planning Advisory Board to consider what services to include. They discussed the value of linking the demographic variables to satisfaction with services.

Summary of model: The survey will gather data on citizen satisfaction with public services, including trash collection, medical facilities, and housing. To see if the town government meets the needs of all residents, the planning staff will

Continued

EXAMPLE 1.2 *Continued*

examine whether residents with different characteristics (gender, age, location of home or job, whether they rent or own) rate services differently.

To organize her presentations, she sketched the model:

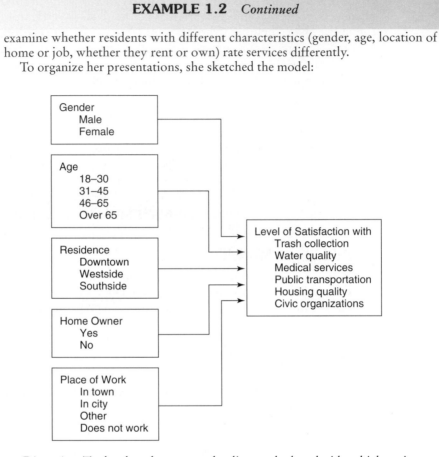

Discussion: To develop the survey, the director had to decide which variables were relevant for the town's planning. To do this she used her own ideas, peer interaction, and the literature. She met with her staff, the manager's staff, an advisory board, and the town council to review and refine the survey's content. The director read the literature to identify possible survey questions and to get ideas on how to construct the sample, how to achieve a higher response rate, and how to analyze the data. Next, she will scrutinize the specific questions, pretest the questionnaire, and pilot the study. As she conducts these steps, she may make some modifications to the preliminary model.

planning with comments such as, "Let's see what the data show," or, "I'll decide after I look at the data." Questionnaires are constructed, subjects are questioned, and data are analyzed with too little attention given to the investigators' objectives. Unfortunately, the investigators may not recognize problems with the model until the end of the research project.

PRESENTING THE MODEL: TYPES OF MODELS

How do investigators present a model's elements and relationships? While many possibilities exist, ranging from physical models, such as mock-ups of buildings, to highly abstract verbal presentations, administrative researchers usually work with two types of models, schematic models and symbolic models. *Schematic models* refer to models that use pictures, lines, points, and similar paper-and-pencil products to designate the elements and illustrate their relationship to each other. The sketches in Examples 1.1 and 1.2 present the model as a schematic, as do blueprints, flow charts, and maps. *Symbolic models* refer to models that use words, equations, or computer programs to represent the elements and describe their relationships.

The type of model chosen depends on the model's purpose, the audience, and the investigator. More than one type of model may be used to present a set of elements and relationships. Consider getting directions to a person's house. Some people distribute maps—a schematic model. Others give verbal directions, listing roads, landmarks, and distances—a symbolic model. Others may give both a map and verbal directions. The choice depends largely on a host's preferences and perceptions of what will be easiest for his guests.

Many investigators build both a verbal model and a schematic model, as is done in Example 1.2. The example's verbal model summarizes the planning director's actual verbal model, which establishes the importance of linking each specific demographic characteristic to the residents' perception of community services. The schematic model sacrifices the detail of the verbal model, but it effectively identifies the model's essential features.

Schematic models work well for illustration purposes. Schematic models with a few elements can be understood quickly and they focus people's attention. Consequently, schematics help an investigator think through the model and explain it to others. A schematic also may serve as an elaborate checklist. For example, an investigator can write down when the data are gathered on an element or when a relationship has been examined. Schematic models are less effective if they include too much detail. Only so much information can be included about an element and its relationship to other elements before a schematic becomes cluttered and confusing.

Symbolic models include verbal models, mathematical models, and computer models. Verbal models use words to describe the elements and define their relations to each other. Verbal models are often found in the introductory or theoretical sections of research articles. A newspaper account of a research study and its findings also may be considered a verbal model.

The verbal model has distinct strengths. The investigators have all the potential offered by language to describe the model, allowing a full and detailed explanation of complex relationships. The researchers are not constrained by requirements to reduce the model to equations or computer code. A fuller range of users can understand and interpret a verbal model than can work with mathematical or computer models. Verbal and mathematical models can complement each other in describing relationships. The verbal model provides the rich details, and the mathematical model looks at the precise nature of the relationships.

Mathematical models use equations to specify relationships. In some areas of interest to administrators, such as operations research or management science, mathematical models guide the model-building process. The mathematical models indicate whether relationships exist, indicate what direction they take, and measure their strength. Mathematical models allow administrators to predict needs, to estimate the impact of policy decisions, and to allocate resources more efficiently.

Computer models extend mathematical models. Particularly complicated mathematical models often are handled best with computers. In such instances a program can quickly manipulate the elements and depict their relationships. Unlike an analyst, the computer can keep track of a large number of elements and the relationships among them successfully and produce "error-free" results. A computer model differs from other models primarily in the amount of information it can manipulate, its speed, and its accuracy. As with other models, the accuracy of a computer model is a function of human judgment that creates the rules for selecting and manipulating elements. No matter how many elements are included, the model still represents a simplification of reality.

LIMITATIONS OF MODELS AND MODEL BUILDING FOR SPECIFIC USERS

Models simplify reality. They represent one view of which elements are relevant to the problem at hand and which elements can be ignored. Differing views may be entertained. The investigators who build a model and the people who critique it are subject to the full range of human weaknesses. Model builders contend with limited time, money, and knowledge. Their viewpoint may be colored by biases, which leads them to ignore others' comments and criticisms.

Users may be seduced by a model's clarity and its apparent usefulness. They may assume erroneously that it is accurate and adequate. Users who read a study or sit in an audience tend to focus on the details of the verbal description, a diagram, or an equation. Users may want to step back and reflect on what the model leaves out.

In initiating a research study, investigators have a similar concern. They do not want to force the administrator or policy maker who requested the study to conform to their way of approaching a problem. For analysts, models serve as a logical mechanism to organize their thoughts and studies, but this is not necessarily the case for their "clients." If a client must adapt to the investigator's methods, the study may be logical and well organized, but it may be ill suited to the client's needs.

Thus, in conducting research for specific users, the investigator works hard to understand why the study is being done and what the users want to do with the findings. Client/investigator conversations may seem far removed from identifying the model's components and relationships. Nevertheless, clients have valuable perspectives on potential models. A researcher also has to deal with the reality of trying to satisfy client demands and/or the clients' individual situation. For example, to evaluate strategies to have toddlers inoculated, the analyst may ask the client to speculate on which factors motivate parents to have their children vaccinated and which factors lead them to ignore or to delay vaccinations. The analyst will then organize the information into a verbal or schematic model.

The researcher may leave many of the research details in the background. A client may receive a list of questions with a strategy for answering them or a description of an experiment. The pilot-test information may be organized so that the user reviews graphs and tables similar to those that will be included in the final report. This strategy mirrors the model-building process. Beginning with the clients' perspective avoids ignoring the observations and concerns of users who cannot articulate their ideas within the context of an explicit model. Focusing on the clients' concerns and needs ensures that a study will be planned to address a specific problem. In the absence of effective interactions, analysts may unconsciously plan a study around their analytical preferences.

In conducting research to answer theoretical questions, such as the nature of organizational leadership, investigators pursue model building as described earlier. They include peer interaction, a literature review, and pilot-test information in building and refining their models. If they report their findings in a scholarly journal, they will use the shorthand afforded by research jargon. In theoretical research, a study evolves from the research that precedes it; in other studies, the literature review may be less systematic and focused more narrowly. Theoretical studies develop a discipline's body of knowledge and set the stage for further empirical research. Consequently, the researchers must provide a detailed discussion of their methodology and conduct extensive statistical analysis of their data.

Applied studies generally are done with intended users in mind. Specific users combine research findings with other information to guide their thinking about a problem or to make a decision. Investigators avoid research jargon in communicating with most administrators and policy makers. The jargon serves as a checklist for the researcher, so he does not overlook the numerous details that can weaken a study. If the terms are unfamiliar to audiences, their attention may shift to understanding the words, and they may ignore the important points that the investigator wants to emphasize. This point is valuable as you read this chapter's next section and Chapters 2 through 5. We introduce a wealth of terminology, but if you read a report you may never see the specific terms. Nevertheless, you still should find ample evidence that the researchers built models and applied standard research procedures in designing their study.

THE COMPONENTS OF MODELS: AN INTRODUCTION TO THE TERMINOLOGY

The elements in models are termed *variables* and *constants.* Variables are observable characteristics that can have more than one value, that is to say, characteristics that vary. Some examples of variables and their values include:

Variable	Values
Gender	Male, Female
Job satisfaction	Very Satisfied, Satisfied
	Dissatisfied, Very Dissatisfied
Salary	Actual dollar amount of salary

If the characteristic has only one value, it does not vary. Elements that do not vary are called constants.

To test a model, researchers examine the relationship between variables linked in the model. The investigators express the relationship between two variables in a simple model called a *hypothesis.* A hypothesis is a statement that specifies or describes the relationship between two variables in such a way that the relationship can be tested empirically. Hypotheses form the foundation of a research effort. A clearly written hypothesis helps researchers to decide what data to collect and how to analyze them. Consider the following three examples of hypotheses:

good H_1: Suicides in jail are more likely to occur during the first 24 hours of incarceration than at other times.

good H_2: The lower the turnover in inventoried stock, the greater the amount of waste caused by spoilage, obsolescence, or loss.

no H_3: Training programs improve the quality of life of the chronically unemployed.

Can you identify the variables in each hypothesis? Frequently, the hypothesis contains only a *value of the variable,* and you must infer the actual variable. In the first hypothesis, the variables are the occurrence of suicides in jail and the length of incarceration. The variables in the second hypothesis are the turnover rate in inventoried stock and the amount of waste. Note that these hypotheses are reasonably specific. We have a good idea of what data to collect to measure jailhouse suicides, length of incarceration, turnover in inventoried stock, and the amount of waste.

Now look at the third hypothesis. Imagine the frustration of the researcher trying to test it. And yet it is not an unreasonable beginning point for a research project. It is just not a useful hypothesis since it is not easily testable as stated here. To what type of training program does the hypothesis refer, and what does its author mean by "quality of life"? We may even debate who qualifies as chronically unemployed. The vagueness of the hypothesis leads us to suspect that its author has a poorly developed model.

The decision on how specific a hypothesis should be is relative. Some elements, such as quality of life and who is chronically unemployed, can be defined, as the researcher decides how to measure a variable and from whom to collect data. Even apparently specific elements may need further definition. Consider jailhouse suicides. What types of penal institutions should the data represent? One could collect data from county jails, state penitentiaries, or detention centers.

A hypothesis typically implies that a change in one variable is caused by a change in another variable. The *independent variable* is used to explain the variation in the characteristic or event of interest. It is sometimes referred to as an "input" or "cause." The *dependent variable* represents or measures the characteristic or event being explained. It also is referred to as an "outcome" or an "effect." One may identify visually the independent and dependent variable with a schematic model; the arrow leads from the independent variable to the dependent variable.

Some people find it helpful to rephrase a hypothesis as an "if–then" statement. For example, "If the age for Medicare eligibility is raised, then the rate of increase in Medicare costs will be slowed." The "if" statement contains the independent variable, that is, age for Medicare eligibility. The "then" statement contains the dependent variable, that is, rate of increase in Medicare costs. In our example hypotheses, the independent variables were length of incarceration, turnover rate in inventoried stock, and training programs. The respective dependent variables were the incidence of jailhouse suicides, the amount of waste in inventory, and quality of life.

We have defined hypotheses as consisting of an independent and dependent variable. Consider a hypothesis with two independent variables. For example, women and older adults use public libraries more often than men and younger adults. Is it necessary that both women and older adults use public libraries more for the hypothesis to be supported? What if women and younger adults more often use public libraries? Or does the independent variable have four values: older women, younger women, older men, and younger men. If this is the case, the hypothesis should make the values explicit. Otherwise, to avoid the ambiguity of having one part of a hypothesis supported and the other part unsupported, it is conventional to have a hypothesis for each independent variable. In our example the hypotheses would be: Women use public libraries more often than men; older adults use public libraries more often than younger adults.

The Nature of Relationships

An important characteristic of a hypothesis is the pattern of the relationships it postulates. *Covariation* refers to the patterned relationship between an independent and a dependent variable. Commonly, covariation between two variables takes one of three forms: *direct, inverse,* or *nonlinear.*

To describe the patterns of covariation, let's consider the relationship between the amount of job training received and salary on the first job after training. The relationship may be direct; that is, as the number of training hours received increases, the amount of salary increases. The relationship may be inverse; that is, as the number of training hours increases, the amount of salary decreases.

The relationship may be nonlinear, in that a distinctive but nonlinear pattern occurs. By way of example, two such patterns might emerge from a study of the relationship between training and salary levels. In the first, salary increases as the number of training hours increases, but only to a point, beyond which it begins to decrease or level off as training increases further. In the second, as the amount of training increases, salary increases to a point, after which the amount of salary received stays constant.

If the independent variable has no discernible effect on the dependent variable, we say that the two variables do not vary together. If two variables do not vary together, their relationship may be described as *random or null.*

In stating and testing a hypothesis, we may wonder about the effects of other variables on a hypothesized relationship. A *control variable* is believed to be related to the independent and dependent variables. It is a third variable that is added to the analysis to see how it alters the relationship between the independent and dependent variables. A control variable may show that the original relationship was in error, e.g., the relationship was false or spurious.

We have two examples that illustrate spurious relationships. First, consider the hypothesis that "arrests for assaults increase with ice cream sales." If subsequent research shows a statistical relationship, should you conclude that ice cream causes physical violence? Of course not; average daily temperatures (a control variable) should reveal that hot weather, not ice cream sales (the independent variable), is associated with more assault arrests (the dependent variable).

Similarly, hospital administrators challenge reports that their hospital has a higher than expected death rate. They contend that their hospital treats sicker patients. Thus they argue that patient prognosis at admission (a control variable), not the hospital itself (the independent variable), causes the higher death rate (the dependent variable).

Control variables, also referred to as *confounding variables,* may alter the hypothesized relationship radically. Consider how noise affects productivity. If a task requires concentration, noise tends to diminish productivity, whereas if a task is monotonous, noise tends to increase productivity because it jolts workers out of their daydreams. In Example 1.3 we show how a control variable is used to interpret the effectiveness of three job-training programs. When the relationship between the training program and student employment is considered, one program appears to be markedly more successful than the other two. When the educational level of trainees is considered, the difference becomes less striking. For students without a high school diploma or with education after high school, two training programs have nearly identical success in placing trainees.

In the example of the relationship between noise and productivity, the relationship does not have the same direction for each value of the control variable. In the example of the relationship between job training programs and student employment, the relationship is notably stronger for one value of the control variable than for the others. The introduction of a control variable can show that: (1) the hypothesis is spurious, or (2) the relationship between the independent and dependent variables is stronger for some values of the control variable than for other values, does not have the same direction for each value of the control variable, or is supported for some values of the control variable and unsupported for other values, or (3) the control variable has little or no impact on the relationship.

EXAMPLE 1.3

Illustrating Variables and Hypotheses

Problem: Identify successful job training programs for hard-to-place individuals.

Hypothesis: On-the-job training programs will be more successful than other training programs in placing participants in permanent positions.

Independent variable: Type of training program.

Dependent variable: Placement in a permanent position.

Control variable: Educational level.

Findings: The data reported in the list below supported the hypothesis that on-the-job training programs had the highest placement success. These data also showed that work-skills training had the lowest placement success.

Placement Success by Job Training Program

Vocational education program (attendance in a school-based training program)
31 percent of participants placed
On-the-job training
41 percent of participants placed
Work-skills training (program to teach basic reading and mathematical skills, attitudes, and behavior needed for permanent, skilled employment)
23 percent of participants placed

Placement Success by Program, Controlling for Years of Schooling (H.S. = high school)

Education	Vocational Training	On-the-Job Training	Work-Skills
<12 years	33%	35%	23%
H.S. graduate	28%	43%	25%
>12 years	38%	39%	25%

Discussion: The examination of the relationship between the independent and dependent variables for all participants shows that on-the-job training is markedly more successful in placing trainees. If education level is controlled and held constant, vocational education and on-the-job training do about equally well in placing participants who did not graduate from high school and those who continued beyond high school. Based on these findings, a counselor would refer trainees who only completed high school to on-the-job training. Other participants may equally do well in either on-the-job training or vocational education. If you funded these programs what decisions would you make? Would you want to look at other control variables? Which ones? Why?

Before you leave this example, make sure you can interpret the figures in the table with the control data. For example, 33 percent means that 33 percent of the people in vocational education who had not completed high school had been placed. Researchers have different ways of presenting control data, so expect to take time to determine exactly what the reported data mean.

If you study human behavior or attitudes, common control variables are age, sex, income, education, and race. If you study agencies, common control variables include agency size, stability, mission or purpose, budget, and region of the country or state. As you read the literature about a particular policy or program, you may locate other control variables that are used regularly to understand the relationship between the independent and dependent variables.

SELECTING A RESEARCH QUESTION

Students may be overwhelmed by seemingly limitless possibilities of topics from which to choose. Analysts face a similar situation as they decide what policies to study and how to study them. Administrators have to motivate themselves to do research; it often is not required in their jobs. Whether one is a student, analyst, or administrator, one wants to study relevant issues, that is, issues that engage public, professional, or agency attention. Recent relevant topics include welfare reform, privatization of public services, the implications of changing demographics, and the consequences of environmental degradation. Other relevant issues can be gleaned from professional journals, professional meetings, and the national media. Once a topic is selected, the research question can be framed by using the questions we listed at the beginning of the chapter—questions that begin "how many," "how much," "how efficient," "how effective," "how adequate," "why."

Students have the most freedom in selecting a topic. A required paper serves as an opportunity to study an unfamiliar topic or to develop new skills. Public administration students may seek projects that introduce them to agency officials or add to their resumés. In selecting a topic and framing the research question, students should be (1) interested in the topic, (2) have, or be able to develop, the required knowledge and skills to conduct the study, and (3) have sufficient time and resources. A student may be encouraged to select a topic simply because it is "hot." Unfortunately, a relevant topic has little value if the research cannot produce a credible study. Students may be hindered by a lack of interest in the topic or insufficient knowledge. For example, a review of the environmental policy literature may require knowledge of economics, statistics, or the physical or biological sciences—expertise that students rarely can develop within a semester. Students may underestimate the time and cost involved in empirical research—data collection and analysis take resources. A small, well-designed study is better than a large study that falls apart because of insufficient time or money.

Analysts' choice of research topics are more limited; topics must be relevant to their agency.[3] Similar to students, they should have requisite knowledge, sufficient time, and adequate resources; however, co-workers or contractors can supplement an analyst's knowledge or skills. In selecting a topic, analysts consider its relevance to the agency and their career. A relevant topic is important to the agency's mission, consumes substantial resources or affects the public's quality of life, and is amenable to change. Studies on inconsequential topics or on policy areas resistant to change are likely to be ignored. A record of producing unused studies is unlikely to lead to career success.

Administrators seldom are required to do research. Nevertheless, research findings are important in identifying problems and evaluating solutions. Administrators use research findings to justify additional resources, to keep existing resources, to monitor programs, and to improve employee performance. An effective strategy for administrators in university towns or with strong alumni ties is to keep a list of research questions. The list is ready whenever a faculty member calls looking for a class project. The students get to work on a relevant project, and the agency benefits from a low-cost study. Even the most modest study teaches administrators more about a particular policy and its implementation.

Administrators may rely on the knowledge and research skills of others. Nevertheless, as we stressed earlier, they should be sufficiently engaged to oversee the project and to question the research strategy and the findings. In our experience working with researchers to define a research question, build a model, and critique the method and the findings contributes to administrators' knowledge of their agency and their programs.

SUMMARY

Effective quantitative research requires that investigators articulate the purpose of a study. With the purpose in mind, the investigators can select the elements or variables of interest and postulate their relationship to each other. These elements and relationships constitute a model. Investigators may find a model aids them in three ways. First, it helps them to explain their ideas to others and to solicit reactions and criticisms. Second, it helps investigators to understand their ideas better. Third, it provides a useful guide to the research. It is particularly valuable in ensuring that all specified elements are measured and analyzed.

In building a model, investigators consider their own ideas and the ideas of colleagues and review existing research. Models may also emerge as investigators work with existing data or examine the results of a pilot test. The specific way investigators use these information sources varies from person to person and requires some creativity. Nevertheless, one can expect to rethink his or her ideas several times as information from different sources is brought to bear.

In our opinion, the review of the literature is the most important source of information. A thorough review of the literature greatly reduces the likelihood of wasting resources. It provides valuable information that can be used in the later stages of research planning. Frequently, it helps investigators to identify strategies they can copy or adapt. Investigators will want to make use of the resources of reference and documents libraries, particularly abstracts, statistical indices, and citation indices.

The preliminary model may be modified several times during the course of planning a study. Once a plan is developed, investigators should conduct a pilot test. It should include the analysis and interpretation of the findings. Pilot-test information can be reviewed by investigators and major study users to ensure that the final study fulfills its purpose.

Administrative researchers primarily use schematic and symbolic models. Schematic models help investigators to illustrate their model and explain it to others, but much of the detail that is needed to understand and test the model may be missing from the schematic. Symbolic models use words, equations, or computer programs to represent the elements and their relationships. Verbal and mathematical models often are complementary. The verbal model presents the model in all its detail; the mathematical model gives precise descriptions of the relationships between elements.

The elements in models are variables, that is, characteristics that vary. A hypothesis is a simple model that states a testable relationship between an independent and a dependent variable. Frequently, an investigator will add additional variables, called control variables, to see whether they alter the hypothesized relationship. Common control variables in studies of human behavior include race, gender, and age. In studies of organizations, size, stability, and mission often are used as control variables.

Once the preliminary model is outlined, the investigators decide when and how often to collect data, how much control to exert over the study, what data to collect, and from whom to collect the data. Chapters 2 and 3 discuss the purpose of a study, how it affects the timing and frequency of data collected, and the investigators' degree of control. Chapter 2 introduces the two most common sources of research information used by administrators—the cross-sectional study and time-series analysis. We also will discuss case studies, which produce in-depth descriptions of events or programs. Chapter 4 considers which data to collect, and Chapter 5 deals with ways to select research subjects.

NOTES

1. Two magazine series that describe how scientists work are: H. S. F. Cooper, Jr., "A Resonance with Something Alive," *New Yorker*, June 21, 28, 1976; H. F. Judson, "Annals of Science: DNA," *New Yorker*, November 1978. A valuable text in this area is *How Does Social Science Work? Reflections on Practice* by Paul Diesing (Pittsburgh, PA: University of Pittsburgh Press, 1992).
2. For a discussion on empirical analysis as part of model building, see J. W. Tukey and M. B. Wilk, "Data Analysis and Statistics: Techniques and Applications," in *The Quantitative Analysis of Social Problems*, ed. E. R. Tufte (Reading, MA: Addison-Wesley Publishing, 1970), 370–390. The authors warn against exploring data with no model in mind and advocate that researchers not take their models too seriously or be unwilling to change them.
3. See A. J. Meltsner's "Problem Selection," in *Policy Analysis in the Bureaucracy* (Berkeley: University of California Press, 1976), 81–113 for a provocative discussion on problem selection.

TERMS FOR REVIEW

models	variables	inverse relationship
elements in a model	constants	nonlinear relationship
relationships in a model	hypothesis	random or null relationship
model building	values of a variable	spurious relationship
literature review	independent variable	control variable
pilot study	dependent variable	confounding variable
schematic model	covariation	
symbolic model	direct relationship	

QUESTIONS FOR REVIEW

The following questions should indicate whether you have a basic competency in this chapter's material.

1. Why should an investigator state a purpose for a model before building it?

2. Why should an investigator build an explicit, preliminary model before beginning a quantitative study?

3. Identify the steps involved in model building, and comment on their importance. Consider the effect on the model if any one step were eliminated.

4. In general, would models built by one person be superior to a model developed by a group? Justify your position.

5. In the following hypotheses, identify the independent and dependent variables, two or three possible values for each variable, and indicate the direction of the relationship. Then identify at least two control variables for each:

    a. Death rates in automobile accidents are higher in less densely populated areas.

    b. The higher the average driving speed on a highway, the higher the automobile death rate on that highway.

    c. Defendants with records of alcohol abuse are more likely to miss scheduled court appearances.

    d. Parents of elementary and high school students are more satisfied with their children's schools than are parents of junior high students.

6. Develop three hypotheses, each with an independent, dependent, and control variables, on a topic of interest to you. Create a schematic and verbal model for each.

7. Consider safety violations as an independent variable, and write three hypotheses. Indicate the direction of each hypothesis.

8. Evaluate the following proposed "hypotheses":

    H_1: School boards should not be appointed.
    H_2: There are more African Americans than Hispanics on U.S. school boards.
    H_3: Appointed school boards are more likely to have African American members than elected school boards.
    H_4: African American school board representation is measured by the percent of school board members who are African American.

9. Identify the independent variables and their values in the hypotheses:

    H_1: Older mothers with a college education are most likely to participate in parks and recreation programs; younger mothers with only a high school education are least likely to participate.
    H_2: Older mothers and more educated mothers are most likely to participate in parks and recreation programs.

    What, if any, changes would you make to H_1 or H_2?

PROBLEMS FOR HOMEWORK AND DISCUSSION

1. Process models or flow charts are often developed to describe and guide a process. One may use a process model to describe ways to build a model. Use a schematic to present a model of what you consider a "good" way to build a model. Show all linkages and their direction. You should have described either a systematic step-by-step process or a dynamic process in which the steps are repeated and the model is revised several times. Defend the process you described.

2. Link the purposes of a literature review with the stages of model building. At what stage(s) of the model would you conduct a review, and what would be the purpose of the review at each stage?

3. Find a newspaper article that presents a verbal model:

a. State the apparent purpose of the model.
b. Draw a schematic to illustrate the model.
c. State a hypothesis included in or implied by the model.
d. Name and identify the independent and dependent variables in your hypothesis.

4. Because of your model-building skills you have been asked to head a committee studying the job training needs of a town's labor force. The committee's purpose is to identify ways to improve the quality of the town's labor force to meet the needs of existing employers and to attract new employers to the area.

   The committee's first meeting is next week. A committee member who has no particular political power wants to survey citizens and community leaders; she has offered to prepare a survey for the meeting.
   a. Would you encourage her to bring a draft survey? Justify your decision.
   b. Outline your agenda for the meeting.

5. Consider the problem of productivity in the United States. Identify recent publications that address the problem. Look at three of these publications. Find a definition for productivity. Note the elements the authors use to study productivity. Create a tentative model to study productivity. First, state the purpose of your model. Sketch a schematic model that incorporates the elements you think are most important.

   In class, work with three to five classmates. Compare your models, and jointly develop and sketch a model that you think should be tested.

6. Many communities must take water conservation measures in the summer. List strategies to get citizens to decrease their water usage. Develop a water conservation model that includes water conservation strategies and strategies for getting citizen compliance.

   In class, work with three to five classmates. Compare your models, and jointly develop and sketch a model that you think should be tested.

7. Consider automobile accidents in the United States. Identify and read a recent publication that studies the problem.
   a. Indicate the elements linked to automobile injuries or fatalities.
   b. Create a preliminary model to arrive at a policy to reduce injuries and fatalities resulting from automobile accidents. State the research question and a purpose for the model. Sketch a schematic model that incorporates the elements that you consider most important.
   c. Prepare a presentation explaining and justifying your model.

   In class, work with three to five classmates. Compare your models, then jointly develop and sketch a model that you think should be tested.

8. Select one of the following topics or a topic assigned by your instructor:

   Teenage pregnancy (incidence, policies, or programs)
   Juvenile crime (incidence, policies, or programs)
   Quality of drinking water
   Welfare reform (policies, effectiveness)
   Municipal finance (innovations)
   Lobbying by nonprofit organizations (policies, activities)

   a. Use a web search engine to locate and explore a relevant site. What information did you find at the site that could help you design or carry out a study?
   b. Go to your university's library or another research library and do a keyword search of the catalogue. How many entries did you receive? How many seem worth consulting? Do the same with a web search engine. Compare your findings.
   c. Go to your university's library or another research library and do a keyword search of an electronic index or database (it should contain entries of research articles). How many entries did you receive? How many seem worth consulting?
   d. With a group of classmates develop a guide to effective on-line searching.

DISK WORK

The disk includes a database, consisting of citizen responses to a survey conducted by Belle County. A random sample of citizens was asked questions about the county's public schools, financial assistance services, and environmental protection regulations. Before analyzing the data, researchers want to know what questions they are trying to answer.

1. Go to the disk and review the list of variables. State three questions that a county administrator could answer by analyzing the data.
2. Go to the disk and review the list of variables. Select two variables and state (1) one hypothesis with a direct relationship and (2) one with an inverse relationship.
3. Use the list of variables to create a model to study variations in citizen satisfaction with county services.

RECOMMENDED FOR FURTHER READING

Information technology is changing rapidly. Many texts exist to help Internet users with research, but most become quickly outdated. Reference librarians are the best source for learning about new technologies and how to use them effectively. One recent text is *Academic Research on the Internet* (Haworth Press, Inc, 2001). Another quite comprehensive text is E. Ackermann and K. Hartman, *The Information Specialist's Guide to Searching and Researching on the Internet and the World Wide Web,* 2d ed., (Chicago: Fitzroy Dearborn Publishers, 2000).

Chapter 2

Designs for Description

In this chapter you will learn

1. criteria for selecting a cross-sectional, time-series, panel, or case study design.
2. the major strengths and weaknesses of cross-sectional, time-series, panel, and case study designs.
3. how to interpret findings from cross-sectional and time-series designs.
4. the value of case studies and how to judge their quality.
5. about using focus groups as study designs.

After formulating a tentative model, investigators need a research plan. They outline how they intend to collect data describing each variable and how they plan to analyze the relationships among the variables. When you study tables, graphs, or other quantitative presentations, you may never think of the decisions and actions required to gather and organize the data used to prepare them. Yet these decisions and actions determine the value of the research, and each step should be conducted carefully. Data collection and analysis include the following steps:

Deciding when and how often to collect data

Constructing measures

Identifying a sample or test population

Choosing a strategy for contacting subjects

Selecting statistical tools

Presenting the findings

These steps constitute *research methodology*. Very often the quality of a set of data is determined by the research methodology, even though little discussion of the methodology is included in the final report. For this reason it is altogether too easy for readers or listeners to underestimate the importance of research techniques and to take for granted the accuracy of reported findings.

Research designs are plans that guide decisions about when and how often to collect data, what data to gather, from whom and how to collect data, and how to analyze data. The term "research design" has a general and a specific meaning. The general meaning of research design refers to the presentation of the plan for the study's methodology. The design should indicate the purpose of the study and demonstrate that the plan is consistent with the study's purpose. Frequently, research designs are described as blueprints for the final research product.

The specific meaning of research design refers to the type of study. Common types of studies are cross-sectional studies, time-series analysis, case studies, and experimental designs. These types of studies or designs guide the decisions as to when and how often to collect the data and how much control an investigator will exert over the research environment.

Cross-sectional studies, time series, and case studies place researchers in an environment where they have little, if any, control over the events. Experimental studies allow the researcher to dominate the research environment. The experimental setting and subjects are selected carefully, and the investigator decides who will be exposed to the independent variable, at what intensity, and for how long. We have labeled experimental designs as designs for explanation and discuss them in the next chapter.

We have labeled and categorized cross-sectional studies, time series, and case studies as designs for description. These three designs for description may be used separately or they may be combined. Cross-sectional studies are often combined with time series, and case studies may incorporate cross-sectional studies or time series.

Descriptive designs are the basic research tools of administrators and policy analysts. They provide a wealth of information that is easy to understand and interpret. The studies can be undertaken to answer the questions that we posed in Chapter 1—how many? how much? how efficient? how effective? how adequate? The designs are used frequently to produce the data needed for planning, monitoring, and evaluating.

The administrator who wants to know what caused a particular event or outcome may find the descriptive designs somewhat limited. Nevertheless, all three designs can eliminate untenable explanations and furnish valuable leads. If the designs are planned and analyzed carefully, they may produce reasonable estimates of an independent variable's effect on a dependent variable.[1] Thus descriptive designs may suggest causality.

Administrators combine findings from quantitative studies with other information and decide what, if any, action to take. From the administrator's perspective, simply describing variables may be sufficient. Consider once again the problem of prison suicides. With stricter enforcement of drunk-driving laws, reports of prison suicides increased.[2] These reports led investigators to collect data on how many prison suicides were occurring and who committed suicide. For each reported suicide, investigators noted whether the prisoner was incarcerated for a violent or nonviolent crime, intoxicated, or held in isolation. Upon analysis investigators found that suicides tended to occur among males incarcerated for drunkenness or kept in isolation.

The analysis did not tell prison officials why one male prisoner chose to commit suicide and another did not. But the data did tell them how widespread the problem of prison suicide was and what characterized the inmates who were more likely to commit suicide.

What could prison officials do with the information? They could identify how many inmates in their institution were at risk of committing suicide. In other words, how many males did they have incarcerated for drunkenness or placed in isolation each day? Were there trends in these cases? Was the number of such incarcerations steadily increasing? Did the number go up on weekends or during certain times of the year?

Officials could propose and evaluate solutions to prevent those prisoners at risk of committing suicide from doing so and determine the feasibility of implementing these solutions. If a solution involves separate facilities or increased staffing, how large a facility is needed to take care of anticipated peak needs? What changes, if any, need to be made in the current staff work schedules? If a solution is tried, its effectiveness can be monitored. Did the rate of suicides drop? If a suicide occurred, had the inmate been identified as being at risk? If identified, had he received the available treatment for a potential suicide?

The number of possible questions goes on. Data are needed to answer them. Other examples would lead to different questions requiring different data. Administrators need data to carry out their tasks. These data are products of research efforts that may or may not have involved the administrators who use the data.

DESIGNS TO FIND RELATIONSHIPS AND SHOW TRENDS

A *cross-sectional design* is one used to collect data on all relevant variables at one time. An investigator decides how to measure each variable in a model. Then data for each variable are collected closely enough to the same time so as to be considered contemporaneous. After the measurements have been completed, investigators use statistical models to examine the relationships between the variables.

The key feature of the cross-sectional design is that its data represent a set of people or other cases at one point in time. Two analogies are often used to explain cross-sectional designs. In one analogy, the design is viewed as a physical "cross section" of the population of interest. In the other analogy, the design is seen as a "snapshot." Both analogies underscore the static, time bound nature of the design. The design depicts what exists at one time interval. Clearly, events may change markedly at a later time, even in the next time interval.

Cross-sectional designs are particularly suited for studies that involve collecting data:

On many variables

From a large group of subjects

From subjects who are dispersed geographically

Any one of these conditions is sufficient justification for using a cross-sectional design.

In addition to the number of variables, subjects, and the location of subjects, other considerations favor cross-sectional studies. They are the design of choice to:

Gather information on people's attitudes and behavior

Answer questions of how much? how many? who? what happened?

Begin exploratory research and identify hypotheses for further research

Cross-sectional studies do not allow the researcher to measure the change in the values of variables over time. A cross-sectional design would allow the director of training to determine the amount of income an individual is earning or the unemployment rate for a city. However, it will not allow her to determine how much average incomes have changed or if the unemployment rate is increasing or decreasing.

Cross-sectional studies generally are inappropriate if investigators want to demonstrate that an independent variable or set of independent variables causes a given outcome. Cross-sectional studies cannot demonstrate causal relationships. Investigators cannot control or manipulate the occurrence of independent variables nor do they have much, if any, control over the environment surrounding the study. Investigators may be unable to rule out alternative explanations as to why something happened. Nevertheless, a major use of cross-sectional designs is to uncover relationships that will be studied further in experimental studies. For example, extensive data on health, diet, and environmental variables have been gathered from individuals. Analysts then look for links between the incidence of cancer or heart disease and other health, diet, or environmental variables. Variables strongly related to the occurrence of cancer or heart disease are identified for further study. Analysts also use statistical models and methods to rule out some alternative explanations, thus obtaining additional evidence necessary for evaluating causality. This technique is known as elaboration.[3] Methods of elaboration are discussed in more detail in Chapters 13 and 14. Analysts use elaboration extensively with large survey data sets to approximate causal research with cross-sectional data.[4]

We normally think of cross-sectional studies in conjunction with surveys, where an individual or a representative of an organization answers a questionnaire. Analysts then compile the data and analyze the variables. Imagine a survey to examine the career backgrounds of city managers. Appropriate measurements for variables, such as sex, age, and professional education, are identified. A questionnaire is mailed to city managers. Later the measurements are analyzed. We can learn how many women or nonwhites are city managers, the average age of city managers, and the types of training city managers receive. We can see if female managers have different career paths than male managers or if professionally educated managers work in larger cities than do managers with only a bachelor's degree or without professional education. More complex analyses also may be performed, depending on the model.

The mass media often sponsor cross-sectional studies on current issues. Interviewers ask respondents about their opinions and their behavior. Then, the magazine, newspaper, or television station reports the percent of respondents in the various categories: how many agreed or disagreed with the stated opinion; how many acted in a particular fashion. The reports may indicate how responses vary according to demographic characteristics: Do women feel differently from men? Do westerners behave differently from easterners? and so on.

We have examples from cross-sectional studies throughout this text. You can find other examples of cross-sectional studies almost daily in newspapers. News stories report surveys studying hunger in America, comparing the achievements of Asian Americans to whites, looking for the causes of premature deaths among African Americans, and seeing whether studying or class attendance is more closely associated with student grades. Undoubtedly as you read this, you also will note the many studies conducted and reported so that we can understand ourselves and our society better.

We use the term "cross-sectional study" to refer to studies that use or approximate survey techniques to collect data. By approximate survey techniques, we have in mind studies in which a researcher compiles data from a variety of sources. For example, to study factors associated with traffic fatalities, a researcher can collect data from several sources for each state on the number of fatalities, road conditions, traffic density, arrests and penalties for various traffic offenses, and so on.

An advantage of well-designed, well-documented, and carefully implemented cross-sectional designs is that researchers with different interests and models often can work with data from a single cross-sectional study. Even a small study can be analyzed in many different ways. The use of data by researchers who did not participate in their collection is called secondary data analysis, discussed in detail in Chapter 9.

The widely used U.S. Decennial Census of Population and Housing may be considered an example of a cross-sectional study, albeit one that has the added advantage of being repeated every 10 years. The 1990 census asked seven demographic and seven housing questions of the entire U.S. population. Roughly 20 percent of the population was asked 45 additional questions. Most of these questions were asked in previous censuses.[5] From the 59 questions, analysts working in governments, universities, and businesses generate a multitude of studies. For example, data on age distribution help communities estimate demands for services. With knowledge of how many young children are in a community, planners can predict how many children will enter its schools each year. Similarly, knowing the number of aged persons and where they live can help to predict levels of service demand and to locate services near concentrations of older residents.

If the Census Bureau changes the wording of the questions from one census to another, the ability to compare the answers over time is reduced. In preparing for the 2000 census, the Bureau was especially concerned with holding down costs, increasing the response from the public, and obtaining accurate and necessary information. At the same time the Bureau had to be sensitive to the comparability of the information from one census to another.

Cross-sectional studies usually investigate the relationships among several variables. When the data are analyzed, cases are divided into different groups based on values of the independent variables. Careful use of multivariate analysis—techniques to investigate the joint relationship of several variables—allows researchers to obtain information on the influence of factors that would be controlled in an experimental study. The researcher can assess the influence of variables other than the independent variable by using statistical control. However, to do so requires obtaining information on the control variables. Basing a cross-sectional study on a carefully developed model helps to ensure that appropriate information is collected and provides a guide for data analysis.

Although cross-sectional studies based on carefully developed models can provide useful information and be effective in testing hypotheses, many seem to suffer from less-than-careful research techniques. Perhaps the greatest weakness of cross-sectional designs rests not in the design but in the implementation. An investigator may attempt to obtain information from too many people, be unable to make return calls or follow-up mailings, and be plagued with a low response rate. Contact may be haphazard. Questionnaires may be constructed hastily without sufficient care to purpose and design. Investigators may fail to pilot test the survey instruments, and relevant variables may be ignored. The measures used may produce the wrong data or data of questionable quality. All these problems are preventable, but administrators should be warned not to collect data without first considering the value of the data and critically evaluating the data collection process.

An interesting example of the use and limitations of cross-sectional designs to suggest causal relationships occurred in 1985, when a noted medical journal published two cross-sectional studies on estrogen.[6] One study examined data on 1,234 postmenopausal women living in a Boston suburb. The researchers related the use of estrogen to chest pains, heart attacks, or death from heart disease. They found estrogen users twice as likely as nonusers to experience heart disease. During this same time period, other researchers surveyed 121,964 postmenopausal nurses and measured how the use of estrogen related to the incidence of heart attack or fatal heart disease. They found that estrogen users were one-third as likely to experience heart disease.

Design features may have led to the different findings. The studies had different sample populations. One study involved women living in a Boston suburb; the other involved nurses living throughout the United States. One study used a mailed questionnaire to collect data; the other relied on personal interviews and physical examinations. One study collected data over a four-year period; the other collected them over an eight-year period.

The results of both studies were plausible theoretically, and neither study's results could be eliminated with information from theories. From biochemical research one model can be built indicating that the estrogen improves cholesterol levels, decreasing the probability of heart disease. A second model can be built from biochemical research indicating that estrogen increases blood clotting, increasing the probability of heart disease. The specific reasons for the different findings were not ascertainable immediately.

The two estrogen studies illustrate the use of cross-sectional studies in setting the stage for later, more controlled research. The studies also demonstrate that statistical association may be insufficient evidence that a certain treatment or independent variable brings about a certain outcome. Experimental studies are designed specifically to produce evidence of causality and the degree of effect that an independent variable has on a dependent variable. Nevertheless, as we noted earlier in this chapter, statisticians and methodologists have created techniques designed to obtain evidence of causality from cross-sectional data. We discuss these techniques briefly in Chapters 13 and 14. Some cross-sectional studies, such as census studies, gather data from a population at regular intervals. The group sponsoring the research has an ongoing interest in obtaining the data. Organizations often require periodic reports to monitor organizational performance and identify organizational needs. These data may be compiled and analyzed on occasion to answer other research questions.

An example in the previous chapter was drawn from a cross-sectional design implemented to learn the placement record of state-funded job training programs.[7] Prior to the study, administrators had no data on the success of training programs in placing participants. The data on job training program participants were collected from state government files. The dependent variable was employment status at the end of the training program. The independent variables were type of training program, sex, race, age, and educational attainment.

For each type of training program, analysts examined placement outcomes by age, sex, race, and educational attainment. They found that participants in on-the-job training programs were most likely to be employed. Males were more likely to be employed than females; employment status did not vary with age, race, or educational attainment. Tables similar to Table 2.1 were produced. Administrators could study the detailed tables to learn whom the programs served and how well a program did in placing its various client groups.

Program administrators combined the research findings with other information to decide on program funding. They had to decide whether the findings were strong enough to warrant a change in current program funding. They also had to consider what was not measured: What salaries were people earning after training? Were their jobs consistent with their training?

Example 2.1 comes from a cross-sectional study conducted by the U.S. General Accounting Office (GAO) to determine the effect of changing Internal Revenue Service (IRS) taxpayer assistance. We look only at the relationship between age and type of assistance. The study, typical of cross-sectional studies, gathered data

TABLE 2.1 AGE AND EMPLOYMENT STATUS OF PARTICIPANTS IN ON-THE-JOB TRAINING PROGRAMS

Age	Employed after Training
16–21 years	40 (51%)
22–24 years	37 (74%)
25–54 years	84 (70%)
>54 years	3 (75%)

EXAMPLE 2.1

An Application of a Cross-sectional Design

Problem: Would changing taxpayer assistance services affect some groups of taxpayers more negatively than others?

> *Hypothesis:* Taxpayer age is associated with the type of taxpayer assistance used.
>
> *Independent variable:* Age of taxpayer.
>
> *Dependent variable:* Type of assistance used.
>
> *Design:* Cross-sectional (a questionnaire administered to taxpayers), to determine the relationship between age and type of taxpayer assistance used.
>
> *Findings:*

TABLE 2.2 DISTRIBUTION OF AGE LEVELS OF TAXPAYERS IN GENERAL AND BY TYPE OF IRS ASSISTANCE USED IN 1982

Age	Taxpayers in General	Type of Assistance Used		
		Telephone	*Walk-in*	*Correspondence*
<21	7.5%	4.0%	1.8%	2.1%
21–34	37.2	27.1	27.1	25.0
35–44	17.5	18.2	15.1	14.9
45–54	11.0	10.9	11.5	16.5
55–64	16.8	15.2	18.2	21.8
>64	9.9	24.0	24.5	18.1
Unknown	0.1	0.6	1.8	1.6

Conclusions: From the data the General Accounting Office concluded that cutbacks in telephone assistance or walk-in assistance would disproportionately affect persons over 64 years old. To interpret this table, one must compare the percentage of taxpayers in general in the particular age group with the percentage who use a service. While less than 10 percent of taxpayers are over 64 years old, 24 percent of taxpayers using telephone assistance are over 64. For other age groups, except those between 35 and 44 years old, the percentage of taxpayers using telephone assistance is less than their percentage in the taxpayer population.

SOURCE: U.S. General Accounting Office, *Need to Better Assess Consequence before Reducing Taxpayer Assistance* (Washington, D.C.: General Accounting Office), April 5, 1984.

on many variables. A large number of variables, by the way, is a mixed blessing. Statistical techniques allow investigators to relate many variables, to identify strong direct or inverse relationships, and to designate relationships worthy of closer study. Nevertheless, information is not free. Each piece of data adds to the costs of collecting, coding, compiling, and storing. The chance of errors increases as data are coded, transcribed, and computerized. Lengthy questionnaires also may discourage some subjects from responding.

Study the data in Example 2.1. Which taxpayers were most likely to seek assistance? Can you tell from Table 2.2 which type of assistance was used most frequently? Can you tell what type of assistance taxpayers under 21 years of age were likely to use? If you cannot answer these three questions, what additional information do you need?

If you tried to answer our questions regarding Example 2.1, you should have found that taxpayers over the age of 64 were most likely to use the available services. Although people over 64 years of age constitute less than 10 percent of the taxpayers, they make up roughly a quarter of the population seeking IRS assistance. Note, however, that you cannot tell which service had the heaviest demand or which service the youngest taxpayers used the most. To learn this you need to know how many taxpayers the various percentages represented. From the data given in the report, the reader did not know how many taxpayers sought help over the telephone, in person, or by mail.

Longitudinal Designs: Studies to Collect Data over Time

Studies using *longitudinal designs* collect information on each variable for two or more distinct time periods.[8] The same or comparable cases are analyzed in each period. This allows the investigator to measure changes in the values of variables over time. Two major types of longitudinal designs are time-series and panel studies. Time-series studies measure variables for a unit, jurisdiction, or group numerous times at regular intervals over a relatively long period. Panel studies obtain data from the same individuals each time and usually involve a large number of cases. Longitudinal studies are used to measure both short-term changes and long-term trends. Ideally, information is obtained with measures repeated frequently at closely spaced, regular intervals. Such is the case with a time series. However, the data to measure trends often come from infrequent, sometimes irregularly timed measures and replications of studies.

A *time-series study* collects data at regular intervals.[9] Most of us are familiar with time series that are regularly reported indicators of some aspect of the nation's economic or social climate. Such time series include consumer price indices, the unemployment rate, and crime rates.

Time series are suited for situations where an administrator wants to:

Establish a baseline measure

Describe changes over time

Keep track of trends

Forecast future trends

Time-series data are neither hard to gather nor hard to arrange for analysis. The data may be gathered by investigators or taken from existing databases. The data come from one or more units, such as a state, county, or office. The data may be collected on the first workday of every month, the fourth Thursday of every November, or any other interval appropriate to the study. An accompanying account of events should be kept and consulted to help explain unexpected patterns: for example, a drop in swimming pool usage may be associated with an unusually cold or rainy summer.

Administrators find time-series data presented in graphs or tables easy to interpret and to combine with other information. They use time series to monitor elements under their jurisdiction. For example, administrators in a social services department may decide to reallocate resources within a department based on the number of clients served, the number of services offered, and length of service time.

A time series may or may not include an explicit independent variable. Time, however, is an implied independent variable. The data are frequently presented in a graph with time along the horizontal axis and the dependent variable along the vertical axis. The reader's attention focuses on the dependent variable and its changes or variations over time. Look at Figure 2.1, which shows two time-series designs—one examines the unemployment rate and the other the crime rate.[10]

Now what do you look for in this time series? Your eye should scan each line to identify the overall patterns and noticeable dips and rises in the line. You look for four types of variations within a time series[11]:

Long-term trends: general movement of a variable, either upward or downward over a number of years.

Cyclical variations: changes in a variable that occur within a long-term trend; cycles recur in one- to five-year intervals.

Seasonal variations: fluctuations traceable to seasonally related phenomena, e.g., holidays, weather.

Irregular (or random) fluctuations: changes that cannot be attributed to long-term trends, cyclical variations, or seasonal variations.

Figure 2.1   U.S. Crime Rate and Unemployment Rate, 1960–1995

SOURCE: *Statistical Abstract of the United States.* Also see N. D. Kristol, "Scholars Disagree on Connection between Crime and the Jobless," *Washington Post,* August 7, 1982.

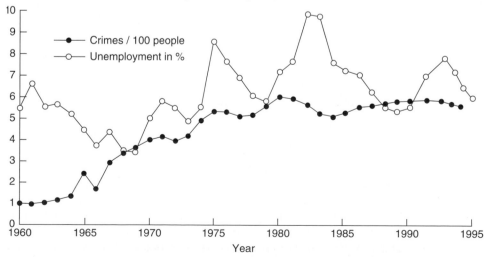

Since our example demonstrates long-term trends, cyclical variations, and irregular fluctuations, we will discuss these first and then consider seasonal variations.[12]

Look first at the change in the crime index from 1960 to 1994. The crime rate seems to have risen steadily from 1960 to 1980 and then to have leveled off between 1980 and 1990. The index drops between 1965 and 1966, 1971 and 1972, 1975 and 1977, and 1980 and 1984. After each drop the crime rate resumed its upward growth. This index depicts a long-term trend in the United States, that of an increasing crime rate. However, about 1980, the crime index drops for several years, rises between 1984 and 1991 but declines again after that. A long-term trend is the underlying movement of a variable either upward or downward over several years. Major forces underlying a long-term trend include population and technological changes. The long-term trend in the crime index seems to have changed in 1980. Perhaps because of the increasing age of the population, the crime rate did not increase as fast after 1980 or possibly has begun to decrease.

Cyclical variations are regularly occurring fluctuations within a long-term trend that last for more than a year; frequently, cyclical patterns recur in one- to five-year intervals. We can detect some cycles in both the unemployment and crime index data. Notice how both time series increase and then decrease about every five years or so. A complete cycle is from "peak to peak" or "valley to valley." Note the unemployment data from 1969 to 1989. Two cycles of about five years each occur between 1969 and 1979. Unemployment increases between 1979 and 1982, but then a longer decline in the unemployment rate begins, disturbing the regularity of the pattern. Try to spot and describe the cyclical variation in the crime index data.

Seasonal variations describe changes that occur within the course of a year. Data must represent time intervals that recur within a year, such as days, weeks, months, or quarters. Seasonal variations include fluctuations traceable to weather, holidays, or similar seasonally related phenomena. The observed fluctuations occur within a single year and recur year after year. An administrator may use seasonal information to decide how to staff public facilities—for example, how many staff to hire for city parks and for how long to hire them (for 10, 12, or 14 weeks). A police department finding that the number of people in jail is highest on Monday mornings can plan ahead for the increased demand. Ignorance of seasonal demands may result in erroneous conclusions. Imagine the disastrous consequences if a merchant assumed that his December sales of toys marked a business upswing that would carry through to January and February. Think of the problems of the jail administrator who orders food based on the number of inmates on Monday morning. Variations not associated with long-term trends, cyclical variations, or seasonal variations also will be observed in a time series. These irregular fluctuations may be the result of nonrandom or random movements. A nonrandom movement is brought about by a condition or set of conditions that can be identified and explain the variation. The conditions may be inferred from an account of concurrent events. For example, changes in a state's criminal code may change what acts are defined as criminal, or a community may be struck by a natural disaster, which impacts employment. Random movements are unexplained variations that most often are relatively minor. The increase in the 1965 crime rate and the drop in the 1966 crime rate depict irregular fluctuations that were relatively inconsequential in the 30-year period. We need more information to determine whether these were nonrandom or random. Records describing other events in 1965 and 1966 might suggest factors causing the increase and the drop. If an explanation was found, the variations would be nonrandom; otherwise, they may be assumed to be random. If we examined the monthly crime-rate data, you would see more unexpected and unimportant fluctuations.

For most administrative purposes, one simply needs to know the types of fluctuations and to recognize evidence of their occurrence in a table or a graph. Otherwise, you may misinterpret the ups and downs in a graphed time series and erroneously attribute changes in a time series to a specific event or administrative action.

Statistical adjustments are applied when investigators use time-series data to forecast future values of a dependent variable—an important use of time series. Several techniques are available for forecasting. The more sophisticated and powerful of them are beyond the scope of this text.[13] However, many of the procedures are straightforward and accessible. Forecasting of some variables can be done by extending the long-term trend. Some procedures involve identifying and separating the types of variations in the time series, and others reduce or eliminate one or more sources of variation in order to bring out the long-term trend. These include a variety of averaging and smoothing techniques. A common technique for forecasting by extending the long-term trend is regression analysis, discussed in Chapter 14.[14]

It is important to draw a graph of the time series and analyze it visually. We will often see graphs with more than one variable, as is the case with Figure 2.1. However, for administrative purposes the clarity of time series diminishes if several variables are being examined together. In Figure 2.1 the graph included two variables: crime rate and unemployment rate. You could scan the graph visually and note where the two varied together and where they went in different directions. From 1962 to 1969, the unemployment rate was going down while the crime rate was going up. From 1969 through 1977, the increases and decreases in the unemployment rate parallel the shifts in the crime rate. Between 1980 and 1988, the two rates seemed to diverge. After 1992, they both appear to be declining. If more variables were placed on the graph, it would become increasingly difficult to follow and interpret.

Time-series data are used frequently in forecasting or in evaluating the effectiveness of a policy. In both cases statistical techniques take into account the fluctuations of a variable. For the most part, these techniques are beyond the scope of this book. Nevertheless, we can make some comments about forecasting that you may find useful. First, quantitative methods of forecasting that depend on time-series data work best for short-term forecasts, e.g., forecasting for up to two years. A parks director or jail administrator may use quantitative techniques to forecast park usage or jail occupancy. This information may help in making staffing decisions or ordering supplies. But forecasts made for longer periods are less likely to be accurate. A major problem is forecasting a change in direction of the long-term trend correctly.

Second, assuming that existing long-term trends may continue unchanged can work reasonably well, but the forecaster must be aware that rates of change eventually will vary and long-term trends will change direction. For example, a town whose population has grown by 10 percent each decade will at some time experience slower growth. An unanticipated slowdown has serious implications if public facilities are planned around the assumption of a much larger population.

Third, identifying regular changes, such as cycles, in time series can be important, especially to guard against mistakenly concluding that a change in a time series is the result of government action or intervention. For example, a short-term decline in unemployment may be the result of a government training program or it may be a cyclic change. However, regular cycles may be difficult to predict and identify. More common are up and down movements that take place but not in a regular pattern.

Fourth, qualitative techniques are important for long-range forecasting. An administrator who wants to identify the types of demands that her agency will face in 10 years may wish to use focus groups or interviews to obtain opinions from citizens and experts. These techniques are discussed later in this chapter and in Chapter 6.

Panel Designs

The *panel design* examines the same cases individually at successive time periods. It combines some characteristics of the cross-sectional design and the time-series design. Panel studies can reveal which individual cases change. This allows the researcher to determine the changes that take place within the group and establish a time order for variables. For example, a training director can organize unemployment data as a time series and note changes in the unemployment rate. However, unless a panel design is used, she cannot tell how individuals in this population changed. That is, some people employed at one time may be unemployed at a later time; some unemployed at the earlier time may be employed later. Since a panel design follows the same individual cases over time, shifts from one condition (employed) to another (unemployed) by individuals can be measured.

Until the late 1960s, poverty was considered to be a relatively permanent characteristic of individuals. Repeated cross-sectional surveys showed the same proportion of Americans living in poverty, and it was assumed that the same people were in poverty each time. These studies showed almost no change from one year to the next in the distribution of income. However, a panel study, the Panel Survey of Income Dynamics, found that roughly one-third of those who were poor one year were not poor the next and were not poor the year before. The number of poor was stable because the number coming into poverty and the number leaving just about equaled each other.[15]

The way that information about the number of elderly receiving institutional care was obtained provides another example of the importance of panel studies. Federal, state, and local administrators have faced an increasing burden of providing care for elderly Americans. Cross-sectional samples of older persons taken at various times had shown consistently that about 5 percent of people aged 65 and older were in a nursing home, hospital, or other long-term care facility. This often was interpreted to mean that any person 65 and older has only a 5 percent chance of being institutionalized. But researchers tracked a panel of individuals over several years and found that many people enter and leave long-term care facilities several times in their later years. At any moment, only 5 percent may be in long-term care facilities, hospitals, or nursing homes, but over a period of years at least 20 percent of the elderly will spend some time in one or more of these places.[16]

Another example of a large-scale panel study is the Framingham, Massachusetts, Heart Study. In this study a large number of residents of a town have been followed for 50 years or more.[17] The study's physician researchers have identified the major risk factors for heart disease. The information from this study is being used to issue advice about diet, exercise, and other factors related to health conditions.

A major problem of panels is in obtaining an initial representative sample of respondents willing to be interviewed at set intervals over an extended time. Panel members also may drop out of the study for one reason or another. This is called panel attrition or experimental mortality, a concept we discuss in Chapter 3. Another difficulty of panel studies is that when people are the cases, the repeated interviews and observations may influence their behavior. When interviewed repeatedly over a period of months or years, people may change the way they answer questions in order to be consistent from one time to the next.[18]

When we follow groups of cases, we often refer to them as *cohorts*. A cohort consists of cases having experienced the same significant event in a specific time period. They may be individuals, organizations, or some other unit of analysis.[19] The event that most often defines a cohort is birth; the term "cohort" usually refers to birth cohort—those cases born or created in a specific year or period. However, cohorts also may be defined in terms of the year of occurrence or exposure to any event such as the year graduated from college or having fought in a particular war. In a panel study, investigators obtain information on the same individuals each time. But a study using cohorts may be conducted in any number of ways. A different sample may be taken from the cohort group each time data are gathered. Remember that a panel design may use cohorts, but not all cohort studies are panel studies.[20]

QUALITATIVE RESEARCH AND DESIGNS TO FILL IN THE DETAILS

The designs described above are used to obtain information on a standard set of items for a large number of cases, as with cross-sectional studies, or information on a single case for many time periods, as with time series. These designs are not useful for obtaining detailed information about the context in which events or behaviors occur, nor do they allow flexibility in the type of data obtained from case to case in the same study. Other approaches used to obtain this type of information are more qualitative and less quantitative in nature. Qualitative research methods have long been important in basic disciplines as well as in applied areas such as administration. Studies using a qualitative research approach typically obtain more in-depth, detailed information on fewer cases than do studies using more quantitative designs. Two important qualitative designs, described below, are the case study and the focus group.

Qualitative Research

Qualitative research methods have received more attention in recent years from both practitioners and researchers.[21] Qualitative research produces verbal data difficult or impossible to convert to numbers. Researchers may draw on both quantitative and qualitative methods in conducting any one study. The qualitative study is defined by its extensive use of verbal information, its preference for developing full information on relatively few cases, and its consideration of the unique features of each case.

Quantitative studies typically involve many cases and many variables that are measured in a predetermined and specific way. The data are numeric and can be summarized numerically. Since an important goal of quantitative studies is to compare cases on different variables, factors unique to individual cases are not included and information about context is often ignored.

Qualitative studies, on the other hand, may include information on the unique features and the environment of each case. Qualitative studies describe specific features of each individual, organization, jurisdiction, or program. Typically, the researcher studies few cases and obtains extensive information on each case and its setting. Qualitative studies may involve extensive fieldwork; the researcher goes to where the cases are located and obtains information on them in their natural setting.[22] In this way the researcher does not attempt to manipulate any aspect of the situation being studied but takes it as it is. Nevertheless, the qualitative researcher's background and personality influence data collection and interpretation. Qualitative studies are often conducted by researchers who are participants or close observers of the phenomena studied. Such researchers are more likely to have the knowledge and interest to design and conduct a sound qualitative study. The researchers use their experiences and insights to design a study and to interpret the findings. A researcher's interactions with subjects affect what he is told and what information he is given.

In qualitative studies the researcher usually works with a flexible design. Although the studies may have a clearly defined methodology and plan of action, the researcher usually has great flexibility. He may alter the design as the research progresses. Typically, he uses several sources of information. Multiple sources give a fuller picture of a case and its setting and help to verify other information.

Researchers using qualitative techniques need different skills than those using quantitative designs. An interviewer in a quantitative study receives a list of questions that she asks every respondent. All other interviewers would use the same set of questions and ask them in the same way. In a qualitative study, the interviewer may have a suggested set of questions but asks them as the situation dictates. Based on the response to one question, the interviewer asks another question; the researcher needs to ask the question, listen, interpret, and phrase a proper follow-up question.[23]

The researcher using qualitative methods must be able to record information accurately, write clearly, divide trivial from important details, and draw appropriate conclusions from the information. Since data from qualitative studies tend to be descriptions, observations, and responses to interview questions, a great deal of information is obtained. To make sense out of it may be difficult. Rather than doing statistical analysis of numerical data as in quantitative studies, the researcher looks for themes and concepts in the analysis of qualitative data.

CASE STUDIES

Case studies are studies that examine in some depth persons, decisions, programs, or other entities that have a unique characteristic of interest. For example, a case study may be designed to study women in nontraditional jobs, a new approach to budgeting by a government agency, or a high school health clinic.

Except for studies that involve a single case within an administrator's jurisdiction, administrators seldom initiate or participate in the design of case studies. Even the single case study may be a by-product of someone else's research needs. For example, some state and local administrators seek out university students to conduct case studies. The studies give the students a "real world" experience, and the administrators learn more about their agency and its programs.

Case studies are the preferred research strategy if one wants to learn the details about how something happened and why it may have happened. Administrators may want a case study to investigate:

A program or a policy that has had remarkable success

Programs or policies that have unique or ambiguous outcomes

Situations where actors' behavior is discretionary

The case must be contemporary and the investigator must have direct access to the people involved. Analysts implementing cross-sectional or time-series designs may never contact program administrators, employees, or clients. An investigator conducting a case study cannot be so detached.

One of the hallmarks of a case study is the combination of several different sources of information. The sources of information used in case studies include documents, archival information, interviews, direct observation, participant observation, and physical artifacts.

The inclusion of information from multiple sources is a major strength of case studies. First, each data-collection strategy affects the types of questions a researcher can answer. For example, from direct observation an investigator learns how people behave. From interviews he hears their explanations of their behavior. The two sources of information give a more complete picture than either piece alone.

Second, the investigator can corroborate information gained from one source with information gathered from another source. For example, staff in a crisis intervention center may report a high level of community support. The claim will have greater credibility if an independent review of agency records confirms extensive community support.

Requiring information from multiple sources also is a drawback of case studies. Typically, different information sources are studied using different research techniques. For example, interviewing skills are needed for face-to-face meetings with subjects, survey research skills are needed to use mail questionnaires, content analysis skills are needed for archival research. Most of us are skilled in only one or two research techniques. Thus a case study may require a larger research team or suffer from unevenness. We suspect that administrators find that they and their staff lack both the training and time needed to do effective case studies.

Each research technique and data collection strategy takes time to design, pretest, and carry out. Incorporating multiple data sources, employing different techniques and possibly multiple researchers, is demanding of time, expertise, and energy. Consequently, researchers who conduct case studies often find that studying multiple cases is impractical because of the effort required.

Case studies may be conducted on a single case or on a set of similar cases. The case study may focus on the case as a whole or on its components. For example, to study a pretrial release program, the investigator may look at the program as a whole: why it was developed, how it was initially organized, what changes it has made, why those changes were made, how defendants are chosen for pretrial release, and how much discretion staff and judges have in making pretrial-release recommendations. Alternatively, the investigator may focus on released defendants: their ages, ties to the community, criminal records, and their compliance with the terms of pretrial release.

Most administrative case studies seem to focus on case components. In program evaluations the broad research question of how effective the program is may be displaced by the more immediate need to know what was accomplished. For example, in a study of a pretrial release program, "successful" defendants, who showed up for scheduled court appearances, were compared with "unsuccessful" defendants, who failed to appear. The study did not look for broader evidence of effectiveness, such as whether released defendants stayed at work or school or whether they pursued criminal activities. Nor did the study try to link the information on released defendants with characteristics of the program as a whole.

Frequently, a case study ends with the collection and reporting of the data. Limiting a case study to an analysis of individual components eliminates the strength of case studies—the value of bringing together diverse pieces of information to explain why and how things happened. The failure to refocus on the case as a whole may appear to be unfortunate, but administrators can fill in the "missing information" with their own knowledge and from informal discussions. The researcher with limited knowledge of the organization and limited resources may not contribute much new information or insight. The researcher who works within the organization may reflect the organization's biases.

Practically speaking, administrators' direct experience with case studies may be limited to their professional reading. Both administrators and researchers may correctly consider the analysis of the components within a single case as time-series or cross-sectional studies.

Because of the potential value of case studies, you may want more information about them. They provide rich details. If you read a case study, you may gain greater insight into how to approach or solve a problem. Case studies may alert you to new management techniques, programs to solve chronic problems, or strategies to improve the quality of agency or community life. If the case study is well done, you should have a good idea of whether you could implement a similar solution. Even if the case study documents a failure or is otherwise inappropriate, it may spur you to think more about your work environment and responsibilities. A creative administrator may read a case study, contact the researcher or program administrator to learn more details, and implement a new program or strategy.

One author, Robert Yin, carefully distinguishes between the case study as a type of design on the one hand and the data collection typically conducted in a case study on the other.[24] He also implies that most people incorrectly assume that any qualitative study is a case study. Although case studies tend to be qualitative, Yin recommends an approach for case studies that follows the scientific method. This approach has the researcher stating a problem; formulating a research question, objective, or hypothesis; identifying the case to be studied; planning the data collection; collecting the data; analyzing the data; and writing a report.

You may wonder if a particular case study is any more than a good story.[25] Sometimes it may not be. The study is as good as the objectivity and training of the investigators. In some disciplines, particularly anthropology, researchers are trained extensively in case-study and qualitative methods. The researcher learns to state the research question and to formulate hypotheses. Without initial hypotheses he may become entangled in the idiosyncrasies of the case. The investigator conducting an exploratory study appropriately may decide to forgo formulating initial hypotheses. Instead, he will develop hypotheses from the case study once it is completed and draw generalizations from later studies.

Once the hypotheses are stated, the investigators decide what evidence to gather. At the same time, they establish specific criteria on how to interpret the evidence. Case-study researchers tend to work with qualitative evidence or limited quantitative data. Thus they need to be particularly careful to follow sound research practice and to specify the criteria for deciding whether data support a hypothesis before collecting the data. Otherwise, the natural wish of researchers to have the data support their hypotheses may bias their interpretation of the evidence.

As part of the design, the researcher must decide what constitutes a case. Doing so may not be easy.[26] Deciding on what is the case to be studied, for example, may be a problem if the case involves a program. Consider an agency program to aid abused children. The agency may have a program for abused children specifically, but it may also have services for abused mothers and for families with a potential for abuse. Should these services be included? The program may have evolved from an earlier program. At what point should the case start? Should the case study include the board of directors, clients, or others in the community? The investigator must answer these questions in order to limit, or set boundaries around, the case study. An inappropriately defined case can be as distorting as a case without predetermined criteria for judging whether a hypothesis is supported.

As an administrator you may want to determine the quality of the design so that you can convince yourself that you are reading more than just a good story. First, you should look for evidence that the investigator had a model before starting the study. Second, you want to know that the investigator decided exactly what were the boundaries of the case. Third, the case study's procedures from design through implementation should be documented thoroughly.

Case studies may involve the investigator intensely in the case and usually require interpretation of qualitative information. Consequently, they are hard to replicate, and great care must be taken to document what was done, how, and why.

Focus Groups

Focus-group methods use group interviews to obtain qualitative data. Researchers have long used group interviews to save time and money by getting a number of people together to provide information.[27] Focus-group procedures have evolved in recent years and include a set of characteristics that distinguish them from other group techniques. Although focus-group research is qualitative, often it is used in conjunction with more quantitative procedures. Survey researchers use focus groups to generate and test the items to be used on a questionnaire or survey instrument. Focus groups also are used to elaborate on data collected in surveys.

Focus groups are semi-structured discussions by small groups of participants about a common topic or experience.[28] They are useful in obtaining information that is difficult to obtain with other methods. A focus-group interview is used to get in-depth information and reactions to a relatively small number of topics or questions, rather than to get answers to a large number of questions. Typically focus-group interviews include fewer than 10 questions and often around five or six.

A study using focus groups usually includes several group interviews. Each group is relatively homogeneous with respect to background characteristics of the participants. The homogeneity helps to ensure that individuals will not be afraid to express their feelings about the issue at hand.[29] What distinguishes focus groups is the presence of group interaction in response to researchers' questions.

The focus-group discussion is led by a moderator who should be an experienced interviewer and who is skilled at group facilitation. The moderator also needs to be familiar with the questions and the purpose of the study. The moderator asks the questions and guides the discussion to ensure that all members of the group participate. The hallmark of focus groups is the explicit use of group interaction to produce data and insights that would be less accessible otherwise.

David Morgan emphasizes the fact that focus groups constitute a research method.[30] Not every group using discussion techniques is a focus group, however. Focus groups have specific defining characteristics; they are created by research teams for well-defined purposes. Focus groups rely on the strengths of qualitative methods, including exploration and discovery; understanding things in depth and in context; and interpreting why things are the way they are and how they got that way. To serve these purposes, focus groups, like other qualitative methods, require a great deal of openness and flexibility.[31]

Although the overall process of focus-group research usually is highly structured, the interviewing must be flexible. The information obtained is qualitative and usually voluminous. The researcher must identify themes, find answers to questions, and summarize the discussion of the group members. Having well-designed questions based on a clearly defined purpose will facilitate the analysis and use of the data. Careful planning should be done prior to assembling the group or groups and the interviewing. Clarifying the purpose of the study and discussing it with colleagues are important. The researcher should be clear about what information is needed, why, who will use it, and how. A written plan, including a schedule and budget, for the entire project should be developed in advance.

Focus groups are used in the public sector in many ways. A manager may find focus groups useful for needs assessments—to identify the services clients need, where they are best delivered, which are not appropriate, and to develop a better understanding of concerns as perceived by relevant participants. A public organization might use focus groups to address such questions as: What are the most important problems of the jurisdiction as perceived by various citizen groups? Why?[32]

Focus groups aid in program design and planning where the objective is to develop ways to deal with a problem or situation. What are the possibilities for dealing with a problem? What options are feasible? How would they be received by the client group? Focus groups can be used to evaluate existing programs and to answer such questions as: How well is a program working? Are clients dissatisfied? Why? What changes will be acceptable? How well do clients think that they would respond to a change if one were instituted? As these situations suggest, the manager would probably want to get more explanation and discussion concerning responses to questions than generally would be possible in a large-scale survey.

The current literature shows how focus groups can be used in applied research projects, such as program evaluation and program development, as well as in qualitative academic research. David Morgan and Richard Krueger say that focus groups are appropriate when the goal is to generate theories or explanations. They also suggest that focus groups are appropriate when the research topic involves understanding the success or failure of a particular program in a specific setting, when those with positions of power and influence wish to gain feedback from those without power, when investigating complex motivations and behaviors, and when wishing to learn more about the degree of consensus on a topic.[33] The focus-group technique can be used as exploratory research in a new topic area, in generating hypotheses to guide the development of structured questionnaires or other research methods, in discovering perspectives and feelings of various groups, in understanding reasons for behaviors or attitudes, and in interpreting previously obtained quantitative results. Focus groups have been used with citizens to assess the quality of city services and to identify priorities for future activities; with groups of clients of anti-poverty programs to assess current services and explore the types of programs that are most effective; with top-level city administrators to obtain input to a planned survey of citizens; with employees to find out about and improve their working environment.[34] Although focus groups often are used in exploratory studies and as adjuncts to other forms of research, they can be used as the major procedure without being supplemented by quantitative methods.

T. Plaut, S. Landis, and J. Trevor report using focus groups for needs assessment and program planning in a rural county of North Carolina. Administrators and researchers chose focus groups as a non-threatening way to obtain perceptions of health, health-related behaviors, and service delivery in the county. The researchers were advised specifically not to use surveys: "These people have been surveyed to death. They're tired of being asked if they are poor."[35]

The county was fragmented by its geography, numerous neighborhoods, and variety of agencies and schools. Researchers conducted 40 focus groups ranging in size from 3 to 37 individuals, greatly exceeding the optimal size of 4 to 12 usually recommended.[36] The sessions were not recorded. A two-person team of facilitators conducted the sessions with one team member moderating and the other taking notes. The focus groups provided important data and also involved residents in the project and helped legitimize the project and its interventions. Members of the groups were asked six questions addressing health problems and potential solutions. Participants were also given a copy of the questions to provide an opportunity for a written and private response. This proved to be useful. The focus-group data were combined with statistics on disease rates; mortality; causes of death and injuries; and with demographic, economic, and social data supplied by state and federal agencies to plan new services and to improve existing services and facilities. Cultural differences among residents and differences in values between the more traditional, long-time residents and the younger health-care professionals were identified in the process.

The use of focus groups has expanded and evolved extensively in the past decade. A large body of literature on how to use focus groups is now available. Some of the practices recommended only a few years ago have changed. For example, the older requirement of having 10 to 12 in a group is no longer important. Practitioners have found that smaller groups work well and offer several advantages. The use of tape recorders to obtain a complete record of the discussion is not considered to be as crucial as it once was.[37] As with other promising research techniques, both quantitative and qualitative, focus-group methods have developed considerably and will continue to be refined.

META-ANALYSIS

Meta-analysis is a systematic technique to locate, retrieve, review, summarize, and analyze a set of existing quantitative studies.[38] Researchers conduct meta-analysis to: draw general conclusions from several empirical studies on a given program or policy; develop support for hypotheses that merit further testing; and identify characteristics of a program, its environment, or its clients that are associated with effectiveness.

Imagine that you want to learn if early childhood education programs for disadvantaged children, such as Head Start, are successful. You probably will begin by reviewing the literature. Assume that you find 10 recent research articles examining the effectiveness of different programs. You identify similar and dissimilar findings among these studies. As you classify the findings, you may compare program clients, note how cases were chosen for analysis, note how program success is defined and measured, and record any unique features in the program or the research. If the findings are dissimilar, you may look for an explanation as to why they differ. Differences in program features or in the conduct of research may account for dissimilar findings. If the findings are similar you may ask whether the program would seem as effective if the research methodology was different. Or you may question whether the program would be as effective with other groups or in other locations.

Proponents of meta-analysis argue that reviews of literature are ineffective for arriving at conclusions about research results such as the effectiveness of Head Start. A researcher cannot summarize a large number of studies effectively, much less integrate them. If a subset of studies is selected for closer analysis, the reviewer's selection of studies may be colored by his own biases. Meta-analysis, on the other hand, enables investigators to review a large body of literature and to integrate its findings. In reviewing even 10 studies, the researcher may be unable to avoid inconsistent judgments. He may focus on sampling problems in one study and errors in data analysis in another.[39] Conversely, meta-analysis requires the researcher to focus on the same specific components of every study analyzed. If you read a description of a meta-analysis, you should be able to repeat the researchers' steps and to come to the same conclusions. Unlike literature reviews, meta-analysis uses quantitative procedures in synthesizing the results of several studies.[40]

In conducting a meta-analysis, investigators record the same information from each study. Their goal is to identify hypotheses that are supported in study after study. In doing this they have to eliminate alternative explanations, such as chance, which may account for the observed relationships. The analysts record the statistical information reported on the dependent variables of interest and the statistical relationships between independent and dependent variables. They also record information on the study itself, such as: the dates of data collection and of publication; who the research subjects were; how they were selected; the research design; evidence that research involved sound measures; and the type of publication, for example, a book, an academic journal, or an unpublished paper.

Once the data are collected, the investigators integrate the findings to create one database. To clarify the meaning of "integrating the findings," we consider two examples. In one meta-analysis, analysts examined 261 citizen surveys. They identified survey questions that asked people to rate specific urban services such as trash collection, and they categorized the questions by the type of service being rated. Neither the question wording nor the possible responses were identical. The analysts ignored variations in question wording and created a common scale so that responses to similar questions from different cities could be combined. After the data were combined, the investigators observed that citizens in cities throughout the United States gave the highest ratings to arts programs and public safety and the lowest ratings to planning.[41]

Integrating study findings goes beyond quantifying specific dependent variables. The second meta-analysis examined studies on survey response rates. Analysts also identify relevant independent variables and incorporate them into a common database. Survey researchers have designed studies to evaluate strategies to improve the response rate for mail surveys. Analysts identified 115 such studies published between 1940 and 1987, which had response rate as the dependent variable. The analysts identified 17 independent variables. Each of these variables had been tested in at least three studies. After detailed analysis, the investigators identified two factors that increased response rate to mail surveys, including a cover letter with an appeal to respond and keeping a questionnaire short (under five pages).[42]

The information on a study's characteristics allows analysts to identify the impact of research strategies. A researcher may be skeptical if a hypothesis is supported only in poor-quality studies. On the other hand, findings may have even greater credibility if a hypothesis is supported no matter what the quality of a study's methodology. Information on the dates of data gathering and publication help identify trends and changes in them. For example, the investigators in the response-rate study found that beginning in the mid-1970s, preliminary notification of subjects improved response rate.

A major problem in meta-analysis is locating a set of studies. At a minimum the topic must have been of interest long enough for a research history to develop. Little or no research may exist on a current, "hot" research topic. The researcher conducting a meta-analysis wants to include all appropriate studies or a representative sample of such studies in his analysis. Consequently, he must do a relatively exhaustive literature search. If he selects articles from a few journals or from a short time period, he runs the risk of working with a biased sample.

Each article selected does not have to include exactly the same dependent variables nor study the same relationships. Of the 261 cities whose citizen surveys were analyzed, 70 percent rated their police. Fewer than 25 percent rated animal control or street lighting. The independent variables used in the response-rate study varied from study to study.

Critics of meta-analysis point to the problems introduced by biased article selection. Let's go back to our early childhood education example where 10 publications were studied. First, we mentioned the problem of bias, introduced if the studies analyzed do not represent the larger body of studies conducted on early childhood education. A critic may raise the related question of the "file drawer." The argument goes as follows. If many studies of a subject are done, chance alone will cause some hypotheses to be supported and the research reporting them to be published. Analysts who only include published studies may have a biased sample because many other unpublished studies on the same topic may be stashed in researchers' file drawers. Researchers put studies aside when preliminary data fail to support the hypotheses, and the study seems to be going nowhere. A statistical solution to this problem requires the analyst to calculate how many unpublished papers have to exist for the findings to be contradicted.[43]

Another criticism of meta-analysis has been termed the "apples and oranges" problem. The critics argue against combining dissimilar studies. Consider the citizen-survey data in which findings based on different question wording and different response patterns were grouped together to create a variable. Glass, a major proponent of meta-analysis, argues that these critics want replication of research not comparison of similar findings. Meta-analysis is intended to mine information from related, but not identical, studies. Furthermore, he argues that combining different studies is not much different from combining responses from different subjects.[44]

Meta-analysis may seem deceptively simple. Yet it is time consuming to identify the appropriate studies and to conduct the data analysis. Understanding the quantitative procedures used to synthesize results requires statistical knowledge. Readers who wish to try their hand at meta-analysis should be familiar with the statistics discussed in this text, particularly in Chapters 12, 13, and 14. Then they should review one or more of the books included at the end of the reference section for this chapter. They should read several meta-analysis studies for examples. We believe that the use of meta-analysis will increase. Given the amount of research literature available and the difficulty and expense of researching some topics, a good meta-analysis may be a very efficient alternative to original research.

SUMMARY

In this chapter we have discussed designs that guide studies describing the occurrence of a variable or the relationship between variables. These designs help a researcher to decide when to make observations and how many observations to make. Administrators may rarely be conscious of these designs, but they are implied in administrators' questions:

What evidence do you have that the program worked?

Do areas where a policy has been implemented see better results than other communities?

Has productivity improved since the program was implemented?

What has been the pattern of usage over the past few years?

What characteristics are associated with success?

The designs help to answer these questions. An administrator may unconsciously apply one of these designs when analyzing a dataset. The design selected may depend on the nature of the dataset or the problem-solving skills of the administrator.

Time-series and cross-sectional designs are particularly effective and efficient designs. Either singly or in combination with each other, they provide valuable information to administrators, legislators, and the public. The data derived from both designs may be organized to communicate information quickly through graphs or tables.

Cross-sectional designs show relationships among variables of interest at one point in time. Cross-sectional designs often call for the collection of many pieces of data. Innumerable investigators may access, manipulate, and analyze the resulting database according to their individual interests.

Longitudinal designs measure variables at two or more time periods and can be used to measure changes in the variables over time. Two longitudinal designs, the time series and the panel, were discussed.

Time-series designs demonstrate long-term, cyclical, and seasonal trends in the occurrence of a variable. A time-series design requires an investigator to collect data on a measure at regular intervals. To interpret irregular fluctuations, a historical record of events that can affect the occurrence of the variable is needed. Time-series designs help a researcher to describe a variable over time. They are used extensively to forecast changes in a variable. For example, forecasting the crime rate can help the courts anticipate their caseloads.

In the panel study, investigators follow individual cases and obtain information on them for several time periods. This design allows investigators to measure the changes taking place within a group as well as to measure the change in a group characteristic over time.

Several qualitative approaches provide useful information for administrators. Case studies provide detail that shows how something happened and why it happened. Case studies usually include information on the natural surroundings of events. One of the strengths of case studies is that they can involve multiple sources of data. Because of the requirement for multiple data sources, we suspect that most administrators and their staff have neither the time nor resources to conduct case studies.

Nevertheless, administrators may be interested in case-study findings and how to use them if a particular case study turns out to be more than just a good story. To determine the quality of a case study, the administrator looks for evidence that the investigator had a model before collecting data, that the case was clearly defined—which can at times be difficult, and that case-study procedures were documented thoroughly.

Focus-group interviewing is used to obtain detailed information from a small group of individuals. A moderator asks a well-developed set of questions and leads the discussion in the focus group. The responses of the participants to the questions and to each other's comments provide data difficult to obtain with other methods. Focus groups often are used to supplement more quantitative studies, such as those using cross-sectional designs, and have many uses in the public sector.

Meta-analysis allows researchers to assemble a set of similar studies, use their data to form a single dataset, and determine what, if any, general hypotheses have been supported consistently. The major difficulty in performing meta-analysis is to identify a representative set of studies. It behooves the researcher to search through many sources to identify appropriate published and unpublished research. The conclusions reached through meta-analysis require thorough statistical analysis in order to provide evidence either supporting a hypothesis or arguing that it could have occurred by chance.

NOTES

1. The issue of causality in cross-sectional and time-series designs is discussed briefly in Chapters 3 and 14, and further references are cited. Robert K. Yin discusses using case studies to infer causality in *Applications of Case Study Research* (Newbury Park, CA: Sage, 1993) and in *Case Study Research: Design and Methods,* 2d ed., (Thousand Oaks, CA: Sage, 1994).

2. M. Specter, "Suicide Rate of Jail Inmates Rising Sharply," *Washington Post,* February 18, 1985, A–1, 18.

3. Earl Babbie, *The Practice of Social Research,* 9th ed. (Belmont, CA, 2001), 417–430.

4. A classic work on this topic is Hubert Blalock, Jr., *Causal Inferences in Nonexperimental Research* (Chapel Hill: University of North Carolina Press, 1964.) Also see Herbert Asher, *Causal Modeling* (Beverly Hills, CA: Sage Series on Quantitative Applications in the Social Sciences, #3, 1976); and O. Hellevik, *Introduction to Causal Analysis: Exploring Survey Data by Crosstabulation* (London: Allen and Unwin, Contemporary Social Research Series, #9, 1984).

5. See C. P. Kaplan and T. L. Van Valey, *Census 80: Continuing the Pathfinder Tradition* (Washington, D.C.: U.S. Dept. of Census, 1980), 278–296; and R. E. Barrett, *Using the 1990 U.S. Census for Research* (Thousand Oaks, CA: Sage, 1994).

6. See J. C. Bailar III, "When Research Results are in Conflict," *New England Journal of Medicine,* October 24, 1985, 1080–1081. Summary of research results reported in "Studies Reach Opposite Conclusions About How Estrogen Pills Affect Heart." *Raleigh News and Observer,* October 24, 1985, 1A, 5A.

7. B. Braddy et al., "An Evaluation of CETA Adult Training Programs in North Carolina Division of Employment and Training" (Raleigh: Department of Political Science and Public Administration, May 1983). Unpublished manuscript.

8. Scott Menard, *Longitudinal Research* (Newbury Park, CA: Sage, 1991), 4.

9. M. S. Knapp, "Applying Time Series Strategies," *Improving Evaluations,* ed. by L. Datta and R. Perloff (Beverly Hills: Sage, 1979), 111–127.

10. Our purpose in presenting these time series is to illustrate different patterns of time series. Do not assume that we are trying to relate unemployment to the crime rate. A similar graph for the years 1960 through 1980 accompanied N. D. Kristol's article "Scholars Disagree on Connection between Crime and the Jobless," *Washington Post,* August 7, 1982, which discusses further the relationship between the two variables.

11. Wayne Daniel and James Terrell, *Business Statistics for Management and Economics,* 7th ed. (Boston: Houghton-Mifflin, 1995), 771–808; William F. Matlack,

Statistics for Public Managers (Itasca, IL: F.E. Peacock Publishers, Inc., 1993), 322.

12. This discussion integrates material from J. E. Hanke and A. G. Reitsch, *Business Forecasting* (Boston: Allyn and Bacon, 1981), chap. 6; R. S. Reichard, *The Numbers Game* (New York: McGraw-Hill, 1973), 123–130.

13. For further information on forecasting, see a management science text such as D. R. Anderson, D. J. Sweeney, and T. A. Williams, *Quantitative Methods for Business,* 5th ed. (St. Paul: West Publishing, 1992), chap. 6.

14. See the following for discussions of forecasting accessible to most students of public administration: Kenneth Meier and Jeffrey Brudney, *Applied Statistics for Public Administration,* 4th ed. (Fort Worth, TX: Harcourt Brace, 1997); W. F. Matlack, *Statistics for Public Managers* (Itasca, IL: F. E. Peacock, 1993).

An interesting and easy-to-understand example using regression analysis with a time series to forecast is given in T. H. Poister, *Public Program Analysis: Applied Research Methods* (Baltimore: University Park Press, 1978), 577–580. Time and season were used as independent variables to forecast ridership on Atlanta's transit system. Matlack, *Statistics,* 312–317 and Daniel and Terrel *Business Statistics, 777–781,* discuss several smoothing techniques, 777–781.

15. Julian Simon and Paul Burstein, *Basic Research Methods in Social Science,* 3d ed. (New York: Random House, 1985), 161–162.

16. Morton Hunt, *Profiles of Social Research* (New York: Russell Sage Foundation, 1985), 209.

17. Ibid., 242. Hunt briefly describes a number of large-scale panel studies. See pages 240–246. Also see David Brown, "Framingham Heart Study at 40," *Washington Post Health,* October 25, 1988, 12–16, for an interesting discussion of the study.

18. Robert F. Boruch and Robert W. Pearson discuss in detail the advantages and disadvantages of panel designs. See "Assessing the Quality of Longitudinal Surveys," *Evaluation Review* 12 (1988): 3–18.

19. Norvelle Glenn, *Cohort Analysis* (Beverly Hills: Sage, 1977), 8; Menard, *Longitudinal Research,* 8.

20. See Glenn, *Cohort Analysis,* for information on analyzing panel data.

21. For example, see M. Patton, *How To Use Qualitative Methods in Evaluation* (Newbury Park, CA: Sage, 1987); and P. Haas and J. Springer, *Case Studies in Applied Policy Research* (New York, Garland Publishing, 1996).

22. J. Creswell, *Research Design: Qualitative and Quantitative Approaches* (Thousand Oaks, CA: Sage, 1994), 145.

23. S. Caudle, "Using Qualitative Approaches," in J. Wholey, H. Hatry, and K. Newcomer, eds., *Handbook of*

Practical Program Evaluation (San Francisco: Jossey-Bass, 1994), 69–95. Also see H. Rubin and I. Rubin, *Qualitative Interviewing: The Art of Hearing Data* (Thousand Oaks, CA: Sage, 1995).

24. Robert K. Yin, *Applications of Case Study Research* (Newbury Park, CA: Sage, 1993) 32–33.

25. For a view of how managers obtain knowledge through the use of stories, see Ralph P. Hummel, "Stories Managers Tell: Why They Are As Valid As Science," *Public Administration Review,* Vol. 51 (January/February, 1991), 31–41.

26. See Charles C. Ragin and Howard S. Becker. *What Is a Case?: Exploring the Foundations of Social Inquiry.* (Cambridge, England: Cambridge University Press, 1992).

27. Robert K. Merton. "The Focused Interview and Focus Groups," *Public Opinion Quarterly 51* (1987), 550–566. R. K. Merton, M. Fiske, and P. Kendall, *The Focused Interview,* 2d ed. (Glencoe, IL: The Free Press, 1990). Richard A. Kreuger, *Focus Groups: A Practical Guide for Applied Research,* 2d ed. (Thousand Oaks, CA: Sage, 1994), 7–15.

28. Ralph Hambrick, Jr., and James McMillan, "Using Focus Groups in the Public Sector," *Journal of Management Science and Policy Analysis 6* (Summer 1989), 44.

29. Ibid., 48.

30. David Morgan, *The Focus Group Guidebook* (Thousand Oaks, CA: Sage, 1997), 29.

31. Ibid., 31.

32. Hambrick and McMillan, "Using Focus Groups in the Public Sector," 44–45.

33. David Morgan and Richard Krueger, "When to Use Focus Groups and Why," in Morgan, ed., *Successful Focus Groups: Advancing the State of the Art* (Newbury Park, CA: Sage, 1993), 3–19. Also see Debra L. Dean, "How To Use Focus Groups," in J. S. Wholey, H. Hatry, and K. Newcomer, eds., *Handbook of Practical Program Evaluation* (San Francisco: Jossey-Bass, 1994), 341.

34. These and other examples cited in Hambrick and McMillan, "Using Focus Groups in the Public Sec-

tor," 46–47. Also see Christopher McKenna, "Using Focus Groups to Study Library Utilization," *Journal of Management Science and Policy Analysis 7* (Summer 1990), 316–329.

35. T. Plaut, S. Landis, and J. Trevor, "Focus Groups and Community Mobilization: A Case Study from Rural North Carolina," in Morgan, *Successful Focus Groups: Advancing the State of the Art* (Newbury Park, CA: Sage, 1993), 205.

36. Ibid., 206.

37. Richard A. Kreuger, *Focus Groups: A Practical Guide for Applied Research,* 2d ed. (Thousand Oaks, CA: Sage, 1994), ix.

38. D. Cordray and R. Fischer, "Synthesizing Evaluation Findings," in Wholey, Hatry, and Newcomer, *Handbook of Practical Program Evaluation,* 202.

39. For more details on the limitations of traditional reviews of the literature, see F. M. Wolf, *Meta-Analysis: Quantitative Methods for Research Synthesis* (Beverly Hills: Sage Publications, *Quantitative Applications in the Social Sciences,* no. 59, 1986), 10–11, and J. E. Hunter, F. L. Schmidt, and G. B. Jackson, *Meta-Analysis: Cumulating Research Findings Across Studies* (Beverly Hills: Sage Publications; *Studying Organizations: Innovations in Methodology Series,* no. 4, 1981), 129–130.

40. D. Cordray and R. Fischer, "Synthesizing Evaluation Findings," in Wholey, Hatry, and Newcomer, *Handbook of Practical Program Evaluation,* 200–206.

41. T. I. Miller and M. A. Miller, "Standards of Excellence: U.S. Residents' Evaluations of Local Government Services," *Public Administration Review* (November/December 1991), 503–514.

42. F. J. Yammarino, S. J. Skinner, T. L. Childers, "A Meta-Analysis of Mail Surveys," *Public Opinion Quarterly* (Winter 1991), 613–639.

43. R. Rosenthal, *Judgment Studies: Design, Analysis, and Meta-Analysis* (New York: Cambridge University Press, 1987), 223–225.

44. G. V. Glass, B. McGaw, and M. L. Smith, *Meta-Analysis in Social Research* (Beverly Hills: Sage, 1981), 220.

TERMS FOR REVIEW

research methodology	cyclical variations	panel design
research designs	seasonal variations	cohort
cross-sectional design	random variations	case study
longitudinal design	nonrandom variations	focus group
time-series designs	quantitative studies	meta-analysis
long-term trends	qualitative studies	

QUESTIONS FOR REVIEW

The following questions should indicate whether you have a basic competency in this chapter's material.

1. What is the value of a research design?

2. (a) List the advantages and disadvantages of cross-sectional, time series, and case studies. (b) When should an investigator use a panel design instead of a time-series design? (c) Under what conditions would a focus group be the best method to use?

3. Select one of the following topics: automobile accidents, water quality, drug abuse, health clinics in high schools, single-parent families, management information systems, personnel training, total quality management, or downsizing. For the selected topic, describe a research question appropriate to a cross-sectional design, a panel design, a time-series design, a case study, a focus group. If you like, also describe a setting or situation in which the research question would be investigated.

4. Update the data in Figure 2.1 using the Statistical Abstract of the United States or an on-line data source. Draw a graph to show the time series as in Figure 2.1.

5. Data have been collected annually on air quality in Smokey for the past 15 years. Explain why the data can be analyzed using a time-series design. What types of trends or variations should a researcher look for? How might a researcher distinguish random variations from nonrandom variations?

6. The Metro Hospital collected data on nurses every three years from 1975 to 1984. Beginning with 1986, the data were collected every year. What limitations would an analyst encounter in studying nursing trends from 1975 to the present?

7. Explain why public agencies are unlikely to conduct case studies.

8. Distinguish between units and components in conducting a case study.

9. For one of the topics in Question 3, generate a list of questions that might be asked of members of a focus group.

10. Why might government agencies use focus groups more now than in the past? What objections might managers have to the use of focus groups?

11. Compare literature reviews to meta-analyses, and discuss why researchers would invest time in conducting a meta-analysis instead of original research.

PROBLEMS FOR HOMEWORK AND DISCUSSION

1. For each of the following studies: identify the variables; state the implied hypothesis(es); identify the research design, and briefly evaluate its appropriateness. (Note: A study may modify a common design or combine features from more than one design.)

   a. A random audit of Unemployment Insurance (UI) sampled eight UI payments per week. If a payment error was found, auditors determined the dollar amount and classified the error by type, source, and cause. Errors were categorized as: overpayment with fraud, overpayment without fraud, or underpayment. Sources of errors were the claimant, employer, or agency. Causes were identified by law or regulation violation.

   b. To evaluate the effectiveness of Head Start, an early-education program, children who had been in Head Start and who were in the first through third grades were given cognitive tests.

   c. Before the adoption of the Magnuson-Moss Warranty Act, the Federal Trade Commission collected data from 4,300 respondents who had purchased a major durable good the previous year. Each respondent rated the performance and servicing of products purchased during the year. The 4,300 members of the sample were randomly selected from a national consumer mail panel. To evaluate the Act, the Commission later asked 8,000 respondents drawn from the same national consumer mail panel the same questions.

d. To develop a statistical base on private foundations, data were gathered from tax records on selected foundations' resources and expenses in 1974, 1984, 1987, and annually beginning in 1989.

e. To assess training needs and how the government could work best with a private agency to meet them, the private agency invited two groups of its clients to participate in discussions led by a moderator from the nearby university.

2. The following figures report the percent of high school seniors who have smoked in the previous 30 days.

Year	Percent of High School Seniors Who Have Smoked
1976	38.8
1977	38.4
1978	36.7
1979	34.4
1980	30.5
1981	29.4
1982	30.0
1983	30.3
1984	29.3
1985	30.1
1986	29.6
1987	29.4
1988	28.7
1989	28.6
1990	29.4
1991	28.3
1992	27.8
1993	29.9
1994	31.2
1995	33.5
1996	34.0
1997	36.5
1998	35.1

Draw a graph to illustrate this trend over time. Comment on the variations found in this dataset. What policy recommendations can be made based on these data? (Data from Institute for Social Research, University of Michigan, Monitoring the Future Project. Website accessed on November 16, 2001.)

3. An administrator for a state employment commission wants to study seasonal variations in the unemployment rate so she can schedule staff vacations and conferences at times when the demand for services (as measured by the unemployment rate) is lowest. The data are shown in Table 2.3.

a. Graph the data.

b. Comment on any trends you notice in these data.

c. What times of year would you prefer for staff vacations and conferences?

4. For each of the following problems, suggest a research design and justify your choice:

a. Identify revenues generated by a county sales tax first adopted in 1966 and increased periodically since then.

b. Learn whether change in state penalties for drunk driving was associated with fewer drinking-related traffic fatalities.

c. Identify what computer hardware and software are used by local governments and how the governments use them.

d. See whether consolidating purchasing by Middletown decreased costs of buying supplies.

e. See whether agency managers who attended a decision-making seminar used the skills taught.

TABLE 2.3 UNEMPLOYMENT RATE (YR.=YEAR)

	Oct.	Nov.	Dec.	Jan.	Feb.	Mar.	Apr.	May	Jun.	Jul.	Aug.	Sep.
Yr. 1	6.8	5.5	5.0	6.4	6.3	6.4	5.4	6.7	6.4	6.5	6.7	8.1
Yr. 2	7.9	7.5	7.3	7.7	7.1	8.6	7.9	7.3	7.7	7.5	7.8	8.2
Yr. 3	9.2	9.5	9.5	10.4	9.5	8.9	8.4	8.7	8.8	8.2	8.2	8.1
Yr. 4	8.6	8.1	7.5	7.4	6.1	5.4	5.7	6.1	6.6	6.8	6.2	6.2

f. Determine whether police personnel involved in a wellness program took fewer sick days and had fewer claims against the department's health insurance plan after enrolling in the wellness program.

5. A state has 10 high school health clinics. These clinics have been opened within the last four years to serve the physical and mental health needs of high school students. Some of the clinics are located within a high school, and others are within a block of the school. The state Department of Education has decided to do a case study of these clinics to evaluate their performance and to see whether similar clinics should be established throughout the state. (In answering the following questions you may make your own assumptions to fill in specific details about the clinics.)

   a. Identify the units and components that could be the subjects of the case study. What information would you want on the units? on the components?

   b. List possible data sources you would use. Indicate the type of information you would want from each data source.

   c. Write a memorandum discussing why a case study would be a valuable research strategy.

6. Look at Example 1.2 in Chapter 1. Assume that you are a management analyst in the department administering the job training program. Write a memorandum to the program manager outlining what actions you would recommend based on these data. Remember that conducting further research can be a recommended action.

7. Locate a study or article that you would classify as a meta-analysis, and attempt to answer the following questions concerning it. What was the topic? How many studies were reviewed? Was a specific hypothesis investigated in the meta-analysis? What did the authors of the meta-analysis conclude from the study?

DISK WORK

1. Load the Belle County data base from the data disk. Analyze the data to see how use of public schools, financial aid services, and environmental regulations vary by income group. Report your findings in a table similar to Table 2.2. To simplifying your task you may want to combine income categories to create four income groups. Write a paragraph summarizing your findings.

2. Cross-sectional data can be reported in tables showing differences in percents or means. Go to the disk and load the Belle County data base. From the income variable, create three categories of income, for example, high, medium, and low.

   a. For each income category, calculate the mean values for the perceived importance of (1) public schools, (2) financial aid services, and (3) environmental regulations. Do the data show that the importance ratings vary by income? What evidence supports your observations? Write a paragraph reporting your findings.

   b. Categorize the variables measuring the perceived importance of public schools, financial aid services, and environmental reg-

   ulation into a high and a low category for each variable. For each of the three income categories, what percent of the observations fall into the various high categories for importance of services? What percent fall into the low categories? Do the data show that the importance ratings vary by income? Do these findings support the findings you had in 2(a)? Write a paragraph reporting your findings.

   c. Of the two options, that used in 2(a), comparing the means, and the one used in 2(b), comparing percents, which way of presenting this information would you recommend using in a report on this issue? Justify your choice.

3. Go to the disk and load the Belle County data base and test the hypotheses that you formulated as part of the Chapter 1 exercise. Do the data support your hypotheses? Cite evidence to support your answer.

4. Go to the disk and load the city homicide data base. Select a city and plot the homicide data as a time series. Describe the variations you see in the data.

RECOMMENDED FOR FURTHER READING

See the references listed at the end of Chapter 7 for information on cross-sectional designs.

A good place to find information on time series, especially as a forecasting tool, is in management science texts. One widely available text is D. R. Anderson, D. J. Sweeney, and T. A. Williams, *Quantitative Methods for Business,* 5th ed. (St. Paul: West, 1992), chap. 6.

For a discussion of various types of longitudinal designs, see Scott Menard, *Longitudinal Research* (Newbury Park, CA: Sage, 1991).

Robert K. Yin, *Case Study Research: Design and Methods,* 2d ed. (Thousand Oaks, CA: Sage, 1994) is an excellent starting point for information on case studies. This chapter's section on case studies made extensive use of Yin's book. Another volume by the same author provides detailed examples of case studies. See Robert K. Yin *Applications of Case Study Research* (Newbury Park, CA: Sage 1993).

For more information on focus groups, see the references listed at the end of Chapter 7, especially Richard Krueger, *Focus Groups: A Practical Guide for Applied Research,* 2d ed. (Thousand Oaks, CA: Sage, 1994).

The reader interested in meta-analysis should review the following books. The best book to begin with is G. V. Glass, B. McGaw, and M. L. Smith, *Meta-Analysis in Social Research* (Beverly Hills: Sage, 1981). It is clear and includes many examples.

J. E. Hunter, F. L. Schmidt, and G. B. Jackson, *Meta-Analysis: Cumulating Research Findings across Studies* (Beverly Hills: Sage, *Studying Organizations: Innovations in Methodology Series,* no. 4, 1981), discuss some limitations of Glass et al.'s procedures. Both the Hunter et al. *Meta-Analysis* and F. M. Wolf's *Meta-Analysis: Quantitative Methods for Research Synthesis* (Beverly Hills: Sage, *Quantitative Applications in the Social Sciences,* no. 59, 1986) focus on the statistical methods associated with meta-analysis.

T. D. Cook, et. al., eds., *Meta-analysis for Explanation: A Casebook* (New York: Russell Sage Foundation, 1992) includes a number of meta-analyses. Also highly recommended is Morton Hunt *How Science Takes Stock: the Story of Meta-Analysis* (New York: Russell Sage Foundation, 1997). Hunt discusses how agencies of the American national government are using meta-analysis more frequently, especially in areas of medical research.

Chapter 3

Designs for Explanation

In this chapter you will learn

1. the evidence necessary to establish that two variables are causally related.
2. the questions to ask to evaluate empirical evidence that a program or treatment caused an outcome.
3. the questions to ask to determine whether findings can be generalized to cases other than the research subjects.
4. the common experimental, quasi-experimental, and observational designs to infer causality.
5. about nonexperimental designs and their value.
6. considerations in inferring causality from cross-sectional designs.

If an administrator wants to go beyond describing the values of a dependent variable and explain why they change or differ from case to case, he needs to show that an independent variable is causally related to the dependent variable. Often the administrator wants to show that some independent variable, such as a program activity, affected a dependent variable, such as nutrition, health care, level of absenteeism, and so forth. For example, the manager of the Women, Infants and Children (WIC) program may want to determine if this program improved infant nutrition. Simply demonstrating a decrease in the percent of malnourished infants is insufficient evidence that the WIC program is responsible. Instead, the manager needs a research design that unambiguously links the WIC program to the outcome of decreased malnutrition.

The administrator may be able to demonstrate with descriptive designs that two variables are linked to each other. That is, he may be able to show that they are associated. However, the administrator may want to go further and demonstrate that one variable caused another. When we say that X has caused a change in Y, we mean that a change in the value of the dependent variable, Y, comes about as a result of a change in the independent variable, X, and not as a result of something else.[1] If one variable causes another, an investigator expects to find a statistical relationship between them. For example, a director of a regional economic development program may believe that the more money the program has the more industries it will attract into the community. To support this belief, he should be able to demonstrate that as program expenditures increase, a corresponding increase in the number of industries locating in the region occurs.

To establish a causal relationship requires more than just a relationship between two variables. One of the real difficulties in determining whether public programs have had their intended impact is to separate the changes that may be due to other factors from changes that are due to the program. For example, a change in state tax laws or the opening of an air-cargo facility may encourage industries to move into the area independent of the economic development program's efforts. Or, to return to the earlier example of the WIC program, if the number of undernourished infants decreased after the WIC program started, the reduction may have been due to something else, perhaps a general improvement in the state's economy and more jobs in the community. To say that it reduced infant malnutrition, an investigator would need to demonstrate that without WIC, infant malnutrition would have been greater than it was with the program.

To claim *causality*, that one variable causes another, requires the following:

1. A statistical association of the two variables: The variables covary with each other or a change in one variable is accompanied by a change in the other.
2. The time order of the variables: The independent variable—the presumed cause—must have occurred before the dependent variable—the presumed result or effect.
3. The elimination of rival independent variables as causes of the dependent variable: Variables other than the independent variable of interest must be ruled out as causes of the dependent variable.
4. A theoritical link between the independent and dependent variable: The analyst should have some logical argument for assuming that two variables covary.

Descriptive designs begin the process of translating administrative concerns and program dynamics into quantitative information. They yield findings that alone or in combination with other information support action or prevent unnecessary further study. Cross-sectional, time-series, and case-study designs produce data that identify variables worth further study. Cross-sectional and time-series designs may incorporate sophisticated analysis to build complex models that provide strong evidence of causal links between variables. Still, policy makers and administrators may want more conclusive evidence that an independent variable causes a dependent variable, especially if they need to determine whether a program has achieved its intended objectives. To gain such evidence, they ask certain questions about the design and incorporate as many components of experimental designs as possible.

An *experimental design* is one in which the researcher can assign subjects to different research groups, control who is exposed to the independent variable, when they are exposed to it, and the conditions under which the experiment takes place. Since this kind of control seldom is possible in administrative work, administrative studies rely on *quasi-experimental designs.* These designs lack some of the characteristics of experiments and some of the control afforded with them. The researcher may need to rely on a naturally occurring independent variable or base her comparisons on groups over which she has no control. Both quasi-experimental and observational designs, used by health researchers, reduce the researcher's ability to judge the impact of an independent variable.

We can never prove that one variable causes another. Nevertheless, having a model and showing that the variables are related statistically, that the independent variable occurs before the dependent variable, and that rival independent variables have been ruled out make a convincing case for a causal relationship. Experimental designs provide a means of obtaining this evidence. When a researcher cannot implement an experimental design, a quasi-experimental design may be tried. In this chapter we present two experimental and three quasi-experimental designs useful in administration and policy research. We also look at two observational designs applied by researchers studying the effects of environmental factors, especially on diseases and other health conditions.

INTERNAL AND EXTERNAL VALIDITY

In evaluating the results of a program, a manager looks for a relationship between the program implementation, the independent variable, and some hoped-for results—the dependent variable. Typically, the manager wants to know if the program caused a change in some condition. As we have already suggested, a change in the target condition or population accompanied by a program change does not mean that the program change was the cause. Thus additional evidence is necessary to determine whether increased expenditures by the economic development program or the efforts of WIC respectively contributed to the location of new industries or less infant malnutrition.

Internal validity refers to the evidence that a specific independent variable, such as a program or policy, caused a change in an observed dependent variable. If an investigator is confident that the independent variable of interest and not something else caused the observed outcomes, the investigator can say that the study was internally valid.

An evaluation of a national 55-mile-per-hour speed-limit law found that a reduction in speed was accompanied by a reduction in traffic deaths. The conclusion that the change in speed limit caused a change in fatalities is internally valid only if the investigators showed that no other plausible factor caused the reduction in traffic deaths. Other factors alone or in combination with the lower speed limit could have caused the reduction.

External validity of a study speaks to the issue of generalizing the findings of a study beyond the specific cases involved. Typically, not all people involved in

generalizable

or affected by a program are studied. Only a portion of them are included in a study, and the investigator wants to know about the entire group. Let us say that we had established for a sample of WIC program participants that the program had reduced undernourishment in children. Would this be true of all WIC participants? Would programs similar but not identical to WIC have the same results? Assume that we determine from a study conducted in North Dakota that the 55-mile-per-hour speed limit reduced fatal traffic accidents. Would these results be true of other states or of the nation as a whole? These examples and questions all concern external validity.

Investigators also are concerned with validity when measuring variables. We refer to this type of validity as operational validity and discuss it in Chapter 4. As a general concept, validity has to do with whether or not we are making correct assumptions about the data and the observed relationships. Internal validity asks whether our study procedures allow us to claim that we have identified the cause of a change in a dependent variable. External validity asks whether the results of a study apply to cases not in the study.

THREATS TO INTERNAL VALIDITY

One cannot conclude that a change in one variable is responsible for changes in another unless one has ruled out the possibility that the observed change in the dependent variable was caused by some factor other than the independent variable. These other factors are known as *threats to internal validity.*[2] They may be categorized and defined as follows:

History: Events other than the independent variable that could have affected the dependent variable.

Maturation: Natural changes taking place in the units being studied.

Statistical regression: If cases for study or action are picked because of an extreme position, such as a low performance score, the instability of extreme scores may cause the observed change.

Selection: The way that cases are selected for a study or a program could affect the way they react to the program. Volunteers, for example, are usually different from those not volunteering.

Experimental mortality: Cases, particularly people, who drop out of a study or program before it is completed. If they are systematically different from those who remain, the results will not be internally valid.

Testing: A situation in which the initial measure or test influences the subjects, which then affects the outcome of the posttest. Employees who score low on a pretest may change their behavior because of this and not because of some program.

Instrumentation: If the measuring instrument used to collect data changes between the beginning of a study and its conclusion, the results may not be valid.

Design contamination: A condition occurring when participants know that they are in a study and act differently because of it or if subjects being compared interact. If study subjects have an incentive to behave in a specific way as to make the program succeed or fail, the design has been contaminated.

The threat to internal validity known as history arises when events or policies other than the independent variable cannot be ruled out as a source of the changes in the dependent variable. Usually such events will have occurred during the same time as the independent variable. In 1973 an oil embargo brought about a gasoline shortage; gasoline prices soared, long lines were found at gas stations, and Americans drove less. To further reduce gas consumption, a national 55-mile-per-hour speed limit was established. Auto fatalities decreased and the national 55-mile-per-hour speed limit continued for more than 20 years. It is entirely possible that the observed reduction in highway fatalities was the result, not of reduced speed, but of less driving.

As we write, commentators are comparing changes in unemployment, consumer confidence, and confidence in government before and after September 11, 2001. Prior to the attacks Americans were receiving tax rebate checks intended to stimulate spending. Policy observers debated if the recipients would spend the rebates or save it. In the latter case the economy would continue to weaken. Nevertheless, the debate became moot and the effects of the attacks could not be separated from other factors effecting the economy. Sometimes changes that occur in variables during the course of the study are due to natural processes. The resulting threat to internal validity is called maturation. People, groups, and other units of observation change over time. These changes occur naturally, rather than as the result of specific, identifiable events or interventions. One may assume erroneously that an independent variable caused a change in a dependent variable when the change involved would have occurred with the passage of time, regardless of whether the independent variable was present. Most juvenile delinquents, for example, decrease their antisocial behavior as they grow older. Thus the apparent success of delinquency programs may result from the aging of the clientele rather than program activities. If one records the behavior of one group of children in the morning and another group in the afternoon, differences between the groups may not be due to a particular independent variable but to the changes in children's behavior during the course of a day.

A third threat is statistical regression. Consider an experience most of us have had during school. Early in our academic career, most of us learn that, on the average over time, we receive roughly the same grade in courses or on exams. But on occasion we may be pleasantly surprised by our score on a test. And we may find that on the next test, our score is noticeably lower than on the first. Or we may have a classmate who scores very low, much lower than expected on an exam. On the second exam, she is likely to do better than on the first. Over time, these students' test scores will approach their average performance. In short, anytime that we observe a test score that is exceptionally high or exceptionally low for a given student, we usually can predict that that student's next score will be closer to her average.

Social problems show analogous patterns. If a program is created in reaction to an extreme situation, then any subsequent change in the desired direction may occur because of statistical regression. A city with an unusually high number of traffic deaths one month may experience a significant improvement the next. So, a program installed in response to a rash of fatal accidents may appear to have been effective, when in actuality the number of traffic deaths had simply regressed toward the average. The result, however, may have been due to statistical regression, not the program. Statistical regression is a threat whenever cases for treatment or study are chosen because of an extreme value on some measure. If the variable is measured again, the cases will be less extreme; they will have regressed toward the average.

Selection is a problem when the basis on which cases are chosen for the study or program is nonrandom. In such instances the group of cases chosen for study may be systematically different from the cases to which they are compared. If so, the difference between the groups rather than the influence of the independent variable may account for any observed change in the dependent variable. Consider the recruitment strategy used by some job training programs when program survival depended on placement rate. The training staff enrolled highly motivated trainees who already possessed good job skills or high aptitudes. Women on maternity leave from typing jobs were recruited into secretarial training programs and placed successfully, sometimes in jobs they had left. Thus the apparent success of the program resulted from recruiting trainees who were eminently employable. As a result, the apparent success of the program was due to the way the recruits were selected, not to the effect of the training program itself.

The threat of experimental mortality arises when people begin a program and later drop out before the study is completed. The difficulty with this is that dropouts may be different from those who complete the program, and the difference may affect the outcome. It may be that those who are successful stay with the program and those who are not leave. Consider the example of a successful delinquency program whose goal was to keep participants in school. Despite the program's apparent success, it may have been that the youths who dropped out of the program were those who had little motivation to remain in school. Those who continued in school might have done so even if the program had not existed.

Testing as a threat to internal validity occurs when an initial measurement changes the dependent variable. In some studies an observation is taken before and after the introduction of an independent variable. The observation taken before exposure to the independent variable is called a pretest. The observation taken after exposure is the posttest. The risk in such a procedure is that the pretest and not the independent variable may have caused an observed change in the dependent variable. For example, a person exposed to a training program to increase knowledge may show increased knowledge from the pretest to the posttest, because the pretest stimulated his interest and he looked up the answers. The pretest, not the program, caused this increased knowledge. Oftentimes people do less well with an unfamiliar task; a pretest serves as practice and may improve later performances on the same or similar test. We observed this when the GREs were first given on computers. Students who had not practiced improved their scores between the first and second testing; most likely their familiarity with the new format led to the improved performance. The effect of testing also is known as the reactivity of measurement; people react to the measuring process and change their behavior because of it.

Instrumentation is a threat to internal validity when the method of measurement changes between the pretest and the posttest. The instrument used may have changed or the definition of the variable may have changed. Suppose that the legal definition of a particular crime changed between two measurements of the crime rate. The change in definition alone may make it appear that the crime rate had changed. If a program to reduce the crime rate were initiated during the period between the two observations, we could not be sure whether any recorded change in the crime rate was due to the way crime was measured, to the program, or to both. Investigators using agency records need to be alert as to how variables are defined and records are kept. Changes in these, if unrecognized, can cause problems of instrumentation.

The final threat to internal validity is known as design contamination. Several types of contamination are possible. Subjects exposed to a treatment may talk to those not exposed, and eventually both groups experience the same program or treatment. Consider the personnel director who wishes to evaluate a program designed to prepare people for retirement. The program has been offered to some employees on an experimental basis. The personnel director wants to know whether employees who participated in the program have fewer economic problems after they retire than nonparticipants. However, if participants had shared the information obtained from the program with their colleagues, both groups might have made similar economic plans, effectively eliminating any difference between participants and nonparticipants. As a result the program would appear to have been unsuccessful. As this example illustrates, one can sometimes falsely assume that an independent and a dependent variable are not related.

A second type of design contamination occurs when participants guess the purpose of the research and alter their behavior so as to achieve an outcome in their best interests. Suppose a researcher wants to learn whether reducing the size of work crews on sanitation trucks from four persons to two persons will increase productivity. Fearing the breakup of their work units and increased job pressures, the workers might alter their behavior with the smaller crews slowing down their work rate and the larger crews increasing theirs.

Yet another type of contamination occurs if a group receiving no treatment changes its behavior in the hypothesized direction because of anger or low morale. Imagine a study to determine if assigning mentors to new employees improves their productivity. Employees not selected to participate may become aware of the program and wonder why they were not included. They may assume they are less valued employees and react by decreasing their own productivity. The researcher mistakenly could assume that the mentoring program explains the difference in productivity; whereas, the difference actually was caused by the poor morale of the control group.

Whenever you, as an administrator, examine empirical research, you will want to raise questions to identify any potential weaknesses in the design and, more specifically, threats to the internal validity of the findings. A list of such questions follows. The purpose of these questions is to help you decide whether you should take action based on such findings. If a study concludes that a causal relationship exists between two variables, then you must be reasonably confident that none of the threats to internal validity account for the apparent relationship. Plausibility should be the key word in determining how much weight to put on the failure of a research design to control for any one threat to internal validity.[3] You should ask whether it is plausible that no factor other than the independent variable is the cause. You also should ask whether it is plausible that some factor other than the independent variable was the case of the dependent variable.

Questions to Ask to Help Evaluate Possible Threats to Internal Validity When Examining Research Reporting a Causal Relationship between Two Variables

1. Based on history: Could an event other than the independent variable have caused this relationship?

2. Based on maturation: Would a similar change in the dependent variable have taken place with the same passage of time without the occurrence of the independent variable? Could the changes found in the subjects have resulted from natural changes such as maturity, aging, or tiring?

3. Based on statistical regression: Were subjects chosen for the study because of a high or low value of the dependent variable?

4. Based on selection: Were the people exposed to the independent variable systematically different from those not exposed? If subjects were volunteers, could this have affected the findings?

5. Based on experimental mortality: Were some people initially exposed to the treatment later assigned to the nontreatment group? Did some people who started the study drop out before finishing?

6. Based on testing: Was a pretest administered that could have affected responses to the posttest? Did the pretest provide practice at performing certain tasks and thus affect the posttest scores?

7. Based on instrumentation: Did the instrument to collect data change between the pretest and the posttest?

8. Based on design contamination: Did the program participants mingle with nonparticipants? Did program participants, nonparticipants, or both have an incentive to change their behavior and make the program succeed or fail?

EXTERNAL VALIDITY

External validity refers to the appropriateness of extending or generalizing research findings to a group beyond that involved in the study. Only the findings of a study that has external validity may be generalized to other cases. Sampling strategy affects the external validity of a design. If research subjects are randomly drawn from a defined group, then the findings should be generalizable to that group, but this by itself is not enough to ensure external validity. External validity also refers to the ability to generalize the results of a study to other places, times, and programs.

An investigator may do a formal study of a program to determine whether the program has had a beneficial or a harmful effect. He wants to know first if the program works. That is the question of internal validity. But he also wants to know if that program will work for others. That is the problem of external validity. The study may be very informal; a manager may simply observe that his program works as he thinks it should. If he or others wish to conclude that the program will work for other groups or in other locations, they must be aware of several external validity problems. Threats to external validity come about because the conditions of the study are not duplicated for cases not in the study. Unique features of the study subjects, the study setting or conditions, and the implementation of the study program itself, as well as the fact that people may know that they are being studied, contribute to problems with external validity.

Threats to external validity include the following:

unique program features

effects of selection

effects of setting

effects of history

effects of testing

reactive effects of experimental arrangements[4]

Sometimes in constructing an experimental study, an entire program is treated as a single independent variable. However, programs typically consist of clusters of several variables. Thus any program may have unique features that affect its results. The program may be unsuccessful in the absence of one or more of the unique features. Creators of experimental programs in a controlled environment may be unable to duplicate the results in a natural, nonexperimental setting where they would be most needed. Consider a demonstration project to enable elderly persons to live independently. The project may have staff who are younger, less experienced, more energetic, and in other ways different from staff usually found in ongoing programs housed in social services agencies. The results of the demonstration project may be atypical and not apply to other programs.

Program managers and investigators need to be aware that programs that appear similar may be different enough in the way they are implemented to affect how they work. A program for reducing drug use among adolescents may appear to work. A program analyst may then infer that all such programs will work. But external validity must be considered. If the programs were only similar, not exactly the same, the analyst may not be able to generalize from one to the rest. Differences in staff, client interactions, activities, or community dynamics may affect program outcomes.

The *effects of selection* arise as a threat to external validity when the subjects in the study are unrepresentative. The group being studied may have responded differently to the program treatment than others who would be likely to participate. The resulting findings are therefore not representative beyond the group being studied. As an example, consider a training program for teachers that is tested on a group of senior career teachers. Even if the results of this experiment are favorable, the program may not work with teachers who are much younger and less experienced.

The project's *location or setting* can threaten external validity. A project based in a hospital may not work as well as one located in a senior citizens' club, simply because the hospital setting may increase feelings of dependency and work against program goals. Or, a program in a New England community may have more success than one in a Southwestern city where community support systems may be weaker.

History can affect external validity in a number of ways. An evaluation of a particular program may be undertaken at a time when clients and the community are unusually receptive to its services. A local scandal about conditions in nursing homes may motivate aged persons and their families to seek alternatives to institutional care. A recent fire in a community may motivate homeowners to respond favorably to an education program presented by the fire department. Other communities whose historical circumstances differ may not respond in the same way. You may think of other conditions that make a program work at one time but not at other times.

If a pretest given for study purposes affects the subject's receptivity to the program, testing poses a threat to external validity. Consider a parent education program. Giving the parents a pretest that asks how to handle a child's behavior may motivate the parents to become involved in the program and achieve its objectives. The pretest may then be a unique feature, and the program will not work in its absence. If a pretest affects the behavior of the study subjects, the results will not necessarily apply to nonpretested clients. *Testing* here differs from the threat it poses to internal validity in that, as a threat to external validity, studied subjects are pretested and other likely participants are not. Testing is a threat to internal validity if studied subjects change their behavior as a result of the pretest, not the program.

Reactive effects of experimental arrangements refers to the fact that study situations often are necessarily artificial, and this study setting itself may affect the outcome. If participants know that they are being studied, they may alter their behavior accordingly. The results of such a study could not be transferred to others who were not being studied. Consider a group of community residents recruited to test participation in a voluntary recycling program. Since they know that they are in a study, they may be especially cooperative and work hard to make the program work. (They may also guess that if the voluntary program does not work, recycling may become mandatory.) If the program were implemented, the results may not apply to other households.

The reader should note that these problems of external validity can occur in combination with each other. A problem of unrepresentative selection also may involve a problem of setting. If an investigator tested a new program by selecting a specialized group, such as Native American children, and conducted the demonstration program in a town in Tennessee, she would have both of these problems. If the program was meant to apply to all minorities, the selection of only Native Americans may bias the results. The geographical setting also may introduce a bias. Something about the particular town may contribute to the success or failure of the program.

External validity can be increased by replicating a program in different settings with different personnel. If a demonstration program seems to have worked in one small town in the state, and a state administrator wants to make sure that it will work throughout the state, his best strategy is to try the same program in other locations. If the program is successful in dissimilar towns, the administrator should feel more confident that it will work statewide.

A program conducted initially with a representative sample of the program's target group should increase external validity. However, replicating a program with a number of smaller, haphazardly chosen samples may offer more external validity than conducting a single study with a carefully drawn sample.[5] This argument rests on the likelihood that some program participants will quit; thus, a study starting with a representative sample may not end up with one. Experimental mortality could render the outcome of a single study externally invalid.

One approach is to select subjects who are markedly different, and infer that if the program works for a wide number of different types of test subjects, then it should work for everybody. This strategy, *deliberately sampling for heterogeneity*, could result in demonstration projects targeted at the elderly in an Eastern city, a rural Southern town, and an urban Indian community. In any one study, problems with internal and external validity are unavoidable. Replication of findings under varying experimental conditions offers reasonably sound evidence of a program's transferability.

Descriptive designs such as sample surveys often have high external validity. Experimental designs, on the other hand, have high internal validity, but often are low on external validity. Administrators want to be sure that a program or policy achieves its desired ends, a matter of internal validity, before identifying the various conditions under which it will work, a matter of external validity. As with internal validity, a series of questions should be asked to help evaluate the external validity of a study. A list of such questions follows.

Evaluating External Validity: Questions to Ask to Determine Whether a Relationship between Two Variables Can Be Generalized beyond the Research Subjects

1. What group did the research subjects represent?

2. Did the program or treatment involve demands that may have affected the representativeness of the subjects, such as excessive commitments of time?

3. Has the program been replicated among different types of subjects, in different settings and locations?

4. Exactly what was the program or treatment? Were unplanned or unexamined features, such as personnel or setting, critical to program success?

5. Was the program as offered to the research group different from what will be offered to others?

EXPERIMENTAL DESIGNS

Experimental designs provide the best means of obtaining the evidence necessary to infer the existence of a causal relationship between two well-defined variables. In an experimental design, the researcher can assign subjects to different groups, manipulate the independent variable, and control most environmental influences. The researcher assigns some subjects to the group that is exposed to the independent variable and other subjects to groups that are not. Subjects are assigned in such a way that there is no systematic difference between the groups. This is *random assignment.* If subjects were randomly assigned to groups, any change in the dependent variable should not be due to differences between the study groups. In evaluating studies claiming to have used an experimental design, you should see whether this procedure was used to help control threats to internal and external validity.

We discuss two experimental designs in this section, the classical experimental design and the randomized posttest-only design. If you understand them, you should have little trouble understanding more complicated variations. The designs we discuss involve one or two treatment groups. A treatment group is a set of research subjects who are exposed to the independent variable and are then compared on the dependent variable to another group, the control group, whose members have not been exposed to the independent variable.

The *classical experimental design* has long served as the model for experimental research. It allows us to control the time order or exposure to the variables under study, to determine statistical association among variables, and to control for other possible causal factors. Properly utilized, it can provide the strongest reliable evidence of a causal relationship. It is also an excellent model for demonstrating the logic of explanatory designs. Its characteristics include the following:

1. Subjects are randomly assigned to an *experimental* or a *control group* so that no systematic difference exists between the two groups. Random assignment provides that each subject has the same chance as any other subject of being in either the experimental group or the control group.

2. A pretest, measuring the dependent variable, is administered to both groups.

3. The experimental group is exposed to the treatment; the control group is not. Both groups should experience the same conditions, except for exposure to the independent variable. The researcher controls exposure to the independent variable, determining who receives it and who does not.

4. A posttest, which again measures the dependent variable, is administered to both groups following exposure to the independent variable.

5. The amount of change in the dependent variable between the pretest and posttest is determined for each group. The difference between the two groups is attributed to the independent variable.

Note that this design yields the three types of evidence needed to demonstrate that one variable causes another. Like other designs it can provide evidence of a statistical relationship between variables. It allows us to determine whether any changes in the values of the dependent variable take place after exposure to the independent variable; with this information and by controlling exposure to the independent variable, the investigator can rule out the possibility that the values of the dependent variable changed before the independent variable occurred. Random assignment of subjects to experimental or control groups eliminates most if not all rival independent variables, although problems associated with experimental mortality and design contamination may persist. This design has very high internal validity. It may not, however, have high external validity.

The classical experimental design is represented symbolically as follows:

$$R \ O_1 \ X \ O_2 \ (\text{experimental group})$$
$$R \ O_1 \quad \ \ O_2 \ (\text{control group})$$

where:

R = randomly assigned subjects

O = observation or measurement of the dependent variable

X = independent variable

With experimental designs it is important to select equivalent experimental and control groups and maintain their similarities throughout the experiment. The preferred method of creating equivalent groups is to randomly assign half of a pool of subjects to the experimental group and half to the control group. The theory underlying random assignment is that if enough subjects are used, differences among groups of subjects tend to disappear as long as no bias enters in the way that subjects are assigned to one group or the other. With random assignment, each subject has the same probability of being in either group. Random assignment allows researchers to begin their study by controlling for the threats to validity associated with nonequivalent research groups. Specifically, random assignment controls for selection bias and statistical regression; however, it only ensures comparability at the initial stage of the research.

An alternative method of assigning subjects is to *match* each individual or unit in the experimental group with an individual or unit in the control group. The researcher identifies characteristics that may affect the dependent variable, gathers data on them in the sample pool, and pairs units with similar characteristics. Subjects that cannot be paired are eliminated from the study. The researcher then randomly assigns one member of the pair to the experimental group and the other to the control group. For example, if she believes that education, sex, and age affect program outcomes, she identifies each subject's education, sex, and race. She then pairs the available subjects; that is, two young (18–29) females who attended college could be a pair, two older males (30–45) with high school degrees could be another pair, and so on. The assignment of the members of the pair to experimental or control groups is random.

Researchers, particularly in the field of medicine, may use matching retrospectively to create comparison groups. For example, researchers match subjects who have a disease with similar persons who do not have the disease. As we discuss later in the chapter, the researchers try to determine why one group developed the disease and the other did not.

Matching can reduce the number of subjects required because it reduces the variation within the treatment and control groups. Nevertheless, methodologists usually prefer random assignment and seldom recommend matching.[6] With more than four relevant characteristics, matching becomes difficult. Matching may reduce internal validity if it focuses on variables actually unrelated to the dependent variable and ignores variables related to it. Matching assumes that the researcher knows which other variables are related to the dependent variable and, hence, knows which to match. The difficulties that stem from this last assumption are virtually eliminated by random assignment, which assumes that the two groups are equivalent in all respects except for exposure to the independent variable.

Experimental designs generally control for other threats to internal validity. To illustrate this characteristic, let's consider history as a threat to internal validity. External events (history) occurring between the pretest and the posttest may not affect internal validity if both groups experience the same event. The event is assumed to have a similar effect on the experimental and control groups. Both groups may change between the pretest and posttest. Changes in the control group may be attributed to history, maturation or another threat. If both groups experience the same conditions and events, other than exposure to the independent variable, changes in the experimental group may be caused by the independent variable and other factors associated with the threats to internal validity. The posttest differences between the experimental and control groups may be attributed to the independent variable.

Example 3.1 summarizes an experiment structured along the lines of a classical experimental design to determine whether a training program increased the empathy of first-year medical students. Students assigned to the control group received the same small-group training immediately after the experiment was over. The strategy of randomly assigning subjects to a group that either receives the treatment first (experimental group) or second (control group) helps resolve the political and ethical problems of deciding whether or not a person receives treatment solely on the basis of random assignment.

In Example 3.1 medical students in both the experimental and control groups showed more empathy on the posttest. Some of the change may have been caused by the lecture on patient interviewing (history), which both groups attended after taking the pretest. Since both groups heard the lecture, it is not a threat to internal validity. History would not be controlled as a threat if only the experimental group heard the lecture, since either the experiment or the lecture may have caused the change. To determine if an experiment controls for history, maturation, or another threat to internal validity requires detailed knowledge of how the experiment was conducted.

EXAMPLE 3.1

Using a Classical Experiment Design in the Field

Problem: Determine if small-group discussions increase medical students' ability to respond to the emotional concerns of patients.

Subjects: 134 first-year medical students registered for Medical Interviewing and History Taking. Students were randomly assigned to a small group (65 students) or a control group (69 students).

Independent variable (treatment): Small groups of approximately 16 students and a professional staff member met four times for a total of 12 hours. The students interviewed simulated patients; the groups discussed the interviews and interviewing techniques.

Dependent variable: Number out of three written scenarios where a student used an emotional term to describe a patient's concern.

Design diagram:

$$R\ O_1\ X\ O_2$$
$$R\ O_1\quad\ O_2$$

Pretest was given at the first class meeting of Medical Interviewing and History Taking. Experimental-group posttest was given at the last small-group session; control-group posttest was given at beginning of the first small-group session (after the experiment was over).

Threats to internal validity: None noted in research report. Random assignment allows us to rule out selection and statistical regression. Use of the same paper-and-pencil test for pretest and posttest allows us to rule out instrumentation and testing. Most likely the threat to internal validity was design contamination, especially if experimental-group members shared information with control-group members. Sharing should decrease differences between the experimental and control groups.

Threats to external validity: None noted; however, possible threats can be assumed easily. For example, the professional staff who facilitated the groups may have been enthusiastic and committed because of their involvement in implementing a new program. Also, a medical school may have its own unique culture, which affects its students' receptivity to classes and other training activities. Best evidence of external validity would be replication of this training in other medical schools.

Analysis and findings: The average number of scenarios where subjects used an emotional word in the response are shown below.

	Pretest	Posttest
Experimental Group	0.68	2.02
Control Group	0.89	1.13

Random assignment does not necessarily result in two identical groups; statistics help researchers decide if differences between groups could have occurred by chance. In the classical experimental design, researchers focus on the change between the pretest and posttest. The researchers compare the change in the experimental group with the change in the control group. Here, the experimental group showed an increase of 1.34; that is, it more than doubled its average use of emotional responses; the control group showed an increase of only 0.24.

SOURCE: Based on F. M. Wolf et al., "A Controlled Experiment in Teaching Students to Respond to Patients' Emotional Concerns," *Journal of Medical Education 62,* (1987): 25–34.

Typically, to determine the amount of change researchers use the same procedure to measure the dependent variable at the pretest and posttest. This is not necessary to ensure internal validity. An experiment may still be internally valid even if the pretest and posttest measuring procedures are not the same, or if the pretest causes a change in the dependent variable. The equivalence of the control and experimental groups neutralizes instrumentation and testing as threats to internal validity. Both groups should respond in the same way to the pretest. Nevertheless, the pretest may sensitize the experimental group to the independent variable and affect the external validity of the design, in which case the pretest becomes part of the treatment or program.

Experimental designs assume the control of the laboratory experiment, a situation that rarely applies to administrative and policy research. Field researchers, that is, researchers who work outside the confines of the laboratory, have markedly less control over subjects and events.[7] Still, researchers conduct field experiments frequently and draw reasonable conclusions from them.

Example 3.2 illustrates an adaptation of the classical experimental design. In this experiment a university housing office created a contest among college residences with cash incentives to try to decrease natural-gas consumption. The independent variable, cash awards, was introduced several times. In a sense, this amounted to doing the experiment six times with the same groups of subjects. We selected this example because it also shows how researchers draw on their knowledge to combine techniques. The researchers' cost-benefit analysis found that the cash awards alone cost more than the fuel savings.

The *randomized posttest design* avoids the possible sensitizing effect of a pretest by eliminating it, which results in a design identical to that of the classical experiment except for the absence of a pretest. The underlying assumption is that a pretest is expendable because random assignment will result in equivalent experimental and control groups. This assumption is most likely to be valid for large study populations. The design is diagrammed as:

$$R \; X \; O_1$$
$$R \quad O_1$$

The randomized posttest design has a number of advantages. Eliminating the pretest reduces costs. The administration of a pretest is often difficult or even impossible. It may not be necessary. The randomized posttest design relieves the researcher of identifying a reasonable pretest. Consider a prison work-release program tested to determine whether it reduced the recidivism rate of prisoners. Qualified prisoners were randomly assigned either to a work-release program or to serve out their full terms. Upon release, all prisoners were followed to determine whether they were arrested for additional crimes. Recidivism rates for the work-release program subjects and full-term subjects were compared.[8] Consider what might happen if the researchers had to obtain pretest data. The data may not exist; the prison may not have reliable records on whether an inmate had been in prison before, how many times, or for how long. Even if sound data exist, confidentiality requirements may prohibit researchers from having access to the data. Finally, researchers may question the value of going to the trouble and

EXAMPLE 3.2

An Adaptation of the Classical Experimental Design

Problem: Determine effective ways to reduce energy consumption by residents in master-meter housing, where individual residents do not pay utility bills.

Subjects: Five university-owned apartment complexes. Analysts paired one set of complexes of comparable size, family mix, and energy source. One complex was randomly assigned to the experimental group, the other to the control group. The remaining three complexes could not be paired.

Independent variable (treatment): Contest with cash awards held six times two weeks apart.

Dependent variable: Savings in natural gas consumption = Cost × (predicted consumption − actual consumption).

Design diagram:

$$R\ O_1\ X\ O_2\ X\ O_3\ X\ O_4\ X\ O_5\ X\ O_6\ X\ O_7$$
$$R\ O_1\quad O_2\quad O_3\quad O_4\quad O_5\quad O_6\quad O_7$$

Threats to internal validity:

History: possible problem because experimental complex also received a 15-page saving guide.

Maturation, statistical regression, selection, testing instrumentation, controlled by the design.

Experimental mortality: none.

Contamination: unlikely; control group members expressed little interest in contest.

Threats to external validity:

Nothing indicated to suggest findings could not be generalized to other university-owned complexes.

Contest Number	Savings in Experimental Group
1	$137.85
2	$79.31
3	$98.35
4	$67.19
5	$66.41
6	$39.19

Conclusion: The contest reduced natural-gas consumption, but not enough to offset contest costs. Questions of history and contamination as threats to internal validity were moot. Findings replicated those found in a study of an apartment complex; the approach worked better in a university that had contests among dormitories.

SOURCE: Adapted from L. McClelland and S. W. Cook, "Promoting Energy Conservation in Master-Metered Apartments through Group Financial Incentives," *Journal of Applied Social Psychology 10,* (1980): 20–31.

expense of obtaining accurate pretest data on recidivism. We assume that inmates with a history of recidivism would not be among the "qualified" prisoners.

If experimental groups are large enough for the investigator to be confident that they are similar, the randomized posttest design is efficient and effective. If a study has relatively few subjects, a researcher needs pretest data to ensure the comparability of the experimental and control groups. Pretest data also are necessary if an investigator needs to determine the extent of change attributable to the independent variable.

Example 3.3 illustrates the application of a randomized posttest design to determine whether coaching improves performance in leaderless groups. In this study, measuring performance in leaderless groups prior to introducing the independent variable would have increased the study's costs. Furthermore, the additional time required may have led to greater problems with experimental mortality and increased the opportunities for design contamination, particularly if members of the experimental and control groups had contact with each other.

Administrators are likely to see experimental designs in conjunction with program evaluation although they are used in other areas as well. A major purpose of program evaluation is to determine whether a planned intervention or program has produced its intended effects. Experimental designs are useful research strategies for determining the effect of the policy or program on a given population. As we mentioned earlier, a major problem encountered when attempting to use experimental designs for program evaluation is the loss of researcher control. This lack of control makes experimental designs impractical for evaluating established programs. Such programs are sufficiently complex with well-established procedures, and researchers cannot expect to spell out who will receive services, exactly what services they will receive, and exactly how the services will be delivered.

Thomas Cook and Donald Campbell have identified other situations in which experimental designs will not work.[9] True experimental research in administrative settings rarely can be done quickly, so an alternative design should be chosen if a decision must be made quickly. Sometimes, important variables such as age, race, or the occurrence of a disaster cannot be manipulated or randomly assigned. The decision to evaluate most programs is made independently of the decision to implement the program and often after the program has begun, making true experimentation impossible, because it is too late to manipulate the intervention (the independent variable) or to assign subjects to groups. True experimental designs also are expensive to conduct in realistic social settings. Preliminary studies should be conducted to avoid premature experimentation.

Experimental designs seem most relevant to the study of new or controversial programs at a time of scarce resources.[10] Programs that are specific, clearly described, and implemented all at once rather than phased in gradually lend themselves to experimental evaluation. The effects of modest treatments, such as changing office accounting procedures, may be more easily and reasonably studied experimentally than ambitious programs to achieve broad social goals. A researcher may have difficulty ensuring that the latter programs are carried out as designed or intended; pressures to participate in the program may make random

EXAMPLE 3.3

An Application of the Randomized Posttest Design

A university placement office wants to learn whether coaching improves performance in assigned-role leaderless groups (a technique used by major employers to select professional employees).

Subjects: Thirty-six female students from introductory psychology classes randomly assigned to one of three groups.

Independent variable: Type of preparation for leaderless group. Two treatments were used, so two experimental groups were set up:

X_1 = Subjects attended two coaching sessions and received feedback on their performance in practice leaderless groups.

X_2 = Subjects saw a short tape of someone giving a biased account about her experience in a leaderless group.

Control group: Subjects did not attend coaching sessions, did not view tape, or have any other preparation.

Dependent variable: Overall performance in an assigned-role leaderless group. Scores on leadership, behavioral flexibility, oral presentation, initiative, and persuasion were averaged for each subject.

Design diagram:

$$R \ X_1 \ O_1$$
$$R \ X_2 \ O_1$$
$$R \quad \ O_1$$

Threats to internal validity:

History: controlled by design and carefully implemented procedures for conducting the experiment.

Maturation, statistical regression, selection: controlled by the design.

Testing, instrumentation: not applicable with this design.

Experimental mortality: none.

Contamination: none documented.

Threats to external validity:

Possible interaction of selection and treatment: These were all college women who might respond to the coaching program differently from the general population of professionals seeking employment.

Possible interaction of setting and treatment: These students had no immediate prospects of using the skills to obtain a job. Thus the experimental setting did not duplicate the natural setting where subjects would be competing for a position.

Findings:

	Group		
	Coached	Viewed Tape	Control
Average performance	5.08	2.83	2.58

Continued

EXAMPLE 3.3   *Continued*

Conclusion: Hypothesis that coaching can improve performance in an assigned-role leaderless group was supported. Tape was meant to duplicate "grapevine" advice; it may not have represented the effect of informal advice. Researchers did not determine whether coaching only makes participants test-wise or whether they later apply learned behaviors to work settings. Also not known was whether coaching would work as well with persons who had management experience.

SOURCE: P. M. Kurecka et al., "Full and Errant Coaching Effects on Assigned Role Leaderless Group Discussion Performance," *Personnel Psychology*, (1982): 805–812.

---

assignment nearly impossible, and subject attrition and design contamination may be inevitable. One objection to the use of experimental designs in the study of social programs has revolved around the question of whether the control group can be offered a treatment. Although traditional experimental design calls for identifying what would happen without "treatment," the resulting practical and ethical problems have made offering alternative treatment to the control group an acceptable practice.[11] Such problems have been particularly prominent in medical research where there has been much debate over the morality of withholding a new medical treatment from a group so that its effects can be verified experimentally.

QUASI-EXPERIMENTAL DESIGNS

The classic experimental design relies on the researcher's ability to control the research setting. The researcher exercises control from the initiation of the experiment to its conclusion, selecting and assigning subjects and exposing the experimental group to the independent variable. As much as possible, she ensures that groups equivalent at the beginning undergo the same conditions during the study, except for exposure to the independent variable. The tradition of referring to the independent variable as a "treatment" emphasizes the objective of manipulating and controlling exposure to the independent variable.

In research conducted outside a laboratory setting, the amount of control required by the classical experimental model may be unattainable. True experiments require (1) the manipulation of at least one independent variable, (2) the random assignment of subjects to groups, (3) the random assignment of the independent variable to groups, and (4) the exposure of the experimental group or groups to the treatment in isolation from other factors. If one of these conditions cannot be met, the appropriate research design is a *quasi-experimental* one. Donald Campbell and Julian Stanley refer to "many natural settings in which the [researcher] can introduce something like experimental design into his scheduling of data collection procedures even though he lacks the full control over the scheduling of experimental stimuli which makes a true experiment possible."[12] In other words, the researcher makes use of as many features of the classical experimental design as possible and adopts other measures to offset threats to internal validity. Unlike the groups in true experimental designs, members of the treatment group and the control group in quasi-experimental designs are not randomly assigned; therefore, the analyst cannot assume that the groups are equivalent at the beginning.

In designing a quasi-experiment, the researcher constructs the best possible approximation of an experiment and controls for as many threats to internal validity as possible. We discuss three of the more commonly used quasi-experimental designs: the comparison group pretest/posttest design, the interrupted time-series design, and the multiple-group, interrupted time-series design.

On the surface, the *comparison group pretest/posttest design* may look like the classic experimental design. However, its subjects are not selected by random assignment but by identifying a group of subjects that seems comparable to the group involved in the test. This is a useful strategy because frequently programs or policies develop in a way that precludes random assignment. Suppose a police department wanted to study the effect of a compressed work week of four 10-hour days. The study may have problems if officers object to being randomly assigned to the experimental schedule. Hence, researchers may prefer to limit the testing of the schedule to units where everyone agrees to participate. The resulting research design would require finding platoons willing to submit to the new schedule, and then designating a comparison group from among the other platoons. One way of constructing a comparison group is to match each platoon in the experimental group on the basis of selected characteristics.[13] Note, however, that unlike true experimental designs, members of the groups here are not randomly assigned, so the analyst cannot assume that the groups are equivalent. Nor is the "experimental" treatment randomly assigned to one of the groups.

Comparison groups also are constructed for contrast with intact experimental groups. This provided a useful strategy for one group of researchers who wanted to study how organic farming affected crop production. Since the researchers were not in a position to convince farmers to switch to organic farming, they identified known organic farms and matched each with a farm of similar size and soil composition. Similarly, in a study of the effects of day care on children, kindergarten students who had been in day care for five years formed the experimental group. Kindergarten children in the same school system who had not been in day care, and whose parents agreed to their participation, formed the comparison group. After the comparison group was selected, researchers studied the characteristics of both groups to identify systematic differences between them.

The comparison group pretest/posttest design is diagrammed as:

$$O_1 \; X \; O_2$$
$$O_1 \quad O_2$$

Sometimes the comparison group design is called "the nonequivalent control-group design," but we prefer to restrict the term "control group" to groups whose members are randomly assigned. The major limitation of the comparison group design is the inability to control for biases introduced by selection. The greater the similarity between the experimental and comparison groups, the more confidence a researcher may have in making inferences from his findings. The design can control for history, maturation, pretesting, and instrumentation, but this must be confirmed. Unless a researcher can keep conditions between the experimental and comparison group the same from pretest to posttest, one group may have an experience that affects its posttest. For example, if the comparison and experimental groups consisted of police precincts, and if the precincts used different criteria for data collection, then instrumentation would be a possible threat to validity. Experimental mortality could be checked by examining records. The analysts could determine whether any platoons discontinued the experimental schedule prematurely.

Statistical regression constitutes a threat to validity in this design. This threat is of particular concern if the experimental group and the comparison group differ systematically on some dimension. Imagine that the pretest turnover rates were higher than usual in the experimental platoons and lower than usual in the comparison platoons. If each group regressed toward its average, a posttest might show a lower turnover rate for the experimental group and a higher rate for the comparison group—both due to a statistical effect, not the difference in scheduling. This is not an unlikely scenario. You would expect administrators to pick the platoon with the highest turnover rate for an experimental program.

The comparison group pretest/posttest design may have high external validity if it replicates a program's effect in a variety of settings. Thus if the change in scheduling reduced turnover in all platoons where it was tried, and the platoons included ones with high morale and low morale, ones in good neighborhoods and ones in tough neighborhoods, ones with easy-going leadership and ones with authoritarian leadership, the administrators would feel confident that shifting the entire police force to compressed scheduling would prove successful. Another application of a comparison group pretest/posttest design is illustrated in Example 3.4.

The comparison group design controls for the threats to internal and external validity in the following fashion:

History, maturation: may be controlled by design. Note possible threat of local history, that is, the event affects one group and not another. Similarly, selection and maturation may interact, that is, independent of the experiment, one group is changing faster than another.

Experimental mortality: not well controlled by design, but can be detected.

Selection, statistical regression, contamination: not controlled by design.

Testing: controlled by design.

External validity: may be reduced since neither experimental nor control group is randomly assigned. However, external validity may be improved greatly by replication in different settings.

In the comparison group pretest/posttest design illustrated in Example 3.4, the experimental group consisted of people who first signed up to have their

EXAMPLE 3.4

An Application of a Comparison Group Pretest/Posttest Design

Problem: Determine whether a home weatherization program for low-income families reduced energy consumption.

Subjects: 59 weatherized homes and 37 homes waiting for weatherization in Minnesota.

Independent variable: Participation in the weatherization program that provided as needed: insulation, weatherstripping, storm doors and windows, glass replacement, repairs.

Dependent variables:

Percentage British Thermal Units (BTUs) saved.
BTUs saved per degree day per square foot of living space. $(O_2 - O_1)$
Dollars saved per degree day. $(O_2 - O_1)$

Design diagram:

$$O_1 \: X \: O_2$$
$$O_1 \quad O_2$$

Threats to internal validity:

History: no apparent threat noted.
Maturation: controlled by design.
Selection, statistical regression: no apparent bias although comparison group had applied later than experimental group for weatherization; both groups had similar amount of floor space, number of occupants, percent owner occupied.
Experimental mortality: various subjects eliminated because of moves, being away from home, or inability to get accurate fuel records.
Testing, instrumentation: controlled by design.
Contamination: none noted.

Threats to external validity: Interaction between history and treatment; interaction between setting and treatment possible. Study took place in Minnesota in the late 1970s, a period of high energy costs.

Findings:

	Weatherized Home (Average)	Nonweatherized Home (Average)
Percent BTUs saved:	10.95	-2.48
BTUs saved per degree day per square foot:	1.68	-0.295
Dollars saved per degree day:	.006	.001

Discussion: On the average, weatherized homes saved 13 percent in fuel consumption; the cost of weatherization was paid back in 3.5 years. Data and design support benefits of weatherization; more evidence needed to support generalizability of findings.

SOURCE: E. Hirst and R. Talwar, "Reducing Energy Consumption in Low-Income Homes," *Evaluation Review,* (October 1981): 671–685. (Copyright © 1981 by Sage Publications. Reprinted by permission of Sage Publications.)

homes weatherized. The comparison group consisted of people who signed up later and were on a waiting list. The researchers gathered data to make certain that the two groups were similar in respect to the size of their homes, the number of occupants, and the ratio of home owners to renters. Other unexamined differences between the groups may have existed. To decide whether such evidence suggests that a weatherization program is effective, decision makers must use their own judgment and experience to decide whether plausible uncontrolled threats to internal validity may have changed the findings.

The *interrupted time-series design* incorporates an independent variable other than time into the time-series design. The design improves greatly upon the before/after design. As contrasted to the simple time series, the interrupted time-series design introduces an independent variable and can be used to trace the effects of that variable upon other variables. The simple time-series design, on the other hand, is used to describe the values of one variable over time and not to explain changes in those values.

The interrupted time-series design calls for several observations before the introduction of the independent variable. These observations help to demonstrate that exposure to the independent variable resulted in a change in the dependent variable that cannot be attributed to long-term trends, cycles, or seasonal events. A series of observations made after the introduction of the independent variable provides evidence specifying the effect of an independent variable. The independent variable may have resulted in (1) an abrupt permanent change in the dependent variable, (2) an abrupt temporary change, which lessens and eventually returns to the baseline level, and (3) a gradual permanent change in which the initial change gradually increases or decreases to a point where it starts to level off.[14] The energy-savings contest described in Example 3.2 seems to illustrate the second situation. Although the data were incomplete, one could imagine that as the weeks passed, the students would revert to their previous energy-consumption habits.

In such designs, the independent variable may be introduced by the researcher. However, it is more likely that the independent variable is something that occurs naturally or is introduced by someone else. In many cases exposure to the independent variable has already occurred when the analyst is in a position to study its possible effects.

The design may be represented as follows:

$$O_1 \; O_2 \; O_3 \; O_4 \; X \; O_5 \; O_6 \; O_7 \; O_8$$

The number of Os and their placement in relation to X dependent on the number of observations made before and after the independent variable was introduced. The design controls best for maturation as a threat to internal validity because the observations illustrate how the dependent variable changes with the passage of time. The design also rules out the effects of statistical regression. Other threats to internal validity may be eliminated after a researcher checks into the probability that each occurred. Fluctuations in a time series may be due to long-term trends, cyclical variations, seasonal trends, and random fluctuations. The interrupted time-series design can eliminate these alternative explanations of what caused changes occurring after an intervention.

A researcher should be especially alert for an interaction between selection and treatment, that is, he wants to be confident that the preintervention data represent a population similar to the postintervention data.[15] For example, to evaluate the effectiveness of a year-round school requires a researcher to determine if the school's student body changed after the year-round school program began. Students who disliked school and dreaded the prospect of losing their long summer vacation may have transferred to other schools and more competitive students may have transferred into the year-round school. Changes in student performance may then be due to changes in the student body and not to the longer school year. A review of the records may suggest other events that could have caused the dependent variable. A researcher should examine program records to determine the extent of experimental mortality. He should make sure that no change in instrument occurred during the time that the observations were made.

The list below summarizes how the interrupted time-series design protects against threats to internal and external validity.

Threats to Validity with Interrupted Time-Series Design
    A. *To internal validity:*

> History, instrumentation: not protected against by the design. Researcher should review records to determine whether other events occurred at the same time as the intervention or whether any change in measurement procedure occurred.

> Maturation, statistical regression, testing: protected against by the design. Changes associated with long-term trends, cycles, seasonal variations, and random fluctuations can be ruled out if the design has a sufficient number of data points (at least 50 data points are recommended for statistical analysis).

> Selection: Researcher needs to make sure that intervention does not coincide with a major change in the population being measured.

> Experimental mortality: not ruled out by design. Researcher should check records to determine whether subjects dropped out after the occurrence of the independent variable.

    B. *To external validity:* The design does not control against threats to external validity. Interaction between selection and treatment in particular is a potential problem.

The interrupted time-series design works best if the independent variable is expected to have a marked and immediate effect. Otherwise, its effect mistakenly may be attributed to long-term trends, cycles, or seasonal effects unless these are removed through statistical procedures. Statistical procedures can help a researcher confirm his impressions that an effect is markedly greater than expected fluctuations.[16] This design also works best if the independent variable can be introduced all at once at a clearly identified time. If it is phased in gradually, its effects may be more difficult to identify.

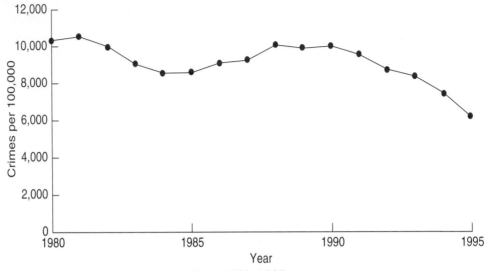

Figure 3.1   New York City Crime Rate, 1980–1995

SOURCE: "Criminal Justice Indicators New York City: 1980–1995," New York State Division of Criminal Justice Services February 13, 1997, (http://criminaljustice.state.nyu.us/crimnet/ojsa/areastate/areastat.cgi").

The interrupted time-series design provides journalists, politicians, and researchers a convenient, easily implemented way to track the impact of a public policy. In 1994 New York's Mayor Rudy Giuliani's newly appointed police chief instituted reforms that emphasized community policing targeted at crime "hot spots." The Mayor's biography cites the program's success, "Under Mayor Giuliani's leadership, New York City has experienced an unprecedented 38 percent reduction in overall crime and 48 percent reduction in murder since 1993."[17] Figure 3.1 supports the Mayor's boast. Although the city's crime rate began dropping in 1989, the crime rates in 1994 and 1995 were the lowest since 1980. The crime rate decreased 11 percent in 1994 and 16 percent in 1995, the greatest drops over the 15-year period. (Disk problem 2 gives New York City's homicide data from 1980–1995.)

As tracking and reporting statistical data becomes a common way to monitor and reward performance, a serious type of design contamination may occur. That is, data collectors, administrators, or analysts will be tempted to manipulate the data to their advantage. For example, one can imagine a police department reconsidering how it classifies some deaths in order to avoid showing an increased homicide rate.

The data eliminate maturation or statistical regression as threats. Yet, they do not confirm the success of community policing or Giuliani's leadership. Other cities also experienced lower crime during the same time period. Other reasons cited for the drop included improvements in the economy, less use of crack cocaine, and relatively fewer teenagers in the population. Furthermore, the re-

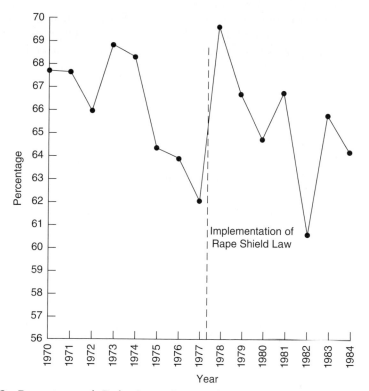

Figure 3.2 Percentage of Defendants Convicted on Rape or Rape-related Charges, Chicago 1970–1984

SOURCE: Data from C. Spohn and J. Horney, "A Case of Unrealistic Expectations: The Impact of the Rape Reform Legislation in Illinois," *Criminal Justice Policy Research 4* (1990): 11.

ported crime rate does not measure the incidence of crime. Cynical citizens may not call the police; burnt out police officers may not file crime reports. To demonstrate the effectiveness of police strategies requires more analysis. Investigators should confirm that reporting patterns were consistent. They should see if changes in the economy, in drug use, or in the population's age distribution coincide with changes in the crime rate. They should compare other cities' data with New York City's data.

To illustrate an interrupted time-series design with more complete analysis, we examined a study on the effect of the Illinois rape shield law. A common legal reform enacted by legislatures in the 1970s and 1980s, rape shield laws restricted the ability of defense attorneys to introduce evidence about the victim's past sexual history into a rape trial. Advocates of rape shield laws argued that a change in existing laws would encourage women to report rapes, press charges, and increase conviction rates. Illinois implemented a rape shield law in April 1978. Figure 3.2, based on data drawn from a more detailed study,[18] shows the yearly data on the conviction rates for rape or rape-related charges in Chicago.

The conviction rate went up in 1978, but in subsequent years the conviction rates dropped and did not look markedly different from the years before the reform. Recall that to implement a time-series design, a researcher should also collect qualitative information. The qualitative information allows the researcher to identify other factors that could have caused an observed change. In this study the researchers interviewed judges, state attorneys, and public defenders. From the interviews and extensive statistical evidence, the researchers concluded that the law "had no impact on the indictment rate, the conviction rate, or incarceration time." The researchers learned that prior to 1978, case law had started to restrict the use of sexual history as evidence; thus, the reform had been more gradual than it appeared. The researchers also observed that the law could have affected only cases that a jury heard and in which a claim of consent was part of the defense. Since less than 10 percent of rape cases were heard by a jury, the potential of the law to affect overall conviction rates was less than its advocates expected.

This example suggests the complexity of interpreting an interrupted time-series design. The graphical information is helpful and easily understood. Often, the graphs are only a first step; they are usually followed by detailed statistical analysis.[19] Tracking a variable and watching its variations raises interesting questions about what actually caused the shift. One strategy is to enrich the time-series design by collecting similar information from an untreated comparison group.

An addition of a comparison time series of an untreated group is seen occasionally with the interrupted time-series design. This design is called *interrupted time series with comparison group* and allows the researcher to compare the dependent variable time series of the treatment group with the same series for a nonequivalent, nontreatment group.

In such a design, a time series, which is interrupted by the occurrence of the independent variable, is developed for the treatment group. In addition, a time series is developed concurrently for another group not exposed to the independent variable. If the groups are equivalent in important aspects, the addition of the comparison group can provide a check on some threats to internal validity. To check the effectiveness of New York City's community policing, one might choose another major American city (Chicago, Philadelphia, or Boston) where community policing was not implemented. To control for selection as a threat to internal validity, the comparison city should have similar populations, e.g., similar variations in age, ethnic background, income, and drug use. One also looks for "local history," that is, events that occurred in one city and not in the other, which could have caused the changes in crime rate.

The interrupted time series with comparison group design is diagrammed as follows:

$$O_1 \; O_2 \; O_3 \; O_4 \; O_5 \; X \; O_6 \; O_7 \; O_8 \; O_9 \; O_{10}$$
$$O_1 \; O_2 \; O_3 \; O_4 \; O_5 \qquad O_6 \; O_7 \; O_8 \; O_9 \; O_{10}$$

Example 3.5 summarizes an interrupted time series with a comparison group design.[20] The researchers were evaluating Arizona's change in drunk-driving laws. To control for history as a threat, they collected data from San Diego, which had implemented a similar law six months earlier. El Paso, which had not enacted similar legislation, served as a comparison group.

EXAMPLE 3.5

An Application of an Interrupted Time-Series Design

Situation: In 1982, Arizona and California implemented drunk-driving laws that carried severe penalties for persons convicted of Driving While Intoxicated (DWI). Research was conducted on the effectiveness of the Arizona law.

Subjects: Cities of El Paso, Phoenix, and San Diego.

Independent variable: Strict DWI law implemented in California in January 1982, and in Arizona in July 1982.

Dependent variable: Number of motor vehicle fatalities.

Design: Monthly data were collected from 1980 through 1984.

Phoenix: $O_1 \ldots O_{24}$ $O_{25} \ldots O_{30}$ X $O_{31} \ldots O_{60}$
San Diego: $O_1 \ldots O_{24}$ X $O_{25} \ldots O_{30}$ $O_{31} \ldots O_{60}$
El Paso: $O_1 \ldots O_{24}$ $O_{25} \ldots O_{30}$ $O_{31} \ldots O_{60}$

Possible threats to internal validity:

History: Data from San Diego and El Paso, two southwestern cities similar to Phoenix, were gathered to control for possible effects such as weather and influx of winter residents.

Instrumentation: assumed that measurement of fatality did not change throughout the data collection period.

Selection: assumed that the DWI law did not change the type of motorists who drove in Phoenix or the other cities.

Maturation, statistical regression: controlled by the design.

Other threats were assumed not to apply.

Possible threats to external validity: This study served to validate the impact of stricter drunk-driving laws, which had been studied by other researchers. In Phoenix the media gave extensive coverage to the spending law change. The law's effect may have been much less without the media coverage.

Findings: Figure 3.3 reports the quarterly vehicular fatalities. (The researchers' monthly data were collapsed to make the data easier to examine.) Fatalities decreased over 50 percent in both Phoenix and San Diego immediately after the implementation of the DWI laws. El Paso, which did not enact strict DWI laws during the period, did not show a similar decrease. In the following months, vehicular fatalities in Phoenix and San Diego gradually increased, approaching the baseline level.

Continued

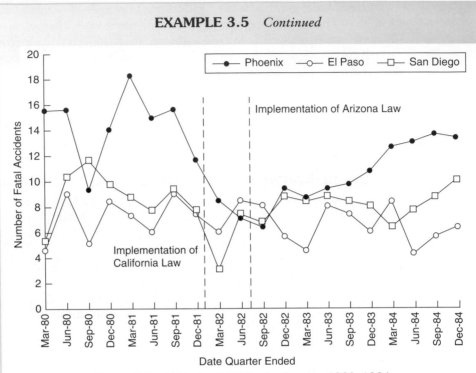

EXAMPLE 3.5   *Continued*

Figure 3.3   Vehicular Fatalities by Quarter, 1980–1984

Discussion: The researchers inspected the graphed raw data and conducted detailed statistical analysis. They concluded that the law's effect was temporary; that is, the decrease in fatalities after the implementation of strict DWI laws did not last. The researchers observed that Phoenix's motor vehicle fatalities started to decrease in January 1982, before the law went into effect. They attributed this decrease to the media's attention to the legislation.

The researcher's qualitative analysis found that the law caused a serious backlog in the criminal-justice system, because motorists were more likely to take legal action to avoid losing their licenses and going to jail.

SOURCE: S. G. West and J. W. Reich, "An Evaluation of Arizona's July 1982 Drunk Driving Law: Effects on the City of Phoenix." *Journal of Applied Social Psychology,* (1989): 1213–1237.

NONEXPERIMENTAL DESIGNS

Nonexperimental designs do not control for threats to internal validity. If an intervention is implemented on randomly selected subjects, which occurs occasionally, the designs have some external validity. The value of nonexperimental designs may be overlooked because of the obvious limitation of drawing conclusions when threats to validity, including history, maturation, statistical regression, and selection, are uncontrolled. The three nonexperimental designs are:

Single group posttest:	X	O_1
Single group pretest/posttest:	O_1 X	O_2

Nonequivalent groups posttest only: $\qquad X \qquad O_1$

$$O_1$$

To illustrate the value and limitation of a single group posttest, we selected research descriptions from two news stories. The design of each study can be inferred from the following quotes:

> About 400 people showed up yesterday to enroll for a special [farecards] available to senior citizens at half price after the Transit Authority sent a news release to three Chinese-language newspapers.[21]

> In a single year [South Carolina's welfare-to-work program] has put 442 welfare recipients on its payroll without creating any new jobs or displacing any state workers.[22]

Although single group posttest studies do not control for any threats to internal validity, only plausible threats need to be considered. In the Chinese-language news release "experiment," history and maturation, the most plausible threats, can be eliminated. The press release announced that a mobile unit would come to New York City's Chinatown to take farecard applications. The mobile unit had been traveling throughout the city for six months; however, prior to the press release relatively few people had used it to apply for farecards. Thus the press release seems to have been a success.

The success of the welfare-to-work program is less certain. People who work in low-paying, low-skilled jobs, rely on welfare during periods of unemployment. The 442 jobs were concentrated in food service, maintenance, and personal services. Maturation or history cannot be eliminated as threats. The 442 jobs normally may be held by people who move on and off welfare depending on their employment status. The state did not know how many welfare recipients it had hired in previous years. Economic growth may have shrunk the pool of job applicants and forced the state to develop new employee sources. The state may have hired welfare recipients because of its inability to find other employees. A good economy, rather than the welfare-to-work program, may have contributed to hiring former welfare recipients.

Even if plausible threats to internal validity cannot be eliminated, the single group pretest provides useful information. First, the design indicates whether an intervention worked as well as expected. The Transit Authority expected 50 people to visit its mobile unit in Chinatown. Its expectations were greatly exceeded. If hardly any people had showed up, the Transit Authority might have concluded that press releases in foreign language newspapers were not helpful. If South Carolina investigators found that the state had hired few welfare recipients, they would question the effectiveness of the welfare-to-work program. Second, the design does not preclude developing valuable, detailed information. In South Carolina, investigators studied the jobs welfare recipients had—the type of work, whether the jobs were temporary or permanent, whether they had benefits. Such information can further demonstrate whether the welfare-to-work program is effective or not.

The single group pretest posttest design does no better at controlling for threats to internal validity, but it does add one useful piece of information. It indicates if something changed between the pretest and the posttest. A pretest/posttest design establishes if program participants changed. Participants are "tested" at a program's beginning and end. The change in their performance may be attributed to the program, but are there alternative explanations? Consider a 10-week course to train new staff how to answer taxpayer inquiries. Participants are tested on their knowledge of the tax code. At the beginning of the course, 30 percent had a score of 85 or better, and at the end, 80 percent had a score of 85 or better. What factors, other than the program, might have brought about the improvement? We can think of four:

If participants work as they attend the training course, the posttest scores may reflect what they learned on the job about the tax code.

People with low pretest scores may have dropped out of the course, contributing to some of the improvement.

The pretest may have motivated people to study the tax code on their own and their "homework," rather than the training, improved their posttest scores.

An unfamiliar format may have lowered the performance on the pretest. Some posttest improvement may be attributed to familiarity with the test format.

Problems of design contamination may arise in studies of programs intended to change attitudes or behaviors. At the time of the posttest, participants may give answers or act in a way that suggests that they have adopted the expected attitudes or behaviors. Nevertheless, their attitudes may have stayed the same, and they have not really altered their behavior.

The single group pretest/posttest has strengths similar to those of the single group posttest. First, investigators can decide if a policy or program meets their expectations. Second, they can gather data to answer specific questions about a program. Third, they can combine their knowledge of the program with other information and make a plausible case that it is effective.

Whether an investigator examines a policy's impact with a single group posttest, a single group pretest/posttest, or interrupted time-series design may depend on the availability of data. As policy agendas change so do data requirements. For example, South Carolina apparently never saw a need to track how many former welfare recipients worked for the state. The single group posttest or single group pretest/posttest may be the best that one can do.

The last nonexperimental design compares two groups: a group that experienced an intervention and a group that did not. The design has the same limitations as the other nonexperimental designs. One cannot tell if differences between groups existed prior to the intervention nor can one tell what, if any, changes took place in each group. Yet similar to the other nonexperimental designs, the nonequivalent group's posttest provides useful information.

Example 3.6 describes a nonequivalent groups posttest design to evaluate the effectiveness of parent training. The information identified the parts of the program

EXAMPLE 3.6

An Application of Nonequivalent Groups Posttest Design

Problem: A program conducts a parent education course for parents charged with child abuse. Program staff want to know how well the program is working.

Subjects: Data gathered from 22 people who had completed the parent training program and 20 people on a waiting list to attend the next training program. Only 20 people were on waiting list; 35 people have completed the course, but only 22 could be reached.

Intervention (Independent variable): Parent education course
Dependent variable: Knowledge of effective parenting strategies
Design:

$$X\ O_1$$
$$O_1$$

Findings:

Strategies for handling a child's temper tantrum

68 percent course participants suggested a positive strategy
40 percent waiting list members suggested a positive strategy

Strategies for handling a child who doesn't want to go to school

59 percent course participants suggested a positive strategy
60 percent waiting list members suggested a positive strategy

Threats to internal validity:

Selection: Waiting list members assumed similar to attendees, but criteria for referring to program or putting on waiting list may have changed over time.

Experimental mortality: Problems in reaching course participants; may have reached only more stable (and more successful) participants.

History: Not controlled

Instrumentation: Controlled, investigators were randomly assigned course participants and waiting list members (which controlled for different interviewing styles)

Maturation, statistical regression, testing: Not applicable

Discussion: The staff used information from the study to assess program components. They identified which concepts needed more emphasis and which needed less. Participants did not seem to give socially acceptable responses. When asked how they handled stress, some parents indicated that they used alcohol or over indulged in their favorite foods. Similarly, parents said they did not agree that they should negotiate with children, even though this was taught in the course.

SOURCE: Adapted from W. Combs et al. "The Evaluation of the Nurturing Program," unpublished evaluation, Department of Political Science and Public Administration, North Carolina State University, (Raleigh, NC, 1996).

that were working and the parts that needed improvement. The particular study had a problem often encountered in collecting data from social service clients, e.g., the inability to keep in contact with former clients. People move, their phones are disconnected, or other household members are careless about taking messages.

OBSERVATIONAL STUDIES

Observational designs, developed in epidemiology, involve no manipulation by investigators; rather, investigators observe outcomes that occur under natural conditions and try to isolate variables that may have caused these outcomes. Observational designs are employed primarily by biomedical researchers, but we mention these designs here because of the widespread public interest in health issues and the policy impact of the health-research findings. Specifically, epidemiologists work with case-control and cohort designs to identify environmental factors that may cause diseases or other deleterious effects.

Case-control designs, also called *retrospective designs,* construct a study group and a comparison group to answer the question, "Why do some people suffer from a specific disease or condition and others don't?" The subjects are identified as either cases or noncases. The study group consists of "cases," that is, subjects with the condition of interest. The investigators trace the subjects' histories to identify a factor that may have caused the condition. The comparison group consists of "noncases." The researchers gather data on the backgrounds of the comparison group members to see if they have been exposed to the same factor and, if so, to what extent.

One author states that case-control studies "constitute the major methodological advance in epidemiological methods in our time."[23] The design markedly improves the efficiency and feasibility of research conducted on relatively rare diseases or diseases that develop over a long period of time. Without this design, researchers would be required to work with large samples over long periods of time.

Nevertheless, the design has serious limitations. Selection as a bias cannot be eliminated. The identification of an appropriate comparison group is particularly difficult.[24] What population should be used as a source of noncases of lung cancer? Other cancer patients? Patients with noncancerous lung diseases? "Healthy" subjects? We assume that each potential comparison group may differ from the study group with respect to more than one potential risk factor. The design is limited further by the need to depend on retrospectively collected information. Needed data may not exist, records may be incomplete or inaccurate, and we cannot assume that subjects will accurately remember what they did in the past. The existence of the disease may cause subjects to "hypothesis guess" or to selectively recall their exposure to a risk factor.

Cohort studies, also called *prospective studies,* follow a study group forward in time to identify subsequent health outcomes. The subjects may represent two populations: those with the risk factor present and those without the risk factor. Alternatively, the subjects may represent varying degrees of exposure to the risk factor. The subjects are followed to determine and compare the frequency of the disease occurring in various cohorts.

Unlike the case-control design, the investigator conducting a cohort study knows that the risk factor occurred before the disease was detectable. This advantage can operate as a limiting factor. To establish that the risk factor occurs before the disease, data on risk factors must be gathered at the beginning of the study. Consequently, researchers cannot add other risk factors once the study is underway.[25] The cohort design does not eliminate selection as a bias. Nevertheless, the greater problem is experimental mortality, that is, subjects may not provide follow-up data because they moved away, lost interest, or died.

The design can be modified and the study carried out retrospectively. Such a modification is most likely to occur in the cases of rare diseases or in studies of occupational groups. To study a rare disease, gathering data prospectively is inefficient; a large number of subjects is required to detect a risk factor's effect. Unlike the case-control study, subjects are selected on the basis of their exposure to the risk factor and not on the development of a disease. When the researcher can obtain sound data, this alteration works reasonably well.[26] Specifically, the researcher needs to have access to data on the risk factor for a population whose health status has been followed for a period of time, such as workers who have regular company-sponsored physical examinations or are participants in longitudinal health studies.

CAUSALITY AND CROSS-SECTIONAL STUDIES

Administrators analyzing a cross-sectional study may want to infer causal relationships from the data. For example, administrators may survey graduates of employment training programs to determine the effectiveness of training. Imagine that the survey finds that persons who received on-the-job training earn more than people who received only classroom training. Can one conclude that on-the-job training caused the higher incomes? The finding of greater earnings for on-the-job participants shows a statistical association between type of training and earnings. We can establish quickly if the training (the independent variable) occurred before reported earnings (the dependent variable). Nevertheless, the concluding piece of evidence, the ability to eliminate alternative hypotheses, is elusive.

When analyzing data from experiments and quasi-experiments, the analyst contends with a limited number of threats to internal validity. In cross-sectional studies a seemingly unlimited number of possible, uncontrolled threats can be identified. The major uncontrolled threat is the inability to control subject selection. The greater earnings of on-the-job training participants may be due to their greater job readiness at the beginning of training or their higher degree of motivation and ambition. If you had more information on the dataset, you could identify other problems with internal validity. For example, if the training programs were conducted in different locations, the on-the-job training participants may be merely benefiting from a more robust economy. Investigators may suggest other plausible third variables, any one of which may demonstrate that the relationship is spurious.

When designing studies to establish causality, researchers prefer experimental and quasi-experimental designs. The deliberate introduction and manipulation of

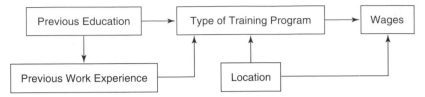

Figure 3.4 Model to Infer Training Effect on Earnings

an independent variable provides much stronger evidence of causality than can a cross-sectional study. Nevertheless, if an experimental or quasi-experimental design cannot be implemented, or if the analyst has to rely on existing cross-sectional data, she may employ sophisticated analytical techniques to make plausible inferences about causal relationships. The adequacy of her analysis depends on her ability to select and use tools accurately to represent complex interactions among variables.[27]

Drawing upon theoretical knowledge and empirical experience, she should build a model, such as the schematic shown in Figure 3.4, which specifies the sequence and direction of relationships. Such a schematic representation places variables in time order from left to right. The most distant event is placed on the left-hand side; the most recent event is placed on the right. Arrows are drawn to identify and give the direction of possible causal relationships. The model will guide her statistical analysis.

The model helps users and critics to analyze a problem better. They can debate whether the model includes the relevant variables and if the effect of included variables has been identified correctly. Whether the model offers a basis for inferring causal relationships depends on its theoretical strength. That is, the analysts should have a coherent, logical explanation justifying the linkages between variables.

SUMMARY

Experimental and quasi-experimental designs provide us with useful models of how to conduct research to establish causal links between independent and dependent variables. Rather than just describing the changes in the values of dependent variables, the analyst uses these designs to help explain those changes. In an experimental design, the researcher has control over the assignment of subjects to groups, the introduction of the independent variable, and the research conditions. Quasi-experimental designs lack one or more of these controls.

With the constraints and resources of a given situation, each experimental or quasi-experimental design must be constructed to minimize possible threats to internal and external validity. An internally valid design is one that eliminates factors other than the independent variable as possible explanations of changes in the dependent variable. The common threats to internal validity are history, maturation, statistical regression, selection, testing, instrumentation, experimental mortality, and design contamination. Experimental designs eliminate most threats to internal validity at the onset of a research study through random assignment of subjects or a combination of matching and random assignment. Nevertheless, simply implementing an experimental design does not protect against subject attrition, nor can it prevent design contamination. If subjects drop out of a study, a researcher should document their attrition and attempt to document whether dropouts are systematically different from continuers. Contamination may be unavoidable in some studies. If participants are markedly affected by the outcome of a study, they can be expected to behave in such a way as to enhance their own interests.

An externally valid design yields findings that can be generalized beyond the test population. Unique features of a program can unintentionally become part of the treatment. A characteristic of the participants, the setting, or the time may interact with the treatment to make the program succeed or fail. Cook and Campbell have postulated that replication of program findings among different populations and settings provides acceptable evidence of external validity even if these studies have poorly designed samples.

An understanding of internal and external validity and the possible threats to each helps an administrator to evaluate the quality of a design and decide whether she is justified in having confidence in a study's findings. An administrator must, therefore, seek to determine whether plausible threats to validity, which could radically change the findings and her decision, have been eliminated. The experimental and quasi-experimental designs discussed here are used widely to minimize threats to validity. Nevertheless, an administrator will want to go beyond identifying the type of design and determine if serious threats were considered and controlled.

Experimental designs depend on random assignment of subjects to a treatment or a control group. The two-group design may be modified to include several treatment groups and to eliminate a no-treatment control group. This modification frequently is necessary to avoid ethical problems of withholding treatment. Researchers will often prefer the ease and efficiency of the randomized posttest design to the classical experiment. The latter design may be necessary, however, if a study includes few subjects or the researcher needs to identify the amount of change brought about by the independent variable. In addition to checking for experimental mortality and design contamination, the researcher should make sure that, save for exposure to the independent variable, the experimental and control groups experience similar conditions from the beginning of the experiment to its end. If program personnel conduct the study, the researcher should ensure that subjects are randomly assigned to groups and that the study is implemented as designed.

Experimentation requires researchers to control the research environment. Frequently, they cannot exert such control and must, as a result, use a quasi-experimental design. In designing a quasi-experiment they try to control as many threats to internal and external validity as possible. The major difference between experimental and quasi-experimental designs is that the latter do not have randomly assigned subjects. Often researchers use comparison groups, but they cannot eliminate the possibility of a selection bias.

Nonexperimental designs lack internal validity. Nevertheless, they can demonstrate if an intervention met expectations. Information gathered using these limited designs may be useful in developing and implementing more effective programs. Existing information may act to eliminate plausible threats to internal validity. A researcher may be able only to implement a nonexperimental design because no pretest data were gathered.

Observational designs primarily are implemented by biomedical researchers. We included these designs because of the importance of epidemiological findings in public policy. The investigator's lack of control over the research environment makes these studies susceptible to problems with internal validity.

In deciding what type of design to use, administrators should define clearly what they want to find out and how they plan to use the information. If they want data on variables that have received little attention, they may want a limited study before authorizing a more extensive experimental study. Whether the design should be quasi-experimental or descriptive depends on the question to be investigated and the availability of data. Occasionally, the inability to control the implementation of a program or the selection of participants requires an analyst to settle for a cross-sectional design. If a cross-sectional design is utilized, analysts must understand fully the interactions among variables and collect data on relevant variables. With a carefully specified model, analysts may use sophisticated statistical tools to infer causality.

Chapters 2 and 3 have discussed research designs—the planning of a study in such a way that the behavior of a variable can be described or explained. The next chapters take up the topics of measuring variables and the procedures for collecting data. Chapter 4 introduces another type of validity—operational validity. This is important for evaluating the measures of variables. The chapter also discusses various levels of measurement for variables. These are especially important in considering the appropriate statistical tests to use in order to analyze the data.

NOTES

1. See T. D. Cook and D. T. Campbell, *Quasi-Experimentation: Design and Analysis Issues for Field Settings* (Boston: Houghton Mifflin, 1979), 9–36 for a discussion of the concept of causality.

2. D. T. Campbell and J. C. Stanley, *Experimental and Quasi-Experimental Designs for Research* (Chicago: Rand McNally, 1966), and Cook and Campbell, *Quasi-Experimentation.*

3. Cook and Campbell, *Quasi-Experimentation,* 55–56.

4. Any of these factors may act in combination with the treatment to produce the particular outcome of the study. Although the treatment may be present for other cases, the particular values of these factors may not be present. Hence, external validity would be affected and the results could not be generalized. Methodologists refer to the combination of these factors with the treatment as interaction.

5. Cook and Campbell, *Quasi-Experimentation,* 73, 75–76.

6. This material on matching is from L. S. Meyers and N. E. Grossen, *Behavioral Research* (San Francisco: W. H. Freeman, 1974), 126–127. For a more detailed, statistical discussion of matching, see D. G. Killeinbaum et al., *Epidemiological Research* (Belmont, CA: Wadsworth, Lifetime Learning Publications, 1982), chap. 18, or S. Anderson et al. in *Statistical Methods for Comparative Studies* (New York: Wiley-Interscience, 1980). S. Isaac, in *Handbook in Research and Evaluation* (San Diego: EDITS Publishers, 1971), 72, recommends A. L. Edwards, *Experimental Designs in Psychological Research,* 3d ed. (New York: Holt, Rinehart & Winston, 1968), chap. 9, for arguments in favor of matching.

7. See M. L. Dennis, "Assessing the Validity of Randomized Field Experiments: An Example from Drug Abuse Treatment Research," *Evaluation Review 14* (1990): 347–373, for a bibliography on the use of randomized field experiments.

8. G. P. Waldo and T. G. Chiricos, "Work Release and Recidivism," *Evaluation Quarterly* (February 1977): 87–107.

9. Cook and Campbell, *Quasi-Experimentation,* 344–382, discuss the limitations of field experiments as well as situations when they are appropriate. P. H. Rossi and H. E. Freeman have a brief discussion on the limitations of randomized field experiments in *Evaluation: A Systemic Approach,* 4th ed. (Beverly Hills: Sage, 1989), 304–307.

10. E. J. Posavac and R. G. Carey, *Program Evaluation: Methods and Case Studies,* 4th ed. (Englewood Cliffs, NJ: Prentice-Hall, 1992), 184–186.

11. Cook and Campbell, *Quasi-Experimentation,* 367–369.

12. Campbell and Stanley, *Experimental and Quasi-Experimental Designs,* 34.

13. Posavac and Carey, *Program Evaluation,* 167–170 discuss the problems associated with selecting comparison groups and give examples.

14. S. G. West and J. W. Reich, "An Evaluation of Arizona's July 1982 Drunk Driving Law: Effects on the City of Phoenix," *Journal of Applied Social Psychology* 19 (1989), 1213–1237. R. McCleary and R. A. Hay, Jr., *Applied Time Series Analysis for the Social Sciences* (Beverly Hills: Sage, 1980), chap. 3, present the statistical analysis procedures for confirming these patterns. Cook and Campbell, *Quasi-Experimentation,* chap. 5, discuss the types of effects, various time-series designs, and how to handle gradual implementation or delayed causation.

15. West and Reich, "Evaluation," 1216, gave an example illustrating this problem.

16. Cook and Campbell, *Quasi-Experimentation,* 225–232 and chap. 6.

17. "Biography of Mayor Rudolph W. Giuliani," NYC Link, New York City's Official Web Site (http://www.ci.nyc.ny.us), February 13, 1997.

18. C. Spohn and J. Horney, "A Case of Unrealistic Expectations: The Impact of Rape Reform Legislation in Illinois," *Criminal Justice Policy Research 4* (1990), 1–18.

19. McCleary and Hay, *Applied Time Series Analysis,* present statistical procedures to statistically analyze time-series data. Alternatively, the reader can consult L. J. McCain

and R. McCleary, "The Statistical Analysis of Simple Interrupted Time-Series Quasi-Experiment," chap. 6, in Cook and Campbell, *Quasi-Experimentation.*

20. Cook and Campbell, *Quasi-Experimentation,* label this specific design as an "interrupted time series with switching replication," 223–225.

21. G. Pierre-Pierre, "Chinatown Crowd Reveals Unexploited Market for Fare Cards," *New York Times,* May 16, 1997, A16.

22. J. Havemann, "Welfare-to-Work Program: A South Carolina Success Story," *Washington Post,* April 21, 1997, A7.

23. A. M. Walker, *Observation and Inference: An Introduction to the Methods of Epidemiology* (Chestnut Hill, PA: Epidemology Resources, 1991), 73.

24. For a discussion of retrospective design and the problems of selecting comparison groups, see Kleinbaum et al., *Epidemiological Research,* especially 67–70, and chap. 11.

25. Kleinbaum et al., *Epidemiological Research,* 65.

26. See Walker, *Observation,* 44, for a brief discussion on data-quality issues in prospective and retrospective studies, i.e., studies in which the data are collected prior to the "disease's" occurrence and studies in which the data are collected after the "disease's" occurrence, respectively.

27. For information on making causal inferences from cross-sectional designs, see H. B. Asher, *Causal Modeling* (Beverly Hills: Sage, Series on Quantitative Applications in the Social Sciences, #3, 1976); O. Hellevik, *Introduction to Causal Analysis: Exploring Survey Data by Crosstabulation* (London: Allen & Unwin, Contemporary Social Research Series, #9, 1984), and Cook and Campbell, *Quasi-Experimentation,* chap. 7. All these works include extensive discussions on statistical techniques. For a discussion that focuses on the validity issues, see L. B. Mohr, *Impact Analysis for Program Evaluation* (Pacific Grove, CA: Brooks/Cole, 1988), chap. 10.

TERMS FOR REVIEW

experimental design	threats to external validity	control group
quasi-experimental design	reactive effects of experimental	comparison group design
internal validity	arrangements	interrupted time-series design
external validity	random assignment	nonexperimental design
threats to internal validity	experimental group	observational design

QUESTIONS FOR REVIEW

The following questions should indicate whether you have a basic competency in this chapter's material.

1. a. What types of evidence are necessary to support a claim that one variable is the cause of a change in another?
   b. Why is each of these types of evidence necessary?

2. Which of the threats to internal validity is likely to be the most common? Why?

3. Which of the threats to internal validity is likely to cause the most trouble or harm? Why?

4. Contrast history with maturation as threats to internal validity.

5. "Internal validity takes precedence over external validity." Evaluate this statement.

6. Discuss three ways to improve external validity.

7. Consider a study on the effects of noise. Fifty subjects will enter data on a computer spreadsheet. The researchers will introduce random noise in the room where the experimental group is working. Data will be gathered on the number of forms each subject processes correctly in an hour.
   a. The experiment will be held in two rooms (a "quiet" room and a "noisy" room) with 25 work stations. Subjects will not know which room is which. Should the subjects decide which room they want to work in, or should they be assigned to one of the rooms? Justify your answer.
   b. The study will begin at 9 a.m. randomly selected experimental group will work for an hour without intermittent noise, and the first hour's data will be collected. From 10 to 11 a.m., the researchers will introduce noise into the room and collect the second hour's data. The control group will work from 1 to 3 p.m. The data will be collected twice, but no intermittent noise will be introduced. Critique the internal validity of this design.
   c. The study will begin at 9 a.m. The experimental and control groups will work in separate buildings from 9 to 11 a.m. In one

of the buildings, a fire alarm (not part of the experiment) goes off and everyone leaves for 20 minutes. The group returns to the room and works until 11:20 a.m. How would the fire alarm affect the experiment?

8. Does the classical experimental design guarantee that the threats to internal validity are controlled? Explain your answer.

9. What conditions should be met for a posttest-only design to work well?

10. A researcher wants to see if question wording affects how much people say they are willing to pay for a program to prevent the deaths of birds from oil spills. He asks 200 people who come into a San Francisco Science Museum to volunteer to answer a questionnaire. The volunteers are randomly assigned to receive one of four versions of a questionnaire.

    Version 1: How much a respondent is willing to donate for the program

    Version 2: How much a respondent is willing to be taxed for the program

    Version 3: How much a respondent is willing to donate for the program (With a reminder that other people will also be donating)

    Version 4: How much a respondent is willing to be taxed for the program (With a reminder that other people will also be taxed)

    a. Use the R X O notation to summarize the study design.
    b. Briefly assess if the author's use of a nonrandom (convenience) sample will affect the internal validity and external validity of the study.

11. Discuss the strengths and weaknesses of the comparison group pretest/posttest design.

12. Why is the interrupted time-series design used so often in administrative and policy research?

13. Summarize the advantages and disadvantages of nonexperimental designs.

14. A newspaper observes that after an "experiment" in cutting the cost of Internet access,

half the residents of Blacksburg, Virginia, were "regular users of the global computer network." Blacksburg, with a population of 37,000, is home of Virginia Tech, a university with a strong engineering program. Infer the study's design. What threats to internal validity seem plausible?

PROBLEMS FOR HOMEWORK AND DISCUSSION

1. To determine if halfway houses improve the transition from prison, 50 inmates who will be released in a month are randomly assigned to one of two groups. One group is sent to a halfway house to participate in a program called "ReEntry." The other group stays in prison until the time of release. Two months after release, data measuring "success in job placement" are gathered on the subjects in both groups.
   a. Use the R, X, O notation to sketch the research design.
   b. Someone says that the design does not control for statistical regression since the subjects are inmates and thus represent an "extreme in their social behavior." Do you agree that the design has problems with statistical regression? Explain.
   c. Define the terms "internal validity" and "external validity" in the context of this study.

2. Three hundred persons working in 40 state offices process X120 Forms.
   a. To evaluate a proposed change in the X120 Form, would you randomly assign offices or individuals? That is, if offices are assigned, 15 offices would use the form with the proposed change, 15 offices would continue to use the form with the proposed change, and 15 offices would continue to use the existing form. If individuals are assigned, roughly 50 percent of the individuals in the office would use the form with the proposed change, and 50 percent would continue with the existing form.
   b. Would you allow subjects to volunteer to test the new X120 Form? Justify your answer.
   c. Would you test the new X120 Form in the three slowest offices and evaluate the change in productivity? Justify your answer.

3. Rye County Hospital's Wellness Center is testing two programs to get smokers to quit. STOP is offered on Tuesday nights and QUIT is offered on Thursday nights. Ninety smokers volunteered to be subjects. They will be randomly assigned to STOP, QUIT, or No Treatment (neither group).
   a. What two threats to internal validity are controlled by random assignment?
   b. About the time the smoking study started, cigarette taxes increased sharply. Would this affect the internal validity of the study? Justify your answer.
   c. Several subjects assigned to QUIT had a schedule conflict with their aerobics class. Before the program began, a secretary let them trade places with subjects assigned to STOP. Comment on how the secretary's action probably affected the study's internal validity.
   d. STOP and QUIT begin and end in the same week. At the last session of the STOP program, data on the subjects' smoking behavior were gathered. The analysts forgot to gather the same data from the QUIT subjects. Three weeks later the oversight was discovered, and the data were collected. Comment on how the oversight may have affected the study's internal validity.
   e. What is the value of having a No Treatment group?

4. A school system conducts a workshop on child abuse and neglect. Attendance is voluntary; 30 percent of school employees indicate that they will attend. To decide whether the workshops should be continued and attendance made mandatory, the staff selects a comparison group from among employees who did not preregister. Before the workshop, both groups are given a questionnaire on the

signs of child abuse and neglect, attitudes about violence, and knowledge of reporting requirements. A similar questionnaire is given to members of both groups after the workshop is over.

a. Name this type of design. Use the R, X, O notation and diagram the design in symbols.

b. Consider each threat to validity, and explain whether it is a problem in this design.

c. Evaluate the external validity of this study.

d. Suggest a design that would provide better evidence for the decision. Would the staff find this alternative design practical to implement? Explain.

5. To reduce crime, a police force tries team policing, which has two officers walk a beat together. If trouble arises, the team calls a patrol car for backup reinforcement.

a. Suggest two different designs to determine the effectiveness of team policing.

b. Indicate how well each design handles the threats to internal validity.

c. Assess the external validity of these designs.

6. A state housing agency director wants to see if changing procedures in the emergency housing assistance program will speed the processing of claims. He selects a sample of 10 counties, then randomly selects five counties to adopt the new procedures and five to continue with current procedures. He measures the length of time required to process claims before and after the changes are adopted.

a. Name and diagram this design in the R, X, O symbols.

b. Revise the design, making it a randomized posttest design. Explain how the study would be conducted; diagram the new design. Would this design have any advantages over the original design?

7. To study organic farming, researchers matched each organic farm with a nonorganic farm of the same size and soil composition. Some agricultural researchers criticized the study design, which they said should have compared small adjacent plots—one exposed to chemical fertilizers and insecticides and the other not exposed. Assess the benefits of the matched study over the classical experimental study to determine the effectiveness of organic farming.

8. A school system will conduct research prior to deciding if to require 9th graders to take Algebra I. (Currently, only 30 percent of 9th graders take Algebra I. Very few students entering 9th grade have completed Algebra; any 9th grader who has passed Algebra I will not be required to take it again.) Three proposed research plans are outlined here:

Plan A: Select a random sample of files of students who complete 9th grade in June. Compare the math achievement scores of students who took Algebra I with students who have not taken Algebra I.

Plan B: Require all 9th graders in a "typical" high school to take Algebra I in this school year. Compare students' math achievement scores at the beginning of the year with their end-of-year scores.

Plan C: Select two similar high schools. Randomly assign one of the schools to require all 9th graders to take Algebra I in this school year. In the other school, students may choose whether to take Algebra I. Compare the two schools' math achievement scores at the beginning of the year with their end-of-year scores.

a. Evaluate the three plans, and recommend which plan the school system should implement.

b. Assume the school system requires all 9th graders to take Algebra I. The school system wants to conduct an interrupted time series to assess the requirement's effectiveness. What features should the time series include to yield useful information?

9. Design an experimental study to see whether administrators make better use of information from graphs or from tables. Your design should indicate, specifically, subject selection and assignment and how you will control exposure to the independent variable. Unless you plan to carry out the experiment, you do not need to select specific pretest or posttest measures, nor do you have to prepare specific tables and graphs. Generally describe the measures, tables, and graphs you would use.

DISK WORK

1. Graduate students on the first day of a research methods class were given a large envelope containing directions, a scenario, and a questionnaire. The students were told to read a description of a crime, then answer questions about what actions they would recommend. Half the envelopes contained a scenario describing a murder. Half the envelopes contained the same scenario with an added paragraph. The added paragraph described how the perpetrator mutilated the victim. The envelopes were arranged so that every other envelope contained the longer (mutilation) scenario. The questionnaire asked respondents (1) how horrible they rated the crime, (2) the length of sentence they would recommend, (3) whether they would recommend parole in the future, and (4) whether they would recommend the death penalty.

   a. Load the murder data base from the data disk. Compare the questionnaire responses between those who received the mutilation scenario and those who received the non-mutilation scenario. How do the answers of the two groups of respondents differ? Do you think that the differences are probably due to the added description of mutilation? Or are the differences probably due to something else? What else?

   b. Can a researcher generalize from these findings to other populations? Why or why not?

   c. What other types of studies would benefit from a similar research design?

2. Go to the disk and load the city homicide data base.

   a. Plot the New York City data. What do the homicide data suggest about the effectiveness of the 1994 change in city policing? Compare and contrast the crime rate and homicide rate as evidence in demonstrating the effectiveness of the change in policing.

   b. Plot the homicide data for Philadelphia and Chicago. Do they add support to the assertion that the 1994 change in New York City policing contributed to a decrease in homicides? Justify your answer.

RECOMMENDED FOR FURTHER READING

T. D. Cook and D. T. Campbell, *Quasi-Experimentation* (Boston: Houghton Mifflin, 1979) is a valuable resource for understanding fully experimental and quasi-experimental designs in field settings. The authors discuss and extend the ideas presented in D. T. Campbell and J. T. Stanley, *Experimental and Quasi-Experimental Design for Research* (Chicago: Rand McNally, 1966).

The recommended text on the statistical analysis of time-series data is R. McCleary and R. A. Hay, Jr., *Applied Time Series Analysis for the Social Sciences* (Beverly Hills: Sage, 1980).

Texts in program evaluation discuss these designs and give cases illustrating their use. See E. J. Posavac and R. G. Carey, *Program Evaluation: Methods and Case Studies,* 5th ed., (Englewood Cliffs, NJ: Prentice-Hall, 1997). P. H. Rossi, H. E. Freeman, and M. Lipsey, *Evaluation: A Systematic Approach,* 6th ed. (Thousand Oaks, CA: Sage Publications, 1999), *Handbook of Practical Program Evaluation,* ed. by J. S. Wholey et al. (San Francisco: Jossey-Bass Publishers, 1994), especially D. J. Rog's "Constructing Natural 'Experiments.'" J. Valadez and M. Baberger, *Monitoring and Evaluating Social Programs in Developing Countries* (Washington D.C.: World Bank, 1994), present 10 quasi-experimental designs with examples of their use.

For information on observational designs, consult an epidemiological methods text, for example, D. G. Kleinbaum et al., *Epidemiological Research: Principles and Quantitative Methods* (Belmont, CA: Wadsworth, Lifetime Learning Publications, 1982). For an overview of epidemiological methods and statistics, we recommend S. Wassertheil-Smoller, *Biostatistics and Epidemiology: A Primer for Health Professionals* (New York: Springer-Verlag, 1990).

Chapter 4

Measuring Variables

In this chapter you will learn

1. terms associated with quantifying or measuring variables: conceptual and operational definitions, measurement, measurement scales, reliability, operational validity, sensitivity.

2. the importance of measurement decisions to data users.

3. strategies for developing reliable, operationally valid, and sensitive measures.

4. strategies for assessing and improving the reliability, operational validity, and sensitivity of measures.

After identifying variables to study, an investigator decides how to define and measure each one. The investigator may begin with concepts and conceptual definitions. A *concept* is an abstraction representing an idea. *Conceptual definitions* indicate what one means by a concept or a variable; they range from brief oral descriptions to thorough detailed statements.[1] Consider alcohol abuse. Alcohol abuse is a concept. Conceptual definitions for alcohol abuse include: physical or physiological symptoms due to drinking; inability to meet work, social, or family obligations due to drinking; binge drinking; or self-identification of a drinking problem. The appropriate conceptual definition depends on a study's purpose. A university, wanting to identify the extent of alcohol abuse, may define it as involving binge drinking. An employer, wanting to identify sources of workplace problems, may define it as drinking that affects work performance. A physician making diagnoses may define it as involving verifiable symptoms.

Next, guided by the conceptual definition, the investigator finds a way to measure the variable. An *operational definition* is formulated. It details exactly how values will be assigned to a variable. Survey items and their responses provide examples of operational definitions. If the conceptual definition of alcohol abuse was whether or not a person indulged in binge drinking, the accompanying operational definition of alcohol abuse might be: "Alcohol abusers are persons who answered 'yes' to the question, 'Did you drink five or more drinks of wine, beer, or hard liquor at one time during the past month?'"

For another example, let us consider one investigator's measurement of work effort.[2] She conceptually defined work effort as the physical demands of work, that is, the speed, hardness, physical effort, manual dexterity, and repetitiveness. Based on this conceptual definition, she drew up an operational definition, which had two major components. First, respondents read five statements describing their work and checked the best response to each statement. Second, to decide how much work effort each person exerted, the investigator assigned each response a numerical value and added up the responses to the five statements. The details of the operational definition are spelled out in Example 4.1.

EXAMPLE 4.1

An Operational Definition of Work Effort

Survey Items and Responses:
  Check the response that best describes what your job requires each day.

1. My job requires that I work very fast
   _____Less than an hour a day
   _____1–2 hours a day
   _____3–5 hours a day
   _____6 or more hours a day
2. My job requires that I work very hard
   _____Less than an hour a day
   _____1–2 hours a day
   _____3–5 hours a day
   _____6 or more hours a day
3. My job requires a lot of physical effort
   _____Less than an hour a day
   _____1–2 hours a day
   _____3–5 hours a day
   _____6 or more hours a day
4. My job requires me to do very repetitious things
   _____Less than an hour a day
   _____1–2 hours a day
   _____3–5 hours a day
   _____6 or more hours a day
5. My job requires skill in using my hands
   _____Less than an hour a day
   _____1–2 hours a day
   _____3–5 hours a day
   _____6 or more hours a day

Continued

EXAMPLE 4.1 *Continued*

Assigning values:

Step 1: Assign values to each response, that is,
Assign 4 to every "6 or more hours" response
Assign 3 to every "3–5 hours" response
Assign 2 to every "1–2 hours" response
Assign 1 to every "less than an hour" response

Step 2: Total the responses to statements 1–5 to determine a respondent's level of work effort. Note: values can range from 5 (least work effort) to 20 (most work effort).

Step 3: Decide whether to group values, for example,
Minimum work effort: scores 5–10
Moderate work effort: scores 11–15
Great work effort: scores 16–20

SOURCE: Adapted from A. H. Hopkins, *Work and Job Satisfaction in the Public Sector* (Totowa, NJ: Rowman & Allanheld, 1983), 42, 135.

Example 4.2 draws upon an incident in which an engineer convinced a budget director to approve a more productive strategy for resurfacing city highways. We assume that the budget director and the engineer never met to discuss either their conceptual definitions of productivity improvement or how the engineer operationally defined it. The engineer formulated an operational definition of productivity based on his conceptual definition of decreasing the cost per lane-mile paved. Using his operational definition, he analyzed alternative highway resurfacing programs. The budget director, who apparently equated productivity with paving more streets without increasing costs, approved the program that cost $2,500 less for each lane-mile paved. Unfortunately, he had also approved a resurfacing program that cost $187,500 over budget.

The misunderstanding in Example 4.2 should convince you of the importance, even to administrators, of conceptual and operational definitions. Some administrators may think they can ignore the details of defining variables. Such a laissez-faire attitude can result in costly mistakes. Studies based on faulty operational definitions may generate misleading or incorrect data. An operational definition may be faulty because it is based on a faulty conceptual definition or there are technical flaws in the operational definition. (This chapter and Chapter 7 focus on the technical issues that affect the quality of an operational definition.)

One reason studies of the same phenomenon arrive at different, even conflicting, conclusions is that they used different conceptual or operational definitions. Administrative participation in formulating operational definitions has at least three benefits. First, administrators can make sure that the operational definition is consistent with their conceptual definition. Second, admin-

EXAMPLE 4.2

Concepts and Operational Definitions

Problem: Increase the productivity of New York City's highway resurfacing program.

Budget director's conceptual definition of productivity: Ability to produce more services with less resources.

Engineer's conceptual definition of productivity: "Efficiency value," i.e., the difference in cost between a more efficient and a less efficient method.

Operational definition of productivity (based on engineer's conceptual definition): Efficiency value = Reduction in cost per lane-mile × number of miles resurfaced.

Analysis: Compared two alternate policies: (1) paving 75 lane-miles; (2) paving 100 lane-miles.

1. Costs
   a. Labor: $10,000 per lane-mile to pave 75 lane-miles
      Labor: $ 7,500 per lane-mile to pave 100 lane-miles
   b. Asphalt: $7,500 per lane-mile
2. Efficiency value calculations
   a. Reduction in cost per lane-mile
      (1) cost per lane-mile for 75 lane-miles = $10,000 + $7,500 = $17,500
      (2) cost per lane-mile for 100 lane-miles = $7,500 + $7,500 = $15,000
      (3) reduction in cost per lane-mile for 100 lane-miles = $17,500 − $15,000
          = $2,500
   b. Efficiency value = $2,500 × 100 lane-miles = $25,000

Action: Budget director accepted the 100 lane-mile proposal assuming a $25,000 cost saving. Note the actual costs for paving 75 and 100 lane-miles.

$$\text{Cost} = (\text{labor/lane-mile} + \text{asphalt/lane-mile}) \times \text{lane-miles}$$

$$\text{For 75 lane-miles} = (\$10,000 + \$7,500) \times 75 = \$1,312,500$$

$$\text{For 100 lane-miles} = (\$7,500 + \$7,500) \times 100 = \$1,500,000$$

Result: Cost was $187,500 over budget.

Discussion: The budget director's conceptual definition of productivity was that the city could produce more services (100 lane-miles resurfaced) with the same resources used to resurface 75 lane-miles. His conceptual definition required a different operational definition: a definition that linked annual program costs with the number of miles resurfaced.

SOURCE: P. D. Epstein, "The Value of Measuring and Improving Performance," *Public Productivity Review* 6 (September 1982): 157–166.

istrators can identify poorly constructed operational definitions that will yield questionable data. Third, they can decide whether the data will allow them to make decisions or take action.

To evaluate an operational definition, an administrator should know why the information is needed and how it will be used. Suppose a personnel analyst wants to identify the causes of employee problems in one unit. He proposes to measure employee job satisfaction. In response to the question, "How satisfied are you with your current job?" employees are asked to select one of the following: very satisfied, generally satisfied, neutral, generally dissatisfied, or very dissatisfied. The choice an employee checks measures his or her degree of job satisfaction. The one question constitutes the entire study (the analyst is a very busy man). The responses will fit into no more than the five categories.

Studying the categories of an operational definition and substituting different number patterns may help an administrator to decide on the adequacy of an operational definition. Would you react differently to the findings reported in column 1 and column 2 shown below? Data in column 2 show that 100 percent of the employees are either very satisfied or generally satisfied with their jobs; whereas, data in column 3 show that 20 percent of the employees fall into each category.

Very Satisfied with Job	70%	20%
Generally Satisfied with Job	30%	20%
Neutral	0%	20%
Generally Dissatisfied with Job	0%	20%
Very Dissatisfied with Job	0%	20%
Refused to Answer	0%	0%

Assume you must solve the unit's employee problems. Do the hypothetical distributions in columns 2 and 3 suggest that the measure will yield adequate data? Do you need more information to take action? Do you have any concerns about its accuracy? Our guess is that you would find the data inadequate. They do not tell you whether pay, supervision, career opportunities, or other factors affect dissatisfaction. So you do not know what you should change and what you should keep.

The adequacy of a measure depends largely on its intended use. The measure might be perfectly adequate if its purpose is solely to pinpoint parts of the organization with particularly high or particularly low employee morale.

You also might have questions about the data's accuracy. An employee who dislikes her rate of pay but likes her job may check "generally satisfied," while another employee with similar complaints and satisfactions may check "generally dissatisfied." Some employees, after all, might fear that a "dissatisfied" response will result in retaliation. If you were the administrator involved, and if the analyst conducted his study without consulting you, in the end you would be stuck with too little information for your purposes. You would also be out the time and money spent collecting and compiling the data.

MEASUREMENT AND MEASUREMENT SCALES

Measurement applies rules for assigning numerals to the values of a variable. Think of something as simple as counting the number of stories in a house. "Stories in a house" is the variable. The operational definition of assigning values to the number of stories should indicate whether attics or basements are considered to be stories. The U.S. Census directs respondents to "count an attic or basement as a story if it has any finished room for living purposes." Not all operational definitions are as simple. For example, to measure the level of air pollution, the operational definition includes precise instructions on how to select an air sample, how many samples to take, requirements for calibrating instruments, and laboratory personnel competencies.[3]

Exactly what value should you assign to an object or event? To determine this, you need to understand *measurement scales* or *levels of measurement.* Most writers on measurement discuss four scales: nominal scales, ordinal scales, interval scales, and ratio scales. Each scale involves categorization. Each object or event observed should be described by one and only one value or category of a scale. In other words, the values or categories should be exhaustive and mutually exclusive. Understanding the differences between levels of measurement is important for choosing the appropriate statistics to use. Many statistical measures are only appropriate if a certain level of measurement is used.

Nominal Scales

Nominal scales measure characteristics by identifying and labeling categories. Nominal scales do not rank categories. You cannot place the different values of a characteristic measured by a nominal scale along a continuum. Individual cases cannot be ordered according to their values on a nominal scale. Even though numbers are sometimes assigned to nominal categories, these numbers have no particular importance beyond allowing one to classify and count the number of cases in each category. One might, for example, classify town employees by department. You could devise the following nominal scale:

1 = Planning
2 = Personnel
3 = Finance
4 = Budgeting
5 = Public Works
6 = Public Safety

Note that if other numbers were assigned to the various categories, the information would remain the same. The numbers are a device to identify categories; letters of the alphabet or other symbols could replace the numbers and the scale would be unchanged. Remember, too, that values of nominal scales are not ranked. In other words, the numbering system does not imply that Finance is more or less important than Budgeting. Typical examples of characteristics measured by a nominal scale are gender, region, and occupation.

Ordinal Scales

Ordinal scales identify and categorize values of a variable and put them in rank order according to those values. They do so, however, without regard to the distance between values. Ordinal scales measure characteristics by determining that one case has more or less of the characteristic than does another case. If you can rank values but not determine how far apart they are, you have an ordinal scale. The numbers assigned to the values must be in the same order as the ranking implied by the scale. For example, the value represented by 3 is greater than the value represented by 2, and the value represented by 2 is greater than the value represented by 1. However, the numbers do not imply an amount of the characteristic measured, only an order of more or less. Let's look at how you could assign numbers to the job satisfaction scale:

5 = Very Satisfied

4 = Generally Satisfied

3 = Neutral

2 = Generally Dissatisfied

1 = Very Dissatisfied

You can try other numbering schemes as long as the numbers preserve the rank order of the categories. For example, you could reverse the order and number "very satisfied" as "1" and "very dissatisfied" as "5." Alternatively, you could skip numbers and number the categories 10, 8, 6, 4, and 2. Because you cannot determine the distance between values, you cannot argue that a "very satisfied" employee is five times happier than a "very dissatisfied" employee. Note that we eliminated the "refused to answer" from the scale. We have no way of knowing where to place the refusals on the scale, nor do we know if all people who refused to answer had similar levels of satisfaction.

Personnel ranking commonly results in an ordinal scale. The supervisor who ranks 10 employees may give the best employee a "10" and the worst a "1." The persons rated "10" and "9" may be exceptionally good, and the supervisor may have a hard time deciding which one is better. The employee rated with "8" may be good, but not nearly as good as the top two. Hence, the difference between employee "10" and employee "9" may be very small and much less than the difference between employee "9" and employee "8."

Interval and Ratio Scales

Interval and ratio scales measure characteristics by ranking their values on a scale and determining the numerical differences between them. The distance between objects whose characteristics have been measured can be determined by using standard intervals. The difference between 10 and 20, for example, measures the same amount of the characteristic as does the difference between 30 and 40. A *ratio scale* has a fixed or absolute zero; an *interval scale* does not. A fixed zero permits one to use ratios to describe relationships between scaled objects. You can add or subtract objects measured by interval and ratio scales. You can multiply and divide the values of the characteristics measured by a ratio scale. Temperature scales are the most common examples of an interval scale. You can state that 50°F is 25 degrees warmer than 25°F, but you cannot state that 50°F is twice as warm as 25°F.

In administrative research, investigators commonly work with ratio scales. Frequently used ratio measures include amount of a total budget or its components, program costs, the population size, or the number of program participants. Very few characteristics in social and administrative research are measured by interval scales that are not also ratio scales. Researchers tend to ignore the distinction between interval and ratio scales and may refer to them both as "interval scales."

The numbers assigned to interval scales correspond to the magnitude of the phenomenon being measured. Thus the numbers assigned could be the actual number of persons working in an agency, the number of public employee strikes in a given year, or the amount of per capita income in a city. If a city's police department has 100 employees and the fire department has 50, we can say that the police department has 50 more employees than the fire department. We can also note that the police department has twice as many employees as the fire department.

In practice, the boundary between ordinal and interval scales may be blurred, especially if the ordinal scale has a large number of values. Some ordinal scales have been created to approximate an interval measure, that is, to estimate the points along an underlying interval scale. For example, ordinal scales, such as IQ scores, suggest the magnitude of differences along the scale, have many categories, and appear to be interval. One can argue that such scales do not have equal distance intervals; for example, one cannot state with certainty that the difference between an IQ of 100 and an IQ of 110 is the same as the difference between an IQ of 120 and one of 130.

Well-known psychometricians have argued that the effect of treating an ordinal scale as interval is largely inconsequential. They argue that statistics designed for interval but not for ordinal measures may be used appropriately to identify differences measured by ordinal scales.[4] In the following analysis, if "very satisfied" has a value of 5 and "very dissatisfied" has a value of 1, the mean level of satisfaction of managers is 4.25 as opposed to 3.4 for non-managers. Thus one can easily summarize the data as showing that managers are more satisfied than non-managers. (Summarizing the data with the median, the measure of central tendency for ordinal data, show that both managers and non-managers are "generally satisfied.")

	Managers (n = 100)	Non-Managers (n = 500)
Very Satisfied with Job	45%	20%
Generally Satisfied with Job	40%	30%
Neutral	10%	20%
Generally Dissatisfied with Job	5%	20%
Very Dissatisfied with Job	0%	10%

The purpose of an analysis affects a decision to treat an ordinal variable as interval. It gives an analyst more options; it may make the analysis easier. On the other hand, the findings may not be intuitively appealing. Reporting a mean satisfaction level of 4.25 is not meaningful without also noting the values assigned to the various responses. An analyst may assume a measure is interval as she analyzes the data and may treat it as ordinal when she reports her findings.

Students often mistakenly assume that groups or categories containing interval or ratio data form an interval scale. They do not. Rather, the new scale is ordinal. For example, the following age categories constitute an ordinal scale: under 21 years old, 21 to 30 years old, 31 to 40 years old, and so forth. The exact distance, that is, the age difference between any two people, cannot be determined. While we know a person who checks off 21 to 30 years old is younger than a person who checks off 31 to 40 years old, the age difference between them could be a few days or nearly 10 years.[5]

Alternative Terminologies

Not all statisticians classify measurement scales as nominal, ordinal, interval, and ratio. Nominal and ordinal scales may be called *categorical variables,* while interval and ratio scales may be called *numerical variables.* The values of categorical variables have labels; the values of numerical variables are numbers that indicate quantities. Categorical variables may be divided further into *ordered categorical variables,* another term for ordinal scales, and *unordered categorical variables,* another term for nominal scales.

Variables also may be described as discrete or continuous. Discrete variables have a limited number of values; continuous variables can take on an unlimited number of values, depending on the precision of the measuring instrument. For example, the number of divisions in an organization is a discrete variable. An agency may have 10 or 11 divisions; it cannot have 10.3 divisions. The amount of time an employee spends on a task forms a continuous variable. An employee may be said to spend 5 hours on a task, 5.4 hours, 5.46 hours, and so on.

The nominal, ordinal, interval, and ratio classification system is widespread and adequate for our purposes. Nevertheless, you may come across the terms "categorical," "discrete," and "continuous" from time to time. Table 4.1 illustrates the relationships among these three classification schemes.

TABLE 4.1   COMPARABLE TERMS FOR LEVELS OF MEASUREMENT CLASSIFICATION SCHEMES

Scheme 1	Scheme 2	Scheme 3
Nominal	Categorical; Unordered Categorical	Discrete; Dichotomous; Unordered Categorical
Ordinal	Categorical; Ordered Categorical	Discrete; Ordered Categorical
Interval and Ratio	Numerical	Discrete; Integer Valued Continuous

The Role of Measurement Scales

Before data are collected, someone needs to ensure that variables are measured at a level appropriate to the planned analysis. Some people may try to collect data at the interval or ratio level, because a greater number of statistical tools can be applied to interval data. Nevertheless, this is not always advisable. First, a shift in measurement level may require a change in the variable. In a study of office automation, for example, you might want to learn what types of computer hardware various agencies own, a nominal measure. By asking how many different types of hardware they own or how much the hardware costs, you could generate ratio level data. In the process, however, you would have changed the definition of the variable radically. Equipment cost is not equivalent to types of equipment. A second reason for not attempting to create a ratio scale is that this sometimes leads to a request for information that respondents are unwilling to provide. For example, respondents may feel that requests for information on their exact age may be combined with other information on an anonymous survey to uncover their identity. Alternatively, a request for precise information that cannot be given without checking records may irritate a respondent. For some studies, such irritation may result in a lower response rate or made up information. An investigator must then decide whether less-precise grouped data are consistent with a study's purpose. Annual income is an example. Although most individuals know their annual income within a range, very few have exact figures at hand. If asked, they may have to check tax records or may give a rough estimate. Questions that ask about income within ranges, such as $10,000 to $19,999; $20,000 to $29,999; and $30,000 to $39,999 often provide more accurate data.

RELIABILITY

The critical factors in selecting a measure and a measurement scale are its reliability, operational validity, and sensitivity. When you ask, "Is the measured difference between subjects or for the same subject over time a real difference?" you are questioning the reliability of the measurement. When you ask, "Does this measure actually produce data on the concept or variable of interest?" you are questioning its operational validity. When you ask, "Is this measure sufficiently precise?" you are questioning its sensitivity.

Reliability evaluates the degree of random error associated with a measure. To understand both reliability and random error, consider the concept of a true score. For any phenomenon being measured, we assume that a true score exists. For example, the actual weight of a person is his true weight, a true score. A scale is an instrument or measuring device to estimate true weights.

No measure is error free. Many errors are random; that is, the measured values may be either greater or lesser than the true value. Errors may occur because a measure lacks stability or dependability. If a measure is said to be "reliable," someone has determined that it is stable or dependable. If you weigh yourself and find that you have gained five pounds, you may react immediately by reweighing yourself. Suppose the second time the scale shows you lost three pounds, an eight-pound difference within seconds. You would consider the scale inconsistent or unreliable. While random error cannot be eliminated completely, the error rate should be kept at a tolerable level. A measure that yields a lot of random error should be judged unreliable and discarded.

Dimensions of Reliability

Reliability has three dimensions: stability, equivalence, and internal consistency. *Stability* refers to the ability of a measure to yield the same results time after time, if and only if what is being measured has not changed. The scale that indicates a different weight for an object each time it is weighed lacks stability. We ask about stability when we ask if an investigator assigns the same number to the same phenomenon each time. If a school counselor examines student files to identify children with learning difficulties, how consistent are her choices? Do her criteria, which constitute her measure of learning difficulties, change with mood changes, fatigue, degree of attention, or other uncontrolled factors? She should check a sample of her work to make sure each case was identified and recorded consistently. Did she identify the same students both times? If she finds relatively few inconsistencies in the sample, she can assume that her measure is reliable.

Equivalence considers (1) whether two or more investigators using a measure assign the same value to the same phenomenon, or (2) whether different versions of a measure assign the same value to a phenomenon. For example, different investigators rating the quality of housing should give the same houses the same scores. To check the reliability of a rating system, each investigator rates all the houses in a sample of houses. The sample should represent the range of housing types and conditions apt to be encountered in an actual survey of housing. If the rating system is reliable, the investigators' ratings for each house should be identical. Nevertheless, some random error must be anticipated, and a decision must be made as to how much error a reliable instrument may contain.

Occasionally, different versions of a measure must be used. This occurs most commonly in testing. Different versions of a test may be created to avoid cheating. Consider written driving tests. If each applicant took the same test, cheating would be a problem, so numerous versions are needed. Equivalence requires that any test taker receives the same score no matter which test version he takes.

Internal consistency applies to measures with multiple items. It considers whether all the items are related to the same phenomenon. For example, in issuing driver's licenses, a state wants to issue licenses to those persons who know state motor vehicle laws and driving practices. Thus if a written test is part of the licensing process, all items on the test should relate to knowledge of safe driving practices or motor vehicle laws.

In general, a measure's reliability increases as the number of questions increases. The importance of using more than one item to measure a variable depends on the underlying concept. A single item is sufficient to measure variables such as a person's age, sex, or similar demographic characteristic. However, measuring individual achievements, attitudes, and aptitudes usually requires multiple items.

Think back to arithmetic tests you took as a child. One problem on a test could not indicate reliably that your class had a knowledge of addition. Instead you and your classmates took tests that asked you to add up problem after problem. Your test score, based on your success in solving a number of problems correctly, gave you and your teacher a good idea of your ability to add and how you compared to your classmates. The following list summarizes the dimensions of reliability.

Dimensions of Reliability

Stability: measure gives same result when applied to the same phenomenon more than one time; that is, different results will only occur if the phenomenon being measured changes.

Equivalence: measure gives same result when applied to the same phenomenon by more than one investigator; different versions of a measure give same result when applied to the same phenomenon.

Internal consistency: all items constituting a measure relate to the same phenomenon.

Establishing a Measure's Reliability

You cannot expect a measure to be completely free from random error. Expecting all applicants with the same level of knowledge to get the same score on a driving test is unrealistic. Mood, test conditions, and other factors can affect performance on any given day. Consequently, we must determine how much error to tolerate with respect to any given measure.

Consider, for example, the high school counselor checking school files to see what percent of students change their schedules during the first week of classes. She wants the information in order to schedule counselors to work during "change week." She may feel that an error rate as high as 15 percent is tolerable. If so, in order to find her data reliable, she would need to place at least 85 students out of every 100 files rechecked in the same category as she did the first time. On the other hand, if the children she identified were going to be assessed for learning disabilities, an error rate of 15 percent would be too high. A far lower error rate would be required to reduce the number of cases incorrectly referred for assessment. The counselor would want to reduce the following two errors. The first error is missing children in need of assessment. The second error is incorrectly referring children for assessment.

To establish a criterion for reliability, an administrator or policy analyst should consider the practical consequences of random error. Minimizing random error may seem desirable, but many measures cannot be refined to meet high standards of precision. Estimating and reducing the level of error may be costly. Procedures to estimate the degree of reliability have their own assumptions and limitations, reducing our ability to establish with certainty a measure's reliability.

To estimate reliability or to apply a measure with known reliability, you should remember that reliability is not only a property of a measure. Reliability also is a function of the conditions under which it is applied. For example, most bathroom scales are unreliable at the extremes of body weight; that is, they do not give consistent weights for infants or very heavy people. Similarly, other measures are designed to work in certain settings. The school counselor may ably select cases from among her caseload. She may be unable to choose cases accurately from the caseload of a counselor with different training or working in another school system. A driver's test may not be reliable for persons with limited knowledge of English or poor reading skills. A housing rating form may not work equally well in a city and in a rural area.

Investigators use qualitative and quantitative methods to estimate reliability. The qualitative method cannot estimate a measure's degree of random error precisely; hence, its importance and value may be underestimated. In practice, the qualitative method can pick up serious problems that will thoroughly discredit a measure. The *qualitative method* requires that the investigators make sure that persons responsible for data collection, assigning values, and entering data are sufficiently trained and supervised, and that the investigators review a measure to decide whether

terms are defined precisely.

ambiguous items or terms have been eliminated.

information is accessible to respondents.

multiple-choice responses cover all probable responses.

directions are clear and easy to follow.

Let us start with the characteristics of the measures to see how the problems of imprecise items, ambiguous items, inaccessible information, poor response choices, and unclear directions affect reliability. Remember that an unreliable measure is one in which observed differences between subjects or in the same subject over time are due to the instrument or data collection procedures rather than to actual differences. Any of the five listed problems can result in similar subjects giving dissimilar responses or dissimilar subjects giving similar responses.

To see the reliability problems associated with imprecise terms, consider trying to measure the number of deaths caused by fires. If you asked city clerks how many people in their towns died in fires during the past calendar year, you may assume incorrectly that each town counts fire deaths the same way. Yet, some jurisdictions may include only deaths that occur within a certain time period, such as within 72 hours of a fire. Other jurisdictions may include only deaths caused by burns or smoke inhalation. Thus a person who died from a heart attack while escaping a fire might not count as a fire death in Town A but will count as a fire death in Town B.

Similar to the problem of imprecise terms is the problem of ambiguity. For one reason or another, an item that seems perfectly clear to the investigators may confuse respondents. The reliability problem caused by ambiguous items may be seen easily by considering the following question and responses:

What is your marital status?

_____ Single

_____ Married

_____ Separated

_____ Divorced

_____ Widowed

As you know, many adults lead complicated lives, and if the word "current" does not appear in the question, a person can accurately check more than one response. Similarly, because many formerly married people consider themselves to be single, the single category should be "single, never married." If just "single" is used, some currently divorced people may check just "single," others "divorced," and others both "single" and "divorced."

If the requested information is not available to respondents, they may guess or use different rules to estimate the correct response. Consider the example of fire deaths. If towns place all fire deaths in one category and keep no records on specific causes, how will they answer a request to indicate how many deaths are caused by smoke inhalation?

If multiple-choice items do not include probable responses, respondents left to their own devices may guess the item's intent. Remember your classroom experiences with multiple-choice tests. What did you do if none of the listed answers seemed remotely related to your answer? Chances are you guessed. So too will some respondents when faced with choices that they find inappropriate. Unclear or complicated directions may cause unreliable data because respondents misinterpret the directions or answer more or less at random because of frustration, anger, or boredom.

Persons involved in data collection must be trained and supervised to reduce problems of reliability, that is, to minimize the number of individual and inconsistent decisions. Thus if investigators are sent to fire departments to collect data, each investigator should define fire deaths the same way and use the same procedures for resolving problems of inaccessible or ambiguous information. Similarly, raters scoring questionnaires may be uncertain how to handle questionnaires on which respondents changed the response categories by combining responses, by embellishing a response category with their own comments, or by adding an alternative response. If individual raters decide on a case-by-case basis how to handle ambiguous responses, the decisions may be inconsistent and the data more unreliable.

Reliability may be estimated with mathematical procedures.[6] Tests of internal consistency establish the homogeneity of the items in a measure. Inter-rater reliability applies to a wide range of administrative data collection projects. Administrators who construct or work extensively with job tests, achievement tests, or personality tests will want to become familiar with other mathematical methods for estimating reliability mathematically.

When a measure includes several items, an analyst should establish its internal consistency. *A test of internal consistency,* easily performed with statistical software, demonstrates if a measure has extensive random errors due to unreliable or heterogeneous items.[7] Example 4.3 applies a test of internal consistency to a measure of police professionalism. The items included citizen ratings of police officers' attitude, competence, performance, and courtesy, and an item about police visibility. The key statistic is alpha, a reliability coefficient. The closer alpha is to 1.0 the more reliable the measure. If alpha is close to 0.0, the measure

---

EXAMPLE 4.3

Establishing Internal Consistency

Problem: Establish the reliability of a measure of police professionalism.
  Procedure:

1. Create a measure of police professionalism by adding respondents' answers to the following items:
   In my most recent contact with a city police officer:

   The officer was courteous (Courteous)
   (1) Agree (2) Strongly Agree (3) Disagree (4) Strongly Disagree

   The officer was competent (Competent)
   (1) Agree (2) Strongly Agree (3) Disagree (4) Strongly Disagree

   The officer displayed a professional attitude (Attitude)
   (1) Agree (2) Strongly Agree (3) Disagree (4) Strongly Disagree

   The officer's overall performance was good (Performance)
   (1) Agree (2) Strongly Agree (3) Disagree (4) Strongly Disagree

   As I move around the city, city police are
   (1) Often visible (2) Sometimes visible (3) Rarely visible (4) Never visible

2. Examine the correlation matrix. The closer a correlation coefficient is to ± 1.00 the stronger the relationship.

	Attitude	Courteous	Competent	Performance	Visible
Attitude	1.0000				
Courteous	.6121	1.0000			
Competent	.6403	.6652	1.0000		
Performance	.6311	.6505	.6675	1.0000	
Visible	.0580	.0298	.0827	.0233	1.0000

   Note that the variable visible has virtually no relationship with any of the other items, i.e., how an individual rates the attitude, courtesy, competence, or performance of the police is unrelated to his perception of police visibility.
3. Note the value of alpha. For these 5 items alpha = .7795
4. Note if alpha can be improved by deleting any one of the items

Continued

EXAMPLE 4.3 *Continued*

Item	Alpha if Item Deleted
Attitude	.6940
Courteous	.6923
Competent	.6749
Performance	.6884
Visible	.8787

5. Decide to eliminate "visible" from the scale. Eliminating "visible" clearly improves the reliability of the scale, e.g., its homogeneity. The low correlation coefficients for "visible" confirm that it is unrelated to the other scale items. Removing any other items would weaken the homogeneity of the scale.
6. Report the reliability test by simply noting the value of alpha. "Police performance was measured by summing respondents' perceptions of police officers' attitudes, courtesy, competence, and performance (alpha = .8787)."

---

has too few items or the items are unrelated to one another. (A negative alpha indicates that the items violate the assumption of homogeneity.) In the example alpha = .7795; deleting the visibility item will increase alpha to .8787.

As is true with many statistics, there are no set criteria for an acceptable alpha. At a minimum, an investigator who reports the results of a test of internal consistency has verified that she performed this reliability test. Furthermore, she has provided information that the reader can use to decide whether the evidence of the measure's internal consistency is weak, strong, or somewhere in between.

Interrater reliability establishes the equivalence of the measures reported by two or more observers. Interrater reliability is established by having trained observers apply a measure to the same phenomena and independently record the scores. The scores are then compared using one of several procedures to determine whether the level of agreement is appropriate.

Example 4.4 outlines the steps researchers took to ensure comparability of observers' ratings of children's behavior. Trainees were qualified as observers after their ratings on type and duration of behavior agreed with 90 percent of the training instructor's ratings.

The equivalence of two or more versions of a measure can be established by the *alternative forms technique*. Two or more versions of a measure are prepared. Subjects are asked to answer both versions. The scores on both versions of the measure are compared. If the measures yield similar scores, the versions are considered to be reliable. In practice, establishing reliability with alternative forms occurs primarily in testing situations, such as in developing tests for driver's licenses.[8]

The *test–retest* technique establishes the stability of a measure. Test–retest requires that an instrument or test be administered to a subject at two points in time. If the results are dissimilar, the measure may be assumed to be unreliable.

EXAMPLE 4.4

Establishing Inter-rater Reliability

Problem: Design a reliable measure for a study on the effects of long-term day care on young children.

   Procedure for data collection: Observers visit classrooms and observe children:

1. planning and organizing work
2. interacting with others
3. carrying out social interactions

   Observer task: Record (a) type of behavior and (b) duration of all of a child's behaviors during a 10-minute interval.

   Observer training:

1. Read about behaviors and how to identify them.
2. Practice observing, timing, and recording children's behaviors at training site.
3. Practice observing, timing, and recording skills in a kindergarten with the training instructor.
4. Complete training when observer's recording of behaviors and their duration agrees with 90 percent of the training instructor's observations.

   Establish reliability of measure of type of behaviors: (a)

$$\text{Reliability} = \frac{A}{A + D} \times 100\%$$

where:
A = number of agreements (trainee records same behavior as instructor)
D = number of disagreements (trainee records different behavior than instructor)

   The equation indicates the percentage of agreements between the trainee and the instructor. For the trainee's data to be considered reliable, the equation must equal at least 90 percent of the time.

   Establish reliability of measure of duration of behavior: (b)

   Compute Pearson's r (a measure of covariation discussed in Chapter 15). To compute r, contrast the duration of each behavior recorded by the trainee with the duration of the same behavior recorded by the instructor. If $r > .95$, the trainee's data are accepted as reliable.

SOURCE: Adapted from D. E. Pierson, "The Impact of Early Education," *Evaluation Review*, 1983: 191–216.

This procedure seems direct and reasonable, but if you think about it, you may recognize its limitations. First, the initial testing may affect the responses to the retest. Suppose you asked people to rate the adequacy of police protection in their community. Responding to this question could focus their attention on policing in their community and eventually lead to a change in their perceptions. Their retest responses would change. Such a change would not mean the measure involved was unreliable. Conversely, they may remember their first response and repeat it. In such a case, the lack of change between Time 1 and Time 2 does not verify the measure's reliability. Second, with practice, respondents' performance may change. They may benefit from familiarity with previously unfamiliar question formats or tasks. Third, an actual change, independent of the first testing, may take place between the two administrations, or tests, of the measure. The more time that passes the more likely an actual change has occurred.

The test–retest procedure is adequate, and useful, if the attribute being measured is unlikely to be influenced by the first test or to change between tests. The review of a sample of files to determine the consistency of measurement is a form of test–retest. If an investigator checks his work by using the test–retest procedure, he should wait long enough to forget how he originally measured specific cases. Obviously, in establishing reliability he would ignore new data placed in the file after the first "test."

From our teaching experience, we know that students underestimate the problems of using test–retest to estimate reliability. For all practical purposes, test–retest is inappropriate for many measures of interest to administrators. As you read management, policy-analysis, or social science articles, notice how rarely the authors indicated that they used test–retest to establish their measures' reliability. The major problem is the influence of the first test. It may cause a change, or respondents may remember and reproduce the first set of answers. Just as the person asked to rate police service may pay more attention to her neighborhood's policing and change her rating, other measures have a similar effect on how respondents observe and evaluate their environment. Alternatively, respondents may mull over the answers and decide another answer would have been more appropriate.

Administrators, depending on how much they work with data and in what capacity, vary in their concern with reliability. At a minimum they want to affirm that data are free of gross errors. If they know a measure's operational definition, they can apply the qualitative method and identify the most serious threats to reliability. In some situations administrators need quantitative information to estimate precisely a measure's error rate. Below we summarize the major features of reliability.

Reliability: A Summary for Administrators

Reliability: evidence that a measure distinguishes accurately between subjects or over time. If a measure is reliable, one can assume that differences between subjects or over time are real differences.

Evidence of a measure's reliability:

Qualitative method: used to evaluate the reliability of any measure. Depending on the purpose of the measure, qualitative evidence of reliability may be sufficient.

Internal consistency: used to demonstrate empirically that several items of a single measure are homogeneous.

Interrater reliability: used if more than one investigator collects data on a measure. Interrater reliability produces empirical evidence demonstrating the equivalence of scores assigned by different raters.

Alternative forms: used to demonstrate empirically that two different versions of a measure are equivalent in assigning scores to subjects. Administrative researchers, other than those who construct tests, rarely use this method.

Test–retest: used to demonstrate empirically the stability of a measure. Test–retest will not produce useful evidence of reliability if the first testing is likely to affect retest responses or performance, or the phenomenon being measured is likely to have changed between the test and the retest.

When to determine reliability: reliability should be determined prior to testing a model, collecting data, or introducing an intervention. Internal consistency may be determined after collecting data but prior to data analysis. Nevertheless, specific problems, such as ambiguous terms, may be overlooked during initial reviews of a measure and only identified after the data are collected or analyzed.

Relative nature of reliability: the degree of accuracy required depends on the purpose of the measure. A measure may be reliable for one purpose and not another.

Once an investigator has amassed evidence of a measure's reliability, he can decide on its operational validity. By definition, an unreliable measure contains an unacceptable amount of random error; therefore, it cannot yield valid data. Data produced by an unreliable measure should be discarded. Depending on degree and source of the unreliability, the measure itself may be discarded or simply revised. A reliable measure can yield reliable, but invalid, data. By example, we know that a bathroom scale may always read five pounds under a person's true weight. Such a scale would provide reliable but not valid data. Demonstrating a measure's reliability is only one step in determining its value.

OPERATIONAL VALIDITY

In addition to knowing that a measure is reliable, we also want to know whether it has been named correctly and that it measures what we intend to measure. Measures that measure what they are devised to measure are said to be *operationally valid.* Operational validity can be a matter of judgment. Consider measures intended to compare and rank the quality of life in American cities. The measures are meant to determine how desirable people consider a community as a place to live. If one investigator were to choose items that focused on cultural and recreational resources, while another selected items that focused on the social climate, such as the crime rate, unemployment rate, and the number of strikes, the results surely would differ. The first investigator would probably conclude that major cities were the best places to live. The second would probably assign higher rankings to smaller, more homogeneous cities. The operational validity of either measure could be challenged by arguing that it does not really measure quality of life.

Measuring the incidence of crime may seem to be a simpler assignment. At first glance one might assume that the number of crimes reported to police would be a clear-cut measure of the crime rate. However, not all crimes are reported. As a result, officials in cities with a high number of reported crimes can argue that reported crime actually measures the vigilance of police officers rather than the actual crime rate. Officials may suggest that in cities with lower crime rates police discourage victims from reporting crimes or that these cities do not have procedures to ensure accurate recording of crimes. A U.S. Department of Health and Human Services publication[9] listed five events that must occur for an actual crime to become part of the crime report:

1. The crime must be known or perceived by someone other than the offender; for example, you must know your home was burglarized.
2. The person perceiving the act or its consequence must define it as a crime; for example, acts of domestic violence may not be defined as a crime by the victim.
3. Someone must report the crime to the police.
4. The police must define the reported act as a crime.
5. The police must record the crime in the appropriate category.

The requirements that a reported crime must be perceived, recognized as a crime, reported to the police, defined by the police as a crime, and recorded correctly imply that the crime report does not constitute an operationally valid measure of crime rate.

Having discussed the importance of operational validity, we have to add that there is no simple way to establish it. Establishing a measure's validity requires judgment. Several techniques can provide evidence of operational validity; however, they cannot prove it. The operational definition must be consistent with the conceptual definition. This assumes that a conceptual definition has been developed and that it accurately captures the concept or variable of interest to the users.

Recall the variable work effort cited in Example 4.1. The researcher conceptually defined work effort as the physical demands of work. Her conceptual definition did not include mental effort. If her operational definition covers the factors that make work physically demanding and ignores factors that make work mentally exhausting she may argue that her operational definition is operationally valid. However, others may question her conceptual definition and challenge the validity of her definition on the basis that she should have gone beyond the physical demands of the job. The investigator can do no better than to provide the best evidence she can that the measure actually measures what it was intended to measure and that it is named correctly.

Operational validity commonly is referred to simply as "validity." We have found that students commonly confuse the validity of measures with the internal and external validity of experimental and quasi-experimental research. Thus, for the purposes of clarity, we prefer to use the term "operational validity" when discussing the validity of measures. The types of operational validity that administrators are likely to encounter are face validity, content validity, and criterion validity. We will confine our discussion to these terms.

A measure that appears to be operationally valid is said to be *face valid*. To construct a face-valid measure, investigators take one or more steps. First, they may simply assume that their operational definition is operationally valid. Second, they may ask colleagues or experts to review an operational definition, comment on it, and suggest improvements. Third, investigators may consult the literature to find measures and discussion of their appropriateness. In practice, face validity is probably the most common form of validation. Methodologists do not define it as a validation technique, and at best it offers only superficial evidence of a measure's appropriateness. Nevertheless, face validity may be valuable to administrators who want to avoid measures that lack credibility.

To determine a measure's operational validity, one develops evidence that it is measuring what it was intended to measure. One may begin by examining its operational definition and deciding if it will produce the needed information. In 1991 the Veterans Administration (VA, now the Department of Veterans Affairs) redefined its definition of "bed." VA hospitals had routinely counted and reported how many beds they had. In counting, the hospitals included beds that were unavailable for patients. For example, because of understaffing, some beds were "closed" and thereby unavailable. At the onset of the Persian Gulf War, the VA found that it did not have the information it really needed. It needed to know how many beds were actually available to care for injured troops, not the number of potentially available beds.[10]

Another source of evidence is demonstrating that the operational definition is consistent with the conceptual definition. This evidence has merit only if potential users agree on the conceptual definition. This might have happened if the engineer and the budget director in Example 4.2 had reviewed and discussed whether the engineer was using the "right" measure of productivity. The lack of consensus suggests problems with the validity of the engineer's measure. Similarly, discussion of economic measures normally will reveal problems with the conceptual definition. For example, measures of a nation's wealth count all production without regard to its social value. Some critics question whether the measures should consider the cost of depleting a nation's natural resources or if production of weapons, tobacco products, or toxic wastes should be viewed as contributing to its wealth.[11]

Content validity provides stronger evidence of operational validity. Just as using several items to measure a variable should reduce random error, using several items should produce a more adequate measure of a concept. Students, who frequently take tests designed to measure their knowledge of subject matter, are only too aware of the importance of content validity. If a test ignores major topics or places undue emphasis on trivial material, one justifiably may complain that the test is not content valid. Students expect a test to emphasize the important material in a course.

To create a content-valid measure, analysts first systematically identify elements integral to the concept of interest. Second, they decide which elements are most important and if any elements need to be weighted. Third, they design a measure that includes the important elements with the appropriate weights. The items may be summed to create a single measure or the items may be analyzed separately. For example, an analyst could report the percentage of respondents who rated the police positively on their attitude, competence, courtesy, and performance (Example 4.3). Alternatively, the analyst could report the percentages who rated the police most favorably, favorably, unfavorably, or most unfavorably when all four items were summed.

To assess a measure's content validity, investigators decide if the items in an operational definition measure the concept adequately. Consider the adequacy of the items making up the measure of police professionalism. As you examine the items and decide if they adequately measure police professionalism, you are judging its content validity. To convince you that a measure is content valid, analysts may do more than simply present the operational definition, they may also describe the process they went through to decide what elements to include and how to weight them.

Content validity underlies many measures used by public administrators. Job tests, official statistics, and performance measurement systems all depend on proper selection of indicators. To create a job test, the elements essential to the job first must be identified. What skills must an employee have? What knowledge does he need? The relative importance of the skills and the knowledge must be determined. Once this is done, the test writer constructs a test blueprint, which outlines the job components and their relative importance. Appropriate measures of job components are developed and reviewed by a panel of experts. The measures may be answers to an objective test, performance in a simulated exercise, or responses to interview questions.[12] Example 4.5 shows how to create a written test of job knowledge in order to hire accounting personnel.

EXAMPLE 4.5

Creating a Written Work-Knowledge Test Based on Job Analysis

Problem: Create a written test of job knowledge to evaluate applicants for accounting positions.

Measure: Knowledge of accounting.

Procedure to establish content validity:

1. Systematically identify elements to include in measure:
   a. Interview job holders and their supervisors about tasks performed by agency accountants.
   b. Review materials discussing accountants' work.
   c. Write a pool of questions covering tasks (identified during steps 1a and 1b):
      (1) Technical experts review questions.
      (2) Eliminate questions if >50 percent of experts said tasks were actually learned on job (50 percent cutoff is an arbitrary standard).

Continued

EXAMPLE 4.5   *Continued*

2. Determine relative importance of these elements:
   a. Ask job incumbents to rate each question using a scale ranging from 0 (lowest) to 7 (highest) on importance, frequency, and relevance.
   b. Keep questions with mean >4.0 and standard deviation >2.5 (arbitrary standards).
3. Create a measure that includes these elements and weights them according to their relative importance:
   a. Identify knowledge needed to perform tasks (repeat steps 1a and 1b).
   b. Write job-knowledge statements.
4. Show how measure incorporates these elements, and account for differences in their importance:
   a. Submit to technical experts.
   b. Keep items if >70 percent of experts consider knowledge essential (arbitrary standard).
   c. Review final measure for consistency with information collected in steps 1 through 3.

SOURCE: G. A. Kesselman and F. L. Lopez, "The Impact of Job Analysis on Employment Test Validation for Minority and Nonminority Accounting Personnel," *Personnel Psychology,* 1979: 91–108.

Performance measures track how well organizations achieve their goals and objectives. To be effective, performance measures must include the appropriate items. A university that focuses on faculty research grants and publications may have faculty members who ignore teaching. A library that only tracks book loans may develop a lopsided collection focused on children's books and best sellers. To be valid, items in performance measures must cover the range of organizational goals.[13]

Personnel selection and promotion procedures must also be valid—they must select and promote personnel for their ability to do the job for which they are applying. Failure to do so exposes the employer to legal challenges. Many employers, public and private, have worked to develop valid selection procedures that do not discriminate against applicants. Content validity is an important part of this development procedure. Example 4.6 illustrates the development of a content valid selection procedure for SWAT team members.[14]

Issues of content validity are particularly relevant in official statistics. To estimate the inflation rate, governments track the costs of a sample of consumer goods and services. A major problem arises when consumer behavior changes. For many years, the typical American diet was heavy on red meat, eggs, and milk. Americans now eat less of these products and more poultry, fruits, and vegetables. So a measure that tracks the cost of foods eaten by a typical American family in 1950 will not reflect accurately the cost of foods eaten by a typical American family today. Why not change the measure? First, establishing the typical American diet requires a costly nutritional survey.[15]

EXAMPLE 4.6

Creating a Content-Valid Personnel Selection Measure

Problem: To develop a physical ability test to select personnel for tactical police units (SWAT Teams)

Procedure:

1. Search the literature for studies identifying tasks critical to the performance of police tactical units.
2. Interview current members of Charlotte Police Department SWAT Units and ask them to identify critical tasks based on experience in actual incidents.
3. Develop questionnaire to be completed by members of SWAT Units in eleven other cities and counties and the State Bureau of Investigation. Questionnaire included a description of each critical task identified and asked respondents to: (a) rate how essential the task was to the successful completion of the duties of a member of a tactical unit (b) rate how important speed was as a factor in the successful performance of the described task (c) list several test items which simulate the described task and rank them according to how well they simulate the described task.
4. Analyze questionnaire data and select critical items and simulated tasks based on ratings and rankings by respondents.
5. Conduct trials of simulated tasks with current SWAT Unit members to establish standards for completion. Standards to be compared with applicants' performance and used for selection.

Discussion: Results of the time trials on the selected simulated items were used to evaluate applicants to SWAT Teams. Managers were satisfied that the selection procedure was content valid and evaluated applicants based on ability.

SOURCE: Glenn R. Jones, "Job Related Physical Ability Test for Tactical Police Units", (University of North Carolina at Charlotte, Charlotte, NC, Masters Thesis, 1993).

Second, if a measure is changed, then comparability with the past is lost. To retain comparability, the revisions may be applied to older data, or both measures may be reported for a time.[16] If a measure is changed in the year 2000, data for earlier years may be adjusted to reflect the change; or beginning in the year 2000, data for both measures may be reported. Third, changes in certain measures inevitably bring charges of political manipulation. Can you imagine a politician advocating a change in a measure that would put his administration in a bad light?

Content validity may seem identical to internal consistency, a dimension of reliability. In addition to being internally consistent, a content-valid measure needs to represent the variable of interest. Hence, internal consistency is not sufficient to demonstrate content validity. To use the test example, a final examination that covers only one section of course material may be internally consistent, but it does not measure adequately what was learned in the entire course, which is what the test is intended to measure. A measure of school vandalism may be internally consistent, but it actually may be measuring the quality of maintenance and not vandalism.

Criterion validity uses statistical evidence to establish validity. A *criterion,* an indicator assumed to measure the same thing as the measure being validated, is selected and related to the measure. The investigator looks for similar response patterns to both measures. There are two types of criterion validity: concurrent validity and predictive validity. *Concurrent validity* is a form of operational validity established by collecting and comparing two different measures at the same time. The concurrent validity of an employment test could be evaluated by having current employees take the test and then comparing their test scores with their supervisors' rating of their performance. If employees with high test scores also have received high proficiency ratings, the test may be considered to have concurrent validity. Example 4.7 illustrates concurrent validity in a study validating employee self-reports of their wages and benefits. The criterion to validate the measure was employer records.

EXAMPLE 4.7

An Application of Concurrent Validity

Problem: Determine whether self-reported information about pay and benefits corresponds to employer records.

Measures to be validated:

Pay: operationally defined as respondent's answer to "How much does your income from your job figure out to be per year, before taxes and other deductions are made?"

Benefits: operationally defined as respondent's answer to "Here are some fringe benefits. Tell me whether or not (employer name) makes each available to you."

Procedures to establish the criterion validity of measures:

1. Select validated measures similar to the measures being validated:
   a. Pay: employer records on individual annual salary.
   b. Benefits: employer policies indicating availability.
2. Administer the measures and criteria to subjects:
   a. Interview 444 employees from three organizations (gathered data on measures).
   b. Review personnel records of the same 444 employees (gathered data on criteria).

Continued

EXAMPLE 4.7 *Continued*

3. Relate the measures being validated to the criteria:
   a. Annual salary reported by employees compared with annual salary found in employer records.
   b. Benefits reported by employees compared with benefits reported in employer policy statements.
4. Examine the relationships and decide whether the criterion and the measure being validated vary together:
   a. Pay: 20.53 percent of the respondents overstated their pay, and 8.57 understated it.
   b. Benefits: for common benefits such as paid vacation, >15 percent did not indicate that they received available benefits. Paid sick leave, medical insurance, and retirement are usually reported accurately.

Discussion: Procedure checked the reliability and criterion validity of measure. Self-reported pay measure is not operationally valid, since the errors tend to be systematic; that is, pay is overstated. The number of errors in both directions of the self-reported pay measure suggests that it has weak reliability. Self-reporting of common fringe benefits seems reliable and operationally valid; self-reporting of less common benefits such as stock options or profit sharing tends to be unreliable. Whether to use self-reports or employer records depends on the purpose of the study; use self-reports for studies of employee perceptions and employer records for studies of behavioral data.

SOURCE: N. Gupta and T. A. Beehr, "A Test of the Correspondence between Self-Reports and Alternative Data Sources about Work Organizations," *Journal of Vocational Behavior*, 1982: 1–13.

Predictive validity requires that a measure correctly predicts a future outcome. For example, a valid job selection test should discriminate between applicants who will perform satisfactorily if hired and those who would not. In such a case, the measure being validated is the job selection test, and future job performance is the criterion. At a minimum, establishing predictive validity requires collecting data at two points in time. Example 4.8 illustrates an attempt to establish the predictive validity of a measure of violent behavior.

You should note the inadequacies of predictive validity in Example 4.8. This is not because we tried to find an example illustrating the problems with predictive validity, but because most measures do not do a good job of predicting behavior. We have tried to convince many public administration students that they should not expect measures to have high predictive validity. One student suggested that a good example of the difficulties in achieving good predictive validity was the experience of drafting college players into professional football or basketball teams. We assume that if researchers could develop a surefire way to determine which draft choices will be stars and which will be duds, the National Basketball Association or the National Football League would pay for the information. We also assume

EXAMPLE 4.8

An Application of Predictive Validity

Problem: Identify a method for predicting dangerous behavior.

Measures validated: Clinical procedures to establish: a person's motivation (M), including history of aggression (H), internal inhibitions (I), and situational factors (S). Then, a method to combine these factors, e.g., $I - (M + H + S)$; if $I > 0$, violent acts are unlikely.

Criterion measure: arrest for a serious assaultive act.

Procedures for validating measure:

1. Clinical assessment to determine whether patients classified as dangerous should be released. Release recommended for 386 patients classified as non-dangerous. Release not recommended for 49 patients; however, court released them.
2. Collection of data on arrest for serious assaultive behavior during the next five years.

Covariation of measure and criterion:

1. Data show 8 percent of those considered nondangerous committed an assaultive act (false negative).
2. Data show 65 percent of those considered dangerous did not commit an assaultive act (false positive).

Discussion: Validity of measure is limited by the number of false positives, which must be evaluated in the context of the consequences of labeling incorrectly a person as "dangerous." Roughly two out of three persons considered too dangerous for release were not found to have committed an assaultive act within the follow-up period. Research critics have questioned the validity of the criterion measure and have asked how many of the false positives committed violent acts without being caught. Also, questions have been raised about the external validity of generalizing from data gathered in an institutional setting in order to predict behavior in an open community.

SOURCES: E. I. Magargee, "The Prediction of Dangerous Behavior," *Criminal Justice and Behavior* 3 (March 1976): 3–21, and J. Monahan, *The Clinical Prediction of Violent Behavior* (Washington, D.C.: Alcohol, Drug Abuse, and Mental Health Administration, U.S. Department of Health and Human Services, 1981). Data and procedures adapted from H. Kozol et al., "The Diagnosis and Treatment of Dangerousness," *Crime and Delinquency 18:* 371–392.

that you as an administrator will be more strapped financially than professional sports teams. Since vast resources cannot produce measures with high predictive validity, you should insist on evidence of predictive validity only if a measure is intended specifically to predict a future outcome. In making personnel decisions, for example, you want job selection and promotion procedures that have predictive validity. Job satisfaction, job performance, and productivity instruments should have content and concurrent validity.

Criterion validity, whether predictive or concurrent, involves empirically checking our assumptions about a measure. Ideally, the criterion and the measure being validated are not collected with the same instrument or even the same data collection method. Using different instruments counters any bias or distortion that might be introduced by relying on a single instrument or data collection method.

Just because the measure and the criterion show the same pattern does not mean that the investigator has named or labeled the measure correctly. For example, if one were to measure satisfaction with police services by asking citizens how satisfied they were with police response time and then to compare these responses with police department data on response time, the two measures might vary together. The researcher may then assume that he had a valid measure of citizen satisfaction with police services. In fact, he would have measured only one component of satisfaction, that is, citizens' attitudes about response time. Thus, while it is up to a researcher to decide what concept a given measure and criterion represent, his or her decision can be wrong.

The best evidence of operational validity includes more than evidence that a measure is content- and criterion-valid. A researcher also will show that the measure behaves as expected, that is, it correlates with theoretically linked variables and does not correlate with other variables. For example, scores on a quantitative aptitude test should be strongly related to math grades but not to English grades. This validation procedure, termed construct validity by psychologists, requires a strong theoretical foundation. Researchers will have defined the components of the concept of interest carefully and developed consistent evidence of how it is linked to other variables.[17]

Naming or labeling a variable correctly may seem trivial, yet the way in which a measure is labeled affects our perceptions and even our behaviors. Out of necessity, administrators deal with summarized information. Often, they have time only to read report highlights or hear brief presentations. Consequently, the label attached to a measure can seduce and mislead administrators. For example, a harried administrator may remember the findings about the "best" American city, without stopping to learn what criteria were used to rank cities. If you plan to act on findings you have read or heard, you should learn more about the measure used. Then you will be in a better position to decide whether your action will get the intended results.

Administrators also need to realize that judgment cannot be eliminated from any effort to establish operational validity. As a result, the validity of any particular measure must be assumed rather than considered as proven. These are matters to which administrators probably devote little attention. Yet administrators who work with data should be concerned with validity and ask themselves appropriate questions: What do these data indicate? Do alternative measures exist? Below we summarize the major features of operational validity.

Operational Validity: A Summary for Administrators

Operational validity: evidence that a measure is named correctly and that it measures what it was intended to measure.

Evidence of a measure's operational validity:

Face validity: evidence that establishes the legitimacy of a measure; those who interpret or act on data accept it as producing appropriate information.

Content validity: evidence that a measure's indicators taken as a whole represent the phenomenon of interest adequately.

Criterion validity: empirical evidence that the measure acts as expected. Concurrent validity compares data produced by the measure of interest to data produced by an alternative measure to see if the data are consistent. Predictive validity applies only to measures produced to predict a future outcome, for example, success in a job or in graduate school.

Construct validity: evidence that measures of a theoretical construct correlate with theoretically linked variables and do not correlate with other variables. Construct validity is primarily of interest to researchers.

Evaluating the evidence: evidence that the measure is content and criterion valid strengthens one's position that an appropriate measure has been used. Nevertheless, whether a measure is accepted as operationally valid or not depends on the user's purpose and conceptual definition.

When to determine operational validity: operational validity should be determined prior to testing a model, collecting data, or introducing an intervention. Because of the role of judgment, if data are being collected for use by administrators or legislators, the validity of the measure should be reviewed with them prior to data collection.

SENSITIVITY

The *sensitivity* of a measure refers to its precision or calibration. A sensitive measure has sufficient values to detect variations among respondents; the degree of variation captured by a measure should be appropriate to the purpose of the study. Measures that are reliable and valid still may not detect important differences. Consider a salary survey. Suppose employees were asked:

What is your salary? (check appropriate category)

_____ Less than $20,000

_____ $20,000 to $29,999

_____ $30,000 to $34,999

_____ $35,000 to $39,000

_____ $40,000 to $44,999

_____ $45,000 to $49,999

_____ $50,000 or more

The categories included in this measure may be adequate for a survey of entry level and mid-level city employees. They probably would not be adequate for a survey of city managers or of department heads. The measure is insensitive to variations in city manager salaries, since most top managers will fall in the last category. Thus, in constructing a measure, an investigator wants to avoid having respondents clustered in a single category. If most responses fall into one category, the measure would be considered insensitive. Insensitive measures do not allow investigators to compare respondents. Some investigators prefer to collect uncategorized data and create categories as needed and appropriate throughout the analysis.

Measures developed to study one type of population may be insensitive to differences in other more homogeneous populations. In the previous example, the problem could be solved by creating more and narrower categories, especially at the higher income levels. With complex measures, such as job-satisfaction scales or intelligence tests, a different set of indicators may be required to ensure sensitivity. For example, a job-satisfaction measure developed for organizations employing unskilled and skilled laborers, clerical workers, technical, administrative, and professional staff may be a poor choice to study a work unit largely made up of professional employees. If individual differences are of interest, then the measure would not be sufficiently sensitive to identify differences among employees in the more homogeneous group. Sensitivity in policy and administrative research is a relative concept, and no standard for an acceptable level of sensitivity exists.

SUMMARY

Measurement is the process of quantification. Quantification makes it easier to compile, analyze, and compare information on phenomena. Nevertheless, the process of measuring sacrifices the richness of a concept. No measure can describe fully job satisfaction, employee competence, quality of life, or level of poverty. The approximations of concepts, represented by measures, have great value, but you also should recognize their limitations.

The measurement process begins with a conceptual definition. The conceptual definition clarifies what the investigator means by a concept, and it serves as a blueprint for the operational definition. The operational definition details exactly how a concept or variable was measured and its values were determined.

A measure can be classified as nominal, ordinal, interval, or ratio. Nominal scales categorize, but do not rank, data. Ordinal scales rank data, but the exact distance separating two pieces of data cannot be determined. Interval and ratio scales indicate the distance between two pieces of data. Ratio scales, unlike interval scales, have a true zero value.

Measures should be reliable, operationally valid, and sensitive. Reliable measures allow an investigator to conclude that differences between subjects or over time are real differences, and not due to the measure or the measuring process. Reliable measures yield the same results time after time if whatever being measured has not changed. Two or more investigators using a measure should give the same score to the same phenomenon. A careful review using the qualitative method markedly improves reliability. The reviewer makes sure that directions are clear and easy to follow, that items are clearly defined, that given responses cover all likely responses, and that the respondent has access to the requested information. People responsible for data collection or data processing should be trained to avoid inconsistent measurement. A review of the measures and staff training may be adequate to determine reliability. If knowing and limiting the amount of random error are important, an investigator should use mathematical procedures to establish reliability. Unreliable data should be discarded.

A reliable measure is not necessarily operationally valid. An operationally valid measure actually measures the concept of interest. Empirical methods provide evidence of a measure's validity. Still, they only complement the judgment of analysts and users; they do not replace it, nor can they offer irrefutable evidence that a measure is operationally valid. Common ways of validating a measure are face validity, content validity, and criterion validity. Face validity relies on the investigator's judgment that a measure is credible. Measurement experts do not consider face validity a validation technique. Content validity uses systematic procedures to ensure that a measure adequately represents the phenomenon being measured. Criterion validity, consisting of concurrent validity and predictive validity, provides quantitative estimates of validity. Concurrent validity compares a measure with a criterion measured at the same time. Predictive validity demonstrates that a measure taken now can predict a future outcome. A sensitive measure sufficiently distinguishes cases from each other so that they can be compared. A valid and reliable measure can be insensitive.

An administrator who includes quantitative information in her decision making may make an inappropriate decision if the data are unreliable or invalid. Quantitative information may be ignored because administrators consider the measures meaningless or inadequate to support decisions. Administrators should not expect researchers to make all decisions about a measure's appropriateness, nor should they base their decisions upon data without questioning the adequacy of the measures that generated them.

Measurement decisions are tied to other research decisions. The level of measurement determines what statistics the investigator can use. The analysis chapters identify the statistics appropriate to data measured at the nominal, ordinal, or interval level. The data collection chapters explicitly discuss measurement. The number of items and their wording must be considered in conjunction with the data collection method. An investigator who uses existing data must determine the measures' reliability and operational validity.

The next chapter is on sampling. In practice, investigators construct measures and samples independently. Implied links exist. Every measure is not necessarily appropriate for all subjects. The degree of precision can affect the cost of data collection or processing; thus, sample size may limit the sensitivity of measures. Investigators may overemphasize sample construction at the cost of developing high-quality measures.

NOTES

1. For an excellent example of detailed conceptual and operational definitions and the relationship between them, see J. E. Royce, *Alcohol Problems and Alcoholism* (New York: The Free Press, 1981), 15–19.

2. This example is drawn from Anne H. Hopkins, *Work and Job Satisfaction in the Public Sector* (Totowa, NJ: Rowan & Allanheld, 1983), 42, 135. Some liberties have been taken in the discussion to meet the needs of the text and its readers.

3. J. S. Hunter, "The National System of Scientific Measurement," *Science 210* (November 1980): 869–874.

4. See Jum C. Nunnally and Ira H. Bernstein, *Psychometric Theory,* 3d ed. (New York: McGraw-Hill, 1994), 22–23.

5. Frequency distributions may be constructed so that the scales can be considered interval. In general, we do not recommend that you use interval statistics on ordinal scales unless you are sufficiently familiar with the scale and the statistic that you feel you can interpret the statistical findings appropriately. For further discussion, see H. M. Blalock, Jr., *Social Statistics,* 2d ed. (New York: McGraw-Hill, 1972), 20–25.

6. See Nunnally and Bernstein, *Psychometric Theory,* chap. 7 for details on mathematical techniques for determining reliability.

7. For more detailed discussion on internal consistency and coefficient alpha, see Anne Anastasi and Susan Urbina's *Psychological Testing,* 7th ed. (New York: Macmillan, 1997), 91–102.

8. Other terms, such as parallel forms, are also used to describe this type of reliability.

9. R. F. Sparks, *Research on Victims of Crime* (Washington, D.C.: U.S. Department of Health and Human Services, 1982), 14.

10. B. McAllister, "VA Finally Decides What Counts as a Bed," *Washington Post,* September 3, 1991, A17.

11. M. H. Maier and Todd Easton, *The Data Game: Controversies in Social Science Statistics,* 3d ed. (Armonk, NY: M. E. Sharpe, 1999), 99–102 discusses problems with Gross National Product (GNP).

12. M. W. Huddleston, *The Public Administration Workbook,* 3d ed. (White Plains, NY: Longman, 1996), chap. 6.

13. For a discussion of performance measures and performance monitoring systems, see James E. Swiss, *Public*

Management Systems (Englewood Cliffs, NJ: Prentice Hall, 1991), chap. 5.

14. Glen R. Jones "Job Related Physical Ability Test for Tactical Police Units" (Unpublished Masters Thesis, The University of North Carolina at Charlotte, Charlotte, NC, 1993).

15. See USDA's Nationwide Food Consumption Survey, GAO/RCED-91-117 (Washington, D.C.: General Accounting Office, 1991), which documents the difficulties in collecting these types of data. The contract for the 1987–1988 survey was $6.2 million; however, the survey was largely discredited because of methodological problems.

16. See J. A. Miron and C. D. Romer, "Reviving the Federal Statistical System," and J. E. Triplett, "Reviving the Federal Statistical System: A View from Within" in *American Economic Review* (May 1990), 329–332 and 341–344, respectively.

17. For a discussion of construct validity, see Anastasi and Urbina, *Psychological Testing,* 153–163.

TERMS FOR REVIEW

concept	stability	content validity
conceptual definition	equivalence	criterion validity
operational definition	internal consistency	concurrent validity
measurement	test–retest	predictive validity
measurement scales	operational validity	sensitivity
reliability	face validity	

QUESTIONS FOR REVIEW

The following questions should indicate whether you have a basic competency in this chapter's material.

1. Indicate whether each statement represents a conceptual definition, part of an operational definition, or a hypothesis.
   a. Co-production consists of voluntary, active, citizen involvement, or participation in the delivery of urban services.
   b. To determine the equity of police services, we asked respondents if they thought there was less, about the same, or more crime in their neighborhoods than in the rest of the city.
   c. The more politically efficacious the respondents, the greater the probability that they will have a favorable attitude toward government services.
   d. Home health care has been defined as an array of therapeutic and preventive services usually provided to patients in their homes or in foster homes because of acute illness or disability.
   e. Controlled inventoried items are those that must be identified, accounted for, secured, segregated, and handled in a special manner.
   f. Uncontrolled, inventoried items have a higher rate of wastage than controlled items.
   g. The rate of school vandalism was measured by counting the number of cracked and broken windows.

2. Why should administrators participate in selecting appropriate operational definitions for a study?

3. What type of measurement scale—nominal, ordinal, interval/ratio—does each describe?

   counties in a state (Ash County, Beach County, Maple County)

   number of participants in food stamp programs

   reputation of colleges

   leadership ability measured on a scale from 0 to 5

   divisions within a state agency

   inventory broken down into three categories: tightly, moderately, or minimally controlled

4. A job training program measures its effectiveness by the number of persons placed in a job. Factors such as salary and length of employment are not considered. Comment on the apparent reliability and operational validity of the program's effectiveness measure. How should the program improve its effectiveness measure?

5. Suggest possible operational definitions to test the hypothesis: Parents of elementary-age school children (5–11 year olds) go to public libraries more often than parents of younger or older children.

6. Evaluate the following statements:
   a. A measure can be reliable for one study but not for another.
   b. A reliable measure will assign the same value to the same subject each time the measure is used.

7. Consider a measure of school vandalism that includes seven indicators of vandalism:
   a. What does a researcher mean when she says that the measure of school vandalism is reliable?
   b. What does she mean if she finds that the measure is stable, equivalent, and internally consistent?
   c. What does she mean if she says that the measure is operationally valid?
   d. What does she mean if she finds that the measure is content valid?
   e. What does she mean if she finds that the measure is criterion valid?
   f. What does she mean if she says that the measure is sensitive?
   g. Can the measure be unreliable but operationally valid? Explain.

8. Consider the measure of school vandalism. In October, the vandalism at eight schools is determined using the measure. Six weeks later, the vandalism at the same eight schools is again determined using the same measure.
   a. What procedure is being used to determine the measure's reliability?
   b. The amount of vandalism between the two applications of the measure increased. Should the researcher assume that the measure is unreliable? Explain.

9. Explain why a measure reliable for one population is not necessarily reliable for another.

10. Explain why operational validity always involves judgment.

PROBLEMS FOR HOMEWORK AND DISCUSSION

1. A city department wants to make sure that its user survey to assess program quality contains reliable and operationally valid measures.
   a. Present one strategy that you can use to determine that the measures of program quality are reliable.
   b. Present one strategy that you can use to determine that the measures of program quality are operationally valid.

2. To gather information on safety violations in factories, a state agency plans to send investigators to selected factories to obtain safety information.
   a. How should the agency determine whether its measure of factory safety is reliable?
   b. What evidence would you look for to decide if the measure of factory safety was content valid?

3. Student observers measure traffic flow through a section of the city. They count the number of vehicles that pass through specified intersections. Each observer works for a four-hour period. An engineer notes that observers become careless in counting near the end of the fourth hour. Is this a problem in reliability, operational validity, or both?

4. A planner wants to assess road quality. He sends a questionnaire to a sample of residents and asks them to evaluate road surfaces, repair quality, and amount of traffic. He finds the results of limited value, so he assigns engineers to travel through the neighborhoods to rate the roads. The engineers are given general instructions but no written rating forms. Still dissatisfied, he develops a rating form that lists the number of potholes per mile, the depth of potholes, the thickness of asphalt, the width of the roadway, and similar measures.
   a. Comment on the reliability and operational validity of each approach.
   b. Comment on the ways each approach could be modified to improve its reliability and validity.
5. A personnel agency administers employment tests to large groups of applicants. To minimize the temptation to cheat, applicants are given different forms of the exams.
   a. Why is it important that the reliability of the test be established?
   b. Briefly describe how the examiners could establish the reliability of the different forms.
6. To develop a licensing examination, two versions of the exam are written and administered. In the morning, one-half of the test takers receives Form A, and the other half receives Form B. In the afternoon, the groups and tests are reversed so that those who took Form A in the morning take Form B and those who took Form B take Form A.

   a. What was the licensing department trying to do?
   b. If later administrators learn that people who had passed either Form A or Form B did not understand traffic laws, is the problem with the examination's reliability or operational validity? Explain.
   c. If the testees retook the tests three weeks later and their scores improved, could the administrators assume the tests were unreliable? Explain.
7. A city council wants to learn what the impact would be if it started issuing "tennis licenses" to allow residents to use the tennis court. A sample of players who use public courts are asked, "If the city charged $10 for tennis licenses, would you still use the public courts?" Discuss the operational validity of this question. Do you think that it would give an accurate indication of the effect of a tennis license?
8. Table 4.2 shows the number of people living below the poverty level as determined by two different operational definitions of poverty. Discuss how you would choose one of these definitions as operationally valid. Do you think that your decision would be the same if you were a legislator, a budget officer, or a provider of social services to clients?
9. Example 4.6 describes the development of a content valid selection procedure. Discuss how the researchers involved could demonstrate that the procedure as a measure also had concurrent and predictive validity.

TABLE 4.2   IDENTIFYING AN OPERATIONALLY VALID MEASURE OF POVERTY

Operational Definition	Number Below Poverty Level (1996)	Percentage Below Poverty Level (1996)
Money income (adjusted by household size; <$16,036 for family of 4)	36,529,000	13.7%
Money income plus subsidized food, housing, medical care (adjusted by family size)	27,133,000	10.3%

SOURCE: U.S. Census Bureau, *Current Population Reports,* March 1996. For information on poverty measures go to http://www.census.gov/ftp/pub/hhes/poverty/povmeas/papers/chinpvup.html

DISK WORK

1. Determine if a set of four questions about people's reaction to a murder are reliable. Using more than one question should improve reliability; however, the questions should be internally consistent. Go to the disk and load the murder data base. Use statistical software and run a program to check internal consistency. (SPSS refers to this procedure as "reliability.") What did the findings tell you about the reliability of the four questions? Can you assume that the questions give an operationally valid indicator of people's reaction to a murder? Why or why not?

2. Load the Belle County database. Identify three to five variables that might be combined to create a single measure, e.g., quality of county's performance or the value of county services. Use statistical software and run a program to check the reliability of these variables. What did you learn about their reliability? Based on these findings would you recommend (a) changing the wording of the questions before the survey is administered again or (b) changing the variables used to create the measure.

RECOMMENDED FOR FURTHER READING

For an extensive discussion of reliability and validity, see Jum C. Nunnally and Ira H. Bernstein, *Psychometric Theory,* 3d ed. (New York: McGraw-Hill, 1994), a sophisticated and detailed work, or Anne Anastasi and Susan Urbina, *Psychological Testing,* 7th ed. (New York: Macmillan, 1997).

Mark H. Maier and Todd Easton, *The Data Game: Controversies in Social Science Statistics,* 3d ed. (Armonk, NY: M. E. Sharpe, 1999), presents an insightful discussion of social science statistics. They identify and critique health, labor, crime, and educational statistics, among others. Their case-study questions are provocative and highly recommended.

Patricia Ruggles, *Drawing the Line: Alternative Poverty Measures and Their Implications for Public Policy* (Washington, D.C.: Urban Institute Press, 1990), examines different conceptual definitions of poverty, how to operationalize these concepts, and policy implications of each operationalization. It is a first-rate case study.

Chapter 5

Sampling

In this chapter you will learn

1. the reasons for sampling.
2. common sampling terminology.
3. how to identify, construct, and interpret common probability and non-probability samples.
4. the guidelines for determining sample size.

Whether you study groups of 100, 1,000, or 1,000,000, drawing a sample is an economical and effective way to learn about their individual members. This applies if your data come from individual respondents, case records, agencies, or computerized datasets. People unfamiliar with sampling may misunderstand it, mistrust it, and feel that studies should include an entire population.

Consider some practical reasons for sampling. For many groups, it is impossible to identify every member. Thus you cannot contact every member and collect data from them. You cannot realistically collect data on every unit of some populations. Imagine an air-quality control agency collecting data on all the air in an area. The cost of gathering data on an entire group may be prohibitive. Contacting all members of a large or widely dispersed population can require tremendous commitments of time and money. Even with a relatively small group, sampling allows one to gather information on members in a much shorter amount of time.

Every 10 years the United States government is required to conduct a census of the nation's population. For the 2000 census, the Census Bureau proposed sampling the population to improve the accuracy of the count and to reduce expenses. The proposal was controversial—members of Congress debated the issue and executive branch agencies as well as professional organizations became involved in providing information. Understanding of the principles of sampling would help most observers appreciate the Census Bureau's proposal although it was ultimately rejected by Congress.[1]

Sampling is used in a variety of settings for a number of purposes. Perhaps the most widespread use of it is in survey research. Sample surveys are used to provide statistical data on a wide range of subjects for research and administrative purposes. A relatively small number of individuals are interviewed in order to gather data that will allow an investigator to find out something about the larger population. Given today's widespread use of surveys, it is somewhat surprising that the sample survey has a relatively short history.[2] Since the 1930s, many advances have been made in all aspects of the survey process but especially in sampling methods. In the early days of this century, statisticians debated whether anything less than investigation of a complete population was acceptable.[3] Sampling has since become widely accepted and a number of techniques developed.

Sampling involves several interrelated factors. These include the type of sample, its size, the population of interest, the accuracy desired, and the confidence the investigator wishes to have in the results. We will discuss these topics in this chapter. Before describing the methods and techniques of sampling, however, we need to introduce and define a number of terms.

SAMPLING TERMINOLOGY

A *sample* is a subset of units selected from a larger set of the same units. The subset provides data for use in estimating the characteristics of the larger set. For example, polling organizations, such as the Gallup Poll, use samples of about 1,500 or fewer people to describe the opinions of over 200 million Americans.

The *population* is the total set of units in which the investigator is interested, that is, the larger set from which the sample is drawn. The population's characteristics and the relationships among these characteristics are inferred from the sample data. A population may be composed of people, but it may also consist of units such as government organizations, households, businesses, records, or pieces of equipment such as police squad cars, and so on.

The *target population* must be specified clearly. The units in a population must conform to a set of specifications, such as "all adults living in Clark County on July 1," so that analysts will know who is considered part of the population and who is not. The interpretation of the results of a study will depend on how the population is defined. Consider a sample survey to assess support for a bond referendum to build a new coliseum in a city. How should the population be defined? Who should be included? Registered voters? Taxpayers? Only people living within the city limits? What should be the minimum age of the population? An investigator may find it useful to start by defining the population as the ideal one required to meet the study objectives. This could be called the target population. This definition would then be modified to take account of practical limitations, and the resultant definition would be the *study population.*

Once the population has been defined, the question arises as to how to draw a sample from it. Many types of samples require a list of all the units in the population. The specific set of units from which the sample is actually drawn is the *sampling frame.* To sample households in a county, for example, one needs a list that names every household in the county. Complete lists seldom exist. Whatever list is used is the sampling frame. In the absence of a list, the frame is some equivalent procedure for identifying the population units.

Sampling frames may include units not defined as part of the population or they may fail to include some members. Suppose a sample of households was drawn from a telephone directory. The directory lists businesses, which are not part of the population, and it does not include households with no telephones or with unlisted numbers. Other potential problems with sampling frames are that some of the listings may be groups of units rather than individual units, and some units may be listed more than once.[4] A list of building addresses, for example, may include apartment buildings in which there are many apartments. If an investigator is interested in individual dwelling units, many would be missed with this frame. We tend to think of sampling frames as being physical lists of units; however, this need not be the case. For example, you could place grids on a map and select a sample of the grids for further study. The sampling frame would be the gridded map.

The term *unit of analysis* refers to the type of object whose characteristics we measure and in which we are interested. If data are collected on fire departments, the unit of analysis is "fire department." If data are collected on fires, the unit of analysis is a "fire." Typically, investigators measure something about the unit of analysis. Frequently, administrative studies use agencies, not individuals, as the unit of analysis. A reader who fails to identify correctly the unit of analysis may reach incorrect conclusions about a study's findings.

A *sampling unit* is that unit or set of units considered for selection at a stage of sampling. The sampling unit may or may not be the same as the unit of analysis. In some sampling procedures, the sampling unit includes several units of analysis.

A *parameter* is a characteristic of the population. These are what investigators want to find out about, and finding out about them is the reason for doing the study. The percent of citizens in favor of a bond issue to finance a new coliseum would be a parameter, as would the average age of new police recruits and the range of ages of retirees. A *statistic* is a characteristic of a sample. We use statistics to estimate parameters. Typically, an investigator will take a sample statistic and estimate that the corresponding parameter of the population is within a certain range of the statistic. For example, the average cost of housing in a sample of residences in the state can form the basis for estimating the average cost of all houses in the state. The investigator does not assume, however, that the statistic exactly estimates the parameter. For the price of housing in the state, he may say that the average cost of all houses in the state is within a certain number of dollars of the average cost of houses in the sample.

The difference between the population parameter and the sample statistic used to estimate it is the *sampling error.* This usually has to be estimated before the sample is drawn or calculated afterwards. It is the expected error in estimating a parameter for any given sample design of a specified size. The *standard error* is a measure of the sampling error. It is based on a theoretical sampling distribution. *Sample bias* is a systematic misrepresentation of the population by the sample. The misrepresentation is in one direction. It usually comes about because of a flaw in the design or implementation of a sampling procedure. Whereas sampling error is random and its size can be estimated, sampling bias tends to be in one direction and is difficult to measure.

A *sample design* is the set of procedures for selecting the units from the population that are to be in the sample. The *sampling fraction* is the percentage of the population that is selected for the sample. The distinction between *probability* and *nonprobability* sample designs is important. With a probability sample, each unit of the population has a known, nonzero chance of being in the sample. Nonprobability designs do not allow the researcher to calculate the probability that any unit in the population will be selected for the sample. In nonprobability sampling designs, other principles take precedence. Properly used probability samples allow us to avoid selection biases, use statistical theory to estimate population parameters and to evaluate the accuracy of these estimates. A variety of probability and nonprobability sampling designs are discussed in the next section. Both types of designs useful are but typically are used for different purposes and in different situations. A weakness of nonprobability designs is that they allow for an element of subjectivity, thereby preventing the investigator from using statistical theory properly. However, these designs are usually more convenient than probability designs and can be very useful to administrators.

The following application illustrates some of the terms defined above.

An Application of Sampling Terminology

Population: All motor vehicles owned by the state in the current fiscal year.

Sampling frame: All vehicles appearing on the state list of Registered Motor Vehicles prepared July 1 of the current fiscal year by the Department of Motor Vehicles.

Sampling design: Probability sampling.

Sample: 300 motor vehicles selected from the sampling frame.

Unit of analysis: Motor vehicle.

Statistic: Passenger cars in the sample were driven an average of 20,000 miles annually.

Parameter: Passenger cars in the state are probably driven, on average, between 15,000 and 25,000 miles annually (estimate derived from sample statistics).

SAMPLING DESIGNS

Probability Samples

With a probability sample, each unit in the population has some chance of being in the sample; that chance is greater than zero and can be calculated. Probability samples permit a precise estimate of parameters. If sample statistics are to be used to accurately estimate population characteristics, probability samples are required. Although the reader need not be familiar with the calculation and interpretation of probabilities, it is important to be familiar with the more common probability sampling designs and recognize the situations in which they are likely to be useful. Our purpose here is to describe these designs so that the reader can determine whether sample findings have been interpreted properly and can participate in discussions of alternative ways of selecting a sample.

We discuss four common probability sampling designs: simple random sampling, systematic sampling, stratified sampling, and cluster sampling. Others exist but readers are most likely to encounter these four. They demonstrate the basic principles of probability sampling. Several variations of each of these designs exist, and you may encounter them in your work. If you undertake a study with a complicated sampling design, you will probably want to consult an expert. There are consultants who design samples for clients and advise them on how to estimate parameters from the sample. A good consultant will probably be able to construct a sample more efficiently than you can.

Simple random sampling requires that each unit of the population has a known, equal, nonzero probability of being included in the sample. The selection of each unit is independent of the selection of any other unit. That is, the selection of one member of the population for the sample should not increase or decrease the probability that any other member of the population will also be chosen for the sample.[5] A common method of constructing a random sample uses either a *lottery method* or a *random number table.* These methods ensure against the inadvertent introduction of a pattern of systematic bias into the procedure. In the lottery method, numbered or named balls, each representing a unit in the population, are placed in a container. The balls are mixed thoroughly, and the number of balls equal to the sample size is removed. For a sample of 100, the investigator would remove 100 balls. The sample then consists of all units of the population corresponding to the selected balls.

While the lottery method is theoretically adequate, usually it is more convenient to use a random number table. To do this, the investigator assigns a number to each unit of the population and consults the table. He then randomly selects a starting place, goes through the table across the rows or down the columns, and lists the numbers as they appear on the table. Members of the population with the selected numbers constitute the sample. The investigator selects a random starting place in order to avoid any preference he may have for beginning at a particular starting spot.

A random number table is a list of numbers generated by a computer that has been programmed to yield a set of random numbers. Computers are used since the typical human is not capable of generating random numbers. For example, a person might have a tendency to list more even numbers or those ending only in 3 or 7. The numbers in a random number table have no particular sequence or pattern. The use of random number tables ensures that the selection will be random and not influenced by any selection bias of the investigator. Computer programs operating on the principle of a random number table for selecting cases are available. Many organizations have computerized records; such records constitute sampling frames, and computer routines can select a simple random sample from them.

EXAMPLE 5.1

An Application of Simple Random Sampling

Problem: County officials want to assess the extent of support for a proposed bond issue to fund construction of a new wing to a high school.

Population: All people eligible to vote in a referendum on the proposed bond issue.

Procedure:

1. Identify the population: The county's registered voters.
2. Identify and obtain a sampling frame: County Board of Election's list of 40,000 registered voters. The list is on the Board's computer, and names are numbered sequentially.
3. Determine sample size: 500.
4. Select a table of random numbers, pick a random beginning point, use a consistent pattern to go through the list, and list the first 500 five-digit numbers from 00001 to 40000.
5. Select each voter whose name appears next to a number selected from the table of random numbers.

Discussion: The sampling frame is an accurate list of members of the population, e.g., citizens eligible to vote in a referendum on a bonding request. A simple random sample can be executed relatively easily. A computer-generated sample would be equally good and less time-consuming. A computer program could have printed out a randomly selected sample of names using its own internally generated table of random numbers. Note that each listed voter had the same chance of being in the sample as every other listed voter, and the selection of any one voter did not affect the chance that any other voter on the list would be included.

In drawing the sample using a table of random numbers, it is possible for a unit's number to be selected more than once. This possibility does not exist with the lottery method because, when the unit's ball was drawn, it was not replaced to be given another chance to be selected. The sampling method is known as unrestricted random sampling or simple random sampling with replacement if a selected unit, or its identifying number, is returned to the population and can be selected again. When the sampling procedures are done without replacement, the method is known as simple random sampling. We will emphasize the method without replacement, as it is used more commonly. Example 5.1 illustrates an application of simple random sampling.

The use of the random number table to select a simple random sample is manageable but can be very tedious. It becomes more so with large populations. Although newer developments for selecting samples, such as random digit telephone dialing, can make the process easier and faster, they cannot be used in many situations.[6] *Systematic sampling* is a widely used alternative to simple random sampling that reduces the amount of effort required to draw a sample and usually provides adequate results. It requires a list of the population units. To construct a systematic sample, the investigator first divides the number of units in the sampling frame (N) by the number desired for the sample (n). The resulting number is called the *skip interval* (k). If the sampling frame consists of 50,000 units and a sample of 1,000 is desired, the skip interval equals 50 (50,000 divided by 1,000). Having determined the skip interval, the investigator then selects a random number, goes to the sampling frame and uses the random number to select the first case. Next the investigator picks every kth unit for the sample. In the example above every 50th case following the starting place on the sampling frame would be chosen. If the random number 45 was selected cases 45, 95, 145 and so on would be in the sample.

With systematic sampling, the list is treated as circular, so the last listed unit is followed by the first. It is important to go through the entire list that constitutes the sampling frame. If the order of the items on the list occur in a regular pattern and the skip interval coincides with this pattern, the sample will be biased. Consider what could happen in sampling the daily activity logs of a sheriff's department. If the skip interval was 7, the activity logs in the sample would all be for the same day, that is, all Mondays or all Tuesdays, and so forth. A skip interval of 14, 21, or any other multiple of 7 would have the same result. Experienced law enforcement officials tell us that certain days consistently have more activity. If the skip interval matched the cycle, the sample would not represent the population of days accurately.

One way to deal with this problem, known as *periodicity,* is to perform the procedure twice, first doubling the skip interval. In our example we would make 100 the skip interval, randomly select a starting point, and go through the sampling frame once. This provides one-half of the sample. We would then pick another starting point and go through the frame a second time, providing the second half of the sample. Another way is to "mix up" the list before selecting the sample, although this may not be practical. The available evidence indicates that periodicity problems are relatively rare in systematic samples.[7]

In order to sample a population whose size is unknown, such as people attending a community event or clients attending a clinic, systematic sampling may be the only feasible type of probability sample. In such cases one can estimate the probable population size, that is, the number of visitors or patients, determine a skip interval, say 50, and pick a random beginning point, say 6. You would then sample the 6th person to arrive (or depart), the 56th person, the 106th person, and so on, until the end of the sampling period.

Systematic sampling does not result in a truly random sample. Although each unit in the population has the same chance of being selected, the selection of one unit affects the probability of selection of other units. For instance, in the above examples, the probability that both units 1 and 2 will be in the sample is zero. There is some nonzero chance that both units 1 and 50 will be in the sample. There is no possibility that adjacent units within the skip interval will be selected.

EXAMPLE 5.2

An Application of Systematic Sampling

Problem: The director of a county Women's Commission wishes to compile a summary describing the characteristics of registrants in the county's Job Bank. The Job Bank has been operating for 10 years.

Procedure:

1. Identify the population: 6,500 women registered with the county Job Bank.
2. Determine the sampling frame: The set of file folders, one for each registrant, kept for the 10 years of the Job Bank.
3. Decide on sample size: 500.
4. Calculate skip interval: $k = 6500/500 = 13$.
5. Select a random number between 1 and 13 for a starting place. The number 7 is selected.
6. Pull files from the filing cabinets for the sample. Start by selecting the seventh file, and continue by selecting files number 20, 33, 46, and so forth, through the entire set of files.
7. The 500 files selected constitute the sample for the study.

Discussion: A systematic sample works well where files are kept. These files were kept in chronological order, providing a useful sampling frame. To go through and number each file and then match them with numbers chosen from a random number table would be tedious. The investigator has no reason to suspect periodicity, so she may pick all members of the sample by going through the sampling frame once. Note: If the skip interval is not a whole number, you may round either up or down. The most important aspects of the procedure are to pick at random a starting place and to be sure to go through the entire list or set of records.

In order to apply sampling statistics to systematic samples, the investigator must make certain assumptions about the sampling frame. The major assumption involved is that the units on the list are randomly ordered, or at least approximately so, with respect to variables under investigation. If this is the case, the systematic sample can be treated as a simple random sample. Lists arranged in alphabetical order usually can be treated this way. Systematic sampling is used widely and works well in practice. You need not be overly concerned about the problems noted here, although it is well to be aware of them. Systematic sampling is also called quasi-random sampling. Example 5.2 illustrates an application of systematic sampling.

Stratified random sampling ensures that a sample adequately represents selected groups in the population. Analysts use stratified sampling if a group of particular interest is a relatively small proportion of the population, or if they plan to compare groups. This technique assumes some knowledge of the population characteristics. Fortunately, we usually know certain things about the population being studied. Information on demographic characteristics, such as the percentage in various racial groups, ages, percentage employed in manufacturing, and so on, often is available.

The first step in drawing a stratified random sample is to divide or classify the population into strata, or groups, on the basis of some common characteristics such as sex, race, or institutional affiliation such as school or agency. The classification should be done so that every member of the population is found in one and only one stratum. Separate random samples are then drawn from each stratum. In a study of Management Information System organizations, Stuart Bretschneider wanted to compare public with private sector organizations and designed a stratified sampling procedure. He developed two sampling frames, one of public sector agencies and the other of private organizations, and drew separate samples from each.[8] The benefits of stratification derive from the fact that the sampler determines the number of each units selected from each stratum. Hence, stratified samples provide for greater accuracy than simple random samples of the same size.[9]

We will discuss two types of stratified sampling, proportionate and disproportionate. In *proportionate stratified sampling* members of a population are classified into strata, and the number of units selected from each stratum is directly proportional to the size of the population in that stratum.

If, for example, an investigator wanted to compare three types of workers—professional staff, technical staff, and clerical staff—she would begin by designating each of these types as a stratum. She would then draw her samples by taking an equal percentage of members from each stratum, say 10 percent of the professional staff, 10 percent of the technical staff, and 10 percent of the clerical staff. The resulting sample would consist of three strata, each equal in size to the stratum's proportion of the total population. A simple random procedure or some other method of probability sampling is used to draw the actual sample from each of the strata. Example 5.3 illustrates an application of proportionate stratified sampling.

The percentage of the members of a stratum selected for the sample need not be the same for each of the strata in the population. In *disproportionate stratified sampling,* a larger percentage is taken from some strata than from others. This is a useful technique when a characteristic of interest occurs infrequently in the population, making it likely that a simple random sample or a proportionate sample may have too few members with the characteristic to allow full analysis.[10] It also is useful when the sizes of important subgroups in the population differ greatly. For example, the State Division of Human Resources wanted to have a sample of employees in all departments of state government. The largest department had over 18,000 employees and the smallest had 50. In disproportionate stratified sampling, the investigator selects a larger percentage of members from groups likely to be underrepresented in the population. In this fashion the investigator assumes that the number of units included in each stratum of the sample will be large enough to allow for separate analysis of each individual stratum. Since many research projects require sample estimates not just for the total population, but also for various subgroups within the population, this is often a useful technique. It must be emphasized that the samples from each stratum constitute subsamples that can be analyzed separately. Since some strata have been sampled at a higher percentage than others—they have been over sampled—a weighting procedure must be applied

EXAMPLE 5.3

An Application of Proportionate Stratified Sampling

Problem: The director of recruitment for the State Law Enforcement Service wanted information about applicants to the service over the previous four years.

Population and sampling frame: All applicants to the State Law Enforcement Service for the past four years.

Procedure: Construct a proportionate stratified sample, using the year of application as strata. Select a random sample of applications from the total group for each year. The same percentage of each year's total is selected. See the accompanying tabulation in Table 5.1.

TABLE 5.1   CONSTANT SAMPLING FRACTION

Stratum	Number of Applications	Sampling Fraction	Number in Sample
Year One	400	15%	60
Year Two	350	15%	53
Year Three	275	15%	41
Year Four	250	15%	38
Total	1,275		192

Discussion: The analyst used his knowledge of the population to stratify along yearly groupings and take a 15 percent sample within each subgroup. The information from each year's group can be compared or combined into one larger sample.

to compensate for over sampling before the subsamples are combined to form one sample. To weight the subsamples correctly, the analyst must know the size of each stratum. Example 5.4 illustrates a disproportionate stratified sample and a weighting procedure. One disadvantage of disproportionate stratified sampling is that it may require a larger sample to achieve the same level of accuracy as simple random or proportionate stratified sampling.

Cluster and Multistage Sampling

In many sampling problems, the units of the population exist in groups or *clusters.* For example, if we wanted to survey state residents on their use of certain state services, the unit of analysis would be individual residents. But they could be grouped in clusters in various ways. Each county, city, planning district, or even city block would contain a cluster of residents. We could also view the city block as a unit, in which case each city would have a cluster of city blocks, and each city block would have a cluster of residents.

EXAMPLE 5.4

An Application of Disproportionate Stratified Sampling

Problem: Identify citizens' transportation needs for a county transportation plan.
   Population: The county's 27,500 residents
   Sampling frame: List of households from county tax records.
   Procedure:

1. Stratify the population by the county's three townships: Tax records are filed by township, and each township differs in its demographic makeup.
2. Note the number of households in each township.
3. Determine sample size: Approximately 500.
4. Decide between proportionate and disproportionate sampling: Note that a 5 percent sampling fraction would yield a 480-household sample with only 26 households from Southwest Township. Because of the importance of location in developing the plan, analysts decide to oversample Southwest Township.
5. Individual households for the sample are randomly selected from the tax records for each township. One resident in each household is interviewed.

See the accompanying tabulation.

Statum	Number of Households	Proportion of Total	Sampling Fraction	Sample Size
North Township	5,760	.60	4%	230
Southeast Township	3,330	.35	4%	133
Southwest Township	510	.05	10%	51
Total	9,600			414

Discussion: Normally, the three groups would be analyzed separately and compared to each other. If the planners wanted to combine the subsamples into one sample, they would weight the subsamples. Specifically, the results of each subsample would be weighted by the proportion of the total population that that strata constituted. The results would then be combined. For example, the average age of residents in North Township would be multiplied by that group's corresponding proportion in the total, .60, Southeast Township by .35, and Southwest Township by .05 to determine the average age of the total population.

In cluster sampling, we select a sample of groups from the sampling frame and obtain information on all the individual units in the groups selected. If all the units within selected clusters are included in the sample, the design is called cluster sampling. If a sample of units is taken from each selected cluster, the design is called multistage sampling.

Drawing a simple random sample or stratified sample of a population, such as state residents, could be very difficult. You may lack a sampling frame of the population, or the frame may be so large as to be impractical to use. A more efficient approach is to use a series of cluster samples. This type of sampling is often called *multistage sampling,* because it proceeds in stages, or *area sampling,* because it is used to sample units dispersed over a large geographic area.

Assume that investigators wanted to obtain data on the use and need for mental health facilities in a five-state region. The following would be a multi-stage, cluster-sampling approach:

1. Stage One: The investigator takes a sample of large units containing clusters of smaller units. In this case, counties would be a likely choice.
2. Stage Two: A sample of smaller areas—townships—is selected from the previously chosen counties.
3. Stage Three: A sample of yet smaller geographic areas, designated by population size, is selected from the townships chosen in Stage Two.
4. Stage Four: Select a random sample of dwelling units—houses, condominiums, and apartments—from the smaller units chosen in Stage Three.
5. Stage Five: At this stage the investigators would go to these selected dwelling units and interview a resident. Of course they would need some procedure for choosing which resident to interview, since many of the dwelling places will have more than one adult resident.

The units selected at each stage are called *sampling units.* The sampling unit may not be the same as the unit of analysis. In this example, the unit of analysis was the resident. However, different sampling units were selected at each stage of the process.

When to Use Cluster Sampling

Cluster sampling is recommended for studies involving a large geographic area. Without the ability to limit the sample to discrete areas, that is, to selected clusters, the costs and logistics would make probability sampling of many widely dispersed populations difficult, if not impossible. If face-to-face interviewing is to be used to collect data, a sample spread thinly over a large area will be extremely expensive to reach. Cluster sampling could help reduce this cost.

Often cluster sampling is used because no sampling frame for the units of analysis exists and one cannot be constructed. Cluster sampling helps to compensate for the lack of a sampling frame. Using cluster and multistage sampling in combination allows the investigator to proceed by developing a sampling frame for just the last stage of the process. Often the final units selected are households, and a listing of these may not be needed. In the description above, for example, the investigators developed a sampling frame by listing the addresses of all dwelling units in the final areas selected. They chose their sample from this list. It would have been very costly and cumbersome if they had begun the process by attempting to find or develop a sampling frame that included addresses of all residents in this five-state region.

Although cluster and multistage sampling reduce travel time and costs, they require a larger sample than other methods for the same level of accuracy. Note that in the multistage process probability samples are selected at each stage. Example 5.5 illustrates a four-stage cluster sample. The research staff applied random sampling techniques four times to select the members of the sample.[11]

EXAMPLE 5.5

An Application of Multistage, Cluster Sampling

Problem: A state health agency needs to obtain information from high school students living in rural areas.

    Population: All high school students attending school in rural areas of the state.
    Sampling frames: List of counties, high schools, classes, and students.
    Procedure: Construct a four-stage cluster sample.

1. Select a simple random sample of counties from all state counties considered to be rural.
2. Obtain lists of high schools in all selected counties and from these randomly select a sample of high schools.
3. Obtain a list of all classes in the selected high schools. From these, randomly select a sample of classes.
4. From the class lists for the selected classes, randomly select a sample of students.
5. Interview the selected students.

    Justification for sampling technique:

1. No obtainable sampling frame of all students attending high school in rural areas existed for the entire state.
2. The study required face-to-face interviews. Cluster sampling allowed research staff to concentrate interviews in fewer locations, thus avoiding costs of traveling all over the state.

What happens if the initial clusters to be sampled have very different sized populations? If one of the clusters contains a significant proportion of the population, a multistage sample could easily miss this cluster and hence a large part of the population. To adjust for this situation, investigators sometimes use a technique called "probability proportional to size" or PPS. A typical application of cluster sampling is a study in which the investigator wants to obtain a statewide representative sample of adult residents. If an accurate list of the number of adults in each county is available, multistage, cluster sampling would be appropriate. A probability sample of 10 counties could be the first stage with a sample of residents selected from these counties for the second stage. However, the investigator would want each adult in the state to have an equal chance of being chosen. If one or a very few large counties contain a significant proportion of the state's population, as is the case in many states, the investigator needs to adjust for this. The adjustment must be done in Stage One or the probability of missing the largest county and much of the population would be high.

The investigator must weight each county by its population. If random numbers are assigned to the counties for the first-stage selection, they would be assigned to the counties in proportion to their population: more numbers assigned to the more populous counties than to the less populous ones. The larger counties would have a greater chance of being selected than the smaller ones. Weighting would ensure that a resident of a large county has the same chance to be selected as a resident of a small county.[12]

Probability sampling designs, when used in conjunction with sound statistical methods, allow us to generalize from the sample to the population. The distinguishing characteristic of probability samples is the random selection of the units for the sample. Randomization eliminates biases that may affect the selection of units. It also allows for the correct use of sampling statistics. Four commonly used probability sampling designs are: simple random, systematic, stratified, and cluster or multistage. The principles underlying simple random sampling form the basis for other probability designs. Although other designs are used more widely, they are attempts to provide a close approximation to simple random sampling when simple random sampling is either difficult or impossible.

NONPROBABILITY SAMPLING DESIGNS

Investigators use a variety of nonprobability sampling designs. In this section we discuss the more common of these. Nonprobability samples can work well for many types of studies, particularly exploratory studies and those used to generate hypotheses to be more fully tested by further research. The usefulness of the information contained in a nonprobability sample depends on the investigator's purpose, the criteria for selecting the units for the sample, and how well they seem to represent the population of interest. These samples are also useful if it is not important to obtain accurate estimates of population characteristics. A visit to one or two homeless shelters, for example, can provide useful information to housing administrators seeking a change in policy governing the provision of services to the shelters.

Nonprobability sampling designs are used widely. They typically are cheaper and easier to carry out than probability designs. Their major weakness is that in using them one cannot estimate parameters from sample statistics. Obviously, investigators attempt to do this in some fashion. However, with nonprobability samples, statistical theory cannot be applied to make these estimates or to evaluate their accuracy. The adequacy of the nonprobability sample can be evaluated only by subjective means; no mathematical evaluation is possible. With non-probability samples, one cannot determine the chance that any unit in the population will be selected for the sample. It is therefore impossible to determine, mathematically, how representative the sample is of some larger population.

The various types of nonprobability samples are named according to the primary criterion used in drawing the sample. *Convenience sampling* involves sampling on the basis of the availability of units. For example, a researcher may ask a classroom of students to fill out an opinion survey. In so doing, he may hope to find out something about a larger population, such as American youth, but in order to do so, will have to assume that his sample is in fact representative, as there is no way to demonstrate this. Convenience samples are inappropriate for generalizing with any degree of certainty. They can, however, provide illustrative case material or serve as the basis for exploratory studies. One could, for example, use the survey described above as a pretest to determine whether any items on the questionnaire were difficult to understand or were inappropriate.

Examples of convenience sampling include: volunteers for a study, interviews conducted in convenient locations such as shopping centers, the respondents to a questionnaire in a newspaper, and telephone calls to a radio talk show. Convenience samples also are known as accidental samples.[13] Although the risk of bias for convenience samples is high, some will be worse than others. Particularly troublesome are those for which subjects select themselves for the sample and in which we would expect only people with particularly strong views to respond. Because of the high risk of bias with convenience samples, it is unwise to use them to make inferences about the general populations. Nevertheless, if the purpose is to identify issues of potential concern to a larger population, to pretest forms to be used by an agency, or for a similar purpose, convenience samples may be economical and appropriate.

A second type of nonprobability sampling is *purposive sampling.* The main criterion for selection of any unit from the population using this sampling procedure is the investigator's judgment that the unit somehow represents the population. Because of this it is also known as judgment sampling. The probability that any unit will be selected is unknown because it depends entirely on the judgment of the investigator. Often units for this type of sample are selected on the basis of known characteristics that seem to represent the population. The investigator assumes that the units selected will represent the population on unknown characteristics as well. Even after collecting the data, an investigator cannot verify the representativeness of the sample on the unknown characteristics. He must therefore be skeptical about the accuracy of estimates.

Local governments create purposive samples when they seek information from cities and counties with a reputation for excellent administration. They may interview the personnel of these governments to ask about their experiences with outsourcing services, what performance measures they use, and how they monitor citizen satisfaction. Similarly, investigators may select for study school systems which have had the most success and those which have experienced failure in implementing charter schools. Example 5.6 illustrates the use of purposive sampling.

A third type of nonprobability sampling is *quota sampling.* In this technique the investigator attempts to structure a sample that is a cross section of the population. It is less costly and easier to administer than a comparable probability sample. The researcher attempts to select a quota of individual units with defined characteristics in the same proportion as they exist in the population. If he thinks that gender and age are important characteristics and the population is 55 percent male and 35 percent are over 40 years old, he will require that 55 percent of the units in the sample be men. He will also require that 35 percent of the sample be over 40. The characteristics used to guide the selection of units for the sample may be independent or

EXAMPLE 5.6

An Application of Purposive Sampling

Problem: A county manager plans to purchase a new computer system and wants to find out what experiences similar counties have had with computer systems, specifically their applications, costs, installation, and maintenance problems.

Population: All counties similar to that of the manager.

Procedure: The manager decides to talk at length with personnel in counties similar to hers that have computerized administrative activities.

1. Based on her knowledge of the area, the manager decides to contact five counties similar to her own in population size and makeup, budget, and services provided.
2. County managers and administrative staff in the five counties are interviewed and asked:
   a. What equipment is owned, leased, or shared?
   b. What alternatives were examined? Why was the existing system chosen?
   c. What does the computer system do?
   d. How well does the system perform? How often does it break down?

Sample characteristics: The representativeness of the sampled counties' population size and makeup, budget, and services are known. The representativeness of their computer-related decisions are not known and cannot be determined by this sampling technique.

Discussion: The manager, familiar with her county and its operation, the counties contacted, and the reputation of possible vendors, may reasonably believe that a limited, nonprobability sample will provide adequate information for a good decision.

they may be interrelated. For example, a researcher seeking to interview members for a quota sample of agency employees may be assigned the following quotas:

10 males under the age of 40, 5 males over the age of 40

6 women who have been with the agency for five years or less

7 women who have been with the agency for more than five years

Quota sampling is sometimes used in surveys in which the interviewer selects the specific individuals to be interviewed. Quota sampling has the advantage of not requiring a sampling frame. It also reduces the need for callbacks. With quota sampling, if an eligible person is unavailable when the interviewer calls, the interviewer simply proceeds to the next dwelling or the next eligible respondent. However, the risk of *selection bias* is much greater.

One purpose in assigning quotas is to reduce the risk of selection biases that might result from giving the interviewer a totally free hand. The biases of the interviewer can reduce the representativeness of a sample since, given a choice, interviewers are likely to interview people with whom they feel most comfortable, who are convenient, or are most willing to be interviewed. However, as a result, such samples are likely either to over represent or under represent traits not specified in the quotas. For this reason stratified sampling is far preferable to quota sampling if it is important that the sample contain an adequate proportion of members of identifiable groups occurring infrequently in the population. Quota sampling is a tempting procedure and at one time was used widely. It gives the appearance of being representative as certain characteristics of the population are structured into the sample. The units may be selected in a biased way, however, and may not be representative of the population on other characteristics. Although quota sampling may appear to be comparable to stratified sampling, it is not. In stratified sampling, the various strata, or subgroups, are identified in advance and a probability sample is selected from each strata, preventing bias.

Snowball or referral sampling is used when members of a population cannot be located easily by other methods and where the members of a population know or are aware of each other. We may want to sample members of professional groups who form informal networks or other elites. Or we may want to sample very small populations who are not easily distinguishable from the general population or who do not want to be identified, for example, drug users. In snowball sampling each member of the population who is located is asked for names and addresses of other members. A bias in snowball sampling is that the more times a given person is mentioned, the more likely that person is to be included in the sample. Those who are most well known may be least typical of the population.

Nonprobability sampling designs have the advantage of being easier, quicker, and usually cheaper than probability sampling. If the purpose is to make accurate generalizations to a larger population, then probability sampling is necessary. If, however, the purpose is to undertake some exploratory investigation, then nonprobability sampling is likely to suffice. If the sample is going to be very small, then a nonprobability sample is likely to be as accurate as a probability sample, and the added inconvenience and cost of a probability sample is not warranted. Here again, this is likely to be the case at the exploratory stages of an investigation.

SAMPLE SIZE

One of the first questions administrators ask about sampling has to do with appropriate sample size. Those unfamiliar with sampling procedures and theory often assume that a major determinant of sample size is the size of the entire population. But to determine the appropriate sample size, the sampling expert needs to know other information. This will be discussed below.

Our intuition tells us that larger samples are likely to give better estimates of population parameters. Generally, this is correct. However, additional units also bring additional expense, and increasing the size of the sample beyond a certain point results in very little improvement in our ability to generalize about the population. Thus, in choosing a sample size, the administrator must balance the need for accuracy against the need to keep costs at a reasonable level. Further, with very large samples, the quality of the data actually may decrease, for example, when a small staff must supervise the interviewing of a large number of people. With a large sample, staff will find it difficult to make many callbacks when respondents are difficult to contact. Each additional case also increases the opportunity for errors in transcribing data.

Note that the following discussion refers only to probability sampling. All of the factors to be discussed here are relevant only when one proposes to use the sample data to estimate population characteristics. Since this cannot be done with nonprobability sampling, the determination of sample size in such cases must be governed by other considerations. In nonprobability sampling, for example, taking a larger sample will not eliminate bias; it may in fact make it worse.

Investigators expect that a sample statistic will not estimate the population parameter exactly. Each possible estimate is likely to be somewhat off its mark. However, if numerous samples were selected, an investigator would expect most of the estimates to be within a specified range of the population parameter; otherwise, the estimate would be of little value. The larger the sample, the closer we would expect these estimates to be.

Both *sampling* and *nonsampling errors* contribute to the difference between the value of the statistic and the parameter that it estimates. Sampling error occurs because sampling has taken place; it is that part of the difference between a parameter and its estimate that is random and due to the probability of selecting one unit rather than another. Because of sampling error, every possible sample is as likely to underestimate as it is to overestimate the value of the parameter. Nonsampling error, also called *bias,* is usually due to some flaw in the design or in the way the design is implemented. If nonsampling error is present, all samples selected in the same way will either underestimate or overestimate the parameter. The sources of nonsampling error are discussed later in this chapter.

The size of the sampling error affects the accuracy of the estimate. Since the investigator usually does not know the exact value of the population parameter—if he did he would probably not need to draw a sample—the size of the sampling error must be estimated. This is done from the sample itself. The formula for doing this is illustrated in Appendix 5.1 at the end of this chapter.

To calculate the appropriate sample size, a sampling expert will be concerned with how large of a sampling error an investigator is willing to accept, since accuracy is an important factor in determining sample size. Greater accuracy usually can be obtained by taking larger samples or by accepting less restrictive values for other factors. Two other factors important in determining the sample size are related to accuracy. These are the confidence the investigator wishes to have in the results and the variability within the population from which the sample is selected.

The formula for calculating the necessary sample size for a study using these factors is shown below. This formula is specific for a dichotomous variable, that is, a variable with only two values such as a respondent being either For or Against a bond issue. A similar formula is used to calculate sample sizes for studies with interval variables as well. An example of the calculations for an interval variable are shown in the appendix.

Formula for Determining Sample Size for Population Characteristic Expressed as a Proportion

$$\sqrt{n} = \sqrt{p\,(1 - p)} \times (\,z\text{-score for confidence level})/\text{accuracy}$$

where:

n = sample size. (Note: A capital N often is used to indicate population size. The factor to adjust for population size is not included here.)

p = proportion of population in one category of a dichotomous variable. The term $\sqrt{p(1 - p)}$ is the standard deviation for proportions and measures the population variability.

z-score = standard score corresponding to the appropriate confidence level. This is taken from the theoretical distribution of all sample statistics. For a 95 percent confidence level, the z-score would be 1.96, or approximately 2. (Standard scores are discussed in Chapter 12.)

The properties of sample statistics may be derived theoretically by considering what the results would be if all possible samples of a given size were drawn. A certain percentage of these possible samples would estimate the population parameter very closely, some would be less accurate, and a few would be very inaccurate. Figure 5.1 illustrates possible outcomes if several samples were drawn from the population. The parameter is 60 percent, and the statistics from four samples are shown. If a large number of samples were selected, the majority of their estimates would be

Figure 5.1   Sampling Error in Estimating Parameters

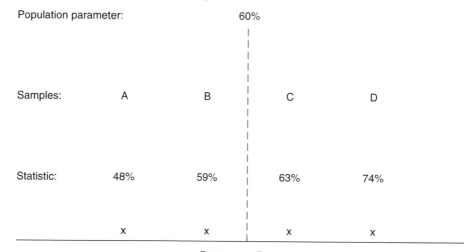

near the parameter. However, as the figure shows, a few would greatly underestimate and some would greatly overestimate the value of the parameter. An investigator, though, draws only one sample. There is always a risk that any single sample will be one of those whose estimate of the parameter is not very accurate. The *confidence level* refers to the confidence that the investigator has that the selected sample is one that estimates the population parameter to within an acceptable range. This confidence usually is expressed as the probability that a parameter lies within this range of the sample statistic. The range is called the *confidence interval* and is usually expressed in terms of units of the standard error, used to measure sampling error. The higher the degree of confidence desired by the investigator, the larger the required sample size if no other factors are changed.

Confidence levels usually are discussed in terms of how confident we are of our estimates. When investigators say that they are 95 percent confident that the parameter falls within a certain range of the statistic, this means that 95 times out of 100, using the same sampling procedure, the population parameter will be within that range of the sample statistic. Conversely, 5 times out of 100, the population parameter will be outside the range specified.

The *accuracy* of a sample is how close the sample statistic is to the population parameter. A measure of accuracy is the standard error. If the standard error is small, then the sample estimates based on that sample size will tend to be similar and will be close to the population parameter. If the standard error is large, then the sample estimates will tend to be different and many will not be close to the population parameter.

If we construct an interval of -1.96 to $+1.96$ standard errors around the sample statistic, we can be somewhat confident that the population parameter is located in that interval. That is, we are 95 percent confident that the population parameter falls within -1.96 to $+1.96$ standard errors of a sample statistic. There will be a 5 percent chance that we are wrong; that is, that the population parameter is not within the interval. The confidence level is the extent to which we are confident that the population parameter is within the confidence interval. Table 5.2 illustrates that as the confidence interval is narrowed, that is, the accuracy desired increases, the investigator's confidence that the parameter is within this interval becomes less.

If the investigator is not willing to accept a 5 percent risk of being incorrect, he can use a different confidence interval. The chance that the parameter will be within -2.58 to $+2.58$ standard errors of the sample estimate is 99 out of 100. But

TABLE 5.2 THE TRADE-OFF BETWEEN CONFIDENCE LEVELS AND ACCURACY

Confidence Level	Accuracy as Shown by Confidence Interval
99%	$-2.58 - +2.58$
95%	$-1.96 - +1.96$
90%	$-1.65 - +1.65$
50%	$- .68 - +.68$

Note: These figures assume that the sample size remains constant.

EXAMPLE 5.7

Application of Sampling Statistics to a Probability Sample

Problem: State officials want to measure the average earnings of participants in a job training program after they complete the training program.

Population: All participants who have completed the job training program.

Strategy: Construct a probability sample of 100 participants and contact members of the sample to learn each member's annual salary.

Finding: The average (mean) salary of the sampled participants is $16,000 yearly. The standard error is estimated from the sample data to be $250.

Interpretation: The state officials can be 95 percent confident that the average salary of all program participants is between $15,510 and $16,490 (1.96 standard errors below the mean and 1.96 standard errors above the mean).

Explanation: If all possible samples of 100 job training participants were drawn, the average salaries found in 95 percent of them would fall between 1.96 standard errors below and 1.96 standard errors above the true average.

note that the sample estimate will not be as accurate with the same size sample. The investigator will be 99 percent confident that the estimate is no more than 2.58 standard errors (se's) off its mark rather than no more than 1.96 standard errors off. The width of the confidence interval can be narrower if the researcher is willing to accept a larger risk of being unable to apply the results to the population. For the same size sample, the investigator can have more accuracy but will be less confident in the results. The researcher could use an interval of –.68 to +.68 standard errors (a very accurate estimate) and have only a 50 percent chance of being correct in assuming that the population parameter is within the interval. To be more accurate without running a larger risk, the investigator needs to take a larger sample.

Usually investigators will say that they want to be at least as accurate as some figure or within a certain number of standard errors of the parameter with their estimate and have a certain level of confidence in their results. That means that a certain size sample is necessary.

The interpretation of confidence levels is difficult because it involves thinking not only about the actual sample but about other samples that could have been drawn. For a 95 percent confidence level, if 100 samples of the same size were selected, about 95 percent of them should produce confidence intervals that include the population parameter. The other 5 percent would not.

Example 5.7 illustrates these concepts. The information shows that members of a sample had an average annual salary of $16,000. The standard error of this estimate was $250. The confidence level indicates how likely it is that the population's average salaries are within 1, 2, or 3 standard errors of the sample's average salaries. For the 95 percent level of confidence, the population average would be within 1.96 standard errors of the sample average. Note that the standard error takes on the same unit of measure as the sample statistic; in this example it is measured in dollars. The standard error goes in both directions; that is, the population average may be below or above the sample average.

If the parameter is a proportion, such as the percent of trainees who had completed high school, the standard error is reported as a percent. If 60 percent of the sample had finished high school and the standard error of this estimate was calculated to be 1.5 percent, then an investigator could report that he was 95 percent confident that the proportion of all trainees who had finished high school was between 57 and 63 percent or within 1.96 standard errors of 60 percent. The specific range depends on the confidence level selected. You would choose the 68 percent confidence level in order to be within 1 standard error of the parameter. To be within 3 standard errors, you would choose the 99 percent confidence level. The standard error of 1.96 corresponds to the 95 percent confidence level. Sometimes 1.96 is rounded to 2. You may be familiar with this measure of accuracy from seeing newspaper reports of the results of polling organizations. Typically, they report the accuracy for a 95 percent confidence level.

If all the units in a population were exactly the same, a sample size of one would be adequate to characterize that population! For example, if everyone in a city earned $45,000 a year, a sample of 1 would be enough to estimate average salary. However, the units within a population usually are somewhat different from each other. *Population variability* is the extent to which members of a population differ from each other on the variables that we want to investigate. The greater this variability, the larger the sample size required to estimate population parameters. A common measure of population variability is a statistic called the *standard deviation*. This measure is used in the formula for determining sample size.

Sample size is a function of the accuracy desired, the confidence level desired, the population variability, and to a much lesser extent, the size of the population. These factors are related to each other. The relationship of each to sample size, if the others remain unchanged, is:

1. Accuracy: The greater the accuracy desired, the larger the sample needs to be. This also means that the smaller the sampling error that an investigator is willing to accept, the larger the sample needs to be.
2. Confidence level: The more confidence desired, the larger the sample required.
3. Population variability: The more diversity among the members of the population, the larger the sample size needed.
4. Population size: The larger the population, the larger the required sample size. However, the population size is only a concern if the population is very small. At a certain point, adding more cases to the sample does not add information.

One common misconception about sample size is that a sample must include some minimum proportion of the population. This implies that if the size of the population is larger, the sample size must be increased by a corresponding amount. This is not the case. As you might expect, however, the members of larger populations usually are more diverse than those of smaller populations. In this indirect way, population size affects sample size. Statisticians use the finite population correction (fpc) factor to adjust for population size. If the population is at least five times the size of the sample, however, this factor usually has little impact on the sample size and often is omitted from the formula for calculating sample size. For samples drawn from very small populations, however, the population correction factor is very important.[14] Appendix 5.1 to this chapter shows an example of calculations for a sample drawn from a population of 100. A table illustrating the sample sizes necessary for small populations for selected accuracy and confidence levels is included in Appendix 5.3.

In order to be more accurate and more confident, an investigator needs to take a larger sample. To increase accuracy without increasing the sample size, the investigator must settle for a lower confidence level. To increase confidence and keep the sample size the same, some accuracy must be sacrificed.

The calculation of sample size for simple random samples is relatively straightforward. Determining sample sizes for cluster and stratified samples requires more complex calculations, although the determination is based on the same factors. We again suggest that you seek expert advice if you plan to implement a complicated design to estimate population parameters.

Although the accuracy and confidence level can be improved by increasing sample size, the amount of improvement realized with additional units becomes less and less. It is a classic case of diminishing returns. When the sample size is small—say 100—an increase to 400 will greatly improve accuracy and confidence. However, an increase in sample size from 2,000 to 2,300 will bring little improvement, although the additional costs are likely to be the same in both cases. Beyond some sample size, the improvements in accuracy and confidence level from increasing the sample size usually are not worth the cost. For this reason, commonly used limits are around 4 percent for accuracy and 95 percent for confidence.

An example using the formula for calculating sample size follows with information for a dichotomous variable. An investigator attempting to determine the proportion of a population supporting a bond issue, for instance, would analyze a dichotomous variable. The responses would be categorized as either "In Favor" or "Not In Favor." The population parameter would be expressed as the percentage "In Favor."

The example shows the calculations required for a variable in which 50 percent of the population favor an issue and 50 percent oppose it; the confidence level desired is 95 percent, and the accuracy desired is ± 4 percent.

$$\sqrt{n} = \sqrt{(.50)(1 - .50)} \times (1.96)/.04$$
$$= (.5) \times (49) = 24.5$$
$$n = 600$$

Table 5.3 shows the relationship of accuracy, confidence level, and sample size for variables that have only two values. In these calculations we assumed that 50 percent of the population was in one category and that 50 percent was in the other. These percentages are expressed as proportions (.50 and .50) and are used to measure the population variability. This is the maximum variability. A population with a smaller percent in one of the categories, say 30 percent, has less variability and therefore requires a smaller sample size to achieve the same degree of accuracy at a given confidence level. If the investigator has little or no information about the population, the easiest and most conservative approach is to assume that the population is split 50/50.

TABLE 5.3   SAMPLE SIZES FOR VARIOUS DEGREES OF ACCURACY AND CONFIDENCE LEVELS

	Confidence Level		
Desired Degree of Accuracy	*99%*	*95%*	*90%*
1%	16,576	9,604	6,765
2%	4,144	2,401	1,691
3%	1,848	1,067	752
4%	1,036	600	413
5%	663	384	271
10%	166	96	68
20%	41	24	71

Computing equation:

$\sqrt{}$Sample size = Population variability $\times$ z-score for confidence level $\times$ 1/degree of accuracy. Where variability is at the maximum for a dichotomous variable, $p = .50$.

Table 5.3 provides conservative estimates of required sample sizes; that is, the size may be larger than is actually needed. If the population split is anything other than 50/50, the population variability will be less, resulting in a smaller required sample size. Note that the commonly used standard of 4 percent sampling error and 95 percent confidence level requires a sample of 600 units, whereas to have a sampling error of only 1 percent and a 99 percent confidence level requires over 16,000 units. The figures in Table 5.3 also assume that the population is large enough that its size can be ignored as a factor in determining sample size. The reader may wish to compare the sample size figures in Table 5.3 with those in Table 5.4, Appendix 5.3.

The approach described here also is used when calculating sample size for nominal and ordinal variables with more than two categories. The investigator treats the variable of interest as if it were a dichotomy and chooses two proportions for the formula, guessing that a certain percent are in one category, and the remainder in all the others. For example, the director of the employment division wants to conduct a study in which one of the variables is occupation. This variable includes the following categories: professionals, managers, and skilled workers. To calculate the appropriate sample size, her statistical consultant assumes that 34 percent of the population is in the professional category and that 66 percent is in the other two categories.

Appendix 5.2 illustrates a calculation of sample size for an interval-level variable. Note that the appropriate sample is relatively small compared to those in Table 5.3, which are for nominal and ordinal variables.

The response rate also affects our choice of sample size. In sample surveys, not all of the units selected for the study respond. A large percent of those receiving mailed questionnaires do not return them. Some respondents contacted by telephone or in person will refuse to be interviewed. The percent of those selected to receive the questionnaire or be interviewed who actually complete and return the questionnaire or agree to be interviewed is called the *response rate.* The calculations in Table 5.3 assume that data will be gathered from every unit selected for the sample. Unfortunately, if some units cannot be found or if individuals refuse to respond, the sample's accuracy will be affected in a way that cannot be determined accurately. Nevertheless, factors such as the anticipated non-response rate need to be considered and the sample size adjusted accordingly. Of course, the amount of time and money available also may set limits on the number to be sampled.[15]

The administrator should keep in mind a study's purpose. Unless the purpose of a study is well defined, and there is reason to be confident that the validity of the measurement of the variables has been established, a preliminary study with a small sample may be more efficient than spending resources on a larger sample. Exploratory studies can be very useful. In quantitative research, just collecting and examining the data frequently give the researcher and the client an opportunity to understand and possibly modify their models. Data collection has its moments of frustration. One is well advised not to spend resources on a large-scale study in the absence of a reasonably well developed model whose critical measures have been tested for reliability, validity, and sensitivity.

Another important factor in determining sample size is the analysis to be undertaken. Specifically, small samples will not withstand extensive statistical exploration; some statistical procedures require a large sample. If, for example, there are a large number of independent or control variables, working with a small sample may result in the analyst's looking at individual cases rather than true samples. Dividing the sample into many small groups will have the same result. A Southeastern state annually conducts a statewide survey of about 1,300 residents. This size sample is more than adequate for estimating characteristics of the population of the state as a whole. However, the sample is not large enough to allow a meaningful analysis at the county level. For example, too few cases exist for analysts to compare the employment experience of males in all 100 counties of the state.

Sample Size for Different Types of Studies

The minimum sample size necessary for credible research differs from study to study. In general, the minimum number of subjects acceptable depends on the type of design. Public-opinion surveys and epidemiological studies rarely use fewer than several hundred subjects, and sample sizes of over 1,000 are common. Surveys of the general population spread over a large geographic area tend to have the largest samples. Studies to discover rare events or conditions also tend to require large samples. Sample sizes for other types of studies, such as controlled experiments, can be much smaller.

Samples for Experiments

In experimental studies, sampling seldom is done in order to be representative of the population at large. What is important is that the subjects are representative of the characteristics relevant to the experiment. Random assignment to an experimental or to a control group in the experiment is equivalent to random sampling. The main interest is in having a sample large enough so that any difference between the control and experimental groups can be attributed to the independent variable.

A rule of thumb for experimental studies is to have at least 30 subjects for each experimental condition, for example, 30 subjects in the experimental group and 30 subjects in the control group.[16] Experimental designs allow for fewer subjects than do cross-sectional designs for a number of reasons. Fewer groups are compared; that is, the sample is not divided into as many subsamples as is done often in the analysis of cross-sectional surveys. The experimenter physically controls for more variables, whereas the survey researcher uses statistical controls in the analysis after the data are collected. The survey analyst divides the obtained sample data into many subgroups whose members are equivalent on important variables and compares the different subgroups. In our example of the statewide survey, if the analyst wanted to compare employment experience for various age, sex, and education groups for different counties, she would need a much larger sample than if she wanted only to analyze employment experience.

If possible, experiments should use more than the minimum sample size. If the difference between groups that is expected at the end of the study is small, it might not show up if samples are small. Statistical techniques can be used to estimate required sample sizes for experimental studies. Using these requires knowing or assuming some facts about the population, such as the difference expected between groups and the variability of the dependent variable in the population. A preliminary study can be most helpful in obtaining initial information on these factors.

Sample Size and Statistical Power

Power refers to the ability of a statistical test to detect correctly from a sample a difference in means between two groups or the strength of a relationship between two variables.[17] The smaller the difference between means or the weaker the relationship between variables, the more difficult it will be to estimate them accurately. There are formulas for computing adequate sample size in order to maximize the power of a given statistical test. Researchers also have developed tables based on sampling principles and experience that relate sample size to generalizability. Tables showing the sample size needed for various levels of accuracy, confidence, and power are available.[18] When testing a hypothesis, the investigator wants to include enough subjects in the sample to demonstrate that the hypothesis probably is true. On the other hand, he does not want to waste resources by sampling many more subjects than needed.

Consider the following two hypotheses:

H_1: City managers are paid higher salaries than county managers with the same length of experience.

H_2: The more hours of training employees receive, the fewer accidents they will have on the job.

To learn whether the hypotheses are probably true in the population of interest, that is, among city and county managers or employees, the investigator may begin by selecting a sample out of the appropriate groups. To decide how many subjects to sample, he needs to decide how great an effect the independent variable is likely to have on the dependent variable.

Let's assume that the investigator anticipates that the difference in pay between city and county managers is relatively small, but he wants to confirm this difference. He also may believe that the impact of longer training on the number of accidents is relatively great, and he may consider his hypothesis to be unsupported if increased length of training brings about only small improvements. In the case of detecting pay differences, then, he will need a larger sample than he will in detecting increased benefits of longer training. Although the concept of power helps in deciding on sample size, the concept and the way to apply it are understood more easily in the context of statistical significance. Thus we discuss power in more detail in Chapter 12, which is devoted to statistical significance.

Nonsampling Errors

Sampling errors are errors that come about because we have drawn a sample rather than studied the entire population. They are due to mathematical chance—the probability that we will select those cases not exactly estimating the population parameter. If a probability sampling method has been used, the size of the resulting error can be estimated with the use of statistical theory. This is one of the powerful advantages of probability sampling. But other types of errors can cause a sample statistic to be inaccurate. Nonsampling errors usually result from a flaw in the sampling design itself or from faulty implementation. These errors cause a distortion in the estimate of the parameter that cannot be evaluated using statistical theory. Unlike sampling errors, nonsampling errors are likely to cause the difference between the statistic and the parameter to be distorted in one direction. This also is called bias. Sometimes we are aware of bias but are not able to estimate its effect, at least not mathematically. Sometimes we are unaware of it. An example of an inappropriate sampling frame causing bias would be the use of the telephone book as a sampling frame for homeowners. Upper-income homeowners are less likely to have a listed number than are middle or lower income homeowners.

Nonsampling errors are serious, and their impact on the results of a study cannot be easily or directly estimated statistically. Taking a larger sample may not decrease nonsampling error; such error may, in fact, increase with a larger sample. For example, if coders rush to code and transcribe data, they may make more mistakes than they would have with fewer forms. Similarly, a larger sample size may result in fewer attempts by interviewers to reach respondents who are not at home, thus increasing the nonresponse rate. In short, a larger body of data generated from a larger sample can adversely affect the quality of data gathering and data processing.

People who do not respond to surveys and questionnaires contribute to the nonsampling error of studies in which they are asked to participate. Some people routinely may refuse requests for information; others ignore questionable or poorly conceived surveys. A researcher may be unable to contact a member of a sample; the person may have moved, missed a telephone call, or be otherwise unavailable. The greater the proportion of sample members who do not respond or who do not give usable responses, the greater the nonsampling error.[19] If members of the sample who respond are consistently different from nonrespondents, the sample will be biased.

Other nonsampling errors include unreliable or invalid measurements, mistakes in recording and transcribing data, and failure to follow up on nonrespondents. If a sampling frame excludes certain members of a subgroup, such as low- or high-income individuals, substantial bias may be built into the sample. And, as we have already said, taking a larger sample will not necessarily reduce these problems. Careful effort must be given to the proper selection and construction of the sampling frame and other steps in the investigation.

Assessing Sample Quality

Administrators should feel confident in their ability to evaluate the quality of samples encountered in their work. They must frequently rely on studies involving limited samples, such as small samples drawn from a narrowly defined population. For example, a researcher who studied falls suffered by elderly people studied only falls in a geriatric facility, perhaps because she did not have the resources or the contacts to study falls reported to private doctors or hospitals. However, as long as one is aware of the limits of a given sampling design, information thus gathered may prove very useful, and one is not likely to make inappropriate generalizations from it.

In evaluating a given sample, an administrator should consider its size, how representative it is of the population of interest, and the implementation of the design.[20] The size of the sample must be evaluated in light of the purpose of the study. Small samples may be reasonable for a small, relatively homogeneous population, especially if the investigators do not want to generalize with great accuracy to a larger population. Nevertheless, sample size partially depends on the extent of analysis; a small sample cannot withstand intensive analysis involving investigation of the joint relationships of many variables. If a population parameter is to be estimated from a sample with accuracy and confidence, a larger sample is needed. Similarly, if an analyst intends to divide the sample into many subsamples, the sample must be larger than otherwise. Consider, for example, the *U.S. Current Population Survey.* This survey, which provides statistical estimates of population characteristics for the nation and each state, uses a sample of over 60,000 households. Still, the sample is too small to estimate the characteristics for a single city or county.

The importance of generalizing from the sample to the population depends on the sample and how an administrator plans to use it. A sample representing just one school will be adequate for the principal. It will be of less interest to the head of the State Department of Education, unless it uncovers something amiss or intriguing about that particular school. Awareness of a study's population and its sampling frame may alert an administrator to findings that cannot be generalized to a similar but unsampled population.

Another important consideration is how well the study was implemented; poor implementation of the sample design will cause avoidable nonsampling errors. Evidence of careless data collection, poor staff supervision, inadequate quality control, and low response rate can seriously undermine the most carefully drawn design. Many people understandably refuse to participate in studies that appear poorly conceived and developed. A well-designed sample cannot overcome the flaws in a poorly designed questionnaire. Although sampling is an important part of a study, an administrator should not assume that a well-designed probability sample will ensure a quality study.

SUMMARY

Sampling is an efficient and effective method of studying a population, whether it consists of people, files, agencies, or other units. Probability sampling normally is the preferred sampling method because with it an investigator can apply statistical methods to estimate parameters, and it helps to control biases that inevitably enter into the construction of samples. The four common probability sample designs are: simple random, systematic, stratified, and cluster. For simple random sampling, the investigator uses a lottery method or list of random numbers to draw the sample. Each member of the sample has an equal probability of being selected, and the selection of one member does not affect the probability that another member will be chosen. In systematic sampling the population size is divided by the desired sample size to determine a skip interval, a random starting point in the list of the population members is selected, and cases separated by the skip interval are chosen.

In stratified sampling the investigator divides the population into classes or strata and randomly selects units from each class for the sample. Stratified samples may be either proportional or disproportional. Proportional samples include members from the strata in the same proportion as they exist in the population. Disproportional samples include a higher proportion of the members of some strata than of others. Oversampling of some strata may occur in order to provide sufficient numbers of units from that stratum for detailed analysis. In cluster sampling the investigator randomly selects units that contain members from the population of interest; then, sample members are randomly selected from the chosen clusters.

Nonprobability samples are suitable for exploratory studies. Purposive and convenience samples rely on an investigator's judgment. These samples may be adequate if they are free of obvious bias; however, sampling statistics cannot be appropriately applied to them. Quota samples, which specify the number of units with certain characteristics to be selected, are less satisfactory and have little to recommend them because stratified sampling provides an unbiased method for ensuring representativeness. In snowball sampling each respondent in the sample is asked to refer the investigator to another member of the population. Although this method has important biases, it can be useful in reaching a population difficult to contact by other methods.

The appropriate sample size for any given study is a function of the desired degree of accuracy, the population's variability, the desired degree of confidence in the results, and the analysis to be done. Population size is sometimes a factor but usually affects sample size only indirectly. Increased precision, that is, a high degree of accuracy and confidence in the data, requires a larger sample size. However, this also will increase a study's cost and may increase the number of nonsampling errors.

Although sample surveys are perhaps the most well-known use of probability sampling, many other endeavors utilize the principles of probability sampling. Experimental designs seldom use samples to represent a general population, but instead have experimental and control groups large enough to allow the investigator to attribute a change in the dependent variable to the independent variable.

Samples are prone to two types of errors. Sampling errors are a product of the sampling process. One cannot reasonably expect any one sample to be a completely accurate representation of the population, nor can one tell with absolute certainty that the sample has only a low degree of error, but statistical theory provides a basis for estimating the extent of sampling error. Nonsampling error also affects the quality of the sample. Common nonsampling errors include nonresponse bias, careless data collection, and careless data processing.

Next, we will begin to examine data collection techniques. Chapter 6 discusses the process of carrying out a sample survey, while Chapter 7 discusses the design and writing of survey instruments.

NOTES

1. Jennifer D. Williams, Census 2000: *The Sampling Debate, CRS Report for Congress* (Washington, D.C.: Congressional Research Service, 2000).
2. Graham Kalton, *Introduction to Survey Sampling,* Sage University Paper Series on Quantitative Applications in the Social Sciences, 07–035 (Beverly Hills: Sage, 1983), 5.
3. L. O'Muircheartaigh and S. T. Wong, "The Impact of Sampling Theory on Survey Practice: A Review," *Bulletin of the International Statistical Institute 49*, (1981): 465–493. Kalton, *Introduction.*
4. Leslie Kish, *Survey Sampling* (New York: Wiley, 1965), 53–59.
5. Ibid., 20–21.
6. Because no new principles of sampling are included in Random Digit Dialing (RDD), we discuss it in Chapter 7 along with other data collection methods.
7. Seymour Sudman, *Applied Sampling* (New York: Academic Press, 1976), 56–57.
8. Stuart Bretschnieder, "Management Information Systems in Public and Private Organizations: An Empirical Test," *Public Administration Review, 50,* (September/October 1990): 536–545.
9. Sudman, *Applied Sampling,* 110, 130.
10. M. Hansen, W. Hurwitz, and W. Madow, *Sample Survey Methods and Theory* (New York: Wiley, 1953), 40–48.
11. Survey Research Center, *Interviewers Manual* (Ann Arbor: University of Michigan, Institute for Social Research, 1969), chap. 8, describes a seven-stage cluster-sampling process used in a nationwide survey.
12. Kalton, *Introduction,* 38–47; E. Terrence Jones, *Conducting Political Research* (New York: Harper & Row, 1971), 61–63 contains a relevant and clear illustration.
13. Kalton, *Introduction,* 90. Kish, *Survey Sampling,* 19. These samples also are called "fortuitous" or "haphazard."
14. See Kalton, *Introduction,* 13, 14, 82–84, and William F. Matlack, *Statistics for Public Managers* (Itasca, IL: Peacock, 1993), 132–135 for discussions of the "finite population correction factor" and when to use it. This correction is important if the sample is a large fraction of the population, say 10 percent or over. This is likely when small populations are sampled. If the population is large and the sample is a very small fraction of the population, the correction factor can be ignored with very little effect.
15. Norman M. Bradburn, "A Response to the Nonresponse Problem," *Public Opinion Quarterly 56* (1992): 391–397. We discuss the issue of response rate and ways to increase it in Chapter 6.
16. L. R. Gay, *Educational Research,* 4th ed. (New York: Macmillan, 1992), 137.
17. H. C. Kraemer and S. Thieman, *How Many Subjects? Statistical Power Analysis in Research* (Newbury Park, CA: Sage, 1987), 22–29.
18. R. J. Krijcie and D. W. Morgan, "Determining Sample Size for Research Activities," *Educational and Psychological Measurement 30* (1970).
19. C. A. Mosher, *Survey Methods in Social Investigation* (London: Heineman, 1969), 139–144. Also see pages 246–250 for further discussion of sources of nonsampling error. G. T. Henry, *Practical Sampling* (Newbury Park, CA: Sage, 1990) discusses formulas to adjust for nonresponse.
20. See Sudman, *Applied Sampling,* page 27 for a more detailed discussion of these points.

TERMS FOR REVIEW

sample	sampling unit	quota sampling
population	simple random sampling	selection bias
sampling frame	systematic sampling	snowball sampling
parameter	skip interval	sampling error
statistic	stratified random sampling	nonsampling error
sampling error	proportionate stratified sampling	confidence level
standard error	disproportionate stratified	confidence interval
sample bias	sampling	accuracy
sample design	cluster sampling	population variability
sampling fraction	multistage sampling	standard deviation
probability sample	convenience sampling	
nonprobability sample	purposive sampling	

QUESTIONS FOR REVIEW

The following questions should indicate whether you have a basic competency in this chapter's material.

1. What are the advantages of probability sampling over nonprobability sampling? Disadvantages?
2. Explain how systematic sampling violates the principles of simple random sampling.
3. Stratified sampling is said to reduce the variability of the population and hence provide for a smaller required sample size. Explain.
4. "Quota sampling is used by people who don't understand or trust probability sampling." Discuss and explain. What is the appeal of quota sampling?
5. Contrast cluster and multistage sampling. Why are they often used together?

6. Describe the factors that are used to determine sample size. Why is population size often not important?
7. How are the factors used to determine sample size related to sample size and to each other?
8. Distinguish among sampling error, nonsampling error, and bias. What are some common sources of nonsampling error for an investigation using government documents such as police crime reports?
9. How might investigators doing different types of studies, such as sample surveys and experiments, approach the issues involved in determining appropriate sample size?
10. Identify the sampling unit in each of the stages of sampling in Example 5.5.

PROBLEMS FOR HOMEWORK AND DISCUSSION

1. From each description identify or infer: the population, the sampling frame, the unit of analysis, and the type of sample. Assess the adequacy of the sampling strategy.
   a. Problem: To study medical factors related to falls by elderly individuals. Sample: A random selection of 150 of the 311 residents who fell in 1990 while in a particular geriatric facility, and 339 randomly selected from the 850 residents in the same facility who did not fall during that year.
   b. Problem: To study intracity travel patterns. Sample: Council of Governments has com-

   puterized dataset of 110,000 trips made in one year; 10 percent of the trips are randomly selected for intensive analysis.
   c. Problem: To see whether employees changed behavior after attending a training program. Sample: Randomly selected five training sessions held in 1993, identified the trainees in the selected sessions, and compared performance reviews of the trainees recorded before the sessions with those developed after.
   d. Problem: To determine the effects of a change in publisher on a newspaper. Sample:

Randomly selected seven U.S. cities, identified and studied all newspapers published in these cities over the past century.

e. Problem: To determine current vacancy rate of rental housing. Sample: Within each planning area, blocks were selected at random, and the rental units on each block identified. Sampling continued until the sample included 32 percent of the rental units in each area. Units were divided into three categories: buildings completed before 1960 with no more than four units; buildings completed before 1960 with at least five units; buildings completed by 1960 or later. Blocks were removed from or added to the sample until the proportion of units in the three categories were similar to their proportion in the city.

f. Problem: To determine the total amount of assistance received by welfare clients. Sample: Thirteen states that represented geographic regions, and payments ranging from high payments to low payments were selected. Selected one to three counties within a metropolitan statistical area within these states. In each selected county, the welfare director was asked to gather data on each of the 50 clients coming in to recertify their eligibility for benefits.

2. You have been contracted by the Office of Continuing Education to construct a sample in order to determine reaction to a public service announcement on your university's night courses. The announcement is intended to attract more adults into night classes. Using publicly available materials:

a. Design a simple random sample. Identify your population and sample frame. Recommend a sample size and justify it. Give specific directions on how members of the sample would be selected.

b. Design a systematic sample. Identify your population and sample frame. Recommend a sample size, indicate the skip interval, and select the first 10 members of your sample.

c. Design a cluster sample. Identify your population and sample frame. Recommend a sample size. Give specific directions on how members of the sample would be selected.

d. For all three samples, discuss the adequacy of the sample frame.

e. What sampling design would you recommend? Explain why.

3. Researchers investigated the impact on total salaries of reductions in force in state government agencies by studying a random sample of 20 of 189 abolished positions. The researchers reported that the sample yielded "an accuracy of ± 9 percent at the 95 percent confidence level." Interpret the researchers' observation.

4. Analysts constructed a random sample of 200 goals and related objectives taken from state health plans in order to evaluate these plans. The analysts reported that 44.4 percent of the sample objectives were specific and quantified; they reported a sampling error of 6.9 percent. The analysts also found that 26.2 percent of the objectives had no recommended strategies for achieving them; they reported a 6.1 percent sampling error. Explain what the sampling error means in the context of these findings. Explain why the sampling errors are different.

5. Select a confidence level and accuracy level for the studies in Examples 5.1 and 5.2. Justify your choices. As part of your recommendation and justification, you should comment on the cost to sample each person or file.

6. For Example 5.1, what size sample would the county need in order to have the findings within ± 5 percent at the 95 percent confidence level if the population split about evenly on the proposition? If the community normally splits 60–40 on bonding issues, how could this information modify the choice of sample size?

7. For Example 5.1, what parameter is the study designed to estimate?

8. The local chapter of the National Urban League wants to find out which type of training or education would be most useful to the city's low-income citizens to enable them to obtain higher-paying jobs. The chapter executives want to have focus groups. Design a snowball (referral) sampling procedure to obtain a sample for the focus groups. Identify the populations and describe the sampling procedure.

9. Construct with your classmates a population of 50 members. Indicate the income of each member of the population. Calculate

the mean income of the population and its standard deviation. Randomly select five samples of 10 members each and five samples of 20 members each. For each sample compute the mean income and the standard error of its estimate (given by the equation: standard error = standard deviation/n). For each sample size, indicate how many samples come within ±1, 2, and 3 standard errors of the mean. What can you conclude?

10. An intern with the city's Division of Employment and Training is designing a study to evaluate whether three training programs impact future wages of Job Training Partnership Act (JTPA) participants differently. She plans to contact between 25 and 40 participants of each program and is concerned because she knows that sample surveys usually have many more study subjects than this.
   a. Write a memo to her explaining why she may have enough subjects for her study. Do you believe that she does have enough? Explain.
   b. The intern has decided that if the differences among the post-program wages of the participants in the different groups is less than 15 percent that the difference is not important. Will this affect her sample size? Explain.
   c. Discuss how the size of the differences among the post-program wages of the participants and the importance of these differences is an issue of the power of a statistical test.
   d. Sketch out a design that the intern might use for the study.

11. Summarize the sampling procedure in the Bretschneider article (Endnote 8). Identify each of the different types of sampling used. Identify or describe each of the following: population, sampling frame, sample size, response rate.

DISK WORK

To see how sample statistics work, load the Belle County data from the disk. Use statistical software to determine the frequency distribution for the respondents' income, perceived importance of public schools, and perceived importance of financial aid services. Request the mean, standard deviation, and the standard error of the mean for each variable. Use the software to get a 20 percent sample from the database and determine its frequency distribution for income, perceived importance of public schools, and perceived importance of financial aid services.

1. Which variable has the most variability? Which has the least?
2. How do the frequency distributions of the 20 percent sample compare to the frequency distributions of the entire sample?
3. Compare the means from the 20 percent sample with the means for the entire sample. For each variable determine if the 20 percent sample means come within 1 standard error, within 2 standard errors, or within 3 standard errors of the mean of the entire sample.
4. How does the variability of a variable effect a sample's accuracy? Cite evidence from this exercise to support your answer.
5. Compare the means from your sample with the means from samples gathered by classmates. For each variable determine how many sample means come within 1 standard error, within 2 standard errors, and within 3 standard errors of the mean of the entire survey sample.

RECOMMENDED FOR FURTHER READING

Leslie Kish, *Survey Sampling* (New York: Wiley, 1965), provides an excellent discussion of sampling designs and sampling statistics.

For a clear and practical discussion of many actual applications of sampling designs, see Seymour Sudman, *Ap-*

plied Sampling (New York: Academic Press, 1976). The author discusses the strengths and weaknesses of the various designs in different circumstances.

Graham Kalton, *Introduction to Survey Sampling*, Sage University Paper Series on Quantitative Applications in the Social Sciences, 07–035 (Beverly Hills: Sage, 1983), provides good descriptions of various sampling designs, including combinations of those presented here, and discusses the calculations for determining sample size and sampling error for them.

Gary T. Henry, *Practical Sampling* (Newbury Park, CA: Sage Publications, 1990) is a short, readable treatment of sampling with well-developed examples from actual applied research.

Steven K. Thompson, *Sampling* (New York: John Wiley and Sons, Inc, 1992) is a very thorough treatment of sampling and sampling designs. Some of the discussion in this book requires knowledge of calculus.

Helena Kraemer and Sue Thieman, *How Many Subjects? Statistical Power Analysis in Research* (Newbury Park: Sage, 1987), discuss the power of statistical tests and provide tables showing sample size for various tests and power. Although much of the book is very technical, Chapter 2 has an excellent general discussion of power for the nonstatistician.

Robert M. Groves, *Survey Errors and Survey Costs* (New York: Wiley Interscience, 1989) is recommended for an excellent treatment of methods to reduce bias, increase response rates, and some of the trade-offs involved.

Jennifer Williams, *Census 2000: The Sampling Debate* (Washington, D.C.: Congressional Research Service, 2000). This reprint discusses several of the issues surrounding the debate about whether sampling should be allowed for the 2000 census. The author cites other reports, relevant court cases, and statutes.

Appendix 5.1

Calculation of the Standard Error

The three examples in this appendix show the calculation of the standard error when the sample size and the standard deviation (a measure of variability) of the variable in the population are known.

Random sampling error is estimated with the standard error formula. One component of the formula is the z-score corresponding to the confidence level desired. For a 95 percent confidence level, the corresponding z-score is 1.96 (often rounded to 2). This also is the most common level of confidence used in administrative and managerial work. For 99 percent and 68 percent confidence levels, the appropriate z-scores are 3 and 1, respectively.

1. The formula for calculating the size of the standard error of proportions is:

$$SEp = \sqrt{p(1-p)/n}$$

where:

SEp = standard error for proportions

p = the proportion of the population in one category of the variable of interest

$\sqrt{p(1-p)}$ = the formula for the standard deviation, the measure of variability of the population

n = the sample size

The reader should note the relationship between this formula and the one for determining sample size presented in the text.

As an example, consider the following situation: A survey was taken to determine the support for city–county consolidation in a city in the Southeast. The following information was developed.

p = the proportion of citizens supporting consolidation = .53

$1 - p$ = the proportion not supporting consolidation = .47

n = sample size = 590

$SEp = \sqrt{(.53)(.47)/590}$ = .0205 or 2.05%

2. The formula for estimating the size of the standard error for means is:

$$SE\bar{x} = s/\sqrt{n}$$

where:

$SE\bar{x}$ = standard error of the mean

s = standard deviation of the sample; this measures the variability of the population

n = sample size

As an example of the use of the standard error of the mean, consider a sample of county managers drawn in a three-state area to estimate the average age of county managers in these states. The following information was developed.

s = 4.5 years

n = 35

$SE\bar{x} = 4.5/\sqrt{35}$ = 4.5/5.92 = .76 years

3. The formula for estimating the standard error when sampling from small populations includes the finite population correction factor (fpc). The following example is from a study in which the investigator took a sample out of a population of 100 counties for a study on nursing home care.

$$SEp = \sqrt{p(1-p)/n} \times (N-n)/(N-1)$$

where:

SEp = standard error for proportions

p = the proportion of the population in one category of the variable of interest

$\sqrt{p(1-p)}$ = the formula for the standard deviation, the measure of variability of the population

n = the sample size

N = the population size

$(N - n)/(N - 1)$ = the finite population correction factor or fpc.

To facilitate comparison with Example 1, assume the following:

$$p = .53$$
$$1 - p = .47$$
$$n = 60$$
$$N = 100$$

Carrying out the calculations, we have

$$SEp = (.53)(.47)/60 \cdot (100 - 60)/(100 - 1)$$
$$= (.064)(.404) = .026 \; or \; 2.06\%$$

For very small populations, investigators may gain little by sampling, even though the fpc has quite an impact. One might wonder if studying all 100 counties wouldn't have been as convenient as taking a sample of 60. In the research from which this example was taken, however, the work involved in studying more counties made the reduction worthwhile. (Again, see Kalton, *Introduction*, pp. 13–16 and 82–84.)

Appendix 5.2

Calculation of Sample Size for Means

The example in this appendix shows the calculation for sample size when the variability in the population is known from previous research or is assumed. Researchers often use a pre-test or pilot test survey to obtain an estimate of the population variability.

A study similar to that in Appendix 5.1, Example 2, is planned by the Center for Public Affairs. The investigators want to calculate the sample size needed for the study. They wish to be 95 percent confident that they have estimated the average age of county managers to within one year of the actual average of all county managers in the area of study. A 95 percent confidence interval can be placed around this estimate by adding and subtracting a number equal to 1.96 standard errors from the mean estimate. (The z-score corresponding to the confidence level desired is also called the reliability factor. In this example it is 1.96.) The amount of error in the estimate is 1.96 times $SE\bar{x}$.

$$\bar{X} \pm 1.96 \times SE\bar{x}$$

The problem for the investigators is to determine how large the sample must be to reduce this error to one year.

The formula for calculating sample size is the one given in the chapter:

$$\sqrt{n} = (\text{variablity}) \times (\text{reliability factor})/(\text{accuracy})$$

The variability is measured by the standard deviation; the population standard deviation is estimated by sample data, previous knowledge, or is assumed to be a certain value. The investigators have the information from the study done in Example 2.

$$\sqrt{n} = (4.5 \text{ years}) \times (1.96)/(1 \text{ year})$$
$$n = 77.79 \text{ or } 78$$

The investigators will need a sample of 78 managers to reach the desired level of confidence and accuracy.

Sample Size for Small Populations

TABLE 5.4   SAMPLE SIZE FOR SMALL POPULATIONS BY SELECTED ACCURACY AND CONFIDENCE LEVELS

| | For 95% Confidence Level | | | | | |
| | Population Size | | | | | |
Accuracy Desired	100	500	1,000	5,000	10,000	20,000
±1%	n.a	n.a	n.a	n.a	*	*
±2%	n.a	n.a	n.a	1,248	1,825	2,113
±3%	n.a	n.a	n.a	839	953	1,010
±4%	n.a	n.a	*	528	564	582
±5%	n.a	*	237	355	369	377
±10%	*	78	87	94	95	96
±15%	24	40	41	43	43	43

	For 99% Confidence Level					
±1%	n.a	n.a	n.a	n.a	n.a	*
±2%	n.a	n.a	n.a	*	2,427	3,287
±3%	n.a	n.a	n.a	1,163	1,503	1,673
±4%	n.a	n.a	n.a	822	930	983
±5%	n.a	n.a	*	575	619	641
±10%	n.a	111	139	161	163	165
±15%	*	63	68	73	73	74

Note: Where variability is at the maximum for a dichotomous variable.

   n.a.: Not Applicable.

*Some statisticians report that in the situation illustrated here, a sample equal to 50 percent of the population will provide the required accuracy or greater. See, for example, Taro Yamane, *Elementary Sampling Theory* (Englewood Cliffs, NJ: Prentice-Hall, 1967), 398–399. Yamane also suggests that some formulas used for sample size do not apply if sample size, n, is more than 50 percent of population size, N.

Chapter 6

Contacting and Talking to Subjects

In this chapter you will learn

1. how to conduct and effectively use mail, telephone, Internet, and in-person surveys.
2. how to deal with low response rates on mail surveys.
3. techniques for constructing a random digit dialing sample.
4. the value of intensive interviewing and focus groups.
5. basic requirements for conducting interviews and focus groups.

After investigators identify the purpose of a study and outline a model, they design a data collection strategy. The design consists of (1) a plan for contacting subjects and obtaining data from them, and (2) a questionnaire or other data collection instrument. Data collection decisions affect the quality of research. Furthermore, in practice, the relationship between the research design and data collection is dynamic. An investigator may change the original research design because of data collection problems. For example, the characteristics of a sample affect the feasibility of conducting face-to-face interviews, telephone calls, or mailed surveys. Question wording determines the reliability and operational validity of measures.

Each discipline has its own way of looking at things and relies on a few data collection methods to answer most empirical questions. Administrative and policy questions can touch on almost any discipline. Consequently, administration students may conclude that they need a background in many methodologies. In practice, administrators and policy analysts rely heavily on survey research, experimental and quasi-experimental designs, or economic analysis. These methods produce evidence to answer diverse administrative and policy questions.

Survey research refers to cross-sectional studies in which investigators use questionnaires, forms, or interview schedules to gather data from individual subjects.

Experiments and quasi-experiments refer to studies in which subjects are exposed to deliberately manipulated treatments. Economic analysis refers to studies in which investigators gather and analyze cost data; its technical details lie outside the scope of this text. Nevertheless, economic analysis depends on reliable, operationally valid, and sensitive measures.

Rather than concentrating explicitly on any one research method, we emphasize the processes of organizing data collection, contacting subjects, enticing their cooperation, writing questions, and designing research instruments. These skills, largely developed by survey researchers, can benefit any empirical investigator. Furthermore, these skills aid even the most basic data collection efforts, such as asking employees to fill out forms reporting unit and individual performance data.

Chapters 6 through 9 provide an overview of basic data collection techniques. These chapters alert you to the decisions and steps involved in empirical research. This chapter looks at how to contact subjects and collect data from them.

Chapter 7 discusses question writing and questionnaire design. The remaining chapters in this section delve into related data collection topics. Chapter 8 examines the ethical concerns with collecting data from, and about, human subjects. Chapter 9 discusses the value of analyzing existing datasets. Chapter 10 shows how to combine several indicators to measure a phenomenon. We included Chapter 10 in the data collection section because of the link between combining indicators and other aspects of data collection. Specifically, the data collection strategy may limit the number and wording of questions.

Administrators should work with investigators to decide how to contact subjects and who will contact them. If subjects view investigators as program representatives, an investigator's behavior can affect agency or program reputation. To avoid violating privacy, administrators may not want investigators to make the initial contact with clients or employees.

Typically, an investigator's first contact with research participants is through the mail, over the telephone, or face-to-face. Contacting and interviewing subjects may occur simultaneously. Alternatively, investigators may telephone individuals and arrange a time and place for a personal interview. Potential subjects may receive a letter informing them that they will be called and interviewed in the near future.

Investigators must locate potential subjects and entice them to participate. A low *response rate* may suggest problems with the study's design or implementation. If a large percentage of potential subjects cannot be found, or if they refuse to cooperate, the research findings may be unrepresentative. To determine the response rate and reasons for non-responses, investigators need the following data:

Total subjects in the original sample

Number of subjects not located (non-existent address or phone number, undeliverable mail, discontinued phone service, unoccupied housing unit)

Number of subjects not contacted (not at home, unable to understand English or other survey language, illness)

Number of subjects ineligible (sample member does not belong to target population)

Number of subjects refusing to provide information

Categorizing an uncontacted respondent can be problematic. A ringing phone or unanswered door does not necessarily mean that the telephone works or that the house is occupied. Persons who were not reached may or may not belong to the target population. Conventions for computing response rate vary. A conservative strategy computes the response rate by dividing the number of subjects who provide data by the total number of subjects minus ineligibles. This calculation implies the sampling frame and the data collection effort were adequate.[1]

The chapter begins with a discussion of mailed questionnaires, a relatively unobtrusive and inexpensive method of data collection. Comments about mailed surveys generally apply to other self-administered questionnaires. We then consider Internet and telephone surveys, increasingly common approaches to contacting and interviewing subjects. The telephone survey section includes an explanation of random digit dialing. Next, we discuss in-person interviewing, including focus groups.

Our discussion concentrates on the relationships between data collection methods and the quality of responses, response rates, and costs. Two data-gathering techniques, random digit dialing and unstructured interviewing, have a direct link to other methodological considerations. Random digit dialing was developed to overcome problems of constructing a probability sample for a telephone survey. Intensive interviewing and focus groups serve as a basis for building models, conducting case studies, and developing and evaluating measures.

MAILED QUESTIONNAIRES

Often when we talk and write about questionnaires, we think of mailed surveys. At home and work, we receive questionnaires from market researchers, professional associations, university administrators, politicians, and not-for-profit agencies. The mail surveyor needn't worry about finding respondents at home or contacting them at an inconvenient time. At the same time, he knows that they might put the questionnaire aside and forget it. They may pass it on to someone else to answer. They may answer questions they really do not understand or give cursory answers without attending to their accuracy or completeness.

Mailed surveys cost less than other data collection methods, and they cause minimal inconvenience to the respondent. The investigator can collect detailed, thoughtful data, especially information requiring reflective answers or perusal of files and records. At the same time, mailed surveys have distinct disadvantages. Designing an unambiguous questionnaire, mailing it, and having it delivered, answered, and returned takes time. Mailed questionnaires normally achieve low response rates. Recontacting nonrespondents markedly improves a survey's response rate. Of course, each follow-up adds even more time and increases costs.

EXAMPLE 6.1

Postcards to Monitor Mail Survey Participation

Problem: Investigators surveyed universities to learn about courses in inventory control. Investigators wanted to know which institutions received surveys, which institutions could not answer the surveys because they were not relevant to the respondent, and which institutions refused to respond.

Solution: Include a postcard enclosure:

Notes:

1. Investigators could assume that universities that did not return postcards did not receive the survey. Investigators could concentrate on trying to successfully contact these universities. This strategy reduces the cost of follow-up.
2. The investigators could determine the percentage of the sample who did not respond because the survey was inappropriate. In addition, the investigators had data on which institutions did not offer inventory control courses.
3. The postcard may have acted as an incentive for appropriate universities to respond. Alternative strategies (such as examination of university bulletins) may be adopted to gather data on nonresponding universities with appropriate courses.

The Survey of Educational Opportunities in Inventory Control has been received.
    (   ) We intend to respond by the end of September
    (   ) We do not intnd to respond
        (   ) because we do not have inventory control courses
        (   ) although we do have some inventory courses

Name
Institution
City and State

Investigators conducting mailed surveys cannot tell why a recipient does not respond. A poor sampling frame, e.g., one with out-of-date listings, may lower the response rate. The recipient may not have received the survey, forgotten about it, or ignored it. The survey may not have applied to the respondent. A postcard enclosure similar to Example 6.1 reduces the uncertainty about why people do not respond. Postcards also keep track of respondents to anonymously answered questionnaires. (Remember, anonymity demands that a specific individual cannot be linked to a specific questionnaire or set of data. Anonymity is different from confidentiality. Confidentiality means that someone on the research team can link an individual to a dataset, but the individual's identity is protected. Only the researcher or the research team knows whom the data refer to.) The postcards are not foolproof. We have had instances where nonrespondents indicated that they had responded and where respondents did not return the postcards.

Writing and designing questionnaires, printing them, and compiling the answers cost virtually the same for each data collection strategy. The data collection method affects personnel expenses. Mail surveyors do not have to pay for interviewer training, travel, and salary. Still, the benefit of lower cost may be canceled out by the time required to mail a survey and receive the responses. If a respondent must consult records to answer the questions, additional time must be allowed. The timing of the mailing also must be considered; for example, a questionnaire arriving at an agency during the midst of budget season will not receive immediate attention. In the United States, the holidays and other year-end activities probably make December a disastrous time to send surveys to either organizations or individuals.

An effective mailed or other self-administered questionnaire should be easy to understand and answer. To achieve clarity, the designer may oversimplify questions, thus sacrificing operational validity. Respondents cannot turn to the investigator and ask him to interpret the questions and clarify misunderstandings.

Poorly worded questions affect all respondents. In addition, not all populations react the same to a questionnaire. Highly educated groups or people accustomed to forms handle mailed surveys most easily. They can understand and follow directions and deal accurately with a variety of question-and-response formats. Some people routinely express their ideas and opinions in writing, whereas others feel uncomfortable expressing their opinions or writing answers to open-ended questions. Aged or less-educated individuals may find mailed questionnaires difficult to read and understand. They may fear making mistakes and appearing foolish. Thus characteristics of the sample can affect response rate as much as the questionnaire itself.

Administrators, managers, and other professionals may prefer mailed surveys to the more intrusive telephone interview. Mailed questionnaires and other self-administered reports, such as monthly, quarterly, and annual reports summarizing unit activities, are part of a professional's work environment. Professionals are busy and occupied with the details of their jobs. The surveyor may find reaching them by telephone a time-consuming and costly exercise in logistics. Furthermore, filling out forms, responding to written requests, and writing memoranda constitute normal parts of administrators' work routine, and they can schedule answering a questionnaire at their own convenience to fit in with their other tasks.

To gather specific information on an agency, such as the number of clients served, their characteristics, and the services received, a mailed questionnaire works well. The addressee may answer parts of the questionnaire and pass it on to another staff member for more detailed completion.

Consciously or unconsciously, an administrator or other respondent decides whether to spend time providing information. Let's assume that most respondents start off willing to answer a survey. What factors may persuade them to ignore it? First, they may postpone answering a survey that seems complicated or asks ambiguous questions. Eventually, the questionnaire sinks to the bottom of a pile. It reemerges months later and is thrown away.

Second, respondents may ignore questionnaires that ask for inaccessible or hard-to-obtain data. Perhaps no one has time to compile the needed data. Perhaps the respondents resent and resist the expectation that they will gather the data. One of our colleagues received an unanswered questionnaire from a municipality along with a note saying that because of budget cuts the town was no longer responding to questionnaires.

Third, respondents may ignore questionnaires that seem biased. For example, some questionnaires assume a state of affairs inappropriate to the respondent. One questionnaire asked respondents why they had left jobs. The available responses stressed job problems or lifestyle changes. People who changed jobs to take advantage of opportunities for professional and personal growth may have been reluctant to associate their job changes with the listed factors. Although they could fill out the "other" category, they may have been disinclined to take the time. Besides, they may wonder about how much attention the researchers will pay to answers of open-ended questions.

Respondents' perception of a built-in bias may largely center on the appropriateness of the response categories. The less appropriate the listed responses, the less likely the respondent is to complete the survey. Similarly, failure to include "neutral," "unsure," or "not applicable" response categories may discourage respondents who feel that an indefinite answer is more appropriate.

Recipients of mail surveys also may react differently according to the survey sponsor and the survey's apparent purpose. The more recipients believe that the survey will help them, the more likely they are to respond—even if they have to spend time compiling data and writing out answers. Conversely, if recipients question whether the survey will help them, then complicated questionnaires with ambiguous response categories and a need to look up or compile data will lead them not to respond.

The sponsorship of a survey can affect the rate of responses. In conducting a study for an agency, we have found that a letter from the agency head endorsing the survey and encouraging the recipient to respond helps to establish the legitimacy of the survey. The endorsements also seem to improve response rates. We once sent a questionnaire to university faculty. The questionnaire's cover letter was from the chancellor. We received a 95 percent response rate. One reviewer of this text noted that he got a 99 percent response rate from Massachusetts' school superintendents when he included a cover letter from the dean of Harvard's School of Education.

Sponsorship also can affect the direction of responses. We suspect that this is a particular problem with surveys of work conditions. If an employer conducts or sponsors a survey to learn about employee satisfaction and other components of the work environment, employees may worry about the confidentiality of their responses, and they may distort their responses in line with their perceived self-interest.

The failure to respond is not a trivial problem. Nonrespondents contribute to nonsampling error, therefore undermining the investigator's ability to infer from the sample. We are surprised and appalled at how many published articles report low response rates. Low response rates occur whether the unit of analysis is an individual or an organizational unit.

In considering response rate, we have focused on substantial research issues, that is, the purpose of the survey, its sponsor, and item validity and reliability. In addition, there are "tricks of the trade" that can lessen people's resistance. The length of the questionnaire, the ease in filling it out, respondent interest in the subject matter, the format and design, and a range of other factors, including the color of the paper and the design of the stamps affixed to the return envelope, have been linked to response rates. Further details of research on how to improve response rates are listed below.

FACTORS AFFECTING RESPONSE RATE

A. Sampling Frame
   1. Accuracy: sample members may not receive a survey if the sample is drawn from an outdated sampling frame
   2. Relevance: survey recipients may not respond if they believe they do not belong to the target population
B. Questionnaire Design
   1. Questionnaire length: research shows mixed results, but when salience and follow-up are held constant, shorter surveys have higher response rates than longer ones
   2. Item content and sequence: items should be logically arranged by topic
   3. Questionnaire layout and format: the questionnaire should be attractive on sturdy, good-quality paper; items should be numbered sequentially, and there should be ample space between items
C. Delivery
   1. Cover letter: response rates improve if the cover letter (a) indicates the importance of the study and the value of the respondent's participation, or (b) offers to provide feedback
   2. Return envelope: stamped or postage-paid envelopes markedly improve response rate
   3. Follow-up: two or more follow-ups are recommended to get higher response rates; including a questionnaire with the follow-up request seems to yield a higher response rate than just a letter follow-up[2]
   4. Incentives: including money or another incentive, e.g., entry in a lottery, donation to a charity, or a token item with the initial questionnaire markedly improves response rates.[3]

The above list was generated as part of a study to improve the response rate to an agency survey. The initial survey had a 34 percent response rate. The respondents were police officers, a profession notorious for its suspicion of researchers. The questionnaire was complicated. It had a matrix, and embedded in each item were five separate questions. It had never been pretested nor was a follow-up conducted.

The revised questionnaire asked respondents to check the appropriate answer. They could easily and accurately answer the items without reading the directions. A group of police officers reviewed the questionnaire before it was mailed. One follow-up reminder was sent to nonrespondents. The revised survey had a 76 percent response rate.

The problem with the initial questionnaire is familiar to us. We have received and read too many inept surveys; they demonstrate poorly thought-out designs, inadequate pretesting, and a simple ignorance of sound procedures. If you plan to do a mail survey, do not rely merely on your instincts. Carefully read a how-to-do-it book, either one of the books cited in the bibliography or a similar text; arrange for a variety of people, including members of the study population, to review and comment on the questionnaire, pretest it, and conduct a pilot study.

To improve response rates, one or more follow-ups are necessary. In anticipation of the year 2000 Census, the Bureau of the Census studied strategies to improve response rates. Just over 40 percent (40.3) of households responded if they received only the initial cover letter, questionnaire, and postage-paid envelope. Follow-up contact, such as postcard reminders and replacement questionnaires, brought the response rate to over 70 percent.[4] The tone and nature of the follow-up depends on the recipients.

Example 6.2 shows a postcard reminder that we sent to alumni. We resisted sending a similar reminder to subjects of a university-sponsored study, since some administrators felt it detracted from the seriousness of the survey.

Postcards can be used as inexpensive reminders to subjects. Nevertheless, either on the first or second follow-up, an additional questionnaire and prepaid envelope should be enclosed. Nonrespondents can be contacted by telephone and asked if they received a questionnaire. An additional survey may be sent, or they may be surveyed over the telephone.

Incentives have a "substantial positive" effect if included with a survey. The groups that received cash, ranging from $1 to $5, had a 19 percent higher average response rate than the control groups. Groups that received a nonmonetary incentive had an 8 percent higher average response rate than controls. Sending an incentive, either monetary or nonmonetary, after a completed survey was received had little or no effect.[5]

Whether an incentive is included with a survey or not, reminders still increase the response rate. Two studies, conducted by the same researchers, found that subjects receiving a $1, $5, or $10 incentive had the same response rate (52 percent) with no follow-up as subjects receiving no incentive and three reminders. On the other hand, subjects that received $20 plus three reminders had a 79 percent response rate.[6]

Not all persons contacted will respond. These people represent the *nonresponse rate.* An investigator should check the assumption that the nonrespondents are similar to respondents. She can sample nonrespondents and make a special effort to persuade them to answer the questionnaire over the telephone or in person. Thus she can determine whether the assumption of random differences between respondents and nonrespondents holds up. At a minimum she should compare respondents' and nonrespondents' demographics, for example, their age, sex, and region of the country, to see whether she can detect a possible bias.[7]

EXAMPLE 6.2

Postcards to Use as Follow-up Reminders

Situation: Investigators needed to send an inexpensive, follow-up reminder to people who had not responded to an alumni survey.

   Solution: We decided that a humorous postcard would serve as a first reminder to alumni.

CENTER FOR PUBLIC AFFAIRS

HAVE YOU FORGOTTEN SOMETHING?
PLEASE SEND YOUR MPA SURVEY TODAY.*
*If you have not recieved a MPA survey, contact Jay Greene
Center for Public Affairs, 555-3926 or 4006.

Notes:

1. Postcards were inexpensive to reproduce and mail. They were not wordy or heavy-handed.
2. Alumni who did not respond to the postcard reminder were sent a short letter with a duplicate questionnaire. If necessary, our next step would have been to telephone nonresponding alumni and to ask key questions.

TELEPHONE SURVEYS

In the past, the value of telephone survey data was limited because a sizeable portion of households did not have telephones, nor could investigators reach households with unlisted numbers. Consequently, surveyors could not expect to telephone a representative sample of individuals.

The conditions for telephone surveying have improved. Current census data indicate that roughly 94 percent of U.S. households have regular telephone service. Households without phone service have been described as "outsiders." They have lower income, tend to move frequently, and have fewer group memberships and community attachments. Some households, about 3 percent, have intermittent phone service. These households, which discontinue phone service from time to time because of money problems or a move, seem to be similar to nonphone households.[8]

Random digit dialing techniques have been developed and refined so that investigators can contact households with unlisted telephones. Random digit dialing also overcomes the limitations of telephone directories as sampling frames. Now investigators can be reasonably assured of telephoning a representative sample, including people whose telephone numbers are not listed in a current directory.

In addition to wider telephone coverage and improved sampling, two factors have given impetus to the spread of telephone interviewing. First, face-to-face interviewing has become less feasible. Interviewer time and travel are costly. In some neighborhoods, residents and interviewers worry about safety. Potential subjects refuse to open their doors to strangers, and interviewers also may feel unsafe. Diverse lifestyles mean that people often cannot be contacted during conventional interviewing hours. Second, telephone interviewing can deliver rapid turnaround from survey conception through reporting the findings. Overnight public-opinion polls reporting reactions to major public events now are commonplace.

Telephone surveying procedures have other distinct advantages. Telephone surveys minimize interview travel time and expense. The interviews can cover a wide geographic area relatively quickly. Interviewers can call from a central location, allowing closer supervision of their work than is possible with face-to-face interviews.

Computerization of surveying processes has accelerated the use of telephone interviewing further. Computers can generate telephone samples and dial the numbers. *Computer-Aided Telephone Interviewing* (CATI) systems have simplified the administration of complex interviews and survey monitoring. The interviewer reads items from a terminal screen and keys in the responses. The computer paces the interview, makes branching decisions for contingency questions, and checks for inconsistent responses. In addition, the computer keeps track of the number of calls made, refusals, completions, and similar data so that at any time, the investigators know the survey's status.

The first questions about telephone surveying center on sampling. How adequate are telephone subscribers as a study population? How can one assemble a representative sample when sampling frames are quickly out-of-date, exclude persons with unlisted numbers, and include households with multiple listings? How does one make sure that the sample contacted coincides with the intended unit of analysis? What has been the nonresponse rate associated with telephone interviewing? The second set of questions centers on questionnaire design. How do telephone questionnaires differ from mailed questionnaires? What types of questions can be asked? How long can telephone surveys be? A third question underlies the other two; that is, how confidential are telephone surveys? Let's consider these questions in turn.

The adequacy of telephone subscribers as a study population depends on the location and the population of interest. Telephone coverage is not the same throughout the country or within a state. Population characteristics and the cost of security deposits and monthly service may affect the proportion of telephone households within a region. Retired persons, single-parent households, rural residents, low-income families, and minority persons have been found less likely to have telephones.[9] Households without telephones may be sufficiently isolated to render them difficult to reach with any data collection technique. All these factors affect the representativeness of a sample reached by telephone.

A telephone directory may seem to be an appropriate sampling frame. Directories of organizations or professionals may be relatively stable and provide few problems. If an investigator plans to draw a sample from a local telephone directory, however, the sampling frame becomes problematic. A telephone directory does not include households with unlisted or unpublished numbers, families who have recently moved into a community, or those who have changed their telephone numbers. Random digit dialing is a technique designed to overcome these problems. In addition, random digit dialing reduces the clerical work required to draw a random sample.

Random Digit Dialing

Random digit dialing produces a sample of randomly generated telephone numbers. The sample is an equal-probability sample of all area telephone numbers—listed and unlisted numbers, residential and nonresidential numbers.

Pure random digit dialing generates a sample of telephone numbers from seven-digit random numbers. The list will include many nonworking numbers, since some of the random number combinations will be for exchanges that are not operating in the community. To reduce the frequency of nonworking numbers, investigators identify all working telephone exchanges in the target geographic area. The investigators assign four-digit random numbers only to working exchanges. In large communities, certain exchanges may be assigned to nonresidential users, including city or state government offices, universities, and businesses. If individuals or households make up the study population, the investigator omits any nonresidential exchanges before constructing the sample.

After the investigators identify the appropriate exchanges, they select an exchange, and complete the telephone number using a variation of random digit dialing. They may select a four-digit random number between 0000 and 9999. Example 6.3 illustrates this procedure. Some telephone companies will provide a list of working exchanges, the number of telephones assigned to each exchange, and an estimate of the proportion of residential telephones assigned to each exchange. With this information the investigator can create a proportional sample as illustrated in Example 6.3.

Completing telephone numbers with four random digits is inefficient. With faxes, pagers, and telephone lines dedicated to computer use, a researcher using four-digit random numbers may reach few appropriate respondents. Since the telephone company usually assigns telephone numbers in blocks, a researcher

EXAMPLE 6.3

Constructing a Random Digit Dialing Sample: A Hypothetical and Illustrative Example

Problem: Surveyors want to telephone 500 households in a community with three telephone exchanges (111, 112, 555).

Strategy: The telephone company gives the surveyors the number of residential telephones in each exchange.

Exchange	Residential Telephones	Percentage of Total
111	2,000	20%
112	3,000	30%
555	5,000	50%

1. Select 2,000 four-digit random numbers.
2. Assign 20 percent of the random numbers to exchange 111. If the first random number is 8,752, the calling number is 111-8752.
3. Assign 30 percent of the random numbers to exchange 112.
4. Assign 50 percent of the random numbers to exchange 555.
5. Select replacement numbers for nonworking or business telephones from the remaining list of random digits.

Notes:

1. Surveyors expect a large portion of the numbers generated in a random digit sample to be nonworking numbers or business telephones. We have assumed that a surveyor needs four calling numbers to successfully reach one household.
2. If we assigned each exchange the same number of calling numbers, 667 numbers, 1 out of 3 households in exchange 111 would be called and 1 out of 7.5 households in exchange 555 would be called. Thus a household in exchange 111 is 2.5 times more likely to be in the sample than a household in 555. Any unique features of the 111 exchange population will be overrepresented in the sample.

may randomly select a residential number from a telephone directory and replace the last digit with a random number.[10]

Professional survey organizations often contract with the telephone company or a private firm to draw a sample meeting certain specifications. For example, only residential telephone numbers may be included in the sample. At least one national firm constructs telephone samples for specific ZIP codes, enabling investigators to study certain population mixes. How representative these samples are depends on the contractor's procedures. Contractors may vary in their policies for including unpublished and unlisted telephone numbers in a sample.

Random digit dialing solves the problem of unlisted numbers but not of multiple listings. A household with more than one telephone or listing has a greater probability of being chosen for a sample. To handle multiple listings, interviewers may ask how many telephone numbers and telephone listings the household has. Later, analysts will weigh the household's responses. For example, responses may be weighted by the reciprocal of the number of telephone numbers or listings; responses from a household with two telephone numbers receive a weight of 0.5. Investigators may decide to ignore this problem.[11] Nevertheless, one should be aware that households with multiple listings are more likely to be selected, and such households may have distinctive characteristics, such as professional employment or teenage children.

Telephone surveys have the household as the implied unit of analysis. Yet, individuals may be the actual unit of analysis. If the surveyor intends to contact individuals, he should not automatically interview whoever answers the telephone. We assume that family members who answer a telephone differ from those who do not answer. For example, researchers have found that women answer a disproportionate number of telephone calls. For some telephone surveys, the interviewer will have the name of the sample member and will ask to speak to that person. Alternatively, the surveyor may be looking for a particular type of person, for example, the person who last had a doctor's appointment.

When the interviewers can theoretically speak to any household member, they need some way to ensure a representative sample. Various techniques have been developed and tested to select a specific household member for the interview. Some of these techniques are too complex to discuss here. One unintrusive method is to ask to speak to the member of the household who most recently celebrated his or her birthday. Other surveys ask to speak with the youngest eligible male because young men are least likely to be home when surveyors call.[12]

The last sample-related question has to do with response rates. In general, telephone surveys have better response rates than mail surveys, although mail surveys with multiple mailings may do nearly as well.[13] Unlike mail surveys, telephone surveyors can distinguish between those they cannot reach (the inaccessible) and those who refuse to participate (the unameniable). As with mail surveys, the response rate to telephone surveys depends on time and money. Because of lifestyle changes, households may be harder to reach than they were in the past. People spend less time at home. They may rely on an answering machine, voice mail, or caller-ID to screen calls, however, just because someone screens calls does not mean that she refuses to answer surveys.[14] Surveyors record machine-answered calls as "not at home," although they may leave a message stating the purpose of the call and the plan to call back.[15] To increase the percent of households successfully reached, a survey organization must conduct calls throughout the week, including weekends, and during daytime and evening hours.

Research on factors affecting telephone refusal rates is limited. A major question that affects survey costs is whether extraordinary efforts to convince respondents to participate biases their responses. A recent study has found that younger and better-educated households are harder to reach; the analysts compared the findings of a five-day survey with an eight-week survey and found few differences in respondents' opinion.[16] Robert Groves, who studies survey research methods, wrote that a high rate of cooperation requires "a population that can be contacted in a reasonable time period, a population measurable using a small set of common languages, a population willing to discuss a wide range of subjects with strangers, and a population trusting of the confidentiality of the answers they supply."[17] These traits may be less common in a nationwide sample. They may be more common in specialized samples, which consist of members who find the study topic interesting or important to them.

Let's turn our attention now to the questioning. Telephone surveys depend on auditory cues. An interviewer has to entice subjects to participate in the study and stay on the telephone to answer the questions. She must rely on her voice and ability to convey key information succinctly. In some locations a pitch to buy real estate or magazines may be proceeded by a request to participate in a "survey." Consequently, legitimate surveyors may encounter high resistance to answering questions put by an unknown caller.

In telephone surveys most refusals to participate occur after the introduction and before the first question is asked; therefore, the introduction must be clear and compelling. Consider the typical telephone survey situation. A householder in the middle of other activities is interrupted by an unexpected call by an unknown caller. The interviewer must persuade the subject that it is worth his time to delay whatever he is doing to answer some questions. The interviewer begins by introducing herself and the survey organization. Next, the interviewer explains how the subject was selected, the purpose of the survey, and its approximate length. (See Example 6.4 for wording presenting this information.) The interviewer should be prepared to answer questions about the survey organization, the survey, and the confidentiality of the answers.

In constructing an instrument for a telephone interview, the writer considers the length of the interview, the order of questions, their length, and complexity. The questions and possible responses must be clear, so the respondents can correctly figure out what they are being asked. The initial questions should reinforce the purpose of the survey stated by the interviewer. The "wrong" questions may arouse respondent suspicion. As the questions proceed, the respondent should sense the underlying logic; otherwise, he may become confused, lose interest, or question the legitimacy of the study.

Unlike the mail survey, the respondent cannot "read ahead," so investigators should consider how question order will affect later responses. The questionnaire should proceed smoothly, so that the interviewer feels and sounds comfortable moving from topic to topic and the respondent can answer easily.

Although the interviewer can repeat questions and responses, and clarify the meaning of words, an overdependence on the interviewer burdens both the interviewer and the respondent. The interviewer does not have visual clues to indicate respondent understanding. The person writing the questions should write short, easily understood questions. The writer must watch for wording that may lead a respondent to misconstrue a question. The investigators should not assume that a respondent will ask to have a question repeated or to say that he does not understand what the interviewer is asking.

Response categories must be carefully considered because the respondent does not have the leisure to read over and consider the responses. The respondent may not remember long lists of alternatives; he may give the last stated alternative just out of convenience. Asking the respondent to rank options does not

EXAMPLE 6.4

Introduction for a Telephone Survey

Situation: A sample of agency employees who participated in the DECIDE management training program were selected for a telephone interview to learn whether they used DECIDE in their work and how they used it.

Step 1: To avoid questions about the legitimacy of the interviewers, a training manager sent a memorandum to the sample explaining that the survey was to find out employee training needs:

> To: xxx
>
> From: Joe Doe, Training Manager
>
> Subject: Training Survey
>
> The Human Resources Development Unit will be conducting a phone survey November 7–14, regarding Management/Professional Development courses.
>
> You have been selected in a random sample to participate. Expect a phone call from one of our interviewers during this period. You will be asked to answer a series of questions regarding training you completed, and we ask that you be candid in your responses. The interview should take no more than 10–15 minutes.
>
> I know each of your schedules is full, but to continue to provide quality training, we need your feedback.

Step 2: Three days after the memorandum was sent, the interviewers began calling. Each interviewer used the following introduction (printed on each survey copy):

> Good morning (afternoon), I am John Cooper. I am calling in conjunction with a memo that you should have received from Joe Doe, the Human Resources Development Manager, regarding a training survey. As the memo stated, the interview should take approximately 10–15 minutes and relates primarily to training you completed with Human Resources. We appreciate your taking the time to work with us. Unless you have any questions I would like to start.

Notes:

1. Introduction does not mention DECIDE, since interviewers did not want to introduce a bias by mentioning it at the beginning. (An early question asked respondents what management decision-making tools they used. If the respondents knew the survey was to study DECIDE, they might have been more likely to mention it.)
2. Interviewer mentioned the probable length of the interview, based on pretest times. This was to prevent being turned down by busy respondents.
3. Introduction was relatively short (as was the memorandum), but interviewer gave respondents a chance to ask any questions.

For Example 6.4 we drew on our work with the DECIDE study and reproduced the memorandum that was sent to members of the sample, and the introductory statement that the interviewers used. An employee from the training division sent a memorandum to the trainees telling them that they would be interviewed. Note that the interviewer mentions the memorandum in his initial comments.

work well, insofar as he has to keep several options in mind prior to ranking them. Instead, a respondent may be asked to rank items on a scale, for example, a scale ranging from a low of 1 to a high of 10.

Open-ended questions work moderately well in telephone surveys if the interviewers can probe beyond a quickly constructed, superficial answer. Open-ended questions work poorly if the interviewers are not well trained about what to listen for, how to probe, and what to write down. On occasion we have tried to analyze completed telephone surveys and have found ourselves bewildered by the cryptic wording recorded by interviewers. This problem is related to problems of reliability where what is noted varies with who conducted the interview.

The length of the study may affect the decision on how to collect data. The research on telephone surveying has found that few respondents terminate the interview after the first questions. Nevertheless, a telephone interview cannot go on indefinitely. Respondents may tire as it drags on. Remember that the typical survey involves question after question with the pace controlled by the interviewer. Tired or bored respondents will give unreliable answers. Similarly, respondents may become anxious to get off the telephone and start giving terse, truncated answers.

With longer interviews, costs, including decreased data quality, may make telephone interviewing less satisfactory. Nevertheless, as with mail questionnaires, no absolute rule on questionnaire length can be formulated. The length depends on the study population, the nature of the questionnaire, the motivation to respond, and the skills of the interviewers. One can imagine keeping a professional respondent on the telephone for much more than 20 minutes answering questions relating to her area of expertise.

Confidentiality is the last aspect of telephone surveying we wish to consider. Random digit dialing approximates anonymity; however, respondents reached through random digit dialing are not more likely to disclose sensitive information.[18] If one is calling from a list, the respondent is known. If we plan to telephone individuals who are agency clients or employees, we have the appropriate agency official write to the individuals explaining the purpose of the study. The letter may discuss provisions for maintaining the confidentiality of the responses. The letter avoids violating the privacy of agency clients, who may not want others to know that they are receiving agency services.

For both clients and employees, the preinterview contact minimizes suspicions about why they were called. Preinterview contact should reduce refusals and avoid lengthy explanations about the purpose of the study and procedures for analyzing and protecting the data.

INTERNET SURVEYS

Internet surveys are posted on the Web or sent as part of an e-mail message. They are faster and cheaper than telephone or mail surveys. No interviewers have to be hired or trained, no postage or printing bills have to be paid, and no one has to enter data from paper questionnaires. Because Internet surveys are a recent phenomenon, questions about their quality remain largely unanswered. Specifically, researchers are only beginning to study ways to improve samples, response rates, and questionnaire design.

Sampling problems are particularly challenging.[19] If a sampling frame with e-mail addresses exists, investigators can choose a sample, send an e-mail message that includes the survey, or give the web address where it is posted. If a list with e-mail addresses does not exist, accessing the target population becomes more difficult. The investigators may publicize the survey through list serves, newsletters, newsgroups, links from relevant webpages, or similar communications.

With a discrete sample response rates may be estimated. Once a survey is disseminated through multiple channels, identifying the represented population and the response rate becomes more difficult. A researcher may not know how many people or what groups of people knew about the survey or accessed it. People outside the target population who happen to visit the website may answer a posted survey. People may send duplicate responses; they may have accessed the survey through more than one link or they may have resubmitted a survey to make sure that it was actually sent out. Researchers will not know how many people begin a survey and then quit without submitting it. Consequently, the researcher may be unable to define the target population or calculate the response rate.

An analyst who designed a Web survey commented on the care that needs to be taken in designing and pretesting the instrument. The respondent to an Internet survey must work within the designer's framework. A respondent cannot ask an interviewer to clarify a question or write in how she interpreted the question. Similarly, unless a comment box is provided, the respondent cannot indicate a more appropriate or precise response. To see if the lessons learned from mail surveys increased the response rate of e-mail surveys, researchers sent a prenotice, letter and survey, reminder, and replacement surveys to randomly selected groups of university faculty. One group received all these materials by e-mail and another group by paper. The response rate for the two groups was virtually identical. E-mail respondents were more likely to complete the survey, to leave fewer items unanswered, to answer open-ended questions and to give longer answers to open-ended questions.[20] Other features associated with effective mail surveys should apply to Internet surveys. They should be easy to access, answer, and return. As is true of any survey, ease of answering and the clarity of the questions should be established through pretesting.

IN-PERSON INTERVIEWING

In-person, or face-to-face, interviews allow researchers to obtain large amounts of data, perform in-depth probing, ask more complicated or sensitive questions, or contact difficult-to-reach populations, e.g., homeless people. There are two major types of in-person interviews: structured interviews, where interviewers each ask each subject the same, closed-ended or short answer questions; and intensive interviewing, where interviewers ask general, open-ended questions.

Studies may combine data collection methods; interviewers may telephone most sample members and meet with sample members who either do not have a telephone or are difficult to interview over the phone. In-person interviewers may give respondents a self-administered questionnaire and thus maintain the confidentiality of their responses.

Studies using in-person interviewing may rely on interviewers to solicit subjects' participation. Interviewers who give vague or erroneous explanations of a study's purpose, including information on confidentiality and use of the data, may discourage participation. Variations in asking questions, probing, or recording can contaminate a measure's reliability or operational validity. Interpersonal dynamics may similarly affect response rate, reliability, and operational validity.

Whether an interview is conducted over the telephone or in person, the interviewer cannot help but interject herself into the research environment. Her presence affects what she sees and hears. Her personality affects her observations. Her need to establish rapport, to interpret questions, and to elicit usable answers may influence a respondent's answers. Telephone interviewers working in a central location under supervision are less likely to bias responses. In-person interviewers work largely on their own with limited supervision. Thus they are more apt to bias an interview.

Structured Interviewing

Structured interviews refer to surveys in which the respondents are asked the same questions in the same order. The investigators want different answers to reflect differences among subjects, not differences among interviewers. To minimize the effect of interviewers on the answers, investigators hire and train interviewers to be consistent in how they[21]

1. explain the purpose of the study
2. ask questions
3. handle incomplete or inappropriate answers
4. record answers
5. deal with interpersonal interactions

In-person structured interviewing works well for studies with lengthy or complex instruments. Researchers have noted that respondents become fatigued if they are kept on the telephone too long; whereas in-person interviews can successfully last several hours. The interviewer may elicit the respondent's trust, thus setting the stage for asking sensitive questions. The interviewer can use visual clues to decide whether the respondent understands a question and whether to continue probing the answers to open-ended questions. The interviewer can use visual aids as part of a question. For example, a respondent can study and rank a list of alternative responses.

Structured interviewing depends on standardized interviewers who: give the same explanation of the study's purpose; ask questions without changing the wording; probe without directing answers; and record answers verbatim. Furthermore, interviewers focus on the survey and avoid talking about themselves or sharing their opinions about the study or the questions.

Computer assistance is an important component of most large scale in-person surveys. It allows for more complex instruments, standardize interviews, reduced data entry costs, and decreased time between data collection and data analysis. Interviewers using Computer-Assisted Personal Interviewing (CAPI) read the questions and enter the data. Interviewers using Computer-Assisted Self-Interviewing (CASI) have respondents read the questions or listen to them. Respondents may key in their answers or reply orally. CASI helps in collecting sensitive information and maintains the confidentiality of a respondent's answers. The interviewers give instructions and answer questions; they take care not to observe or overhear a respondent's answers.[22]

Intensive Interviewing

Another type of in-person interviewing is more similar to a conversation, with the interviewer working with a list of general questions. The questions asked, their wording, and order vary from interview to interview. When individuals are interviewed, this type of interviewing is called *intensive interviewing.* Researchers may apply intensive interviewing techniques when interviewing a group. Focus groups, which we discuss in the next section, refer to a similar process, but they are distinguished by their makeup. A *focus group* consists of a small group of people who share some characteristics, but who usually do not know each other.

For administrative researchers, either type of interview accesses rich data to improve the research design or to elaborate on the statistical findings. Before we discuss the interviewing process, let us illustrate its value to a research design. First, both individual and group interviews help develop hypotheses. One of us studied centers for victims of sexual assault; the centers grew out of the radical politics of the 1960s. She began her study of the organization of the centers strongly convinced of the value of unstructured, leaderless organizations. From an interview with staff at a highly structured, traditional social services organization, she learned that it had a large pool of peer counselors. Other centers had scarcely enough volunteers to answer their telephone crisis lines. Furthermore, the traditional center seemed to serve the needs of a wider segment of the community; the unstructured centers rarely worked with children, older victims, or the families of victims. After the interview, she changed her model and postulated that traditionally structured groups were better at providing victim services and that unstructured groups were better at raising the social and political issues associated with sexual assault and victim services.

Second, interviews help identify appropriate measures, especially in program evaluations. Once we did a short study to see the effects of discontinuing free transportation on low-income patients receiving renal dialysis. The administrators wanted to know "if anyone had died as a result." We constructed a sample and called patients or their families to learn whether patients had missed dialysis sessions and their current health status. We spoke with staff at the dialysis centers. One employee mentioned that health status was the wrong outcome measure, "since the patients would do anything to avoid dying." She argued that dietary status and adherence to medication schedules were more valid measures of the impact of termination. Her observation led us to reevaluate how we designed program evaluations; we began to include interviews with program constituents or stakeholders as part of a design.[23]

Interviews help program evaluators to learn about the background of the program, its objectives, its processes, its accomplishments, and its failures. The evaluators identify whom they want to talk with and what they want to learn. They compose general questions or outline topics that they want to explore in the interview. The interviewer might ask why the program was started, what its objectives were, how the program operates to achieve its objectives, how the objectives have changed, and so on.

Effective interviewing requires practice and careful preparation. Specific populations may present special challenges. One colleague, for example, tells about interviewing members of a white supremacist group. He arranged to meet them on street corners, after going through extensive questioning to assure them that he was not conducting a criminal investigation. Furthermore, the respondents insisted on anonymity, which required elaborate procedures for conducting the interviews.

You may occasionally read studies based on intensive, unstructured interviews. Typically, the interviewers have training in clinical interviewing, for example, in counseling, social work, psychology, or a similar therapeutic discipline.

The interviewing we advocate here is far more modest. Nevertheless, the interviewer borrows some clinically developed techniques, such as good listening skills. The interviewer needs to have a good understanding of the subject matter of the interview. Finally, the interviewer needs to have had a sufficient amount of interview experience and practice to avoid wasting a subject's time, overlooking important material, or distorting responses.

Whom to interview and when to interview them depends on the study and logistics. Some simple guidelines apply to most interviews. First, the interviewer should not speak with the most important respondents first. By most important, we mean the persons whose information, opinions, and insights are expected to be most valuable. Normally, an interviewer can identify her important respondents. They may be more difficult to reach and more protective of their time. She does not expect them to provide basic descriptive or factual information. The rule not to interview important respondents first arises from the logic that one does not want to throw away an important interview by asking the "wrong" questions.

Factual questions covering widely known or easily attainable information constitute a type of question that may be "wrong" for some respondents. Evaluators often start with knowledgeable program staff or constituents willing to describe program operations and accomplishments. These early interviews bring the interviewer up-to-date on the program, its operations, and current issues.

After she has practiced her interview skills for the specific project, identified current issues, and begun to formulate hypotheses, she can learn more from later respondents. She can test out her hypotheses with these respondents. Furthermore, she may bring insights and observations to the interview that the respondent will find valuable. We often forget that an interview can benefit the respondent. Frequently, in their day-to-day work, managers have no time to reflect upon their programs, why they developed as they did, how they work, and how they could be changed.

Second, interviewers should not avoid talking with respondents who have a different, even hostile, point of view. However, one does not want to interview them first. The first interviews serve as a learning period during which the researcher seeks respondents who will be sympathetic to gaps or errors in her information. Nevertheless, delaying interviews with difficult respondents has its costs. During the initial interviews, the interviewer is most open and flexible. Later, as the interviewer becomes more convinced of the correctness of her hypotheses, people with a different point of view may be considered "exceptions" and their insights may be ignored or overlooked. Diverse respondents are especially recommended to identify unexpected outcomes of programs or policies.

An interviewer needs good listening skills to tap the insights of respondents. Otherwise, she may misinterpret their comments or override them with her own point of view or agenda. Common listening errors include reaching a premature conclusion about the correctness of a respondent's observations. An interviewer who does this stops listening. Alternatively, the interviewer may become anxious during periods of silence and either begin to fire questions or put words in the respondent's mouth. In both cases the interviewer loses opportunities to learn from the respondent. Other common complaints about interviewers are: the interviewer did not know enough; the interviewer did not use the right vocabulary; and the interviewer interrupted with irrelevant comments or had to have too much explained. These errors tend to put respondents off, and they will become less involved with the interview.

Example 6.5 summarizes a project based on interviews with women police officers. One of us worked with a colleague to learn how women officers participated in a police department: How did they learn about their jobs? What policing activities did they gravitate toward? What were their career goals? How were they planning to achieve them?

We interviewed the women in small groups. We decided on small groups because we wanted to minimize the wariness police typically show toward researchers. We felt that the small groups would lessen the tension and encourage free discussion and interaction among the officers. The group interviews seemed to work well for this exploratory study.

At the beginning of the interviews we introduced ourselves and the purpose of the study. We mentioned our criminal justice experience. With most of the officers, the interview proceeded smoothly. We asked the basic questions and followed up with specific questions as needed. Generally, before asking the next question, we glanced at the interview schedule to make sure we had covered all the planned topics. Occasionally we interjected with comments such as, "Could you explain that?" or "Can you give me an example?" to encourage the officers to expand upon their answers. Also, to ensure against projecting our own professional experiences into the answers, we often repeated what the women had said. For example, one of us might say, "Let me repeat what I think you said to make sure I got it right."

EXAMPLE 6.5

Interviews with Women Police Officers

Problem: Academic researchers wanted to learn about the socialization of women police officers, particularly their attitudes toward using force and the military.

Procedure:

1. Obtained permission from the police chief to interview officers.
2. Arranged to interview two or three officers together for approximately 1 hour.
3. Developed an interview schedule:
   a. How are women different from men in their approach to police work?
      (1) Different emphases in law enforcement, service, community relations?
      (2) More/less likely to deviate from department rules?
      (3) More/less committed to a career in police work?
      (4) More/less integrated into the social aspects of police work as a profession?
   b. Once you were out of the academy, who helped you become experienced as a police officer?
      (1) What kinds of partnership arrangements did you have?
      (2) What role did other women play?
      (3) Was your immediate supervisor involved?
      (4) What kinds of problems arose most frequently? Who showed you how to handle them?
      (5) Did you sense antagonism to women as police officers?
   c. What have been your major problems as a police officer?
      (1) Work problems—dealing with public, other officers, supervisors, handling physical or other aspects of assignments.
      (2) Personal problems—family, social image.
   d. We found that in a survey of this department, most officers who answered said that force was one of the things about policing they liked least. Some people who have studied police, however, have found that the best police officers are those who do not avoid the use of force and are not uncomfortable about the fact that it is sometimes necessary.
      (1) Can you explain why the officers in this department answered that force was the part of the job they liked least?
      (2) Have you ever had to use force in your work?
      (3) Do you think that men handle this part of the job better?
      (4) Is this a problem for policewomen?
   e. How will this job make a difference in your total career?
   f. In your police training and in your work, does the subject of being "professional" come up? What do they mean by that term?
   g. What is most attractive/least attractive about police work for women?

Continued

EXAMPLE 6.5 *Continued*

4. Scheduled interviews: placed specialized and senior officers midway in the interviews; scheduling depended on officer availability.
5. Conducted interviews:
   a. The two researchers introduced themselves and the purpose of the study.
   b. Interviews were largely conversational.
   c. Both researchers took notes during the interview and wrote up their notes immediately following.

Before interviewing, an investigator must decide how to take notes. A method that the interviewer is comfortable with works with most subjects. For example, interviewers who use tape recorders report little subject resistance. Nevertheless, an interviewer who uses a tape recorder may want to jot down the important points of the interview. Transcribing or even listening to an entire interview can be costly in money or time. We still take notes and leave plenty of time immediately after the interview to amplify and organize our notes. Unless we do this promptly, the details fade quickly. The interviewer should not conduct back-to-back interviews. The interviewer may become fatigued, and the content of one interview may merge into the next.

Focus Groups

Investigators assemble focus groups to get in-depth information and reactions to a few topics. Surveyors, program evaluators, and program planners often construct focus groups. Surveyors use focus groups to identify appropriate survey questions or to supplement survey findings. Program evaluators use them to delve into the experiences of program clients. Program planners use them to get reactions from potential service recipients. The hallmark of focus groups is the group interaction, which investigators believe produces data and insights that would be less accessible if data were collected from individuals.

No one focus group represents a population; however, studies include several focus groups to ensure that their insights and observations extend beyond any one group. Recall that the best evidence of external validity is replication, that is, achieving similar results under somewhat varying conditions. Similarly, if several focus groups express similar attitudes or experiences, the investigators may persuasively argue that the groups represent the opinions and experiences of a larger population.

A focus group study involves four major phases: preparation, forming groups, conducting interviews, and analyzing and reporting the results. Preparation for a focus group is similar to any other empirical research project. The investigators clarify the study's purpose, what information is needed, why, and by whom. They write a limited number of open-ended questions for the group to discuss.

Everyone in a focus group should have a chance to discuss each question and to react to each other's comments. Thus the questions must be carefully thought out to ensure that they will spark interest and develop the needed information.

Focus groups bring together a small group, ranging from four to 15 members, of unacquainted people who agree to meet for a focused discussion. The group should be small enough for everyone to have a chance to participate but large enough to provide some diversity. In larger groups, some members may dominate the discussion; some members may have little or no chance to talk because there never is a pause long enough for them to speak. Small groups may lack enough diversity to move beyond listless conversation.

Focus group members are homogeneous on some important characteristics. They may have the same occupation, the same income level, receive services from a public agency, or have a common experience, such as recently losing a job or having heart surgery. Group members must be sufficiently similar to encourage open discussion. If a group represents widely different socioeconomic levels or lifestyles, social dynamics may inhibit free or productive conversations. People with markedly different experiences may not work together effectively in a group. For example, large-scale farmers and family farmers may have an interest in the implementation of new farm legislation, but their different perceptions, concerns, and needs may cause the group to spend most of its time clarifying and overcoming differences.

Focus group members are selected from lists of persons with the desired characteristics. Potential members are contacted by letter or telephone and are asked if they wish to participate. Potential members are again screened, often in more depth, to make sure that they meet the criteria for participation. For example, each focus group of farmers may consist of farmers who are actually responsible for running the farm, who work on similar-size farms, and whose farms generate similar amounts of revenue annually.

The staff needed to conduct a focus group consists of a moderator and one or two persons to take notes and set up any recording equipment. Other researchers may observe, either behind a one-way mirror or off to the side of the room. The moderator should be familiar with the study's topic; however, she may be less knowledgeable than an intensive interviewer. She may be "brought up to speed" by learning about the questions she will ask and their purpose.

A focus group usually meets for less than two hours. The meeting begins with the moderator's brief description of the study. Then, in a somewhat spontaneous fashion, she leads the group through the list of questions. Her job is to keep the group going and to prevent it from bogging down on unproductive conversations. As soon as the focus group session ends, the moderator and any observers meet to discuss and record their impressions of the group and the interview.

Example 6.6 highlights the focus-group segment of an evaluation of a program offering college courses in prisons. The program director wanted to learn what the inmates thought of the program. Focus groups seemed to be the best way to develop this information.

The team that worked on this project had no previous experience in running focus groups or in prison research. They found that the focus groups provided

EXAMPLE 6.6

Focus Groups with Prison Inmates

Problem: The director of a prison program to provide college education to inmates wanted to know if the program was meeting their expectations. The evaluators decided to survey the prisoners who had taken college courses in the program and to supplement the surveys with information collected in focus groups.

Procedure:

1. Survey forms were created, focus group questions were written, and necessary permissions and authorizations were obtained.
2. The evaluators met with inmates at three prisons. At each prison the evaluators met with the group at one location. The evaluators introduced themselves and the purpose of the study, then the inmates filled out a questionnaire.
3. Randomly selected inmates were asked to stay for a discussion of educational programs.
4. A research team member acted as a moderator and led the inmates through a discussion based on the following questions:
   a. What do you think about the survey?
   b. What do you consider the value of education to be?
   c. What do you think will be the value of the courses you are taking?
   d. What benefits do you expect from taking courses here?
   e. How do prison administrators view the program?
   f. What kinds of courses would you like to see offered?
   g. How would you explain to "John Q. Public" that his taxes help pay for someone who committed a crime to take college courses?

      The discussions proceeded smoothly with inmates commenting on or reacting to each other's remarks. Security restrictions prevented recording the focus group at the maximum-security prison; the other groups were recorded.
5. The research team met after each session to discuss and record the information; the tapes also were transcribed for further study.
6. The focus group data were included in both the written and oral evaluation reports. Some of the comments supplemented survey data. Discussions on the value of education and the types of courses desired delved into concerns that could not be easily addressed or ascertained by the questionnaire. Comments on the hostile attitudes by the custodial staff addressed an issue that was completely ignored by the survey items.

Discussion: This study violated the focus group model that the participants should not be acquainted. The focus groups elucidated inmates' opinions of the program, and group interaction yielded information that would not have been picked up by a survey or individual information. The survey helped to focus the discussion and to provide summary data.

far superior information than they would have obtained with just a survey. Their judgment mirrors our experience that focus groups add immeasurably to investigators' knowledge of how a program is perceived and how well it is working.

Analyzing Data from Intensive Interviews and Focus Groups

In later chapters we will discuss quantitative analysis. Since our discussion of qualitative information is largely confined to this chapter, this seems to be the appropriate place to include a few comments about analyzing qualitative information.

Analysis of information from focus groups and intensive interviews depends on the quality of the investigator's records. The investigator should have thorough and accurate notes or recordings of the interviews. He may want to have both. In addition he should leave time after each interview or focus group to write down his observations and to fill in any gaps in his notes. An interview or focus group produces extensive data. When he reviews his notes or recordings, he looks for trends and patterns that reappear among various participants or groups.

The analysis must be systematic and verifiable. Systematic analysis follows a prescribed sequential process. The analysis is verifiable if another researcher can use the same process, information, and documents to reach a similar conclusion.

Analysis of data from focus groups and intensive interviews is driven by the purpose of the study. It also is directly related to the questions asked. Throughout, the analyst must keep the purpose of the study in mind. The objectives should guide the analysis. Researchers clarify and state objectives and ask questions to obtain information according to the purpose of the study. The questions elicit the material that will be analyzed. Clear, well-stated questions will make the analysis easier. Complex or confusing questions will be difficult, if not impossible, to analyze. The analyst typically examines each question separately and summarizes the information. He also should consider the context within which comments were made and what triggered the comments.

To begin with, the analyst may focus on general trends and patterns. He may then do a more detailed analysis in which he codes topics and even phrases and groups them. He also will consider the range and diversity of information that he heard. After the information is summarized, the analyst tries to interpret it. Of course, the quality of the interpretation relies heavily on the analyst's insights, intellectual talents, and previous experience with the subject matter and with analyzing qualitative data.[24]

SELECTING A METHOD OF DATA COLLECTION

The nature of the study should determine the data collection method. The study topic and the sample interact to suggest the appropriate method. For example, an investigator should consider mailing a complicated questionnaire, or one with many open-ended questions, only to an articulate and highly motivated sample. Studies with inarticulate or socially isolated populations require face-to-face interviews. If the research question requires extensive qualitative information, intensive interviewing or focus groups work best. To explore how stakeholders view program plans or how clients react to an existing program, focus groups may be most effective.

Researchers have compared structured data collection methods, that is, mail, telephone, Internet, and in-person surveys. Their findings suggest that no one factor alone, with the possible exception of cost, automatically points to the desirability of one method over another. Problems such as response rate, questionnaire length, complexity, or sensitivity can be resolved to accommodate the constraints of the data collection method. In our presentation we identified some general advantages and disadvantages of each type of data collection technique. We have summarized these characteristics below.

Comparing Mail, Telephone, Internet, and In-person Surveys: A Review

Costs:

Mail: Relatively low cost (printing, mailing, and postage, incentives for responding)

Telephone: Higher cost (personnel, equipment, telephone charges)

Internet: Low cost

In-person: Highest cost (personnel, travel)

Sampling Issues:

Mail: Requires a good sampling frame; can distinguish nonrespondents from nonrecipients if undelivered questionnaires are returned

Telephone: Provides a reasonably good initial sample of general public with random digit dialing, must have a mechanism for selecting respondents within a household to assure generalizability

Internet: Does not provide a reasonably good sample of general public; a good sampling frame may allow access to specific populations

In-person: No distinctive issues

Response rate:

Mail: Low (follow-up required)

Telephone: Higher (may need to vary calling times to get a representative sample)

Internet: Lowest response rate

In-person: Highest (problems with not-at-homes)

Turnaround time:

Mail: Slowest

Telephone: Quick

Internet: Quick

In-person: Slow (depends on sample size and dispersion)

Respondent issues:

Mail: Convenient, especially for hard-to-reach professionals; poor if subjects are elderly or poorly educated

Telephone: Most intrusive; allows easy access to dispersed populations

Internet: Requires Internet access, awareness of survey, motivation to access and answer survey

In-person: Convenient, if appointment scheduled; allows access to hard-to-reach populations

Content:

Mail: Highly motivated respondents can look up information, write detailed answers; other respondents require clear, easily-answered questions

Telephone: Avoids biases caused by respondent reading ahead; allows for probing and elaboration of answers; may give socially acceptable answers; respondent fatigue if too long

Internet: May have some of the benefits of computer-assisted interviewing; may encounter privacy concerns; respondents limited in their ability to communicate if questions seem ambiguous or responses inappropriate

In-person: Allows for in-depth, probing questions; good source for qualitative detail; valuable for exploratory studies; respondent–interviewer interaction may introduce bias; use of self-administered interviewing may encourage disclosure of embarrassing information

Prior to selecting a data collection technique, the investigator should carefully consider the appropriateness of conducting a survey. The rate of refusals of the general public has increased since 1950.[25] Refusal rates of 40 percent for telephone surveys are not uncommon. The ability to successfully contact respondents may further decrease response rates. Overnight and one-day polls may have response rates of less than 30 percent.[26]

Another trend researchers have noted is the incidence of multiple participation; that is, a respondent who participates in more than one sample survey a year. As this chapter was written, one of the authors was asked to participate in three telephone surveys within a month. One was a political survey and the other two were marketing surveys. Her opinion of how long a telephone survey should take changed when she saw how an interview can interrupt family routine and inconvenience family members who are waiting for a call or who want to use the telephone.

A 1984 study on survey participation, which has not been updated, found that 23 percent of the respondents interviewed had been surveyed during the year; over half of them had been interviewed more than once during the year. The interview subjects were more likely to be female, and younger, wealthier, and better educated than subjects who were not interviewed. The investigators concluded that these differences reflected sampling techniques designed particularly by market researchers to capture the opinions of certain segments of the population. They suggest that over surveying may increase both refusal rates and repeat participation.[27]

The problems with repeat participation have not been explicitly studied to date. Investigators wonder whether cooperative subjects overrepresent some characteristics measured in a survey or if multiple participants evolve into "professional respondents," thereby affecting the representativeness of the data.

From our own experience, an analogous case can be made with organizational studies. Just as market researchers target certain populations, trends in administrative studies focus on certain organizations and professions. Imagine how many questionnaires are sent to city managers, municipal police departments, and public administration faculty by students and faculty doing academic research. Add to this professional associations and government agencies that compile statistical data or conduct studies to answer specific questions. Furthermore, city managers and police departments have to contend with inquiries from the public, public officials, and journalists. You may begin to see how repeated requests for information may overwhelm and annoy the most cooperative individual.

Before deciding to conduct an original survey, investigators, especially academic researchers, should attempt to identify and locate existing databases. If no appropriate existing data can be found, the decision to survey should proceed only after carefully pretesting the data collection instrument. The less experience the investigator has with the problem at hand, the more modest should be the research effort. If investigators limit their survey efforts to well-thought-out and carefully designed instruments that respect the time and experience of respondents, refusals to respond by organization members and by members of specific samples should decrease, and the quality of the data should improve.

SUMMARY

The data collection strategy is integral to implementing a research plan. How an investigator contacts potential subjects and obtains data from them may determine the success of a project. Mail, telephone, Internet or in-person surveys have their own strengths and weaknesses. Nevertheless, no one characteristic, with the possible exception of cost, automatically recommends one survey collection method over another. Rather, investigators should consider both the study and its population and choose the data collection method best suited to their objectives.

Mail surveys generally cost the least of any survey method, but the time required for data collection offsets the benefit of lower cost. Mail surveys allow motivated respondents time to look up requested information and to provide detailed answers to open-ended questions. Mail surveys require the investigators to take time to make sure that the final questionnaire is free from confusing or ambiguous items, because no one will be there to answer the respondent's questions about what information is wanted. Contingency questions also must be kept to a minimum to avoid complex questionnaires.

Mail surveys work best with educated respondents, who are used to working with forms. These respondents will not be intimidated by open-ended questions where they have to express their ideas in their own words. Mail surveys seem appropriate for many organizational studies in which data must be looked up, and more than one person may be involved in answering the survey. Furthermore, in organizational research the mail survey can be squeezed into the respondents' schedule, whereas telephone or in-person surveys may be disruptive and hard for the investigator to schedule.

The major weakness of mail surveys has been their low response rates. Investigators have found that even in surveys of the general public, who are the least motivated to respond to most surveys, mail surveys perform as well as telephone or in-person surveys if the researchers follow up with nonrespondents. To check the assumption that the nonrespondents are similar to respondents, researchers should compare the known demographic characteristics of the nonrespondents and the respondents. Also, with mail surveys, a random sample of nonrespondents may be telephoned or visited and asked to answer the questionnaire. Their answers may be compared with the other respondents'.

Telephone surveys have spread as the cost of in-person surveys has increased and the telephone has become commonplace in American homes. In addition, random digit dialing solves the inability to reach homes with unlisted telephone numbers and reduces the cost of selecting a representative sample. Telephone surveys can provide rapid turnaround in data collection time and make full use of computerization. Computer-Assisted Telephone Interviewing relies on the computer to help administer a survey. The interviewer keys in the answer; the computer then selects the appropriate next question, reducing the logistic problems associated with making sure the interviewer finds the right contingency questions. The computer keeps track of inconsistent responses, stores the data, and monitors the interviewer's performance. The cost of acquiring the equipment, programming each survey, and training interviewers makes computer-assisted interviewing feasible only for organizations that constantly conduct large telephone surveys.

Telephone surveys are most limited in their ability to reach segments of the population who do not have ready access to a telephone. They may not be appropriate for organizational research, where information must be looked up or more than one respondent contacted. Managers and other professionals may be difficult to reach on the telephone, seriously increasing the cost and time involved.

Other limitations of telephone surveys are their length and inability to elicit information on sensitive subjects. Although most nonrespondents have already refused to participate in a survey before the questioning commences, length is the most common complaint about telephone surveys. Long surveys may lead a respondent to refuse later requests for information. In addition, answer quality may degenerate toward the end of a long survey.

Internet surveys may work well in surveying a discrete group with easy Internet access. The low cost of Internet surveys may be offset by the more common problems of finding a good sampling frame, making potential respondents aware of a survey, and motivating them to answer it.

In-person interviews, which approximate telephone interviews, have limited use, insofar as costs and improvements in telephone surveying methods are making them less desirable. Nevertheless, in-person interviews seem to work best for complex studies where interviewer–subject rapport is necessary.

Structured interviewing depends on standardized interviewers. Without standardized interviewers a researcher does not know whether the answers obtained are a product of respondent characteristics or of those of the interviewer. To conduct structured interviews, interviewers must be consistent in how they explain the study's purpose, ask questions, handle inadequate answers, and record information. Above all, the interviewer should not draw attention to his own experiences and opinions.

Intensive interviewing, a type of in-person interviewing, and focus groups can greatly improve administrative studies. The interviews allow investigators to consider the adequacy of their models and the appropriateness of their measures. Furthermore, interviews produce important background information necessary for understanding a problem, how it came to be, what solutions have been tried, and how they have worked.

Effective intensive interviewing requires practice. Some simple steps can minimize common errors. The first interviews usually are informational and focused on factual information. The interviewer normally avoids asking the "most important" subjects for relatively common information and waits to interview key subjects until she has a fuller understanding of the program or the problem at hand. Similarly, the interviewer avoids limiting her early interviews to people who share her own point of view. Unless people with another viewpoint are interviewed early, their insights and information may be inadvertently filtered out.

The interviewer must listen carefully to the subject. Interviewer training often works toward eliminating listening habits that cause interviewers to ignore or misunderstand what a subject is saying. Similarly, interview preparation includes familiarizing oneself with the topic of the interview and the applicable terminology or jargon; otherwise, the subject tends to spend too much time explaining.

Focus groups have the same benefits as intensive interviewing. They also foster group interaction and discussion, which can provide even more information for program evaluation and program planning. Focus group research requires more than one investigator; the responsibilities of moderating and recording should not fall on one person. A major challenge in conducting focus groups is to identify a discrete number of open-ended questions that will elicit discussion consistent with the study's purpose. Because focus group studies involve relatively few individuals who agree to participate, the findings cannot be unambiguously generalized to a larger population.

Probably more important than selecting a method of data collection is asking the question, "Are original data needed?" As the number of researchers grows and the value of research findings spreads, people are asked for more and more information. Market researchers target certain groups known to have more discretionary money to spend. Academic and administrative researchers have analogous target groups. The result of all this survey activity may be multiple requests for information, which raises questions as to whether multiple respondents are truly representative and whether in the long run they will continue to answer questions willingly. We assume that the problem is not how many times one is asked, but how worthwhile respondents feel their participation is. If a subject questions the worth of a study or his participation in it, we assume that he either will not answer or will give cursory answers.

In the next chapter, we examine strategies for writing questions and questionnaires. It links questionnaire design to a study's purpose, its model, and the reliability and operational validity of items. Questionnaires that contain unneeded, unreliable, or invalid items waste resources. Failure to include key variables can also waste resources. Consequently, the chapter stresses the need to pilot test any survey and evaluate each question, the proposed data analysis, and planned use of the findings.

NOTES

1. This categorization of potential sample members is drawn from M. A. Hidigoglou, J. D. Drew, and G. B. Gray, "A Framework for Measuring and Reducing Nonresponse in Surveys," *Survey Methodology 19* (1993): 81–94. See pages 82–84 for a discussion of components and calculations of various rates.
2. See F. J. Yammarino, S. J. Skinner, and T. L. Childers, "A Meta-Analysis of Mail Surveys," *Public Opinion Quarterly 55* (1991): 613–639 for a more thorough discussion of research on response rates.
3. A. H. Church, "Incentives in Mail Sureys: A Meta-Analysis," *Public Opinion Quarterly 57* (1993): 62–79.
4. D. A. Dillman, K. K. West, and J. R. Clark, "Invitations to Answer by Phone in Mail Surveys," *Public Opinion Quarterly 58* (1994): 557–568.
5. A. H. Church, "Incentives in Mail Sureys," p. 71.
6. J. M. James and R. Bolstein, "Response Rates with Large Monetary Incentives," *Public Opinion Quarterly 56* (1992): 442–453; and J. M. James and R. Bolstein, "The Effect of Monetary Incentives and Follow-up Mailings on the Response Rate and Response Quality in Mail Surveys," *Public Opinion Quarterly 54* (1990): 346–361.
7. For a discussion of nonresponse in surveys and how to handle the problem of nonresponse, see N. Bradburn, "A Response to the Nonresponse Problem," *Public Opinion Quarterly 56* (1992): 391–397. Bradburn suggests R. M. Groves, *Survey Errors and Survey Costs* (New York: Wiley Interscience, 1989) for a description of methods for weighting the responses of a sample of "converted" nonrespondents. Also I-Fen Lin and N. C. Schaeffer evaluate two models for estimating information from nonrespondents in "Using Respondents to Estimate Nonresponse Bias," *Public Opinion Quarterly 59* (1995): 236–258.
8. Information on nonphone households and households with intermittent service are from S. Keeter, "Estimating Noncoverage Bias from a Phone Survey," *Public Opinion Quarterly 59* (1995): 196–217. The comment about nonphone households being outsiders is from T. W. Smith, "Phone Home? An Analysis of Household Telephone Ownership," *International Journal of Public Opinion Research 2* (1990): 369–390, cited by Keeter, 198. The estimate of 3 percent households with intermittent phone coverage is based on *1992–93 Current Population Surveys* data cited by Keeter, 199.
9. C. H. Backstrom and G. Hursh-Cesar, *Survey Research,* 2d ed. (New York: Wiley, 1981), 115.
10. A popular random digit dialing method is described in J. Waksberg, "Sampling Methods for Random Digit Dialing," *Journal of the American Statistical Association 73* (1978): 40–46. A random number is constructed by adding a two-digit random to a phone bank (a phone bank is the first eight digits of a phone number starting with the area code). The number is called. If it is a residential number, several other random numbers using the same phone bank are called. If the first phone number is not residential, the phone bank is discarded. J. M. Brick et al., "Bias in List-Assisted Telephone Samples," *Public Opinion Quarterly 59* (1995): 218–235, identify commercially available lists that categorize phone banks according to whether or not they contain any residential numbers.
11. Backstrom and Hursh-Cesar, *Survey Research,* 115. D. S. Voss, A. Gelman, and G. King, "Review: Preelection Survey Methodology," *Public Opinion Quarterly 59* (1995): 98–132, gathered data from eight organizations that do presidential polling. Only two organizations reported weighting by the number of phone lines, and

both organizations used a weight of 1 for homes with only one phone line and .5 for homes with more than one phone line.

12. See Frey, *Survey Research by Telephone,* 2d ed. (Newbury Park, CA: Sage, 1989): 78–85, for a discussion and evaluation of strategies for selecting persons to interview. See Voss et al., 110–112, for information on practices of specific polling organizations. "Review: Preelection Survey Methodology."

13. D. A. Dillman, *Mail and Telephone Surveys: The Total Design Method* (New York: Wiley, 1978), 248.

14. M. W. Link and R. W. Oldendick, "Is Call Screening Really a Problem?" *Public Opinion Quarterly 63* (1999): 577–589.

15. Backstrom and Hursh-Cesar, *Survey Research,* 115, suggest that more than three callbacks are inefficient and not worth the benefit of an increased response rate. Dillman, *Mail,* 47–49, has an excellent discussion on substituting sample members in telephone surveys. For how to handle answering machines, see R. W. Oldendick and M. W. Link, "The Answering Machine Generation," *Public Opinion Quarterly 58* (1994): 264–273; T. Piazza, "Meeting the Challenge of Answering Machines," *Public Opinion Quarterly 57* (1993): 219–231; and M. Xu, B. J. Bates, and J. C. Schweitzer, "The Impact of Messages on Survey Participation in Answering Machine Households," *Public Opinion Quarterly 57* (1993): 232–237. The Piazza study, based on California data, considers the probability of getting through, the best times to get through, and the effect of multiple callbacks.

16. S. Keeter et al., "Consequences of Reducing Nonresponse in a National Telephone Survey," *Public Opinion Quarterly 64* (Summer 2000): 135–148.

17. Groves, *Survey Errors,* 238. See Groves, *Survey Errors,* chap. 5 for a thorough discussion on refusals to cooperate, efforts to increase cooperation, and research on noncooperation.

18. W. S. Aquilino and D. L. Wright, "Substance Use Estimates from RDD and Area Probability Samples," *Public Opinion Quarterly 60* (1996): 563–573.

19. This section relies on the observations and findings reported by B. K. Kaye and T. J. Hohnson, "Research Methodology: Taming the Cyber Frontier," *Social Science Computer Review 17* (1999): 323–337.

20. D. R. Schaefer and D. A. Dillman, "Development of a Standard E-Mail Methodology," *Public Opinion Quarterly 62* (1998): 378–397.

21. F. J. Fowler, Jr., *Survey Research Methods,* 2d ed. (Newbury Park: Sage, 1993), chap. 7.

22. Current research is focusing on survey mode and willingness to report sensitive information. Respondents using self-administered surveys seem more likely to disclose embarrassing information. CASI administered in school settings may compromise the accuracy of the responses, if the respondents are physically close to one another. See R. Tourengeau and T. Smith, "Asking Sensitive Questions," *Public Opinion Quarterly 60* (1996): 275–304, which also summarizes previous research relating survey mode to disclosure of sensitive information; D. L. Wright, W. S. Aquilino, and A. J. Supple, "Comparison of Computer-Assisted and Paper-and-Pencil Questionnaires in a Survey on Smoking, Alcohol, and Drug Use," *Public Opinion Quarterly 62* (1998): 331–353; Y. Moon, "Impression Management in Computer-Based Interviews: The Effects of Input Modality, Output Modality, and Distance," *Public Administration Quarterly 62* (1998): 610–622.

23. See E. O'Sullivan, G. W. Burleson, and W. Lamb, "Avoiding Evaluation Cooptation," *Evaluation and Program Planning 8* (1985): 255–259.

24. For additional information and examples on analyzing and reporting results from focus groups, see Richard A. Krueger, *Focus Groups: A Practical Guide for Applied Research* (Thousand Oaks, CA: Sage, 1994), chap. 8.

25. See C. G. Steeh, "Trends in Nonresponse Rates, 1952–1979," *Public Opinion Quarterly 45* (1981): 40–57. For confirmation that these trends are continuing, see P. Farhi, "How Would You Answer This One?" *Washington Post,* April 14, 1992, A1, A4; R. Rothenberg, "Surveys Proliferate," A1, A6; and T. W. Smith, "Research Notes: Trends in Non-Response Rates," *International Journal of Public Opinion Research 7* (1995): 157–171.

26. Farhi, "How Would You Answer," A4.

27. S. Schleifer, "Trends in Attitudes toward and Participation in Survey Research," *Public Opinion Quarterly 50* (1986): 17–26.

TERMS FOR REVIEW

response rate	Computer-Aided Telephone	structured interviewing
non-response rate	Interviewing	intensive interviewing
random digit dialing	Internet surveys	focus groups

QUESTIONS FOR REVIEW

The following questions should indicate whether you have a basic competency in this chapter's material.

1. Why would a low response rate to a survey concern a researcher?

2. What is the value of being able to distinguish between the response rate and refusal rate? Can researchers distinguish between response rates and refusal rates on mail surveys? on telephone surveys? on Internet surveys? on in-person interviews? Explain.

3. Assess the advisability of investigators' assuming that respondents are similar to nonrespondents. What is the value of telephoning a sample of the nonrespondents to a mail survey?

4. Explain what random digit dialing is and its value for telephone surveys.

5. Compare and contrast information you would collect to pretest a mail survey, a telephone survey, an Internet survey.

6. When should structured, in-person interviewing be used instead of telephone interviewing?

7. What is the value of intensive interviewing? What type of people would you most likely target for an intensive interview? Why?

8. Some students tend to "wing it" if they have to do intensive interviewing. Assess the dangers of this strategy.

9. What would be the advantage of using focus groups to learn
   a. alumni opinion about the program you are studying?
   b. parents reactions to a proposed county-wide, after-school program?

10. For each of the following studies, suggest and justify a data collection method
   a. to find out how many agency employees are attending continuing-education classes.
   b. to understand how parole board members make parole decisions.
   c. to estimate the portion of the voters likely to vote in a referendum who favor issuing a school bond.
   d. to identify the demographic characteristics of city managers in a state.
   e. to find out what corrections officials consider an appropriate measure of "successful rehabilitation."
   f. to learn what constitutes community standards of pornography.

PROBLEMS FOR HOMEWORK AND DISCUSSION

1. Examine an issue of a journal such as *Public Administration Review* or *Administrative Science Quarterly*. For each article based on data collected from individuals or organizations, note
   a. who the research population was.
   b. how the subjects were contacted (mail, telephone, Internet, in person).
   c. what the response rate was.
   d. how the investigators handled subjects who did not respond to the first contact, that is, the number of follow-ups.
   Compare your results with your classmates'. Can you make any generalizations linking the nature of the study population to the method of contacting subjects, and linking the number of follow-ups to the response rate?

2. Try your hand at constructing a telephone sample. Estimate the number of listings in one section of a local telephone directory, for example, listings for one community or residential listings for the city. Develop a procedure for selecting five telephone numbers to serve as the roots for the telephone numbers you will call. (Do not develop a procedure that requires you to count each listing.) Select the five telephone numbers. Note how long it takes you to select the five numbers.

3. Two Internet surveys are designed. Survey 1 asks state, city, and county managers what benefits they offer employees. Survey 2 asks public employees about the benefits they receive from their employer. How would you access respondents for each survey? Con-

trast the quality of the samples for the two surveys.

4. You want to learn more about research: how projects are selected, models are built, measures are operationally defined, and new data are collected.
   a. Outline what you would ask in an unstructured interview of a faculty member at your university.
   b. Videotape a member of your class interviewing a faculty member. Critique the interview.
5. You decide to construct a study of the effectiveness of your academic program. What data collection method reviewed in this chapter would you use? Whom would you interview or survey (give general characteristics of the potential interviewees or respondents)? How many people would you include? How would you select them? If you tried to cover different groups, say students and faculty, in what order would you interview or survey them? What questions would you ask? Sketch out a research plan for this study. Compare and discuss the research plans in class. Would you base the entire study on your chosen method? If not, what alternative data collection methods would you use, and when would you use them?

A CLASS PROJECT

Do you think participatory or autocratic groups produce better results? Under what conditions might one management style work better than another? For this project, three groups of students will prepare reports on these questions, using a word factory scenario that is acted out by a fourth group. While the participants act out the word factory, one group of students will observe, one group will prepare a survey, and one group will prepare to interview the factory workers.

1. A group will be assigned to participate in the word factory. Each person brings to the factory one vowel and one consonant. The factory will operate for 20 minutes with a goal of making as many words as possible. (The instructor, class, or factory members set the rules—for example, how members select what letters to bring, whether a letter may be used more than once in a word, and restrictions on permissible words.)

2. One group of about three persons should observe the factory. After the factory ceases operation, they should write a report describing its leadership style.
3. While the factory is operating, another group writes a questionnaire to learn about the group's leadership style and its output. (The questionnaire may have been assigned previously.) After the factory ceases its operations, the members answer the questionnaire. The group then analyzes the answers and writes a report describing the factory's leadership style.
4. While the factory is operating, the third group of students will decide how to interview members on the subject of the factory's leadership and output. After the factory ceases operations, conduct the interviews and write up a report describing the group's leadership style. Now compare the three reports. What are your conclusions?

RECOMMENDED FOR FURTHER READING

There are many sound how-to-do-it books on survey research. One, which goes through the entire process from designing a study to analyzing the results, is Louis M. Rea and Richard A. Parker's *Designing and Conducting Survey Research: A Comprehensive Guide,* 2d ed. (San Francisco: Jossey-Bass, 1997). Also recommended for public administrators is: David Foltz, *Survey Research for Public Administration* (Thousand Oaks, CA: Sage Publications, 1996). A classic reference on surveys is D. A. Dillman's *Mail and Telephone Surveys* (New York: Wiley, 1978).

An excellent resource book examining and comparing errors in mail, telephone, and in-person interviewing is: R. M. Groves, *Survey Errors and Survey Costs* (New York: Wiley Interscience, 1989).

For information on unstructured interviewing, a classic text is L. A. Dexter's *Elite and Specialized Interviewing* (Evanston, IL: Northwestern University Press, 1970).

For a how-to-do-it guide on focus groups, see R. A. Krueger's *Focus Groups: A Practical Guide for Applied Research* (Thousand Oaks, CA: Sage, 1994).

Readers interested in focus groups also should consult *The Focus Group Kit* by David L. Morgan and Richard A. Krueger (Thousand Oaks, CA: Sage Publications, Inc., 1998). The entire kit contains six volumes covering all aspects of focus-group research including planning, question development, moderating, and analyzing and reporting results, among other topics. The volumes are available individually.

For up-to-date research findings on surveying strategies, see *Public Opinion Quarterly,* the journal of the American Association of Public Opinion Research, published by the University of Chicago Press. *Social Science Computer Review,* published by Sage Publications, provides timely information on web-surveying and data collection software.

Chapter 7

Data Collection: Questions and Questionnaires

In this chapter you will learn

1. the role of model building and the model in designing a survey.
2. proper roles for open-ended and closed-ended questions.
3. how question content and wording affect reliability and operational validity.
4. ways to avoid asking unnecessary questions and forgetting important ones.
5. pretesting methods to prevent wasting resources on surveys.

Writing questions and designing questionnaires are important research skills for administrative investigators. Agencies use questionnaires in program planning, monitoring, and evaluation. Surveys help the agency to plan programs by identifying problems, assessing support for policy alternatives, and learning what services are needed. Agencies use questionnaires to monitor programs by compiling information on client characteristics and what services clients use, when, and how often. Evaluators use questionnaires to gather information from clients about their satisfaction with a program, its actual practices, and its effectiveness. Social scientists rely on questionnaires to collect a wide range of data on individuals and organizations.

Writing questionnaires seems easy. Yet, as we implied in our discussion of cross-sectional designs, poor-quality questionnaires are common. Poor questionnaires may result in low response rates, unreliable or invalid data, or inadequate or inappropriate information. In our classes we have observed that students identify a problem for which they need data and begin immediately to write a questionnaire. Potential questions flow quickly as they brainstorm. We believe that similar behavior occurs in offices, when someone wants information about other people or organizations.

207

What is wrong with a questionnaire that comes out of such a session? The questionnaire may be inappropriate for the study's purpose. It may ask too few questions or the wrong questions. Unless it is adequately pretested, serious errors affecting reliability, such as ambiguous questions or confusing directions, may not be detected. The underlying concepts may not be clarified resulting in invalid measures.

Quality questionnaires require well-worded questions, clear responses, and attractive layouts. In addition, investigators must use systematic procedures to decide exactly what to ask. First, the investigators must clarify the study's purpose, ascertain that the proposed questions are consistent with its purpose, and determine whether the administrators believe that the survey information will be adequate. Second, the investigators want to make sure that the questions and the overall data collection strategy will yield reliable and operationally valid data. Third, they want to verify that the data meet the needs of the intended users.

Investigators may meet with intended users to confirm that the study will produce appropriate and adequate information for their needs. For example, a city may contract for a citizen survey to find out what services citizens most want and who wants them. Staff who plan to use the survey data should meet with the survey designer to discuss how they want to use the data and to review the survey draft. If a survey designer fails to ask respondents where they live or how old they are, staff will not know if demands for better recreational facilities vary by neighborhood or age group. Alternatively, a designer may ask about potential services that the city has no intention of providing. Unneeded questions increase the burden on respondents. The questions may falsely imply planned changes in city services, angering those who feel the city is doing too much and misleading those who think the city is not doing enough.

This chapter examines strategies for developing questionnaires that yield useful data. It begins by considering strategies for making sure that an instrument asks the right questions. It presents techniques for writing effective questions and questionnaires. It suggests a strategy for mapping out the questionnaire to confirm that it is complete. The chapter discusses how to pretest questionnaires. Investigators cannot accurately assess the clarity of the questionnaire or its completeness without a pretest. This chapter stresses the necessity of thoroughly pretesting all questionnaires and similar instruments before using them to collect data.

QUESTIONNAIRE AND QUESTION CONTENT

A questionnaire with short, easily answered questions may seem to have required little effort to write. But in fact, questionnaire writing can be tedious, involving several drafts and more than one pretest. A clear, uncluttered questionnaire may be a testament to the time and effort of its writers. Questionnaire writing involves: deciding what variables to measure; writing questions that accurately and adequately measure the variables; assembling the questions in a logical order on a questionnaire; and pretesting the questions and questionnaire.

In deciding what to include in a questionnaire, researchers need to identify the variables they want to measure, the type of questions that will measure the variables, and the number of questions needed to ensure reliability and operational validity. Many analysts, including ourselves, have labored on questionnaires only to discover later that they asked questions they did not use. Some questions were not needed; others were useless because the respondent misunderstood them. Researchers also fail to ask questions critical to the study. Over time, we have become philosophical about this failure—nobody is perfect.

The first component that defines a survey's content is the model. We are certain that many surveys are written with no reference to a model. It may have faded into memory, but more likely, no one ever constructed an explicit model for the study. We wish that we could convince everyone that model building is not just for academics and management scientists.

Model building requires investigators to identify and link variables needed to answer a question or solve a problem. Prior to building a model, investigators need to know why it is being built, that is, its purpose. Similarly, investigators need to know a survey's purpose. They also should be convinced that a study is necessary and that a survey is better than alternative methods of data collection.

The investigators identify those variables for which data are needed. They must find or develop measures for each variable in the model. Other variables should be included only if they serve a clear purpose. Next, the investigators decide what linkages among variables need to be studied. Explicitly listing the variables and the linkages of interest should guide the debate about whether a specific question is necessary.

As useful as we find model building, for some projects developing a coherent, integrated model may be inefficient. Some users may actively resist efforts to build a fully articulated model. Investigators conducting a study for a specific user, for example, an administrator or a legislator who wants the information to help make a decision, may prefer to focus on the specific questions that the user wants to have answered. Michael Patton, in a classic program evaluation text, suggests that investigators first identify the purpose of the study and its primary users. Next, the investigators ask the primary users to indicate how they plan to use the study to answer their questions or to solve a problem.[1] The discussion between the investigators and primary users should detail exactly what information they need, how they will use it, and whether it will be adequate. With this information, questions can be formulated to yield the needed data.

Decisions on what questions to include may extend over the planning period. Later in the chapter, in Example 7.7, we show a procedure to track how each question in a questionnaire will be used. The procedure should prevent asking unneeded questions and failing to include necessary questions. The investigators also should analyze the data gathered during the pretest or pilot study. The data analysis may help the investigators and users to evaluate the adequacy of the questionnaire.

The second component of content is the type of question being asked. Knowledge of question type can help you decide the operational validity of a measure. Survey analysts may categorize questions as gathering information on:

Facts

Behaviors

Opinions

Attitudes

Motives

Knowledge

Factual questions elicit objective information from respondents. The most common factual questions are demographic questions, such as sex, age, marital status, education, income, profession, and occupational history. Factual questions may be asked about anything on which someone wants information. How much does a public library collect in fines? How long does it take a city to issue a building permit? How many miles of highway does a state pave annually?

Behavior questions, which are a type of factual question, ask respondents about things they do or have done. For example, citizens may be asked how far they travel to work or whether they have ever attended a public hearing. We suspect that most administrators work with data concerning facts and behaviors.

Opinion questions ask people what they think about an issue or event. Opinions are said to be the verbal expressions of attitudes. *Attitude questions* try to elucidate more stable, underlying beliefs or ways of looking at things. *Motive questions* ask respondents to evaluate why they behave in a particular manner or hold certain opinions or attitudes.

Knowledge questions, which are similar to test questions, determine what a person knows about a topic, the extent, or accuracy of the information. Knowledge questions may act as filters to eliminate the answers of uninformed respondents. Knowledge questions commonly appear in evaluations of training programs to find out whether subjects learned what was taught. Knowledge questions can measure what a population knows about a policy or issue. They can indicate whether citizens know that a particular service or program exists.

Investigators who know a model's purpose and understand how different types of questions produce different information avoid collecting the "wrong" data. Consider a problem in program evaluation. Program participants may be asked their opinion of a program. For example, trainees may be asked to rate the quality of a training program. Yet, administrators may want to know whether training affects the trainees' knowledge or behavior on the job. The administrators may question retaining a program that does not produce results. They may find opinions interesting, even helpful. Respondent opinions may lead to future program changes. Still, the opinions do not indicate whether the program has performed as desired.

Question wording, emphasis, and order have a greater effect on opinion and attitude questions than on factual questions. For any type of question, the respondent must understand what information is wanted. For example, in a housing survey, respondents may report fewer bedrooms than their houses contain because they do not think of a den, a playroom, or a home office as a "bedroom." If the questionnaire writer wanted to count such converted rooms as bedrooms, she may be stuck with invalid data.

The third component of content is the number of questions to be asked to measure each variable. Recall that the number of questions or indicators affects a measure's reliability. To avoid burdening respondents, we should keep the number of questions to a minimum. Thus we have to consider the trade-off between lower reliability and higher response rates.

The number of questions also affects operational validity, specifically the content validity of a variable. Many variables cannot be adequately measured with only one indicator. For example, measures of socioeconomic status normally combine data on education, occupation, and income. Measures of citizen satisfaction consider different components of a service. Examining satisfaction with a police department may involve asking citizens to rate: the department's response time; its ability to prevent crime and to solve crimes quickly; how fairly officers treat all citizens, especially young people and minorities; and the department's general competency.

The number of questions and operational validity problems are of special concern when gathering organizational data. To determine organizational or program effectiveness requires more than a single indicator. Imagine if the only information collected on the performance of a job training program was the percentage of trainees placed. Relying on this one piece of data may inaccurately measure program effectiveness. Information on the quality of trainees' jobs —for example, pay rate, skills required, and stability of employment—gives a more complete and valid picture. Furthermore, measures that are not content valid may seriously distort staff behavior. Staff members may focus on the one indicator, percentage placed, and accept only trainees with a high placement potential, or they may place graduates in low-paying or temporary jobs to keep the placement rate up.

QUESTIONNAIRE STRUCTURE

Open- and Closed-ended Questions

Questions may be either open-ended or closed-ended. *Open-ended* questions require the respondent to answer in her own words. *Closed-ended* questions ask the respondent to choose from a list of responses. For example, respondents may check whether they "strongly agree," "agree," "disagree," or "strongly disagree" with a statement, or they may indicate a number representing the most appropriate answer. Open-ended questions are valuable. Nevertheless, they have two major drawbacks, which limit their use. First, they are often unanswered. Respondents with little time or limited communication skills may ignore them. Second, they complicate data compilation. Categorizing and counting the answers can be a formidable task.

Researchers ask open-ended questions for at least five reasons. They help a researcher identify the range of possible responses. They avoid biases that a list of responses can introduce. They yield rich, detailed comments. They give respondents a chance to elaborate on their answers. Just as "a picture is worth a thousand words," a comment can add immeasurably to an investigator's information. Finally, respondents can more easily answer some questions with a few words rather than selecting an answer from a long list of possible responses. For example, the question, "In what state do you live?" is easier to answer by writing a state name than by looking for the state on a list.

Open-ended questions are useful in exploratory research and during the early stages of decision making. When we studied how trainees used DECIDE, a management training program, we did not know what applications were prevalent nor did we know whether trainees had found unique uses for the technique. We asked trainees for an example of how they applied DECIDE on their jobs. Some respondents could not give a work-related example, but they did give examples of using DECIDE to make personal decisions. If we had written a list of responses, we would not have included personal applications, and we would have overlooked one reason why the course was popular with employees.

From the examples, we categorized and summarized how employees used DECIDE. With the uses identified and responses categorized, we could later write appropriate closed-ended questions. We could ask, "How do you use DECIDE?" and the respondent could check off the appropriate responses from a list of common uses.

If we wished, we could then create a series of closed-ended questions from the responses. For example, we might ask, "How often do you use DECIDE to help you make budget request decisions?" "How often do you use DECIDE to help you make purchasing decisions?" "How often do you use DECIDE to help you make personnel allocation decisions?" In constructing the questions, we select specific decisions from our list of common uses.

In political polling the movement from open-ended to closed-ended questions is well established. Long before American political parties and voters express any formal preference for a presidential candidate, pollsters ask respondents to name whom they prefer for the next president. This procedure allows pollsters to identify candidates with early support. It avoids the possibility that respondents will simply choose a familiar name, in which case the poll is measuring name recognition rather than support. As election day approaches, open-ended questions have long since disappeared, replaced by closed-ended questions that focus on actual, active candidates.

A similar pattern occurs as decision makers study policy alternatives. Administrators may ask constituents to indicate policies that they want adopted. Example 7.1 presents several open-ended questions from a state health planning survey of county health directors. State health planners asked the directors to suggest programs and policies to address the problem of teenage pregnancy. Question 1 asks for a description of the problem of teenage pregnancy in the director's county. From the descriptions, the planners can learn about local conditions and programs, agency attitudes about teenage pregnancy, and acceptable programs. For example, what data are selected to show that teenage pregnancy is a problem? What, if any, causes of teenage pregnancies are cited? Are the needs of young teenage parents distinguished from the needs of older teenage parents?

Question 2 asks directors to suggest programs or policies to address problems of teenage pregnancy in their counties. From the comments, the planners can hypothesize which programs will be acceptable and which ones will be unacceptable. Innovative solutions or programs may be suggested, and unantici-

EXAMPLE 7.1

Application of Open-ended Questions

Problem: State planners are developing policies and programs to address the problem of teenage pregnancy. County health agencies will administer the programs. To make sure planned programs are acceptable, the planners survey county health directors.

Strategy: Write a series of questions to get needed information. The following questions are included:

1. Describe the problem of teenage pregnancy in your county.
2. In your opinion, what programs or policies would help with the problems of teenage pregnancy? Make any additional comments on the strengths and weaknesses of these solutions. Your comments will help us formulate statewide plans.
3. What is the size of your annual budget?

Discussion: Initially, planners informally reviewed the answers to select the most feasible programs and policies. The planners also compiled the answers and presented them systematically in a report. The answers to Question 1 disclose how the directors view teenage pregnancy; the question avoids distortions introduced by a set of responses. The answers to Question 2 may reveal innovative programs or policies; later closed-ended questions and responses may be developed from the answers. Categorizing the answers can be tedious. Reliability problems may occur if directors either describe similar programs with different terms or use similar terms to describe different programs.

Question 3 was open-ended because the planners did not know the range of possible responses. A list of responses could have been either insensitive to actual variations or too long. The answers are relatively easy to categorize and present quantitatively.

pated benefits or costs of possible programs may be mentioned. The answers to Questions 1 and 2 help the planners find out more about the policy environment. They may learn: how much time county directors have spent thinking about and learning about teenage pregnancy programs; whether any programs have been planned or implemented; and what local conditions would affect the success of a program.

Open-ended questions provide investigators with additional information. The questions allow respondents to elaborate on their answers. Investigators may ask respondents to explain what a term or issue means to them. Terms and their meanings change quickly. For example, the concept of terrorism changed for Americans after the September 11, 2001 attacks on New York and Washington. In a similar vein, when we originally wrote this chapter, President Ronald Reagan was promoting "star wars defense." The policy had a futuristic ring and promised a future in which wars would be fought in outer space, not on earth. In a later edition we wrote, "Now as we update this chapter, nuclear war seems more remote, and the idea of fighting in space seems unrealistic or silly." As we write this edition, the concept has been resurrected, but relabeled "strategic defense initiative (SDI)." An open-ended question would indicate whether the population surveyed understands that "strategic defense initiative" refers to military defense. A respondent may be asked, "What do you understand by the term 'strategic defense initiative?'" The survey should not ask about "SDI." Abbreviations are easily misunderstood. For example, SDI also refers to Steel Door Institute, a business association located in Cleveland, Ohio. Consider how the answers can be studied. An investigator can learn what percentage of the public correctly identifies the term as referring to military defense. Investigators can go further and examine how much or how well the public understands SDI proposals. The answers can be used to separate the responses of "informed respondents" from "uninformed respondents." Investigators may ask respondents to explain their answers to a preceding question. For example, respondents may be asked whether they are doing better, worse, or about the same economically this year as last. Then, they will be asked to explain why they answered the way they did. From the explanations, investigators learn how respondents evaluate their economic situation and what factors they believe contribute to their economic well-being.

A survey gives the respondent the ear of the investigator or study sponsor. The respondent may wish to comment on related issues and bring them to the attention of others. We ended our survey of DECIDE trainees by asking respondents whether they had comments that they wanted us to pass on to the training department. Several did; one respondent had a lengthy complaint about problems with computer training. In community surveys, respondents can comment on the policies being considered, add to the list of policies, or mention related concerns they have about local government or agency operations.

The answers to broad, open-ended questions may add to the administrator's general information. They may contribute to respondents' positive feelings about surveys. Soliciting a respondent's opinion may serve as minimal compensation for his time, effort, and cooperation.

Answers to open-ended questions provide the rich detail that puts a mass of collected data into context. If a policy is being planned or evaluated, a comment may add immeasurably to an investigator's understanding about the policy and the public's attitude toward it. Comments from open-ended questions are normally incorporated into a report. The answers may demonstrate the operational validity of a measure, or they may help explain the findings. Comments taken from open-ended questions add to the readability of a report and keep the interest of less quantitative readers.

You can infer the problems of open-ended questions from Example 7.1. First, a respondent must be motivated to spend the time and effort to answer an open-ended question. We may assume that the survey about teenage pregnancy was important to the directors and that they took the time to write thorough, thoughtful answers. The directors were probably motivated by more than the content of the survey. Since the survey was sponsored by a state health department, the directors may have assumed that their answers would affect state policy. More often than not, respondents will not be so motivated.

We may assume that in many studies, the investigators have more at stake in the survey and its findings than the individual respondents. Thus investigators tend to overestimate the importance of their work and respondents' willingness to provide detailed answers. We assume that generally respondents prefer to avoid questions that require a long written response. This assumption may not apply if the answers will affect a policy decision important to the respondent.

Respondents may answer open-ended questions more readily if an interviewer collects information. The interviewers must be well trained. Otherwise, they may add their own interpretation to respondents' answers, amplify the question in a way counter to the investigator's intentions, or fail to record the comments accurately.

The other problem of open-ended questions is how to use the information effectively. If relatively few people are surveyed, the answers may be carefully read, analyzed, and quoted. If many people are surveyed, the probability of carefully reading the answers diminishes. One solution is to select a random sample of open-ended responses for detailed analysis.

Whether all the answers or merely a sample are studied, categorizing and counting the answers is difficult, time consuming, and requires thoughtful attention. A perusal of the questionnaires by someone familiar with the study's model should help create appropriate categories. The difficulty rests in assigning responses accurately and consistently. To ensure reliable data based on open-ended questions, the investigators should apply a test/retest procedure to a random sample of cases. If several analysts are categorizing responses, interrater reliability also should be established. To do so, each analyst categorizes the same sample of cases. Then, an investigator compares the work of the analysts to see if they reported similar results.

Closed-ended questions come in several formats. All closed-ended questions require a respondent to select one or more appropriate responses from a list. The reliability and operational validity of closed-ended questions partially depends on the list provided.

A list may include several options with instructions to "check all that apply." While such a list may burden respondents less, they may not actually check all that apply. An unchecked item may (1) not apply or (2) have been overlooked. More items may be reported if a respondent is asked to check an appropriate response for each item, for example, "yes" or "no."[2]

Including an "other" category does not guarantee that additional appropriate responses will be mentioned. Some respondents may limit themselves to the list. They may do this out of laziness because they have identified a desirable response, or because the list has led them to accept the investigators' frame of reference. Even if they answer the "other" category and write in a response, the investigator may be stuck interpreting and categorizing these responses.

Some response lists do not include "other," "no opinion," "not sure," or "not applicable" as choices. Such questions are called *forced choice questions*. Of course, respondents cannot be forced to choose, and some will pen in their own answers or ignore the question.

EXAMPLE 7.2

Application of Closed-ended Questions

Situation: A state employee association (SEA) wants to survey its members to learn their opinions about SEA and state employment.

Strategy: Develop a closed-ended questionnaire to survey members. Format should be chosen to facilitate quick responses by members and easy tabulation. The questions include:

1. What is your opinion of why some employees do not join SEA? Check all that apply.
   _____Money (dues)
   _____Dislike organizations
   _____SEA doesn't adequately represent employees
   _____Don't consider their jobs permanent
   _____Don't care
   _____Don't know
2. How much influence do you believe the average SEA member has in SEA?
   _____Very much
   _____Quite a bit
   _____Some
   _____Very little
   _____None
   _____Don't know
3. Number the following in order of priority, 1 being highest, 2 next highest, etc. SEA should work for
   _____payment of sick leave upon separation from the service.
   _____collective bargaining.
   _____payment of time and one-half for overtime.
   _____reduction in retirement contributions.
   _____dental insurance.
   _____higher salaries.
   _____increased mileage and per diem rates.

   _____ _____
   _____
   _____

Another type of closed-ended question asks the respondent to rank or rate items. Look at Question 3 in Example 7.2. Respondents are asked to rank organization activities proposed for an employee association. Inevitably, some respondents select several items and rank each item with a "1." A few may appear to reverse the rating scale. In the example they would give a "7" to the highest-priority item and a "1" to the lowest-priority item. Some will rate all items, others will ignore all but a few items. Similar to ranking questions are questions that ask people to assign percentages to how much time they spend on a list of activities. A surprising number of people assign values that add up to well over 100 percent.

The limitations of closed-ended questions are best understood by thinking of the strengths of open-ended questions. Closed-ended questions encourage the respondent to accept the investigator's response categories. Investigators may assume that they and the respondents interpret the questions and response choices the same way. Once we asked agency heads about volunteer characteristics. The question asked respondents to note how many volunteers in their agency had certain characteristics. Included among the response categories was "Native Americans." When we wrote Native Americans, we were referring to American Indians, Hawaiians, Eskimos, and Aleutians. Only after we received several surveys indicating that "all" volunteers were Native Americans did we realize that our terminology was interpreted differently by our respondents.

To minimize misinterpretation of responses, and inadequate or inaccurate response lists, closed-ended questions should be carefully pretested. Investigators also should satisfy themselves that their testing included procedures to review item reliability and operational validity.

Example 7.2 takes a selection of questions from a survey that a state employees' association (SEA) sent to its members. The questions illustrate some common formats used in closed-ended questions. You should visualize how easily an investigator can compile the responses. At the same time, you may think of how the responses could be misinterpreted. For example, some respondents may answer the questions on why others do not join the association by reflecting their own dissatisfaction with SEA or a similar organization. Members who have tried to recruit others to join may have more accurate perceptions. As the questionnaire is written, the analyst cannot separate the two types of respondents, and their answers will be grouped together.

The decision as to whether to choose an open-ended question over a closed-ended question depends on the type of information needed, who is supplying the information, the data collection method, and the time available for completing the study. The type of information needed dominates the decision to use open-ended questions. The type of respondent and the data collection method may affect the choice. Questions that require longer, thought-out answers, such as in Example 7.1, may work best on mail surveys if the survey is sent to a targeted sample of interested respondents. Less-interested and less-motivated respondents may avoid answering open-ended questions that require more than a few words. Interviewers may be more successful in getting complete responses to open-ended questions; however, unless the interviewers are well trained, the information may be unreliable or invalid. Closed-ended questions can be compiled and analyzed far more quickly. Investigators should not waste respondents' time by asking open-ended questions unless they have budgeted time for the proper analysis of the answers.

Contingency and Filter Questions

Contingency and *filter* questions separate respondents and direct them to the appropriate parts of a questionnaire. Contingency questions apply only to a subgroup of respondents. Whether or not a respondent should answer a contingency question is determined by his or her answer to a preceding question called a filter question. Filter questions, also called screening questions, identify respondents who should answer the contingency question that follows. Filter questions are nearly always closed-ended. A filter question in a housing survey might be:

Do you own or rent the house in which you now live?
      _____Own (answer question 10)
      _____Rent (answer question 11)

Can you imagine one or more questions that apply to homeowners but not renters? For example, questions on mortgages, interest rates, and property taxes would apply to owners but not directly to renters.

Formats for filter and contingency questions vary. An effective format leads a respondent to the questions he should answer. It should prevent him from missing questions that apply to him and from answering questions that do not apply to him. The above filter question has written directions next to each response category, telling respondents what is the next question they should answer. Visual coding seems especially effective. Contingency questions may be boxed and set apart from the other questions. Arrows may direct the respondent to the appropriate questions. Example 7.3 is an example of visually coded filter and contingency questions.

Rather complicated contingency question forms can be used in interviews, especially in telephone interviews where the interviewer does not need to maintain eye contact. Computer-Assisted Interviewing facilitates complicated contingency-question sequences. The software leads the interviewer through the questionnaire, "automatically" going from the initial question to the proper follow-up questions. Contingency questions can cause confusion on mailed questionnaires or other self-administered forms. If a questionnaire cannot be kept simple and the instructions clear, then contingency questions should be eliminated.

QUESTION AND RESPONSE WORDING

Question Wording and Formatting

Respondents must see the value of a question. Respondents providing information for performance appraisals, program evaluations, or other management studies may resist spending time collecting and recording data that they do not value. They may distort data that they believe can adversely affect them. They may estimate or make up data to conform to management expectations or to get a form off their desk. Administrators and others who are frequently surveyed may show a similar resistance. They may start to answer a questionnaire and stop if it is too time consuming or if they perceive it will produce worthless information. We suspect that respondent perceptions are shaped as they read the specific questions.

Each question should be worded so that the respondent accurately understands its meaning and answers honestly. An investigator wants to make sure that she and the respondent view a question as asking for the same information.

EXAMPLE 7.3

Visually Coded Filter and Contingency Questions

Situation: A state survey of citizens includes questions on educational policy. Questions check compliance with requirements for periodic testing, contact between parents and teachers, and support for education-related policy.

Strategy: Questions on testing apply only to families with children in certain public school grades, questions on parent/teacher relations apply only to families with children in school, and questions on education-related policy apply to all respondents. The survey is conducted over the telephone. The arrows save time as the interviewer selects the appropriate questions based on a respondent's answer.

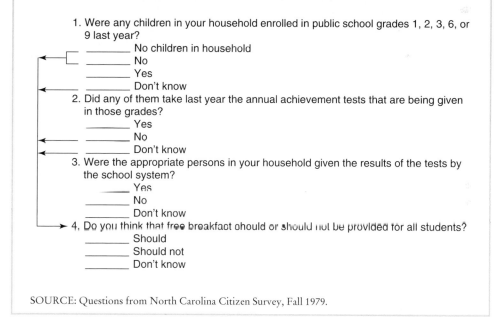

1. Were any children in your household enrolled in public school grades 1, 2, 3, 6, or 9 last year?
   _____ No children in household
   _____ No
   _____ Yes
   _____ Don't know
2. Did any of them take last year the annual achievement tests that are being given in those grades?
   _____ Yes
   _____ No
   _____ Don't know
3. Were the appropriate persons in your household given the results of the tests by the school system?
   _____ Yes
   _____ No
   _____ Don't know
4. Do you think that free breakfast should or should not be provided for all students?
   _____ Should
   _____ Should not
   _____ Don't know

SOURCE: Questions from North Carolina Citizen Survey, Fall 1979.

Imagine a question asking, "Do you own stock?" People can interpret stock as an investment instrument, livestock, or broth. We have discussed misunderstood questions in the context of reliability and operational validity. The ambiguity of the term "stock" illustrates the importance of precisely defining critical terms.

Questions should be clear, short, and specific. Words in common usage and not subject to different interpretations add to question clarity. Long questions tend to be complicated and confusing; they may be easily misinterpreted. Frequently, a respondent will consider part of a long question in his answer and ignore the question's broader meaning.

Specific questions leave little room for interpreting the time, place, or amount involved. For example, to estimate clinic usage in a town, investigators may ask, "How many visits did you make to a medical clinic in Middletown

---

EXAMPLE 7.4

Two Strategies for Defining Ambiguous Terms in a Survey

Strategy 1: Key terms are defined as part of the instructions. Actual wording and format included on cover page:

The following terms are used in the survey:

TOP ADMINISTRATION means the President/CEO and Vice Presidents, or Senior Administrators

SUPERVISOR means the person to whom you report on a daily basis

WORK GROUP means the people you work with on a daily basis

Strategy 2: Define terms as part of the question. Actual wording and format included in question:

How often, if at all, does your supervisor, that is, the person to whom you report on a daily basis, overrule the findings or conclusions of a report and require that changes be made?"

1[ ] Never, or almost never
2[ ] Some of the time
3[ ] About half the time
4[ ] Most of the time
5[ ] Always, or almost always

SOURCE: Strategy 2 item adapted from *Federal Personnel Management: OPM Reliance on Agency Oversight of Personnel System Not Fully Justified* (Washington, D.C.: General Accounting Office, GAO/GGD–93–94, December 1992), 51.

---

between September 1 and December 31 of this year?" If "Middletown" did not appear in the question, respondents might count out-of-town clinic visits. If the question said "recently" instead of "between September 1 and December 31," each respondent could answer the question with a different time interval in mind. Some respondents may think of the number of visits within the last month; others may think of the number of visits within the past year.

The advice to keep questions short and specific may conflict. A vague term may confuse respondents and lead to unreliable data. Asking teenagers how many hours they worked, or asking adults how many hours they exercise, may raise questions about what constitutes work or exercise. The researchers must know exactly what they want to measure. They must know if their conceptual definition defines baby-sitting as work or not, or if working in the yard constitutes exercise. To solve this problem, the definition may be incorporated into the instructions. Alternatively, the definition may be incorporated into the body of the question. Example 7.4 illustrates (1) including definitions in the instructions, and (2) including a definition in the question. A longer example would include parallel questions about the behavior of top administration and the work group.

Separate questions may be written to create a content-valid measure. Example 7.5 illustrates a list of separate questions used to ask employees to rate their

---

EXAMPLE 7.5

Dividing a Question into Separate Questions

Strategy: Rather than ask one broad question, the investigator may divide a question into a series of questions. The following questions ask respondents to indicate their level of satisfaction with various employee benefits. The survey directions told respondents to X-out the number that corresponded to their response. The directions included a sample item with an X covering one of the numbers.

Actual wording and format: In these questions, please indicate how satisfied you are with each of the following employee benefits (1 = very dissatisfied; 2 = dissatisfied; 3 = slightly dissatisfied; 4 = indifferent; 5 = slightly satisfied; 6 = satisfied; 7 = very satisfied).

How Satisfied Are You With:

Medical—Employee coverage	[1]	[2]	[3]	[4]	[5]	[6]	[7]
Medical—Family coverage	[1]	[2]	[3]	[4]	[5]	[6]	[7]
Dental insurance	[1]	[2]	[3]	[4]	[5]	[6]	[7]
Life insurance (Employee)	[1]	[2]	[3]	[4]	[5]	[6]	[7]
Dependent life insurance	[1]	[2]	[3]	[4]	[5]	[6]	[7]
Long-term disability	[1]	[2]	[3]	[4]	[5]	[6]	[7]
Pension plan	[1]	[2]	[3]	[4]	[5]	[6]	[7]

Notes: This question did not include a "Not applicable" category, which may affect the accuracy of the results. Employees who have neither dependent medical insurance nor life insurance may check "indifferent" or not answer the question. Either response is subject to misleading interpretations.

---

satisfaction with employee benefits. An alternative format has respondents react to specific statements. For example, employees may indicate their degree of agreement with the statements such as, "I am satisfied with the medical benefits I receive on my job," "I am satisfied with the life insurance I receive on my job," "I am satisfied with the pension benefits I receive on my job." Possible responses may range from "strongly disagree" to "strongly agree." Asking people about their satisfaction with various components of their benefits package yields a content-valid measure. Nevertheless, at some point the cost of obtaining more accurate information must be weighed against the benefits.

An example of erring by seeking too much specific information occurred in the Nationwide Food Consumption Survey. Respondents were asked to keep a two-day record of what they ate and whether it was eaten at home or away, how it was prepared, and the size of the portion. Data were collected on extensive checklists, which included 350 foods. By putting the responses together, the investigators could learn that one day Jane Doe ate at home and had a boneless, roasted slice of chicken breast, 2-by-1$\frac{1}{2}$-by-$\frac{1}{4}$-inch. The survey's low response rate of 34 percent was partially blamed on the burdensome questionnaire.[3]

In constructing a list of responses, investigators need to list all probable responses. Recall that this is a qualitative indicator of reliability. Respondents may resent response categories that seem to exclude them. For example, listed responses may not allow a young adult to report that her job is only temporary or a disabled respondent to indicate that he depends on public transportation. The respondents may become frustrated or annoyed; they may toss out the questionnaire. Agencies may react similarly. For example, an agency that has volunteers deliver client services may question the motives of a surveyor who lists fund raising and office work as volunteer tasks but does not mention delivering services.

The question or the list of responses should indicate how precise an answer is expected. A county official wanted to estimate how user fees would affect the use of county recreational facilities. He surveyed recreation department heads and asked them, "How much did the implementation of user fees impact the use of recreation facilities and programs?" The answers received were "very much," "very little," and so forth. A closed-ended question that gave the possible responses "less than 10% decrease in use of facilities," "10–25% decrease in use of facilities," and so forth, would have avoided this problem.

Related to amount specificity is the need to ask a respondent for information she has or can easily get. A demand for specific information may require a respondent to calculate or search out data with which she could give a reasonably accurate estimate. The questioner needs to keep in mind the purpose of the research and the trade-off between precision and the cost of information gathering.

Writing Questions for Self-Reports of Behavior and Opinions

Question and response wording are especially important in surveys that ask people to report their behavior, attitudes, or motives. Clearly defined questions requesting accessible information can produce reasonably accurate organizational information, for example, the number of full-time staff or the size of the budget. Furthermore, investigators can verify the accuracy of such information. Verifying self-reported information is harder or even impossible; consequently, investigators have far less confidence in its reliability and operational validity.

People have models of how they should act, and their answers may be more in line with how they think they should act than with how they actually act. Alternatively, the answers people give may depend on how they store and retrieve information. Consider information on who votes. From time to time, researchers check voting records to establish the concurrent validity of the self-reports of voting. They have found that roughly 15 percent of the people surveyed after an election misreport whether or not they voted, and a higher percent of those polled after an election report having voted for the winning candidate than indicated by actual votes.

The direction of misreports is not random. Typically, nonvoters "erroneously" report voting. Three reasons have been proposed to explain why misreporting occurs. First, misreporters may wish to give a socially desirable answer. Second, they may be people who usually vote, and they forgot that they did not vote in the most recent election. Third, voting records may be in error. For example, a check of records may miss a voter whose name on the voters' rolls differs from the name she gave to the surveyor.[4] The accuracy of voting information has been studied extensively, because self-reports can be validated and because the relatively large number of misreports may have distorted knowledge of American voting behavior. Because an act as straightforward and uncontroversial as voting is consistently misreported, we recommend interpreting all self-reported information with caution.

Similar problems of social desirability and misreporting occur with opinion questions. Uniformed or disinterested respondents may express an opinion. Including "don't know" as a response choice may alleviate this problem; however, investigators cannot infer what a "don't know" indicates. Respondents may answer "don't know" because they have problems answering the question. They may be ambivalent, that is, they have thought about the issue but have yet to reach a firm opinion. They may be uninformed or disinterested in the topic. Some respondents may become distracted while hearing a question or have trouble understanding it. They will answer "don't know" to avoid the trouble of having the question repeated or trying to decipher its meaning. Thus investigators must examine any question that generates a high proportion of "don't knows" to make sure it is not ambiguous or otherwise flawed.

To get a snapshot of the public's opinion, the distinction between disinterested and ambivalent respondents may be less necessary.[5] If an investigator wants to identify disinterested respondents, she may ask a filter question. For example, respondents may be asked, "How interested are you in the bond referendum to build a civic center?" An alternative solution, illustrated below, asks a dichotomous question and follows up with an intensity question. Since asking a series of questions may tax respondents' patience, respondents may be simply reminded that "not interested" is an appropriate response.

1. Do you support or oppose the bond referendum to build a civic center?

    ____Support
    ____Oppose
    ____Don't know

2. How interested are you in the bond referendum to build a civic center?

    ____A lot
    ____Some
    ____Not much
    ____None

Among the respondents who answered "don't know" to Question 1, investigators may assume that disinterested respondents answered "not much" or "none" to Question 2, and ambivalent respondents answered "a lot" or "some" to Question 2. If a question is forced choice with no follow-up intensity question, responses closest to the midpoint will group ambivalent, disinterested, and less intense respondents together.

Some researchers argue that offering people a "don't know" option encourages them to avoid stating their position. Others believe that "don't know" represents a midpoint between positive and negative attitudes. Including "don't know" as a possible response discourages disinterested respondents from making up an opinion on the spot.

Questions asking respondents how often they do something should cover a limited time span. Someone may accurately remember how many times he used a library in the past month. If he is asked about the past year, he may multiply the number of visits in the past month by 12. He is unlikely to adjust his estimate to indicate that he used the library more than usual or less than usual. A response list may serve as a frame of reference, and a respondent may alter his answers if they seem atypical. Hence, questions about frequency may be kept open-ended.[6]

If a measure includes a series of questions with similar answers, such as "agree" and "disagree," the respondent may answer all questions in the same way regardless of content. Serious distortions may occur if a respondent guesses the purpose of the questions. For example, a survey to identify opinions about community development may have a number of questions about types and levels of development. A respondent who is generally opposed to development may answer all questions with a "disagree" and ignore the content of the specific questions. This problem can be reduced if all questions do not go in the same direction. In other words, for some questions a "disagree" would be a pro-development choice and for others a "disagree" would be an anti-development choice. Nevertheless, the respondent may become annoyed or confused with a questionnaire in which questions change direction capriciously. Some questions may be misread or misunderstood simply because the respondent missed a key word such as "not."

The items below, taken from a client satisfaction survey, illustrate how questions are worded to avoid set responses. Investigators conducted the survey to see how agency clients rated support staff. The respondent ranked each statement on a scale ranging from "strongly agree" to "strongly disagree."

1. The agency staff can answer my questions.
2. The agency staff is polite when I telephone.
3. The agency staff is accessible by telephone.
4. The agency staff is rude when questions are asked.
5. The agency staff interrupts me when I talk with them.

A person who is pleased with agency staff should agree to items 1 through 3 and disagree with items 4 and 5. The shift from "agree" to "disagree" is referred to as a change in direction. The shift is achieved without resorting to awkward wording. A respondent should quickly and accurately grasp the meaning of each question.

A major problem with changing the direction of items may occur when the data are compiled. The direction should not be changed when the data are coded and entered into a computer file. By keeping the original direction, the analyst reduces the risk of data-entry errors. Instead, she can easily change the direction as part of the computer programming.

Biased Questions

A *biased question* is worded so that it encourages respondents to give one answer over another, eliciting inaccurate information. Although questions may be intentionally worded to lead the respondent to give a specific answer, biases also may be introduced unintentionally. A response list is often a source of question biases. Responses should cover the range of plausible options. One error is to use a rating scale with a disproportionate number of positive (or negative) ratings. For example, a four-point rating scale with responses of "excellent," "good," "satisfactory," and "poor" has three positive responses out of four possible responses. This increases the probability that a person will express some degree of positive satisfaction. The failure to include a particular response on a list of responses also may create biases. Instead of penning in the appropriate information, a respondent may settle for checking off the next-best answer.

Loaded questions are worded so that a respondent gives an acceptable answer. Some adjectives or phrases tend to have a positive or negative value, thus leading a person to ignore the major content of the question. For example, labeling a proposed policy as "liberal," "permissive," or "bureaucratic" will tend to measure respondents' reactions to these words and not their general opinions about the policy. Also, questions may include an assumption affecting answers. For example, if we ask people whether they agree or disagree that the "state should build more prisons in order to decrease violent crimes," we are assuming that building prisons will decrease violent crime. The question may unwittingly lead respondents concerned about violent crime to support building more prisons.

Another common, unintentional bias is to ask two questions in one. These questions are easily identified by the conjunction "and." Consider the question, "Are you in favor of tightening the state's DUI (Driving Under the Influence) laws and making it illegal for parents to serve liquor to minors in their homes?" A person may favor tightening up the DUI laws but not agree with making it illegal for parents to serve liquor to their minor children. How should the person accurately report his attitude?

Another source of bias occurs if the available responses do not fit the question asked. For example, we received a questionnaire with the following item:

Do you think that state annexation statutes need to be changed, or do you think that they are appropriate as they are?

_____Yes

_____No

The question writer was following the professional practice of wording the question so that it did not favor either changing the statutes or leaving them alone. Unfortunately, the responses were not appropriate. There was no way we could accurately report our opinion unless we went to the trouble to write an answer. This problem is easily solved by altering the response wording. The two responses to this item could be:

_____Yes, statutes need to be changed

_____No, statues are appropriate as they are now

Other Considerations

Whereas inexperienced question-writers unintentionally write biased questions, special-interest groups may intentionally word items to encourage a particular answer. A *New York Times* article reported on a study contrasting an interest-group question with questions written by professional surveyors.[7] An example of a leading question and a balanced version of the same question is:

> *Version 1:* Should laws be passed to eliminate all possibilities of special interests giving huge sums of money to candidates?

> *Version 2:* Should laws be passed to prohibit interest groups from contributing to campaigns, or do groups have a right to contribute to the candidate they support?

The differences in wording should leap out at you. The first question has charged phrases "special interests" and "huge sums of money." It also lacks the feature of stating a contrasting choice in the question in order to keep the item neutral. Of course, Version 2 could not "work" if the response categories were "yes" and "no." Rather, response choices included "laws should be passed to prohibit interest groups from contributing to campaigns" and "groups have a right to contribute to the candidate they support."

We cannot contrast the responses to the two questions because the first question was answered by a voluntary sample. Version 2, which was administered to a random sample, found 40 percent favored prohibiting contributions. Another version of the question that asked, "Please tell me whether you favor or oppose the proposal: The passage of new laws that would eliminate all possibility of special interests giving large sums of money to candidates," found 70 percent favored prohibiting contributions. The example suggests how question wording can affect the response pattern and how fragile one question is at measuring attitudes and opinions.

Questions that ask respondents how much they would be willing to pay for something are particularly sensitive to wording. If the respondent feels that her answer will affect service cost, she may cite an amount lower than what she would pay. Consider a question that asks people whether they would pay $10 for a tennis license to play on the city's public courts. A tennis player, who may be quite willing to pay $10, might try to influence the policy outcome by answering "no." Alternatively, people asked how much they would pay for various environmental programs are likely to overestimate their willingness to pay.[8]

Some studies involve sensitive subjects, and one must be aware of the probability that a respondent will distort his or her answers. Questions on drug use and other activities that are illegal or widely criticized may bring about inaccurate responses. A naive schoolchild may report drug use to make herself appear knowledgeable, whereas a drug user fearful of the consequences of accurately reporting her behavior will deny or underreport her drug experience.

Each of us has feelings about what we have accomplished and how we have failed. Surveys to learn about individuals undoubtedly will have questions that make some respondents uncomfortable. Questions that seem likely to create respondent discomfort should be carefully considered. First, such questions may raise ethical concerns; that is, the research may harm the subjects. (Ethics and the avoidance of harming human subjects are discussed in Chapter 8.) Second, the questions may cause respondents not to participate in a study and may even result in a negative attitude toward research in general. Third, the questions may lead respondents to give inaccurate information.

Knowing which questions are potentially threatening requires a knowledge of the subject population. Observers should not assume that their perceptions of what is a sensitive subject or a threatening question agree with a respondent's perceptions. An acquaintance from India observed that Americans seemed to talk freely about their feelings toward family members but refused to discuss their salaries. Conversely, he noted that Indians talked about their earnings openly but virtually never discussed their feelings about family members.

Stating a question so that it suggests to the respondent that any possible answer is acceptable not surprisingly helps reduce threat. For example, such questions may be introduced with the phrase, "Some people find . . ." Question order also can reduce the discomfort associated with a question. Potentially threatening questions should not be asked at the beginning of a questionnaire or interview, where they may make a respondent suspicious and less willing to cooperate. On the other hand, a sensitive question should not be placed at the end either, where it may cause a person to finish a survey feeling anxious and wondering if the survey had a hidden purpose. Finally, as we discussed in Chapter 6, respondents are more likely to share sensitive information on self-administered questionnaires, including those that a respondent answers on a computer or with paper and pencil while an interviewer waits.

QUESTION SEQUENCING AND QUESTIONNAIRE DESIGN

Question Sequencing

Obviously, one cannot put questions on a form in random order. Questions should be logically ordered. The initial questions can affect a respondent's willingness to answer a questionnaire. If the early questions are confusing, threatening, or time consuming, a respondent may not complete the survey or cooperate with the interviewer. Self-administered questionnaires and interview schedules follow a general sequence.

Introduction

An introduction states the nature and purpose of the survey. It identifies the person or organization conducting the survey. The introduction should be short and to the point. An overly long explanation of the purpose of a survey may bias results.

Subjects must be told what, if any, risks may be associated with participating in a study. With very few exceptions, e.g., providing data to the U.S. Census Bureau, research participation must be voluntary. Subjects must understand that

---

EXAMPLE 7.6

Examples of Survey Introductions

Sample 1: The introduction is from a survey given to town employees. The surveys were given directly to employees, and they could mail their responses back to the investigators.

Actual wording: This questionnaire is designed to find out how you and others feel about the Town of Oaks as a place to work. The data collected will provide information needed to better understand how people feel about the quality of working life in the organization.

If this questionnaire is to be useful, it is important that you answer each question frankly and honestly. There are no right or wrong answers to these questions. We are interested in what you think and feel about your life at this organization.

Your answers to these questions are completely confidential. All questionnaires will be taken to State University for analysis. No one in the Town of Oaks organization will ever have access to your individual answers.

For analysis and data collection purposes, a number has been put on this questionnaire that can be matched with your name on a list at the university. It would be appreciated if you would leave this number intact.

Thank you in advance for your cooperation and assistance.

Sample 2: This survey introduction is from a telephone survey of community residents. The purpose of the survey was to learn their opinion of the town police force.

Actual wording:

INTRODUCTION: Hello, my name is (interviewer name), and I'm calling from the Town of Oaks.

PURPOSE: In conjunction with State University, we are calling about 500 homes in Oaks to find out how you feel about police services in Oaks. (TO INTERVIEWER: IF CALLING BETWEEN 5 and 6:30 P.M., ADD: Is this a convenient time to call you, or should I call back later this evening?)

CONFIRMATION: Do you live within the town limits of Oaks? (If the answer is no, END THE CALL.) Is this a home phone or a business? (If a business, END THE CALL.)

---

their participation is voluntary, they may decline to answer any question, and they can withdraw from a study at any time. Regulations on "protection of human subjects" cover requirements for informing subjects of their rights and the risks of participation. The regulations and related ethical issues are discussed in Chapter 8.

Example 7.6 illustrates two questionnaire introductions. The first is from a survey given to town employees. The second is from a phone survey of the general public. Each introduction indicates the purpose of the study. Each introduction encourages respondents to participate by indicating the importance of their answers. Each introduction implies voluntary participation. In the case of mail or telephone surveys, voluntary participation is often implied because subjects usually feel no compunction about not returning the survey or hanging up the phone.

The introduction to the survey sent to employees fully detailed how the investigators planned to protect respondents' confidentiality. Such surveys are particularly sensitive because employees are suspicious about what will be done with the information. The other survey informs the respondent that the survey is anonymous.

Sampling frames are not perfect. A sample may include inappropriate respondents who should be screened out immediately. The introduction or the first question should establish whether the respondent should complete the survey. In Example 7.6, Sample 2, the respondents were asked whether or not they lived in the town. In Example 6.1, an enclosed postcard allowed inappropriate respondents to quickly excuse themselves from replying. Respondents who do not fall within the sample population are usually asked to return the uncompleted questionnaire. An interviewer will have a parallel set of directions telling him if and how he can replace an ineligible respondent.

First Questions

Following the introduction, relevant, easily answered questions appear. These involve the respondent in the study. During an interview, this section builds rapport between the interviewer and the respondent. In a self-administered questionnaire, the questions draw the respondent into making a "psychological commitment" to complete the questionnaire.

For the recipient of a mailed survey, the first questions keep him from putting the survey aside and forgetting it; however, if the survey becomes unduly complex or confusing, the benefits of good first questions may be lost. In a telephone survey, the first questions may be important in getting cooperation from a wary respondent who may suspect that the caller is really going to sell him something. In the police survey, the first questions asked the respondents about their contacts with police officers during the previous 12 months.

In the questionnaire sent to employees of the town of Oaks, the first three questions, each answered on a strongly agree to strongly disagree scale, were:

1. I get a feeling of personal satisfaction from doing my job well.
2. I work hard on my job.
3. If I had the chance, I would take a different job within this organization.

Major Questions

The distinction between the initial questions and the major questions may be virtually nonexistent. Many questionnaires ask a few introductory questions, then group questions in sections addressing the major issues of the survey. In the sections, the question order may be important. In-person interviewers start with more general questions followed by specific questions. Care must be taken to avoid sequences that can bias answers.

The introduction of the DECIDE study told respondents that the survey's purpose was to learn more about management training needs. The questionnaire started with questions about respondents' management responsibilities. The next grouping of questions asked respondents about management decision-making tools: What tools were they familiar with? What tools did they commonly use? What were some of the problems with the tools? The following section asked about DECIDE as a decision-making tool.

In Question 5 respondents were asked, "What decision-making tools do you commonly use?" A note to the interviewers told them, "If a prompt is needed, use value analysis." The first mention of DECIDE was in Question 7 after respondents had been asked about management decision-making tools. Nearly 90 percent of the respondents who said they used DECIDE several times a month had mentioned it earlier as a decision-making tool. If we had mentioned DECIDE early in the study, we would have been more suspicious of the level of reported use.

Sequencing to avoid bias is not as effective in self-administered questionnaires. The respondent can read the entire questionnaire before answering any questions, or he can go back and change answers.

Demographic Questions

The final section typically asks personal questions about income, age, race, education, or employment. Analogous questions are asked in organizational surveys. By the end of the interview, the respondent may feel less reluctant to answer personal questions. Personal questions at the beginning of a survey may make a person wonder about its real purpose. We suspect that this reaction is especially likely in areas where telephone salespersons use the guise of a survey to keep a potential customer on the telephone.

Some investigators get into the habit of asking a standard set of demographic questions at the end. For example, they may routinely include questions about age, sex, race, education, and income. These questions may go unanalyzed and contribute little to the database. Surveying consumes resources, including respondent goodwill. Thus we prefer to stick to information appropriate to the study and to eliminate questions that are not in the analysis plan. In addition, too many personal questions may disturb respondents who worry about the anonymity of their answers.

Questionnaire Design

Question wording and sequencing are elements of questionnaire design; they affect the clarity and validity of the responses. The physical layout of the questionnaire or interview schedule affects its utility. In organizing a questionnaire, the designer must consider its impact on the person filling it out and the person compiling or coding the information.

An interviewer needs a form that is easy to read and to follow while speaking to a respondent and recording responses. A respondent needs a questionnaire that is easy to follow and does not overwhelm him. A questionnaire that can be easily and quickly answered reduces the possibility that it will be put aside and forgotten. Factors such as the design of the pages also may affect the response rate and the quality and quantity of the information obtained. Furthermore, a well-designed questionnaire may communicate to the respondent the seriousness of the research effort and favorably affect his inclination to respond.

We have listed below a partial "instrument checklist" to guide you in constructing a survey. You may wish to add to this checklist as you read other materials or review various data collection instruments:

A Checklist for Constructing Surveys

Self-administered surveys:

The purpose is clearly stated in the introduction

Directions on how to answer are clear

Recipients who do not belong to the target population are identified, for example, by the use of a screening question, and are told what to do with the survey

Survey instrument deadline date and return address should appear on survey instrument

Interviewer-administered surveys:

Interviewer's introduction clearly indicates the purpose

Directions on how to ask questions and record answers are clear

Recipients who do not belong to the target population are identified, and interviewer instructions indicate if and how he should look for a replacement respondent

On all surveys and data-collecting instruments:

Critical terms are defined

Abbreviations are not used

Conjunctions, such as "and," are avoided, because an answer may not apply to both parts of the question

Response choices must be adequate and appropriate

Requested data must be easily accessible

Item groupings are logical

For opinion questions:

Question wording should be neutral, such as, "Do you favor or oppose?"

Responses should be balanced, for example, an equal number of positive and negative responses

Questionnaire Efficiency

Trying to make certain you need every question you ask and ask every question you need is difficult. The more you can visualize the information a survey will produce and how you will use it, the better off you are. Working with a model serves as a beginning point in deciding what questions to ask and how to ask them, yet it may be insufficient. Identifying the output the survey will produce should improve its efficiency and suggest ways to improve it.

The researchers describe how they plan to analyze the data. Then, they link the plan with the questionnaire to double-check that each question is needed. The team can review the plan with the study users to show them what information the study will produce. The review should help users identify gaps in the planned survey as well as information not needed. After the data are collected, the researchers can refer to the plan to guide their data analysis.

Example 7.7 shows a partial outline produced to help design a questionnaire to learn how agency managers, trained in a decision-making technique called DECIDE, used the technique. The DECIDE training program required two licensed trainers to conduct week-long training seminars of 16 agency managers. During the week, teams of trainees systematically analyzed problems, identified and evaluated possible solutions, selected a solution, and developed an implementation plan. The agency needed the information to help it decide whether the benefits of the training justified the costs.

Planning, Pretesting, and Piloting Surveys

Good data collection instruments that yield useful and used information emerge from an iterative process. The first stage, which has been the focus of the chapter, involves planning and writing the instrument. As ideas are fleshed out to form an

---

EXAMPLE 7.7

Using Planned Output to Guide Questionnaire Content

Situation: Investigators plan to survey managers who received DECIDE training and ask them how they used the training in their jobs.

Step 1: Describe planned analysis. Indicate what outputs will be produced, identify the questions that will be included to produce each output, and indicate the value of each output to the study. Note the number of categories that are used to perform analysis.

Outline of Planned Output:

Univariate Output: Trainees' use of DECIDE

Frequency of use (Question 3)
Impact on present job (Question 5)

Continued

EXAMPLE 7.7 *Continued*

Types of use (Question 4)
Specific examples of use (Question 4; categorize and analyze open-ended responses)

Bivariate Output: Factors associated with how often trainees use DECIDE, how they use it, and problems with the use. Tables will be created to examine the following relationships:

1. Frequency of use by
   a. years since training
   b. management functions
   c. position
   d. division
   e. education
2. Type of use by
   a. years since training
   b. management functions
   c. position
   d. division
   e. education
3. Problems with use by
   a. years since training
   b. management functions
   c. position
   d. division
   e. education

Value and use of bivariate output on use: If patterns of use are related to years since training, the pattern may be attributed to decay (training forgotten over time); changes in the types of persons trained over the years; changes in trainees' jobs. (Note: should we include variables to measure the latter explanations?)

If patterns of use are related to management functions, the number of employees supervised or position pattern may show whether variations in use are associated with either a specialized or generalist management focus. Information could be used to limit training to groups identified as frequent or effective users of DECIDE.

If patterns of use are related to work unit, the pattern may suggest that DECIDE is more suited to the work of specific units, or that some unit managers are more supportive of the technique. Information could be used to limit training to units identified as frequent or effective users of DECIDE. If supervisor training in DECIDE is related to frequent or effective use, managers may suggest the need to train supervisors before training their staff.

Step 2: Check outline against draft questionnaire to make sure it contains all items needed for analysis; consider deleting questions that are not noted on outline.

Step 3: Review questionnaire and outline with study users to see if they can identify unnecessary information or overlooked information.

actual survey, investigators better understand the purpose of the study and what it can find out or accomplish. The planning process brings critical actors together to decide what information they want, whether a survey is needed, and if it will yield the desired information. From the various discussions, the investigators should be able to identify a list of variables. With this list they can develop measures and design an instrument. Finally, the contents of the questionnaire are outlined as in Example 7.7 to evaluate if all the proposed items are needed and if all needed items have been included. Once it is outlined, further feedback may be solicited from critical actors.

Next, the questionnaire should be reviewed by researchers and their colleagues. They should determine if the questions seem reliable: Are there any ambiguous items? Are the response choices appropriate? Is the information easily available to respondents? Human nature may lead the writers to disagree with their critics and argue that an item is not ambiguous, that the response choices are fine, or that the respondents will be motivated to find the information. Nevertheless, in our experience, reviewers tend to identify the same items that study subjects find troublesome.

Writing questions takes time and effort. Participants need a thick skin because good questionnaires emerge only after a lot of criticism and argument. Good questionnaire design takes place among equals, with everyone's comments getting consideration. In our experience, not only do participants act as equals, but they become intense and pointed in their comments. To illustrate the process of question writing, we have selected just one question from the DECIDE survey. Example 7.8 shows the changes that question underwent through various drafting sessions.

After the questionnaire is redrafted, it should be *pretested.* To conduct a pretest, one asks a small group to answer the proposed questionnaire. These pretest subjects should represent common variations found in the target population. For example, a survey of city employees should be pretested on employees ranging from unskilled laborers to senior management. The investigators also may want pretest subjects who represent various city departments, such as public works, public safety, planning, and finance.

Pretests normally involve face-to-face contact with the subjects. The investigators determine if subjects understood and could answer the questions, and if their answers showed enough variation for the planned analysis to be conducted. The investigators should record how long it took individuals to answer the survey and if it held their interest and attention. If a survey does not engage respondents, the information may be less reliable, incomplete questionnaires may be more common, or, in the case of mail questionnaires, the response rate may be lower.

After answering the questionnaire, the pretest subjects may be interviewed or debriefed about their answers and reactions to the questions and the survey as a whole. The investigators use their own observations, the subjects' comments, and their responses to the survey questions to determine how coherent the questionnaire is: Are directions clear? Is the question order logical?[9] The survey should be redrafted based on the pretest findings. Common changes include changing or clarifying unclear terms, rewording or dropping ambiguous questions, changing response categories, and shortening instruments.

The final stage is the *pilot study* or dress rehearsal. One text in questionnaire design contains the statement, "If you do not have the resources to pilot test

EXAMPLE 7.8

The Evolution of a Question

Situation: Questionnaire on DECIDE training was designed to learn how trainees felt it affected their jobs.

Stage 1: Group of three wrote a questionnaire. First questionnaire had several questions on DECIDE's effect and use on job. Questions 1 and 2 were both open-ended.

1. Were DECIDE course objectives related to your job needs?
2. Do you use any DECIDE processes on the job? If not, why?

Stage 2: Questionnaire map drawn up and questionnaire redrafted by another team member.

1. In general how would you rate DECIDE's impact on your present job? (responses: excellent, good, fair, poor, no impact, unsure)
2. About how often do you use any DECIDE process on your job? (responses: 1 time a week, several times a month, about once a month, several times a year, rarely or never, don't know)
3. Let me know if DECIDE helps you think about any of the following: (responses included: setting priorities, setting objectives, identifying alternatives)
4. Give me a specific example of how you have used DECIDE approach on your job.
5. In applying DECIDE process, what, if any, problems have you encountered?

Stage 3: Team of seven reviewed the draft and made the following changes:

1. In general, how would you rate DECIDE's effect on your job performance? (changed "no impact" response to "no effect")
2. Question kept the same. Placed "rarely and never" responses into separate categories. Respondents who answered "never" were directed to a later question.
3. Question kept the same. Deleted two response categories.
4. Give me a specific example of how you have used DECIDE process on your job.

Stage 4: Questionnaire pretested. Sample of 10 called. Frequency of responses to each question reviewed. The only change in the above questions was to further reduce the number of response categories for Question 3.

your questionnaire, don't do the study."[10] In modest studies the pilot study and the pretest may overlap, but at a minimum investigators should test the instrument on potential subjects, check that items have sufficient variation, conduct minimum analysis to assess whether the survey will produce useful information.

We wish that everyone who tried to conduct a survey believed the preceding quote. The amount of resources wasted on poorly designed or inadequate questionnaires is staggering. More astonishing is how many questionnaires are sent out without a commitment of resources for data analysis. Consider an actual survey that resulted in 33,000 responses. The office, which did not normally conduct or process surveys, spent a frantic few weeks simply coding 21 closed-ended and two open-ended questions. Each questionnaire took approximately one minute to code for a total of 550 hours. Staff also read the responses to four other open-ended questions. The data analysis was less of a drain on resources; the questionnaire's content didn't allow for much analysis beyond counting and categorizing the responses to each question. Two questions could not be analyzed; because of ambiguous wording, the responses were uninterpretable. We assume that the poor ratio between the survey's cost and the meager amount of information it yielded could have been avoided if the survey had been pretested and piloted. It wasn't.

The pilot study involves conducting the entire study as planned on a small sample representing the target population. The questionnaire is administered as planned, that is, either in person, through the mail, or over the telephone. The planned analysis is conducted on the returned surveys. Any special procedures to be used in collecting or compiling data, for example, computer-assisted interviewing, are used during the pilot study.

By the time of the pilot study, questionnaire problems should be minimal. Investigators pay closer attention to the feasibility of the sampling, data collection, and analysis procedures. The dress rehearsal should identify any problems in contacting sample members and getting their cooperation. The time involved in data preparation can be estimated, and the adequacy of data preparation and analysis plans checked. Previously unnoticed, unreliable, or invalid measures may be detected. Problems encountered in the pilot study should be resolved prior to implementing the final study design.

Earlier in this chapter, we mentioned the Nationwide Food Consumption Survey, which had a response rate of 34 percent. The problems with that survey illustrate two common situations. First, identifying problems in a pretest or dress rehearsal is not enough. An effective solution to the problems identified in the pilot study must be put in place. Second, without a dress rehearsal the serious problems may be missed or underestimated. Two pretests of the food consumption survey had been conducted. Interviewers and subjects complained of fatigue with a survey that took as long as $5\frac{1}{2}$ hours to complete. As a result, the computer-assisted interviewing procedures were supposed to be improved. The pretest of the improved computer-assisted interviewing methods found that interviewers required rigorous training. To save money, the planned dress rehearsal was canceled. Note that the dress rehearsal would have evaluated the effectiveness of the interviewers' training. The long survey was not shortened, and interviewer training was not sufficiently rigorous. As a result, a study that cost $7.6 million yielded seriously flawed data.

SUMMARY

Questions and questionnaires constitute basic elements of data collection. Writing questions and designing questionnaires require one to understand their effect on the implementation of a research design. Each question or series of questions has implications for reliability and operational validity.

A first step in questionnaire construction is to outline its content. An investigator wants to avoid a questionnaire that asks trivial questions or fails to ask important ones. To prevent a mismatch between the research purpose and a survey instrument, each question's role in the research should be explored and justified. One also should determine whether the types of questions asked elicit the desired information. Asking the wrong type of question, for example, asking an opinion question where a behavior question is needed, affects operational validity. Common question types ask about facts, behaviors, opinions, attitudes, motives, and knowledge.

A second step is deciding on whether to ask open-ended or closed-ended questions or to include contingency and filter questions. Open-ended questions require respondents to write their answers. These questions work well during questionnaire development when investigators want to learn the range of possible responses. Open-ended questions provide rich, detailed information; they may be asked in conjunction with closed-ended questions. Because open-ended questions are difficult to quantify, may unnecessarily tax respondents, and may lower the response rate, researchers prefer closed-ended questions. Closed-ended questions have a respondent select an appropriate response from a list. These questions work well if the questionnaire has been carefully pretested to ensure that the questions are understood and the response categories are appropriate.

Filter questions or screening questions direct subgroups of respondents to appropriate contingency questions. For example, renters may answer one set of contingency questions and owners another set. On mailed questionnaires boxes or arrows may direct respondents to applicable questions. Interviewers may use the same tools or they may use computer software that "automatically" goes to the appropriate follow up questions.

Question wording is a major component of measure reliability and operational validity. In general, questions should be clear, short, and specific. The respondent should understand what information is needed. Questions can be biased, either intentionally or unintentionally. A biased question increases the probability that a respondent will choose one answer over another. Words that respondents perceive as positive or negative may bias answers. Response lists that have disproportionately more positive or negative alternatives also introduce bias. Questions on sensitive subjects must be handled with special care. Respondents may distort their answers; furthermore, such questions can raise ethical concerns if they expose the respondent to acute discomfort.

The order in which questions are asked affects response rate and the operational validity of the questions. Nevertheless, ordering questions to avoid bias works better if subjects are being interviewed. Respondents answering self-administered questionnaires can read ahead or change their answers, reducing the value of the sequence.

Questionnaires start with an introduction and end with any needed demographic questions. Some researchers get in the habit of routinely asking a set of demographic questions, without considering which demographic variables are needed for the planned analysis. Asking needless questions should be avoided;

furthermore, demographic questions may raise the distrust of respondents who wish to remain anonymous.

One would be well advised to approach any survey asking, "Is this survey necessary?" To assure oneself that it is and that it does not squander resources, one should first determine that the needed data do not yet exist. If the data do not exist, then the survey should proceed only after a pilot study. A pilot study rehearses the research plan, including the analysis. In analyzing a pilot study, researchers may focus on question wording and sensitivity of the response categories. Researchers may be tempted to ignore the opportunity to evaluate their planned analysis. Yet, a review of the planned analysis may be most helpful in avoiding unnecessary surveys or questions.

The next chapter looks at the ethical concerns raised by gathering data from human subjects. We will review some key incidents that led to federal regulations and professional guidelines for protecting human subjects. The regulations dominate data collection. The requirement for informed consent dictates what potential research subjects must be told about a planned study and its effects. Furthermore, the provision that research participation must be voluntary challenges researchers to design studies that respect the respondents' privacy and entice their participation.

NOTES

1. M. Q. Patton, *Utilization-Focused Evaluation,* 3d ed. (Thousand Oaks, CA: Sage, 1997).

2. K. A. Rasinski, D. Mingay, and N. M. Bradburn, "Do Respondents Really 'Mark All that Apply' of Self-Administered Questions?" *Public Opinion Quarterly* 58 (Fall 1994): 400–408.

3. *USDA's Nationwide Food Consumption Survey,* Washington, D.C.: General Accounting Office, GAO/RCED–91–117. The GAO report on why the survey yielded poor-quality data is highly recommended; it vividly points out several errors that can occur in a major survey project.

4. Most of the information on validating voting data are from S. Presser and M. Traaugott, "Correlated Response Errors," *Public Opinion Quarterly* 56 (Spring 1992): 77–86. For a discussion on voter records as a source of error, see P. R. Abramson and W. Claggett, "The Quality of Record Keeping and Racial Differences in Validated Turnout," *Journal of Politics* 54 (August 1992): 871–880.

5. Researchers have reported that the ratio of positive to negative responses remains the same whether or not "don't know" is offered as a response alternative. For further discussion of "don't know," see L. F. Feick, "Latent Class Analysis of Survey Questions That Include Don't Know Responses," *Public Opinion Quarterly* 53 (1989): 525–547, J. M. Converse and S. Presser, *Survey Questions: Handcrafting the Standardized Questionnaire,* Sage University Paper Series: Quantitative Applications in the Social Sciences 63 (Beverly Hills: Sage Publications, 1986): 35–39, and M. Gilljam and D. Granberg, "Should We Take Don't Know for an Answer," *Public Opinion Quarterly* 57 (Fall 1993): 348–357.

6. S. Sudman, N. M. Bradburn, and N. Schwarz, *Thinking about Answers.* (San Francisco: Jossey-Bass, 1996), 225.

7. D. Goleman, "Psychologists Offer Aid on Bias in Polls," *New York Times,* Sept. 7, 1993, B5, B7. The article relies heavily on information included in an article in the June 1993 issue of *The Public Perspective.*

8. See P. Passell, "Polls May Help Government Decide the Worth of Nature," *New York Times,* Sept. 6, 1993, for an example of a question to ask how much a respondent would be willing for the government to pay to clean up an oil spill.

9. S. Sudman and N. M. Bradburn, *Asking Questions: A Practical Guide to Questionnaire Design* (San Francisco: Jossey–Bass, 1982) 283.

10. For a thorough discussion on pretests and pilot studies, see Converse and Presser, *Survey Questions,* 51–75 and F. J. Fowler, Jr. "Presurvey Evaluation of Questions," *Improving Survey Questions: Design and Evaluation* (Thousand Oaks, CA: Sage, 1995), chap. 5. Fowler discusses the use of focus groups, intensive interviewing, and field pretests.

TERMS FOR REVIEW

open-ended questions	contingency questions	loaded questions
closed-ended questions	filter questions	pretest
forced-choice questions	biased questions	pilot study

QUESTIONS FOR REVIEW

The following questions should indicate whether you have a basic competency in this chapter's material.

1. List the steps required to write a questionnaire.
2. How would you decide the content of a questionnaire?
3. Imagine you are writing a questionnaire to evaluate training given to new employees in your agency. (The training introduces employees to the agency, its purposes, and major policies.)
   a. Write a factual, behavior, opinion, motive, and knowledge question that you could include on the questionnaire.
   b. How valuable do you imagine each type of question (factual, behavior, etc.) would be to determine the quality of the training?
   c. On reflection, would you include all the questions you listed in part a?
4. A young researcher believes that questionnaires tend to be too long and adopts a rule of asking only one question to measure a variable. Evaluate the advisability of such a rule.
5. Compare and contrast the value of open-ended questions and closed-ended questions.

6. In general, would you recommend asking respondents ranking questions? Justify your answer.
7. What characteristics of question wording affect reliability? Explain.
8. Should you always include questions asking for demographic information? Why or why not? If you choose to include them, where would you place them in the survey?
9. Compare and contrast pretesting and piloting a questionnaire.
10. An investigator has written a questionnaire asking police officers about their career satisfaction. She pretests the questionnaire on students in an undergraduate criminal justice class. Comment on the adequacy of her pretesting strategy.
11. You are interested in neighborhoods and communities. You find a questionnaire that was used in metropolitan New York. The questionnaire covers topics that you are interested in studying in a moderate-size midwestern city. What would you do in order to decide that the questionnaire was appropriate for your study?

PROBLEMS FOR HOMEWORK AND DISCUSSION

1. The following is from an actual town survey. Identify the different parts of the survey. Identify the type of questions asked. Consider the value of findings from this questionnaire. Assess the wording of the questions.

   Questions a–d could be answered "yes," "no," or "no opinion." Questions f–h were open-ended.

   Hi, I am ———. I am helping to conduct a census for Wind Valley. Would you mind answering a few questions? It will take only a few minutes.
   a. Are you a resident of Wind Valley? (if yes, continue; if not, thank him/her and leave)
   b. Would you support redevelopment of the downtown business area?
   c. Would you favor once-a-week garbage collection in order to keep service charges down?

d. Would you be willing to accept fewer services for a reduced tax rate?

e. If city services had to be reduced in one area, which would you choose? (responses were: streets, fire, sanitation, parks and recreation, police, library, other, none)

f. How long have you lived in Wind Valley?

g. How many people are living in this household?

h. How many people are over 60 years of age?

2. The following questions are taken from a draft of a survey to identify stereotypes that social service workers may have of American Indian people. Review each question and then the five questions together. Assess the wording of the questions. Consider whether the questionnaire seems to risk a set response pattern problem. Note: all questions were to be answered "yes" or "no."

a. Do you put down Indians for their lifestyle?

b. Are the Indian people losing their culture?

c. Do you feel white society in general has labeled Indians to be lazy, uneducated, and drunk?

d. What is it to you to be an Indian today?

e. Do you provide support through staff who have knowledge and understanding of reservation or urban Indian needs?

3. Evaluate questions a and b from a "Job Turnover Questionnaire" sent to public administrators. What changes would you recommend?

a. Most important reasons for leaving your last job (check two only):

_____ Lack of job satisfaction (e.g., lack of achievement, recognition, growth potential)

_____ Disagree with agency policy/administration

_____ Poor interpersonal relations on job

_____ Salary insufficient

_____ Poor physical conditions

_____ Discrimination

_____ Work load

_____ Sexual harassment

_____ Continue education

_____ Family reasons (e.g., spouse moving, birth of child)

_____ Termination (end of contract, position defunded, reorganization)

_____ Other, specify

b. Type of job (check one only):

_____ Administration

_____ Counseling/social work

_____ Research/technical

_____ Secretarial/clerical

_____ Teaching

_____ Other, specify

4. A community survey sent interviewers to residents' homes. The respondent, any adult living in the household, was asked to supply the following information for each person in the household. Evaluate this question.

The Major Source of Income

	Person 1	Person 2
Salary	_____	_____
Hourly wages	_____	_____
Investments	_____	_____
Retirements/ pensions	_____	_____
Parent support/ inheritance	_____	_____
Welfare	_____	_____
Self-employment	_____	_____
Refusal	_____	_____
Don't know	_____	_____

5. Evaluate the following question: "Do you oppose measures promoting the abolition of the death penalty?"

6. Evaluate the following question and response categories on a survey given to nursing home residents. What changes, if any, in wording would you recommend?

How much do you use or participate in the following services or activities?

a. The Beauty and Barber Shop

_____ Often

_____ Occasionally

_____ Rarely

_____ Never

b. Crafts
_____ Often
_____ Occasionally
_____ Rarely
_____ Never

c. Card and Game Night
_____ Often
_____ Occasionally
_____ Rarely
_____ Never

d. Religious Services
_____ Often
_____ Occasionally
_____ Rarely
_____ Never

7. Draft a survey to determine needs and preferences of part-time students enrolled in your degree program. The survey should identify changes the program could make to better serve the needs of part-time students. Create and use the mapping forms to determine what questions to ask, how they will be used, and the value of the information.

8. Imagine 600 members of a statewide professional association responded to a survey. It included an open-ended question on the effectiveness of the association's activities. Perusal of the questionnaires suggests that most members answered the question.

   a. You are asked to make an initial report on the survey findings. You will not have time to examine all the open-ended questions. Suggest a strategy so that you can include information from the open-ended questions in your report.

   b. Describe how you would analyze the question for your final report.

9. Contrast the value of (a) finding questionnaires that have questions you can adapt and (b) writing questionnaires with a group of colleagues.

10. Investigators are often tempted to add questions that they may or may not get around to analyzing. Evaluate this strategy.

11. Review and evaluate a software package to design questionnaires.

DISK WORK

Limitations of a questionnaire may become obvious only as you analyze the data. To get a feel for this role of analysis, this exercise asks you to conduct a study on the Belle County data set. Since analyzing even a small number of variables can quickly become tedious, this exercise works best if you work with a group of classmates. The Belle County manager wants to learn how familiar residents are with county services and the extent to which they use the services. Load the Belle County data set and analyze whether:

a. Knowledge of county services varies with respondent characteristics.

b. Use of county services varies with respondent characteristics, knowledge of county services, or attitudes toward county services.

c. Based on your analysis write a memo (no longer than 3 pages) to the manager presenting your key findings. Make appropriate recommendations for action or further study.

d. Based on your analysis what changes would you suggest if the questionnaire were to be used again? Write a memo "to the record" summarizing your suggestions.

RECOMMENDED FOR FURTHER READING

There are a number of excellent books on survey research and questionnaire design. We recommend:

Don A. Dillman, *Mail and Telephone Surveys: The Total Design Method* (New York: Wiley, 1978).

Floyd J. Fowler, Jr., *Survey Research Methods,* Sage Applied Social Research Methods Series, 3d ed. (Thousand Oaks, CA: Sage, 2001).

Seymour Sudman and Norman M. Bradburn, *Asking Questions: A Practical Guide to Questionnaire Design* (San Francisco: Jossey–Bass, 1982).

Ellen J. Westland with Kent W. Smith surveys research on response accuracy and a meta-analysis in *Survey Responses: An Evaluation of Their Validity* (San Diego: Academic Press, Inc., 1993).

Professional associations and research publish guides for designing questionnaires and conducting surveys. Two guides that review major points covered here and provide additional examples are: H. P. Hatry et al., *Customer Surveys for Agency Managers: What Managers Need to Know* (Washington, D.C.: The Urban Institute, 1997), and Thomas I. Miller and Michelle A. Miller, *Citizen Surveys: How to Do Them, How to Use Them, What They Mean*, ICMA's Special Report Series, 2d ed. (Washington, D.C.: International City Management Association, 2000). Other how-to-do-it books can help refresh your memory of key points, for example see Mildred L. Patten, *Questionnaire Research*, 2d ed. (Los Angeles: Pyrczak Publishing, 2001); and a very helpful basic brochure series called *What is a Survey* provided by the American Statistical Association's Survey Research Section.

To keep up-to-date with current research on survey research topics such as question wording, questionnaire design, data collection, and data analysis, see *Public Opinion Quarterly,* the journal of the American Association for Public Opinion Research, published by the University of Chicago Press. S. Sudman, N. M. Bradburn, and N. Schwarz, *Thinking about Answers* (San Francisco: Jossey-Bass, 1996), provide a good review of research findings.

Chapter 8

Protection of Human Research Subjects and Other Ethical Issues

In this chapter you will learn
1. some of the major cases informing ethical practices in conducting research on human subjects.
2. elements of ethical practice in conducting research on human subjects.
3. requirements for obtaining informed consent from a research subject.
4. what to consider in protecting confidential information.
5. federal requirements for protecting human subjects.
6. what administrators should consider before permitting research on their employees or agency's clients.

The nature of research creates a special relationship between researchers and their human subjects. Researchers require the cooperation of humans to conduct investigations. At the same time, subjects rely on researchers to treat them respectfully and ethically. Subjects do not expect to be harmed by merely participating in research. Nevertheless, some research projects may expose participants to risks, including physical injury, psychological discomfort, or loss of privacy.

Administrative students may believe that administrative or policy research rarely puts a *subject at risk*. While the subjects seem unlikely to experience life-threatening or permanently harmful effects, the risks may be more than trivial. Apparently innocuous studies may leave participants feeling angry, upset, humiliated, or otherwise worried. They may be less willing to participate in other studies. They may tell others of their experience and further decrease support for research endeavors. Sound, ethical research practices can greatly lessen such negative effects.

Administrators should be sensitive to the issues surrounding research with human subjects and recognize how research participation can cause a subject distress. Otherwise, administrators may fail to adequately protect agency employees or clients. Administrators, who decide whether to provide investigators requested access to subjects, want to authorize studies that conform to ethical research practice and do not harm participants or reflect badly on the agency. Administrators who work in hospitals, schools, prisons, and social service agencies should be vigilant, since their employees and clients often interest researchers.

In this chapter we begin by highlighting some well-known cases. The cited cases are dramatic examples, but they were not necessarily aberrations from contemporary research practices. For one reason or another, they achieved notoriety and shaped current thinking about ethical research on human subjects. Since the last cited case occurred in 1963, you may reasonably conclude that ethical missteps no longer occur. This is not true. From 1993 to 2001 four different medical studies resulted in the deaths of eight research subjects. As a result, bio-ethicists began to review policies intended to protect research volunteers.[1] Ethical concerns are not limited to medical research. In 1999 parents filed a lawsuit claiming that a student survey to "identify community assets and resources" violated their children's privacy.[2]

As you read the cases, put yourself in the place of the judges, hospital administrators, or others who have a role in approving research. Put yourself in the position of the patient, juror, or an observed citizen. Imagine how you would react to a survey asking about your management style. As you think about these different scenarios, you may realize that protection of human subjects can directly involve you even if you never conduct research in your professional career.

The second part of the chapter focuses on principles of ethical treatment of human subjects, e.g., obtaining informed consent. The administrator familiar with what constitutes informed consent has a firm foundation for deciding on the appropriateness of research involving agency personnel or clients. The chapter considers privacy and confidentiality and presents strategies to protect confidentiality. Next, the chapter summarizes current federal regulations on protecting human research subjects. The chapter concludes with a discussion on administrative concerns, which should guide a decision whether or not to cooperate with a research effort.

ILLUSTRATIVE CASES

The Tuskegee Syphilis Study is the best known U.S. example of an egregious abuse of human subjects.[3] Begun in 1932 by the U.S. Public Health Service, the researchers monitored the health of two groups of African American males. One group had untreated syphilis; the other group was free of syphilis symptoms. The research documented the course of untreated syphilis. At the time the study began, treatments for syphilis were potentially dangerous, so denying treatment might have been rationalized. However, from the mid-1950s on, penicillin was known to be an effective treatment for syphilis and was widely available. Yet by 1973, when the study was discontinued, the participants had not received penicillin and were actively discouraged from seeking treatment elsewhere.

The failure to treat the subjects was particularly disturbing because the study continued unchallenged despite the findings of the Nuremberg Trials and a later lawsuit against the Jewish Chronic Disease Hospital. At the end of World War II, disclosure of Nazi atrocities included reports of abuses committed by doctors and scientists performing human experiments. The Nuremberg Military Tribunal judgment against these doctors and scientists listed 10 principles of moral, ethical, and legal medical experimentation on humans. The principles, referred to as the "Nuremberg Code,"[4] formed the basis for later regulations protecting human subjects.

The Tuskegee study did not comply with the Nuremberg principles. The violated principles included free and informed consent from the subjects, the researcher's obligation to avoid causing unnecessary physical suffering, the subject's ability to terminate his or her participation at any time, and the researcher's obligation to discontinue an experiment when its continuation could result in death.

In 1963 the issue of informed consent again received public attention. A lawsuit and investigation questioned whether 22 patients at Brooklyn's Jewish Chronic Disease Hospital (JCDH) had given informed consent when they agreed to be injected with live cancer cells.[5] The patients were asked if they would consent to an injection for research on immune system responses. They were not told that the experiment was unrelated to their disease or its treatment. They were not told that the injection contained live cancer cells. The investigation concluded that asking a patient to consent to a vaguely described procedure could not be considered informed consent. Still the publicity surrounding the JCDH case did not change the course of the Tuskegee study, which continued until 1973, when an ad hoc advisory committee to the Secretary of Health found that the study did not meet requirements for informed consent.

The knowledge of Nazi medical experiments, the Tuskegee study, and other reported cases has had a lasting effect. Most notably, withholding beneficial treatment from control-group subjects is considered unethical. Several controlled studies have been discontinued when a marked improvement occurred in the experimental group. Alternatively, if some treatment may be beneficial, but the most beneficial treatment remains unknown, the control-group subjects are assigned to a form of treatment. For example, in a study of depression, all subjects were assigned to some form of treatment. Each form of treatment was believed to be better than no treatment, but the relative effectiveness of the treatments was unknown. In addition, the Tuskegee study left as a legacy African Americans' distrust of medicine. African Americans are less likely to participate in medical research or to donate their organs for transplant. Polls conducted in 1990 found that roughly a third of African Americans thought it was at least possible that AIDS was a genocidal plot to infect them.[6]

The lack of informed consent is a theme that runs through most of the reported abuses of human subjects. The following cases illustrate other themes that have helped define ethical research practices. In 1954, researchers from the University of Chicago Law School secretly recorded jury deliberations. The investigators wanted to learn more about the jury processes, processes that were known only by anecdotes, post-trial interviews with jurors, and jury simulations. The researchers believed that open recording would affect and distort the deliberations. They conscientiously developed procedures to obtain undistorted information while protecting the rights of the parties involved. Only juries deliberating civil cases were studied, and the presiding judge and the attorneys representing the litigants gave their permission for the recording. After the recordings were made, they were kept with the judge until the case was closed.

As word of the jury study spread, a U.S. Senate subcommittee held a hearing to learn more. Despite the researchers' precautions to protect the jury members and other parties to a case and to avoid influencing the judicial processes, the research severely compromised the secrecy of jury deliberations. The potential harm was identified in a comment of the subcommittee's chairman, "Would a member of a jury hesitate to frankly express his opinion if he thought there might be a microphone hidden, taking down what they said? . . . [H]ow is he going to know whether in that particular case there is a microphone or not?"[7]

Research participants may lose their privacy. Privacy refers to an individual's ability to control the access of other people to information about himself. A loss of privacy may occur in deceptive research, where a participant is not told a study's real purpose. While few public administrators become directly involved in deceptive research, it is an issue associated with social science research. In a well-known deceptive study, a doctoral student, Laud Humphreys, studied men who engaged in casual, anonymous, sexual activities with other men. He found that these men were indistinguishable from other members of the community, rather than stereotypical deviates.

Humphreys offered to act as a lookout for men who were using a public rest room for sexual encounters. He recorded the license plate numbers of the unsuspecting, and unconsenting, subjects. He traced the licenses and linked them to the subjects' names and addresses. A year later he changed his hairstyle and manner of dress and took on the role of surveyor. He visited the homes of the previously identified subjects and asked them to participate in an anonymous public-health survey.

Critics questioned whether the benefits of Humphreys's research outweighed the costs.[8] Even if the risks of disclosing the subjects' identities were negligible, the extent of other risks was unknown and inestimable. Given the publicity surrounding the study, one can imagine the men figuring out that they were the subjects, experiencing a loss of privacy, and feeling used and betrayed by Humphreys.

Some social scientists argued that Humphreys had a right to pursue knowledge, that his strategy was appropriate to the question at hand, and that the subjects benefited from the revelation that they did not fit any commonly held, unsavory stereotype. Others believed that deceptive practices were morally wrong and demeaning to subjects. Some critics worried that knowledge of deceptive research studies might result in a general reaction against social science research.

Another deceptive research study illustrates the possibility that research subjects may gain unwanted information about themselves. Psychologist Stanley Milgram designed a study to see how ordinary people could be induced to obey authority. The research question was sparked by his interest in understanding how the Holocaust happened. The subjects were told that the experiment was to study learning theory. As part of the experiment, the subjects were told to administer what they believed were electric shocks to other participants. The other participants were actors, who vividly acted out the pain of the (nonexistent) "shocks."

Some subjects refused to continue administering the shocks and withdrew from the study. Others continued but were clearly distressed at their participation. The ethical problem that critics noted was that the subjects had learned that they would follow orders and seriously harm others. This self-knowledge may have never been gained without their participation in the experiment.

In addition, without their knowledge, subjects were forced to choose between two strong and competing values. On the one hand, they had an implied contract with the researcher to carry out the research as designed. On the other hand, they held the value of not harming another person.

Milgram was conscious of the study's potential to disturb the subjects, and his study included a careful debriefing procedure. A sample of participants was interviewed by a psychiatrist who was experienced in outpatient treatment; he reportedly found no evidence of injurious effects.[9] Milgram's own and others' follow-up research found that the self-knowledge had no lasting ill effects, and that some participants reported benefiting from the insight. Nevertheless, the case stands as a landmark in the history of deceptive research.

PRINCIPLES OF ETHICAL TREATMENT OF HUMAN SUBJECTS

In response to these and other reported abuses, The Belmont Report, written by the National Commission for the Protection of Human Subjects of Biomedical and Behavioral Research, identified three basic ethical principles: respect for persons, beneficence, and justice. Respect for persons requires that subjects enter into research voluntarily and with adequate information. Beneficence requires doing no harm and maximizing possible benefits and minimizes possible harm. Justice requires that research subjects are not selected "simply because of their easy availability, their compromised position, or their manipulability, rather than for reasons directly related to the problem at hand." To implement these principles requires that subjects give informed consent, that benefits and risks be identified and weighed, and that selection of subjects be fair.[10] Informed consent demonstrates respect for persons; assessing risks and benefits demonstrates beneficence, and fairly selecting subjects demonstrates justice.

Informed Consent

Informed consent is a cornerstone of ethical research practice. A subject must be given adequate information so he can make an informed, voluntary decision to participate. First, potential subjects need to know the general purpose of the study. This information provides a foundation for the subject's assessment of his costs and benefits. One author[11] suggested that in deceptive studies the subject may be told that deception is part of the research and that he is being asked to agree to participate without knowing the full details of the study's purpose.

Second, federal guidelines require that subjects be informed about the procedures, their purposes, and possible risks, including risks that are unknown. In other words subjects should be told what they will be expected to do and what will be done to them. This information should include information on discomfort, anxiety, unwanted information about oneself, or inconvenience.[12] In many studies subjects may be more concerned about inconveniences than they are about the procedures.

Third, potential subjects should be told why they were selected. While this is not required or even implied in the federal regulations, this practice strengthens the subject's understanding of a study's purpose, his importance to the study, and the fairness of the selection process.[13] We suspect that it also suggests to subjects questions they might want to ask about the confidentiality of the study.

Fourth, potential subjects should be told what will be done with the collected information. Who will receive the information from the study? What type of information will be disseminated? What steps will be taken to protect the identity of the subject? If photos, movies, recordings, or similar research records are being produced, the subject should know what will be done with them. We know of one student who was shocked to learn that an interview tape, produced as part of an experiment, was being shown to classes at her college.

Providing information about a study's purpose, procedures, and risks is only part of assuring voluntary participation. Other factors can compromise the voluntary nature of research participation. First, the subjects must understand the potential risks and the probable benefits. The way the risks and benefits is communicated must be appropriate to the subject population and the study. For example, in a research project that puts a subject at risk, oral consent is not adequate. Nor is just signing a statement adequate. Rather, the researcher needs to select words and techniques to ensure that subjects actually appreciate what is being asked of them.

Second, the relationship between the researcher and the potential subject may cloud the subject's judgment. For example, imagine a teacher who asks students to participate as research subjects. The teacher may state that participation is voluntary and will have no effect on class grades. Nevertheless, students may volunteer because they imagine that declining to participate may influence the teacher's feelings about them. The question is not whether a decision to participate or not to participate affects the teacher's grading or other class-related behaviors. Rather, if a student feels that his or her academic progress could be affected, then the decision to participate may not be voluntary.

Third, specific circumstances may impede a subject's ability to make a voluntary decision. Prisoners, members of the military, and schoolchildren, all of whom are in controlled settings, may interpret requests for information or participation as commands. Research involving prisoners is closely scrutinized.[14] Among prisoners, even modest benefits may act as inducements to participate, and these inducements will preclude a voluntary decision to participate.

Patients may mistakenly believe that their research participation will have a therapeutic benefit. Voluntary research participation requires clear, realistic information on the benefits and risks of participation. Participants should be told how research interventions may affect their present treatment. Still, the ability of seriously ill persons to give informed consent, no matter what they are told, is questionable. A *New York Times* article summed the problem as follows:

> Potential participants are often desperately ill and may grasp at any straw—even signing a document without reading it. For this reason, many say there is no such thing as informed consent only consent.[15]

Fourth, care must be taken in working with vulnerable populations, such as, children, aged people, and mentally disabled people, who may not be fully capable to make an informed decision or to protect their own interests. In general, researchers try to get informed consent from such subjects and from a legal guardian.

Finally, voluntary participation requires the ability to withdraw from a study at any time. The potential subject must be told this as part of informed consent. Furthermore, potential subjects must be told that other benefits they are entitled to will not be affected by their decision to participate or to discontinue their participation. For example, a client receiving public assistance must be told that his continued eligibility for assistance does not depend on participating in a research study.

Identifying and Weighing Costs and Benefits

People may not agree on the costs and benefits of research participation. Individuals' commitment to research, and their educational, social, and professional backgrounds contribute to what they see as risks and benefits and their importance. Consequently, informed consent requires that researchers, impartial reviewers, and potential subjects separately assess a proposed study and decide if the benefits outweigh the risks. Researchers may incorrectly assume that a proposed study presents minimal or no risk. They may overestimate the benefits of a study. Researchers are expected to be especially vigilant if potential subjects represent a distinctly different population from themselves. In such cases the researcher is more likely to misjudge what constitutes a risk or a benefit for a participant. She may erroneously assume that the way she requests consent is unbiased and informative.

To minimize the potential of overlooking risks, overestimating benefits, and assuming consent is informed and voluntary, an investigator should solicit the opinion of others. Most university-based research or biomedical research is reviewed by an Institutional Review Board (IRB), which determines that a proposed project adequately protects its human subjects. (IRBs are discussed in more detail later in this chapter.)

What are the benefits of participating in research? Sometimes the research involves a treatment that may relieve a physical or psychological problem. Sometimes the research may seem to benefit a group that a potential subject values.

For example, alumni may agree to participate in research on the effectiveness of their education because they believe that the findings will help future students. For some studies, perhaps most, the subject may participate because the research question seems somewhat interesting and the inconvenience is minimal. For some studies, remuneration is a valuable benefit. We know of a few graduate students who subsidized their incomes by participating as subjects for biomedical research projects. Paying subjects for the inconvenience of participating is not unethical, unless the remuneration is so large that it may be considered as a bribe or questionable inducement to participate.

What are the risks of participating in research? The most commonly cited risks are physical harm, pain or discomfort, embarrassment, loss of privacy, loss of time, and inconvenience. Other risks, alluded to in the illustrative cases, include undermining confidence in public institutions and lessening interpersonal trust. As part of informing a subject, he must be told what risks may occur during the study or as a result of the study. If the risks are unknown, or if researchers disagree on the risks, this information must be communicated to the subject.

Both risks and benefits may apply beyond individuals to include participants' families as well as society in general. Terminally ill patients may agree to participate in a study that promises to lead to a future cure. Nevertheless, a researcher must inform potential subjects only of benefits that can be reasonably expected. Theoretically, a study may be groundbreaking; however, most studies are not. Consequently, a subject should not be told that a study has a probability of generating significant knowledge. Nor should potential subjects be led to believe that they will gain benefits that are possible but unlikely. The jury study example suggested a project that would neither harm nor benefit its participants, but which could have had a serious negative effect on an important social institution.

Informed consent should give a potential subject the information she needs. The subject then is free to make her own decision about whether she wishes to participate or not. The greater the risk to a subject, the more extensive the informed consent procedures are required. For projects where a subject experiences no risks beyond the risks of everyday life or ordinary professional responsibilities, informed consent may be inferred. For example, mail and telephone surveys normally include some elements of informed consent primarily to entice respondents to participate, but detailed, signed statements may be reasonably viewed as unnecessary.

Selection of Subjects

Selection of research subjects should be unbiased and take into account who will benefit from the study. Examples such as the Tuskegee study and the Jewish Chronic Disease Hospital raised questions about studying vulnerable populations. Subsequently researchers and IRBs were expected to be especially diligent in reviewing work that relied on subjects from vulnerable populations and to make sure that appropriate measures were taken to solicit informed consent. The perspective on selection of subjects has shifted from exclusion to inclusion. Excluding certain groups from studies is also viewed as ethically questionable. For example, prior to the 1990s women were routinely excluded from clinical trials. Consequently, much more was known about men's health and how males reacted to various therapies than was known about women's health.[16]

The key principle in the ethical selection of a study population is distributive justice, e.g., the equitable distribution of research benefits and risks, treating like situations the same way, and offering equal access to participate in research.[17] Currently, the ethical debate on subject selection is confined to bio-medical research where both the individual risks and benefits can be quite high. Because each population is different, a general rule will not cover different racial and ethnic groups, institutionalized people, and international studies. Rather researchers should be aware of why they are studying a particular group and the ethical dimensions of their choice.

Selection of individual subjects should be fair. For example, in medical experiments people assigned to a placebo group may feel cheated and lobby to receive the experimental treatment. Placing a favored subject in a more beneficial treatment group or placing a disliked subject to a more risky treatment group is unethical. Note, in this example good research practice coincide with ethical practice.

The Ethical Guidelines of the American Statistical Association include sample size as an ethical consideration. Both an excessive number of subjects or an inadequate sample presents ethical problems. Similarly statisticians are asked to consider the value of the "data elements to be collected."[18]

PROTECTING PRIVACY AND CONFIDENTIALITY

Understanding the terms privacy, confidentiality, anonymity, and research records provides a basis for ethical research practice.[19] As we noted earlier, *privacy* refers to an individual's ability to control the access of other people to information about himself. *Confidentiality* refers to protection of information, so that researchers cannot or will not disclose records with individual identifiers. *Anonymity* refers to collecting information, so that researchers cannot link any piece of data to a specific, named individual. *Research records* refers to records gathered and maintained for the purpose of describing or making generalizations about groups of persons. Unlike administrative or clinical records, research records are not meant to make judgments about an individual or to support decisions that directly and personally affect an individual.

The requirements of voluntary participation and informed consent uphold the individual's right to have control over information about himself. While researchers may promise anonymity or confidentiality, a potential subject may not necessarily trust her to follow through. Guarantees of confidentiality neither ensure candor nor increase propensity to participate in research; rather, limited research has found that respondents tend to view promises of confidentiality skeptically.[20] Nevertheless, researchers must respect participant's privacy and maintain confidences as part of their professional responsibilities to subjects.

The need for trust may be greater with Internet surveys. The potential subject may not know the researcher, and in some cases wonder if the researcher has honestly identified herself, her affiliation, and her purpose. The potential subject may wonder what will happen to the information he provides, especially if he has no clear idea if anonymous responses are anonymous or how confidentiality will be maintained. For Internet surveys providing standard informed consent information on how respondents' identity will be protected and how their data will be used may be an ethical practice. It has the added benefit of increased response rates.[21]

Some research questions may seem unduly intrusive. Questions may stir up unpleasant recollections or painful feelings. Such topics include research on sexual behaviors, victimization, or discrimination. People who read pornography, have poor reasoning skills, or harbor controversial opinions may prefer to keep this information to themselves. Disclosure of behaviors such as drug use, child abuse, or criminal activity may cause a respondent to fear that she will be "found out." For a study of a sensitive topic to be ethical, (1) the psychological and social risks must have been identified, (2) the benefits of answering the research question must offset the potential risks, (3) the prospective subjects must be informed of the risks, and (4) promises of confidentiality must be maintained.[22]

In their thoughtful work on confidentiality,[23] Robert F. Boruch and Joe S. Cecil argue that asking for individual information encroaches upon people's privacy; consequently, researchers should seek methods to reduce the need to acquire data on identifiable individuals. Boruch and Cecil suggest that survey sampling and questioning techniques can "conserve privacy." Survey sampling reduces the number of people questioned. Surveyors may also reduce the number of questions each respondent answers. In large studies, all respondents may not be asked all questions. For example, a survey may have two forms. Some questions are on both forms, but many of the questions appear on just one of the forms. Fifty percent of the respondents are randomly given Form A, and 50 percent are given Form B. The smaller sample size and fewer questions asked of each respondent lessen the infringement on the target population's privacy.

To avoid the problems of confidentiality, the researcher may gather anonymous information. Anonymous participation occurs if no records are kept on the identity of subjects, and data cannot be traced back to a specific individual. An approach that approximates anonymity is to have the agency collect information and delete any information that directly identifies the respondents. This approach may be taken if revealing a client's identity to outsiders compromises the client's privacy. An agency may select the sample, distribute questionnaires, or collect data from agency files. Alternatively, an agency may ask clients' permission to give their names to the researchers.

Often anonymity is impossible. Researchers must know and record subject names to follow up on nonrespondents or to compare respondents and nonrespondents; to combine information from a subject with information from agency records; to carry out follow-up studies and collect information from an individual at different points in time; or to conduct a study audit to verify that the research was done and that accurate information was collected and reported.

Auditors may need access to identifiable records. Auditing can present problems of confidentiality, but without the possibility of conducting an audit, incompetence or malfeasance may go undetected and potentially cause even greater harm.

A researcher may keep a list with subjects' names separate from information collected on them. If information is obtained from more than one source, each person may be assigned an alias so that the information can be combined. The list of names and aliases should be kept separately from the collected data. A similar procedure may be used with longitudinal data, or the respondent may choose her own alias, that is, information that others could not easily obtain, such as her mother's birth date. The success of the latter depends on the subject's ability to consistently report the requested information.

Exactly how much care to take in protecting the identity of respondents varies from topic to topic. Some topics and some information require stringent safeguards. For the most part, social science researchers record individual information only to keep track of respondents and their data. They should take adequate safeguards to prevent disclosing identifiable information about an individual. Normally, such disclosure may be disquieting rather than harmful. Removing identifying information from the data and strictly limiting access to lists with subject names are sufficient for studies requiring stringent safeguards to protect confidentiality.

When reporting data, one should be sensitive to inadvertent disclosures. For example, if a state has very few female city managers, tables distinguishing between the responses of male and female city managers may compromise the confidentiality of the female managers. Similarly, case studies may require more elaborate procedures to protect identities, including pseudonyms, and alteration of some personal information, such as occupation.

Sharing research records constitutes special problems for confidentiality. As we discuss in the following chapter, data sharing and secondary analysis may reduce research costs and increase research quality. Nevertheless, once records leave the control of the researcher, issues of informed consent and confidentiality become a particular concern. In regard to informed consent, the subject may have agreed to participate in research for a specific purpose without giving blanket authorization for other uses. Researchers should inform potential subjects of anticipated future uses of the data, including their availability for independent verification of the study's implementation and replication of its analysis.[24] Before releasing data, the researcher should remove identifiers such as names, addresses, and telephone numbers.

A more formidable problem is that of *deductive disclosure.* If the names of participants in a research project are known, someone may be able to sort through the data to identify a specific person. Imagine a study of employee satisfaction in a state agency. With a list of respondents, someone may sort the data by age, race, sex, and position and deduce a respondent's identity. One way to protect against such abuses is to not disclose the list of respondents.[25]

Federal laws covering privacy and confidentiality are equivocal. The Privacy Act of 1974 regulates federal agencies' collection, management, and disclosure of individual information. Individuals must give written permission for identifiable records to be transferred to a person or another agency.[26] The act applies only to data collected directly by federal agencies; it does not cover data collected by state or local governments or federally funded projects.

The Privacy Act includes exceptions to the requirement for written permission. The exemptions allow for the transfer of records if individual identifiers have been removed and the individual's identity cannot be disclosed through deduction. Records may be transferred to the General Accounting Office in order to audit federal programs. Records may be transferred for law enforcement purposes. This proviso underscores the point that even if a researcher has promised confidentiality, research records are not automatically exempt from subpoena.

Government efforts to supersede promises of confidentiality are rare. An article published in 1983 identified 13 cases in which researchers had been subpoenaed.[27] As federally funded research began to include studies of sensitive subjects involving drug abuse and mental illness, laws were enacted to protect confidentiality. Boruch and Cecil speculate that problems of confidentiality are much more likely to occur in private research; for example, market researchers may disclose individual information to a client.[28]

FEDERAL POLICY ON PROTECTION OF HUMAN SUBJECTS AND INSTITUTIONAL REVIEW BOARDS

In 1991 a uniform federal policy, the Common Rule, for the protection of human subjects was published.[29] Its hallmark was a requirement that every institution receiving federal money for research involving human subjects create an *Institutional Review Board* (IRB) and appoint its members. The IRB determines if a proposed project meets the following requirements: (1) risks to subjects are minimized, (2) risks are reasonable in relation to anticipated benefits, (3) selection of subjects is equitable, (4) informed consent will be sought and appropriately documented, (5) appropriate data will be monitored to ensure the safety of subjects, and (6) adequate provisions exist for ensuring privacy of subjects and confidentiality of data.[30] Two of these criteria merit further mention. First, the long-range effects of the knowledge gained from the research are explicitly excluded in determining the risks and benefits of participation. Second, the policy reflects concern with possible abuses of vulnerable populations. IRBs are reminded to consider whether research on a specific population is consistent with an equitable selection of subjects and to make sure that these populations' vulnerability "to coercion or undue influence" has not been exploited.

To perform these tasks, an IRB as a whole should be professionally competent to adequately review the proposals it commonly receives and sensitive to general ethical issues, especially issues affecting "vulnerable" populations, for example, prisoners, children, pregnant women, people with mental or physical disabilities, and otherwise disadvantaged people. An institution should consider each appointee's training, race, gender, cultural background, and sensitivity to community attitudes.

Failure to comply with the Common Rule can result in termination or suspension of federal support, which is a powerful incentive to ensure that the IRBs are created and follow through on their responsibilities.

An IRB reviews all research involving human subjects under the purview of the institution. To review only publicly or privately supported research implies that only funded projects have to conform to ethical practices. To understand what an IRB does requires knowledge of what constitutes research and what constitutes a human subject.

Covered research is "a systematic investigation, including research development testing or evaluation, designed to develop or contribute to generalizable knowledge."[31]

A *human subject* is a "living individual about whom an investigator (whether professional or student) conducting research obtains (a) data through intervention or interaction with the individual, or (b) identifiable private information."[32]

The IRB chair first determines if a project is exempt from further review, appropriate for an expedited review, or must be subject to full review. Exempt and expedited projects receive less close scrutiny. These categories allow research involving minimal risk to avoid the long delays associated with a full IRB review. Minimal risk applies to those projects where the risks of participating in the research are similar to the risks of daily life.

When the Common Rule was developed, social scientists pointed out that policies rooted in biomedical research did not readily apply to three categories of research: surveys (questionnaires, interviews, and standard educational and psychological tests), observations of human behavior in public places, and demonstration projects.[33] Neither surveys nor observations of behavior in public places seemed to warrant obtaining and documenting informed consent. Survey participation involved very low risk, and consent could be inferred from respondents' willingness to participate and answer questions. A requirement for informed consent would virtually eliminate observation of public behavior as a research strategy.

The U. S. Department of Health and Human Services wanted demonstration projects exempt because needed studies could not be conducted if subjects could withdraw at any time or if they could receive entitled benefits if they refused to participate. A 1972 study required an experimental group of employable welfare recipients to accept public-sector employment; if they refused to work, their benefits were discontinued. Clearly, such a study would have problems with internal validity if subjects could change their experimental-group status at will. The study ended up in federal court, which ruled that the experiment was acceptable because it was consistent with the Social Security Act's objective to remove people from the welfare rolls and into gainful employment.[34]

The Common Rule exempts demonstration projects that study or evaluate public benefit or service programs, procedures for obtaining benefits or services under these programs, changes in or alternatives to the programs or procedures, and changes in the level or method of payment.[35] It implicitly allows IRBs to waive written documentation of informed consent for surveys and observation of public behaviors. Waivers are not permitted if responses could be traced to a specific individual and if disclosure could result in civil or criminal liability or damage subjects' financial standing, employability, or reputation.

The adequacy of the IRB system has recently been questioned and policy revisions are underway. A key motivator for examining the existing system was the 1999 death of an 18-year-old participant in a federally funded gene therapy study. He suffered from a disorder that was controlled by diet and drugs; he was not terminally ill. One of the immediate reactions was to pay more attention to informed consent forms, and to stress that having people sign informed consent forms was not sufficient evidence that they understood the information, especially the risks. Subsequently, federal agencies, advisory commissions, and research organizations have drafted and reviewed policies, which may culminate in "a unified, comprehensive federal policy embodied in a single set of regulations and guidance . . . that would apply to all types of research involving human participation." The policies have been drafted by persons in the fields of bio-ethics and bio-medical research. Nevertheless, these proposed policies will affect social science research, and social science organizations are monitoring and evaluating them.

To what extent do you have to concern yourself with IRB review? Federal policies protecting human subjects require compliance by Federal agencies, institutions, and individual researchers. These policies are more detailed than we have presented here. Furthermore, they are still evolving.[36] If you are a student or an employee of a university, a medical facility, or other institution that receives federal research funds, you should consult with your IRB before proceeding to conduct research that has you interacting with people, manipulating them, or using identifiable private information. Public administration students and professionals are most likely to conduct "research on individual or group characteristics or behavior . . . or research employing survey, interview, oral history, focus group, program evaluation, human factors evaluation or quality assurance."[37] All of which may be eligible for an expedited review.

BEYOND INFORMED CONSENT AND CONFIDENTIALITY: ISSUES OF INTEREST TO ADMINISTRATORS

As an administrator, the research studies you conduct or participate in may never involve risks beyond those experienced in everyday life. Nevertheless, you may be approached by researchers who want to study your clients. Administrators who work in educational, penal, or health-care institutions are especially likely to be approached by researchers. In considering the ethical aspects of research, the administrator's major interest is to make sure that the researcher implements standard procedures to reduce risks.

First, an administrator should get an overall picture of the planned study. Why does the researcher want to study her agency's clients or employees? How will the research subjects be chosen? Will they be anonymous or confidential? What steps will be taken to protect their identities? What will they be asked to do? How much time will it take? What are other potential risks? She will want to make sure that selection of research subjects or assignment into different experimental groups is fair and will be seen as equitable to both participants and non-participants.[38] To protect the identity and privacy of clients and employees, an agency representative should contact the affected people, explain the nature of the research, and seek their permission to give their names to the researchers. The researchers should not initiate contact with clients. Public announcements, such as posters, may be used to recruit employees or clients. Voluntary participation is less likely to be compromised with posted announcements than by personal solicitation.[39]

Second, the administrator should make certain that contacted clients understand that their eligibility for agency programs or services will not be affected by a decision to participate. Research with employees may be problematic. For employee participation to be voluntary, whether or not they decide to participate should not affect performance ratings or pay decisions, and this should be clearly communicated to the employee.[40]

Third, the administrator should review the informed-consent procedures. If subjects will be at risk, the administrator should remember that signing an informed consent form is not sufficient evidence that the subjects understood what was asked of them and the risks involved. The administrator may want to learn whether the researcher has submitted the research for review to the sponsoring institution. Universities and other institutions involved with human-subjects research have Institutional Review Boards (IRB), which review all research involving human subjects. We have found that some institutions have lax controls on reviewing unfunded research. The administrator may wish to check that a review has been held, simply to determine whether the researcher has sought the advice of others on ethical issues that could be raised by the research.

The administrator may want to engage the researcher in a discussion of potential risks. This lets the administrator decide whether the researcher has considered the ethical implications of the research. The administrator may learn more about research risks and improve his or her ability to judge the risks involved in later projects that come to the agency. Related to this, the administrator should check to see that subjects will be debriefed, if appropriate, at the end of their participation. For example, subjects who perform some task may be disappointed or frustrated about their performance. A debriefing offers the researcher an opportunity to observe any negative effects of the research and to answer questions or concerns that a subject may have.

Fourth, if the study involves creating a program, the administrator may want to find out what the researcher plans to do when the research is finished. In prisons or psychiatric hospitals, the subjects may participate in a research project, such as a therapy group, that seems to end prematurely because the researcher's data collection has ended. Employees or students may participate in an experimental course only to find that their new skills are not wanted by their employer or do not fit into their school's curriculum.

A sticky issue is what will become of the findings. If the agency feels that it should receive the research data, it should work out the details beforehand. This must be done if the researcher is going to act ethically and inform subjects of what will become of the information. If the agency, whether it employs the subjects or provides them with benefits, is going to get individual information, then the subjects must be told this as part of giving their informed consent.

The American Psychological Association guidelines recommend that subjects be informed if the researcher plans to release anonymous data to a databank. The guidelines also recommend that even if researchers are confident the participants' identities will be protected, they should not release data that could reasonably be expected to violate the participants' agreement to participate. For example, we can imagine data gathered on union workers going into a data bank and later being analyzed by someone in order to support a strong anti-union position. The original participants may have cooperated in good faith to benefit members of their profession and resent it if the information was used for ends that they consider repugnant.

Fifth, the administrator should consider how the proposed research may affect the agency's reputation. No matter what the agency's role, its reputation may be enhanced by research that others consider valuable and harmed by research that they consider worthless or intrusive. An administrator may question whether a planned study will unduly infringe on respondents' privacy or abuse their time. He should decide if a study requiring agency resources, including time, represents a good use of the public's money. He should be convinced that a study will yield valued information. Unreliable items and items that serve no clear purpose cannot yield valued information. Studies that assume that others will act on the findings should be reviewed by relevant actors, or at least the investigators should try to anticipate their reactions realistically. Unreliable items, unwanted items, or unwanted studies waste respondents' time. Items that are not operationally valid may abuse respondents' goodwill, insofar as their responses contribute to incorrect or misleading conclusions. To ensure that a proposed study provides usable and useful information, administrators should review research instruments, make sure that the researchers pretested all instruments, and established their reliability and operational validity.

The detrimental effects of an unwanted or poorly designed study go beyond the respondents. Future studies also are affected. Seeking too much information or seeking it too often can build resistance to future requests for information. Consider the complaints of businesses and state and local governments that must churn out data only to meet federal information requests. A similar outcome may occur if respondents perceive that the data are merely collected but not used.

SUMMARY

The specific regulations of protecting human research subjects may seldom impinge on the day-to-day data collection and analysis efforts of public administrators. Most research conducted by administrators does not put subjects at more than minimal risk. Nevertheless, administrators may participate in research efforts that have ethical implications. In addition, administrators may cooperate with researchers who want to study agency employees or clients. While such researchers may be covered by existing regulations, the administrator still must protect the rights of his or her employees or agency clients.

Obtaining informed consent is central to most research on humans. Informed consent means that a subject agrees to participate after receiving information on the purpose of the study, the potential risks associated with participating, and the probable benefits associated with participating. The information should be clear; the investigators should not oversell the benefits of participating nor discount social or psychological discomfort. Subjects must be told what will be done to them and what will be expected of them. Although informed consent may need to be documented, this should not take precedence over making sure that subjects understand what is being asked of them.

The participation of subjects must be voluntary. Participants may receive incentives, but they should not be so large or attractive that they act as an inducement. Researchers who maintain a professional or personal relationship with potential subjects must be aware that the relationship may make a request to participate in research exploitive and preclude the possibility of voluntary participation. Potential subjects must be told that their eligibility for benefits, other than benefits associated directly with participation, does not depend on participation. Similarly, their continued eligibility for benefits cannot be affected if they decide to withdraw from a study. As part of the informed-consent process, the potential subject must be informed that he or she can withdraw from the research at any time.

Potential subjects should be told what will be done with the information after the study is completed. The research records should not be made available to others, including a subject's parents, physician, or employer without the subject's explicit permission. This prohibition does not preclude allowing authorized auditors to examine records to verify the integrity of the research; however, the procedures for an audit must take proper precautions to maintain confidentiality, and disclosure to auditors should be part of the informed consent. If data are to be sent to a databank, the researcher should remove identifying information and take precautions to prevent deductive disclosure of a person's identity.

Agencies that receive federal money for research involving human subjects must have an Institutional Review Board (IRB), which reviews and approves all research involving human subjects. The IRB may expedite review of research involving minimal risk to subjects and waive certain aspects of informed consent for research involving surveys, observations of human behavior, and social experiments sponsored by a government agency or government officials. Whether IRB approval is required or not, researchers and project sponsors should satisfy themselves that a study adequately protects human research subjects.

The administrator who agrees to have research conducted with an agency's cooperation should interview the researcher and ascertain that the researcher will employ standard ethical practices and use appropriate procedures to get informed consent. Procedures for selecting subjects and assigning them to experimental groups must be perceived as fair by both participants and non-participants. Care must be taken that clients recognize that participation will not affect services they receive from the agency, and employees must know that their participation does not affect their working conditions. The administrator will want to learn, as appropriate, whether subjects will be debriefed and how research programs, such as therapy groups, will be terminated. If the agency expects to have access to the research data, this must be worked out beforehand and included in the information given to obtain a potential subject's informed consent.

Chapter 9 discusses the use of data that have been gathered earlier and stored. Acquisition of preexisting, or secondary, data eliminates the time and cost required to design and implement a data collection instrument. Use of existing data also decreases the burdens placed on the people and agencies that are queried for information. The chapter covers: how investigators may locate secondary data; what information is required to acquire, verify, and document them; the content of some major studies conducted by the Bureau of the Census. While secondary data have distinct benefits, they may be inadequate or inappropriate for the planned study. Furthermore, as this chapter has indicated, ethical considerations may rule out the use of existing data.

NOTES

1. L. K. Altman, "Volunteer in Asthma Study Dies After Inhaling Drug," *The New York Times,* June 15, 2001.
2. K. Sucato, "Education; Student Survey's Unexpected Lessons," *The New York Times,* Feb. 5, 2001.
3. N. Hershey and R. D. Miller, *Human Experimentation and the Law* (Germantown, ND: Aspen Systems Corporation, 1976), 8–10, summarizes the bureaucratic history of the Tuskegee study. Hershey and Miller made the observation that the Tuskegee study continued during this period when protection of human subjects was receiving so much attention.
4. For the text of the Nuremberg Code, see Jay Katz, *Experimentation with Human Beings* (New York: Russell Sage Foundation, 1972), 305–306.
5. Katz, *Experimentation,* 10–65, reproduced a slightly edited version of the record from the investigation. Hershey and Miller, *Human Experimentation,* on 6–7, summarize the issues.
6. J. H. Jones, *Bad Blood: The Tuskegee Syphilis Experiment* (New York: Free Press, 1993), 221.
7. Katz, *Experimentation,* 68–103, reproduced material from the hearings. The subcommittee chairman was Senator James O. Eastland. His quote is found on page 80 of Katz's book.
8. This summary of the critics' points of view is based on information from T. L. Beauchamp et al., *Ethical Issues in Social Research* (Baltimore: The Johns Hopkins University Press, 1982), 11–15. Edited versions of key criticisms also are found in Katz, *Experimentation,* 325–329.

9. Katz, *Experimentation,* 358–365, reprints Milgram's description of the study; on pages 403–405 Katz has reprinted some of the reactions to the Milgram study.
10. *The Belmont Report: Ethical Principles and Guidelines for the Protection of Human Subjects of Research.* (Washington, D.C.: The National Commission for the Protection of Human Subjects of Biomedical and Behavioral Research, April, 1976), 4–6.
11. See Hershey and Miller, *Human Experimentation,* 31, 68–70. Also see *Ethical Principles in the Conduct of Research with Human Participants* (Washington, D.C.: American Psychological Association, 1982), Principle E.
12. See *Protecting Human Research Subjects: Institutional Review Board Guidebook* (Office for Protection from Research Risks, National Institutes of Health, U.S. Dept. of Health and Human Services, 1993), 3-2–3-7 and 3-11–3-13.
13. This suggestion is made by Hershey and Miller, *Human Experimentation,* 33.
14. On May 19, 2000, the Division of Human Subjects Protections issued a memorandum "OPRR Guidance on Approving Research Involving Prisoners." The memo is at the Office for Protection from Research Risks website (ohrp.osophs.dhhs.gov/humansubjects/guidance/prison.html).
15. L. K. Altman, "Fatal Drug Trial Raises Questions about 'Informed' Consent," *New York Times,* Oct. 5, 1993, B7.

16. N. Kass, "Gender and Research," in J. P. Kahn, A. C. Mastroianni, and J. Sugarman, eds., *Beyond Consent: Seeking Justice in Research* (New York: Oxford University Press, 1998), 67–87.

17. C. R. McCarthy, "The Evolving Story of Justice in Federal Research Policy," in J. P. Kahn, A. C. Mastroianni, and J. Sugarman, eds., *Beyond Consent: Seeking Justice in Research* (New York: Oxford University Press, 1998), 11.

18. American Statistical Association, Ethical Guidelines for Statistical Practice (1999). The Guidelines are available on the association's website (www.amerstat. org/profession/ethicalstatistics.html).

19. R. F. Boruch and J. S. Cecil, *Assuring the Confidentiality of Social Research Data* (Philadelphia: The University of Pennsylvania Press, 1979), 23–27.

20. A. G. Turner, "What Subjects of Survey Research Believe about Confidentiality," in *The Ethics of Social Research: Surveys and Experiments*, ed. J. E. Sieber (New York: Springer-Verlag, 1982), 151–165.

21. H. Cho and R. LaRose, "Privacy Issues in Internet Surveys," *Social Science Computing 17* (Winter 1999): 421–434.

22. For an extensive discussion of procedures to protect privacy, applicable federal laws, and an extensive bibliography, see *Protecting Human Research Subjects*, 3-27–3-37, 3-56. Readers interested in strategies for identifying and questioning subjects about sensitive topics may wish to read the cases in C. M. Renzetti and R. M. Lee, eds., *Researching Sensitive Topics* (Newbury Park: Sage Publications, 1992).

23. R. F. Boruch and J. S. Cecil, "Statistical Strategies for Preserving Privacy in Direct Inquiry," in *The Ethics of Social Research: Surveys and Experiments*, ed. J. E. Sieber (New York: Springer-Verlag, 1982), 207–232.

24. T. E. Hedrick, "Justifications and Obstacles to Data Sharing," in *Sharing Research Data*, eds. S. E. Fienberg, M. E. Martin, and M. L. Straf (Washington, D.C.: National Academy Press, 1985), 136. Hedrick cites sources that discuss this issue in more depth. See also the Ethical Guidelines in Statistical Practice D4.

25. For strategies to prevent deductive disclosure, see J. Steinberg, "Social Research Use of Archival Records: Procedural Solutions to Privacy Problems," in *Solutions to Ethical and Legal Problems in Social Research*, eds. R. F. Boruch and J. S. Cecil (New York: Academic Press, 1983), 249–261, and Boruch and Cecil, *Assuring the Confidentiality of Social Research Data*, chap. 7.

26. For detailed information on the Privacy Act, see an annual copy of Freedom of Information Act Guide and Privacy Act Overview (Washington, D.C.: Office of Information and Privacy, U.S. Department of Justice); J. S. Cecil and E. Griffin, "The Role of Legal Policies in Data Sharing," in *Sharing Research Data*, eds. S. E. Fienberg, M. E. Martin, and M. L. Straf (Washington, D.C.: National Academy Press, 1985), 161–167. Boruch and Cecil, *Assuring the Confidentiality of Social Research Data*, 245–249, have a good summary of the act and its implications for research.

27. C. R. Knerr, Jr., "What to Do Before and After a Subpoena of Data Arrives," in *The Ethics of Social Research: Surveys and Experiments*, ed. J. E. Sieber (New York: Springer-Verlag, 1982), 191–206. In addition to citing cases, the author provides an overview of legal protections. No major new developments have occurred since then (C. M. Renzetti and R. M. Lee, "Overview and Introduction," in *Researching Sensitive Topics*, 9–10).

28. Boruch and Cecil, *Assuring the Confidentiality of Social Research Data*, 26.

29. U.S. Science and Technology Policy Office, "45 Code of Federal Regulations 46 (45 CFR 46) Federal Policy for the Protection of Human Subjects: Notices and Rules," *Federal Register 56*. (June 18, 1991): 28002–28018.

30. 45 CFR 46 Section 46.111

31. 45 CFR 46 Section 46.102(d)

32. 46 CFR 46 Section 46.102(f)

33. A discussion of the problems with the initial guidelines issued by DHHS is found in M. J. Breger's "Randomized Social Experiments and the Law," in *Solutions to Ethical and Legal Problems in Social Research*, eds. R. F. Boruch and J. S. Cecil (New York: Academic Press, 1983), 97–144.

34. Breger, "Randomized Social Experiments and the Law," 104–105, citing material from *Aguayo v. Richardson*, 352 F. Supp. 462 (S.D.N.Y. 1972).

35. 45 CFR 46 Section 46.110

36. An excellent source of current activity is the Office of Human Research Protections Web page (http://ohrp. osophs.dhhs.gov). For social science concerns see J-P Hauck, "Reforming Human Subjects Protection: The Beat Goes On," *PS: Political Science and Politics*, (June 2001), and C. Shea, "Don't Talk to the Humans: The Crackdown on Social Science Research," *Linguafranca 10* (September 2000).

37. "Categories of Research that May be Reviewed by the Institutional Review Board (IRB) through an Expedited Review Procedure." (Washington, D.C.: Office of Human Research Protection), November 1998 63 FR 60364-60367.

38. For a more detailed discussion on recruiting volunteers, employees, and vulnerable populations, see *Protecting Human Subjects*, chap. 6 and A. J. Kimmel, *Ethical Issues in Behavioral Research* (Cambridge, MA: Blackwell Publishers, 1996), 215–235.

39. *Protecting Human Subjects*, 6–53.

40. Ibid, 6–55.

TERMS FOR REVIEW

subjects at risk
informed consent
voluntary research
    participation

privacy
confidentiality
anonymity
deductive disclosure

research records
Institutional Review Board
human subject

QUESTIONS FOR REVIEW

The following questions should indicate whether you have a basic competency in this chapter's material.

1. What four main pieces of information must a potential research subject have to give informed consent? Explain why for each.

2. How are informed consent and voluntary participation related to each other?

3. To learn if traumatic events are associated with drug abuse, researchers propose to interview drug abusers about their childhood and adolescence. The researchers know that the interview may be painful and cause participants emotional distress. What should an IRB consider before allowing the research to be conducted?

4. What types of benefits should a potential participant be told about? How expansive should an investigator be when informing potential participants about the benefits of participation?

5. What types of risks should a potential participant be told about? How expansive should an investigator be in informing potential participants about the risks of participation?

6. Why is debriefing subjects important? What is the role of debriefing in lessening the risks to the subject? of teaching the researcher more about the risks of participation?

7. Explain why the following may be considered inappropriate:
    a. A principal asking teachers in her school to participate in a study she is doing for a graduate class
    b. Giving each return envelope in an "anonymous" survey a different box number so that each participant can be identified
    c. Explaining in English the planned research to potential participants who recently immigrated from Asia
    d. A social agency turning over a list of clients to researchers who are studying how clients view agency services
    e. Conducting research on developmentally disabled adults based on the consent of their guardians and not the subjects

8. Explain the difference between collecting confidential and anonymous information. Under what circumstances will a researcher prefer confidential information? Under what circumstances will a researcher prefer anonymous information?

PROBLEMS FOR HOMEWORK AND DISCUSSION

1. Imagine you head a large agency, such as a school district. Outline a protocol for approving research involving agency employees and/or clients.

2. How does a researcher identify the risks associated with his or her studies?

3. A researcher proposes testing an accelerated math program on talented third-graders in a school system. The program will last for one year, although data collection on participants may continue through elementary school. What risks do you foresee for children who participate in the program?

4. A young researcher contends that never putting subjects at risk is the only ethical way to conduct research. Comment on this position.

5. The American Statistical Association ethical guidelines imply that having too many subjects or too few are ethical concerns. Why do you think that this is so?

6. Does your college or university have an IRB? Who is on it? Obtain a copy of its policies for human-subjects research. How is survey research handled? How is research involving agencies (such as program evaluations) handled?

7. Find a consent form and identify the components critical to giving informed consent. Are any pieces of critical information missing?

8. A researcher is studying the effectiveness of educational programs offered to prisoners. In his interviews with prisoners, he learns that several of them smuggle drugs. Should he inform the prison authorities? Why or why not?

9. A researcher conducts genetic tests on subjects. One genetic test shows that Mary Doe carries the gene for Huntington's Disease. What should the researcher tell Mary Doe?

10. Investigators are conducting a 24-month demonstration project to study the effectiveness of a job-training project. The investigators propose to randomly assign persons eligible for job training to either an experimental or control group. Control group members will neither receive training nor will project staff inform them of other training opportunities. Comment on the ethics of this proposal.

11. Why is debriefing subjects important? What is the role of debriefing in lessening the risks to the subject?

RECOMMENDED FOR FURTHER READING

For excellent sources on cases and issues that define ethical treatment of human subjects, see Jay Katz, *Experimentation with Human Beings: The Authority of the Investigator, Subject, Professions, and State in the Human Experimentation Process* (New York: Russell Sage Foundation, 1972); T. L. Beauchamp et al., *Ethical Issues in Social Research* (Baltimore: The Johns Hopkins University Press, 1982); A. J. Kimmel, *Ethical Issues in Behavioral Research* (Cambridge, MA: Blackwell Publishers, 1996). *The Final Report of the Advisory Committee on Human Radiation* (Washington, DC: Government Printing Office, 1996), is a history of human-subject experimentation that includes previously classified documents. Also see James H. Jones, *Bad Blood: The Tuskegee Syphilis Experiment,* new and expanded edition; (New York: Free Press, 1993).

For up-to-date information on federal policies affecting human subject research the following home pages are recommended: Office of Human Subjects Research, National Institutes of Health (http://ohsr.od.nih.gov) and the Office for Human Research Protections, U.S. Department of Health and Human Services (http://ohrp.osophs.dhhs.gov). The OHRP section on "Policy Guidance" contains copies of regulations and other documents. The section on educational materials includes an on-line copy of the IRB Guidebook as well as self-instructional materials.

The APA's *Ethical Principles in the Conduct of Research with Human Participants* (Washington, D.C.: American Psychological Association, 1982) is a basic source listing and explaining guidelines for ethical work with human subjects. The ethical guidelines of other professional associations including historians, anthropologists, statisticians, sociologists, and program evaluators have ethical guidelines (available on their professional societies home pages), which are worth consulting to get a better understanding of the ethical issues.

R. F. Boruch and J. S. Cecil, *Assuring the Confidentiality of Social Research Data* (Philadelphia: The University of Pennsylvania Press, 1979), cover issues associated with confidentiality, strategies for maintaining confidentiality, and legal issues.

Comprehensive books and papers on ethical issues include: R. F. Boruch and J. S. Cecil, *Assuring the Confidentiality of Social Research Data* (Philadelphia: The University of Pennsylvania Press, 1979); *The Ethics of Social Research: Surveys and Experiments,* ed. J. E. Sieber (New York: Springer-Verlag, 1982); J. P. Kahn, A. C. Matroianni, and J. Sugarman, eds., *Beyond Consent: Seeking Justice in Research,* (New York: Oxford University Press, 1998, which focuses on equitable selection of subjects and relies on bio-medical concerns; and *Solutions to Ethical and Legal Problems in Social Research,* eds. R. F. Boruch and J. S. Cecil (New York: Academic Press, 1983).

Chapter 9

Secondary Data Analysis: Finding and Analyzing Existing Data

In this chapter you will learn

1. strategies for identifying, accessing, and evaluating the quality of secondary data.
2. advantages and disadvantages of secondary data analysis.
3. the general content of major U.S. Census Bureau population surveys and vital records.
4. about using census data.

In our eagerness to get a study under way, we may overlook the possibility that appropriate data may already be available. Similarly, we may avoid examining problems with data needs that exceed our data-gathering capacity. Secondary data can provide inexpensive, high-quality data adequate to define or solve a problem.

Secondary data are existing data that investigators collected for a purpose other than the given research study. Secondary data may result from the research efforts of an individual researcher, a research team, an agency division, or a research organization. The data may have been collected for a specific study, as part of a database, or to monitor agency performance. Other investigators with differing backgrounds, needs, and questions regularly consult and use secondary data.

An individual researcher or research team may have gathered, compiled, and analyzed the data and written the report. Typically, researchers collect more data than they analyze. They ask questions that turn out to be unreliable or not operationally valid. Investigators drop questions from the analysis because they do not improve the solution, or they are simply overlooked. In writing a questionnaire, the investigators may act as if information is free. They add questions with vague plans to analyze them later, but typically investigators run out of time and their interests shift.

Organizations collect and store data for many purposes. Managers consult data to monitor spending, personnel activity, resources acquired and spent, and productivity. Managers review specific pieces of data, such as performance indicators, at regular intervals as part of their management responsibilities. Managers depend on data to track the performance of agency subdivisions. They use existing data to estimate demand for services and the resources needed to meet the demand. No matter why data are collected and stored, they may be retrieved and combined to answer a range of questions beyond those originally asked.

Statistical organizations, including the U.S. Census Bureau, state offices of vital statistics, public-opinion polling firms, and university research groups, such as the InterUniversity Consortium for Political and Social Research, exist to collect, compile, and interpret data. Professional associations, such as the International City/County Management Association (ICMA), and public-interest groups routinely collect and publish survey data on topics of interest to their members. Investigators with differing backgrounds, needs, and questions consult and use such data regularly.

In this chapter we survey the benefits and costs of using secondary data and how to identify appropriate databases, gain access to them, and evaluate their quality and applicability to a study. Next, we introduce you to a few important data sources. The chapter gives an overview of the contents of the Census of Governments and two population surveys that the U.S. Census Bureau conducts.

WORKING WITH SECONDARY DATA

The Benefits and Costs of Secondary Data Analysis

Secondary data analysis markedly reduces a researcher's costs. He can dispense with the costs of instrument design, data collection, and compilation. It has other benefits as well. Secondary data analysis enables researchers to conduct studies that are otherwise unfeasible. It opens up research to public scrutiny, thereby allowing for verification, refinement, or refutation of the original results. It can improve research quality.

Secondary data analysis may be necessary if investigators want comparative or longitudinal data. Consider a study to analyze the feminization of poverty, that is, the perception that women and children make up a disproportionate segment of the poor. The investigators examined patterns of women's labor force participation, the availability of social welfare, and the diffusion of single-parent households in the United States and other industrialized nations.[1]

The investigators could not have conducted their study without government statistics. The investigators would have had to dig through records, some in languages other than English, to compile the data. Searching records requires time and money; hiring translators adds even more expenses. One also must locate the appropriate records and get permission to review them. If records do not exist, a cross-sectional study might have been tried. Logistic requirements would have restricted the study population. Including time-series data seems out of the question.

Relying on government statistics has limitations. The researchers have to determine that the data are sufficiently reliable and comparable. The design may have to be modified if data for certain years or for some countries are missing or unattainable. Such modifications may introduce bias. For example, we assume that there is a difference between those countries that share their data and those that do not.

Secondary analysis is a necessary component for an open science; it allows others to scrutinize a researcher's work. In the field of public policy, scrutiny can be especially important. Secondary analysis may be undertaken if the investigator's veracity is questioned; however, it is more likely to occur within the context of challenging and improving research that affects policy decisions.

M. H. Maier's book, *The Data Game,* demonstrates the use of secondary analysis to investigate policy questions and the value of scrutinizing reported findings. The book includes thumbnail sketches of policy controversies fueled by analysis of publicly available data, for example, "Does capital punishment deter murder?" "Are the rich getting richer?" "Is the work place safe?" Maier concludes that the misuse of statistical data, for example, treating a short-term change as a long-term trend, and different conceptual definitions of phenomena, such as white-collar crime, illiteracy, and a nation's economic health, contribute to such policy debates.[2]

Analysts working with existing data may reexamine the findings by including supplemental data, adapting the measures, or applying different statistical models. Their efforts may confirm and extend the research findings. If their work contradicts the original research, their findings may contribute to greater insight into the complexity of the policy issue and its solution.

Ideally, secondary analysis should improve the quality of data collection and documentation. The researcher who knows that her work will be scrutinized may pay more attention to documenting the research process: the decisions that were made about which variables to include and how to measure them; the results of pretests; the sampling design and possible nonsampling errors; and the details of how data were compiled and analyzed. An investigator working with secondary data may have his mind jogged. He may think creatively about the research design and have insights on better ways to measure the concepts or to analyze the data. His experience is analogous to most researchers' reactions when they analyze their own data, and they find themselves rethinking the research design, including their model and how they measured the variables.

While secondary data reduce the costs of the secondary analyst, they can increase the costs to the initial investigators.[3] They may incur costs in increased data preparation and documentation. In modest studies many of the details are carried in the investigator's memory. Modest studies have their place, but public administrators and investigators should not absolve themselves of proper documentation and retention of research records. Later analysis of existing data can prevent needless requests for information from subjects or replication of earlier mistakes.

Finding Secondary Data

If you want to find out whether data exist to meet your needs, where do you begin? Technology is rapidly changing search techniques, and the number of databases available electronically is constantly expanding. Official statistics, national surveys, and other data can be accessed through the Internet. Internet search engines may help identify potential databases. Nevertheless, any given search engine may "miss" obvious websites. A search engine can direct you to an out-of-date, biased, or poorly maintained database. As we write, no surefire, efficient method exists to locate needed data. (For example we spent several hours searching for smoking data for a homework problem in Chapter 2.) With the changing technology, such as improvements in constructing and maintaining Web pages, and variations in licensing agreements, a reference librarian may be the best source of suggestions on how to conduct an on-line search.

Published works should indicate where their data came from, alerting you to databases that you may wish to examine. Some works cite privately held data, that is, data owned by the researcher or a private organization. You may infer that a database contains variables of interest from the description of its sample, purpose, general content, or from the identity of the agency sponsor(s). You may or may not have access to these data, depending on the willingness of the researcher or her sponsors to make them available or to perform requested analyses for you. Even your access to public data may be limited by confidentiality guarantees to the respondents.

Reference librarians can alert you to other resources for locating databases. Some databases are located almost by luck. Throughout agencies and universities, there are individuals who hold data. Administrators or analysts may conduct a survey, analyze the data, and write up the findings. The data may have been entered into a computer file with little or no formal documentation of their existence, or paper questionnaires may be stored on an office shelf. Inventories of agency databases may reduce the waste of underanalyzed data and redundant studies; however, the cost of documenting, storing, and protecting confidentiality may offset the benefits.

Database Access

Identifying a database is only half the battle. The researcher must determine whether he can access it, and he must review its documentation. Poor documentation or the inability to access a database may eliminate it from consideration.

For some research questions, investigators may be able to confine themselves to aggregated and published data. Example 9.1 shows how a researcher compiled information from four published sources to study factors associated with public-employee work stoppages. The researchers studied variations in work stoppages among the states because local government statistics were not published at the time the research was conducted.

Compiling aggregated data can be tedious. A researcher who relies on aggregated and summarized data is limited in the analysis he can perform. For maximum

EXAMPLE 9.1

Combining Aggregated Databases

Problem: Academic researchers wanted to identify factors associated with work stoppages from strikes, walkouts, and lockouts.

Strategy:

1. Collect data for one year (1973) measuring: number of public-employee work stoppages, number of public employees involved, and number of public employee-days lost.
2. Identify sets of variables measuring: state social and economic characteristics; local government structure and finance; local government workforce characteristics; state policies regarding local government collective bargaining.
3. Identify data sources measuring variables.
4. Conduct analysis: use factor analysis to combine variables into summary measures (see Chapter 10); covary summary measures with numbers of work stoppages, employees participating in work stoppages, and employee-days idle from work stoppages.

Unit of analysis: States of the United States.
Sample: All 50 states.
Variables measuring state social and economic characteristics:

1. Percentage of state population urban, 1970
2. Percentage of nonagricultural workforce that has union membership, 1972
3. Right-to-work law
4. Percentage of state population below low-income level, 1969
5. State per capita income, 1973
6. State median family income, 1969
7. Percentage of state population of African Americans, 1970
8. Percentage of state population employed in nonagricultural establishments, 1973
9. Employee-days idle/million nonagricultural employees, 1972
10. State population density, 1970

Data sources for variables in study:

1. Council of State Governments, *The Book of the States* (Lexington, KY: Council of State Governments).
2. U.S. Dept. of Labor, *Summary of State Policy Regulations for Public Sector Labor Relations* (Washington, D.C.: U.S. Government Printing Office, 1973).
3. U.S. Census Bureau, *Public Employment in 1972* (Washington, D.C.: U.S. Government Printing Office, 1973).
4. ———, *Statistical Abstract of the United States* (Washington, D.C.: U.S. Government Printing Office).

Continued

EXAMPLE 9.1 *Continued*

Illustration of data compilation procedures for Alabama:

1. From *Summary of State Policy Regulations,* determine whether Alabama has right-to-work law; code "yes" or "no."
2. From *Public Employment in 1972,* copy data for Alabama on: percent non-agricultural workforce that has union membership and employee-days idle/million nonagricultural employees.
3. Copy Alabama data on other variables from specified data sources.

Discussion: First, actual study collected data on 40 variables. Second, all data were collected or aggregated at the state level. A preferable unit of analysis would have been local governments. The researchers did not sample local governments because statistics on some variables of interest were not published for local governments. Third, all the dependent variable data were for 1973, and independent data variables were for 1973 or earlier. Earlier data were the most recent available statistics and were assumed to be the best estimate of 1973 values.

SOURCE: J. L. Perry and L. J. Berkes, "Predicting Local Government Strike Activity," *Western Political Quarterly 30*(4): 1977.

flexibility, investigators require access to individual records for their analysis. They may get access in one of three ways:

1. Through extracted files, containing a portion of the data
   a. a sample of cases, or
   b. a subset of variables on all cases
2. Through direct access to the database
   a. a purchase of the computer tape(s), CD-ROMs, or other electronic media
   b. a direct link allowing the investigator to access the database
3. Through an agreement for the database holder to perform the requested manipulations

Of course, the investigator has no guarantee that he can access the database at all, especially if it is held by a nonpublic agency. Agency policy and his affiliation with the agency affect whether he can access data stored on an agency information system. The goodwill of the original researcher largely determines whether he can access individually held data. Contractual agreements may either guarantee or prohibit public access. Furthermore, confidentiality considerations may limit his access to the database or his ability to perform certain tabulations.[4]

Locating and accessing public data is becoming easier all the time. The University of Michigan's Document Center (http://www.lib.umich.edu/libhome/Documents.center/stats.html) has a comprehensive list of publicly available data and databases organized by subject matter. The user should be able to easily locate needed data and receive information on how to access them. Some databases can be analyzed or downloaded on-line. Other databases are available for purchase. FedStats (http://www.fedstats.gov) is similar to the Michigan site. FedStats directs users to publicly available Federal data. Users can easily track trends and access official statistics. Each state has a state data center that provides users with technical assistance in accessing and using Census and other public data.

Accessing data involves more than locating the database and receiving authorization to use it. The documentation accompanying the database affects the ability of a researcher to access it, manipulate it, and interpret the results. To access a database with a computer, an analyst needs specific information, such as the file name, and to know how the data are organized and structured.

Verifying the Database

After a database is downloaded or arrives at a research site, its content and scaling should be verified. We know of instances where investigators put a dataset aside until they were ready to do the analysis, only to discover the dataset was seriously flawed. To verify a database's content, an analyst confirms that: (1) the number of cases or records conforms to the number indicated in the documentation; (2) variables listed in the documentation have actually been downloaded or are on the tape, disk, or CD-ROM; and (3) summary statistics reported in the documentation can be confirmed. Any discrepancies should be resolved. An error may have been made in downloading the data, or the wrong data may have been sent. Furthermore, the possibility that errors can be traced and resolved decreases as time passes, and people involved in the collection, documentation, and compilation of the original database can no longer be reached.

Next, the scaling should be verified. This may have been done as part of documenting the content, but, if not, the researcher should review the variables of interest or a sample of variables. He should check that codes appearing on the computer printout conform to the codes found in the documentation. For example, if the documentation indicates that males are coded as "1," females as "2," and missing as "9," no other codes should appear on the printout. Also, the frequency of each code should conform to the frequency found in the documentation. For example, if the documentation states that 49 percent of the sample was male, 50 percent female, and 1 percent unknown or missing, the printout should report the same percentages for each category. We have found that discrepancies occur because of errors in transferring the data into the computer file or typographical errors in the documentation. Typographical errors may be especially serious since an analyst may be manipulating the wrong variable or assuming the wrong values for a variable.

If an analyst is unfamiliar with the database, or unsure about the quality of the original survey or the accuracy of the documentation, he may wish to verify the accuracy of the sample. The analyst may apply techniques to answer the question, "Could the data on this tape have been produced by the methodology described in the documentation?" The analyst may want to note the frequency of nonresponses and missing data. Sample verification may be especially important when databases are being merged and the study will be used to estimate parameters. In merging databases the number of cases may be reduced, altering the representativeness of the original samples. The techniques for sample verification can become quite complex. The reader interested in learning more about how to verify a sample should consult the article by J. C. Fortune and J. K. McBee[5] and the references they cite.

Evaluating the Database

Quantitative researchers are continually reminded about their vulnerability to having "the tail wag the dog." They may unconsciously define a problem so that they can solve it using their methodological skills. Similarly, they may radically alter a problem to make it conform to available secondary data. In working with secondary data, some shifts in the original research question will be necessary. Nevertheless, a researcher should determine the impact of the shift and whether the change will undermine his ability to accomplish the study's purpose.

In working with secondary data, a researcher must first remember that the secondary data can be no better than the research that produced it. Analytical sophistication cannot compensate for poorly conceived measures and sloppy data collection. Investigators may be wary of working with data accompanied by haphazard documentation. To decide whether the secondary data meet his needs, the researcher needs to know the following:

1. What constituted the sample?
    a. What was the population?
    b. What was the sampling frame?
    c. What sampling strategy was used?
    d. What was the response rate?
2. When were the data collected?
3. How were the data collected?
4. How were the data coded and edited?
5. What were the operational definitions of measures?
6. Who collected the data and for what purpose?

Information on the sample population lets the researcher know whether the data represent the population of interest. If the population of interest and the database's population do not coincide, the researcher must decide the impact of the difference. In the research on work stoppages, the researchers decided to settle on state data rather than collect local data; they reasoned that state data would uncover patterns of association that could be investigated later.

Information on the sampling frame, sampling strategy, and response rate all affect the quality of the sample. Furthermore, a low response rate may render the data inadequate for the researcher's purpose. He also may decide that a low response rate indicates low research quality.

Knowing when the data were collected can be extremely important in correctly interpreting some study findings. Consider school data. Achievement scores gathered on fourth-graders in October should be interpreted differently from achievement scores gathered in May. Time can affect public-opinion data. Investigators examining public concern about environmental warming may hypothesize that the public's opinion is linked to weather patterns. Consequently, investigators would want to know when surveys were conducted, so they could learn if, and how, extreme temperature or weather-related disasters were associated with variations in the public's opinions.

Information on how the data were collected helps an investigator make inferences about data quality. He wants to know if respondents were surveyed by mail, telephone, or in person, and how interviewers were trained and supervised. Information on data coding and editing procedures also relates to data quality. Specifically, the investigator wants to know whether someone checked for errors in coding data or entering them into a computer. He also wants to learn how miscellaneous responses and atypical answers were handled. In evaluating the information, the investigator uses his own judgment to decide whether the evidence suggests sound research procedures.

Knowing the operational definitions of measures allows the investigator to determine the reliability, operational validity, and sensitivity of the measures. Ideally, the documentation explains and evaluates the measures used. Studies generated with the database also may provide evidence of the quality of the measures. Finally, a copy of the instrument used to collect the data helps the investigator to reach his own conclusions.

Data published by the Bureau of the Census are accompanied by fairly detailed documentation. In Example 9.2 we have quoted sections of the appendices of an issue of *Current Population Reports*. The purpose of the example is to show you what to look for in reviewing documentation and to provide you with a model of what to include when you write up your own research.

Knowing who collected the data and why can be valuable. Imagine that you find data that support the health benefits of eating chocolate. Would you be skeptical if the report was from a trade association of chocolate manufactures? What information would convince you that the data were not biased or misleading? The answers to questions about the sample, the operational definitions, and how the data were coded and analyzed might lessen your suspicions.

U.S. CENSUS DATA

Official statistics, statistics collected by governments, are a major source of secondary data. In the United States, most federal cabinet-level agencies regularly collect data needed for policy making. Important agency producers of statistical series include the Departments of Education, Health and Human Services, Agriculture, Justice, Labor, and Commerce. Maier's book, *The Data Game*, and Jean S. Stratford and Juri Stratford's *Major U.S. Statistical Series* identify and evaluate major federal databases.[6]

The U.S. Census Bureau conducts periodic and special studies to describe the characteristics of the American people, their governments, and their businesses. The periodic studies include:

Census of Governments

Decennial Census of Population and Housing

EXAMPLE 9.2

Documenting Secondary Data: An Example from the Annual Demographic Survey

Situation: Each March the Current Population Survey (CPS) conducts an Annual Demographic Survey, which supplements its monthly data on labor force participation with data on money received the previous calendar year, education, household and family characteristics.

Population and Sample: The Annual Demographic sample consists of the CPS sample of 60,000 housing units, 2,500 additional units with at least one Hispanic member, and members of the Armed Forces, which are excluded from the CPS labor force survey.

Sampling frame and strategy: The sampling frame was selected from 1990 census files and updated to reflect new construction. Current CPS sample is located in 754 areas; an area consists of a county, several contiguous counties, or minor civil divisions in New England and Hawaii.

Response rate: About 50,000 occupied households were eligible for interview. Interviews were not obtained from about 3,200 occupied units, because the occupants were not found at home after repeated calls or were unavailable for some other reason. Between 92 and 93 percent of households provide basic labor force information; between 80 and 82 percent complete the Annual Demographic Survey supplement.

When data were collected: March 19–March 27, 1996.

How data were collected: Face-to-face interviews, with the interviewer using a laptop computer, were conducted with households that had not been interviewed previously, with poor English-language skills, or without telephone access. Telephone interviews were conducted with other households.

Conceptual definition of involuntary part-time: Individuals who give an economic reason for working 1 to 34 hours during a week. Economic reasons include slack work or unfavorable business conditions, inability to find full-time work, and seasonal declines in demand. Those who usually work part-time must also indicate that they want and are available to work full-time to be classified as part-time for economic reasons.

Operational definition (partial): In the weeks that (name/you) worked, how many weeks did (name/you) work less than 35 hours in 1995? What was the main reason (name/you) worked less than 35 hours per week? (1) Could not find a full-time job, (2) Wanted to work part-time or only able to work part-time, (3) Slack work or material shortage, (4) Other reason

SOURCE: Information drawn from Current Population Survey Web Site (http://www.bls.census.gov)

Current Population Survey (CPS)
Survey of Income and Program Participation (SIPP)
Census of Agriculture
Economic Censuses

We limited this chapter to U.S. Census Bureau surveys because of the extensive use of Census data and the Bureau's longstanding efforts to reduce nonsampling error. The data are critical to political and policy decisions. Census data users include federal agencies, state and local governments, nonprofit associations and businesses, and private citizens pursuing business and personal interests.

This chapter discusses the Census of Governments and the Bureau's two major population surveys. We summarize how the Bureau decides on questionnaire content and documents data. The methodological discussion should improve your knowledge of data collection and your appreciation of Census Bureau procedures. You may wish to note that the Census Bureau and other federal agencies do not do public-opinion polling. Official statistics document information about governments, other organizations, and individuals.

The U.S. Bureau of the Census

The U.S. Bureau of the Census traces its origins back to the Constitutional requirement that the U.S. population be counted every 10 years. The head count forms the basis for reapportioning the number of seats a state holds in the U.S. House of Representatives. By law, within nine months of "Census Day," the Census Bureau must give the President a count of state populations so that congressional delegations can be apportioned. Within a year, state legislatures must receive population totals for specified political subdivisions so they can draw legislative districts.

A hallmark of the Census Bureau has been its record for protecting the confidentiality of the information it collects. The principle of confidentiality has contributed to its success in getting people and businesses to answer questions about themselves. Current law on confidentiality states:

Census data may be used only for statistical purposes.

Publication of census data must not enable a user to identify individuals or establishments.

Only authorized employees of the Department of Commerce or Census Bureau may examine individual census forms.

The Bureau releases its information on an individual only with that person's specific consent. For example, some individuals have asked for census records to corroborate their ages and demonstrate their eligibility for Social Security benefits. Census officials must anticipate how computer users can manipulate data to uncover the identity and private information on specific individuals or establishments.[7]

The Census Bureau is not restricted to collecting data on and from individuals. It also collects data on the nation's economic activity, including manufacturing, agriculture, transportation, and government. The Bureau protects the confidentiality of business information. Data on governments are based on public records and are not confidential.

After census data are compiled, the immediate interest is in the snapshots they supply of the nation and its economic activity. Nevertheless, the real importance of the census statistics is their role as time-series data. Thus the Bureau is concerned with producing high-quality data and ensuring their comparability over time.

Censuses of Governments

In years ending with two or seven, the Census Bureau's Government Division conducts a Census of Governments. It conducts annual sample surveys to gather data on government finances and public employment. Data from the censuses are used to estimate the government-sector economic activity in the United States. These estimates are incorporated into the National Income and Product Accounts, the account that measures the Gross Domestic Product.[8] The census collects information on four major areas—governmental organization, taxable property values, governmental employment, and governmental finance.

Public officials and scholars may cite these data when comparing governments or looking for patterns of fiscal health. Regularly reported data can answer questions such as:

How much revenue does California realize from state-run lotteries? What percentage goes to prizes? How does its profitability compare with New York's state-run lotteries?

How many highways are administered as special districts? How much of their revenues come from taxes? tolls and charges?

What percentage of state and local government employees work in corrections? What percentage of payroll goes to corrections? How does this differ by state?

Rules governing statistics collected by the Government Division differ from typical census operations in two respects. First, as mentioned, governmental information is not confidential; the Bureau regularly publishes statistics for individual governments. Second, the sovereignty of the American states exempts them and their subdivisions from the U.S. code (Title 13) requirement to supply the Bureau with requested information.

A major challenge for the Bureau's Government Division is to procure comparable data. Achieving high response rates and receiving comparable information necessitate developing data collection procedures that do not burden respondents. The Bureau collects some data from reports submitted to other federal agencies. The Bureau receives some financial data for individual local governments from state governments. Both strategies avoid having a state or local government receive more than one request for the same information.

To further decrease respondent burden, staff review existing documents, partially customize survey forms, and conduct site visits. State governments and major local governments send public documents, including financial statements, to Washington, where analysts extract the needed data. The Bureau solicits basic data through mailed surveys. Several versions of a survey may be created so that the questions can be tailored to the size and type of the respondents' government.

If data cannot otherwise be obtained from a major general-purpose government census, staff may compile the data on-site.[9]

Staff manually review responses for completeness and consistency. A computer check is performed to identify improbable data and to show differences from previous years. Staff may conduct extensive follow-ups with the governments to fill in incomplete data, to clarify ambiguities, or to verify questionable responses.

Publication of the data is relatively quick. For example, the annual survey of government employment collects data on the payroll period that includes October 12; the data are published by October of the next year. The more complicated annual survey of government finances is available 18 months after the end of the fiscal year. Because the data are not confidential and largely consist of publicly available information, errors are constantly being identified and the data refined. A city manager or mayor who sees her city's revenue has been misreported is unlikely to let it pass without comment.

The Census of Population and Housing

The mainstay of the Census Bureau is the *Decennial Census of Population* and Housing, the constitutional reason for its existence. As we have suggested, counting the population is neither an easy task nor one that is done with complete accuracy. From the first census, government officials added to the work of census takers and asked them to collect additional information about the population. Thus the Census Bureau has had to develop procedures to accurately count the population and to determine what additional information to gather and from whom.

The Census Bureau, government officials, and researchers have given considerable attention to how the census can obtain an accurate population count. In 1990 census forms were returned by 74 percent of occupied housing units, as compared to an 83 percent response rate in 1980. The lower rate of cooperation increased costs and decreased quality. More census takers had to be hired and trained.[10] Plausible explanations for the low response rate included: reluctance of people living in nontraditional households to disclose household composition, an aversion to surveys instilled by repeated telephone and mail surveys, increased concern with privacy, and a growing non-English-speaking population.[11]

In preparation for the 2000 Census, the Census Bureau focused on containing costs and increasing the response rate. The Bureau studied ways to increase the return rate for the mailed Census form.[12] Follow up questionnaires were mailed out. Citizens could fill out and mail back the questionnaires, answer on line or over the telephone. States and advocacy groups urged citizens to respond. The following statement from the State of Ohio's home page illustrates the appeals made to citizens and some of the official uses of Census data.

> Census 2000 is critical to assuring Ohio's success in the next millennium. Census data will be used to allocate federal funds for communities throughout the State of Ohio. Results of the 2000 census are crucial to planning local community services including: schools, employment services, housing assistance, road construction, hospital services and special programs for children and the elderly.

Businesses will decide where to locate and to invest with assistance of Census 2000 data. An accurate 2000 census will guarantee Ohio is properly represented and prepared for the future.

The phenomenon of missing people completely is referred to as the *undercount*. The problem of undercounting goes beyond underestimating the total size of the U.S. population. Certain groups, particularly urban minorities, are more likely to be missed, and their need or demand for services may be seriously underestimated. Urban areas with a sizeable uncounted population may end up shortchanged in their number of legislative representatives or in the size of their allotment of government program funds. To address the problem of the undercount and to keep costs in line, the Bureau recommended sampling a portion of the households that did not return their forms. The plan to sample, however, ran into Congressional resistance, and in 2000 the Bureau was stuck with the costs of attempting to contact every non-responding household.[13]

What to include in the Census requires negotiation and evaluation. Other federal agencies, state and local government users, interest groups, and individual citizens suggest questions. To decide what additional questions to ask, census officials assess whether the proposed information will serve a broad public interest. Census officials approach the issue of the public interest by deciding whether the information justifies the expenditure of public monies. The criterion of public interest commonly leads to the elimination of questions primarily of interest to businesses, such as information on the number of pet owners in the United States.

One way the Census Bureau avoids overburdening respondents is to limit the number and content of questions so that a respondent can complete the form within a reasonable amount of time. The Decennial Census has two forms. One form asks all households to answer no more than two facing pages of questions; this form is referred to as the *100 percent count*. A sample of approximately 20 percent of all households receives a longer form. The longer form asks the same questions as the 100 percent count, plus one-and-a-half pages of housing questions and two additional pages for information on each household member. Thus space limits the total number of questions asked.[14]

The 100 percent count asks a member of a household to give each household member's name, relationship to the respondent, sex, race, ethnicity, and age. In asking its questions, the Bureau considers historical comparability. If a question is reworded or response categories are altered, the change affects the answers. The Bureau must weigh whether the benefit of a change balances the loss of comparability of information from one census to another.

In the first edition of this text, we traced the history of the race and ethnicity questions, as shown in Example 9.3, to illustrate the trade-off between consistency and the need to make question changes that reflect current social conditions. From this abbreviated summary, you can infer the social conditions that gave rise to the particular data-gathering strategy and the problems in comparing racial or ethnic changes from one census to the next. For example, note that until 1960 racial classification was not based on self-identification; rather, by asking specific questions on parentage or by observation, census takers decided a household's

EXAMPLE 9.3

Comparability among Censuses

Summary of the Recent History of Racial and Ethnic Questions

1920: Census taker decided appropriate category. Categories: White, Negro, Mulatto (Black–White mixture), Chinese, Japanese, Indian, Other

1930: Mulatto category dropped; a person identified as Mulatto counted as Negro

1940: Mexican (Mexican birth or Mexican parents) added; persons who qualified as Mexican but who were identifiable as Negro, Chinese, Japanese, or Indian were no longer counted as Mexican

1960: Self-identification of race on mailed census forms. If data collected by a census taker, the census taker observed and filled in the racial data

1970: Combination of self-identification and census taker observation continued. Categories: White, Black or Negro, Japanese, Chinese, Filipino, Korean, Vietnamese, Indian (Amer.), Asian Indian, Hawaiian, Guamanian, Samoan, Eskimo, Aleut, Other

1980: Question added to 100 percent count, "Is this person of Spanish/Hispanic origin or descent? Categories: No (not Spanish/Hispanic); Yes, Mexican-Amer.; Yes, Chicano; Yes, Puerto Rican; Yes, Cuban; Yes, Other

1990: Changed the "other" response category in both the race and Hispanic questions to allow the respondent to name the specific Asian or Pacific Islander or Spanish/Hispanic group

2000: Allowed respondent to check more than one racial group

SOURCE: C. F. Citro and M. L. Cohen, eds., *The Bicentennial Census: New Directions for Methodology in 1990* (Washington, D.C.: National Academy Press, 1985), 205–214; 1990 Census Questionnaire. 2000 Information from Census 2000 form available on Census Bureau website.

race. In 1960 and 1970, households that received a mailed form identified their own race, but if a census taker collected data, he or she decided, based on observation, the appropriate racial category. By 1980 the race question included 15 categories, mixing traditional concepts of race with ethnic or geographic identities. Also, in 1980, respondents in all parts of the country could identify themselves as Eskimos or Aleuts; previously, these groups were listed only on census forms distributed in Alaska. The 2000 form simplified the directions on how to identify the applicable Hispanic group, e.g., Columbian or Peruvian. An analysis of the New York City data found a sharp increase in the number of "other Hispanics" since 1990. At the same time, city agencies had over-estimated the size of specific Hispanic groups. Explanations for the change, other than the wording, could not be ruled out. One critic speculated that younger, U.S. born Hispanics might not identify with a specific nationality.[15] Deciding on racial categories was a major controversy in planning for the 2000 Census.[16] People who had more than one racial background expressed their resentment at having to choose one racial group over another. Adding "bi-racial" and "multi-racial" as categories was considered. This strategy was opposed by those who feared that many African Americans would choose these categories and diminish the ability of analysts to identify patterns of discrimination. The final decision was to allow respondents to check more than one racial group.[17] The longer form asks for information that the Census Bureau decides is important but unnecessary to count precisely. The development of a longer form allows the census to reduce the costs of data collection. First, the short-form information can be processed earlier to meet deadlines for releasing data. Second, the short form relieves roughly 80 percent of the respondents from a more burdensome questionnaire. Third, the Census Bureau can trade off the problems of missing data, associated with longer questionnaires, with the desirability of gathering more information. In recent censuses the longer form has asked questions about education, language, place of birth, previous residence, employment, and income. The housing questions gathered more complete data on the physical nature of the housing stock (including mobile homes and boats), residential stability, and housing quality and adequacy.

Approximately five years before "Census Day," a series of census pretests begin. The pretests gather data on diverse aspects of the census process. Analysts evaluate the questionnaire, any computer assisted interviewing techniques, and response rates.[18]

The Bureau conducts post-census evaluations of the census coverage and content. The evaluation findings indicate data quality and suggest future changes. Post-census evaluations largely consist of information supplied by respondents, who are reinterviewed. The Bureau also checks administrative records. For example, public-utilities records have been compared with respondents' reports of utility expenditures. Medicare, income tax returns, and similar governmental records have been used to improve the accuracy of the population count.[19]

Reinterviews and administrative records have their flaws. Reinterviewing has some of the problems associated with using test–retest to estimate item reliability. First, answers between testings may not change because respondents remember and duplicate their answers, or interviewers, who know the original answers, fit ambiguous answers into the originally selected categories. Second, answers between interviews may change because a household member other than the person who originally answered the census may be reinterviewed. Third, the value of administrative records largely depends on the accuracy of the records themselves and the ability to correctly match administrative records with a completed census form.

The Census Bureau does not escape data-collection problems, but in general it does as well as or better than other organizations that collect data. The Bureau's resources, including its reputation, add to its advantage. In general, people are more willing to respond to government requests for information; consequently, census surveys have lower nonresponse rates than similar surveys conducted by nongovernment agencies and researchers.

Current Population Survey (CPS)

The *CPS* is a monthly household survey to gather current population and labor-force data. The U.S. Bureau of Labor Statistics releases the CPS data each month in its report on the nation's employment and unemployment rates. The Census Bureau analyzes the population data and reports them in *Current Population Reports*.

The data describe the personal characteristics of the labor force, including the age distribution, race, and sex of American workers. Data on who works, who works full-time, who works only part-time, and who is unemployed give us a picture of who gets ahead or falls behind in the labor force. For instance, the CPS reports separately the employment patterns for whites and African Americans, for men and women, for teenagers and adults, and for rural residents and urban dwellers. What will be done with this information depends on one's responsibilities. Interest groups, journalists, and legislators cite data to document social problems or to advocate policy changes. Program managers, especially in education and job-training programs, consult the data to structure programs to meet their clients' needs or simply to give their clients accurate information and advice.

Planners in programs that deliver services to specific age groups, such as school children or the elderly, need current data on the population's age distribution so that they can estimate demands for services. Business analysts examine the data to identify population trends that may change the demands for products and services; administrators can undertake similar studies to improve their program planning or implementation.

Census analysts construct the CPS sample, consisting of approximately 50,000 housing units, so that it is representative of the nation's population. The sample is large enough that one can estimate parameters for individual states, Los Angeles, New York City, and the District of Columbia.[20] Example 9.4 reviews sampling statistics and illustrates why you may be able to use a given database to estimate parameters for a state but not for its communities.

In reviewing Example 9.4 you may wish to note what a small standard error means at the national level. In 2001 the size of the civilian labor force was 141.8 million. If the unemployment rate was estimated to be 5 percent, then 7,090,000 persons were believed to be unemployed. If an analyst assumed a 95-5 split between employed and unemployed, at the 95 percent confidence level the standard error would be .0009 (0.09 percent). This means that the estimate of the percent unemployed would be off by plus or minus 0.18 percent (0.09 × 1.96). The actual number of unemployed could be as high as 5.18 percent, e.g., 7,345,240 or as low as 4.82 percent, e.g., 6,834,760. Thus a very low standard error of less than 0.1 percent can yield an estimate that is off by as many as 510,480 persons.

USING CENSUS DATA

The Census Bureau aggregates and releases data from the Decennial Census by political and statistical areas. The political areas are states, counties, minor civil divisions (such as townships and New England towns), and incorporated places.

EXAMPLE 9.4

Estimating Parameters from the CPS: A Hypothetical Example

Problem: Can an analyst use CPS data to estimate the proportion of a city's households with a certain characteristic? What will be the amount of sampling error if the characteristic is split 50–50? 75–25?

Sample	n	SE 50–50	95% Confidence Interval	SE 75–25	95% Confidence Interval
National	50,000	.0022	49.55–50.45%	.0019	74.63–75.37%
Regional	11,000	.0048	49.06–50.93%	.0041	74.19–75.81%
State	1,700	.012	47.65–52.35%	.0105	72.94–77.06%
City	85	.054	39.37–60.63%	.047	65.79–84.20%

Discussion: Recall that to establish a 95 percent confidence interval, the *SE* is multiplied by 1.96. The sampling error will be larger for interval data because they are more variable. This example assumes that the analyst is manipulating data for all city households included in the subsample. The sample sizes become considerably smaller, and the sampling error larger, when one tries to estimate the distribution of the characteristic among a specific group, for example, income of Hispanic families.

Statistical areas have been created to describe functionally integrated areas that are relatively homogeneous in population characteristics, economic status, and living conditions. Most important of these are the *census tract* and the *block*. Census tracts are large neighborhoods, averaging 4,000 in population and generally with a population between 1,500 and 6,000. Census tracts are not to cross county lines. Every metropolitan area has been mapped with census tracts. In rural areas data are provided for the equivalent spatial unit, the block numbering area. The block is the smallest statistical area. It is a well-defined piece of land bounded by a street, railroad, or similar physical feature.[21]

Traditionally, census data have been publicly available as *macrodata,* that is, aggregated by political or statistical area. Beginning with the 1940 census, samples of individual records have been made available for public use. These samples are called *microdata* samples and are systematic, stratified samples of the long questionnaires filled out by individuals. A microdata record includes the responses reported to the Census Bureau with all personal identifiers removed. Information on geographic locations and data on very small and visible subgroups also may be eliminated to protect the confidentiality of respondents. Macrodata are available in books, on microfiche, and electronically. Microdata are only available electronically.

The advantages of the microdata are that the user can access individual records and design cross-tabulations of the variables in these records. Users can analyze variables in any combination they choose, something not possible with the summary data files. Since the microdata represent a sample, users must deal with the issues associated with making inferences from samples to populations. These files also are large, and users need adequate computer support to do the analysis.

The most immediate and obvious uses of the decennial data are for legislative reapportionment, funding allocations, and policy decisions. The national, state, and local government data give politicians, administrators, and journalists a snapshot of the nation's population on one day. The population can be viewed cross-sectionally or longitudinally. Cross-sectional studies look at the patterns among variables in the census dataset; longitudinal studies measure changes from one census to another.

One outstanding feature of census data is that the same types of data are provided in the same format for so many different places. Users can analyze any state in the nation, any of its over 3,000 counties, or any city or neighborhood. Data are in a standardized format for every place, so the same analysis can be easily repeated for any jurisdiction. Another important characteristic of census data is its coverage of small geographic areas. As we implied in our discussion of the CPS, at best, national surveys at best estimate population characteristics of individual states and large metropolitan areas. Example 9.5 illustrates how a smaller community can use census data to select an area for a pilot project serving impoverished preschoolers.

Census data are important components of demographic analysis, such as studies of patterns of fertility, mortality, and the population's age distribution. Public services rely on demographic data to help with planning. School planners attempt to provide advance notice that school capacity is greater or less than needed for the anticipated number of children that the community must educate. In recent years communities have paid more attention to the needs of their aging populations. Communities with an increasing proportion of elderly persons may experience a marked change in demand for certain services—for example, an increased need for nursing homes and specialized medical care.

An obvious problem with decennial data is its timeliness. Over the course of a decade, the accuracy of the counts declines substantially. Population changes at the block level can be rapid and dramatic. Within a matter of months, vacant lots, fields, and wooded areas may be replaced by residential housing. Conversely, housing of marginal quality may be condemned and disappear. Mid-decade censuses have been suggested; one was planned for 1985 but was never funded. The Census Bureau periodically develops post-census estimates of state populations. The Bureau adjusts the states' census population with data on state births, deaths, and migration. Birth and death data are obtained from the state office of vital statistics. Migration data are estimated by "symptomatic indicators"—for example, unexpected changes in school enrollments.[22] Several states have agencies that update the population count for the state and major subdivisions, such as counties and cities. These states also project or estimate the state's future population and that of its subdivisions, particularly counties.[23]

Each state has an agency called a State Data Center that helps disseminate census data to other state agencies and local governments and aids those wishing to use census data. State data centers are the main contact between the Census

EXAMPLE 9.5

Using Census Data on Census Tracts to Select a Site for a Program

Situation: A local human services program plans to launch a pilot program for impoverished preschoolers. The program will combine a full-day nursery school program with nutritional and health services. A human services analyst has reviewed data on city census tracts to identify communities where the program could be located; see Table 9.1.

TABLE 9.1   HOUSEHOLDS BELOW POVERTY LEVEL IN SELECTED CENSUS TRACTS

	Census Tract				
	A	B	C	D	E
Population below poverty level	4,390	3,458	2,670	5,262	3,417
Number of related children less than six years old	151	114	91	173	41
Number of related children less than six years old in a household with no husband	77	51	56	63	12
Percentage population below poverty level	28	25	29	21	16

Decision: Look for a site in Census Tracts A or D. Indicators for both communities show a high level of need: number of young children living in poverty; number of young children living in a female-headed household; large percentages of population below poverty level. Census Tract E is an inappropriate site for the community project because of the small number of children in the target population and a distinctly lower level of need evidenced by indicators.

Bureau and state and local governments. Many of these centers also coordinate the collection, documentation, and dissemination of data by all state government agencies. If you have good reason to believe that an agency in your state collects certain data, chances are that the state data center can tell you if it is available and how to obtain access to it.

We have only scratched the surface in our description of census data and their uses. We have only touched on data gathered in the census of governments and the economic censuses conducted every five years. And we have not mentioned many of the products derived from the Decennial Census. Similarly, we have ignored many other important statistical collections and agencies. Federal agencies regularly gather statistics describing the nation's health, education, agriculture, crime, and criminal justice systems.

We had three reasons for writing at length about census data. First, we wanted to alert you to their availability and potential. Second, the Bureau of the Census continually appraises its data collection and compilation procedures; thus, it is an important source of information on current developments in survey research methodology. Third, the information accompanying Census Bureau data serves as a model for documenting primary data, so researchers can decide whether the data are suited to their needs. The Census Bureau continually strives to make the census data more available and easier to use. With the Internet and other advances in technology, more people can access this important source of secondary data.

VITAL STATISTICS

Vital records are another important secondary data source used by investigators from different disciplines and with different interests. Vital records and the resulting *vital statistics* give information on births, deaths, marriages, divorces, abortions, communicable diseases, and hospitalizations. Most countries have a system for recording vital statistics. These data were among the first collected by governments and nongovernmental organizations. Before national censuses were conducted, these records were used to estimate populations.

In the United States, federal, state, and local government agencies cooperate to collect, compile, and report vital statistics. Data are collected by individual counties and states. The state data are forwarded to the National Center for Health Statistics, which compiles the data. The center publishes U.S. vital statistics reports and provides technical assistance to state agencies and other data users.

Investigators use vital statistics to assess the state of a community's mental and physical health. Policy makers can examine vital statistics to evaluate the effectiveness of current programs, change policies or programs to better meet existing needs, and forecast future needs.

Typically, a county collects data required by state statute and reports them to the state. Hospital administrators, physicians, funeral directors, and medical examiners may collect the actual data. In most states the state health department maintains vital records and releases them to the public in printed form or on computer media after removing information that identifies individuals. State offices of vital statistics also issue periodic statistical reports describing the health of the states and their communities.

The information gathered on a live birth illustrates the extensive information included in vital records:

where birth occurred
institution of delivery
mother's residency
mother's marital status

mother's race

mother's total pregnancies

mother's previous number of live births

mother's previous number of fetal deaths

date of mother's last live birth

date of mother's last fetal death

outcome of mother's last delivery

mother's number of previous children still living

prenatal care

baby's Apgar score (a medical rating scale done at birth)

complications with this pregnancy

congenital malformations

At first vital records may appear to be objective, and a user may not doubt the quality of the data. Actually, the accuracy of any one vital record is subject to many possible errors. Think of distortions that can occur in the information on a live birth. For example, information on previous pregnancies may be misreported. Fear of censure may cause a woman not to tell her physician or midwife about previous pregnancies that resulted in an abortion, miscarriage, or adoption. Many women may not have recognized miscarriages early in a pregnancy. Added to the problem of misreporting are possible errors in recording the data and different standards in diagnoses; considering these factors you can begin to appreciate the difficulties of maintaining data quality.

Similarly, social values affect death reports. Vital statistics on causes of death are obtained from death certificates and are coded according to an international code. Consider the current problems in getting accurate data on deaths from AIDS. AIDS patients and their families may fear the social stigma attached to the disease. Physicians sensitive to the feelings of patients and their families have admitted to indicating cancer or another related disease on the death certificate rather than AIDS. Similarly, accurate reporting of suicide varies widely. Societies that consider suicide a shameful act are likely to underreport its occurrence. Depending on community mores, then, a physician may decide to attribute a death to diseases or events that cause a family less embarrassment.

Vital statistics and some other health records are based on complete counts of all relevant individuals. The Center for Health Statistics attempts to count all births and deaths, and the Centers for Disease Control and Prevention attempts to collect a complete count of many diseases and causes of death. However, a great deal of useful health-related information is collected with sample surveys. The National Center for Health Statistics, several other U.S. government agencies, and many private organizations conduct extensive surveys on health-related topics. Large amounts of health survey data are available.[24] To locate health statistics, a good beginning point is either the website maintained by FedStats or the University of Michigan library.

SUMMARY

Secondary data are existing data that investigators collected for a purpose other than the given research study. Secondary data can be inexpensive, high-quality data adequate to define or solve a problem. Analyzing an existing database requires fewer resources than collecting original data. Some databases have higher-quality data than a researcher can hope to gather. Organizations that specialize in collecting data typically have well-trained, professional staff to check the reliability and operational validity of measures; to design, implement, and document a sound sampling procedure; and to collect and compile data.

One may argue that secondary analysis contributes to the quality of primary databases. First, secondary analysis requires that the original researchers fully document a database. Second, secondary analysis enables researchers to see whether they can replicate the original researcher's findings. The need to document and the ability to check findings will encourage researchers to attend to research quality.

As documentation becomes routine, data archives are kept, and access to secondary data becomes easier, investigators may increasingly turn to existing data to conduct preliminary research and to hone their research questions. Whether or not secondary data are appropriate for the final research question depends on the question and the data. As investigators work on a research problem, they begin to understand what population and what measures are needed to answer their questions. Sometimes they may modify the question so that it is consistent with the existing database. Such adjustments should be made only after the investigators fully consider what is lost in making such a shift.

The U.S. Bureau of the Census is a major source of data on the country's population, governments, and businesses. Investigators find census data valuable because of their content and the quality of the data collection. Census data may be analyzed by geography, by demographic characteristics, and over time. Maintaining comparability and reducing respondent burdens have been especially challenging in a changing society.

Other federal bureaus, state offices of vital statistics, survey organizations, and professional associations routinely collect data that others study. Virtually any organization is a potential source of data, as are individual researchers. Internet sites may help you locate existing data. Occasionally, by asking agency personnel, individual investigators may uncover a fugitive or unknown database.

Once investigators locate a database, they have to find a way to access it. Some questions can be answered by working with published statistics, but often one needs access to the database. Depending on who holds the database, and the contractual provisions for releasing data, a researcher may either access the database or a portion of it directly or have the database holder perform the analysis. Nevertheless, researchers cannot assume that access to a database is guaranteed. Organizational policies, contractual guarantees, and researcher inclination may become important factors in any agreement to allow someone to access data.

If access is obtained, the investigators need to verify the content of the database. Occasionally, the wrong database is accessed or information about a variable and its coding is incorrect. The researchers also need to review information on the sample, the measures, when the data were collected, how they were collected, and coding procedures to infer data quality.

Chapter 10 examines techniques to combine indicators to form a single measure. Data are collected on each indicator and stored as separate variables in a database. Investigators may, and often do, analyze each variable separately. Nevertheless, as you should observe, combining variables can give a more accurate, fuller picture of the phenomenon under consideration. Examining a long list of single variables can easily mislead a busy decision maker, who may be mistakenly impressed by one or two striking findings.

NOTES

1. G. S. Goldberg and E. Kremen, *The Feminization of Poverty: Only in America?* (New York: Praeger, 1990).
2. M. H. Maier with T. Easton, *The Data Game,* 3d ed. (Armonk, NY: M. E. Sharpe, 1999).
3. For more discussion of the costs of secondary analysis, see Committee on National Statistics, Commission on Behavioral and Social Sciences and Education, National Research Council, *Sharing Research Data,* eds. S. E. Fienberg, M. E. Martin, and M. I. Straf (Washington, D.C.: National Academy Press, 1985), 15–18.
4. J. S. Cecil and E. Griffin, "The Role of Legal Policies in Data Sharing," in *Sharing Research Data,* discuss laws that affect researchers' access to data.
5. J. C. Fortune and J. K. McBee, "Considerations and Methodology for the Preparation of Data Files," in *Secondary Analysis of Available Data Bases,* ed. D. J. Bowering (San Francisco: Jossey-Bass, New Directions for Program Evaluation, 1985).
6. J. S. and J. Stratford, *Major U.S. Statistical Series: Definitions, Publications, Limitations* (Chicago: American Library Association, 1992).
7. For a further discussion of confidentiality, see C. P. Kaplan and T. L. Van Valey, *Census '80: Continuing the Factfinder Tradition* (Washington, D.C.: U.S. Bureau of the Census, 1980), 65–79; "Plenary Session V: Confidentiality Issues in Federal Statistics," *First Annual Research Conference Proceedings* (Washington, D.C.: U.S. Bureau of the Census, 1985), 199–233. Summary of current law is based on material found on page 71 of *Census '80.*
8. For information on the National Income and Product Accounts, see Stratford and Stratford, *Major U.S. Statistical Series,* 64–66.
9. Each major Government Division report includes a section on data collection including any sampling in its introduction. The fiscal surveys are more complicated and tend to use the full array of strategies described here.
10. *Decennial Census: 1990 Results Show Need for Fundamental Reform* (Washington, D.C.: General Accounting Office, GAO/GGD-92–94, 1992), chaps. 2–5.
11. Ibid, 37–38.
12. *2000 Census: Progress Made on Design, but Risks Remain* (Washington, D.C.: U.S. General Accounting Office, GAO/GGD-97–142, July 14, 1997).
13. To learn more about the politics surrounding the Census Bureau's plans to sample, see M. J. Anderson and S. E. Fienberg, *Who Counts? The Politics of Census-Taking in Contemporary America* (New York: Russell Sage Foundation, 1999). I. I. Mitroff, R. O. Mason, and V. P. Barabba, *The 1980 Census: Policymaking Amid Turbulence* (Lexington, MA: Lexington Books, 1983), detail the political, legal, and statistical aspects of the undercount.
14. C. F. Citro and M. L. Cohen, eds., *The Bicentennial Census: New Directions in Methodology in 1990* (Washington, D.C.: National Academy Press, 1985), 49.
15. J. Scott, "A Census Query is Said to Skew Data on Latinos," *New York Times,* June 27, 2001.
16. For an excellent discussion of the issues involved in the racial categories, see L. Wright, "One Drop of Blood," *New Yorker,* July 25, 1994, 46–55.
17. A March 14, 2001 press release, "Questions and Answers for Census 2000 Data on Race," discusses issues associated with categorizing racial data and comparing the races over time. The press release is available at the Bureau's website, www.census.gov/Press-Release/2001/raceqandas.html.
18. *The Bicentennial Census,* 104–114, discusses the pretesting program for the 1990 Census. Information on the dress rehearsals for the 2000 Census can be found on the Census Bureau's Website.

19. N. L. Stevens, *Census Reform: Major Expansion in Use of Administrative Records for 2000 is Doubtful* (Washington, D.C.: General Accounting Office, GAO/ T-GGD-92-54, 1992), 4–6.

20. *Design and Methodology: Technical Paper 63* (Washington, D.C. Current Population Survey, March 2000): H–1.

21. Dowell Myers, *Analysis with Local Census Data: Portraits of Change* (San Diego: Academic Press, 1992), 16–17. Those interested in doing research with census data, particularly for the investigation of local areas, should see this book. Beginners as well as those with considerable experience working with census data will find it useful.

22. For a full description and evaluation of estimation methodology, see *Estimating Population and Income of Small Areas* (Washington, D.C.: National Academy Press, 1980), 12–19.

23. For example, see North Carolina Office of State Planning, *NC State Data Center Newsletter* (Raleigh, NC: January 1992 and October 1992). Also see North Carolina Office of State Budget and Management, "North Carolina Population Projections 1988–2010: Assumptions and Methods" (Raleigh, NC, n.d). The Internet address for the North Carolina State Data Center is: http://www.ospl.state.nc.us/sdn/

24. ICPSR, the Inter-University Consortium on Political and Social Research, is another good source for computer-accessible secondary data. Its Web address is www.icpsr.umich.edu.

TERMS FOR REVIEW

secondary data
Current Population Surveys
Decennial Census of Population and Housing

census undercount
100 percent count
census tract
macrodata

microdata
vital statistics

QUESTIONS FOR REVIEW

The following questions should indicate whether you have a basic competency in this chapter's material.

1. What is the value of secondary data? When would you recommend collecting original data instead of relying on secondary data?

2. A regional agency plans to study the relationship between highway features and accident rates.
   a. Briefly describe how you would go about locating existing databases.
   b. Briefly describe how you would decide whether existing databases were adequate for the planned study.
   c. Assume that you have obtained a computerized copy of a database. What information would you need to be able to use and interpret the data?

3. You analyze a computerized database. You examine it and note that it reports 70 managers and 200 nonmanagers. The documentation indicates the data represent 60 managers and 210 nonmanagers. What would you do?

4. Why is an undercount of the population during the Decennial Census treated as a serious problem?

5. In conducting a survey regularly, such as the Decennial Census, what are the trade-offs between changing a question's wording or its responses and keeping the wording the same?

6. How can local government planners use Decennial Census data?

7. Briefly contrast the two forms used in the Decennial Census (the 100 percent count and the long form). Defend the use of two forms as opposed to asking everyone all the questions included on the long form.

PROBLEMS FOR HOMEWORK AND DISCUSSION

1. Refer to Example 9.5. In Census Tract A:

    53 percent of the adults are high school graduates

    100 percent of the population over 5 years of age speak English

    1,105 rent housing

    Median family income of female householder with no husband present and children under 18, $8,774

    Median family income in census tract, $12,580

    a. A program in Census Tract A compiles information on community services. Which of the following should receive highest priority—information on tenants' rights, high school equivalency requirements and resources, or English language resources? Justify your recommendation.

    b. Based on the above data, what types of eligibility requirements would you initially suggest to make sure that those needing the services the most will receive them?

    (Your recommendations will be tentative, and they will be refined as you become more familiar with the community.)

2. Use the Internet or your university's library to obtain census data for the state in which you live, and find data on the following for the state and city of your choice:

    a. Number of people over age 65

    b. Number of people under age 5

    c. Number of households with incomes between $35,000 and $75,000

    d. Median value of owner-occupied homes

    e. Percent of labor force employed in public administration

3. Assume that a hospital located in your community is assessing the need to open a long-term care facility (nursing home). Gather census data on no more than five variables. Based on these census data, what would be your initial recommendation? What other data would you want?

DISK WORK

1. The state legislature has funded a limited project to aid the state's poorest areas in economic development. You work for the agency that will implement and oversee the project monies. You have been asked to select no more than six counties to receive project funds. The primary criterion for the selection must be based on income. Load the NC State Census Database.

    a. Your first task is to come up with an operational definition for county poverty. The data set contains several possible variables: median family money income; percent households with money income less than $15,000; per capita money income; percent families with income below poverty level; percent of persons with income below poverty level. Identify your operational definition of county poverty. Make a preliminary argument for its operational validity.

    b. Use your operational definition to select the project counties.

    c. For the recommended counties, present data on: population size; infant mortality, serious crime rate, percent of adults with a high school degree, percent of labor force unemployed.

    d. Write a short memo identifying your choices and providing evidence to justify them.

    e. Compare your recommendations with those of your classmates. Can the class as a whole reach a consensus on which counties should receive funding?

2. We have found that students make some common errors when working with macrodata. To illustrate these errors load the NC County Census Database, perform the requested analysis, and answer the accompanying questions.

    a. Examine the relationship between median family money income and percent of families with income below poverty level.

(1) Is there a relationship between these variables?

(2) Evaluate the value of postulating and analyzing the relationship.

(3) State a lesson one can draw from this exercise.

b. To test the hypothesis that female headed households are at the root of social problems, examine the relationship between number of female householders (no spouse present), family households, and serious crimes per 1,000 population. Now examine the relationships between crime rate and percent of female householders (no spouse present) in the population.

(1) Which analysis serves as the most appropriate test of the hypothesis? Explain why.

(2) State a lesson one can draw from this exercise.

c. Examine the relationship between median family income and percent of births to women under 20 years old.

(1) Can one conclude from the evidence that young women from poorer families are more likely to become teenage mothers? Justify your answer.

(2) Can one conclude from the evidence that poorer counties have higher rates of teenage pregnancy?

RECOMMENDED FOR FURTHER READING

For information on secondary analysis, see *Secondary Analysis of Available Data Bases,* ed. D. J. Bowering (San Francisco: Jossey-Bass, New Directions for Program Evaluation, 1984). This collection includes J. C. Fortune and J. K. McBee's detailed essay on merging and verifying databases.

The Committee on National Statistics, Commission on Behavioral and Social Sciences and Education, National Research Council, *Sharing Research Data,* eds. S. E. Fienberg, M. E. Martin, and M. I. Straf (Washington, D.C.: National Academy Press, 1985), includes the committee's report and essays. Its essays discuss data sharing in the social sciences, with a list of data-sharing facilities and legal policies covering data sharing.

M. H. Maier with T. Easton, *The Data Game,* 3d ed. (Armonk, NY: M. E. Sharpe, 1999), is an excellent compendium of some commonly used databases and their limitations. The book is especially strong in identifying common problems of misinterpreting data.

J. S. and J. Stratford, *Major U.S. Statistical Series: Definitions, Publications, Limitations* (Chicago: American Library Association, 1992) is another work that identifies major databases and measures.

Descriptions of Census Bureau products, data, and methodology may be found at its website (www.census.gov). The reports prepared by the General Government Division of GAO are a good source of various details (www.gao.gov). Census staff also report on census research activities at professional conferences, including the American Statistical Association's sections on survey research methods. Stephen E. Fienberg and Margo J. Anderson, *Who Counts? The Politics of Census-Taking in Contemporary America* (New York: Russell Sage Foundation, 1999), have an up-to-date discussion of the controversy surrounding the undercount and sampling and racial classifications.

Dowell Myers, *Analysis with Local Census Data: Portraits of Change* (San Diego: Academic Press, 1992), writes an excellent source for those wishing to use census data. He discusses the various collection procedures, data sources and media, and methods of analysis, and has a good section on presentation.

Chapter 10

Combining Indicators: Index Construction

In this chapter you will learn about

1. the reasons for using indices.
2. issues involved in the development of indices.
3. some common methods of developing indices.
4. ways to standardize measures for use in indices.
5. the uses of index numbers.

Administrators often find it useful to combine several indicators to form a single measure. One indicator is rarely adequate to measure a community's need for health services, the amount of crime in a neighborhood, or the level of sanitation. To measure the health status of a neighborhood, an administrator would want to use more than one indicator of a disease or condition and would combine several indicators into a composite measure called an index. *Index* is a term for a set of variables used as a measure for a more abstract concept. Each variable is called an item or indicator; an index will be composed of two or more items or indicators.

We are all familiar with a number of commonly used indices, such as the consumer price index (CPI), the Dow Jones Index, and students' grade point averages (GPA). The consumer price index is used to measure the prices of goods that consumers purchase. Obviously, the price of more than one good needs to be included to obtain an accurate and valid measure. The prices of a basket of representative goods are combined to arrive at a value for the CPI. The Dow Jones Index provides an indicator of the performance of the stock market by providing a combined measure of the performance of a set of selected stocks. And we are all familiar with the grade point average illustrated in Table 10.1. Grades are given a numerical value and are combined to provide a measure of academic performance.

The value of the index is computed using an equation that includes all the items that are part of the index. The resulting number is a composite of two or

TABLE 10.1   EXAMPLE OF AN INDEX: THE GRADE POINT AVERAGE (GPA)

Course	Letter Grade	Numerical Grade	Credit Hours	Points (grade × hours)
Math	C	2.0	3.0	6.0
History	A	4.0	3.0	12.0
Economics	B	3.0	4.0	12.0
Total			10.0	30.0

GPA = Total points divided by total credit hours
     = 30/10
     = 3.00

more numbers, each representing an item in the index. A more operationally valid and reliable measure can usually be obtained if several components of an attribute, rather than only one, are used. A measure of crime in a neighborhood that combines the rates of several different crimes including burglaries, assaults, homicides, and robberies, will be more valid and reliable than one that uses only one crime, such as the rate of home burglaries. Indices are often constructed so that seemingly different things can be combined and described by a single number. For example, one can combine income, occupation, and place of residence to obtain an index of social class (Social Economic Status).

Scales refer to a type of index. Researchers often do not distinguish between indices and scales and use the terms interchangeably. A *scale* combines indicators according to rules that are designed to reflect only a single dimension of a concept.[1] Strictly speaking, a scale assigns a number to a case based on how that case fits into a previously identified pattern of indicators. An index usually refers to any combination of indicators. Indexes need not be one dimensional and may measure more than a single concept.

True scales can be difficult and complex to construct and their operational validity and reliability difficult to establish. Scales differ from indexes by the greater rigor in their construction. Whereas indexes are constructed by the accumulation of values, greater attention is paid in scales to testing validity and reliability. Numerous published scales are available for the study of attitudes, opinions, beliefs, and other mental states. They range from ad hoc indices developed for specific uses to standardized (and copyrighted) scales for the measurement of common concepts, such as managerial stress and job satisfaction. Readers interested in these or in the various types of scaling procedures should consult the books listed at the end of the chapter. In our discussion we will be concerned only with constructing indices and will not delve into scaling as such.

Some indices have been validated through long and varied experience. Before constructing a new index, analysts should see what indices that others doing similar kinds of research have developed. We will discuss four important issues in developing indices. These are:

1. Defining the concept to be measured
2. Selecting the items to be included in the index

3. Combining the items to form an index
4. Weighting the separate items

DEFINING THE CONCEPT

A clear understanding and definition of the concept to be measured is needed. The analyst should be able to explain what the concept means and, theoretically, what its components are. In Chapter 4 we discussed conceptual and operational definitions. The first step in developing a measure is to define and describe the concept to be measured. The literature should be reviewed to find any definitions of the concept used by others. We should define a concept in the same way that others have unless there is good reason for not doing so.

An operational definition of a concept details how the concept is to be measured, and this is done in the remaining steps. However, the conceptual definition will determine the appropriateness of each possible measure of the concept. We want the correspondence between the conceptual and operational definitions to be close. When selecting items for a measure, the analyst should be able to discuss how each item measures the concept as defined.

SELECTING THE ITEMS

Choosing items for a composite measure is critical. This process is associated with content validity. The analyst should be concerned about four things. First, use the right items—those that represent the dimension of interest and no other. Second, include enough items to distinguish among all the important gradations of a dimension and to improve reliability. The emphasis here is on thinking of lots of items. Third, decide whether every item is supposed to represent the entire dimension in which you are interested or whether each is to represent just part of the dimension. Fourth, keep costs down by excluding items that provide no extra information—use only the items you really need. In other words, use as many items as you need but no more.

The items selected for the index should cover the characteristic being measured in a balanced way. An analyst constructing an index to measure management performance for an agency would include those aspects that he felt were important. For example, if personnel turnover, absenteeism, and the number of grievances were all thought to be important, a measure leaving out any of these may be biased. In terms of content validity, the analyst would want to verify that the content of the items reflected what he wanted to measure.

One's knowledge of the subject matter related to a topic being measured can be very important in selecting items. Items should not be picked arbitrarily; they should be theoretically or conceptually related to what the analyst wants to measure. Those that logically relate to the concept being measured should be given top priority. Evidence from other sources that indicates an item is related to the concept being measured should be considered. For each item the analyst should be able to write at least a few sentences explaining why he thinks it should be included.

Analysts use several methods to choose items; the choice can be made with unaided judgment, or expert opinion may be used. They talk to people who are knowledgeable in the area and to potential users of the index to determine what they think is important. One danger in talking to too many users, however, is that if they think that they will ever have a use for an item, they may suggest including it. You must guard against including unneeded items.

Analysts may prefer methods that make it possible to assess how well a set of items "hangs together"; that is, whether the set of items contributes significantly to the reliable measurement of a well-defined concept. Items hang together when each of them reflects the underlying dimension in roughly the same way. They also hang together when several measures are all associated—highly correlated—with each other. When this happens the separate measures may all be tapping the same concept. One method for reducing a large number of associated items and combining them into fewer indices is factor analysis. Later in the chapter we discuss factor analysis and how it can be used to select among variables to be included in an index.

The validity of a measure is greatly dependent upon the items selected for the index. Content validity of an index can be evaluated by reviewing the items involved in measuring the concept. In developing an index to measure performance of personnel, a supervisor would want to be sure that the items in the index represented the content of the performance being evaluated. That is, the content of the index should match what is thought to be important about the employee's performance. In an example in Chapter 4, the content validity of a measure of employee performance was discussed. Example 10.1 similarly illustrates the importance of content validity to index construction.

EXAMPLE 10.1

Content Validity and Index Construction

Problem: A supervisor wants to develop an index to appraise the performance of her subordinates.

Procedure: After reviewing her agency's personnel policies and the job descriptions of those she supervises, and discussing the task with other supervisors, she determines that the following characteristics are most important: accuracy in filling out standard forms, production (the number of forms completed and entered in the offices database in a week's time), knowledge of her office's filing system, ability to use the filing system in her office, and facility with computer software. The supervisor then selects items for the index to measure the employee's performance in these areas.

Comment: The items that the supervisor selects must measure the employee's performance in these areas in order for the index as a measure to have content validity. If one or more of these criteria were not included in the index, the measure would not be valid. If evaluation of other characteristics were included, such as the employee's attitude or dress, this also would affect the validity of the index.

COMBINING THE ITEMS IN AN INDEX

The administrator can use a variety of methods to combine the values for separate measures into an index. The simplest and most common procedure is simply to add the values of the separate items. A City Stress Index provides an example of simple adding, using rankings on four separate items. The authors of this index obtained data on four indicators of psychological stress for cities. These were the rates for each of the following: alcoholism, divorce, suicide, and crime. They then ranked the 300 largest cities in the nation on each of the four indicators and added the ranks together for a composite ranking for each of the cities.[2] Another common procedure is to find an average of the values of the separate items. Items for an index also may be combined by a more complicated equation to compute a single value. The individual values may be multiplied or divided by each other, for example.

The values of each separate item may need to be transformed so that they can be combined. Often the separate items will be measured in different units and have different ranges of values. In an index to determine grant eligibility for a community, for example, one cannot meaningfully add the percent of unemployed adults to the per capita income of residents. Methods of transforming measures so that they can be combined to accurately measure the characteristic of interest are discussed later in the chapter.

WEIGHTING THE SEPARATE ITEMS

Each item should contribute to the index in proportion to its importance. For some indices we will want each item to have the same influence as all other items. For others we may feel that some items are more important and want them to have greater influence on the final index. We can *weight* the separate items differently if we want them to have different influence on the index. You may create an index to evaluate the desirability of different job offers, for example, and decide that the following items are important: salary, location, and vacation time. Assume that you need to decide between two jobs and construct the following index.

Job Offer A	Job Offer B
Salary = 1	Salary = 2
Location = 2	Location = 1
Vacation = 1	Vacation = 2

The numbers are the ranks of each of the items for each job offer; the higher the number the better the job. The number 2, for example, means that the job ranks higher on that item than the other job does. Salary for Job B is preferable to the salary for Job A, but the location for Job A seems better to you than the location for Job B, and so on. You also decide that salary is by far the most important thing that you are looking for in a new job and that the amount of vacation time is not nearly as important. So you decide to weight each item by how important it is and multiply the rank of each item by its weight.

TABLE 10.2   THE CRIME RATE INDEX FOR TWO CITIES

City A		City B	
Crime	*Rate*	*Crime*	*Rate*
Homicide	5	Homicide	8
Manslaughter	7	Manslaughter	6
Rape	13	Rape	10
Burglary	35	Burglary	36
Total	60	Total	60

The index provides a higher measure for Job B than for Job A. If you have included the proper items and weighted them accurately, you would choose Job B over Job A.

Job Offer A	Weights	Job Offer B	Weights
Salary = 1	×4 = 4	Salary = 2	×4 = 8
Location = 2	×2 = 4	Location = 1	×2 = 2
Vacation = 1	×1 = 1	Vacation = 2	×1 = 2
Total Index Value	9		12

The Uniform Crime Index adds together the number of crimes per 100,000 people for each of a wide variety of crimes including murder, manslaughter, rape, and burglary. Table 10.2 gives an example of the crime rate index for two cities. Note that the level of crime in the two cities is the same on the index, although the cities have different rates for each of the crimes in the index. Each crime in the index is treated as having the same importance. Since the Crime Index is dominated by property crimes, changes in the rates of other, more violent crimes have less impact on it.[3]

In many cases administrators may want to assign varying weights to separate items when combining several into an index. The weight is determined by the importance of an item to the attribute being measured. When an index is described as being "unweighted," this typically means that each item comprising it is weighted the same.

We need to be careful that we do not unintentionally allow some items to have undue influence on the index. This might be the case if we tried to combine items whose values had much different scales or ranges. An item with values that range from 1 to 50 differs considerably from an item whose values range from 1 to 10. The difference between 5 and 10 on the first item is probably not as important as the difference between 5 and 10 on the second. However, if we simply added them together, they both would have the same influence on the index. The index to measure financial stress in communities, discussed in Example 10.2, gives an example of this situation. In Item 1 of the index, the range of values obtained went from 10 to 50, and in Item 2 the range was from 1 to 10.

CREATING STANDARDIZED INDICATORS FOR INDICES

Separate items in indices must be included in such a way that each is in comparable units and each contributes appropriately to the composite measure. It is often

EXAMPLE 10.2

Community Financial Stress Index

Item 1. Percentage of population applying for any kind of public assistance. Lowest community = 10; highest = 50; Community C = 14; Community D = 20.

Item 2. Percentage of increase in the number of business failures from previous year. Lowest community = 1; highest = 10; Community C = 7; Community D = 1.

Financial Stress Index Values:

	Item 1	Item 2	Total
Community C =	14%	7%	= 21
Community D =	20%	1%	= 21

Both communities have the same total value on the index. However, the difference between the values for Item 1 is likely to be much more important than the difference between the values for Item 2. Although both items are measured in the same units—percentages—they have greatly different ranges and simply adding them together gives greater weight to the first item.

necessary to *standardize* the individual measures so that each is based on the same scale and items measured in different units may be combined. If this is not done, an unimportant measure may contribute more to the final index than an important one simply because of different values or ranges.

Combining, transforming, and weighting the separate items in an index are related issues. Transforming the items will often reduce the risk that any one item will have undue influence on the index. We can then decide how we want to weight the separate items; if we want some to have more weight, we can multiply the values of those items by a factor before combining them, as in the job-offer example. In building an index the analyst should address the two issues of transforming the measures and weighting the items separately.

As an example, consider an index that created a measure of intercity hardship by combining a number of measures, such as the unemployment rate and dependency that is the percentage of persons under 18 or over 64.[4] Although the second figure could vary greatly among cities, the first may be more important, and a few points' difference in the unemployment rate may be very important. To measure each variable using the same units and to prevent the second measure from having undue weight, researchers needed to standardize the variables. Example 10.3 presents a detailed example drawn from the research mentioned above.[5]

Indices like the one described above have been developed to measure city stress and community need to determine allocation formulas for grants. Each of the indicators in this index was standardized and weighted equally. However, different weights could have been assigned to each if desired. Another method of creating standardized measures is to use the z-scores of each of a series of separate measures and then to add the z-scores. An example of this approach is included in Appendix 10.2 at the end of this chapter.

EXAMPLE 10.3

Creation of an Intercity Hardship Index

Quantifiable Measures and Definitions

1. *Unemployment:* percent of civilian labor force unemployed
2. *Dependency:* percent of persons under 18 or over 64
3. *Education:* percent of persons 25 years of age or older with less than a 12th-grade education
4. *Income level:* per capita income
5. *Crowded housing:* percent of occupied housing units with more than one person per room
6. *Poverty:* percent of families below 125 percent of low-income level

Note that the range of each of these variables could differ considerably. Also, the income level variable is not a percentage as are the other five. In order to standardize them, each of the variables was treated in the following manner: The lowest value of the variable was assigned the value 0, the highest was assigned a value of 100. The value for cities in between was determined by the following formula:

$$x = ((y - y_a)/(y_b - y_a)) \cdot (100)$$

where:

x = standardized value to be created for each city
y = value on a specific measure of need for each city
y_a = value of y indicating least need
y_b = value of y indicating greatest need

Thus, for each measure, the city with the greatest need (the highest unemployment, the lowest per capita income, and so on) was assigned a score of 100, and the city with the lowest need was assigned a score of 0. Consider unemployment and per capita income as examples.

Unemployment: The city having the lowest unemployment is Raleigh, with 3.0 percent; the highest rate occurs in El Paso with 11 percent. Determine the standardized value for Newark with an unemployment rate of 6 percent.

$$x = ((\text{Newark rate} - \text{lowest})/(\text{highest} - \text{lowest})) \cdot 100$$
$$= ((6 - 3)/(11 - 3)) \cdot 100 = 37.50$$

Income: Per capita income: highest = Raleigh, at \$17,000; lowest = Vilas, at \$6,000. Lower per capita income indicates greater need. Determine standardized value for Newark, with per capita income at \$9,500.

$$\text{Standardized measure of income for Newark} =$$
$$((\$9,500 - \$17,000) \div (\$6,000 - \$17,000)) \cdot 100 = 68.18$$

Since a higher income level is considered to be more desirable than a lower one, the lowest value for income is given the value of 100. This city then has the highest value of need on the per capita income measure. Both variables are now standardized to a range of 0 to 100 and are measured in the same units. (The units, of course, are percents. They are not the amounts of unemployment or of income.)

Continued

> **EXAMPLE 10.3**   *Continued*
>
> **TABLE 10.3   DEVELOPING STANDARDIZED VALUES FOR THE ITEMS IN AN INDEX FOR CITIES**
>
> | | | | Newark | |
> | --- | --- | --- | --- | --- |
> | Variable | *High* | *Low* | *Unstandardized* | *Standardized* |
> | 1 | 11% | 3% | 6% | 37.50 |
> | 2 | 25% | 7% | 13% | 33.33 |
> | 3 | 15% | 5% | 7% | 20.00 |
> | 4 | $6,000* | $17,000† | $9,500 | 68.18 |
> | 5 | 40% | 10% | 25% | 50.00 |
> | 6 | 35% | 15% | 22% | 35.00 |
> | Total | | | | 244.01 |
>
> *greatest need
> †lowest need
>
> The standardized measures for each variable can be added together to obtain an index value for each city.
>
> Each separate variable in the index is standardized in the fashion described and summed for each city. Table 10.3 shows the low and high values for each variable and the standardized value for the example city, Newark.
>
> Note that the highest possible value for the index would be 600. A city would have this value only if it were the highest on each of the separate variables.
>
> The separate factors in an index such as this can be averaged. That is, the total value for each case is divided by the number of factors in the index. For this index, the total for each city would be divided by six. For Newark the six-item average would be 244.01 ÷ 6 = 40.67. The maximum average for the index would be 100.

EXAMPLES OF CREATING INDICES

Likert Scaling

A common method of building indices is called *Likert scaling.* Despite its name, it is usually used to create indices rather than scales.[6] An index combines values from two or more separate measures of a characteristic. A scale assigns a value to a case based on how that case fits into a pattern of responses. Likert scaling accomplishes the former. Likert scales also are called summated rating scales. The procedure is relatively easy to use. To develop an index using Likert scaling, the analyst selects a set of statements, each of which reflects favorably or unfavorably on some aspect of the characteristic that he wants to measure. A rating form is provided for each item with several ranked responses. The dimension is then rated on each item according to the responses provided. A numerical value is assigned to each response, and the values are summed to obtain a single numerical value. An alternative is to sum

EXAMPLE 10.4

An Example of a Likert Scale Index

The following was developed to assess client satisfaction with a public agency.

Item 1. The staff of this agency always treat me with respect.

_____Strongly Agree   _____Agree   _____Neither Agree nor Disagree
     (5)   (4)   (3)

_____Disagree   _____Strongly Disagree
     (2)   (1)

Item 2. I never have to wait longer than 20 minutes for service at this agency.

_____Strongly Agree   _____Agree   _____Neither Agree nor Disagreee
     (5)   (4)   (3)

_____Disagree   _____Strongly Disagree
     (2)   (1)

Item 3. I am often told to come on the wrong day by staff of this agency.

_____Strongly Agree   _____Agree   _____Neither Agree nor Disagree
     (1)   (2)   (3)

_____Disagree   _____Strongly Disagree
     (4)   (5)

Item 4. I am not satisfied with the services provided by this agency.

_____Strongly Agree   _____Agree   _____Neither Agree nor Disagree
     (1)   (2)   (3)

_____Disagree   _____Strongly Disagree
     (4)   (5)

The numbers under the responses are the values for each item. They can be added together to obtain a value for the index. Of course, more items would usually be included. The numbers representing the values of each response category would not necessarily appear on the questionnaire. Notice that the direction of Items 3 and 4 is reversed from that of Items 1 and 2. Items 1 and 2 are positive statements, and if the client agrees with them a higher value is given. Items 3 and 4 are negative statements, and if the client agrees with them a lower value is given. People often get into the habit when answering questions of this nature by either agreeing or disagreeing without giving the item adequate thought. It is therefore wise to change the direction of some of the items so that the client is more likely to think through an answer before responding. Note also the "Neither Agree nor Disagree" category. This response is often included in Likert scaling.

    Two alternatives are used to combine the responses to these items into an index. The first is to add the numerical value of the response to each item. Assume that a client gave the following responses to the questionnaire in this example.

Continued

EXAMPLE 10.4 *Continued*

Item	Response	Numerical Value of Response
1.	Agree	4
2.	Agree	4
3.	Strongly Disagree	5
4.	Strongly Disagree	5
Total		18

The total would be the index value. If one of the items did not apply to this agency, or if the client did not respond to one or more of the items, adding the total responses would be inappropriate. The alternative is to add the total values of each response and divide by the number of items answered. This would give an average value for each item and would be more accurate if some items were not answered. Using this approach for the client above would result in an index value of 18/4 = 4.5.

If we used the index in another agency where Item 3 did not apply, we might find a client giving the following responses:

Item	Response	Numerical Value of Response
1.	Agree	5
2.	Agree	4
3.	(No answer. Clients come in at their convenience.)	NA
4.	Strongly Disagree	5
Total		13

To compare this total to the total for the first agency would be inappropriate and inaccurate. Dividing the total by the number of items answered gives a more accurate value and one that can be compared to the average of the first agency.

Total/number of items answered = 13/3 = 4.33.

the separate ratings and divide by the number of items to provide an average of the responses to each item.

Likert scaling is often used to measure opinions or attitudes of individuals. If it is used in an interview or survey, respondents are asked to indicate on the rating scale the degree to which they agree or disagree with each statement. The agreement scale may have only two choices (Agree–Disagree), or it may have more choices, permitting an indication of the level of agreement or disagreement. Five categories are commonly used: Strongly Agree, Agree, Neutral or No Opinion, Disagree, and Strongly Disagree. Some forms omit the neutral category, and some add even more categories to permit finer distinctions. An equal number of positive and negative statements is recommended. An unequal number of positive or negative response categories may bias responses. For positive statements the categories are scored 1, 2, 3, 4, 5, with 1 indicating "Strongly Disagree" and 5 indicating "Strongly Agree." If the statement is unfavorable toward the subject, the scoring is reversed, as in Example 10.3. The respondent's index value is the sum of

EXAMPLE 10.5

Example Index

A city's Public Works director wishes to evaluate the cleanliness of neighborhoods surrounding the city's solid-waste transfer and materials recycling stations. He prepares an index for inspectors to use once a month. Inspectors are to check one rating for each item.

Neighborhood Cleanliness Index

1. The entire area looks like a pleasant residential neighborhood.
   _____Very much   (A)
   _____Somewhat   (B)
   _____Not at all   (C)
2. Loose trash such as paper, bottles, and cans are visible.
   _____Not at all   (A)
   _____Somewhat   (B)
   _____Very much   (C)
3. Grass is neatly trimmed and weeds are kept out.
   _____Very much   (A)
   _____Somewhat   (B)
   _____Not at all   (C)
4. Streets and sidewalks are dusty or dirty.
   _____Not at all   (A)
   _____Somewhat   (B)
   _____Very much   (C)

Numerical values are assigned to each response in the following manner:

$$A = 3; B = 2; C = 1.$$

If an inspector rated a neighborhood as shown below, the corresponding numerical values would be assigned:

Item	Rating	Numerical Value
1.	B	2
2.	A	3
3.	A	3
4.	B	2

The total would be 10. The inspector could divide this by 4—the number of items—to obtain a cleanliness index value of 2.5 for the neighborhood. This number could be used to compare the cleanliness of the neighborhood with other neighborhoods or with the same neighborhood at some previous time. Note that the higher the value of the index, the cleaner the neighborhood. If the value of the index falls below a certain level, the director would probably wish to address the problem and take corrective action.

The operational validity and reliability of the index also should be determined. If the items comprising the index were known to be the factors that most concerned nearby residents, then it would probably be a content-valid measure. However, the director would need to verify that each inspector used the index in the same way and that the index allowed the inspectors to assess cleanliness accurately.

the values on the separate items. Example 10.4 shows an example of a typical Likert scale used as an index to assess clients' satisfaction with agency service.

The first stage of constructing a Likert scale is the selection of the items. Although no definitive set of procedures exists, we offer the following general suggestions. First, understand the concept to be measured. The analyst should be able to write a few paragraphs about the concept and why each item is chosen and explain how he thinks each item relates to the concept being measured. Much of what applies to writing good questions for questionnaires applies to the construction of items for Likert scales. Once statements have been selected, they should be pretested. The relationship of each item to the total score should be examined. In general, one wants items that are highly associated with the total scores. The items in a Likert scale need not be weighted equally. However, in practice most Likert scales treat items with parity. One criticism of Likert-type indices is that the same total score can be obtained in a variety of ways. One of the main advantages is that they are easily constructed.

Indices based on the Likert scaling technique do not always use the "Strongly Agree" to "Strongly Disagree" continuum. And although each item has the same number of response categories, every item may not have the same responses. Example 10.5 shows such an index.

A Likert-type index represents an ordinal level of measurement. The items do not really measure the quantity of a characteristic, but we can use the items to rank the cases. However, by adding together the numbers assigned to the response categories for each item, we are treating the measurement as if it were interval. This practice allows us to use more statistical techniques for analysis. Many analysts feel that treating Likert-type scales as if they were interval measures provides more advantages than disadvantages.

FACTOR ANALYSIS

Factor analysis is a technique used to investigate the relationship between theoretical concepts and empirical indicators. It also is used to reduce a large number of items to a smaller, more manageable number of indices. Analysts use it to select items and determine their importance to an index. One method of factor analysis transforms a set of variables into a new, smaller set of composite variables. It can show which items should be used in an index and how they should be weighted. The technique involves a large number of calculations. However, numerous computer programs are available to carry out the computations and provide the necessary information. You are likely to see the application of factor analysis in reports using or developing indices.

Factor analysis was developed to help construct indicators of abstract concepts. The basic ideas were developed in the context of using examination grades as an indicator of general intelligence. Suppose we have a large number of students' exam grades on six courses taken during a semester. We would expect that a student's exam grades would be related to each other. The original investigators suggested that the link among the exam grades was the individual's general level of intelligence and was not directly observable. The investigators suggested that grades in all subject areas would depend to some extent on this factor. General intelligence could be considered a factor common to the performance on all of the tests. The several exam grades can then be used as a measure of this factor.

Factor analysis can be used to condense a large number of items into a smaller number of indices. The composite should have greater reliability and operational validity than the items taken separately. Factor analysis also can be used to identify individual variables to combine in order to measure a complex concept and can help select the variables to include in an index. Factor analysis calculates how closely a large number of variables, assumed to be associated with each other, are related to a common dimension or factor. The analyst can pick those that seem to be most closely associated with that factor and then use those variables in the index.

For example, assume an analyst has data on several characteristics of counties in his state. These might include utilization of public services, such as hospitals; measures of conditions, such as prevalence of diseases, the number of high school graduates and dropouts, and the number of handicapped; and measures of per capita income, employment, types of jobs, assessed evaluation of county real property, and so on. The analyst wants to develop indices of human service needs and financial condition. A factor analysis could help determine which of the separate indicators best measure these two dimensions. It would show the analyst how the individual measures are related to the two conceptual dimensions of human service needs and financial condition. The analysis will help him pick out the indicators to use in the two indices and in the weighting of these indicators.

Factor analysis is based on the concept of association. Associations among variables are assumed to reflect the extent to which the variables are measuring the same trait or factor. Factor analysis begins by calculating association measures between each pair of variables of interest. Then, a factor that maximizes the associations among the variables in the set is created mathematically. Next, coefficients measuring the association between each variable and the factor are calculated. These coefficients, called *factor loadings*, vary between 0 and 1; the closer the loading is to 1, the more closely the variable is associated with the factor. Variables showing high loadings with a factor are considered to be measures of that factor. The analyst using factor analysis to help build an index would use as items in that index those variables that had the highest loadings with the factor.

Factor analysis also is used to determine which underlying dimensions are measured by a group of separate indicators. In an effort to learn more about which local governments were likely to suffer strikes by public employees, James Perry and William Berkes conducted a factor analysis of a large number of government characteristics of communities.[7] This case differs from the Need Index presented in Example 10.6, in that Perry and his colleagues did not know what factors would emerge from the analysis. They had a large number of separate variables and wanted to use them to create indices to predict how likely it was that localities would experience strikes.

These authors analyzed the following "public-employment variables":

a. Ratio of local government employee earnings to private-sector employee earnings

b. Ratio of local employee earnings to teacher earnings

EXAMPLE 10.6

Need Index

Factor	Composite Variables	Factor Score Coefficients
Health needs	1. Local suicide rate	.73
	2. Infant mortality rate	.64
	3. Birth rate	.55
	4. Death rate	.51
	5. Families with income below $7,500	.44

The composite value computed for each city on the index, the factor score, is obtained by multiplying the coefficient for each variable by the value that the city has for that variable. The formula that is applied in each case is:

factor score = .73 × (value on variable 1) + .64 × (value on variable 2)

+ .55 × (value on variable 3) + .51 × (value on variable 4)

+ .44 × (value on variable 5).

In combining the values for each separate item, it is usually necessary to use the cities' z-scores for each variable rather than the cities' actual value. Appendix 10.1, at the end of this chapter, shows how to do this and calculates the index value for an example city. The z-score is used to account for different units of measurement and different ranges of the separate items.

---

   c. Local government employment as a percentage of nonagricultural employment

   d. Ratio of local employee legal policy to teacher policy

   e. Number of teacher strikes in one year

   f. Number of public employees involved in work stoppages over a 10-year period

   g. Public-sector employee-days idle, 10-year period

The factor analysis generated two factors from these variables. The authors named the factors based on the variables with the highest loadings on that factor. The first factor was called "Local Employee Status"; the second was called "Past Strike Activity." The factors with the factor loadings of the variables on each are shown in Table 10.4. The authors used these loadings to create indices of "Local Employee Status" and "Past Strike Activity." These composite indices were used to assess how likely it was that any local government would experience a public-employee strike in the near future.

An analyst also can use the results of factor analysis to determine a value for each case for the index. The factor-analysis program provides a second coefficient, called a *factor score coefficient,* for each variable. These are the weights to be used; the analyst multiplies each by the original value of the case on that variable. The results are added to obtain the index value for each case. This value is

TABLE 10.4 PREDICTING PUBLIC-EMPLOYEE STRIKE ACTIVITY: DETERMINING AND MEASURING THE IMPORTANT FACTORS

	Factors and Factor Loadings*	
Variable	*Local Employee Status*	*Past Strike Activity*
a	.97	−.01
b	.99	−.02
c	.93	−.02
d	.69	.05
e	−.05	.46
f	.05	.99
g	.08	.97

*Remember that the factor loadings are measures of how closely a variable is associated with the underlying factor.
SOURCE: James Perry and William Berkes, "Predicting Local Strike Activity," *Western Political Quarterly* (Spring 1979), p. 501–517.

called a *factor score.* Example 10.6 shows an index developed with factor analysis and the factor score coefficients used.

In an effort to develop several indices of urban needs, Gregory Schmid and others used factor analysis to select items for each index. They wished to develop indices of health, social service, recreation, environmental, public safety, and transportation needs and analyzed a large number of separate measures of community characteristics.[8] The factor analysis showed how the individual variables were associated with five different factors. Five indices were developed from the loadings on these five factors. Example 10.6 shows the items selected to form an index of health needs for cities because of the high loading of each of these items with the factor named "Health Needs." The factor score coefficients also are shown. Computer programs that perform factor analysis also will produce the factor score coefficients and can also calculate the composite value, the factor score, for each city.

Factor analysis requires interval level measurement, although analysts sometimes use it when the variables are measured at ordinal and even nominal levels. To develop reliable factors, a large number of cases is also needed.

INDEX NUMBERS

Index numbers express the relationship between two figures, one of which is the base, and are used to describe changes over time in such things as prices, production, wages, and unemployment. Indices, such as the CPI, are used extensively in the analysis of economic conditions. The CPI combines prices for a large number of separate items to measure the cost of living and to describe changes in economic variables over time. This index produces a summary statistic called an *index number.*[9] The CPI, as an index number, provides information on (1) a composite price of a standard set of goods and services, and (2) the percent change that has occurred in the composite over a given time. To facilitate comparison, the index is expressed as a percentage, a proportion, or a ratio.

The CPI is probably the most commonly used and well-known index number and has many subcomponents. It groups the prices of more than 400 commodities and services into eight categories.[10] The index measures price changes from a designated reference date, which is set equal to 100. An increase of 50 percent, for example, is shown by the index as 150. This change also can be expressed in dollars as follows: the price of a set of goods and services in the CPI has risen from $10 in the base year to $15. One can treat the index number as a percent to determine by what percent the price of goods and services has increased since the base year. Currently, 1982 is used as the base year for most of the components of the CPI. Table 10.5 illustrates how index numbers show the relative increase in a factor of interest, such as prices. The index number for year 5, for example, shows that the prices of goods and services have increased by 11.2 percent since the base year.

Administrators often wish to assess growth in the amount of money spent by the organizations they direct. However, they usually like to separate increases in expenditures due to increased services and activities from growth due to inflation. An index number helps them to do that. For example, the administrator of a county hospital can use a component of the CPI to compare increases in the cost of hospital and health-care goods and services to increases in the hospital's budget.

TABLE 10.5   CHANGES IN THE CPI OVER TIME

Year:	1 (Base)	2	3	4	5	6	7	8
Index:	100	101.9	105.5	109.6	111.2	115.7	121.1	127.4

SOURCE: U.S. Department of Labor, *CPI Detailed Report for March 1993* (Washington, D.C.: Bureau of Labor Statistics).

SUMMARY

When a single indicator is inadequate to measure a concept, investigators often use multi-item measures called indices. Three important, related issues in constructing indices are: (1) selecting items to be included in the measure, which involves being very clear about what you want to measure and not omitting any important aspect; (2) combining items to form an index, which requires you to think about strengths of indices, the categories of the index, and type of index; (3) weighting the separate items so the index satisfactorily represents the concept you had in mind when you started. Procedures and methods for accomplishing each of these were discussed. These include Likert scaling, factor analysis, and procedures for standardizing variables.

Likert scaling is most likely to be used when the cases can be rated on several items. It is easy to do and can be done even if only a few items are available. Although each item represents an ordinal scale, by assigning a numerical value to each category and adding the values for each, analysts treat the index as an interval-level measurement. The resulting index value is often treated as an interval value as well. This has the advantage of allowing the analyst to apply statistics that assume interval-level measurement.

If the separate items measure the case's attributes on an interval scale, you may prefer one of the other methods. Factor analysis is used to reduce a large number of measures to a few underlying common factors. The variables associated with each factor can be combined in a composite index. The factor analysis provides information to help in choosing the variables for the index and weights to use for each variable. Factor analysis requires a large number of cases and requires that the measures be interval level.

If separate items in the index are measured in different units, the measures must be standardized. Even if the items are measured in the same units, if the range of values for the items differs greatly, the scale or range should be standardized. If not, the greatly differing ranges may cause some of the items to have a greater impact than others, contrary to the intent of the analyst.

In constructing indices, one should determine whether each item measures the variable appropriately and then decide how to weight each item. If the ranges or units of items are different, the analyst should apply a standardization procedure first and then separately apply a weighting procedure.

The consumer price index (CPI) is an example of an index number. Index numbers typically express the change in some factor relative to a designated date called the base year. The CPI is set to 100 for the base year, and the number for each succeeding year indicates the percent change in prices since that year.

The previous three chapters have discussed data collection and related issues. The next chapters consider what to do with the data from a study once they have been collected. Chapter 11 discusses managing data and analyzing single variables, Chapter 12 covers statistical significance, and Chapters 13 and 14 deal with measures of association.

NOTES

1. R. A. Singleton, B. C. Straits, and M. M. Straits, *Approaches to Social Research*, 2d ed. (New York: Oxford University Press, 1993), 397.

2. Robert Levine, "City Stress Index: 25 Best, 25 Worst," *Psychology Today* (November 22, 1988), 52–58.

3. The Uniform Crime Reports are described in the Federal Bureau of Investigation, U.S. Department of Justice, *Crime in the United States 1987* (Washington, D.C.: U.S. Government Printing Office, 1988). Also see Mark H. Maier, *The Data Game*, 3rd ed. (Armonk, NY: M. E. Sharpe, 1999), chapter 6. Maier discusses the Crime Index and how reporting methods can cause

it to be biased. He also reports on other sources of crime statistics as well as their shortcomings.

4. See Robert W. Burchell, David Listokin, George Sternlieb, James W. Hughes, and Stephen C. Casey, "Measuring Urban Distress: A Summary of the Major Urban Hardship Indices and Resource Allocation Systems," in *Cities under Stress: The Fiscal Crises of Urban America*, eds. R. Burchell and D. Listokin (Rutgers: The State University of New Jersey, 1981), 159–229. The specific index on which Example 10.3 is based was developed by Richard P. Nathan and Charles F. Adams, Jr. They measured city hardship us-

ing 1970 Census data in "Understanding Central City Hardship," *Political Science Quarterly 91* (1), 1976, and updated the study with 1980 Census data in "Four Perspectives on Urban Hardship," *Political Science Quarterly* 104 (Fall 1989), 483–508.

5. Nathan and Adams, "Four Perspectives," 504–506; Burchell et. al., *Cities Under Stress*, 159–229.

6. We do not discuss other common scaling methods, such as Thurstone, Guttman, and the semantic differential. Although these are used in basic research, most administrators are not likely to use them very often. We believe that it is more important to be aware of some principles of constructing indices. However, those interested in pursuing these topics will find them discussed in: Andy B. Anderson, Alexander Basilevsky, and Derek P. J. Hum, "Measurement: Theory and Techniques," in *Handbook of Survey Research,* eds. Peter H. Rossi, James D. Wright, and Andy B. Anderson (New York: Academic Press, 1983), 231–287. For a discussion and an example of the distinction between indices and scales, see Earl Babbie, *The Practice of Social Research,* 9th ed. (Belmont, CA: Wadsworth/Thompson Learning, 2001), 149–152. Other sources for these topics are listed in "Recommended for Further Reading" at the end of this chapter.

7. James Perry and William Berkes, "Predicting Local Strike Activity," *Western Political Quarterly* (Spring 1979), 501–517.

8. Gregory Schmid, Hubert Lipinski, and Michael Palmer, *An Alternative Approach to General Revenue Sharing: A Needs Based Allocation Formula* (Menlo Park, CA: Institute for the Future, 1975).

9. Wayne Daniel and James Terrel, *Business Statistics,* 7th ed. (Boston: Houghton-Mifflin, 1995), 69–81. See David S. Moore, *Statistics: Concepts and Controversies,* 5th ed. (New York: W. H. Freeman and Company, 2001), 308–327, for a thorough but accessible discussion of the CPI, trends, and how to convert the purchasing power of a dollar at one time to another. The reader should note that the CPI received a great deal of criticism in 1997, and a major revision of the methodology for calculating it was discussed and researched. CPI data can also be found at http://www.bls.gov/cpi.

10. For a more detailed discussion of the Consumer Price Index, see U.S. Department of Labor, Bureau of Labor Statistics (BLS), *Handbook of Methods,* Vol. II, "The Consumer Price Index," Bulletin 2134–2, April 1984; and "The Consumer Price Index: 1987 Revision," BLS Report 736, January 1987. Also see the Department of Labor's monthly publication *CPI: Detailed Report and the Department of Commerce's Survey of Current Business* for current and historical values of the CPI and other indexes. See David Ammons, *Administrative Analysis for Local Government,* (Athens, GA: Vinson Institute of Government, 1991) for a discussion of the Implicit Price Deflator (IPD), an index number appropriate for use by local governments. Ammons has clear instructions for using the IPD.

TERMS FOR REVIEW

index	factor analysis	factor score
weighing	factor loading	index number
Likert scaling	factor score coefficient	

QUESTIONS FOR REVIEW

The following questions should indicate whether you have a basic competency in this chapter's material.

1. What benefits does using an index to measure a characteristic provide to an investigator?

2. Why is content validity important to index construction?

3. Explain why an index should provide a more valid and reliable measure than the use of a single indicator.

4. Give an example of an index for which using unweighted items is not likely to cause any problem. (Unweighted items means that all items are weighted the same.)

5. Give an example of a second index for which unweighted items are likely to result in an invalid measure.

6. Explain why transforming variables so that they are in comparable units and weighting the items are usually accomplished separately.

7. Consult a library to obtain a recent copy of the United States Department of Labor's *CPI: Detailed Report* or access the Department's

website at http://www.bls.gov/cpi. Determine how much goods and services costing $50,000 in 1982 would cost in the current year or in the year of the report. What is the CPI for the year used?

PROBLEMS FOR HOMEWORK AND DISCUSSION

1. Develop a Likert index to rate the quality of a public transportation system. List 10 items that could be included. Use the index to evaluate the bus system in a town or city with which you are familiar.

2. Refer to Example 10.4 to answer the following: Assume that a client gave the following responses to the items in the index: Agree, Disagree, Strongly Disagree, No Opinion.
   a. Calculate the index value for this client.
   b. What other item(s) would you consider adding?

3. In Example 10.3, work out the calculations for Items 2, 3, 5, and 6. (Items 1 and 4 are done in the text.) Check your answers against those listed in the example.

4. Pick a sample of five cities in your state, and apply the index discussed in Example 10.3. Remember that the lowest and highest levels of need will be based on the values from your sample, not on those in the example.

5. Name five indicators of health needs that may have been included in the set of measures factor-analyzed in the research reported in Example 10.6. Which of these indicators do you think would be most closely associated with a factor called "Community Health Needs"?

6. Find examples of indices using each of the following:
   a. Likert scaling
   b. Factor analysis
   c. Different weights for at least some of the items
   d. A method of standardizing items that measure characteristics in different units such as dollars, years of education, and percent unemployed.

   Describe how each was used and what it was intended to measure. Do you think that another technique would have been better? If so, why?

7. Consult a recent edition of the County and City Data Book and develop an index of "city hardship" using three of the following indicators: percent unemployed, average level of education, income level, amount of crowded housing, percent of residents under age 18 and over age 64. Copies of the Data Book can be found on the Internet at http://fisher.lib.Virginia.edu/ccdb. Most academic libraries also have printed copies.

8. For one of the examples found for Question 6, discuss the validity and reliability of the index. Evaluate the index in general. What criticisms, if any, do you have of the index?

9. If your class updated and gathered the James Perry and William Berkes data as suggested in Chapter 9, do a varimax factor rotation on the dataset, and compare your findings with those of Perry and Berkes.

DISK WORK

Use the Belle County Questionnaire Data Set to develop Likert Scales for Problems 1, 2, and 3.

1. A measure of knowledge by respondents of services of Belle county. Combine the values of the responses of KNOWAID, KNOWSCH, KNOWENV.

   Generate a frequency distribution for the responses for this scale. Compare these to the distribution for the responses to KNOWSERV. Would it be useful to include KNOWSERV as an item in this scale? Why or why not?

2. A measure of respondents' opinion of the Belle County Schools. To do so add together responses to the following: JOBSCH, QUALSCH, VALSCH.

Generate a frequency distribution for the responses. Write a brief memo describing the results.

3. A measure of how good a job respondents think Belle County is doing in delivering services. Use the following items: JOBAID, JOBSCH, JOBENV.

    Generate a frequency distribution and compare it to a frequency distribution for JOBSERV. Which do you think provides the more reliable and valid measure? Explain.

    What other items would you recommend for a scale to measure the over-all opinion of respondents' toward services provided by Belle County.

4. Use the variables in the Census Data Base to create your own county hardship index. Select indicators to measure three of the following: unemployment, educational attainment, income, crowded housing, dependency (percent of residents under 18 and over age 64). Load the Census Data Base and apply your index. Based on your index, which five counties have the greatest hardship; which five counties have the least hardship?

5. Use the variables in the Census Data Base and apply the hardship index in Example 10.3 to the counties in the Census Data Base. Before carrying out this exercise, you should have worked out Problem 3 in Problems for Homework and Discussion, and you should be able to use a spreadsheet or statistical software package to combine variables and mathematically transform existing variables. Load the data base, identify the relevant variables (use the variable measuring percent population over 75 years old to measure dependency, and percent families below poverty level to measure poverty), create standardized values for each variable, and create the hardship index.

    a. For each variable in the index, identify the county with the least need and the county with the greatest need.

    b. Using a spreadsheet or statistical software package and the formula from Example 10.3, calculate x for each of the six variables for each county. (You will be creating a new variable from each in the index.). Total the x values for the six variables for a hardship index value for each county.

    c. Produce a frequency distribution for the hardship index.

    d. For each of the three counties with the greatest hardship and the three counties with the least hardship, identify the percent of labor force employed in: agriculture, forestry and fisheries; manufacturing; wholesale and retail trade; and public administration. Put your findings in a table similar to Table 9.1. Do these data suggest what types of economic development would be most beneficial? Write a brief (no more than a two-page memo) suggesting types of economic development activity which should be explored in more depth to benefit less-well-off counties.

RECOMMENDED FOR FURTHER READING

D. C. Miller, *Handbook of Research Design and Social Measurement: A Text and Reference Book for the Social and Behavioral Sciences,* 5th ed. (Newbury Park, CA: Sage, 1991), 323–581. Miller lists and reviews many existing indices covering a variety of subjects. Although the majority of these are used in basic research, many others reviewed are likely to be of interest to managers and administrators. These include measures of organizational structure, organizational effectiveness, community services, leadership in the work organization, morale, and job satisfaction.

For an extensive discussion of job-satisfaction scales and similar indices, see J. P. Robinson, R. Athansiou, and K. Head, *Measures of Occupational Attitudes and Occupational Characteristics* (Ann Arbor: Institute of Social Research, 1969). A publication similar to Robinson et al. reviews and discusses a large number of scales and indices measuring social, psychological, and related attitudes. See J. P. Robinson and P. P. Shaver, *Measures of Social Psychological Attitudes* (Ann Arbor: Institute for Social Research, 1973).

I. McDowell and C. Newell, *Measuring Health: A Guide to Rating Scales and Questionnaires* (New York: Oxford University Press, 1987), review and evaluate several indices of health and well-being.

For an extended discussion of the development and application of a new index, see *Methods and Applications in Mental Health Surveys: The Todai Health Index,* eds.

S. Suzuki and R. Roberts (Tokyo: University of Tokyo Press, 1991).

Guttman scaling is discussed in R. L. Gordon, *Unidimensional Scaling of Social Variables* (New York: Macmillan, 1977).

N. Nie, C. H. Hull, J. Jenkins, K. Steinbrenner, and D. H. Bent, *SPSS: Statistical Package for the Social Sciences,* 2d ed. (New York: McGraw-Hill, 1975), 468–514. This book provides references for important sources of factor analysis. Guttman scaling also is discussed on pages 528–539.

Factor analysis also is discussed in the following (Kim and Mueller booklet is more technical than the others):

B. B. Jackson, *Multivariate Data Analysis: An Introduction* (Homewood, IL: Richard D. Irwin, 1983).

J. Kim and C. W. Mueller, "Factor Analysis: Statistical Methods and Practical Issues," Sage University Paper Series on Quantitative Applications in the Social Sciences, 07–014 (Beverly Hills and London: Sage, 1978).

M. Hamburg, *Basic Statistics,* 2d ed. (New York: Harcourt, Brace, Jovanovich, 1979). Chapter 14 discusses index numbers and procedures for combining and weighting items.

For more information on the CPI—Consumer Price Index—see the Bureau of Labor Statistics Web site: www.stats.bls.gov/cpihome.htm and David S. Moore, *Statistics: Concepts and Controversies*, 5th ed. (New York: W.H. Freeman and Company, 2001).

Calculation Factor Scale Scores

In Example 10.6, factor score coefficients were used to construct an index. This appendix gives more detail on that procedure and calculates the index value for a city using the items in the example. The z-score is calculated:

z value for each city = ((city's value for a variable) − (average value of the variable for all cities))/(standard deviation of the variable)

The z-score is a standardized measure for each variable. The mean and standard deviation for each variable are provided by the factor analysis program, and most programs also will calculate the z-scores. Commonly used factor analysis programs also have routines that will provide the factor scores for each of the cases so that this does not have to be done separately by the investigator.

The following calculates the factor score for one city.

Variable	City A's Values	z-Scores for City A	z-Score × Coefficient
1.	3 per 1,000	.5	.5 × .73 = .365
2.	5 per 1,000	−.2	−.2 × .64 = −.128
3.	9 per 1,000	1.0	1.0 × .55 = .550
4.	2%	.5	.5 × .51 = .255
5.	5,000	2.0	2.0 × .44 = .880
Total			1.922

City A's value on the index is 1.922.

Appendix 10.2

Using z-Scores to Standardize Measures for Indices

The z-score is calculated by the following formula:

((value of a case for a specific measure) − (average value of the measure for all cases))/(standard deviation of the measure)

In an index developed to measure the fiscal strain of cities, five quantifiable variables were used, and z-scores for each city on each of the measures were calculated. The variables were:

Population change, 1972 to 1976

Per capita income change, 1969 to 1974

Own-source revenue burden change, 1969 to 1974

Long-term debt burden change, 1972 to 1976

Change in local full market property value, 1971 to 1976

Statistical z-scores were developed for each city for each indicator. The five z-scores were summed for each city to obtain a Total Fiscal Strain value.[1]

You should note that each standardized measure can be given greater weight than others if desired. In the example used here, some of the z-scores were given greater weight as the ana-lysts thought that these indicators were more important than others. The z-scores for each city were multiplied by the following weights before summing:

Variable	Weight
population change	.37
per capita income change	.27
revenue burden change	.12
long-term debt burden change	.12
change in full market value	.12

Population change was given more weight than any other indicator in the index.[2]

Notes

1. Robert W. Burchell, David Listokin, George Sternlieb, James W. Hughes, and Stephen C. Casey, "Measuring Urban Distress: A Summary of the Major Urban Hardship Indices and Resource Allocation Systems," in *Cities under Stress: The Fiscal Crises of Urban America*, eds. R. Burchell and D. Listokin (Rutgers: The State University of New Jersey, 1981), 159–229.
2. Ibid.

Chapter 11

Univariate Analysis

In this chapter you will learn

1. how to prepare and organize data for analysis.
2. about computer programs for managing and analyzing data.
3. about displaying data in graphs, tables, and charts.
4. about statistics for analyzing a single variable.
5. to calculate and interpret measures of relative frequency.
6. to calculate and interpret measures of central tendency and measures of dispersion.

One of the first steps after collecting and assembling a set of data is to get a sense of its nature: What are the values of individual variables? How similar are the values for different cases? How different are the cases? Over what range are values distributed? Even if the analyst wishes to evaluate associations between variables, he also should describe the values for individual variables. Often the main purpose of a study is to obtain data on individual variables, for example when the fire chief or city manager want to find out the dollar amount of fire damages in the city over the past year.

Many of the questions we ask as administrators, analysts, and researchers require us to describe the distribution of a single variable: How many individual programs were funded last year by the county budget? What percent of welfare recipients have lived in the county for less than two years? How much do the per capita expenditures for police differ among cities in the state? How does the tax rate in my county compare to the most common rate?

Two important distinctions in statistics are (1) between descriptive and inferential statistics, and (2) between statistics for univariate and those for multivariate distributions. *Descriptive* statistics are used to summarize and describe the data on cases included in a study. *Inferential* statistics are used to make inferences to larger populations, to use data from the cases studied to conclude something about the cases not studied. *Univariate* statistics tell us about the distribution of the values of one variable. *Multivariate* statistics measure the joint distribution of two or more variables and are used to assess the relationships between and among variables. *Bivariate* distributions are special cases of multivariate distributions; they are the joint distributions of two variables.

In this chapter we discuss descriptive statistics for univariate distributions and several other quantitative measures for describing single variables and their distributions. We also discuss tables and graphs—important tools for analyzing and illustrating the nature of variable distributions—and computer programs for managing, analyzing, and presenting data.

The availability of computers has eased the burden of calculating statistical measures. However, the full potential provided by statistical packages for computers to aid in understanding and using statistics often is not realized. Although more people are likely to use computers to obtain statistical measures, they may not understand the statistics or use them correctly. All users need to understand basic statistics. We discuss several—such as the arithmetic mean, the median, and the mode—useful to administrators and analysts. These measures are often misunderstood and misused. New analytical techniques allowing for useful visual presentations of data have been combined with the power of personal computers to provide additional tools.

Our purpose in these chapters on statistics is to discuss application in a way that is useful. We do not intend for these chapters to substitute for courses in statistics. We provide formulas for the statistics and, in some cases, worked-out examples. However, the main reasons for providing these examples are to clarify the nature and purpose of statistical measures and to illustrate their applications. An appendix to this chapter includes additional information and worked-out examples of many of the statistics.

Data usually must be coded if a computer program will be used for statistical analysis. A chapter appendix includes an example and discussion of data preparation for computer analysis.

COMPUTER SOFTWARE FOR DATA MANAGEMENT AND ANALYSIS

A variety of computer programs are available for managing and analyzing data. These include statistical analysis programs, spreadsheets, database managers, and geographic information systems (GIS). The most powerful and versatile types of software for statistical analysis are *statistical software packages.* These were developed to analyze large datasets and include numerous statistical routines. After the data are prepared, the database file defined, and the data entered, the user can easily conduct many types of analysis. Statistical packages calculate numerous statistics and allow the user to subdivide the dataset, combine the values of different variables, create new variables from earlier calculations, and change the values of variables. Two of the most widely used statistical packages for administrative and social science data are: *SPSS,* Statistical Package for the Social Sciences, and *SAS,* Statistical Analysis System.[1]

Administrators are more likely to have spreadsheets and database managers available on their desktop computers than they are to have a statistical package. Spreadsheet programs are used extensively for managing numerical information. They can be used to calculate many of the statistics discussed in this and the following chapters.

A *spreadsheet* is a rectangular matrix of rows and columns. A spreadsheet program shows on the computer screen a form in which data can be entered in a rectangular array with each row as a case and each column as a variable. The user can enter labels for columns and rows and can enter mathematical formulas. He can change column widths to accommodate lengthier pieces of information, enter and manipulate data, and perform statistical and other mathematical analysis. Numbers, text, formulas, and logical statements are used. A spreadsheet is useful for entering datasets, for recording budget and expenditure data, and in doing arithmetic and algebraic calculations. The data input form for some statistical programs also uses a spreadsheet format.

While spreadsheet programs generally do not perform advanced statistical calculations, most have built-in functions for basic statistics. Users can write formulas to perform others. Managers and students who have never used a statistical program but have considerable experience with spreadsheets often ask why university instructors require them to learn how to use a statistical program. The answer is essentially this—although spreadsheets provide for some statistical analysis, this capacity is limited. Statistical software packages are faster, permit easier alteration of variables and their values, provide a wider range of statistical analysis, and allow more sophisticated data analysis. Spreadsheets, however, are especially useful for managing small datasets, calculating univariate statistics, providing graphics, and entering data. After a data set has been entered into a spreadsheet program, a user can move it into a statistical analysis program such as SPSS or SAS for extensive analysis.

Even fairly large data files are sometimes made available as spreadsheets.[2] Some datasets released by U.S. government agencies are made available in spreadsheet format. Others, including some census data files, are released in a database format, which can be transferred to a spreadsheet program and then to a statistical package.

A *database management system* (DBMS) is a program through which the user enters and stores large amounts of data under different headings. These systems can store textual information for each case. Forms containing the outline of a questionnaire or other data-collecting instruments can be shown on the screen. Information stored in a database can be edited and manipulated easily and specific information located quickly. Database management systems can sort and report large amounts of data quickly. They can handle text, numbers, labels, and formulas and manage related files. If the database has more than one file, the files must be related to each other. A database with two or more files with common variables, or fields, that allow information to be linked across files is called a *relational database.* The most powerful and useful database managers for personal computers are relational database managers. These help the user manage information in new ways and can be used to organize data from separate files for reports and statistical analysis.

Relational databases have several advantages. Old information does not have to be reentered when a new file is created. The first file does not have to save space for records in succeeding files that might have blank fields. Databases are often developed for multiple purposes and the data shared by many users. For example, a county government may have records on personnel, financial information (such as revenues and expenditures), and budget information in a large database accessible to all departments. Several different files may contain information about employees. One may contain employment history, another may contain benefit records, and a third may contain information on training and volunteer activities. Many include a data dictionary function that names and describes each piece of information and its location in the database. The dictionary aids users by letting them know what information is available and how it can be obtained.

Relational database managers can produce summary information, basic statistical analysis, and graphs. Database managers are not powerful tools for statistical analysis. For this reason, analysts often transport the data to a statistical analysis package. If data from more than one file are used, transporting usually requires that the analyst create a new file containing those variables that he wishes to analyze further. The database manager program will do this easily. The resulting file is then transported (exported) to the analysis program.

The major statistical analysis programs provide for easy transfer of data from spreadsheet and database programs. SPSS, for example, can read the files from several different spreadsheet and database programs and accept raw data values for variables and variable names, data types, input field widths, and so on. SAS can convert back and forth between database and spreadsheet program formats and SAS datasets.[3]

Separate data dictionaries should be developed for each file in a database. The planning for this should be done before data entry. The quality of the data is paramount to a good database. The structure of the database makes little difference if the quality of the data or the documentation is poor. Throughout this book we have emphasized the importance of ensuring high-quality data. As data files are linked in databases and their use expands, the quality of the data becomes even more important.

A *geographic information system* or *GIS* is a special type of relational database. Its unique and defining characteristic is that it records data that can be displayed geographically. Many of the data records stored by government agencies include important geographic location information. A few examples are property valuation and taxes, residence information, locations of streets, water mains, buildings, utility lines, and crimes. A GIS has the ability to display this information on maps produced by the computer.

Examples of location information collected by governments and private organizations include data on individuals: taxpayers, clients of various services, school-age children, homeowners, and users of public facilities. Such information may be kept in separate files in a relational database. With the addition of geographic location information, a GIS can show these data in various ways on maps and provide an important method for analyzing them.[4]

The method of analysis provided by a GIS is called analytic mapping.[5] GIS can present data so that the analyst can literally see the relationship between region and values of a variable. The strength of a GIS is not in its capability for statistical analysis but in its ability to map on a geographic display the values and distributions of variables. For example, a GIS can show the locations of users of services, of existing and proposed school district lines, and numbers of school-age children. An important and powerful use of GIS is in combining census data with the mapping capability of GIS. GIS software can be interfaced with statistical packages for a more thorough statistical analysis of variables.[6]

Analytic mapping using geographic databases has developed rapidly in recent years with advances in microcomputer technology, software, and improved collection and dissemination of geographic data. It has many applications in public policy making and administration as well as to a broad range of social science topics. With this tool the analyst can relate the values of variables to areas or locations. Although a GIS map shows the relationship of variables to locations rather than to each other, the distribution of several variables can be overlaid. For example, a city analyst working with a GIS could map crime data and unemployment data on the same map. The same map could also show where the city government spends its money.[7]

We cite four of the many books describing GIS now available. G. David Garson and Robert Biggs discuss the uses of GIS in social science, public administration, and public policy. They also discuss several sources of geodata and GIS products available as well as the relationship of statistical analysis to GIS and analytic mapping. Garson and Biggs emphasize that statistical and GIS approaches are complementary. Given the importance and growth of this technology in the public sector, we agree with them that a generalist knowledge of research methods should include information about this tool.[8]

ANALYZING AND PRESENTING THE DATA

Tabular Presentation

A straightforward way to present data is to report the measurements associated with each case. This is done in an *array*—a listing of each case along with the classification or value for each of the variables measured. An array provides useful information concerning the individual cases but does little to facilitate the analysis of the variables. For example, a researcher may be less concerned with the fire rates of individual cities than with how many cities have high rates and an average rate for the group of cities. The frequency of high or low values or what constitutes a typical rate cannot be easily ascertained from a data array with a large number of cases. Table 11.1 is a data array for three variables and 20 cases from an Injury Protocol (See Appendix 11.2). It would be unusual, by the way, to see a data array included in a report except as an appendix. Data arrays are often so large that they are only included if it is likely that readers may want to analyze the data further.

TABLE 11.1 DATA ARRAY FOR THREE VARIABLES: COUNTY, CAUSE, AND SEVERITY OF INJURY

Case	County	Cause	Severity
01	Baker	Fall	3
02	Charlie	Car	4
03	Charlie	Violence	6
04	Able	Car	4
05	Charlie	Violence	5
06	Baker	Fall	9
07	Charlie	Car	10
08	Baker	Fall	1
09	Able	Violence	5
10	Charlie	Violence	5
11	Charlie	Fall	7
12	Able	Car	4
13	Charlie	Car	7
14	Baker	Fall	6
15	Able	Fall	3
16	Baker	Car	5
17	Charlie	Car	5
18	Baker	Fall	6
19	Able	Car	4
20	Charlie	Violence	7

The first step in organizing the data for analysis is to group cases in an array with the same or similar values and count them. This process is called enumeration and is the starting point for analysis. If the analyst's concern is with the variable distribution itself, rather than with the value of individual cases, then developing a frequency distribution is the next step. A *frequency distribution* lists the values or categories for each variable and the number of cases with each of the values. A *univariate distribution* is the distribution of a single variable. If the variable is the number of fires per 1,000 households per year and the population is the 340 towns and cities of a state, then the distribution consists of the 340 separate fire rates as shown in Table 11.2. Remember, however, that one table may include several univariate distributions.

The categories in the frequency distribution must be exhaustive and mutually exclusive. The categories for any variable must be defined or set up in such a way that each case will be counted in only one category. Also, there must be a category into which each case will be counted.

Percentage or relative frequency distributions are often combined in the same table with frequency distributions, as in Tables 11.2 and 11.3, and show what proportion of the total number of cases has a particular value or set of values. A frequency distribution should show the total number of cases. If a percentage distribution is presented without the accompanying frequency distribution, enough information should be given so that the reader can determine the number of cases represented by each of the percentages.[9]

TABLE 11.2 FREQUENCY DISTRIBUTION OF FIRE RATES FOR CITIES IN SOUTHEASTERN STATES 1998

Fire Rates (Number of fires per 1,000 buildings)	Number of Cities	Percentage
0–1.99	49	14.4
2–3.99	87	25.6
4–5.99	112	32.9
6 and above	92	27.0
Total	340	100.0

Percentages do not add up to 100% because of rounding.

The letter f, for frequency, indicates the number of cases with each value or category of the variable. The letter N stands for the total number of cases in the distribution and equals the sum of the category frequencies. Developing a frequency distribution for a variable often requires the analyst to decide how many categories of the variable to present and how wide to make these categories, called *class intervals*.[10] If there are a large number of cases and many individual values, the values may be grouped into a smaller set of class intervals. A distribution for income, for example, could have so many values that presenting them all separately would not be very useful. Rather an analyst would group, or collapse, the cases into a smaller number of income categories.

In the example of the fire rates for a number of cities, the investigator may have nearly 340 different values, because the rates include decimal values—for example, 5.75 fires per 1,000 buildings. The analyst needs to reduce the large number of separate rates, presented in a data array, to a much smaller number of categories for the frequency distribution. Table 11.2 shows how this might be done.

The intervals should allow the reader to make comparisons among them. If the variable being grouped is discrete, the highest value of one category is clearly distinct from the lowest of the next. If the variable is continuous, the values of the categories overlap. For continuous variables, class intervals include the left endpoint but not the right. In Table 11.2, the first interval contains 0 and up to, but not including, 2; a city with a fire rate of 1.99 would be in the first group, whereas a city with a fire rate of 2.0 would be in the second group. The intervals should not be so broad that important differences are overlooked. Nor should they be so narrow that too many

TABLE 11.3 FREQUENCY AND PERCENTAGE DISTRIBUTION FOR COUNTY OF INJURY

County	Frequency	Percentage
Able	5	25
Baker	6	30
Charlie	9	45
Total	20	100%

intervals are required. The number of cases in the data array and the range of values in the data suggest to the researcher how to set up the class intervals.[11] Table 11.3 is a frequency and a percentage distribution for the variable "county of injury" developed from the array in Table 11.1. The frequency distribution lists each value or category of the variable in one column and the number of cases with that value—the frequency—in another. Note how this table is fully labeled.

Cumulative Frequency Distribution

A cumulative frequency distribution shows how many cases are below a certain value of the variable. Table 11.4 shows a frequency and cumulative frequency distribution for the ages of a number of employees.

The entries in the cumulative frequency column are obtained by adding the number of observations in an interval to the total number of observations from the first interval through the preceding one. For example, Table 11.4 shows that 39 employees are under 50 years of age.

TABLE 11.4   FREQUENCY AND CUMULATIVE FREQUENCY DISTRIBUTION OF AGES OF EMPLOYEES

Age in Years	Frequency	Cumulative Frequency
20–29	9	9
30–39	14	23
40–49	16	39
50–59	21	60
Total	60	

VISUAL PRESENTATION OF DATA

Visual presentations of data often can illustrate points more clearly than do verbal descriptions. Tables, charts, and graphs help the analyst see what is in the data as well as to present them to an audience. The analyst should prepare a picture of the data for his own use. Visual presentations can be more precise and revealing than conventional statistical computations. Maps showing the distribution of variable values and frequencies are also very useful and easily produced with GIS software. The injury data from Table 11.1, for example, could be shown on a map of the counties involved.

Visual displays should:

show the data.

entice the reader to think about the substance of the information.

avoid distorting what the data have to say.

make large datasets coherent.

encourage the eye to compare different pieces of data.

serve a clear purpose—to describe, explore, tabulate, or elaborate.

enhance the statistical and verbal descriptions of the data.[12]

Tables

Tables are a familiar visual presentation. Students have produced and interpreted tables since grade school. However, tables can be easily misinterpreted and are sometimes confusing. Analysts must make certain that their tables can be understood easily and correctly. Administrators must make sure that they interpret correctly the various tables they are presented.

Conventions important in constructing tables are:

1. Provide a descriptive title for each table. This applies as well to charts, graphs, and figures.
2. Label variables and variable categories. All rows and columns should also be fully labeled.

Develop the habit of fully labeling each table, graph, or other display. Although each graph, table, and figure in a report should be discussed, if only to identify it and its purpose, readers should be able to comprehend and interpret each without reference to the discussion.

Several conventions have been developed for tables showing the joint distribution of two variables. Usually the independent variable is the column variable with its label and categories along the top of the table. The dependent is the row variable with its categories forming the rows. The frequencies in each column of the independent variable are then totaled at the bottom. The frequencies in each row of the dependent variable are added across and shown at the right side of the table. We discuss two-variable tables in more detail in Chapters 12 and 13.

Bar Graphs and Histograms

Bar graphs are a particularly effective and simple way to present data. A *bar graph* shows the variable along one axis and the frequency of cases along the other. The length of the bar indicates the number of cases possessing each value of the variable. Figure 11.1 is a bar graph for the variable "county of injury" from Tables 11.1 and 11.3. It is a graphical representation of the frequency distribution for that variable.

The bars in a bar graph should be of the same width for all categories of the variable. It can be misleading to show the bars of different widths for different categories. In fact, that technique is used at times to intentionally mislead the reader.[13] Bar graphs also are used to present percentage distributions for variables.

Bar graphs are sometimes developed with the bars displayed horizontally so that the frequency is indicated by the length of the bar. In this case the value labels for the variables would be placed along the side of the vertical axis as in Figure 11.2. Many computer programs generate bar graphs with horizontal rather than vertical bars, and some authors prefer this. Whether the bars are presented vertically or horizontally depends on several factors, including the

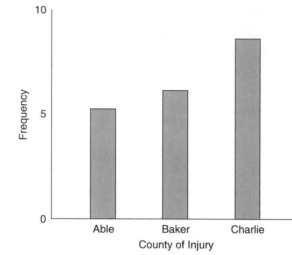

Figure 11.1 Bar Graph for County of Injury

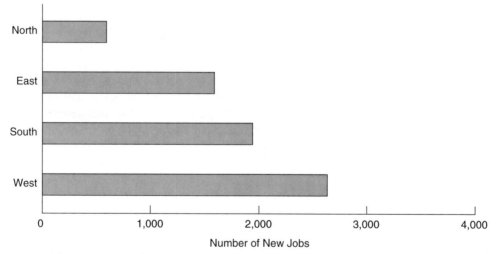

Figure 11.2 Number of New Jobs by Sector, 1984–1990

number of categories of the variable, the length (or height) of the bars, and the amount of variation in frequency that must be displayed. The choice of horizontal or vertical bars depends on which display communicates more effectively and clearly.

A *histogram* is a bar graph made by plotting frequency of occurrence against the values obtained for interval- and ratio-level variables. It is the common way of representing frequency distributions in statistics and also is used for relative frequency distributions, that is, those showing percents. With the histogram, the width of the bar also portrays information so that the width of the bar and its length or height are related.[14] Each column of the histogram represents a range of

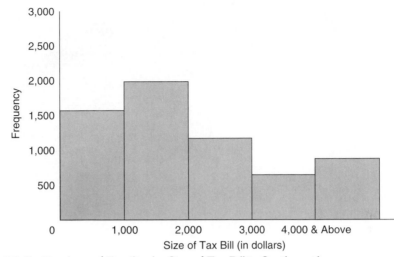

Figure 11.3 Numbers of Families by Size of Tax Bill in Southwood

values, and the columns adjoin one another because the range of values is continuous. The variable and its values are displayed along the horizontal axis, and the frequency or percentage is displayed along the vertical axis of a histogram. Figure 11.3 is an example of a histogram. A histogram represents numbers by area, not height. Histograms differ from bar graphs in that the width of the bars represents specific quantitative values or ranges of values. Although histograms are used for percentage distributions, the percents are not plotted unless the class intervals are equal in length.[15]

Pie Charts

A *pie chart* represents a complete circle—indicating a quantity—that is sliced into a number of wedges. This graph conveys what proportion of the whole is accounted for by each component and facilitates visual comparisons among parts of the whole. The portions usually are expressed as percentages of the whole. Financial information, such as source of revenue, category of expenditure, and so on, is often displayed in this manner. The circle represents 100 percent of the quantity of the resource or other factor displayed. The size of each wedge or "slice of the pie" corresponds to a percent of this total. Consult the budget document for your city or county and you are likely to see information displayed in one or more pie charts. Figure 11.4 is a pie chart showing the sources of revenue for a city government. Some authors advise that when possible the largest slice of the pie should begin at the 12 o'clock position, and the other slices should follow in a clockwise direction according to size, with the smallest slice last. Analysts may violate this rule when two pie charts are used for comparison.[16]

The same information also can be shown by a bar graph, as in Figure 11.5; however, the pie chart—sometimes called a circle graph—more effectively

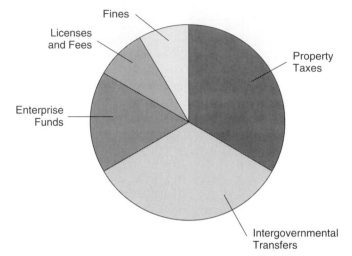

Figure 11.4 Pie Chart: Sources of Revenue for West City

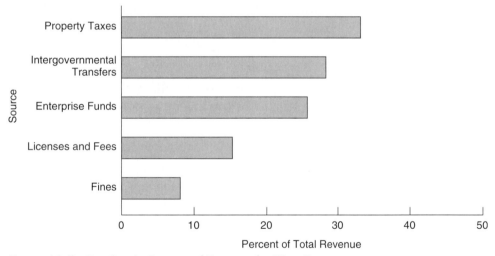

Figure 11.5 Bar Graph: Sources of Revenue for West City

illustrates the relationship of parts to the whole and allows the reader to more readily see the relative sizes of various categories. Pie charts are commonly used to enhance presentations. Many computer programs, such as spreadsheets and data analysis programs, can generate them.[17]

Note on Figure 11.5 how the bars are arranged in declining order of magnitude. The longest bar is at the top, indicating the largest source or frequency, and the other bars become shorter as we look down the chart. This makes it easy to spot the largest and smallest revenue sources. Arranging bars this way is particularly effective in charts with numerous bars.

Line Graphs

Line graphs used for displaying frequencies are primarily of two types: the frequency polygon and the time series. We will discuss each here, but recall that we introduced the time series in Chapter 2.

Frequency Polygon

A *frequency polygon* has as its horizontal axis a scale showing the values of an interval- or ratio-level variable. Frequencies or percentages are placed on the vertical axis. The frequency polygon is closely related to the histogram in the type of information and in the way that it is presented. The area under the line—the polygon—has important implications. The line is formed by marking a position, a "dot" over the value of the variable at the height corresponding to the number of cases—frequency—possessing that value. The line is formed by connecting these dots. For a distribution with many individual values, the line will appear continuous and smooth. Alternatively, the height of the line could indicate the percentage of cases possessing any value of the variable. The values of the variable indicate quantities measured with an interval or ratio scale.

Figure 11.6 is a frequency polygon illustrating the distribution of the variable "severity of injury" from Table 11.1. We can read the frequencies from the figure by going vertically over the value of interest to the polygon and then to the left to determine the number of cases with that value. For example, there are five cases of injury with a severity rating of 4, one with a severity rating of 9, and none with severity of 8. Figure 11.6 does not look much like a polygon. However, with more and more cases, a smoother curve, such as that in Figure 11.7, would result.

The polygon in Figure 11.7 is an example of an important type of distribution, the normal curve. It can be described by a mathematical formula that allows analysts to make precise observations about this population.[18] The normal curve will be discussed in more detail near the end of this chapter.

Time Series

In a time series, the units of time are displayed along the horizontal axis, and the frequency of some occurrence or the values of a variable are scaled along the

Figure 11.6   Frequency Polygon for Severity of Injury

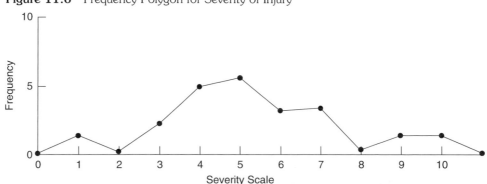

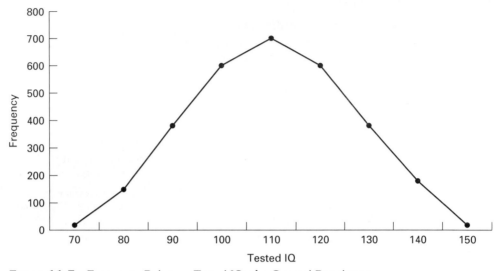

Figure 11.7   Frequency Polygon: Tested IQ of a General Population

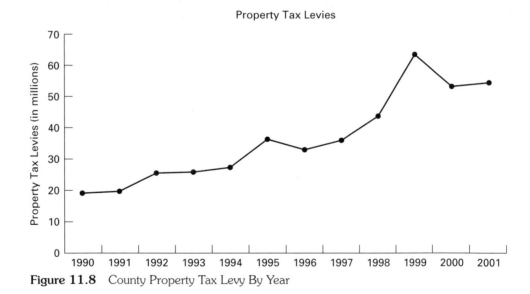

Figure 11.8   County Property Tax Levy By Year

vertical axis. The time scale marks the passage of time in units such as days, months, or years. Figure 11.8 shows a line graph of a time series—county property tax levy by year.

For many time series, the occurrences being enumerated are given in *rates.* Time-series graphs of accident rates, crime rates, unemployment rates, and so forth, allow the analyst to compare these factors from year to year without worrying about changes in population, because these changes are accounted for in the process of calculating rates.

QUANTITATIVE MEASURES

Numerous measures are available for summarizing and comparing data sets as well as for measures of individual quantities. These include traditional statistical measures such arithmetic means as well as newer measures use for specific purposes.

Percentage or Relative Frequency Distribution

The most well-known relative frequency is the percentage. Almost everyone is familiar with percents and can quickly understand presentations based on them. A *percent* reports the number of units as a proportion of 100. It is calculated by dividing the frequency of one category of the variable by the total number of cases in the distribution and multiplying the result by 100. Percents are especially useful when the analyst wants to compare the frequency of the part to the whole or compare frequency distributions with different numbers of cases.

Proportion

Parts of a whole are sometimes given as proportions. A *proportion* is the same as a percentage, except we do not multiply it by 100. The formula for a proportion is: proportion $= f/N$. For example, the proportion of all injuries in the distribution in Table 11.3 that occurred in Able County is .25.

Percent Change

Analysts are often interested in the degree of change in the frequency or amount of something over time. The changes in budget amounts, tax collections, population, unemployment, and so forth, are important to track over time. A relative frequency that provides a useful measure of change is the *percent change.* This converts to a percentage the amount of change in the value of a variable between two points in time for a case. The formula is:

$$\text{percent change} = ((N_2 - N_1)/N_1) \cdot (100)$$

The value of the variable at the earlier time (N_1) is subtracted from the value at the later time (N_2), and the difference is divided by the earlier value. The result is multiplied by 100 to produce a percent. For example, the population of Mecklenburg County increased from 511,433 in 1990 to 695,454 in 2000. This is a 36 percent increase in population.

$$N_1 = 511,433; N_2 = 695,454$$
$$\text{percent change} = ((695,454 - 511,433)/511,433) \cdot 100$$
$$= (184,021/511,433) \cdot 100 = 35.98 = 36\%$$

Of course, the percent change could be negative, indicating a decrease in the frequency or value. Recently in one small city in Texas, property-tax collections declined from \$13,300,000 to \$12,700,000 from one year to the next. This is a 4.5 percent decrease.

Do not attempt to find an average yearly rate of change by dividing the percentage change over a period of time by the number of years involved. Think of the percentage change as an interest rate that is compounded at the end of each year. The base on which each succeeding year's growth is calculated changes. In the previous example of population change in Mecklenburg County, for example, it would not be accurate to calculate an average yearly growth rate by dividing the total percent change for the decade by 10. The appropriate statistical measure to use in this case is the geometric mean. We will discuss this after discussing the arithmetic mean. Logarithms can also be used to determine the yearly average growth.

Ratio

A *ratio* compares the frequency of one variable category to the frequency of another variable category. Patient-to-physician ratios and student-to-teacher ratios are common. Often the denominator is reduced to 1; for example, the patient-to-physician ratio for a state may be 240 to 1, or the student-to-teacher ratio for a school system is 30 to 1. Administrators can compare these ratios for different years or for different communities. We may also compare the number of cases in one category of a variable to that in another. For example, assume that we found that an organization employed 45 men and 15 women; we would express this as a ratio of men to women employees of 3 to 1.

Rates

Rates are defined as the number of actual occurrences of an event divided by the number of possible occurrences of that event over some period of time. To compare the number of occurrences of an event, such as crimes or traffic accidents in a year for different cities or states, the number of occurrences must be evaluated by standardizing the measure. This is usually done by dividing the frequency of the occurrence of an event in a jurisdiction by the total population of that jurisdiction.

For example, in 1990, Perth County had only 24 automobile accidents, whereas Maltiby County had 384. Which county has the greater accident problem? Directly comparing the number of accidents would not be useful since Perth County had only 14,800 inhabitants, while Maltiby County had 307,700 inhabitants. A more useful comparison is the frequency of automobile accidents in each county relative to the population of the county.

Dividing the number of automobile accidents by the population for each county results in ratios of 24 to 14,800 or .001621 to 1 for Perth County and 394 to 307,700 or .00128 to 1 for Maltiby. The large imbalance between the numerator and the denominator makes it difficult to comprehend these figures. The decimal values are so small that readers, and analysts, find it hard to attend to and interpret them. These problems can be corrected by multiplying by a base number that will convert the numerator from a decimal to a whole number. Multiply-

TABLE 11.5   AUTOMOBILE ACCIDENTS FOR TWO COUNTIES, 1990

County	Number of Accidents	Population	Rate
Perth	24	14,800	1.62 per 1,000 of population
Maltiby	394	307,700	1.28 per 1,000 of population

ing by 1,000 as a base number produces 1.621 accidents per 1,000 of population for Perth County and 1.28 per 1,000 of population for Maltiby County. This is clearer and makes the comparison of these rates between counties or over time much more meaningful. Table 11.5 illustrates this.

A *rate* divides one frequency count N_1, by another frequency count, N_2, and multiplies the result by a base number. The numerator, N_1, in the rate formula contains the count for the variable of interest; for an accident rate, it is the number of accidents; for the murder rate, it is the number of murders. The denominator, N_2, is the population size or another indicator of the number of cases at risk. The formula for a rate is as follows:

$$\text{rate} = (N_1/N_2)(\text{base number})$$

The selection of the denominator for the rate is very important but somewhat arbitrary. For many rates the denominator is the size of the population. However, an analyst could compare the frequency of automobile accidents in a county relative to the number of automobiles in the county. Automobile death rates also are expressed in terms of millions of miles driven. Rates also are given for the size of the population at risk. The rate of a childhood disease, for example, means more if it is given relative to the number of children in the population rather than for the entire population. Example 11.1 illustrates how the choice of a denominator for the rate can influence our perspective of the subject variable.

The following conventions apply in selecting an appropriate base number. Remember that these are conventions, not absolutes.

1. Be consistent with rates already in general use for given properties. Be consistent in your own use of rates for the same properties. Crime rates, for example, are usually given as crimes per 100 of the population. Birth and death rates, however, are usually given per 1,000 of the population.

2. The base number should produce a rate with a whole number of at least one digit and not more than four digits.

3. The base number is usually an exponent of 10 (10, 10^2, 10^3, and so forth).

4. Use the same base number when calculating rates for comparison. For instance, in the above case, you would not use a base number of 1,000 for Maltiby County and a base number of 100 for Perth County.

Rates are reported for birth, death, crime, accident, illness, unemployment, and countless other variables. Note that a rate is meaningful only if it is specified for a particular time period, usually a year.

EXAMPLE 11.1

Selecting a Denominator for a Rate

Policy analysts in a large southeastern state investigated the potential impact of a proposed law requiring hunters to wear orange reflective clothing. Opponents of the proposal pointed out that the rate of hunting deaths in the state was very low and did not differ from states with a reflective-clothing law. They used the state's population as the denominator for the rate calculation. A more useful denominator might have been the number of hunting licenses issued. This would provide a more useful rate to compare with other states having a law requiring hunters to wear orange clothing.

Consider the following information from states A and B.

State	A	B
"Wear orange" law:	No	Yes
Number of hunting fatalities:	9	5
State's population:	5,500,000	3,200,000
Number of hunting licenses issued:	18,100	16,900

Calculate the following rates for both states (use 100,000 as the base number):

1. Number of hunting fatalities per population
2. Number of hunting fatalities per licensed hunter

Do you think that the "wear orange" law is a good idea? Do you see how the choice of a denominator for the rate calculation influences the perspective?

Rate calculation answers:

1. **A.** 16 per 100,000 population   **B.** 15 per 100,000 population
2. **A.** 49.7 per 100,000 hunters   **B.** 29.6 per 100,000 hunters

SOURCE: *The Charlotte Observer* (Charlotte, NC, December 28, 1986).

Special Uses of Rates: Health Care

Health-care professionals use rates extensively and have developed a number of commonly used measures. Many of the terms used in the discussion of rates come from the various fields of health care. Four such terms are morbidity, incidence, prevalence, and mortality rate.

Morbidity is a measure of disease frequency or the number of persons with one or more specified health conditions. The rate calculations discussed in the previous section apply to morbidity measures: We want to know how many people have a disease, were robbed, were involved in an accident, and so on. Incidence and prevalence are the two most commonly used measures of morbidity.[19]

Incidence is defined as the number of people who get a disease over a specified period of time, usually a year. *Prevalence* is defined as the total number of people who have a disease at a given time. We can apply these concepts to the occurrence of conditions other than disease, for example, being a victim of a crime, having an accident, and so on. Incidence is calculated according to the following formula:

incidence rate = number of new cases of a disease in a population over a specific period of time divided by the total population at risk of the disease in the same period of time

In calculating incidence, only the new cases for the time period in question are included. If we are investigating the incidence of a chronic disease, such as diabetes for 2001, we would include in our rate calculations only the number of new cases occurring in 2001. Cases carrying over from 2000 or previous years would not be counted.

In measuring prevalence, cases carrying over from previous years are included in the count. Those individuals who developed diabetes in 1999 and still had the condition would be included in the 2001 prevalence count. Incidence and prevalence as well as mortality rates are usually calculated for a year's time. The number of people in the population of interest at midyear is then used as the denominator. Prevalence rates can be determined using a cross-sectional design; incidence rates typically require a longitudinal design. Usually a panel or a cohort design is used, with cohort design the more common. Ideally, to determine incidence, an analyst would follow a population over time.

The formula for a prevalence rate is:

prevalence rate = total number of cases of a disease in a population at a specific time divided by the total population at risk of the disease in the same period of time

All of us are aware of the danger of AIDS. Public-health and other officials are concerned with both the number of new cases each year and the total number of people with AIDS. The first of these concerns involves incidence and the second involves prevalence. Another example is the statistics on epilepsy in Olmsted County, Minnesota, where one year the incidence was 30.8 cases per 100,000 of population and the prevalence was 376 cases per 100,000 of population.[20]

A *mortality rate* is an expression of the observed number of deaths per unit of a specified population in a defined period of time. Mortality rates are given for all causes for the total population, for specific causes, and for specific components or parts of the population. They are typically given as the number of deaths per 1,000 of population. To make better use of mortality rates, analysts adjust them by the age, race, and sex composition of the populations studied. The unadjusted, or crude, mortality rate is calculated according to the following formula:

mortality rate = (all deaths in the population during a calendar year divided by the population size at midyear) × 1000

CHARACTERISTICS OF A DISTRIBUTION

In summarizing a distribution of values, analysts usually want to provide several kinds of information. They want to indicate how similar the individual values are to each other and also how different they are. Two types of statistics are ordinarily used to describe the distribution of one variable: (1) measures of central tendency, and (2) measures of dispersion. These categories represent two important things that an analyst usually wants to show about a group of values: how similar the individual values are and how different they are. Several measures are included in each of these categories. The choice of which to use depends on the level of measurement of the variable and the information the analyst wants to obtain. Other types of measures also are used by statisticians, but we do not discuss them here.

The measures of central tendency indicate what a typical value or case in the distribution is like. One might ask how well the measure of central tendency reflects the overall nature of the distribution. This leads to measures of the variability of the values in a distribution. Measures of variability include those of spread, variation, and dispersion. These, along with measures of central tendency, are useful for measuring and comparing groups.

Measures of Central Tendency

Measures of central tendency are used to indicate the value that is representative, most typical, or central in the distribution. These measures include: mode, median, and arithmetic mean.

Mode

The simplest summary of a variable is to indicate which category is the most common. The *mode* is that value or category of the variable that occurs most often. In a frequency distribution it is the value with the highest frequency. Table 11.6 shows the distribution of a nominal-level variable. The mode for this variable is "Council manager": More cities in the table have this form than any other. Remember that we find the mode by determining which category or value has the highest frequency. The mode can be determined for all levels of data: nominal, ordinal, interval, and ratio. A mistake that students often make is to confuse the frequency of the modal category with the mode. For instance, the mode for Table 11.6 is "Council manager"; it is not 45. For nominal and many ordinal variables, the category that occurs most often will have a name; for interval and ratio variables, the value of mode will be a number.

TABLE 11.6   FREQUENCY AND PERCENTAGE DISTRIBUTION FOR TYPE OF CITY GOVERNMENT

Type of Government	Frequency	Percentage
Strong mayor	22	25
Council manager	45	51
Weak mayor	17	19
Commission	4	5
Total (*N*)	88	100

Median

The *median* is the value or category of the case that is in the center of the distribution. It is the value of the case that divides the distribution in two; one-half of the cases have values less than the median and one-half of them have values greater than the median. The median requires that variables be measured at the ordinal or interval level. It can be determined only if the values can be ordered. It makes no sense, by the way, to find the middle case if the cases have not been ordered according to their values on the variable of interest.

To find the median, we must locate the middle case in a distribution. To find the middle case we add 1 to the number of cases and divide by 2, or: $(N + 1)/2$. If the number of cases (N) is odd, then the median will be the value of a specific case. If N is even, then the median is estimated as the value that is halfway between two cases. For example, if N is 21, then the median is the value of the 11th case. If N is 22, then the median would be halfway between the value of case number 11 and case number 12. Several examples follow.

Table 11.7 shows the distribution of an ordinal variable from a sample survey. The table also includes a column showing the cumulative percent, that is, the percent of cases with a particular value or less. The middle case is the case $(629 + 1)/2 = 315$. This case is in the rating category "Good." The median for this variable, then, is "Good." One-half of the cases rated county government as "Good" or better, and one-half rated it as "Good" or worse. Note that the cumulative percent reaches 50 in the "Good" category. Cumulative percent information allows us to quickly locate the category containing the middle case.

TABLE 11.7   RATING OF COUNTY GOVERNMENT

Rating	Frequency	Percentage	Cumulative Percentage
Poor	36	5.7	5.7
Fair	206	32.8	38.5
Good	287	45.6	84.1
Excellent	100	15.9	100.0
Total (N)	629	100.0	

Table 11.8 shows a small distribution of values—the yearly incomes of a number of employees. We will discuss how to calculate the median income for this group. The first part of Table 11.8 shows the income data as it was collected; that is, the values are not in any particular order. To find the median, the cases must be ordered according to increasing or decreasing values. Sometimes, people unfamiliar with calculating the median overlook this. The second part of Table 11.8

TABLE 11.8   YEARLY INCOMES OF SEVEN EMPLOYEES (IN DOLLARS)

(1) Unordered:	17,000	25,000	30,000	12,000	24,000	18,000	27,000
(2) Ordered:	12,000	17,000	18,000	24,000	25,000	27,000	30,000

TABLE 11.9   YEARLY INCOMES OF EIGHT EMPLOYEES (IN DOLLARS)

12,000	17,000	18,000	24,000	25,000	27,000	30,000	58,000

orders the incomes from lowest to highest. The median is the income of the fourth case, which is the middle case in the ordered set. Since the number of cases N in the distribution is 7, the middle case is $(N + 1)/2 = 8/2 = 4$. The value of the median is the income of that case, $24,000.

Consider how the median would be affected if one more case were added. Table 11.9 shows the same distribution as does Table 11.8 with one income figure added. In Table 11.9, N is 8, an even number, so the middle of the distribution is between case number 4 and case number 5. We would place the median value halfway between the values of these cases. This value would be

$$(24,000 + 25,000)/2 = 24,500$$

Notice how little the extreme value of the highest income in the distribution affects the median. In Table 11.9, the one income of $58,000 is substantially higher than any of the other incomes. However, the median is only $500 higher than the median of the distribution in Table 11.8. This is one of the most important characteristics of the median. An additional property is that when used with interval and ratio variables, the median is closer to all other values than any other point in the distribution.

The median should be used as the measure of central tendency for ordinal variables. It is also useful for interval variables if the distribution has a few extreme values, as in Table 11.9. A distribution such as this with a few extreme values is said to be skewed. The most serious problems of skewing seem to occur with variables measuring resources. These include income, in particular, but also the values of stock, land, and other real estate owned by individuals and families. Since the median is affected little by extreme numerical values, it gives an accurate picture of central tendency even for highly skewed distributions.

Computing the Median from Grouped Data   It is often necessary to compute the median from grouped data, that is, data already organized and presented in a frequency distribution with class intervals more than one unit wide. Table 11.10 shows such a distribution. Since the individual values in the frequency distribu-

TABLE 11.10   AGES OF EMPLOYEES IN CENTRAL AGENCY

Age (in years)	Frequency	Cumulative Frequency
20–29	9	9
30–39	14	23
40–49	16	39
50–59	21	60
Total	60	

tion are not identifiable, we cannot find the exact value of the median. One method of estimating the median is to find the class interval containing the middle case and take the midpoint of that interval as the median. The middle case is in the third class interval, the interval with ages 40–49. The midpoint of this interval is 44.5 years; thus 44.5 is the estimated median.[21] A more exact procedure for estimating the median from grouped data is illustrated in the appendix to this chapter.

Arithmetic Mean

A third way of measuring central tendency is with the arithmetic average or arithmetic mean. This is probably the most commonly known measure of central tendency. The *arithmetic mean* (mean or $\overline{X}$) is the arithmetic balance point or center of the distribution. By that we mean that the sum of the differences from the mean for values above the mean is equal to differences from the mean of the values below the mean. Although the mean is sometimes the middle of the distribution and has the same value as the median, we cannot always expect this to be so. To use the mean requires variables to be measured at the interval or ratio level.

The mean is created by mathematical calculations involving the values of each case. It is useful by itself as a measure of central tendency but is also an important component of many other statistical formulas. To calculate the arithmetic mean, add the value of the variable for each case and divide by the number of cases. The following is the formula for the arithmetic mean.

$$\text{arithmetic mean} = \overline{X} = \Sigma X_i / N$$

The symbol Σ means to sum the value of the variable for each individual case. X_i is the value of the variable for each case. The distribution in Table 11.9 would have the arithmetic mean as follows:

$$\Sigma X_i = 12{,}000 + 17{,}000 + 18{,}000 + 24{,}000 + 25{,}000 + 27{,}000$$
$$+ \ 30{,}000 + 58{,}000$$
$$= 211{,}000$$
$$\text{arithmetic mean} = 211{,}000/8 = \$26{,}375$$

For a frequency distribution, the following formula is more useful:

$$\overline{X} = (\Sigma f_i x_i)/N$$

This directs you to multiply each value of the variable by the frequency of that value (f), then add these values and divide by the total number of cases (N).

Calculate the mean for the distribution in Table 11.8. You should obtain $21,857. This illustrates how a few extremely high or low values will greatly affect the value of the mean. The reason that the mean for distribution 11.9 is so much higher than the mean for distribution 11.8 is the one very high income of $58,000. If a distribution has a few extreme values, the mean is not as useful a measure of central tendency, and the median is the preferred measure. Providing both the mean and the median for distributions of interval and ratio variables is often useful, and we recommend it.

TABLE 11.11   AGES OF EMPLOYEES IN CENTRAL AGENCY

Age (in years) (X)	Frequency (f)	Midpoint of Interval (m)	(f) × (m)
20–29	9	24.5	220.5
30–39	14	34.5	483.0
40–49	16	44.5	712.0
50–59	21	54.5	1,144.5
Total	60		2,560.0

Computing the Mean from Grouped Data   As with the median, analysts often want to have the mean for data grouped in class intervals and presented in tables. In this situation the analyst multiplies the value of the midpoint of each interval of the variable by the frequency of that interval.[22] The resultant values are added and divided by the total number of cases to obtain the mean. The procedure is demonstrated in Table 11.11, which reproduces the data from Table 11.10. The arithmetic mean for this distribution is 42.7. The reader should compare this to the value of the median.

Geometric Mean

The *geometric mean* is used to average ratios and rates of change. Assume that an agency's budget increased from $100,000 to $150,000 over a period of five years. The change is 50 percent during this time. But how much has the budget grown on a yearly basis? If we used the arithmetic mean and divided the total percentage change by the number of years—5—the average yearly change would be 10 percent. However, this would be too high. If you start out with the beginning budget of $100,000 and increase it by 10 percent each year, the ending budget will be larger than $150,000. (It is a useful exercise to do this.) The actual average yearly growth is less than 10 percent. The geometric mean is used to calculate this. Several sources are available for those who wish to pursue this topic.[23] Our concern here is that the reader understand that the geometric mean is used with ratios and rates of change, especially in calculating the mean percentage change over time, giving the annual average growth rate.

Guidelines for Selecting an Appropriate Central Tendency Measure

Spindel County was applying for a Community Improvement Grant for one of its low-income neighborhoods. "But the average income in that neighborhood is over $15,000," said County Commissioner Crane. "Yes," agreed Hap, the county's grants manager, "but one-half of the families earn less than $7,000." Charlie, a member of the neighborhood, commented, "The most common income level here is $9,000." The grant application required the reporting of an "average income figure." Which average or measure of central tendency should the grants manager include?

   The analyst needs to be aware of which appropriate measure of central tendency to use. Since each of the measures provides somewhat different information, she must take care to choose the proper one. The appropriate measure of central tendency depends on the level of measurement, the nature of the resulting distribution, and the information the analyst wants to present. The following guidelines should be considered[24]:

1. The median and the mean require ordinal and interval levels of measurement, respectively. If the variable is nominal, only the mode can be used. Nevertheless, the mode is appropriate when the purpose is to report an actual typical figure. In Spindel County, Charlie is reporting that $9,000 is a typical income. If the distribution has two or more modes, both of these should be reported.

2. In a distribution of an interval or ratio variable, if the distribution is unimodal and symmetrical, or nearly so, the mean is the preferred measure of central tendency. In such a distribution, the mode, median, and mean will be the same or nearly so. If, however, the distribution has a few extreme values, either high or low, the mean will be distorted, and the median should be used. Such a distribution is said to be *skewed.*

   Distributions of the measures of income tend to be skewed. For example, in any community, most people will have relatively low or moderate incomes. But a few people, or families, will have very high incomes. These high values will distort the mean. This has probably happened in the neighborhood in Spindel County. The grants manager would want to report the median, as it will be affected less by any extreme income values.

3. The geometric mean has an explicit application. It is used primarily to average rates of change and does not apply to the Spindel County example.

Unimodal distributions that are not symmetrical are skewed. Extremely high or low values in a skewed distribution pull the mean away from the median toward the extreme value. The more the degree of skew, the greater the difference between the values of the mean and the median. The mean may give a misleading figure for a skewed distribution. The median also should be given, and the analyst should compare the median and the mean to judge if the distribution is skewed.

Figure 11.9(a) shows a distribution positively skewed or skewed to the right. The mean is higher than the median and the mode. The distribution in Figure 11.9(b) is negatively skewed or skewed to the left. The mean is lower than the median and the mode.

Measures of Variation and Dispersion

Two distributions may have similar means yet very different values overall. So in addition to measures of central tendency, analysts present measures of dispersion and variation that indicate the extent to which individual values in a distribution are different from each other. *Measures of dispersion* describe the uniformity of the data. Relatively smaller values on the measure of dispersion for a variable imply more uniformity, whereas relatively larger values imply more diversity or variation.

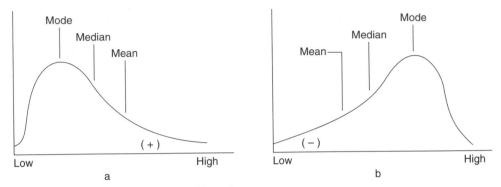

Figure 11.9   Examples of Skewed Distributions

Some measures indicate only the difference between two observations in an ordered set of values. Other measures consider all observations in a distribution.

In comparing distributions of income for two groups of employees, measures of central tendency would be used. The average incomes of the two groups shown in Table 11.12 are nearly equal, but, as a visual inspection of the data will confirm, the individual incomes are very different. Measures of dispersion must be calculated to provide complete information.

Maximum variation for ordinal, interval, and ratio variables is defined as occurring when all cases are equally divided between two extreme categories or values. Maximum variation for nominal variables occurs when cases are evenly distributed across all categories. The more the cases are clustered in one category, the less the variation. If all cases were in one category, then variation would be zero.[25]

Common measures of dispersion for interval and ratio variables are the range, midranges (such as the interquartile range), standard deviation, and variance. Somewhat less common but useful as quantitative measures are the average deviation and median absolute deviation.

Range

The simplest measure of dispersion is the *range.* It is the difference between the highest value and the lowest value in a distribution and indicates the range over which the values are spread. However, it has many disadvantages, since one extreme value will greatly affect its size. Note the ranges for the income distributions from Employee Groups A and B from Table 11.12.

TABLE 11.12   DATA AND ARITHMETIC MEANS FOR INCOMES OF TWO GROUPS OF EMPLOYEES (IN DOLLARS)

Group A: 12,000; 17,000; 18,000; 24,000; 25,000; 27,000; 30,000; 58,000
$\overline{X} = 26,375$

Group B: 22,500; 24,500; 25,000; 26,000; 27,000; 28,000; 28,500; 29,000
$\overline{X} = 26,312.50$

Group A Range = Highest value − Lowest value = $58,000 − $12,000
= $46,000

Group B Range = Highest value − Lowest value = $29,000 − $22,500
= $6,500

These range figures make it obvious that although the two distributions have similar arithmetic means, they are different in other respects.

Because the extreme values in a distribution affect the size of the range, statisticians have developed a number of midrange measures that eliminate some portion of the low and high ends of a distribution. Whereas the range is very sensitive to extreme values, the midrange measures are not. The most common of these is the *interquartile range.* It is also known as the midspread.[26]

Interquartile Range (IQr)

This specifies the range of values within which the middle 50 percent of the observations are found. The first quartile is that value below which 25 percent of the cases are found. The third quartile is that value below which 75 percent of the cases are found. The second quartile, of course, is the median. In determining the interquartile range, the lowest 25 percent of the observations and the highest 25 percent are omitted. The resulting range is less affected by extreme values than is the range. Note the interquartile ranges for the incomes of the two groups of employees shown in Table 11.12.

IQr (distribution A): Range of the middle 50 percent of values, e.g., the four values between $18,000 and $27,000. To find the first quartile drop the lowest 25 percent of the cases, that is, the two cases with the lowest values. To find the third quartile drop the upper 25 percent of the cases, that is, the two cases with the highest values. For this distribution the Interquartile range − $27,000 − $18,000 = $9,000. The spread of the middle 50 percent of the cases is $9,000. Compare this to the IQr for distribution B.

IQr (distribution B): $28,000 − $25,000 = $3,000. The middle 50 percent of the cases are spread over a range of $3,000.

The interquartile range indicates the extent of variation among individual values. It is useful as a means of comparing the variation or spread of two or more distributions measuring the same variable. Many analysts use it to compare distributions over time or to compare the distributions for two or more groups. For example, in a quality-improvement program, we might record the number of errors made by accounting clerks. To show success, we would expect that the interquartile range would become smaller over time and that those involved in the program would show a smaller variation than those not involved. By itself, however, without a context or perspective, the interquartile range has little meaning. A more precise method for calculating quartiles and the interquartile range is shown in the appendix to this chapter.

In reporting on frequency distributions with a large number of cases, investigators often quote percentiles of the distribution. A *percentile* is a value below which a certain percent of the ordered observations in a distribution are located. The 90th percentile of a distribution of applicants' job-registry ratings is the rating value below which 90 percent of the applicants fall. Only 10 percent of the applicants equal or exceed the 90th percentile. The 50th percentile, of course, is the same as the median: 50 percent of the values are lower and 50 percent are higher. The 25th percentile and the 75th percentile are the first and third *quartiles*, respectively, and mark the endpoints of the interquartile range. Students are usually familiar with instructors "curving" the exam scores from large classes to assign grades. Those students at the 90th percentile or above get As; those between the 80th and 89th get Bs, and so forth. *Quartiles, percentiles,* and similar measures are called location parameters because they help locate a distribution on the axis showing the variables' values when the distribution is graphed.[27]

Standard Deviation and Variance

Analysts also need a measure that includes all values in a distribution. Two such measures for quantitative variables are the standard deviation and the variance. The *standard deviation* is a measure of the average distance of values in a distribution from the arithmetic mean of the distribution. The *variance* is the square of the standard deviation. Both of these measures are used in higher-level statistical measures and tests; they are two of the most important statistical measures. Unfortunately, it is difficult to obtain an intuitive understanding or interpretation of them. The following calculations will help explain them.

The formula for the variance is given first, as we usually calculate the variance and then take its square root to find the standard deviation:

$$S^2 = \text{variance} = \frac{\Sigma(X_i - \overline{X})^2}{N}$$

The formula for the standard deviation is the square root of the variance:

$$S = \sqrt{\Sigma(X_i - \overline{X})^2/N}$$

The steps for calculating the variance and standard deviation are these:

1. Subtract the mean $(\overline{X})$ from each individual value $(X_i - \overline{X})$. This shows how much the value of each case deviates from the mean of the distribution.
2. Square each deviation value $(X_i - \overline{X})^2$.
3. Add the squared deviations $\Sigma(X_i - \overline{X})^2$.
4. Divide the total of the squared deviations by the number of cases $\Sigma(X_i - \overline{X})^2/N$. This is the variance.
5. Take the square root $\sqrt{\Sigma(X_i - \overline{X})^2/N}$. This is the standard deviation.

The variance and standard deviation of the salaries in Group A, Table 11.12, are $173.23 and $13.16, respectively.

The formulas presented above are to be used with a population. If you are working with a sample, the denominator, N, is replaced with $N + 1$. Many calculators and computer packages have both N and $N + 1$ programmed in the equations used for the variance and standard deviation.[28] If the means of two distributions are about the same and the standard deviations differ, the larger standard deviation indicates greater dispersion in the distribution.

Alternative formulas for calculating the standard deviation and variance are given and illustrated in the chapter appendix. Although they do not demonstrate as well the principles underlying the measures, the alternative formulas are easier to use with calculators than is the one shown here.

Other Deviation Measures

The *average deviation* and the median absolute deviation are two useful quantitative measures, although they lack mathematical properties necessary for other statistics. Unlike the standard deviation, which is used as a component in the formula for many other statistical measures, the average and median absolute deviations are not used in formulas for other statistics.

Average Deviation

The *average deviation* measures how far, on average, the cases deviate from the arithmetic mean. To calculate it, add the absolute value of the deviation of each case from the mean of the distribution and divide by the number of cases. The formula is:

$$\text{Average Deviation} = \frac{\Sigma \left| X_i - \overline{X} \right|}{N}$$

For most people the average deviation is more intuitively appealing than is the standard deviation. Forecasters use it to estimate the accuracy of models. In a normal distribution, the average deviation is about 20 percent smaller than the standard deviation.[29] The average deviation is less sensitive to extreme values than is the standard deviation.

Median Absolute Deviation

This measure calculates the average deviation of a set of cases from the median of the distribution. A property of the median is that the total deviations and the average deviation from the median are smaller than from any other point in the distribution. This fact makes the median absolute deviation useful in some financial applications, such as measuring the uniformity of property tax assessments of local governments.[30]

The Standard Deviation and the Normal Curve

The standard deviation is used extensively in inferential statistics. It allows us to estimate population parameters, such as means and variances. From our knowledge of the distribution of sample means, we can use the standard deviation to estimate how close any particular sample characteristic is to the corresponding population parameter.

The standard deviation is a key part of an important type of distribution in statistical analysis. This distribution is the *normal curve* and has the following characteristics:

1. It is bell-shaped and symmetrical.
2. The mode, median, and arithmetic mean have the same value at the center of the distribution.
3. A fixed proportion of the observations lie between the mean and any other point.[31]

This last characteristic is very useful. If a distribution is normal, or approximately so, we know what proportion of observations found in it lie between any two values of the variable measured. Typically, these values are measured in standard deviation units above and below the mean. This is illustrated in Figure 11.10.

The mean of the distribution divides it exactly in half: 50 percent of the observations are above it and 50 percent are below. Between the mean and one standard deviation above it lie 34.13 percent of the observations. The same proportion is between the mean and one standard deviation below the mean. Between one standard deviation below the mean and one standard deviation above the mean are included 68.26 percent of all observations in the distribution.

Standard or z-scores are used to measure the value of the observations. Standard scores express the values in terms of units of the standard deviation. A z-score of 1.5, for example, indicates that a case's value is 1.5 standard deviations above the mean; a z-score of −2.0 shows that the value is two standard deviations below the mean, and so on. An observation with a z-score of −2.0 would be an

Figure 11.10 Proportions for the Normal Curve

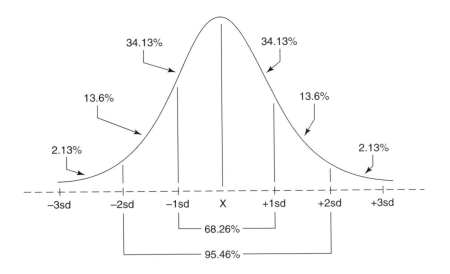

unusually low observation relative to the rest of the observations. Standard scores are calculated by the following formula:

$$Z = \frac{X_i - \overline{X}}{S}$$

where:

Z = standard or z-score = number of standard deviation units
X_1 = an observation
$\overline{X}$ = arithmetic mean of the distribution
S = standard deviation of the distribution

For example, if the mean of the distribution in Figure 11.10 is 100, the standard deviation is 20, and an individual observation, x, has the value 115, the z-score for that individual would be:

$$z = (115 - 100)/20 = .75.$$

If the observations in the distribution are the means of all possible samples, we can determine how likely it is that any particular mean is within a certain distance of the center of the distribution. The center of such a distribution is the mean of all sample means; it also is the population mean. This information is very useful in inferential statistics. It allows us to calculate the size of the standard error and to determine how likely it is that the confidence interval around any particular sample estimate encompasses the population parameter.

EXPLORATORY DATA ANALYSIS

The topics of central tendency and variability are among the oldest in statistics. In addition to traditional ways of treating them, newer techniques have been developed in recent years. Based on the work of statistician John Tukey and others, applied statistics has developed many techniques of exploratory data analysis, often abbreviated as EDA.[32] EDA emphasizes becoming thoroughly familiar with a set of data, rather than just computing one or two summary statistics. The adherents of this approach have introduced new terms and devised new measures of center and spread. New diagrammatic and graphical means of displaying distributions also have been developed and adapted for personal computers.

New measures of central tendency include order-based measures and some variations of the arithmetic mean, such as *trimmed means*.[33] These measures are helpful in understanding the central part of the distribution of a variable. Variations of the arithmetic mean are not influenced by cases with extreme values, or outliers, as these means are calculated after adjusting or removing such cases. The 5 percent trimmed mean, for example, drops the top 5 percent and the bottom 5 percent of cases before calculating the mean. The midmean uses only the middle 50 percent of the cases. Although these means are useful in comparing the centers of distributions without influence from outliers, some authorities feel that they pay too little attention to extreme values. Also, remember that these measures do not enter into the calculation of other statistics.

Several new graphic procedures have been created for data exploration in recent years. These appear to have been motivated both by developments in EDA and by the enhanced graphics capabilities of computers. These techniques and computers provide opportunities for visual analysis of distributions in ways not generally used before.[34]

One popular technique is the *box plot*, also called a box and whisker diagram. This shows in the same graphic the median of a variable, its minimum and maximum values, quartile locations, interquartile range, and in some cases, outliers. Box plots give a quick and clear view of both central tendency and spread.

Figure 11.11 illustrates a box plot for the 1999 murder rates from 23 western and southern states in the United States. The horizontal axis gives the possible values of the variable. The extreme left part of the plot, the end of the whisker, shows the minimum value in the distribution. The maximum value is marked by the extreme right of the plot. The box enclosed by two vertical bars and two horizontal bars marks the middle 50 percent of the cases in the distribution. This, of course, is the interquartile range, with the left vertical bar marking the first quartile and the right vertical bar marking the third quartile. The median is marked within the box by an asterisk. Some graphics programs will show the median as another vertical bar.

The minimum, maximum, median, first quartile, and third quartile values are called the *Tukey five-number summary* after the statistician who developed several EDA measures. These are readily shown on the box plot and often are included in the computer output. For the set of data illustrated by the plot in Figure 11.11, these values are:

minimum = 2.0; maximum = 10.7; median = 6.0;

first quartile = 3.4; third quartile = 7.8.

Figure 11.11 Box Plot of 1999 Murder Rates in Western and Southern States

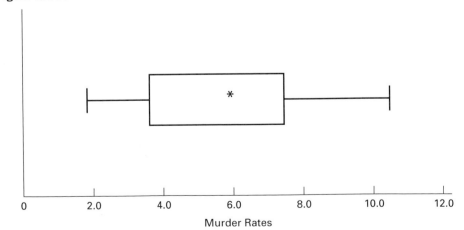

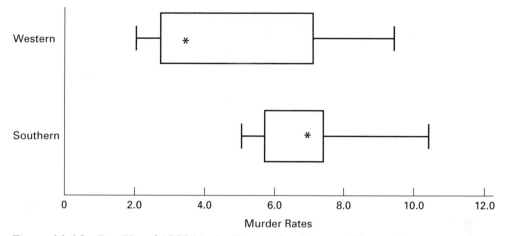

Figure 11.12   Box Plot of 1999 Murder Rates in Southern and Western States

Figure 11.12 shows two box plots on the same diagram—one for western states and the other for southern states. Comparison of the two reveals much about murder rates in the two groups of states. The data for these box plots are included in Problem 9 at the end of the chapter.

SUMMARY

After data are collected, appropriate ways of managing and analyzing them must be found. This chapter discusses preparing and organizing the data for analysis. Data are usually coded and entered into a computer file. A data dictionary enables the user to interpret the meaning of the data codes without having to go back to the original collection forms.

With the increased availability and use of personal computers, hundreds of programs to manage, analyze, and store data are available. Three types of computer software available for the administrator and the analyst to manage and analyze data are: statistical packages, spreadsheets, and database managers. Statistical packages are perhaps the most useful for thorough statistical analysis of large datasets. Spreadsheets can assist in the entry of small datasets, as a medium of data transfer between application programs, and for some simple statistical calculations. Geographic Information Systems (GIS) include geographic data and allow users to show the distribution of other variables on maps produced by the computer.

Investigators typically organize data in frequency distributions for further analysis and presentation. In frequency distributions, cases are grouped by their variable value and the number of cases with each value is shown. Relative frequencies, especially percents, also are included in frequency distributions. Percents, rates, rates of change, ratios, and proportions communicate information about a variable quickly and effectively. Most people can easily visualize and interpret percentage data. Ratios facilitate comparisons between groups or jurisdictions, whereas percent changes and rates of change indicate how the values of a variable change over time.

Various graphs and tables are used in analyzing and presenting data. Bar graphs and histograms show the frequency of cases for each variable value with a bar whose height or length indicates the number of cases. Histograms are limited to interval and ratio variables. Line graphs also are used to summarize and display interval- and ratio-level variables. Time-series and frequency polygons are two types of line graphs. Frequency polygons show the frequency of cases with each value of a variable. Time-series graphs show how the value of a variable changes over time.

Measures of central tendency describe one aspect of a frequency distribution. The mode, a nominal measure, is the most frequently occurring value in a distribution. The median, an ordinal measure, is the value of the center of a distribution's cases. It should be used with interval and ratio variables when the distribution is skewed, as its value is not affected by extreme values. The arithmetic mean, an interval measure, is preferred to summarize those interval variables that are neither bimodal nor skewed. The mean has properties that make it an important measure for many statistical procedures.

Measures of dispersion indicate how well the measure of central tendency describes a variable. A number of measures of spread, such as the range and interquartile range help assess the configuration of a distribution. The variance and standard deviation describe the degree of variation in the distribution of interval and ratio variables. The variance and standard deviation are important components of other statistical measures and are useful in estimating population parameters.

Recent work in statistics has produced measures for exploratory data analysis. This approach emphasizes the benefit of becoming thoroughly familiar with a set of data. Graphic techniques, such as box plots, based on this approach are readily produced by computers, providing additional visual means of analyzing data.

Chapter 12 discusses hypothesis testing and the concept of statistical significance. Chapter 13 discusses the analysis of relationships between variables. It discusses contingency tables and presents statistics for analyzing the relationships among variables in contingency tables. In addition, in Chapter 13 we discuss analysis of variance, a method for analyzing the differences between groups as measured by the arithmetic means of variables. Chapter 14 treats correlation and regression analysis—techniques for the analysis of relationships among interval and ratio variables.

NOTES

1. L. B. Bourque and V. Clark, *Data Processing: The Survey Example,* Sage University Paper Series on Quantitative Applications in the Social Sciences, series no. 07–085 (Newbury Park, CA: Sage, 1992), 45–48. For an excellent, brief introduction to SPSS see *SPSS Base 10.0 Brief Guide* (Upper Saddle River, NJ: Prentice-Hall, Inc, 2000).

2. Larry D. Hall and Kimball Marshall, *Computing for Social Research* (Belmont, CA: Wadsworth, 1992), 230–232.

3. Bourque and Clark, *Data Processing,* 46–47.

4. Andy Mitchell, *Zeroing In: Geographic Information Systems at Work in the Community*, Environmental Systems Research Institute Press; (Redlands, CA, 1997–98).

5. G. David Garson and R. S. Biggs, *Analytic Mapping and Geographic Databases,* Sage University Paper Series on Quantitative Applications in the Social Sciences, series no. 07–087 (Newbury Park, CA: Sage, 1992), 2–3.

6. Ibid., preface.

7. Ibid., 2.

8. Ibid., 76.

9. Remember that the percent is calculated by dividing a part by the whole and multiplying by 100. For example, the percent of injuries in Table 11.3 occurring in Able County is the number of injuries in that county divided by the total multiplied by 100:

$$(5/20) \times 100 = 25\%$$

10. Wayne Daniel and James Terrell, *Business Statistics for Management and Economics,* 7th ed. (Boston: Houghton-Mifflin, 1995), 19.

11. See Daniel and Terrell, 18–21, for discussion of a formula, Sturges' Rule, used to guide analysts in deciding on the number of intervals.

12. Edward R. Tufte, *The Visual Display of Quantitative Information* (Cheshire, CT: Graphics Press, 1983), 13.

13. Ibid., 54–58; Darrel Huff, *How to Lie with Statistics* (New York: Norton, 1954) is an entertaining and informative treatment of techniques used intentionally and unintentionally to mislead and misrepresent data.

14. David Freedman, Robert Pisani, and Roger Purvis, *Statistics* (New York: Norton, 1978), 25–31.

15. Ibid., 30–31.

16. Ibid., 39–40.

17. For example, see "Microsoft Excel" in Gary Shelley, Thomas Cashman, and M.E. Vermaat, *Microsoft Office 97: Introductory Concepts and Techniques* (Cambridge, MA: Course Technology, 2000).

18. Frequency polygons of a particular shape are called normal curves or normal distributions. These have characteristics that are extremely useful in statistics. See Freedman, Pisani, and Purvis, *Statistics,* 69–87, and Joseph F. Healey, *Statistics: A Tool for Social Research,* 3d ed. (Belmont, CA: Wadsworth, 1993).

19. For information on measures of morbidity and discussion of formulas, see a basic text in epidemiology, for example, Gary D. Friedman, *Primer of Epidemiology* (New York: McGraw-Hill, 1980), especially chaps. 2 and 6, or Charles H. Hennekens and Julie E. Buring, *Epidemiology in Medicine* (Boston: Little-Brown and Company, 1987). For a comprehensive list of concepts and definitions used in epidemiology see John Last, ed., *A Dictionary of Epidemiology*, 3d ed., (New York: Oxford University Press, 1995).

20. Rochester, Minnesota, the home of the Mayo Clinic, is in Olmsted County. The medical conditions of its population are among the most thoroughly studied of any county in the nation.

21. H. F. Weisberg, *Central Tendency and Variability* (Newbury Park, CA: Sage, 1992), 26–27.

22. In the calculation of the median we assumed that the lower limit of the class interval was the whole number ending in 0. We make that assumption here as well. In this case the midpoint of the interval is then halfway between two numbers. If the true lower limit of the interval 20–29 is 20, for example, then the midpoint of the interval is 24.5.

23. See Weisberg, *Central Tendency,* 41–43 or one of the other "Recommended for Further Reading" suggestions for a formula to calculate the geometric mean. Logarithms also can be used, and readers familiar with the mathematics of finance will have used present-value and interest-rate tables that can be used to determine the geometric mean.

24. These criteria consider the major properties of measures of central tendency but are not the only ones. See Weisberg, *Central Tendency,* 35, for a more extensive list.

25. Healey, *Statistics: A Tool for Social Research,* 93–97, discusses the calculation of IQV, a measure of variation for nominal and ordinal variables.

26. Weisberg, *Central Tendency,* 63–64.

27. Daniel and Terrel, *Business Statistics,* 65–66.

28. For a more detailed discussion of the difference between N and $N - 1$ in the formulas for computing the variance and standard deviation, consult one of the statistics texts listed under "Recommended for Further Reading"; see especially Hubert Blalock, *Social Statistics* (New York: McGraw-Hill, 1972), 81, 185–193.

29. Richard Chase and Nicholas Aquilano, *Production and Operations Management: A Life Cycle Approach,* 5th ed. (Homewood, IL: Irwin, 1989), 250–254.

30. See Weisberg, *Central Tendency,* 66, for more information about this measure and its calculation. For application to property tax procedures, see John Mikesell, *Fiscal Administration: Analysis and Applications for the Public Sector,* 5th ed. (Fort Worth, TX: Harcourt-Brace College Publishers, 1999), 409–418.

31. For more discussion of the normal curve, see the "Recommended for Further Reading" section, especially Freedman, Pisani, and Purvis, *Statistics,* 69–87, and Healey, 120–130.

32. See the following for discussions of exploratory data analysis. John Tukey, *Exploratory Data Analysis* (Reading, MA: Addison-Wesley, 1977); D. Hoaglin, F. Mosteller, and J. W. Tukey, eds., *Understanding Robust and Exploratory Data Analysis* (New York: Wiley, 1983); Frederick Hartwig and Brian E. Dearing, *Exploratory Data Analysis* (Newbury Park, CA: Sage,

1979); Herbert Weisberg, *Central Tendency and Variability* (Newbury Park, CA: Sage, 1992).

33. Tukey, *Exploratory Data Analysis;* Hartwig and Dearing, *Exploratory Data Analysis;* Weisberg, *Central Tendency.*

34. See Tufte, *The Visual Display of Quantitative Information.* Two recent books by William S. Cleveland also are recommended: *Visualizing Data* (Summit, NJ: Hobart Press, 1994) and *The Elements of Graphing Data* (Summit, NJ: Hobart Press, 1994).

TERMS FOR REVIEW

descriptive statistics
inferential statistics
univariate statistics
multivariate statistics
bivariate statistics
statistical software packages
spreadsheet
database management system
relational database
SPSS
SAS
GIS
array frequency distribution

univariate distribution
class interval
bar graph
histogram
frequency polygon
pie chart
rate
incidence
prevalence
ratio
percentage change
mode
median

arithmetic mean
measures of dispersion
range
interquartile range
percentile
quartile
standard deviation
variance
average deviation
normal curve
box plot
data dictionary

QUESTIONS FOR REVIEW

The following questions should indicate whether you have a basic competency in this chapter's material.

1. How does a bar graph differ from a histogram?

2. Describe the differences between a frequency polygon and a graph of a time series.

3. Why are pie charts used so often in budget documents?

4. Compare percentages to rates. How are they similar? How are they different?

5. When would the median be preferred to the arithmetic mean as a measure of central tendency? In what situations would you recommend using both?

6. "The standard deviation can be used as a measure of how adequate the arithmetic mean is as a measure of central tendency." Explain.

7. Compare the uses of the standard deviation and midrange measures of variation or dispersion. What are the advantages and disadvantages of each?

8. When would an analyst use the interquartile range for interval or ratio level data instead of the standard deviation?

9. When is the average deviation best used?

10. Discuss the criteria to use for choosing a measure of central tendency.

11. What statistics are used to construct a box plot? When would you use box plots to present your data?

PROBLEMS FOR HOMEWORK AND DISCUSSION

1. Develop a data dictionary for the following data collection instrument. You will need to anticipate the responses to Part E, an open-ended question.

Library Users' Study

A. Do you currently have a County Public Library card?

Yes. 1   No. 2

B. How often have you visited the Public Library within the past 12 months?

At least once a week. 1

Less than once a week but at least once a month. 2

Less than once a month but at least once every three months. 3

Less than once every three months but at least once a year. 4

C. Which of the following keeps you from using the Public Library more frequently?

Hard to find parking. 1

Hours are inconvenient. 2

Too far away from home. 3

I use another library. 4

Lack of time. 5

No need for library services. 6

Library doesn't have what I need. 7

I'm not a reader. 8

Other (please specify). 9

D. Do you usually find the materials you need?

Yes. 1   No. 2

E. What subject area or types of materials would you like to see the library add to its collection? (please specify)

F. What is your age?

16–20 years. 1

21–30 years. 2

31–50 years. 3

51–65 years. 4

Over 65 years. .5

G. What is your gender?

Male. 1

Female. 2

2. Write the data record for a case having the following answers to the Library Users' Study survey.

Item	Response
A	Yes
B	At least once a week
C	Hours inconvenient
D	Yes
E	Architectural history
F	31–50 years
G	Female

3. Obtain a copy of a recent budget for a city, town, or county and answer the following questions concerning it. Which types of graphical presentations are used? For what purposes? Which type is most effective? Would you change any of them in order to improve them? How?

4. Change one of the graphical displays from the budget you obtained by using a different format. That is, change a pie chart to a bar graph. Or change a bar graph to a pie chart to show the same information.

5. A users' survey to determine the number of personal computers owned by government agencies in a five-county planning region generated the data shown in Table 11.13. Construct a frequency polygon using these data. Write a short paragraph describing the results of the survey.

TABLE 11.13 DATA ARRAY FOR NUMBER OF PERSONAL COMPUTERS

Agency ID Number	Number of Computers	Agency ID Number	Number of Computers
01	1	16	3
02	4	17	4
03	9	18	2
04	7	19	5
05	7	20	8
06	7	21	11
07	10	22	6
08	6	23	6
09	4	24	4
10	5	25	8
11	9	26	5
12	10	27	7
13	5	28	3
14	1	29	5
15	2	30	3

6. Use the data array given in Table 11.14, which is a slightly revised version of Table 11.1, to work the following:

a. Calculate injury rates for Able and Charlie counties. (The population of these counties is 15,300 for Able and 79,200 for Charlie.) Which is the most dangerous county in which to live?

TABLE 11.14 DATA ARRAY FOR THREE VARIABLES: COUNTY, CAUSE, AND SEVERITY OF INJURY

Case ID	County	Cause	Severity Index
01	Baker	Fall	3
02	Charlie	Car accident	4
03	Charlie	Violence	6
04	Able	Car accident	4
05	Charlie	Violence	5
06	Baker	Fall	9
07	Charlie	Car accident	10
08	Baker	Fall	1
09	Able	Violence	5
10	Charlie	Violence	5
11	Charlie	Fall	7
12	Able	Car accident	4
13	Charlie	Car accident	7
14	Baker	Fall	6
15	Able	Fall	3
16	Baker	Car accident	5
17	Charlie	Car accident	5
18	Baker	Fall	6
19	Able	Car accident	4
20	Charlie	Violence	7

b. What is the ratio of injuries due to violence to those due to falls in Charlie County?

c. What is the mode for "cause of injury"?

d. For "severity index," calculate the following: mode, median, arithmetic average, range, 90th percentile, variance, and standard deviation. Also calculate the z-score for case 07.

7. The population of Mecklenburg County in 1970 was 354,000. In 1980 it was 404,270. Calculate the percent change in population during this time. Compare the change in population in this period to the change from 1990 to 2000. (The 1990–2000 percent change was worked as an example in the text.)

8. Draw box plots illustrating how the distributions from the following figures in the chapter might look: Figure 11.9 (a) and (b); Figure 11.10.

You will not be able to get precise values from the figures. The purpose is to approximate the distribution by drawing a box plot to show the various locational measures of center and spread.

9. Table 11.15 shows murder rate data for 12 southern and 11 western states for 1997 and 1999. These include murder and nonnegligent manslaughter and show the number of crimes per 100,000 of population.

a. Calculate the arithmetic average for the data for each year, and determine the following: minimum, maximum, median,

TABLE 11.15 MURDER RATE DATA FOR SELECTED STATES, 1997 AND 1999

State	1997 Murder Rate	1999 Murder Rate	State	1997 Murder Rate	1999 Murder Rate
Alabama	9.9	7.9	Montana	4.8	2.6
Arizona	8.2	8.0	Nevada	11.2	9.1
Arkansas	9.9	5.6	New Mexico	7.7	9.8
California	8.0	6.0	North Carolina	8.3	7.2
Colorado	4.0	4.6	Oregon	2.9	2.7
Florida	6.9	5.7	South Carolina	8.4	6.6
Georgia	7.5	7.5	Tennessee	9.5	7.1
Idaho	3.2	2.0	Utah	2.4	2.1
Kentucky	5.8	5.4	Virginia	7.2	5.7
Louisiana	15.7	10.7	Washington	4.3	3.0
Maryland	9.9	9.0	Wyoming	3.5	2.3
Mississippi	13.1	7.7			

SOURCES: FBI " Uniform Crime Reports for the United States–1997 edition" (U. S. Government Printing Office, November, 1998) and *Statistical Abstract of the United States*.

first and third quartiles, and interquartile range. Draw a box plot for the data set from each year and label the components corresponding to the Tukey five-number summary.

b. Construct a frequency distribution of the rates for 1997. Group the values into intervals of 5, that is, 0–4.99; 5.0–9.99; and so on. Draw a histogram from the frequency distribution.

c. Review the box plots in Figure 11.12, and write a page describing the differences between the two groups of states in their murder rates.

d. Draw separate box plots for southern and western states for the 1997 rates.

e. Write a memo comparing the rates in southern and western states. Discuss how these rates have changed from 1997 to 1999 (See Figures 11.11 and 11.12).

DISK WORK

These exercises require you to become familiar with statistical software and its outputs. Begin by loading the Belle County data set from the disk.

1. This exercise requires you to use a statistical software package or spreadsheet to learn about variations in respondents' education.

a. Get the following information on respondents' education: frequency distribution, relative frequency distribution, and cumulative percents.

b. Produce a bar graph (for both number of respondents and percent of respondents) and a pie chart describing respondents' education. Which would you include in a report? Justify your choice.

c. If you were including the information on education in a report what class intervals would you use? Justify your choice.

d. Get information on the mode, median, and mean for respondent education. Use the procedure "Computing the Mean from Grouped Data", described in the chapter to calculate the estimated mean. Compare this with the mean on the output. Can you conclude that either mean is accurate? Why or why not?

e. To review sampling statistics estimate the percent of Belle County adults who have at least a college degree. Use a 95 percent confidence level.

2. This exercise asks you to analyze variations in attitudes about the importance of financial aid and environmental services.

a. Produce a histogram and frequency polygon for the variables, IMPTAID and IMPTENV. (Create these visuals for both number of respondents and percent of cases.) Which would you be most likely to include in a report? Justify your choice. Would you consider using bar graphs or pie charts to present these data? Why or why not?

b. For the variables IMPTAID and IMPTENV produce a frequency distribution and obtain the following statistical information: mode, median, mean, minimum, maximum, range, first quartile (25th percentile), third quartile (75th percentile), standard deviation. What do these statistics tell you about the similarities and differences between the two distributions.

3. To see if the attitudes of newer county residents differ from those of other residents recode years into two groups: residents living in the county for five years or less and other residents.

a. Create two sets of box plots. Have one set of box plots compare newer and longer-term residents' attitudes on the importance of financial aid services. Have the other set of box plots compare newer and longer-term residents' attitudes on the importance of environmental services.

b. Write a one-page memo, "How New Residents Differ from Other Residents in Their Priorities for County Services." Your memo should report your findings and their implications.

RECOMMENDED FOR FURTHER READING

H. M. Blalock, Jr., *Social Statistics,* 2d ed. (New York: McGraw-Hill, 1972) is the standard source of details on statistics commonly used by social scientists.

J. F. Healey, *Statistics: A Tool for Social Research,* 3d ed. (Belmont, CA: Wadsworth, 1993) is an excellent introductory statistics text covering a wide range of topics.

K. J. Meier and J. L. Brudney, *Applied Statistics for Public Administration,* 4th ed. (Belmont, CA: Wadsworth, 1997) presents excellent examples and problems suggesting how administrators can use statistics in decision making. The calculations for statistics are worked in detail and are easily followed.

Several works discuss preparation of charts and graphs, theory of graphic design, visualization techniques, and the research supporting these principles. The following four are recommended: C. F. Schmid, *Statistical Graphics: Design Principles and Practices* (New York: Wiley, 1983); E. R. Tufte, *The Visual Display of Quantitative Information* (Cheshire, CT: Graphics Press, 1983); William S. Cleveland, *The Elements of Graphing Data* (Summit, NJ: Hobart Press, 1994); William S. Cleveland, *Visualizing Data* (Summit, NJ: Hobart Press, 1994).

J. W. Tukey, *Exploratory Data Analysis* (Reading, MA: Addison-Wesley, 1977), discusses several techniques for exploratory data analysis, illustrates their use, and provides examples.

H. F. Weisberg, *Central Tendency and Variability* (Newbury Park, CA: Sage, 1992) is a thorough and accessible discussion of these two topics.

For preparing survey data for analysis by a statistical package, see L. B. Bourque and V. Clark, *Data Processing: The Survey Example,* Sage University Paper Series on Quantitative Applications in the Social Sciences, series no. 07–085, (Newbury Park, CA: Sage, 1992); and D. H. Folz, *Survey Research for Public Administration* (Thousand Oaks, CA: Sage, 1996) chaps. 5 and 6.

For GIS see the following: Laura Lang, *GIS For Health Organizations* (ESRI Press, Redlands: CA, 2000). Lang has numerous examples of how GIS is used to map and analyze health conditions and improve service delivery. This inexpensive book includes a tutorial compact disk for the beginner. ESRI (Environmental Systems Research Institute) has numerous publications describing GIS applications (www.esri.com).

Stan Aronoff, *Geographic Information Systems: A Management Perspective* (Ottawa, Canada: WDL Publications, 1989), chap. 6; and William E. Huxhold, *An Introduction to Geographic Information Systems* (New York: Oxford University Press, 1991), chap. 2.

Huxhold is a good source for a discussion of the development of a GIS for urban government applications. Huxhold and Aronoff describe various types of computer files and the similarities and differences among them. David Garson and Robert Biggs, *Analytic Mapping and Geographic Databases,* Sage University Paper Series on Quantitative Applications in the Social Sciences, series no. 07–087 (Newbury Park, CA: Sage, 1992), discuss the application of GIS to public policy and administration.

For a brief yet more detailed overview of the following types of applications programs—word processing, statistical packages, spreadsheets, and database managers—see L. D. Hall and K. P. Marshall, *Computing for Social Research* (Belmont, CA: Wadsworth, 1992).

D. B. Wright, *Understanding Statistics: An Introduction for the Social Sciences* (London: Sage, Inc., 1997) is a very readable text in which the author integrates output from SPSS with his discussion of a variety of statistics.

Statistical Calculations

Estimating the Median from Grouped Data

The distribution from Table 11.10 is reproduced below in Table 11.16.

TABLE 11.16 AGES OF EMPLOYEES IN CENTRAL AGENCY

Age	Frequency	Cumulative Frequency
20–29	9	9
30–39	14	23
40–49	16	39
50–59	21	60
Total	60	

In dealing with the median for such data, we make a distinction between the rough median and the exact median. The rough median is the value corresponding to the midpoint of the interval containing the middle case. We find the class interval containing the middle case by looking for case $N/2$. Note that for grouped data, we do NOT use $(N + 1)/2$ as we do with ungrouped data. Since $N/2$ equals 30 for this frequency distribution, the middle case is in the third class interval, the interval with ages 40–49. The midpoint of this interval is 44.5.

To find the exact median, we can use the following formula:

$$\text{Exact median} = L + j/f(W)$$

where:

L = the true lower limit of the class interval in which the median is located

j = the number of values needed to reach the median after the lower limit of the interval containing the median has been reached

f = the frequency in the class interval containing the median

W = the width of the class interval containing the median

In this example we find that 23 cases have values lower than 40, the beginning of the interval containing the median. To find the middle case, we need to go through 7 more cases out of the 16 in that interval. The interval is 10 units wide so we go 7/16 (10) units into this interval to find the location of the median. This value is added to the value of the beginning of the interval to equal 40 + 4.4 (rounded) or 44.4 years. To compute the median this way assumes that the cases in the class interval are distributed evenly throughout the interval. We must assume that there are as many cases aged 40–42 as aged 44–46 and 47–49, and so on.

Calculating the median from grouped data also requires making assumptions about the true limits of the intervals into which values are grouped. The procedure outlined here assumes that the true lower limit of an interval is the whole number. That is, the lower limit of the interval 40–50 is 40.0. This in turn makes the midpoint of the interval 44.5. Other lower limits can be used as long as the placement of cases with decimal values is consistent with these limits. See Herbert F. Weisberg, *Central Tendency and Variability* (Newbury Park, CA: Sage, 1992), p. 11.

Finding Quartiles

The following is a more precise method than the one discussed in the text for determining the value

TABLE 11.17 YEARLY INCOME OF EIGHT EMPLOYEES (IN DOLLARS)

12,000	17,000	18,000	24,000
25,000	27,000	30,000	58,000

of quartiles of a distribution. For ungrouped data, as in the example array shown in Table 11.17, reprinted from Table 11.12, the first and third quartiles may be found as follows:

First Quartile or Q1:

Value of the ordered observation number
= $(N + 1)/4$

For the array in this example, this would be $(8 + 1)/4 = 2.25$. This would put the value of the quartile between two observations. Case number 2 has the value 17,000, and case number 3 has the value 18,000. The quartile would be 25 percent of the way between 17,000 and 18,000, or 17,250.

Third Quartile or Q3:

Value of the ordered observation number
= $3(N + 1)/4$.

For this example it would be $3 (8 + 1)/4 = 6.75$. This value also comes between two observations, cases number 6 and 7. The third quartile would be 75 percent of the way between the values of these two cases, 27,000 and 30,000. This would make it 29,250.

The interquartile range is the distance between the third and the first quartiles and would be $29,250 - 17,250$, or 12,000.

From this it follows that the formula for the second quartile, the median, also may be written:

Median = Q2 = value or ordered observation
number = $2(N + 1)/4 = (N + 1)/2$.

Variance and Standard Deviation Calculation

The following illustrates the calculation of the variance and standard deviation. Formula 1 is the formula given in the text and is the definitional formula for each. Formula 2 is an alternative that works better if you have a large number of cases and a calculator. Of course,

many calculators have a standard deviation routine built in.

Find the variance and standard deviation of the distribution in Table 11.19. The calculation table setup is useful.

TABLE 11.18 CALCULATION TABLE FOR VARIANCE AND STANDARD DEVIATION

X	X^2	$(X - \overline{X})$	$(X - \overline{X})^2$
13	169	−14.4	207.36
18	324	−9.4	88.36
19	361	−8.4	70.56
25	625	−2.4	5.76
26	676	−1.4	1.96
28	784	.6	.36
31	961	3.6	12.96
59	3,481	31.6	998.56
Σ 219	7,381		1,385.88

Formula 1:

$$S^2 = \frac{\Sigma(X - \overline{X})^2}{N}$$

$$S = \sqrt{S^2}$$

$$S^2 = \frac{1385.88}{8} = 173.2$$

$$S = \sqrt{173.2} = 13.2$$

Formula 2:

$$S^2 = \frac{\Sigma X^2 - \frac{(\Sigma X)^2}{N}}{N}$$

$$S^2 = \sqrt{\frac{\Sigma X^2 - \frac{(\Sigma X)^2}{N}}{N}}$$

$$S^2 = \frac{7381 - \frac{47961}{8}}{8} = 173.2$$

$$S = \sqrt{173.2} = 13.2$$

If the data are from a sample, then $N + 1$ replaces N in the denominator.

Appendix 11.2

Data Preparation

Data are usually coded for storage and analysis by computers. Before collecting the data, project staff should consider how it will be coded, stored, and analyzed, as these concerns may affect the number of variables included in the study and their operationalization. Coding should be kept simple. Data must be in a form that can be entered in a computer file and the desired analysis can be done easily. Usually, this means assigning a number to each value of a variable.

For an example, consider a data collection form used by a state-supported regional emergency medical service (EMS). Individuals suffering head injuries in a multi-county area were taken by ambulance to the emergency room of a regional hospital associated with the EMS. An attendant recorded several pieces of information on each case, including the county where the injury occurred, the cause of the injury, the severity of the injury, and other information about the individual who was injured.

Preparing a data dictionary, also called a codebook, is an important step in organizing and preparing the data. In a *data dictionary,* the analyst lists the items, labels the valid codes for a variable's values, names each variable, and gives the location of the variable in the file. Given the data and the dictionary, an analyst should not need to consult the original data collection forms. Coding all information as numbers is useful for statistical analysis, although it is not always necessary. However, data analysis with a statistical package will be easier with numerical coding.

Data dictionaries typically contain the following information:

1. *Item number*

2. *Item description* This may include the actual question from a questionnaire or the instructions that were used for collecting a particular piece of data.

3. *Item codes* This is the most important part of the dictionary. These show the numbers, letters, or other codes assigned to each possible value of the item. It is a good idea to assign a code for unavailable data. Analysts usually try to use the same code, such as 9 or 99, for missing information for all items. Similarly, the same code may be assigned to all "Don't Know" responses. In a survey, for example, the number 8 might be consistently used to code an answer of "Don't Know," and 9 to indicate missing information.

4. *Variable or field name* Most statistical computer programs require that a name be assigned to each variable. The variable name is used in instructions to the program for manipulating and analyzing the data. Sometimes the variable name is determined early in the process and printed on the data collection form.

A dictionary for the Injury Protocol Data Collection Form is represented in Table 11.19. This questionnaire and the data from it were used for some examples and exercises in this chapter. Note that the unit of analysis for this example is the injured individual.

An identifying number should be assigned to each case and placed on the data collection form for that case. This number should be included in the data record and in the data file.

Computerized data collection systems display a collection form on the computer screen, and the researcher enters the data directly. When complete, the information on the form is transmitted directly into the computer and stored, and a blank form takes its place on the screen. One form is used for each case. This system is often used in telephone surveys and is called CATI—computer assisted telephone interview.

TABLE 11.19 DATA DICTIONARY FOR INJURY PROTOCOL DATA COLLECTION FORM

Item	Description	Codes	Variable Name
1	Case identification number	001-total	ID
2	County of injury	01 = Able	County
		02 = Baker	
		03 = Charlie	
		.	
		.	
		.	
		99 = Unknown or not answered	
3	Cause of injury	1 = Car accident	Cause
		2 = Fall	
		3 = Violence	
		.	
		.	
		.	
		9 = Unknown or not answered	
4	Severity scale	Include actual score: 1–10	Severity
		1 = Least severe	
		10 = Most severe	
		99 = Unknown or not answered	

Chapter 12

Examining Relationships among Variables: Tests of Statistical Significance

In this chapter you will learn

1. the meaning of the terms "null hypothesis," "statistical significance," "Type I" and "Type II" errors, and "power."

2. how to determine the statistical significance of research results.

3. when to use chi-square and *t*-tests.

4. how to apply and interpret tests of statistical significance.

5. the distinction between statistical significance and practical significance.

———————

Deciding how to analyze data involves many choices. The researcher chooses from an array of analytical tools and statistics. The choice is based on her knowledge of specific tools and statistics, the questions she wants to answer, and the properties of the variables and the sample. She learns the tools common to her profession on the job and in her professional reading and training. Investigators have identified certain tools as appropriate for typical questions and data in her profession. Consequently, planners, psychologists, engineers, financial analysts, and administrators may prefer different approaches to analysis and work with different statistics. In carrying out management and policy-making tasks, public administrators rely on analytic approaches favored by social scientists. They use the tools of sociologists and political scientists in working with cross-sectional data, the tools of economists and statisticians in working with time series, and the tools of psychologists in working with experimental and quasi-experimental designs.

The following three chapters should guide public administrators in selecting methods of data analysis and interpreting statistics. We include only the statistics commonly encountered by administrators. Chapter 12 focuses on tests of statistical significance. Chapter 13 looks at two major approaches to examining the relationships among variables: contingency tables and measures of association, used to study cross-sectional data; the basic analysis of variance model, used to study experimental findings and to compare means among groups. Chapter 14 discusses linear regression. Our discussions are not intended to teach you statistics. Rather, we emphasize what you need to consider in selecting a data analysis method or in interpreting statistical findings. In effect, we are interested in the reader's understanding of the applications of statistics. The chapters focus on the questions that a statistic helps to answer, its data requirements, and its correct interpretation and application.

In examining data, the researcher may have two general questions: (1) What is the probability that a particular finding arose by chance? and (2) How strong is the relationship between an independent and a dependent variable? To answer the first question, the researcher works with tests of statistical significance. To answer the second, he works with measures of association, comparison of means tests, analysis of variance, and regression.

Before you start reading, we want to alert you that respected social science researchers argue that tests of statistical significance are overrated and misunderstood. We agree. Nevertheless, we decided to begin our discussion of statistical analysis with them. We did this because introductory statistics courses typically focus on testing the null hypothesis. Consequently, you may be familiar with the steps in significance testing, and the chi-square and t-test statistics. You may encounter these statistics in professional reports and research journals.

Statistical significance can be difficult to understand. We have found in our classes that students feel frustrated and angry if we rush through it during the last week of classes. Furthermore, the term "significance," the time spent on hypothesis testing in statistics courses, and the frequent appearances of significance tests in research reports all suggest that tests of statistical significance are extremely important. To counter this misperception, we point out the limitations of significance tests and suggest alternative statistical information and procedures that provide more information about a hypothesis test.

Tests of statistical significance are a type of inferential statistic. *Inferential statistics* allow an investigator to infer population characteristics from sample data. To use inferential statistics correctly, the investigator must have a probability rather than a nonprobability sample. (The reader may find it useful to review parts of Chapter 5 before completing this chapter.)

Recall that inferential statistics are used to estimate parameters. A parameter can be estimated for a single variable or a relationship among variables. Recall also that with sample data, one can state the probability that a parameter falls within a specified range, called the *confidence interval.* From a sample, one cannot tell exactly what portion of the population has a certain characteristic. Nevertheless, one can say with 95 percent confidence that the parameter falls within ±1.96 standard errors of the sample's estimate.

Another use of inferential statistics is to learn the probability that the observed relationship between variables in a sample could have occurred if the two variables are *randomly related* in the population. Randomly related means that the two variables are independent of each other or not related to each other. Asking if variables are randomly related in the population is the same as asking, "Could this relationship have occurred by chance?" If we examined the entire population or another sample, would a relationship between the variables still be found? The two variables are the independent and dependent variables of a hypothesis. If a statistical test suggests that in the population the relationship between the two variables is nonrandom, the relationship is said to be *statistically significant.*

Just because the relationship between two variables is statistically significant does not mean that the relationship is important or strong. Nor does it mean that all or any of the previous research steps were conducted correctly. An important, valuable, or useful research finding is said to have *practical significance.* Just because a finding is statistically significant does not mean that it is practically significant.

Statistical significance simply tells us something about the statistical relationship between variables. For example, with a large sample, many relationships will be statistically significant. Yet, the amount of explanation associated with the independent variable may be trivial.

The traditional process of determining if two variables have a nonrandom relationship requires the researcher to carry out four steps:

1. State the null and research hypotheses
2. Select an alpha level
3. Select and compute a test statistic
4. Make a decision

You may have learned this four-step process or a similar one in a statistics course. We use it here to organize our discussion. Nevertheless, strict adherence to these steps may not be appropriate in social science research.[1] The term "significance" and the logical process in applying tests of statistical significance imply that these tests are more informative than they are. They provide evidence that may support a hypothesis, but they may be inadequate for making a final decision whether to accept or reject a hypothesis.

Before we explain each step, we want to assure you that many people are bewildered the first time they study hypothesis testing. It is probably one of the most complicated topics in statistical analysis. Furthermore, hypothesis testing has its own terminology. Hypothesis testing has developed from careful statistical and epistemological thinking, and this attention is reflected in the terminology. Nevertheless, the phrases may seem convoluted.

With careful reading you should be able to follow the reasoning behind hypothesis testing and to interpret a finding of statistical significance. Rather than slowly reading, digesting, and thoroughly understanding each section, you may find it better to read through the chapter and then go back and review the specific sections.

STATING THE NULL HYPOTHESIS

A *hypothesis* states a relationship between two variables. The *research hypothesis* is the hypothesis that an investigator is studying. Typically, through model building, the investigator formulates a plausible research hypothesis; then he initiates research to see if it is supported. The *null hypothesis* postulates no relationship, or a random relationship, between the same two variables. Stated on the next page are three sets of research (H_1) and null (H_0) hypotheses:

Examples of Research and Null Hypotheses

H_1: Some job training programs are more successful than other programs in placing trainees in permanent employment.

H_0: All job training programs are equally likely to place trainees in permanent employment.

H_1: The more clearly written a research report, the more likely it will be used.

H_0: The clarity of a research report is not related to the probability that it will be used.

H_1: Male planners earn higher salaries than female planners.

H_0: Gender is not related to planners' salaries.

To "prove" that a hypothesis is true requires two types of evidence: confirming evidence, based on inductive reasoning, and disconfirming evidence, based on deductive reasoning. Consider the hypothesis that participants in on-the-job training (OJT) programs are more likely to find jobs than are nonparticipants. If one study is conducted, and it shows that OJT participants have higher placement, can a researcher say she has proved the hypothesis to be true? Evidence confirming her hypothesis would include her ability to demonstrate that the study design satisfies the criteria for establishing causality, including eliminating alternative hypotheses, and replication.

The subjects of one study represent one sample. If investigators consistently find higher placement rates among OJT trainees, the hypothesis receives stronger support. When just one study is conducted, one has to entertain the possibility that sampling error accounts for the higher placement rates of OJT trainees. One must entertain the possibility that another sample from the same population may not show a higher placement rate for OJT participants.

Hypothesis testing and tests of statistical significance rely on disconfirming evidence to support a hypothesis. An investigator does not directly assert that her data support the hypothesis. Rather, she states that her data show that the null hypothesis is probably false. She confirms the research hypothesis by disconfirming the null hypothesis.[2] Let's outline that process:

Stage 1: Investigator states research hypothesis that OJT has higher placement rates

Stage 2: Investigator states null hypothesis of no relationship between OJT training and placement rate

Stage 3: Sample data show that a relationship exists

Stage 4: Investigator rejects the null hypothesis as false

Stage 5: Investigator argues that because the null hypothesis is false, OJT affects placement rate

If her data did not show a difference in placement rates, she notes that she failed to reject the null hypothesis. For the same reasons that she cannot prove the research hypothesis, she cannot prove the null hypothesis. She cannot use failure to reject her null hypothesis to argue categorically that OJT training does not affect placement rates.

In conducting a hypothesis test, the researcher selects a statistical test to determine the probability that the hypothesized relationship in the population is random. The investigator uses sample data to make a guess about the population. In our example, the investigator found higher placement rates among OJT trainees; she selects a hypothesis test to determine the probability that OJT training does not affect placement rates in the population.

In guessing about what is true in the population of interest, a researcher risks making one of two types of errors. She may decide to reject the null hypothesis, when in reality the null hypothesis is true, or she may decide not to reject the null hypothesis, when in reality the null hypothesis is untrue. Each of these errors has a name. Rejecting a true null hypothesis is a *Type I* error. Failure to reject a false null hypothesis is a *Type II* error. Table 12.1 illustrates the linkage among the researcher's decision, the state of nature (what is "really" true), and the types of errors.

With a Type I error, we have concluded from sample data that the research hypothesis is true, when in fact the research hypothesis is untrue. In general, researchers try to minimize the probability of a Type I error. This bias rests in their desire to minimize the risk of promoting research findings that may have occurred by chance. Conversely, researchers want to accept only findings that were unlikely to have occurred by chance. A Type I error may be thought of as a false alarm; in other words it alerts one to the possibility of a relationship or situation, yet in reality the relationship or situation does not exist. A Type II error may be thought of as a failure in signal detection; it fails to alert the researcher to an existing relationship or situation.

Prior to beginning the analysis, the investigator decides on a criterion for rejecting a null hypothesis. This criterion is a probability value and is referred to as the *alpha (α) level.* The alpha level is a number between 0 and 1. Common alpha levels for hypothesis testing are .05, .01, and .001.[3]

The interpretation of the alpha levels is as follows:

$\alpha = .05$, 5% chance of committing a Type I error

$\alpha = .01$, 1% chance of committing a Type I error

$\alpha = .001$, 0.1% chance of committing a Type I error

If alpha is set at .05, and an investigator tests 100 hypotheses where the null hypothesis is true, he can expect to make five Type I errors.

TABLE 12.1   TYPE I AND TYPE II ERRORS

Decision Based on Sample	State of Nature	
	H_0 *True*	H_0 *Untrue*
Reject H_0	Type I error	Correct decision
Do not reject H_0	Correct decision	Type II error

Closely related to Type I and Type II errors is the concept of power. Just as we know that not all of the hypotheses we accept are true, some of the null hypotheses we do not reject are untrue. *Power* refers to the probability that a test of significance results in the rejection of false null hypotheses. To illustrate this, Table 12.2 reorganizes the information in Table 12.1. The cells identify the term used to describe an outcome and the probability of the outcome occurring. No specific term describes the acceptance of a true null hypothesis.

The power of a test of significance is 1 minus the probability of a Type II error (β); if the probability of a Type II error is 20 percent, the power of the test of significance is 80 percent, or .80. If the power of the test is .80, an investigator knows that 80 times out of 100 she will correctly reject the null hypothesis, and 20 times out of 100 she will fail to reject an untrue null hypothesis.[4] Determining the probability that the null hypothesis is false requires calculating the probability of a Type II error, a tedious procedure. The hypothesis must be exact, that is, the hypothesis states the strength of the anticipated relationship. In the absence of an exact hypothesis, an administrator can consider sample size and the anticipated magnitude of the effect to estimate the power of the test. For example, a sample of 1,300 will detect a very slight effect 95 percent of the time at an alpha level of .05. A sample of 50 will detect a moderate effect only 46 percent of the time if alpha is set at .05.[5]

The power of a test is related to sample size and the strength of a relationship. If we hypothesize that OJT programs have higher placement rates than other training programs, how big a difference do we think there is? If we expect that the difference is very small, we may need a relatively large sample; otherwise, we risk failing to reject a false null hypothesis. If we expect to find a large difference, a relatively small sample may be adequate. In Chapter 5 we pointed out that as the costs of sampling rise, investigators are more likely to consider power in deciding on the appropriate sample size.

If a test has high power, a researcher may state that he has strong evidence supporting the null hypothesis. For example, if a test has power of .90, there is only a 10 percent probability that a false null hypothesis will be accepted. There is a 90 percent probability that a true hypothesis will be accepted. Thus a researcher who has such high power and still cannot reject a null hypothesis may be justified in arguing that his data support the null hypothesis.[6]

TABLE 12.2   TERMS AND PROBABILITIES OF OUTCOMES ASSOCIATED WITH TESTS OF STATISTICAL SIGNIFICANCE

	State of Nature	
Decision Based on Sample	H_0 *True*	H_0 *False*
Reject H_0 (probability)	Type I error (α)	Power ($1 - \beta$)
Do not reject H_0 (probability)	($1 - \alpha$)	Type II error (β)

SELECTING AN ALPHA LEVEL

The specific alpha level selected depends on the practical consequences of committing a Type I error or a Type II error and on the anticipated strength of the relationship. Sorting out the consequences of Type I and Type II errors involves thinking through the hypothesis and the null hypothesis and the actions that will result from accepting or rejecting the null hypothesis. Example 12.1 describes how one might think through the practical consequences of committing a Type I or Type II error.

The examples should lead you to question the wisdom of accepting a specific, rigid criterion, such as $\alpha = .05$, and applying it to a wide range of studies. The examples also illustrate that acceptable levels of Type I or Type II errors are affected by point of view and other practical concerns.

The alpha level is one of four parameters that should be considered in testing statistical significance. The other parameters are the power of the test, the sample size, and the size of the effect. A small effect is unlikely to be detected with a small sample and the traditional $\alpha = .05$ cutoff. Manipulating the alpha level can change the probability of Type I and Type II errors. If the alpha level is raised, the probability of Type I errors will increase, and the probability of Type II errors will decrease. If the alpha level is lowered, the probability of Type I errors will decrease, and the probability of Type II errors will increase. Type I and Type II errors both decrease with added cases.

How do these considerations apply to public administrators? While administrators may want to know the probability that an observed relationship is nonrandom in the population, the size of the effect is of far greater concern. For some situations, reacting to a "false alarm" or even responding to minor, nonrandom, differences may be undesirable. Segments of the population may differ in their opinions about public policies or their experiences with public services. Nevertheless, administrators may prefer to ignore small differences. If older people are less satisfied with recreational facilities than other respondents, or if the police respond less quickly to calls from the south side of town than from other parts of town, administrators may not address these variations if they do not suggest great anger or indisputable patterns of discrimination. The political and economic costs may render resolving small differences infeasible or undesirable.

On the other hand, ignoring small effects may be troublesome in evaluating programs. A test of significance is an inadequate criterion of a program's effectiveness. Evaluations based on small sample sizes and programs with modest effects may result in the erroneous conclusion that an effective program is ineffective. When social programs were first evaluated, researchers were disappointed in how little such programs accomplished. The disappointment was misplaced. It now seems naive to assume that a limited social program is going to markedly change behavior. We may have to be satisfied with smaller changes, albeit changes in the desired direction.

To limit research costs and disruptions to a program, program evaluations may involve relatively few subjects. If a study has few subjects, and the program's effect is not expected to be strong, the probability of a Type II error is larger. If the measures are not perfectly reliable, more random error will be introduced, further increasing the probability of a Type II error.[7] If a discrete number

EXAMPLE 12.1

Practical Consequences of Type I and Type II Errors

Case 1

H_1: Gamma cars are less safe than other cars

H_0: Gamma cars are as safe as other cars

Situation: You have an opportunity to buy a Gamma car for an excellent price. You collect accident data on a sample of Gamma cars.

To select an alpha level, you need to think through what will happen if you commit a Type I error or a Type II error. If you conclude from the data in your sample that Gamma cars are less safe than other cars when in fact Gamma cars are as safe as other cars, you will commit a Type I error. The practical significance? You miss out on a bargain.

If you conclude from the data in your sample that Gamma cars are as safe as other cars when, in fact, they are less safe, you will have committed a Type II error. The practical consequence? You may purchase and drive a car that is less safe than other cars. Eventually, this decision may lead to a serious personal injury that could have been avoided.

Your decision in this situation? In analyzing the data you collect on cars and safety, you want to minimize the probability of committing a Type II error. Specifically, you will select a higher alpha level, that is, a value closer to zero. Alternatively, you will select a test with high power, that is, a low probability of accepting a false null hypothesis.

Case 2

H_1: Some job training programs are more successful than others

H_0: All job training programs are equally successful

Situation: Data on job training programs and placement outcomes are gathered and analyzed. What happens if a Type I error is committed? Some job training programs are erroneously assumed to be more successful than other programs. What are the practical consequences? Program continuation or cessation may depend on the findings. Programs that in reality are as successful as other programs may come to an end.

What happens if a Type II error is committed? Less effective programs will continue to offer training.

Your decision? It may depend on your point of view. If you represent training programs, you may want to minimize Type I error, which could result in effective programs closing. If you are a trainee, you may be concerned about being assigned to a less effective program. If you are a legislator, you may want evidence of the success of the programs you have supported.

The findings may reduce ambivalence about minimizing one type of error or the other. A small, but significant, difference in placement rates may not be worth the disruption of discontinuing programs.

of measures are used, other effects may be missed. Let's imagine an evaluation of a job training program. If a Type II error occurs, which is far more likely than a Type I error, a program that has a modest impact on participants may be judged to make no difference. If the program is canceled or phased out, trainees lose tangible benefits associated with program participation. They also may become more cynical or discouraged if a program that seemed to offer a brighter future no longer exists. Because of the higher probability of a Type II error and its consequences for program clients, evaluation students have been encouraged to consider the need to minimize Type II errors.

If the evaluation is typical, investigators can easily calculate a test of statistical significance and determine the probability that the null hypothesis is true.

SELECTING AND COMPUTING A TEST STATISTIC

In this text we discuss two common tests of statistical significance. If you need only a basic understanding of the research findings, you should find the information provided here adequate for your needs. The first test statistic we consider is *chi-square* (χ^2). Chi-square is a statistic for nominal level data usually applied to contingency tables. (Contingency tables are covered in Chapter 13.) The second test statistic is the *t-test*. *t*-tests examine the differences between the means of two groups, that is, the relationship between an interval dependent variable and a nominal independent variable.

Chi-Square

The chi-square test compares the observations contained in a dataset showing the joint distribution between two variables with the observations expected if the relationship between variables is random in the population. Table 12.3 contains data gathered to test a hypothesis that specific job training programs achieved different outcomes. Table 12.3 (top) compares three job training programs and outcomes; the table contains the frequencies observed (f_o) in the collected data. Table 12.3 (bottom) shows what the data would look like if there were no relationship between a program and trainees' outcomes. The figures in Table 12.3 (bottom) represent the frequencies expected (f_e) if the null hypothesis were true.

Nearly 50 percent of the subjects were working. If the work status and program categories were not associated, the same percentage of participants in each program would be working. Hence, in Table 12.3 (bottom) nearly 50 percent of the clients of each program are assigned to the category "working." Somewhat less than 25 percent are assigned to the "in school" category, and somewhat more than 25 percent to the "unemployed" category. The footnote in Table 12.3 explains how the values for the table of expected frequencies are calculated.

The next step is to calculate chi-square. Each cell from the table of frequencies observed is subtracted from its counterpart in the table of frequencies expected ($f_o - f_e$). The result is squared and divided by the frequency expected

TABLE 12.3   OBSERVED AND EXPECTED FREQUENCIES

CURRENT STATUS BY TRAINING PROGRAM ATTENDED: OBSERVED FREQUENCIES (f_o)

	Program			
	Vocational Education	*On-the-Job Training*	*Work Skills Training*	*Total*
Working	19	109	164	292
In school	19	82	31	132
Unemployed	26	82	54	162
Total	64	273	249	586

CURRENT STATUS BY TRAINING PROGRAM ATTENDED: EXPECTED FREQUENCIES IF PROGRAM AND STATUS ARE UNRELATED (f_e)

	Program		
	Vocational Education	*On-the-Job Training*	*Work Skills Training*
Working	31.9	136.0	124.1
In school	14.4	61.5	56.1
Unemployed	17.7	75.5	68.8

Note: To calculate frequency expected (f_e) for each cell multiply the column total and the row total for that cell and divide by the table total. f_e (cell 1,1): $(64 \times 292)/586 = 18{,}688/586 = 31.9$.

$((f_o - f_e)^2/f_e)$. For example, for the cell "working" and "attended Vocational Education," the calculation would be $(19 - 31.9)^2/31.9 = 5.22$. Chi-square ($\chi^2$) equals the sum of these figures. Thus the equation is

$$\chi^2 = \Sigma(f_o - f_e)^2/f_e$$

for the example $\chi^2 = 50.57$.

The "significance level" of a χ^2 value is typically reported by statistical software programs. The programs perform the calculations and report the χ^2 value and its "significance level." This significance level is the *associated probability*, that is, the probability that the specific value of χ^2 will occur if the null hypothesis is true in the population. Alternatively, a researcher can calculate chi-square, find its value in a chi-square distribution table and identify the associated probability. (We have more details on calculating chi-square and looking up its value in the appendix to this chapter.) In interpreting a printout or reading a chi-square table, the investigator determines if the associated probability level is equal to or smaller than the alpha level he set. In this example, for if $\alpha = .01$, then $\chi^2 = 50.67$ is statistically significant. Chi-square is a widely used and understood test of statistical significance. You should be aware of three of its characteristics. First, because chi-square is a statistic for variables measured at the nominal level, it does not provide information on the direction of any association. In our example, the chi-square evidence indicates that the relationship between type of training program attended and current status is probably nonrandom. It does not indicate which program is the most effective.

Second, the numerical value of chi-square tends to increase as the sample size increases. Thus the chi-square value is partially a product of sample size. It does not directly measure the strength of the association between variables and should not be used as a measure of association. Some statistics to measure the strength of a relationship are based on chi-square, but they take into account and adjust for sample size. We present one such statistic, Cramer's V, in Chapter 13.

Third, chi-square does not reliably estimate the probability of a Type I error if the expected frequency of a cell in a table is less than 5. Recent research has found that violating the expected frequencies criterion causes relatively small errors; a researcher can easily ignore this problem if it occurs in relatively few cells. If most cells have few cases, the investigator may consider combining categories.[8]

Let's review with an example the steps taken thus far to test the hypothesis that the training program was related to program outcomes:

1. State the hypothesis and the null hypothesis:

   H_1: The job training programs achieved different outcomes

   H_0: The job training programs did not differ in their achievement of outcomes

2. Select an alpha level: set $\alpha = .01$ because of the relatively large sample size and desire to detect only a marked difference between program outcomes (making changes based on small differences would be costly)

3. Select a test statistic: chi-square is selected because the table had nominal data

4. Determine the value of test statistic: $\chi^2 = 50.57$

5. Determine if the value of χ^2 meets alpha-level criterion: From associated probability on printout, associated probability must be less than or equal to .01; from a table of χ^2 values, for $\alpha = .01$, χ^2 must be greater than or equal to 13.277

6. Decide if statistical evidence supports the research hypothesis: If associated probability is no more than .01 or if χ^2 is at least 13.277, (using the alpha-level criterion), the statistical evidence supports the research hypothesis

t-Tests

Assume that you want to learn whether men earn more than women or whether children at School A obtain higher state achievement test scores than children at School B. One way you could test these hypotheses is to rearrange the data into contingency tables and perform a chi-square test. Of course, in this process you must change the dependent variable information from interval to ordinal and would lose information. And you might rightfully wonder whether the finding of significance or lack of significance was associated with how the variables were collapsed.

Alternatively, you could consider the hypothesis that the groups had different means. You could hypothesize that the average earnings of men are higher than the average earnings of women. You could hypothesize that the average achievement test grades at School A are higher than at School B.

The *t*-test is an interval statistic that can test hypotheses that two groups have different means. Each group is considered a sample, and the test is a two-sample *t*-test. The *t*-test can also test a single sample hypothesis, for example, that a group's mean is greater or less than a specified value. The single sample *t*-test is useful for staffing studies.[9] For example, a university library may assume that its reference desk handles an average of 25 inquiries per hour on weekends. The assumption determines the level of staffing at the reference desk on weekends. Periodically, data may be gathered and the average number of inquiries per weekend calculated. A single sample *t*-test is performed to evaluate the hypothesis that the average number of inquiries is greater or less than 25.

The *t*-test can test a hypothesis that two groups have different means or that one group's mean is higher than the other's. The first type of hypothesis has no direction; a two-tailed *t*-test is used to test nondirectional hypotheses. The second type of hypothesis has direction; such hypotheses are tested with a one-tailed *t*-test.

Different formulas are used to calculate the *t*-value depending on the situation. One formula is used if the variances of both populations from which the sample groups are taken are assumed to be equal. Another formula is used if the populations are assumed to have unequal variances.

A third formula is used if data for both groups come from the same subjects. For example, a researcher may compare analysts' error rates when entering data on laptop computers as opposed to desktop computers. A single group of analysts would enter data into both laptop and desktop computers. The dependent variable would be error rate, and the independent variable would be type of computer.

To illustrate a *t*-test, we test the hypothesis that male planners earn higher salaries than female planners. We assume unequal variances of the salaries of the two groups.

Step 1. State the hypothesis and the null hypothesis.

H_1: The average salary of male planners is higher than the average salary of female planners.

H_0: The average salary of male planners is the same as or less than the average salary of female planners.

The above hypothesis requires a one-tailed test. In a one-tailed test, the null hypothesis is expanded to include a finding in the "wrong" direction. Thus, if the data showed that the average salary of female planners was more than that of male planners, the researcher would not reject the null hypothesis. Alternatively, with a two-tailed test, the hypothesis only indicates a difference in salaries. It does not specify which gender earns more. The null hypothesis only notes no differences in the average salaries of male and female planners. So a researcher could find that the average salary of female planners is greater than that of male planners and still reject the null hypothesis.

Step 2. Select an alpha level: set $\alpha = .01$. With the large sample size, .01 should be adequate to pick up at least a moderate effect.

Step 3. Select a test statistic: A *t*-test is selected because the hypothesis postulates that the two samples have different means. A one-tailed test is selected because the hypothesis postulates which sample mean is greater than that of the other.

Step 4. Calculate the test statistic. An assumption about the variances must be made. The formula for unequal variances will produce slightly higher associated probabilities. Consequently, it is the more conservative test and can be assumed. For the study, an assumption of unequal variances seems reasonable. Women have entered planning and similar professions at a high rate for a relatively short period of time. Thus women are less likely to have salaries consistent with extensive experience, and one can expect that the salaries of female planners have less variance. With this assumption the formula to calculate t is:

$$t = \frac{\overline{X}_1 - \overline{X}_2}{\sqrt{\dfrac{s_1^2}{n_1 - 1} + \dfrac{s_2^2}{n_2 - 1}}}$$

where:

For the Male Sample

$n_1 = 403$

$\overline{X}_1 = 17{,}095$

$s_1 = 6{,}329$

$s_1^2 = 40{,}056{,}241$

For the Female Sample

$n_2 = 132$

$\overline{X}_2 = 14{,}885$

$s_2 = 4{,}676$

$s_2^2 = 21{,}864{,}976$

$$t = \frac{17{,}095 - 14{,}885}{\sqrt{\dfrac{40{,}056{,}241}{402} + \dfrac{21{,}864{,}976}{131}}}$$

$$= \frac{2210}{\sqrt{99{,}642 + 166{,}908}}$$

$$= \frac{2{,}210}{\sqrt{266{,}550}}$$

$$= 4.28, \; df = n_1 + n_2 - 2 = 533$$

Step 5. Determine if the value of t meets the alpha-level criterion: From associated probability on printout, associated probability must be less than or equal to .01; from a table of t values, if $n = 535$ and the t-test is a one-tailed test, for $\alpha = .01$, t must be equal to or greater than 2.326.

Step 6. Decide if statistical evidence supports the research hypothesis: If associated probability is no more than .01 or if t equals at least 2.326, alpha-level criterion, statistical evidence supports the research hypothesis.

The Normal Distribution

Students who have studied statistics may wonder why we do not use the normal distribution (z-scores) to test hypotheses about sample means. To use z-scores properly, the population variance must be known. If the population variance is not known, it is estimated by the standard deviation, in which case t-tests as opposed to z-scores are appropriate. While using z-scores introduces little error with larger samples ($n \geq 60$), social scientists tend to rely on t-tests.

MAKING A DECISION

Making a decision based on a test of statistical significance is relatively straight-forward. The strategy we have presented thus far has the investigator (1) finding the minimum χ^2 or t value needed for the selected alpha-level criterion; (2) comparing the calculated value of χ^2 or t to the minimum value; (3) rejecting the null hypothesis if the calculated value is equal to or larger than the minimum value, otherwise, the null hypothesis is not rejected. In our examples an investigator would reject the null hypotheses and accept the research hypotheses that different job-training programs achieved different outcomes and that male planners earned more than female planners. The values of χ^2 and t are greater than the values required for an alpha level of .01.

An alternative strategy begins with the associated probability. The investigator looks up the specific probability (p) associated with the calculated value of χ^2 or t. If this associated probability is no larger than the alpha-level criterion, the researcher rejects the null hypothesis and accepts the research hypothesis. Statistical software programs usually report associated probabilities. Example 12.2 reproduces a printout from a popular statistical software program, SPSS, and identifies the relevant χ^2 information. Note that if an investigator had decided on an alpha level of .05 or .01, she would accept the research hypothesis. If she had decided on an alpha level of .001, she would not reject the null hypothesis.

The associated probability does not indicate the probability of a Type I error, nor does it imply that a relationship is "more significant" or "stronger." Its contribution is more modest. It indicates the probability of a specific χ^2 or t-value occurring if the null hypothesis is true.[10] Researchers combine information on the associated probability with the other evidence to make inferences about hypotheses. Such evidence may include evidence of internal validity or findings from previous studies.

Tests of statistical significance may appear to constitute a "pass/fail" test. Should they play this role? No, not in our examples or in similar situations. The investigator is only testing a statistical model. The data represent many decisions, including whom to sample, how to sample them, what information to gather, how to gather it, and when to gather it. The investigator applies statistical tests to a set of numbers; he obtains an answer even if he violates all the statistical assumptions and ignores sound methodological practice.

If the methodological decisions are sound and the statistics are applied correctly, the data still represent a single sample out of all the possible samples from the population. A test of significance alone should not bear the burden of demonstrating the value of a hypothesis. It is far more realistic and reasonable to consider each statistical finding as part of a body of evidence supporting the truth or error of a hypothesis. We doubt that any administrator would decide the effectiveness of a program or the fairness of salaries based on one piece of statistical evidence.

EXAMPLE 12.2

Interpreting χ^2 Information on an SPSS Printout

Situation: A probability sample of 830 citizens graded a city's police department. The investigators hypothesized: The younger the respondent, the lower the grade he or she gave the police department. (The null hypothesis was that age had no relationship to the grades given.)

Findings: An SPSS program is run, and Table 12.4 and statistics are reported. Note that relatively more of the oldest respondents gave the department an A or B, and that relatively more of the youngest respondents gave the department a D or F.

TABLE 12.4   GRADE BY AGE

Col Pct Grade		Age			
		Under 18	*18–59*	*60 or older*	
		1.00	2.00	4.00	Row Total
A or B	1.0000	50.0	72.7	82.0	615
					74.1
C	2.0000	41.7	22.0	14.8	174
					21.0
D or F	4.0000	8.3	5.3	3.3	41
					4.9
	Column	24	623	183	830
	Total	2.9	75.1	22.0	100.0

Chi-Square	Value	DF (Degrees of Freedom)	Significance
Pearson	13.90036 [calculated value of χ^2]	4	.00762 [associated probability]

Notes:

1. "Pearson" refers to "Pearson's chi-square," which is the chi-square equation used in this text.

2. The χ^2 information would be reported as follows: "$\chi^2 = 13.9$, $df = 4$, $p = .00762$." One may round p to .008.

3. The column labeled "significance" is actually reporting the associated probability. Some researchers do not report the specific associated probability; instead, they indicate if the hypothesis was supported based on the preset alpha level. For example, if the researcher set $\alpha = .01$, he would report "$\chi^2 = 13.9$, $df = 4$, $p < .01$."

4. If the researcher changes the number of rows or columns in the table, chi-square must be re-calculated.

In some situations, investigators can appropriately use tests of statistical significance to make definite decisions. The tests establish interrater reliability, verify whether shifts in time series can be assumed to be random, and demonstrate the probability that respondents and nonrespondents are similar to one another.[11]

Tests of statistical significance have been particularly valuable in quality control, where a sample of "products" is inspected to locate systematic problems. For example, a quality control unit may review a sample of public-assistance cases. An analyst reads a case record and notes any errors. Working with small samples, she applies tests of statistical significance to determine the probability that the errors she finds are random. If the errors are not random, the agency should take corrective action, such as retraining the caseworker.

REPORTING TESTS OF STATISTICAL SIGNIFICANCE

In most reports, tests of statistical significance may be inconspicuous. The reader unfamiliar with them may scarcely notice that they are mentioned. Readers with a serious interest in the research topic refer to them to evaluate research and its findings.

The researcher should report the test statistic used and its value, the degrees of freedom, and the associated probability. Citing the statistic allows readers trained in statistics to determine whether the researcher used the appropriate statistical test. The statistic's value and degrees of freedom (df) are needed to determine the associated probability. With this information, a reader can identify mathematical or recording errors, and she can visualize how the data were analyzed. The associated probability allows the reader to make her own independent determination of the findings' "significance." To report this information in the text, the researcher encloses the statistical details in parentheses. For example:

> The type of job training received is related to participants' current employment status ($\chi^2 = 50.57$, $df = 4$, $p < .001$).

> The average salary of male planners is higher than that of female planners ($t = 4.28$, $df = 533$, $p < .001$).

If contingency tables are included in a report, the same information is reported immediately beneath the last row of table cells. Table 12.5 illustrates a common format for presenting a series of t-tests, which compares means for two values of an independent variable. The table reports the average (mean) values for male and female planners on nine variables. Underneath the mean values are the values of the standard deviation. The third column reports the values of the t-test. Note, that marital status and race are dichotomous variables and the means represent the percent of married planners and the percent of white planners. The interested reader has all the information she needs to compute the values of t herself. The asterisks next to the t values direct the reader to the table footnotes, where she can find the associated probability rounded to the nearest usual alpha level. One asterisk represents $p = .1$, two asterisks represent $p = .05$, and three asterisks represent $p = .01$. The relationship between the number of asterisks and value of p varies from author to author. Usually, the more asterisks, the lower the value of p.

TABLE 12.5 TESTS COMPARING MEN AND WOMEN IN PLANNING	Men $\overline{X}$ (s)	Women $\overline{X}$ (s)	t
Individual characteristics			
Age	32.43 (8.28)	30.11 (7.72)	2.93***
Marital status	.75 (.41)	.61 (.49)	3.00***
Race	.93 (.26)	.81 (.34)	2.05**
Organization characteristics			
Agency size	4.78 (2.88)	5.29 (2.99)	−1.70*
Centralized management	5.01 (2.61)	5.25 (2.73)	−.85
Career behavior			
Job turnover	.51 (.37)	.60 (.39)	−2.19***
No. of roles	7.98 (1.67)	7.88 (1.79)	.53
Yrs. experience	3.67 (5.31)	3.42 (2.57)	7.26***
Career attainment			
Income	17,095 (6,329)	14,885 (4,676)	4.28***

*Significant at the .10 level.
**Significant at the .05 level.
***Significant at the .01 level.
SOURCE: M. Mayo, Jr., "Job Attainment in Planning: Women Versus Men," *Work and Occupation* (May 1985): 152. (Copyright © 1985 by Sage Publications, Inc. Reprinted with permission: Sage Publications, Inc.)

At the present time, no one convention for reporting associated probability has emerged. Using a preset alpha level to report the significance of all values is least common. In Table 12.5 the author distinguished among three levels of significance rather than reporting all the significant findings as significant at $p = .10$. Whether the specific associated probability is reported or not seems to depend on the researcher's ability to present the information in an uncluttered table. The asterisks in Table 12.5 would not work if the author wanted to report the exact associated probability. This author's strategy is the most common, that is, to round the associated probability up to .10, .05, .01, or .001 and report the rounded up p value.

A researcher may simply note that a relationship was found to be "statistically significant." This observation merely means that the value of a specific statistical test met the researcher's alpha-level criterion. If the value did not meet the alpha-level criterion, the relationship is said to be "statistically insignificant." In order for such information to have any value, the researcher must indicate the statistical test and alpha level that he used.

MODIFICATIONS AND ALTERNATIVES TO TESTS OF STATISTICAL SIGNIFICANCE

Let us reiterate some important misconceptions about tests of statistical significance.[12] They cannot remedy a flawed design. They only test a statistical hypothesis not the theoretical hypothesis. The analyst applies an equation to a set of numbers, comes up with a statistical value, and makes a decision. Nothing prevents someone from dividing a set of random digits into groups, calculating a test statistic, and finding a statistically significant relationship. One researcher summed up the situation aptly with the phrase "the numbers don't remember where they came from."[13] The numbers do not know if the data represent a carefully designed study with reliable measures and a sample free of nonsampling errors.

The information produced by a test of statistical significance is modest. It demonstrates the probability that a null hypothesis of no difference occurred by chance. Depending on the sample size and the α-level, statistically significant differences may be too slight to be of theoretical interest or practical use. Social scientists have recommended four alternatives to the traditional significance test. First, the null hypothesis can include a specific difference. Let's go back to an earlier example. We will assume that administrators do not want to fund more on-the-job training programs unless they place at least 10 percent more of their trainees than other training program. To test this preference the hypothesis and null hypothesis would be stated as:

H_1: On-the-job training programs place at least 10 percent more of their trainees than other training programs.

H_0: On-the-job training programs place less than 10 percent more of their trainees than other training programs.

Second, instead of reporting significance researchers may report confidence intervals. (To refresh your memory on the standard error and computation of confidence intervals see Chapter 5). Proponents argue that confidence intervals are more informative. They provide information on the size of parameters, differences between them, and the direction of the differences.[14] To illustrate how this works, Table 12.6 is based on the data comparing male and female planners.[15]

Table 12.6 shows that male planners on average are older and earn more than female planners. These differences continue even when sampling error is taken into account. The confidence interval avoids implying that the sample means provide a precise estimate of the differences. Rather the population means probably fall somewhere within the range indicated by the confidence intervals.

The third strategy is to report a measure of association. Chapters 13 and 14 cover statistics that quantify the effect of an independent variable on a dependent variable. These statistics, not tests of statistical significance, measure the strength of a relationship.

The fourth alternative is replicating studies. One author states, "The results from an unreplicated study, no matter how statistically significant . . . are necessarily speculative . . . Replications play a vital role in safeguarding the empirical literature from contamination from specious results."[16] Replications do not have

TABLE 12.6   MEAN AGE AND INCOME OF MALE AND FEMALE PLANNERS

Age	Mean	95% Confidence Interval
Males ($n = 300$)	32.43	31.49–33.37
Females ($n = 132$)	30.11	28.8–31.42
Income		
Males ($n = 300$)	17,095	16.379–17.811
Females ($n = 132$)	14,885	14.087–15.683

to duplicate previous research exactly. Investigators may implement the research using a different population or another setting and see if the findings generalize to other populations or settings. Findings that go in the same direction, whether or not they attain a specified a-level, or that have overlapping confidence levels provide more confirmation than a simple significance test.

With the exception of measuring the size of the effect of the independent variable on the dependent variable, each alternative has constraints. A researcher may have inadequate knowledge or understanding of the question at hand to specify a relationship beyond anticipating some difference. Confidence levels work with interval data, but setting confidence levels for proportional data can become unwieldy. Replication requires the opportunity and resources to repeat a study.

Tests of statistical significance can serve as a provisional test of a hypothesis. The term "provisional" avoids inferring that any one hypothesis test is definitive. On the other hand investigators may use them as an initial screen to filter out the weakest relationships and to identify relationships meriting closer examination. In using significance tests as a filter, an investigator should recall that with an alpha level of .05 and a small sample, a test of statistical significance will have low power and will probably identify strong relations as statistically significant.

One author surveyed the technical and theoretical arguments for and against using tests of statistical significance. While he found little support for the tests, he gave two justifications for their continued use. First, the tests allow a researcher to argue that random error or chance has been ruled out. Second, since the tests yield "pure numbers," they standardize findings, allowing researchers to easily scan findings to identify results that are too weak for further study.[17]

Neither a test of statistical significance nor an alternative approach can indicate that a supported hypothesis is interesting or of any apparent importance. The findings may have no practical significance. Statistically significant findings may be uninteresting and unimportant. A practically significant finding is one that piques people's interest and leads to follow-up investigations, spurs policy decisions, or causes change in behavior. The term "practical significance" is what most people mean by the term "significant" in everyday conversation.

Over the years professionals have become more educated about statistics and more sophisticated in using them. Researchers typically report statistical significance along with measures of association. The readers are given sufficient information to decide whether they agree with the researcher's conclusions or to apply different statistical criteria and reach other conclusions. The researcher and the reader are both likely to understand that statistical significance is not the same as practical significance.

SUMMARY

Tests of statistical significance allow a researcher to determine the probability that variables related in a random sample are not related in the population. A test of statistical significance cannot indicate that a relationship is strong or important; it may not even indicate if the direction is as hypothesized. Nor does a finding of statistical significance imply that other parts of the research were carried out correctly. The test only makes a statistical statement about the nature of a relationship.

To carry out a test of statistical significance, a researcher

1. states the null and the research hypotheses.
2. selects an alpha level.
3. selects and computes a test statistic.
4. makes a decision.

The null hypothesis postulates that an independent and a dependent variable are not related. For some statistical tests, the null hypothesis may state that the relationship goes in a certain direction or does not exceed a specific value.

In hypothesis testing, a researcher runs the risk of making two errors. First, he may reject a null hypothesis that is actually true. The researcher, then, has accepted an untrue research hypothesis. This error is called a Type I error. Second, the researcher may accept a null hypothesis that is untrue. The researcher has failed to accept a true research hypothesis; that is called a Type II error.

In practice, researchers are more likely to make a judgment about a hypothesis based on the associated probability, the sample size, the magnitude of the effect, the power of the test, and the practical consequences of their decisions than they are to decide on a specific alpha level set a priori. The associated probability is the probability of a specific χ^2 or t value occurring if the null hypothesis is true. The power of a test refers to its ability to make sure that untrue null hypotheses are rejected. A researcher may be concerned about power if a study has a relatively small sample and a modest effect is expected. This is most likely to occur in program evaluations. To detect small effects, the investigator will tend to set higher alpha levels or to accept higher associated probabilities. With a larger sample and an interest in detecting moderate or strong effects, the investigator will want to work with lower alpha levels or prefer lower associated probabilities.

Depending on the nature of the data and the hypothesis, the researcher selects a test of significance. Chi-square and t-tests are two commonly used tests. The major piece of information needed is the probability that a given statistical value would occur if the null hypothesis were true, indicated by the xx value in the notation $p < xx$.

Tests of statistical significance are easily misinterpreted and produce modest information. Researchers are urged to put aside the traditional process of testing a null hypothesis of no difference. Rather, they should provide alternative or additional information supporting the merits of a hypothesis. Researchers may include a specific difference in the null hypothesis, report confidence levels, and report measures of the strength of the relationship between variables. Replication of studies provide the best test of a hypothesis. Occasionally, administrative investigators base a decision on a single test of significance, for example, in deciding whether respondents and nonrespondents are similar, or if shifts in a time series are greater than shifts that can be attributed to long-term trends, cycles, seasonal effects, or random fluctuations.

NOTES

1. For discussion on uses of tests of statistical significance in social sciences, see J. Cohen, "Things I Have Learned (So Far)," *American Psychologist 45* (December 1990), and M. Oakes, *Statistical Inference: A Commentary for the Social and Behavioral Sciences* (New York: Wiley, 1986).

2. For clear explanations of the epistemological reasons for working with and rejecting null hypotheses, see A. Kaplan, *The Conduct of Inquiry* (San Francisco: Chandler, 1964), and R. E. Henkel, *Tests of Significance* (Beverly Hills: Sage, *Quantitative Applications in the Social Sciences,* 07–004, 1976), 34–40.

3. See D. B. Wright, *Understanding Statistics: An Introduction for the Social Sciences* (London: Sage Publications, 1997), 42–43, for a short but informative discussion of the nature and philosophy of probability or *p* values and the link to power analysis.

4. Wright, *Understanding Statistics,* 42–43; 77–83.

5. J. Cohen, "Things I Have Learned," 1309.

6. Ibid. 1308–1309.

7. E. J. Posavac and R. G. Carey, *Program Evaluation: Methods and Case Studies,* 5th ed. (Englewood Cliffs, NJ: Prentice-Hall, 1997), 97.

8. Henkel, *Tests,* 48–49.

9. T. H. Poister, *Public Program Analysis* (Baltimore: University Park Press, 1978), 213–214, illustrates the one sample *t*-test with a worked-out example.

10. For a discussion on how to interpret the associated probability, see M. Oakes, *Statistical Inference,* (New York: Wiley, 1986), 15–19.

11. Statistical tests in time-series analysis are key in model building, and the findings from a specific test determine subsequent decisions. See R. McCleary and R. A. Hay, Jr., *Applied Time Series Analysis for the Social Sciences* (Beverly Hills: Sage, 1980), 97–100. Homework Problem 5 shows how tests of statistical significance are used to compare respondents and nonrespondents.

12. This section is based on the several works critiquing tests of statistical significance. The consulted works were: *What if There Were No Significance Tests?* Edited by L. L. Harlow, S. A. Mulaik, J. H. Steiger (Mahwah, N.J.: Erlbaum Associates, Publishers, 1997), especially "Significance Testing Introduction and Overview" by L. L. Harlow; M. N. Branch, "Statistical Inference in Behavior Analysis: Some Things Significance Testing Does and Does Not Do," *The Behavior Analyst 22* (1999): 87–92; Hubbard and Ryan, "The Historical Growth of Statistical Significance Testing in Psychology—and Its Future Prospects," *Educational & Psychological Measurement 60* (2000): 661–681.

13. This phrase is cited by Oakes, *Statistical Inference,* 173 and Cohen, "Things I Have Learned," 1310. Curiously, the citations differ slightly. Oakes quotes it as "don't remember" and Cohen as "don't know." The original is found in F. M. Lord, "On the Statistical Treatment of Football Numbers," *American Psychologist 2* (1953): 750–751.

14. Observations about the value of using confidence intervals are not covered here. For information on using confidence intervals see H. Rothstein and M. C. Tonges, "Beyond the significance test in administrative research and policy decisions," *Journal of Nursing Scholarship 32* (2000): 66–70. For a critique of using confidence levels see J. M. Cortina and W. P. Dunlap, "On the logic and purpose of significance testing," *Psychological Methods 2* (1997): 161–172.

15. The standard error, used to compute the confidence level, was estimated by dividing the standard deviation by the square root of the respective samples.

16. Hubbard and Ryan, "The Historical Growth of Statistical Significance Testing in Psychology,"

17. Henkel, *Tests,* 87. On pages 78–87 he summarizes the literature on the utility of tests of statistical significance. He divides the literature into two categories: technical issues and philosophy of science issues.

TERMS FOR REVIEW

randomly related	null hypothesis	chi-square
statistical significance	Type I error	*t*-test
practical significance	Type II error	associated probability
hypothesis	power	

QUESTIONS FOR REVIEW

The following questions should indicate whether you have a basic competency in this chapter's material.

1. What is meant by statistical significance? How is it different from practical significance?
2. What are the steps in hypothesis testing?
3. Distinguish among Type I error, Type II error, and power. What two strategies are available to reduce the probability of a Type I error? What two strategies are available to reduce the probability of a Type II error? As the power of a test is increased, does the probability of a Type II error increase or decrease?
4. The common wisdom among social scientists is that tests of statistical significance are overrated. What is the value of tests of statistical significance? What are their limitations?
5. Evaluate the soundness of using an alpha level of .05 as a minimal cutoff point for rejecting a null hypothesis.
6. Discuss the adequacy of tests of statistical significance as evidence supporting a hypothesis.

PROBLEMS FOR HOMEWORK AND DISCUSSION

1. A parents' group has charged that minority students are more likely than other students to be suspended for breaking school rules. For example, minority students are more likely to be suspended for fighting. The school superintendent has a random sample of 200 cases drawn from the list of all students in grades 7 through 12 who have been cited for serious school infractions. For each sample, student data are gathered on the student's racial or ethnic group, nature of offense, and action taken.
   a. State a hypothesis that the superintendent may have tested.
   b. What would be the practical consequences of committing a Type I error? What would be the practical consequences of committing a Type II error?
   c. Should the superintendent seek to minimize a Type I or a Type II error? Justify your answer.
   d. What contribution would power make in deciding if the parents had a legitimate concern?

2. The data given in Table 12.7 are reported in a study of soup-kitchen users. (Note: Soup kitchens serve free meals to homeless or very poor people.)
   a. State the hypothesis and the null hypothesis that these data may have been testing.
   b. If you set $\alpha = .05$, what is the probability that you committed a Type I error? Would you reject the null hypothesis?

TABLE 12.7   NUMBER OF MEALS EATEN DAILY BY SOUP-KITCHEN USERS

	Age of Soup-Kitchen User		
Number of Meals Eaten Daily	Less than 31 Years Old (n = 66)	31–54 Years Old (n = 213)	Over 54 Years Old (n = 144)
1	37.9%	29.1	27.1
2	47.0	49.3	40.3
3	15.2	21.6	32.6

Note: $\chi^2 = 10.4$, $df = 4$, $p < .05$.

TABLE 12.8   PERCENTAGE OF CORRECT ANSWERS BY GRADE LEVEL

	6th (265)	9th (125)	12th (120)	χ^2 probability
Lung cancer is higher among pipe smokers	10.2	5.6	10.8	.593
Smoking constricts blood vessels	38.2	70.8	57.7	.0001
Smoking helps circulation	43.3	65.8	61.3	.0001
Smokers live longer than nonsmokers	77.0	90.8	84.9	.0189

SOURCE: T. T. L. Chen and A. E. Winder, "When is the Critical Moment to Provide Smoking Education in Schools," *Journal of Drug Education 16* (1986): 121–132.

c. If you set $\alpha = .01$, what is the probability that you committed a Type I error? Would you reject the null hypothesis?

d. What is the value of knowing whether age is related to the number of meals a soup-kitchen user eats daily? Assess the adequacy of using only the information provided by a χ^2 test to decide if these two variables are related.

3. The data given in Table 12.8 were reported in a study of children's knowledge of the effects of smoking. The column headed "χ^2 probability" reports the associated probabilities, not the actual χ^2 value.

   a. How many hypotheses are being tested?

   b. Explain what information the associated probabilities reported in the chi-square analysis provide.

   c. State the hypotheses that you would probably accept based on the associated probabilities results.

   d. What other information would you include, if any, to support your hypotheses? Justify your answer.

4. Consider the data in Table 12.9:

   a. How different are male and female planners?

   b. What alpha level would you suggest for this dataset? Why did you select it? Which null hypotheses would you fail to reject?

   c. What information does a *t*-test give that chi-square doesn't?

5. A random sample of 407 adults was asked to participate in a study; 283 agreed to participate.

TABLE 12.9   COMPARISONS BETWEEN MALE AND FEMALE PLANNERS ON SELECTED CHARACTERISTICS

	Men $\overline{X}$ (s)	Women $\overline{X}$ (s)	*t*
Age	32.43 (8.28)	30.11 (7.72)	2.9**
Agency size	4.70 (2.88)	5.29 (2.99)	−1.7*
Job turnover rate	.51 (.37)	.60 (.39)	−2.19**
Number of planner roles	7.98 (1.67)	7.88 (1.79)	.53
Years of professional experience	3.67 (5.31)	3.42 (2.57)	7.26**
Income	17,095 (6,329)	14,885 (4,676)	4.28**

*Significant at the .1 level.
**Significant at the .01 level.
SOURCE: J. M. Mayo, Jr., "Job Attainment in Planning: Women Versus Men," *Work and Occupation* (May 1985): 152. (Copyright © 1985 by Sage Publications, Inc. Reprinted with permission: Sage Publications, Inc.)

Can the researchers conclude from the data in Table 12.10 that the participants were similar to the nonparticipants? Justify your answer.

6. Use $\alpha = .05$ to interpret the findings in Table 12.11.

TABLE 12.10 COMPARISON BETWEEN PARTICIPANTS AND NONPARTICIPANTS ON SELECTED CHARACTERISTICS

Race	Participated	Did Not Participate
White	70% (186)	30% (81)
African American	88 (97)	12 (13)
$\chi^2 = 14.25, df = 1, p < .001$		

Gender		
Male	85 (115)	15 (21)
Female	70 (168)	30 (73)
$\chi^2 = 10.36, df = 1, p < .005$		

Education		
12 years or less	73 (101)	27 (37)
13–15 years	82 (80)	18 (17)
16 years or more	72 (102)	28 (39)
$\chi^2 = 3.52, df = 2, p < .25$		

Age		
18–39 years	80 (177)	20 (43)
40 years or older	67 (105)	33 (51)
$\chi^2 = 8.36, df = 1, p < .005$		

SOURCE: D. Linz et al., "Estimating Community Standards," *Public Opinion Quarterly 55* (Spring 1991): 93.

TABLE 12.11 DIFFERENCES BETWEEN EARLY AND LATE ADOPTERS OF SPREADSHEET SOFTWARE

	Early Adopters		Late Adopters			Significance
	Mean	s	Mean	s	t-value	Level
Age	28.3	(7.3)	30.3	(10.1)	−1.91	.059
Years of education	16.2	(1.7)	15.4	(1.8)	3.06	.002
Number in prof. assoc.	2.6	(3.5)	2.6	(4.9)	.05	.956
Number of professional journals read	8.2	(4.5)	6.7	(5.3)	2.21	.028
Size of work group	2.6	(1.2)	2.5	(1.1)	.65	.516

SOURCE: J. C. Brancheau and J. C. Wetherbe, "The Adoption of Spreadsheet Software: Testing Innovation Diffusion Theory in the Context of End-User Computing," *Information Systems Research 1* (June 1990): 129.

DISK WORK

1. Test the hypothesis that use of county services varies by income level.
   a. State the research hypothesis and null hypothesis
   b. To test the hypothesis would you use chi-square or a *t*-test? Justify your choice.
   c. Load the Belle County data set and carry out the appropriate statistical procedure.

Based on the analysis would you reject your null hypothesis? Why or why not? What evidence did you use to make your decision?

2. Analyze the Belle County data to see if use of financial aid services, environmental services or public schools vary by age. To conduct your analysis categorize age into three categories.
   a. Report your findings in a table similar to 12.7
   b. State the hypotheses you tested.
   c. Which hypotheses were supported, e.g., which null hypotheses did you reject? Give evidence to support your decision.

3. Analyze the Belle County data and use the *t*-test (independent samples) to see if time in county (new residents vs. other residents), income (wealthier residents vs. less wealthy residents), sex, race (white vs. nonwhite), or age (younger vs. older residents) vary in the importance they give to financial assistance. Remember that to perform a *t*-test the independent variable must be dichotomized. Report your findings in statements similar to those found in the section on reporting tests of statistical significance.

4. Load the murder data base.
   a. Use tests of statistical significance to compare the questionnaire responses of those who received the mutilation scenario and those who received the non-mutilation scenario. Do the statistical findings support the hypotheses that differences between two groups did not occur by chance? Give evidence to support your conclusion. Do the statistical findings support the hypotheses that the wording of the scenarios affected the responses? Give evidence to support your conclusion.

   b. Test of statistical significance are affected by sample size. To observe this phenomenon categorize the variable "parole" into three categories (combine the "likely" and "very likely" values). Create contingency tables for each year to analyze the relationship between the scenario and "parole." (i) For each year note the associated probability and what it tells you about the relationship between scenario and "parole." (ii) For each year note how strong the relationship between the scenario and "parole" seems to be (Examine the percent differences between columns; the greater the difference the stronger the relationship.) (iii) What lesson might one draw from this exercise?

   c. An assumption of experimental design is that random assignment controls for differences between groups. Consider the assumption that the attitude of death penalty was associated with unique characteristics of each year's class. Use year as an independent variable and the death penalty item as a dependent variable.
      i. State the research hypothesis and null hypotheses.
      ii. Is the researcher hoping to reject the null hypothesis or not? Explain your answer.
      iii. What is the associated probability? What does it indicate about the relationship between attitudes toward the death penalty and each year's class?

RECOMMENDED FOR FURTHER READING

Theoretical orientation for this chapter was drawn from the insights of Michael Oakes in *Statistical Inference: A Commentary for the Social and Behavioral Sciences* (New York: Wiley, 1986). This book will challenge and reward readers interested in statistical inference.

What if There were no Significance Tests? Edited by L. L. Harlow, S. A. Mulaik, J. H. Steiger (Mahwah, N.J.: Erlbaum Associates, Publishers, 1997). An excellent source on current thinking about tests of statistical significance. "Significance Testing Introduction and Overview" by L. L. Harlow is especially recommended.

J. Cohen, "Things I Have Learned (So Far)," *American Psychologist 45* (December 1990): 1304–1312, is an accessible work that identifies common misconceptions in interpreting and working with tests of statistical significance.

See D. B. Wright, *Understanding Statistics* (London: Sage Publications, 1997), for a very accessible discussion of power.

Helena Kraemer and Sue Thieman, *How Many Subjects? Statistical Power Analysis in Research* (Newbury Park: Sage, 1987), discuss the relationship between sample size and the power of statistical tests.

Appendix 12.1

Calculating Chi-Square and Two-Sample *t*-Tests

This appendix reviews the equations for chi-square and *t*-tests and how to use the tables for their respective distributions.

Chi-Square

The equation for chi-square is

$$\chi^2 = \Sigma(f_o - f_e)^2/f_e$$

The data contained in Table 12.12 show the values for the observed frequency (f_o) and the expected frequency (f_e). The symbol f_e is the fre-

quency expected if the independent and dependent variables are randomly related. To obtain its value for a cell, the frequency of the row total is multiplied by the frequency of the column total and divided by the total n represented in the table. For the three cells under "vocational education," the calculations to derive f_e are:

$$f_e \text{(voc. ed. \& working)} = (64 \times 292)/586 = 31.9$$
$$f_e \text{(voc. ed. \& in school)} = (64 \times 132)/586 = 14.4$$
$$f_e \text{(voc. ed. \& not working)} = (64 \times 162)/586$$
$$= 17.7$$

TABLE 12.12   OBSERVED AND EXPECTED FREQUENCIES

CURRENT STATUS BY TRAINING PROGRAM ATTENDED: OBSERVED FREQUENCIES (f_o)

	Program			
	Vocational Education	*On-the-job Training*	*Work Skills Training*	*Total*
Working	19	109	164	292
In school	19	82	31	132
Unemployed	26	82	54	162
Total	64	273	249	586

CURRENT STATUS BY TRAINING PROGRAM ATTENDED: EXPECTED FREQUENCIES IF PROGRAM AND STATUS ARE UNRELATED (f_e)

	Program		
	Vocational Education	*On-the-job Training*	*Work Skills Training*
Working	31.9	136.0	124.1
In school	14.4	61.5	56.1
Unemployed	17.7	75.5	68.8

The next step is to subtract the value of f_e from the value of f_o for each cell, square this figure, and divide it by f_e. For the three cells under vocational education, these calculations are

Cell 1,1 $(f_o - f_e)^2/f_e = (19 - 31.9)^2/31.9 = 5.22$
Cell 1,2 $(f_o - f_e)^2/f_e = (19 - 14.4)^2/14.4 = 1.47$
Cell 1,3 $(f_o - f_e)^2/fe = (26 - 17.7)^2/17.7 = 3.89$

To obtain the value of chi-square, all the values for $(f_o - f_e)^2/f_e$ are summed. For this example, $\chi^2 = 50.57$.

The degrees of freedom (df) equal the number of columns minus 1 multiplied by the number of rows minus 1 ($(C - 1)(R - 1)$). For the example, the degrees of freedom $= (3 - 1)(3 - 1) = 4$. Next, the investigator consults a chi-square distribution table, such as Table 12.13.

If the investigator has selected a specific alpha level, for example, $\alpha = .05$, he notes the value in the column headed ".05" and the row for 4 degrees of freedom (df), that is, 9.488. For $\alpha = .05$, he will reject the null hypothesis if the value of chi-square is equal to or greater than 9.488.

Alternatively, he can find the associated probability for $\chi^2 = 50.57$. He goes to the row for 4 degrees of freedom and looks for the value that is closest to, but not greater than, 50.57, that is, 18.467. He identifies which column 18.467 is in, .001; thus, .001 is the associated probability for $\chi^2 = 50.57$ with 4 degrees of freedom.

If he includes the table in the report, he puts the χ^2 value, the degrees of freedom, and the as-

sociated probability underneath the table. (For an example, see Tables 12.6 and 12.10.) If the investigator combines two columns or makes another change in the table, he must recompute chi-square.

Two-Sample *t*-Tests

To test hypotheses that compare two means, an investigator chooses between two equations of t. If she assumes the variances for the two groups are unequal, she calculates t using the equation

$$t = \frac{\overline{X}_1 - \overline{X}_2}{\sqrt{\frac{s_1^2}{n_1 - 1} + \frac{s_2^2}{n_2 - 1}}}$$

If she assumes the variances of the two groups are equal, she calculates t using the equation

$$t = \frac{\overline{X}_1 - \overline{X}_2}{\sqrt{\frac{n_1 s_1^2 + n_2 s_2^2}{n_1 + n_2 - 2}} \cdot \sqrt{\frac{1}{n_1} + \frac{1}{n_2}}}$$

How does she decide between the two models? She may prefer to assume unequal variances, since the appropriate use of the equation does not require unequal population variances[1]. If she wishes, she can test the hypothesis that the variances of the two groups are unequal. If she fails to

[1]For a discussion of these two equations, see H. M. Blalock, *Social Statistics* (New York: McGraw Hill, 1972), pp. 220–228.

TABLE 12.13   CHI-SQUARE DISTRIBUTION

	Probability			
df	.10	.05	.01	.001
1	2.706	3.841	6.635	10.827
2	4.605	5.991	9.210	13.815
3	6.251	7.815	11.345	16.266
4	7.779	9.488	13.277	18.467
5	9.236	11.070	15.086	20.515
6	10.645	12.592	16.812	22.457

SOURCE: Adapted from R. E. Walpole and R. H. Myer, "Critical Values of the Chi-Square Distribution," *Probability and Statistics for Engineers and Scientists*, 3d ed. (New York: Macmillan, 1985), 577.

reject the null hypothesis (**H$_0$:** the variances are equal), she will calculate t with the second equation; if she rejects the null hypothesis, she will use the first equation.

For either equation, the degrees of freedom equals the sum of the number of observations in the two samples minus 2. Next the investigator

consults a t-distribution table, such as Table 12.14. If she has hypothesized a direction, she uses the columns reporting probabilities for a one-tailed test. Otherwise, she uses the columns reporting for a two-tailed test.

Let's consider the example of planners' salaries. We hypothesized that female planners would have

TABLE 12.14   DISTRIBUTION OF t-VALUES

df	Probability for One-Tailed Test		Probability for Two-Tailed Test	
	.05	.01	.05	.01
1	6.314	31.821	12.706	63.657
2	2.920	6.965	4.303	9.925
3	2.353	4.541	3.182	5.841
4	2.132	3.747	2.776	4.604
5	2.015	3.365	2.571	4.032
6	1.943	3.145	2.447	3.707
7	1.895	2.998	2.365	3.499
8	1.860	2.896	2.306	3.355
9	1.833	2.821	2.262	3.250
10	1.812	2.764	2.228	3.169
11	1.796	2.718	2.201	3.106
12	1.782	2.681	2.179	3.055
13	1.771	2.650	2.160	3.012
14	1.761	2.624	2.145	2.977
15	1.753	2.602	2.131	2.947
16	1.746	2.583	2.120	2.921
17	1.740	2.567	2.110	2.898
18	1.734	2.552	2.101	2.878
19	1.729	2.539	2.093	2.861
20	1.725	2.528	2.086	2.845
21	1.721	2.518	2.080	2.831
22	1.717	2.508	2.074	2.819
23	1.714	2.500	2.069	2.807
24	1.711	2.492	2.064	2.797
25	1.708	2.485	2.060	2.787
26	1.706	2.479	2.056	2.779
27	1.703	2.473	2.052	2.771
28	1.701	2.467	2.048	2.763
29	1.699	2.462	2.045	2.756
30	1.697	2.457	2.042	2.750
60	1.671	2.390	2.000	2.660
∞	1.645	2.326	1.960	2.567

SOURCE: Adapted from R. A. Fisher and F. Yates, *Statistical Tables for Biological, Agricultural, and Medical Research,* 6th ed. (New York: Hafner, 1968), Table III, 46.

lower salaries than male planners; thus, we would want to perform a one-tailed *t*-test. If we select a specific alpha level, for example, $\alpha = .01$, we note the value in the column headed ".01" and the row for the appropriate degrees of freedom (*df*). In the example, the degrees of freedom was 533. So we go to the row marked with ∞ (infinity) and find that if the value of *t* is equal to or greater than 2.326, we will reject the null hypothesis.

t-values may be negative. The negative sign indicates which group has the larger mean. In reading and interpreting the *t*-distribution tables, the associated probability is the same whether *t* is negative *t* or positive *t*.

Chapter 13

Examining Relationships among Variables: Contingency Tables with Measures of Association, Analysis of Variance

In this chapter you will learn

1. how to construct and interpret contingency tables with two or three variables.

2. how to select and interpret common measures of association for variables measured at the nominal or ordinal level.

3. how to analyze data from experiments.

4. a technique for determining the statistical significance and strength of a relationship between a nominal independent variable and an interval dependent variable.

This chapter discusses two alternative approaches to data analysis: contingency tables with measures of association and analysis of variance. In practice, analysts tend to work with one or the other approach. Investigators who conduct surveys and work with cross-sectional designs tend to rely on tests of statistical significance, contingency-table analysis, and measures of association. Depending on the level of measurement, they select specific statistics appropriate to their data. The measures of association generated from contingency tables or from regression analysis, discussed in Chapter 14, provide evidence of the strength of a relationship.

Analysis of variance is frequently encountered in connection with the analysis of experimental data. Its primary output is a test of statistical significance, the F-test. With one additional calculation, a measure of association, eta, also can be produced. We discuss analysis of variance in this chapter for four reasons. First, it parallels contingency-table analysis. A researcher who chooses analysis of variance seldom uses contingency-table analysis to analyze a dataset. The reverse also is generally true. Second, contingency-table analysis and regression dominate research conducted by social scientists doing non-experimental research. Analysis of variance dominates research conducted by experimental researchers. Researchers may be familiar with one set of techniques and virtually ignorant of the other.

While the discussion in this chapter does not give a balanced coverage of both techniques, it should give you a better idea of their separate roles.[1] Third, analysis of variance involves a specific statistic to determine the significance of a relationship and a specific statistic to determine its strength. Consequently, separating these discussions into two chapters seems inefficient. Fourth, analysis of variance can be used to compare means of several groups, that is, to analyze the relationship between an interval dependent variable and a nominal independent variable.

If you are reading this chapter before the material on tests of statistical significance, you may wish to concentrate only on the contingency-table section. The analysis of variance discussion will be of more value if you understand tests of statistical significance.

AN OVERVIEW OF CONTINGENCY TABLES AND RELATED MEASURES OF ASSOCIATION

Often the analyst wants to investigate the joint occurrence and distribution of the values of two or more variables. He may want to know how the distribution of the values of one variable differs for different levels or categories of a second variable. To find out he may organize his data into a contingency table. A *contingency table* shows the frequency or relative frequency of each value of the dependent variable for each value of the independent variable. An analyst may use measures of association to summarize the relationship depicted in the contingency table. *Measures of association* are statistics that indicate the strength of the relationship between a dependent and an independent variable.

Contingency tables and measures of association help test hypotheses. Chapter 12 suggested that accepting a research hypothesis required empirical evidence that the relationship between variables was (1) nonrandom, (2) in the anticipated direction, and (3) sufficiently strong given the sample size. Contingency tables indicate the direction of the relationship and provide information so one can judge the strength of the association. Measures of association serve as standardized indicators of the strength of a relationship; some measures also indicate the direction of the relationship. Tests of statistical significance indicate the probability that a relationship occurred by chance.

CONSTRUCTING AND INTERPRETING CONTINGENCY TABLES

Table 13.1 shows how residents of Large County reacted to a proposal to consolidate the county government with the government of the county's largest city. Analysts wanted to display how residents of the large city and residents outside of the city differed in their responses.

By convention, the values of the independent variable head the columns and the values of the dependent variables head the rows. If the variables are ordinal, the values are arranged along a continuum. In this table, "no opinion" was put in the middle or neutral position. The research model guides analysts in deciding which values to include and how to include them. The study's purpose should dominate

TABLE 13.1   SUPPORT FOR CITY–COUNTY CONSOLIDATION BY RESIDENCE

	Residence			
	Inside City		Outside City	
Support for Consolidation	N	%	N	%
For	273	54	54	37
No opinion	134	27	34	23
Against	98	19	57	39
Total (% rounded)	505	100	145	100

Note: Percentages may not add up to 100% because of rounding.

their decisions, but other factors, such as the distribution of the values and the clarity of the table, may be considered as well. In Table 13.1 the analysts examined the values "inside city" and "outside city" and "for," "against," and "no opinion." Consolidation opinions originally included "strongly for" and "strongly against." The analysts defended combining "strongly for" with "for" and "strongly against" with "against" on the grounds that their job was to estimate the proportion of residents for and against consolidation, and that more specific information was not needed. If relatively few residents were strongly against consolidation, the analysts may appropriately decide to report four categories: "strongly for," "for," "no opinion," and "against." Depending on the purpose of a report such an arrangement may provide full adequate information without adding to a table's clutter.

The percentages are computed "in the direction of the independent variable." The analysts were interested in the differences between city and non-city residents. Each group's total was treated as 100 percent, and the relative frequency of each group who responded "for," "no opinion," and "against" was shown.

To interpret contingency tables, analysts focus on the percentages. In Table 13.1 the population of city residents is so much larger than that of non-city residents that directly comparing the frequencies for any particular response would be inappropriate. Using percentages corrects this. The *percentage difference,* the difference in percentages when subtracting across the rows, indicates the strength of relationship between two variables. The analyst begins by reading across a row and noting how the percentages change. The difference can range from 0, for no difference, to 100, indicating maximum difference. The analysis is clearest when there are only two columns, that is, two columns for the independent variable.

In comparing the two groups in Table 13.1, we find that 54 percent of city residents supported consolidation, but only 37 percent of non-city residents did, a percentage difference of 17. Nineteen percent of city residents and 39 percent of non-city residents were against consolidation, a percentage difference of 20. We can conclude that city residents differ from non-city residents in the distribution of opinions toward consolidation.

The joint distribution of the values of two variables is a *bivariate distribution.* Table 13.1 shows the bivariate distribution between residence and support for consolidation. In Example 13.1, Table 13.2 shows the bivariate distribution between the evaluation of city services and support for consolidation. The table

EXAMPLE 13.1

Organizing and Interpreting Contingency Tables

Situation: City and county residents were surveyed about their evaluation of local government services and whether they favored city–county consolidation. The researchers' implied hypothesis was: Support for city–county consolidation is directly related to respondents' evaluation of their local services.

Analysis: The data are organized into a contingency table, Table 13.2. The values of the independent variable head the columns, and the values of the dependent variable head the rows. Either the highest or lowest value can go in the first column or first row. To avoid clutter, only the percents are shown in the body of the table.

TABLE 13.2 SUPPORT FOR CONSOLIDATION BY EVALUATION OF LOCAL SERVICES

	Evaluation of Local Services			
Support for Consolidation	*Excellent or Good (%)*	*Fair (%)*	*Poor (%)*	*Total (N)*
For	55	47	36	331
No opinion	24	25	34	161
Against	21	28	31	155
Total (N)	387	224	36	647

Note: Percentages may not add up to 100% due to rounding.

To determine the direction of the relationship, an analyst looks across the rows: from left to right along the "for" row the percentages drop, and from left to right along the "against" row the percentages increase. The data are consistent with the hypothesis. The higher the rating that respondents give to local services, the more likely they are to favor consolidation; the lower they rate local services, the less likely respondents are to favor consolidation. Another way to view the table is to look at how the "center of gravity" changes along the values of the independent variable. The "excellent or good" column has the highest center of gravity and the "poor" column the lowest. This strategy helps to quickly identify nonlinear relationships, where a middle value will have the highest or lowest center of gravity.

A test of statistical significance establishes the probability that the distribution in the contingency table occurred by chance. The percentage distributions provide further support for a hypothesis. Although whether one judges the relationship strong enough to support the hypothesis based on the percentage distributions is a matter of judgment.

shows that those who gave a higher evaluation to city services were more likely to support consolidation. The example's discussion spells out how the table was constructed and interpreted.

Earlier in this book we addressed control variables. This refers to a situation in which a third variable is included in the analysis to see if it influences

TABLE 13.3 SUPPORT OF CONSOLIDATION BY RATING OF LOCAL SERVICES BY PLACE OF RESIDENCE

	Residence					
	City Service Rating			*Noncity Service Rating*		
Support for Consolidation	Good (%)	Fair (%)	Poor (%)	Good (%)	Fair (%)	Poor (%)
For	65	46	30	1	49	35
No opinion	20	25	35	45	25	34
Against	15	29	35	54	25	31
Total (N)	329	161	15	59	63	21

the relationship between the other two variables. For example, we may wish to see whether the relationship between service rating and support for consolidation is the same for city residents as it is for non-city residents. We would divide the original group of cases into two subgroups—city residents and non-city residents—and create two additional tables, one for each group. We would then analyze the relationship for each subgroup. In doing so, we would have controlled for place of residence. Table 13.3 shows the relationship among three variables: support for consolidation, rating of local services, and place of residence. Inspection of the percentages in the table shows that those in the city were likely to be in favor of consolidation if they rated service as "good" (65 percent), whereas non-city residents were very unlikely to be for consolidation if they rated service as "good" (1 percent). The number of variables displayed in a table can be expanded to three, four, and even more. Although occasionally we see a table with four variables, very few tables show the relationships among more than three.

Tables also are described by their *size* and *dimensions.* A table's size is indicated by the numbers of rows and columns in the table. The number of rows is the number of categories of the dependent variable, and the number of columns is the number of categories of the independent variable. The dimension of a table refers to the number of variables whose joint distribution is being displayed. A table showing the joint distribution of two variables is a two-dimensional table; one with three variables is a three-dimensional table, and so on.

SELECTING AND USING MEASURES OF ASSOCIATION

The percent distributions in a contingency table suggest the strength of the relationship between two variables; however, what constitutes a "strong" or a "weak" relationship partially depends on the observer. Measures of association do not eliminate the effect of perception, but they help by providing a standard criterion to summarize the relationship in a table. They are most useful when investigators want to see the effect of a control variable or if they want to compare several tables at one time. Direct comparisons may be difficult if the number of cases or the number of cells varies from table to table. Even if the number of cases and cells remains the same, comparing a large number of tables quickly becomes tedious.

For example, an analyst asked city employees to rate the performance of their human resources department in carrying out 28 activities. The analyst wanted to identify characteristics associated with employee ratings. Just to find out whether employees in different departments had similar attitudes, he had to study 28 tables with 21 cells in each table. His task of screening the tables was greatly simplified by relying on a statistical measure of association. It let him quickly decide how strong a relationship was and whether he wanted to look in more depth at the table and its cells.

Measures of association are descriptive statistics that indicate the strength of a relationship between two variables. Statisticians have developed measures of association to summarize the relationships between nominal, ordinal, and interval variables. Nominal and ordinal measures of association are primarily used to eliminate from further study weak or null relationships between variables. Measures of association may be used to compare the strength of relationships among tables of similar size. However, researchers seldom report nominal or ordinal measures of association without including the contingency tables, thus allowing readers to assess the relationships and reach their own conclusions.

Perfect and Null Relationships

Each measure of association has a criterion for *perfect relationship*. A perfect relationship is one in which a change in the independent variable is always associated with a change in the dependent variable. An analyst may observe a direct relationship in which an increase in the value of the independent variable always coincides with an increase in the dependent variable. Alternatively, she may observe an inverse relationship in which an increase in the value of the independent variable always coincides with a decrease in the dependent variable. Typically, measures of association designate a perfect relationship with an absolute value of 1.00.

Similarly, each measure of association has a criterion for a *null relationship*. A null relationship occurs if a change in the independent variable is as likely to coincide with an increase as with a decrease or no change in the dependent variable. Typically, measures of association designate a null relationship with a value of 0.00.

The values of nominal measures of association vary between 0.00 and 1.00. The values of ordinal measures of association vary between 0.00 and ±1.00. The closer a measure of association is to 0.00, the weaker the association; the closer it is to 1.00, the stronger the association. The sign, a plus or a minus, indicates the direction, not the strength or weakness, of a relationship. A +1.00 represents a direct relationship, and a −1.00 represents an inverse relationship.

Tables 13.4 and 13.5 illustrate two models of perfect relationships. Table 13.4 illustrates a perfect direct relationship, and Table 13.5 illustrates a perfect inverse relationship. A nominal measure of association for both of these tables would have a value of 1.00; an ordinal measure of association would have a value of 1.00 for Table 13.4 and −1.00 for Table 13.5.

Table 13.6 illustrates a model of a null relationship. Measures of association for the table would have a value of 0.00.

Tables 13.4 through 13.6 do not include all the models of perfect and null relationships. Most, if not all, readers would agree that Tables 13.4 and 13.5 represent perfect relationships and that Table 13.6 represents a null relationship. What about Table 13.7? Does this seem to be a null relationship? Most readers would probably argue that it shows a direct relationship between length of job training

TABLE 13.4   LENGTH OF JOB-TRAINING PROGRAM AND PLACEMENT SUCCESS

Placement Rate (%)	Length of Job-Training Program		
	≤1 Month	2–3 Months	>3 Months
Low (<50)	100%		
Moderate (50–75)		100%	
High (>75)			100%

TABLE 13.5   LENGTH OF JOB-TRAINING PROGRAM AND PLACEMENT SUCCESS

Placement Rate (%)	Length of Job-Training Program		
	≤1 Month	2–3 Months	>3 Months
Low (<50)			100%
Moderate (50–75)		100%	
High (>75)	100%		

TABLE 13.6   LENGTH OF JOB-TRAINING PROGRAM AND PLACEMENT SUCCESS

Placement Rate (%)	Length of Job-Training Program		
	≤1 Month	2–3 Months	>3 Months
Low (<50)	20%	20%	20%
Moderate (50–75)	40%	40%	40%
High (>75)	40%	40%	40%

TABLE 13.7   LENGTH OF JOB-TRAINING PROGRAM AND PLACEMENT SUCCESS

Placement Rate (%)	Length of Job-Training Program		
	≤1 Month	2–3 Months	>3 Months
Low (<50)	40%	30%	20%
Moderate (50–75)	40%	40%	40%
High (>75)	20%	30%	40%

and placement rate; however, some measures of association may designate this relationship with a value of 0.00.

Using Measures of Association as a Screen

One way that analysts use measures of association is to separate trivial relationships from stronger relationships. Table 13.8 illustrates such a use of a measure of association.

The analyst wanted to learn if previous experience in the private sector was related to respondents' ratings of the city human resources department. He chose a nominal measure of association because previous private sector experience is a nominal variable. He had a number of measures from which to choose. He chose Cramer's V because he was familiar with the statistic and because its criteria for evaluating the strength of a relationship was appropriate to his purposes. (We discuss criteria for selecting a measure of association and basic characteristics of measures of association later in this section.)

The measure shows that previous management experience is most strongly associated with the ratings of the human resources department's performance in administering the performance appraisal system and most weakly associated with the ratings of its performance in updating department heads on personnel policies. The analyst can rank the strength of the relationships. He would place administering the performance appraisal system first, visiting departments to learn about their working conditions second, explaining personnel policies and actions third, and so on. Updating department heads is placed last.

The analyst would try to visualize the response patterns. For example, he suspects that .36, .38, and .42 depict relatively similar relationships. Still, he rarely stops with his list of measures of association. He closely examines the tables representing the stronger relationships and glances at the tables representing weaker ones. If he studied all the tables, the measure would not be an efficient screen.

Look at the tables with the strongest and weakest relationships. Table 13.9 suggests that respondents' previous experience is related to their ratings of the

TABLE 13.8   VALUES OF A NOMINAL MEASURE OF ASSOCIATION: RATINGS OF HUMAN RESOURCES DEPARTMENT PERFORMANCE BY RESPONDENT PRIOR EXPERIENCE

	Measure of Association (Cramer's V)
Explain policies	.36
Advise departments	.30
Respond to applicants	.20
Recruit personnel	.22
Visit departments	.38
Run affirmative-action program	.16
Administer performance appraisals	.42
Administer safety program	.14
Update department heads	.11

TABLE 13.9 RATINGS OF THE PERFORMANCE OF HUMAN RESOURCES DEPARTMENT IN ADMINISTERING PERFORMANCE APPRAISAL SYSTEM BY PRIOR EXPERIENCE

	No Management Experience ($n = 59$)	Management Experience ($n = 12$)
Poor	70%	17%
Satisfactory	22%	50%
Good	8%	33%

Note: Cramer's V = .42.

administration of the performance appraisal system. Those without management experience are distinctly more critical than those with management experience. Employees without management experience are far less likely to rate the human resources department's administration of the performance appraisal system as "good." Instead, they tend to rate it as "poor." You also can see this relationship by comparing the percents reported for those without management experience to the percents for those with this experience. One can confirm the strength of the relationship by computing a percentage difference. There is a 53 percent difference between the percentage of those without management experience and the percentage of those with management experience rating the human resources department as poor. The percentage difference for small tables such as this can effectively substitute for a measure of association.

Table 13.10 shows a similar, but far weaker, trend. Those without management experience are more critical of the human resources department's performance in keeping department heads up-to-date, but their attitudes are not markedly different from that of those with management experience. In this case, there is a 5 percent difference between the percentage of those with management experience and those without who rate the human resources department as poor. Although the opinion of the person identified as "other" is included in the calculation of statistics, analysts avoid drawing conclusions from only one case.

The analyst's use of the information from the measures of associations and the tables depends on his model. Often the findings lead to other questions. For example, are those without management experience more critical because they have unrealistic expectations of the human resources department? Or do those

TABLE 13.10 RATINGS OF THE PERFORMANCE OF THE HUMAN RESOURCES DEPARTMENT IN UPDATING DEPARTMENT HEADS ON PERSONNEL POLICIES BY PRIOR EXPERIENCE

	No Management Experience ($n = 56$)	Management Experience ($n = 11$)	Other ($n = 1$)
Poor	43%	38%	0%
Satisfactory	29%	27%	100%
Good	29%	36%	0%

with management experience feel more invested in the city government employment system or are they more realistic because of their experience elsewhere? Other questions may occur to you. Some of these questions can be answered by introducing a control variable. Others require additional information.

In the example, the analyst used the measure of association as a screen. Instead of trying to examine the detail in each table, he ranked the relationships according to the values of a measure of association and then decided which tables to study in more depth. Alternatively, he could have set a cutoff point and examined only the tables with measures of association equal to or greater than the cutoff value.

Selected tables are studied carefully to ascertain the direction of relationships and to make sure that they confirm the relationship described by the statistical measure. A small number of cases in the table or the clustering of data in one category, such as "do not know" or "neutral," may suggest that an apparently strong statistical relationship is actually trivial.

In writing up a report, analysts seldom mention the measure of association. Instead, their reports present and discuss findings in prose, tables, and graphs, which are familiar and easily understood by a wide range of readers. The text may refer to percentages in the tables; however, measures of association, if reported, are included parenthetically or placed in table footnotes.

Selecting a Measure of Association

In working with measures of association, students normally have two questions. How do I choose a measure of association? What constitutes a strong relationship?

The first criterion for choosing a measure of association is the consistency between the statistic and the level of measurement. If the variables are measured at the nominal level, the analyst must use a nominal statistic. If they are measured at the ordinal level, the analyst may use a nominal or an ordinal statistic. If the relationship includes one nominal and one ordinal variable, the analyst may use a nominal statistic or choose a measure of association designed to examine a relationship between nominal and ordinal variables. It would not be appropriate to use a measure designed for ordinal variables.

Note that dichotomous nominal variables, variables with two categories, may be analyzed using ordinal measures of association. The two categories may be visualized as endpoints of a continuum. For example, male and female may be categorized as male and non-male (or female and non-female). Conventionally, one category of the variable is assigned a "1," and the other category is assigned a "0."

The second criterion for selecting a measure is its criteria for a null and perfect relationship. The analyst should choose a statistic that is consistent with her theoretical purposes. She should select a measure that assigns a "1" to relationships that she considers perfect and assigns a "0" to relationships that she considers random or null.

The third criterion for selecting a measure is its sensitivity. A *sensitive measure of association* is a statistic that detects small differences between the strengths of relationships. When we introduced measures of association, we argued that they helped the investigator quickly distinguish between stronger and weaker relationships. An insensitive measure assigns the same or nearly the same numerical value to relationships that an investigator would judge differed in their strength. A sensitive measure assigns different numerical values to relationships that may have slight, even subtle, differences in strength.

The fourth criterion is familiarity with the statistic. An analyst needs to be familiar with a statistic to know how sensitive it is and to decide if he agrees with its criteria for a null and perfect relationship. Furthermore, familiarity helps an analyst to judge the strength of a specific relationship.

The answer to what constitutes a strong relationship depends on the statistic and the research question. First, because of having different criteria for null and perfect relationships, some measures of association tend to have much lower values than others. Second, the factors affecting some dependent variables are well known. If a researcher were analyzing such a well-studied dependent variable, even moderate associations might be of limited value because stronger relationships may have been identified and explained. On the other hand, some dependent variables are not well studied or understood, and even relatively weak relationships may suggest research questions worth pursuing.

To compare one relationship with another, we use a single measure of association, but such comparisons should be done with caution. Some statistics are intended only for 2×2 tables or square tables; hence, some comparisons may be impossible. Some ordinal measures of association may underestimate or miss nonlinear relationships, so a measure that identifies strong direct or inverse relations may completely miss a strong nonlinear relationship. Exact comparisons between tables of different sizes should be avoided. The number of rows and columns in a table can affect the value of a measure of association.

We cannot directly compare two different statistics measuring association as each has its own criteria for perfect and null relationships. These criteria as well as the strength of the association affect the numerical value. Thus we cannot assume that a relationship with a Cramer's V of .10 is weaker than a relationship with a gamma of .45. If, however, different measures of association all suggest a strong or weak relationship between two variables, we can be more confident in our conclusions.

The Logic of a Measure of Association

Rather than survey specific nominal and ordinal measures of association, we closely examine one nominal measure of association to give a better idea of what a measure of association does. We also outline the major features of an ordinal measure of association to demonstrate how ordinal measures incorporate the additional information contained in ordinal variables and to alert you to some common problems encountered in working with ordinal measures of association. With this understanding you can refer to a statistics text to study and select a measure appropriate to your needs. In addition, you can find the calculations for the nominal and ordinal measures mentioned in this chapter in the chapter appendix.

We look at lambda, a simple nominal measure, to illustrate measures of association. Lambda is a *proportional reduction in error (PRE) measure* and is based on the mode. All PRE measures indicate how much that knowledge of the distribution of the independent variable reduces the error in predicting the distribution of the dependent variable. How much error is there in predicting the distribution of the dependent variable without knowing the independent variable? Lambda calls this error *original error.* Original error for lambda is equal to the number of non-modal responses.

Consider an analysis of the ratings of the performance of a city's human resources department produced in Table 13.11. Imagine that you were to meet all 95 survey respondents but only knew the total number giving each rating. You know that 38 of the respondents rated the human resources department as "poor," 32 rated the department as "satisfactory," and 25 rated the department as "good." You guess how each individual rated the human resources department. To meet the assumptions of lambda, you guess that each person rated the department as "poor." In other words you guess the most common response or the mode for each individual. With this guessing rule, you are wrong 57 times. Fifty-seven is the original error—the sum of the non-modal responses. If you guessed that everyone gave the department either a "satisfactory" or "good" rating, you would be wrong more than 57 times.

Does including data on an independent variable reduce the original error? Lambda considers the error for each category of the independent variable as *new error.* New error for lambda is equal to the non-modal responses for each category of the independent variable. Let's return to our example. Note that the table gives you the distribution of the independent variable, that is, the distribution of ratings given by each department's respondents. You use this additional information and ask each respondent in which department he or she works. You then guess that a respondent's rating was the same as the modal response for his department. You guess a police department employee rated the human resources department as "good," fire and planning employees rated it as "poor," and public works employees rated it as "satisfactory." In our example, you have incorrectly labeled 15 police employees, 15 fire employees, 10 public works employees, and 2 planning employees. With knowledge of a respondent's department, you made 42 errors. The 42 errors, based on the distribution of the independent variable, is the new error.

TABLE 13.11   RATINGS OF THE HUMAN RESOURCES DEPARTMENT'S PERFORMANCE BY RESPONDENT DEPARTMENT

	Police	Fire	Public Works	Planning	Total
Poor	10	15	5	8	38
Satisfactory	5	10	15	2	32
Good	15	5	5	0	25
Total	30	30	25	10	95

To compute lambda, subtract the new error from the original error and divide the result by the original error. The solution for our example is:

$$\text{lambda} = (\text{original error} - \text{new error})/\text{original error}$$
$$= (57 - 42)/57$$
$$= .263$$

The .263 indicates that by knowing respondents' departments, we have reduced the error in guessing the ratings by 26.3 percent.

Lambda tends to be a relatively insensitive measure. That is, it does not detect small shifts or differences in the strength of a relationship. You can infer this by looking at its criterion for a null relationship. Lambda is calculated in such a way that many relationships with a discernible pattern between the independent and dependent variables have a lambda equal to 0.00. Consequently, even though lambda equals 0.00, an analyst or audience may see a relationship between the variables. Let's illustrate this by arranging our dataset on perceptions of the human resources department a little differently. In Table 13.12, do you see any departmental trends in the perception of the human resources department?

Look at the median for each value of the independent variable. The majority of respondents in the planning and fire departments rate the human resources department as "poor." Fewer than half the employees in the police and public works departments give a similar rating; in fact, 40 percent of the police employees rated human resources as "good." Lambda for these data equals 0.00. The lesson is not that your perception was wrong. Rather, it is to demonstrate that lambda is insensitive and ignores relationships if the mode of every value of the independent variable is the same category of the dependent variable.

Salient Features of an Ordinal Measure of Association

Ordinal measures of association summarize relationships between ordinal independent and dependent variables. These measures take into account the additional information provided by data measured at the ordinal level. An ordinal measure of association indicates whether a change in the value of an independent variable is associated with a linear change in the value of the dependent variable. If an analyst has hypothesized a direct relationship, an increase in the value of the independent variable should be associated with an increase in the value of the dependent variable. If she has hypothesized an inverse relationship, an increase in

TABLE 13.12   RATINGS OF THE PERFORMANCE OF THE HUMAN RESOURCES DEPARTMENT BY RESPONDENT DEPARTMENT

	Police	Fire	Public Works	Planning	Total
Poor	12	15	9	8	44
Satisfactory	6	10	8	2	26
Good	12	5	8	0	25
Total	30	30	25	10	95

the value of the independent variable should be associated with a decrease in the value of the dependent variable. Ordinal measures can effectively estimate the strength of direct and inverse relationships but not the strength of nonlinear relationships. If the analyst has hypothesized or suspects a nonlinear relationship, she may prefer to use a nominal measure of association.

Ideally, the measure of association will be positive for a direct relationship and negative for an inverse relationship. In practice, specific decisions on how to organize a variable's values along a continuum determine if the statistic has a positive or negative sign. Analysts should always inspect tables on which the measures were calculated to be sure they understand how the values were ordered and that the sign is consistent with the observed relationship.

The analyst may choose among several ordinal measures of association. The measures vary in their statistical models of what constitutes a perfect relationship. We limit our discussion to one measure, gamma. Gamma illustrates the salient characteristics of ordinal measures and is a sensitive measure. It has a generous criterion for detecting perfect relationships. An analyst who wishes to avoid screening out potentially interesting relationships may prefer to work with gamma, which will give her more options than other ordinal measures.

Gamma shares two characteristics with other ordinal and interval measures. First, its sign depends on the order of the numerical values of the variables. Second, it is insensitive to nonlinear relationships, and it may seriously underestimate their strength. In addition, gamma's generous standard for a perfect relationship may overestimate the strength of the relationship between two variables.

Look at Table 13.13. Do you consider this to be a perfect relationship? Chances are that you think that the relationship is strong but less than perfect. You would probably consider the relationship to be perfect if all 12 respondents who had worked in the police department for one to five years were in the satisfactory category. Yet, gamma for these data equals +1.00. Gamma's generous criterion for a perfect relationship affects other values of gamma, so gamma assigns higher values to a relationship than other ordinal measures of association.

Does the table show a direct relationship, which is implied by the +1? No, we see an inverse relationship between the rating and years of employment. To designate the inverse relationship, gamma should equal −1.00. The +1.00, then, results from the way that the variables' numerical values were ordered. Starting at the upper left-hand cell, the independent variable was ranked from low to high values, that is, from <1 year to >5 years, whereas the dependent variable was ranked from high

TABLE 13.13   POLICE DEPARTMENT RESPONDENTS' RATINGS OF THE PERFORMANCE OF THE HUMAN RESOURCES DEPARTMENT BY YEARS OF EMPLOYMENT

	<1 year	1–5 years	>5 years	Total
Good	12	0	0	12
Satisfactory	0	6	0	6
Poor	0	6	12	18

to low values, that is, from "good" to "poor." This inconsistent arrangement of values caused gamma to have the "wrong" sign. Remember, the sign a computer program assigns to an ordinal measure of association depends on the consistency in ranking values of the independent and dependent variables. The signs will be "correct" if the numerical values of both the dependent and independent variables go from the lowest value to the highest or from the highest to the lowest. To prevent an error in deciding the direction, check the table and make sure that it is consistent with the sign of the statistic. When writing up findings, remember that the reader should be able to quickly and accurately interpret the direction implied by the finding. For example, one could report a $+1.00$ gamma for the hypothesis that as seniority increases, disdain for the human resources department increases. However, readers can easily miss such subtle wording variations and be misled.

In reporting your findings do not simply say that a strong association exists. Describe the relationship. If we were reporting on the relationship between length of tenure with the police department and perceptions of the human resources department, we might write one of the following statements:

> *Sample statement 1:* Length of tenure in the police department and ratings of the human resources department are strongly and negatively related (gamma $= -1.00$). The longer a respondent had worked with the police department, the more likely he was to give the human resources department a poor rating.
>
> *Sample statement 2:* The longer a respondent had worked with the police department, the more likely he was to give the human resources department a poor rating (gamma $= -1.00$).
>
> *Sample statement 3:* The length of time a respondent had worked with the police department was strongly and negatively associated with the rating of the human resources department. Respondents who had worked with the police department longer tended to give the human resources department a poorer rating.

In selecting and interpreting an ordinal measure of association, you should be aware that ordinal measures underestimate strong nonlinear relationships. Table 13.14 relates years of working experience to perceptions of the human resources department's effectiveness.

Note the nonlinear pattern. Employees with the least working experience are most likely to rate the human resources department as "poor." Employees

TABLE 13.14 RATINGS OF THE PERFORMANCE OF THE HUMAN RESOURCES DEPARTMENT BY YEARS OF FULL-TIME WORKING EXPERIENCE

	<2 years	2–5 years	>5 years
Poor	20	0	5
Satisfactory	10	10	20
Good	5	20	5

Note: Gamma = .29.

with between two and five years of working experience are most likely to rate the department as "good." Employees with more than five years experience are most likely to rate the department as "satisfactory." The data indicate a relationship that is neither distinctly direct nor inverse. The gamma value, suggesting a weak direct relationship, underestimates the strength of the relationship because it ignores the nonlinear pattern.

The problem of underestimating non-linearity illustrates the value of starting out with an explicit model. The model may have postulated a nonlinear relationship. Even if a nonlinear relationship was not expected, the analyst has anticipated what relationships are important. A good analyst will examine tables analyzing an important relationship even if the measures of association suggest a weak relationship.

A nominal measure may be best to uncover nonlinear relationships between ordinal variables, whether they were expected or not. Nominal measures evaluate each category of a variable without assuming a rank ordering, and they will assign the same numerical value no matter how the categories are arranged. Ordinal measures assume a monotonically increasing or decreasing pattern; that is, two variables either steadily increase or decrease together.

Symmetric and Asymmetric Measures of Association

Measures of association can be characterized as symmetric or asymmetric. *Symmetric measures* have the same value no matter which variable is designated as the independent variable. *Asymmetric measures* may have different values depending on which variable is designated as the independent variable. Lambda is an asymmetric measure. Gamma is a symmetric measure of association. Cramer's V, which appears in several examples in this chapter, also is a symmetric measure.

Some Common Nominal and Ordinal Measures of Association

Nominal measures of association can be categorized as chi-square–based measures and Proportional Reduction in Error (PRE) measures. Chi-square, an inferential statistic discussed in Chapter 12, is the basis for several nominal, symmetric measures, including Cramer's V. Lambda is a PRE measure.

PRE measures tend to have lower values for a given relationship than do chi-square–based measures. We might choose a chi-square–based measure to screen a set of contingency tables for further analysis. It will normally result in more tables being reviewed, and the investigator is not apt to miss an interesting relationship.

PRE measures are less likely to overestimate the strength of an association. In fact, PRE measures may underestimate them. An investigator summarizing the effects of a large number of independent variables might choose a PRE measure. Investigators tend to prefer measures that are more likely to indicate a null relationship for this purpose. In general, researchers would rather bias their studies so that they do not assume that a trivial or nonexistent relationship is important.

Ordinal measures also are called rank order measures. Three common ordinal measures for contingency tables are *gamma, tau,* and *Somers' d*[2]. Gamma and tau are both symmetric measures while Somers' d is asymmetric. If the variables in a contingency table are ordinal, researchers normally prefer ordinal measures of association over nominal measures. They are more likely to detect relationships,

TABLE 13.15   COMMON MEASURES OF ASSOCIATION FOR DATA MEASURED AT THE NOMINAL OR ORDINAL LEVEL

Measure	Type Data	Characteristics & Comments
Lambda (λ)	Nominal	Asymmetric, PRE measure; may report 0.00 even if variables are statistically related
Cramer's V	Nominal	Symmetric; chi-square-based; values of .20–.40 range suggest a moderate relationship, values over .80 are rarely encountered[1]
Gamma (γ)	Ordinal	Symmetric; reaches ±1.00 for relationships that seem less than perfect; values of .30–.40 range suggest a moderate relationship[2]
Tau (τ)	Ordinal	Symmetric; tau_b used for square tables, tau_c for rectangular tables (tau_b cannot reach ±1.00 for nonsquare tables); values of .30–.70 range suggest a moderate relationship[3]
Somers' d	Ordinal	Asymmetric; values normally fall between gamma and tau[4]

[1]Interpretation of values is from T. H. Poister, *Public Program Analysis: Applied Research Methods* (Baltimore: University Park Press, 1978), 443.
[2]Interpretation of values is from Poister, *Public Program Analysis,* 456, citing J. A. Davis, *Elementary Survey Analysis* (Englewood Cliffs, NJ: Prentice-Hall, 1971), 49.
[3]Interpretation is from B. D. Bowen and H. F. Weisberg, *An Introduction to Data Analysis* (San Francisco: W. H. Freeman, 1977), 76.
[4]Poister, *Public Program Analysis,* 457.

since they make fuller use of a table's information. Nominal statistics ignore the ranking inherent in an ordinal scale. However, in a table with one nominal and one ordinal variable, the analyst usually must rely on a nominal statistic.

Table 13.15 summarizes major characteristics of common measures of association for data measured at the nominal and ordinal levels. As you review this table, remember that the measures of association should add information to a contingency table. If the independent and dependent variables are ordinal, then gamma, tau, or Somers' d should be examined; however, if the relationship is nonlinear, these measures underestimate the strength of the relationship. Recall that what constitutes a "strong" or "moderate" relationship partially depends on the study topic. If an investigator has found few independent variables that are associated with the dependent variable, a weak relationship may merit attention. Furthermore, while ordinal measures of association assign negative values to inverse relationships, the sign indicates only the direction, not the strength, of the relationship.

MEASURES OF ASSOCIATION WITH CONTROL VARIABLES

Depending on the model, an investigator may add a control variable to eliminate a rival hypothesis or to explore further the original relationship. Including a control variable in a contingency table is relatively easy. The dataset is divided into subsets.

Cases are assigned to subsets on the basis of their values of the control variable. For example, for the variable gender, the subsets are male and female. All the females in the dataset are assigned to one subset and all the males are assigned to the other.

The model guides the number of subsets created and studied. For some variables, such as gender, the content of subsets is clear-cut. For other variables, the analyst may have to decide what categories are appropriate for the planned study. He needs to avoid having so many subsets that they contain too few cases for meaningful analysis. He may limit the subsets to the values of interest or combine similar values. The control variables he chooses and the way he arranges them depend on the purpose of the model. For example, if education were the control variable, with the values less than 12 years, high school graduate, bachelor's degree, and graduate degree, the analyst does not have to study each category. He may use all the existing values, combine some values, or examine select values. Listed below are three possible ways of treating education as a control variable:

Option 1: (1) Less than 12 years, (2) high school graduate, (3) bachelor's degree, (4) graduate degree

Option 2: (1) Less than 12 years, (2) high school graduate (includes those with college degrees)

Option 3: (1) Less than 12 years, (2) high school graduate (excludes those with college degrees)

A relationship between two variables is considered spurious if it disappears when a control variable is added to the analysis. A *spurious relationship* is one where the independent variable has been falsely assumed to cause the dependent variable.

Example 13.2 gives a vivid, homey example of a spurious relationship. Table 13.16 lends credence to the hypothesis that storks deliver babies. Counties with large numbers of storks have high birth rates; conversely, counties with few storks have low birth rates. Undoubtedly, no reader of this text believes the hypothesis to be true. An alternative hypothesis that explains why the relationship was observed is that population density is related to both the independent and dependent variables. Specifically, rural areas may have both large numbers of storks and high birth rates, and urban areas may have few storks and low birth rates. Table 13.17, introducing the control variable, county population density, shows that most rural counties have high birth rates no matter how many storks are present and most urban counties have low birth rates. You may be familiar with similar examples, such as ice cream sales being related to violent crimes (the control variable that explains the association is outdoor temperature).

Administrators usually want to learn how a relationship changes if other variables are considered. This is referred to as *specifying* or *elaborating* a relationship. They want to understand how three variables interact. In other words, they want to learn if the original relationship changes under different conditions. The conditions are represented by the values of the control variables.

An analyst normally looks for one of four outcomes in elaborating a relationship. First, the original relationship may continue with little change in each category of the control variable. Second, the original relationship may become

EXAMPLE 13.2

An Example of a Spurious Relationship. *Hypothesis:* Storks Deliver Babies (Data Given in Table 13.16)

TABLE 13.16   BIRTH RATE OF COUNTY BY NUMBER OF STORKS SIGHTED IN COUNTY

	Stork Count	
Birth Rate	**High (n = 100)**	**Low (n = 100)**
High	82%	18%
Low	18%	82%

Note: lambda = .36; Cramer's V = .64; gamma = .91; $\chi^2 = 82$; $df = 1$, $p < .001$.

Control variable: County population density.
   Values: Rural counties; urban counties (data given in Table 13.17).

TABLE 13.17   BIRTH RATE OF COUNTY BY NUMBER OF STORKS SIGHTED BY POPULATION DENSITY OF COUNTY

	Rural Counties Stork Count			Urban Counties Stork Count	
Birth Rate	**High (n = 90)**	**Low (n = 10)**	**Birth Rate**	**High (n = 10)**	**Low (n = 90)**
High	90%	90%	High	10%	10%
Low	10%	10%	Low	90%	90%

Note: For statistics involving rural and urban counties, lambda = 0.00; Cramer's V = 0.00; gamma = 0.00; $\chi^2 = 0$, $df = 1$, $p > .90$.
SOURCE: J. B. Williamson, D. A. Karp, and J. R. Dalphin, *The Research Craft* (Boston: Little, Brown, 1977), 417–418.

stronger or weaker in some, but not all, categories of the control variable. Third, the original relationship may disappear in some or all categories of the control variable. Fourth, the relationship may change direction in some or all categories of the control variable.

An investigator may find that the relationship disappears in all categories of the control variable, in which case the relationship is considered spurious. Occasionally, the control variable may reveal an association between two variables that was not observed when the relationship between only the independent and dependent variables was analyzed.[3]

Measures of association decrease the work required to determine the effect of a control variable. By looking at a measure of association, an analyst can quickly visualize how the control variable affects the original relationship. The analyst looks at the measure of association between independent and dependent variable for each value of the control variable to see how it varies among the categories and how much it differs from the original relationship. To illustrate this role of control variables, we analyzed data on municipal employees to identify characteristics associated with the type of position employees held. The dependent variable, position type, was assigned three values: administrator, supervisor, and non-manager. Four independent variables that might account for employee positions were examined: employee department, number of years with the city, sector of previous job (private or public), and education. The analyst controlled for the variable gender to see if it affected the relationship between any of the independent variables and the dependent variable, position type.

Table 13.18 reports the statistical findings. The column "among all employees" shows the relationship between each independent variable and whether a person worked as an administrator, supervisor, or non-manager. The Cramer's V suggests that an employee's department and the years worked with the city are most closely related to the employee's position type. If we could examine the individual tables (not shown here) we could learn the details of this situation, we would find that employees of the finance and planning departments were most likely to be administrators. To learn the details of the relationships the tables must be examined. Employees of the finance and planning departments were most likely to be administrators. Police and fire department employees were most likely to be supervisors. Employees with master's degrees were more likely than employees without master's degrees to hold either administrative or supervisory positions. Whether a person had previously worked in the private sector or public sector had little relationship to whether he or she currently held a managerial position.

The columns "among males" and "among females" report the relationship between the dependent variable (position type) and the four independent variables. The column "among males" shows the values of Cramer's V for the relationship between the dependent variable and each independent variable when only the data on men are analyzed. Similarly, the column "among females" shows the values when only the data on women are analyzed.

When gender was controlled, the relationships generally stayed the same. The relationship between education and position type changed the most. The difference between the values of Cramer's V for males and females for the relationship between education and position type should encourage an analyst to inspect the contingency tables (not shown here) for these relationships. The tables show that for

TABLE 13.18   ASSOCIATION BETWEEN POSITION TYPE AND SELECTED EMPLOYEE CHARACTERISTICS CONTROLLING FOR GENDER

	Measure of Association (Values of Cramer's V)		
	Among All Employees	*Among Males*	*Among Females*
Department	.26	.30	.36
Years with city	.30	.30	.22
Sector of previous job	.09	.10	.10
Education	.17	.19	.08

the male employees, those with advanced degrees were no more likely to be administrators or supervisors than those without advanced degrees. For the female employees, education made a difference; women with master's degrees were more likely than those without to hold management positions. The years spent working with the city seemed to benefit the women less than men; men were more likely to advance into an administrative position the longer they worked for the city.

For the male employees, the relationship between position type and department was virtually unchanged; that is, employees in finance and planning were more likely to be administrators, and public-safety employees were more likely to be supervisors. Among women the relationship between department and position type was stronger. Only finance and planning departments had women administrators. Women were most likely to work as supervisors in public safety and public works departments.

An analyst can quickly determine the influence of the control variable by reviewing a measure of association. Nevertheless, to describe the nature of the relationships in this example, we had to examine the actual tables. Since Cramer's V is a statistic for nominal data, we had to check the tables to understand the exact nature of the relationship. Without having the tables to look at, we can only guess which departments had relatively more administrators or supervisors and whether certain departments were more likely to employ women in managerial positions.

With an ordinal measure, an analyst can more clearly visualize the content of the table by just reviewing the measure of association. Let's look at the relationship between years with the city and management position in more detail. Table 13.19 shows the relationship separately for men and women.

The tables show that for both men and women, the longer they work with the city the more likely they are to have a managerial position. Nevertheless, both the tables and gamma values imply that men are more likely than women to be promoted the longer they stay with the city. The tables and measures of association are said to show an interaction between gender and length of city

TABLE 13.19   MANAGEMENT POSITION BY YEARS EMPLOYED WITH CITY BY GENDER

	Males: Years Employed by City				
	<1 (72)	*1–2 (153)*	*3–6 (208)*	*7–10 (243)*	*>10 (830)*
Non-manager	81.9%	79.7%	79.8%	68.5%	35.5%
Supervisor	12.5%	16.3%	13.5%	27.2%	57.0%
Administrator	5.6%	3.9%	6.5%	4.5%	7.5%

Note: Gamma = .56.

	Females: Years Employed by City				
	<1 (19)	*1–2 (45)*	*3–6 (41)*	*7–10 (51)*	*>10 (72)*
Non-manager	100.0%	91.1%	87.8%	84.3%	76.4%
Supervisor	0.0%	6.7%	12.2%	5.9%	22.2%
Administrator	0.0%	2.2%	0.07%	9.8%	1.4%

Note: Gamma = .39. Percentages may not add to 100% due to rounding.

employment. Being both male and employed by a city for more than 10 years increases the probability of working as either an administrator or supervisor.

While ordinal measures have the advantage of helping the investigator visualize a table's data, the table must be examined. First, as we pointed out earlier, measures of association for ordinal data do not detect nonlinear relationships. Second, the specific statistic may be an artifact of the number of rows and columns. Collapsing a variable, that is, combining the categories, differently may yield a different value for the statistic. Comparing measures of association may lead to incorrect assumptions about the strengths of relationships.

Recall the early chapters of this text in which we wrote about the importance of an explicit research model. At the same time, we encouraged you to consider a model as tentative. The tentativeness of a model is apparent during contingency-table analysis. The analyst examines table after table of bivariate relationships. Then he or she explores the *effect of control variables.*

For many analysts the process is compelling. Each table raises more questions and possibilities. The analyst might wonder where to stop. The purpose of the model should suggest which control variables are worth examining. The purpose also may imply how exhaustive an investigation is warranted. Furthermore, an analyst should remember that a control variable will not affect a relationship if it is not related to both the independent and dependent variables.

TESTS OF STATISTICAL SIGNIFICANCE AND MEASURES OF ASSOCIATION

Measures of association summarize the strength of the relationship between two variables; that is, a measure of association indicates the magnitude of the effect. It serves as a criterion for labeling an effect as weak, moderate, or strong. A measure of association that suggests a weak relationship may motivate a researcher to discount a relationship found to be statistically significant. Indeed, a relationship may be nonrandom, but it also can be too small or trivial to merit any action. Recall that what constitutes a weak effect or a strong effect depends on the statistic, its criteria for a perfect relationship and a null relationship, and the degree of existing knowledge about the research question. Effect size is related to the power of a statistical test. Power depends on the size of the effect that has been measured and on the number of cases in the data set being studied. Other things being equal, the larger the effect and the larger the sample, the more powerful the test. When a test with low power fails to show a statistically significant relationship, one should not necessarily conclude that there is no effect.[4]

Tests of statistical significance are inferential statistics. They indicate the probability that an observed relationship occurred by chance. A researcher uses inferential statistics to infer from a sample to the population. Appropriate use of tests of statistical significance requires a random sample. Measures of association are descriptive statistics. A researcher uses descriptive statistics to summarize data, whether or not they represent a random sample. Taken together, measures of association and tests of statistical significance produce evidence supporting or disconfirming a hypothesized relationship.

The more knowledge an investigator has about an entire research effort and the details contained in a contingency table, the more confident he can be in interpreting the study's statistics. The tests of statistical significance and measures of association may confirm his conclusions or lead him to look at some of the evidence more carefully. The statistics can elucidate the research findings, reinforce decisions about their implications, and help to summarize and communicate them effectively to an audience.

COMPARISON OF MEANS AND ANALYSIS OF VARIANCE

For many situations contingency-table analysis is inadequate. It ignores the statistical advantages of experimental designs, misses the clarity of comparing the means of two or more groups, and fails to utilize information available when means and variances can be calculated. For example, suppose school system administrators wanted to compare the number of days missed by children who attend schools outside their neighborhood with the number of days missed by children attending neighborhood schools. An analyst can create several categories of days missed, for example, none, 1–5, 6–10, and so on, and construct a contingency table. Alternatively, the analyst can average the number of days missed by children who attend schools outside their neighborhood and compare it with the mean number of days missed by neighborhood children.

The primary statistical tool for analyzing experimental data and the differences between group means is analysis of variance, abbreviated ANOVA. *ANOVA* provides information on both the strength and statistical significance of a relationship. Analysis of variance was developed early in the 20th century by R. A. Fisher, a British statistician, who wanted a method for analyzing data collected in carefully structured experiments. He primarily studied agricultural practices. Hence, many of the early textbooks and experts treated analysis of variance in the context of agricultural research. The main statistical test used in ANOVA, the *F*-test, is named for Fisher.[5]

In an experiment the subjects may be drawn from the same population and randomly assigned to an experimental or control group. The experimental and control groups constitute separate samples with identical population means and variances. Just as differences between a random sample's statistics and its parameters are due to chance, pretest differences between the means and variances of the experimental and control groups should be due to chance.

Analysis of variance has the following assumptions: (1) dependent variables are interval or ratio level; (2) variances and standard deviations for each group are equal or close to it; (3) the independent variable or variables should be normally distributed for each group; (4) the values of the dependent variables are independent of each other.[6] Correctly designed experiments fulfill these assumptions.

After the experimental intervention takes place—the independent variable of the experiment—the means of the groups may differ. Experimenters expect an experimental intervention to cause differences between the experimental and control groups. ANOVA is designed to determine whether the posttest differences between the experimental and control groups are large enough that they occurred for a reason other than chance.

Analysis of variance examines two types of variances: within-groups variances and between-groups variances. *Within-groups variances* refers to how each member within an experimental or control group varies from the group mean. *Between-groups variances* refers to how the mean and variances of each group differ from those of other groups. If experimental and control group subjects are assigned correctly, the between-groups and within-groups variances of pretest groups should be equivalent. If the experimental treatment had no effect, the statistics for the posttest groups also will be equivalent.

ANOVA begins by establishing whether the differences between the experimental and control groups could have occurred by chance. Analysis of variance has the following basic research and null hypotheses:

H_1: The arithmetic means of two or more groups are unequal.

H_0: The arithmetic means of two or more groups are equal.

In experiments the investigators compare the means of the posttest experimental and control groups to see whether the data support the research hypothesis. Analysis of variance determines whether differences between the groups (variations between groups) are greater than differences within any of these groups (variations within groups).

To judge whether the difference between two means is large enough to be statistically significant, we use the *F-test,* which is based on the following ratio:

Between-groups variance/Within-groups variance

If the value of the ratio is much greater than 1, the difference between group means is likely to be statistically significant. The ratio will be greater than 1 if the difference between group means is a relatively large value, and the variability within groups is relatively small. If the researcher obtains a large enough value for the *F*-ratio, he rejects the null hypothesis of the equality of the means and accepts the research hypothesis.[7]

ANOVA has widespread applications apart from experimental designs. It is used to assess the results of multiple regression, a topic covered in the next chapter.[8] It may be used to analyze cross-sectional data if the dependent variable is interval or ratio and the independent variable is nominal.[9] Remember that an ordinal variable can be treated as a nominal variable. To use ANOVA appropriately, the data must come from random samples. The assumption that variances in all groups in the population must be equal is often ignored if the number of cases in each group is similar. The analyst may wish to check this assumption, especially if the group sizes are markedly different.[10]

To clarify the points we have made thus far, let us consider a study conducted by an analyst with Majesty City's Division of Training and Job Placement.[11] The analyst wanted to compare three programs sponsored by the agency: (1) Basic Skills, (2) Classroom Training, and (3) On-the-Job Training (OJT). The agency assigned clients to one of the three programs. At the end of the training program, clients were placed in jobs.

The analyst wanted to see if clients trained in the OJT program were earning more than clients trained in either of the other two programs. Previous research

TABLE 13.20   AVERAGE MONTHLY EARNINGS BY PROGRAM

		Program		
		Basic Skills	*Classroom Training*	*On-the-Job Training*
Average monthly income ($)	$\overline{X}$	433.5	528.7	765.1
Sample size	n	11	21	8

Note: Average for all participants = grand mean = 549.8; total number of participants = 40.

suggested that OJT participants were more successful. Furthermore, from her own observations, she knew that OJT participants were normally more "job ready" than other trainees, and therefore were more likely to receive better job placements. The analyst collected data on trainees' monthly earnings during their first year of work. Her research and null hypotheses were:

H_1: The average earnings of OJT trainees will be greater after one year than the earnings of trainees in the basic skills and the classroom-training programs.

H_0: The average earnings after one year will be equal for trainees in all three programs.

A sample of clients attending each program was selected from agency records. Interviewers telephoned the members of the samples and asked them for wage information. Table 13.20 shows the average monthly earnings for each group. The grand mean refers to the average monthly earnings for all 40 persons included in the study.

Figure 13.1 supplements the table information and visually represents the data. The graph shows the average earnings and the range, a measure of variability, for each group. The asterisk indicates the average income, and the ranges are

Figure 13.1   Average Monthly Earnings by Program

enclosed with the boxes. Analysts also often graph the mean and the 95 percent confidence interval for each group on an error bar diagram.[12]

The data in Table 13.20 and the graph support the research hypotheses. To supplement these findings, the analyst uses statistics to answer two questions:

1. Are the differences among average salaries for the groups statistically significant? That is, are the differences larger than would be expected to occur by chance?
2. How strong is the relationship between type of program and average income?

The *F*-test answers the first question. A measure of association, *eta,* answers the second question.

If all three groups were equal on the dependent variable (earnings), then the between-groups and within-groups variances would be equal and the value of the *F*-ratio would be 1. If the *F*-ratio is larger than 1, the investigator determines its statistical significance by consulting a table of *F*-values or obtaining the statistics from a computer program. To use a table of *F*-values, the analyst must know the value of the *F*-ratio and the degrees of freedom for the numerator and the denominator. In our example the degrees of freedom for the numerator is 2, the number of groups minus one, and for the denominator it is 37, the total sample size minus the number of groups.

The data from the Majesty City study were analyzed by a computer program, SPSS, using analysis of variance. Figure 13.2 shows the printout from this program. The "Source" column identifies the two types of variance, between groups and within groups. "D.F." is the degrees of freedom for each group. The "Sum of Squares" measures the between-groups variation and the within-groups variation. The total sum of squares represents the squared deviation of all cases from the mean of cases. The between-groups sum of squares represents the sum of the squared deviations of each case from its group's mean. The within-groups sum of squares is the difference between the total sum of squares and the between-groups sum of squares. The mean square is the sum of squares divided by the degrees of freedom. The *F*-ratio is between-groups mean square divided by the within-groups mean square. The "*F*-prob." refers to the associated probability

Figure 13.2 Analysis of Variance Table

ONEWAY

	Variable	MWAGE	Monthly salary and wages
By	Variable	PROGRAM	Program participant enrolled in

ANALYSIS OF VARIANCE

SOURCE	D.F.	SUM OF SQUARES	MEANS SQUARES	F-RATIO	F-PROB.
BETWEEN GROUPS	2	528,965	264,482.5	5.2	.0100
WITHIN GROUPS	37	1,869,230	50,519.7		
TOTAL	39	2,398,195			

of *F.* In this case the probability that an *F*-ratio as large as 5.2 would have occurred if the means of the three groups were equivalent is .01 or 1 percent.

The *F*-test, in this example, tells the investigator that at least two of the groups differ significantly from each other. To learn which pairs of means are significantly different, separate *t*-tests must be performed. *t*-tests of the example's data found a significant difference between the earnings of trainees who received basic skills training and those in the OJT group.

An *F*-test does not measure the strength of the relationship between variables. A measure of association, eta or *E*, based on analysis of variance is used for this purpose. Eta can vary between 0.00 and 1.00. The formula for eta is:

$$E = \sqrt{SS_b/SS_t}$$

where:

SS_b = Between-groups sum of squares
SS_t = Total sum of squares

For the example's data:

$$E = \sqrt{528,965/2,398,195}$$
$$= .47$$

Analysts square eta to interpret it[13]. In the example $(.47)^2$ equals .22, which indicates that 22 percent of the variation in monthly income after one year of work is associated with the independent variable, that is, the program in which the client was trained.

This discussion focused on the basic analysis of variance model. In one-way analysis of variance, the analysis involves one independent variable and each case contributes one score to the analysis. In the school example mentioned at the beginning of this section, the independent variable was whether a student attended school in the neighborhood or elsewhere and the piece of data contributed by each subject was the number of days missed from school. In the job training example, the independent variable was type of job training program, and the contributed score was each subject's monthly earnings.

The basic model can be adapted to include other variables. Analysis of variance models including more than one independent variable are called multivariate analysis of variance (MANOVA) or, depending on the number of independent variables, two-way analysis of variance, three-way analysis of variance, and so on. Analysis of variance models also may include more than one measure on a subject; these are called repeated measures models.[14]

SUMMARY

Administrators are normally comfortable with contingency tables and the information conveyed by percents. They also may be familiar with tests of statistical significance, especially chi-square, which indicate the probability that the relationship occurred by chance. Measures of association associated with contingency tables are less familiar to administrators and generally are of interest only to the analyst.

Contingency tables illustrate the relationship between variables by showing the joint distribution of two or more variables. Comparisons between groups to see whether the distribution of one variable differs for different values of the second or third variable are easily made with carefully constructed tables.

Nominal and ordinal measures of association are most commonly used to screen contingency tables for further study. To choose a measure of association, one should consider the level of measurement of the variables and the measure's criteria for a perfect and a null relationship. Familiarity with the measure helps in evaluating a particular value. All measures of association indicate a null relationship with a value of 0.00. Nominal measures of association indicate a perfect relationship with a value of 1.00. Ordinal measures of association assign +1.00 or −1.00 to a perfect relationship.

To compare contingency tables with measures of association, an analyst must use the same measure for all comparisons. The closer a measure is to ±1.00, the stronger the relationship. The closer a measure is to 0.00, the weaker the relationship. Comparisons must be made with caution. The specific statistic may be inappropriate for some tables, or the value may be an artifact of the number of rows and columns. Ordinal measures of association will miss or underestimate the strength of nonlinear relationships.

The criteria for a strong or weak relationship depend on the measure of association and the nature of the research question. In general, ordinal measures produce higher values than nominal measures. Symmetric measures produce higher values than asymmetric measures. Similarly, some variables have been extensively studied, and moderate associations without a theoretical basis may not add to our knowledge. Other dependent variables are poorly understood, and weak relationships may generate some productive leads.

Measures of association help an analyst to determine the effect of control variables. If a relationship between an independent and dependent variable completely disappears with the addition of the control variable, the relationship is said to be spurious. More often the control variable elaborates the relationship by showing how a relationship changes for different values of a control variable. The relationship may remain the same in all categories of the control variable—it may become stronger for some values, it may disappear for some values, or it may change directions in some or all values.

The analyst should be guided by the research model in deciding what control variables to add. Furthermore, he should remember that to change the original relationship, the control variable must be related to both the independent and dependent variables.

Analysis of variance is primarily intended to take advantage of the strengths of experimental designs, the random assignment of subjects, and the assumed equivalence of experimental and control groups. Analysis of variance also may be used to analyze hypotheses with an interval dependent variable and a nominal independent variable from non-experimental studies. The subjects must constitute a random sample, however.

Analysis of variance provides information on both the statistical significance and the strength of a relationship. To determine statistical significance the *F*-ratio is calculated. If it is markedly larger than 1, the relationship probably is statistically significant. The statistic eta is calculated to measure the strength of association. The values of eta range from 0.00 (a null relationship) to 1.00 (a perfect relationship). Eta squared indicates the amount of variation in the dependent variable that is explained by the independent variable.

One way analysis of variance applies in designs with one independent variable in which each subject contributed one piece of data. Other models of analysis of variance are used to analyze designs with more than one independent variable or which collect data from the subjects more than once over the course of the study.

Chapter 14 parallels this chapter and examines techniques for studying the linear relationship between variables measured at the interval level. Nominal and ordinal measures of association act primarily to identify relationships for closer study. Interval statistics are widely reported and provide investigators with valuable information to explain, describe, or predict relationships.

NOTES

1. D. B. Wright, *Understanding Statistics: An Introduction for the Social Sciences* (London: Sage Publications, 1997) discusses the relationship between ANOVA and regression and cites seminal work in the social sciences on this topic. See page 132 especially.

2. There are other useful measures for ordinal variables in situations where there are many cases and many categories of the variables but data are not in contingency tables. We do not discuss these measures of association here. See Sidney Siegal, *Nonparametric Statistics for the Behavioral Sciences* (New York: McGraw-Hill Book Company, 1956), 202–239 and Hubert M. Blalock, Jr., 2d ed. *Social Statistics* (New York: McGraw-Hill Book Company, 1972), 415–421

3. For a complete discussion on how a control variable can affect the relationship between an independent and dependent variable, see T. Poister, *Public Program Analysis: Applied Research Methods* (Baltimore: University Park Press, 1978), 153–171. Also see M. Rosenberg *The Logic of Survey Analysis* (New York: Basic Books, 1968).

4. R.S. Pindyck and D.L. Rubinfeld, *Econometric Models and Economic Forecasts*, 4th ed. (Boston: Irwin/McGraw-Hill, 1998), 43–45.

5. Poister, *Public Program Analysis*, 463.

6. Wright, *Understanding Statistics: An Introduction for the Social Sciences*, 131–133; G. W. Bohrnstedt and D. Knoke, 2d ed., *Statistics for Social Data Analysis* (Itasca, IL: F.E. Peacock, Inc., 1988), 232–233. These assumptions are for between subjects ANOVA. Other models require somewhat different assumptions; see Wright, 141.

7. L. Meyers and N. Grossen, *Behavioral Research: Theory, Procedure, and Design* (San Francisco: W. H. Freeman, 1974), 78–79. Also see Bohrnstedt and Knoke, 232–233.

8. Wright, *Understanding Statistics: An Introduction for the Social Sciences* (London: Sage, Inc., 1997), 132, 183–84.

9. See Bohrnstedt and Knoke, *Statistics for Social Data Analysis,* 240–244.

10. J.F. Healey, *Statistics: A Tool for Social Research*, 3d ed. (Belmont, CA: Wadsworth, 1993), 287–293. Wright, 131–133 discusses using SPSS to test for equality of variances.

11. H. Livengood, *JPTA: Follow Up and Evaluation of Selected Programs in Charlotte, N.C.* (Charlotte: University of North Carolina at Charlotte, 1993).

12. Wright, *Understanding Statistics*, 116–119. To help visualize the data and the model, you also could draw a box plot for each group and indicate in it the location of the mean instead of the median. Remember that ANOVA requires the calculation of the arithmetic mean.

13. Bohrnstedt and Knoke, *Statistics for Social Data Analysis*, 234–236 and 290–294 discuss eta.

14. Wright, *Understanding Statistics,* 116–145 is recommended for an introductory discussion of ANOVA and MANOVA models. Wright includes the SPSS printout for several of these.

TERMS FOR REVIEW

contingency table
measure of association
percentage difference
bivariate distribution
perfect relationship (between 2
   variables)
null relationship
sensitive measure of association

proportional reduction in error
(PRE) measure
original error
new error
symmetric measure
asymmetric measure
spurious relationship
specification (of a relationship)

effects of a control variable
ANOVA
F-test
within-groups variance
between-groups variance
eta

QUESTIONS FOR REVIEW

The following questions should indicate whether you have a basic competency in this chapter's material.

TABLE 13.21 DATA ARRAY FOR THREE VARIABLES: COUNTY, CAUSE, AND SEVERITY OF INJURY

Case ID	County	Cause	Severity Index
01	Baker	Fall	3
02	Charlie	Car accident	4
03	Charlie	Violence	6
04	Able	Car accident	4
05	Charlie	Violence	5
06	Baker	Fall	9
07	Charlie	Car accident	10
08	Baker	Fall	1
09	Able	Violence	5
10	Charlie	Violence	5
11	Charlie	Fall	7
12	Able	Car accident	4
13	Charlie	Car accident	7
14	Baker	Fall	6
15	Able	Fall	3
16	Baker	Car accident	5
17	Charlie	Car accident	5
18	Baker	Fall	6
19	Able	Car accident	4
20	Charlie	Violence	7

1. Use the data array in Table 13.21 to:
   a. Create a contingency table showing the relationship between county and the causes of injury. Write a sentence describing the relationship.
   b. Create a contingency table showing the relationship between cause of injury and its severity. Note that you will have to group together values of the severity index. Write a sentence describing the relationship.
2. Table 13.22 was constructed in an evaluation of a pilot project conducted by a city to encourage citizens to recycle more of their trash. Calculate percentages for this table. Write a short report to the head of the Engineering Department summarizing the results.

TABLE 13.22 RECYCLING PARTICIPATION BY NEIGHBORHOOD

Neighborhood	Number of Times Participated in Recycling Program			
	0–2	*3–6*	*7–10*	*11–13*
Steel Creek	13	16	8	5
Hidden Valley	6	15	17	12
East Side	2	5	14	19

3. In a related activity, the city obtained information regarding the support of a sample of citizens for bond financing for a waste-to-energy facility. Table 13.23 shows support by income level. Table 13.24 shows the support for two areas of the city.
   a. Calculate the percentages for Table 13.23 and use the percentage difference to describe the variations in support.

TABLE 13.23 SUPPORT FOR BONDS TO FINANCE WASTE-TO-ENERGY FACILITIES BY INCOME LEVEL

Support for Bonds	Income Level Below $14,500	Over $14,500
Oppose	185	153
Favor	95	167

b. Calculate the percentages for Table 13.24 and describe what happens.
c. What control variable was used in this analysis? What was its effect?

TABLE 13.24 SUPPORT FOR BONDS FOR WASTE-TO-ENERGY FACILITIES BY INCOME AND PLACE OF RESIDENCE

Support for Bonds	West Side Income Level Below $14,500	Over $14,500	East Side Income Level Below $14,500	Over $14,500
Oppose	158	79	27	74
Favor	42	21	53	146

4. List the criteria one should use to choose a measure of association.
5. The gamma value for Table 13.13 is +1.00. This indicates a "perfect" relationship. In what sense is the relationship perfect? In what sense is it not a perfect relationship? Explain. Compute percentages for the table. Does this affect your answer to the other parts of this question? Explain.
6. Consider the hypothesis: "Employers who are trained during their second quarter on the job make the greatest use of computer software." The variables were categorized as: extent of use (limited, moderate, extensive) and time of training (1st quarter of employment, 2nd quarter, 3rd quarter, or 4th quarter).

a. If time of training and extent of use have a perfect relationship, what would the data look like?
b. If time of training and extent of use have a null relationship, what would the data look like?
c. Would you be more likely to consider using a nominal or an ordinal measure of association to study this hypothesis?
7. Explain why a rule of thumb such as the following is poor: "any measure of association with a value greater than .45 depicts a strong relationship."
8. For Example 13.2, explain what Table 13.16 shows. What happens when a control variable is included in the analysis? What could explain this outcome?
9. Tables 13.25 through 13.27 present data collected on soup-kitchen users. The tables related age to the number of meals eaten in a day.

TABLE 13.25 NUMBER OF MEALS EATEN DAILY BY RESPONDENT'S AGE

Number of Daily Meals	Age <30 (66)	31–54 (213)	>55 (144)
1	38%	29%	27%
2	47%	49%	40%
3	15%	22%	33%

Note: Cramer's V = .11; lambda = .002; gamma = .18.
Percentages may not add up to 100% because of rounding.

TABLE 13.26 NUMBER OF MEALS EATEN DAILY BY AGE FOR RESPONDENT MALES

Number of Daily Meals	Age <30 (48)	31–54 (172)	>55 (108)
1	35%	32%	31%
2	50%	48%	41%
3	15%	20%	29%

Note: Cramer's V = .09; lambda = .000; gamma = .12.
Percentages may not add up to 100% because of rounding.

TABLE 13.27   NUMBER OF MEALS EATEN DAILY BY AGE FOR RESPONDENT FEMALES

Number of Daily Meals	Age		
	<30 *(18)*	*31–54* *(38)*	*>55* *(35)*
1	44%	18%	17%
2	39%	53%	40%
3	17%	29%	43%

Note: Cramer's V = .21; lambda = .070; gamma = .34.
Percentages may not add up to 100% because of rounding.

a. Write a sentence describing the relationship depicted in each table.
b. What is the control variable? How does it affect the original relationship?

c. Which measure of association did you use to compare the tables? Why did you select it?
10. Discuss when an investigator would use analysis of variance and eta to evaluate a relationship instead of Cramer's V or gamma. When would she use analysis of variance instead of a *t*-test?
11. The average murder rate for western states is lower than the average murder rate for southern states. Is murder rate in states related to region? Explain.
12. Draw a graph similar to Figure 13.1 that would illustrate that (a) the average murder rates for regions decline in the following order: South, Northeast, West, Midwest, and (b) the variance in murder rates declines in this order: Northeast, West, Midwest, South.

PROBLEMS FOR HOMEWORK AND DISCUSSION

1. An investigator is curious about whether respondent characteristics were associated with completion of a lengthy questionnaire. Seven contingency tables were produced; their measures of association are given in Table 13.28.

TABLE 13.28   ASSOCIATIONS BETWEEN COMPLETION OF SURVEY AND RESPONDENT CHARACTERISTICS

	Lambda	Cramer's V	Gamma
Years worked for city	.00	.12	.14
Department	.00	.14	−.19
Sector of previous employment (public, private, first job)	.00	.00	−.01
Age	.00	.08	−.14
Gender (M/F)	.00	.01	−.04
Position (management, nonmanagement, unskilled, clerical)	.00	.14	−.375
Degree (MPA, BS/BA, Other)	.00	.09	.18

a. Which characteristics of respondents seem clearly to be randomly related to completion of the survey?
b. Which characteristics appear to be associated with whether a person completed the questionnaire?
c. What criterion did you use to answer a and b?

d. For what relationships (independent variables), if any, does lambda appear to be an inappropriate measure of association? Explain.
e. For what relationships (independent variables), if any, does gamma appear to be an inappropriate measure of association? Explain.

f. For this particular study, do you think that the investigator should use lambda or Cramer's V as a screen to identify tables for further examination? Explain.

g. Do you need to consult the tables to interpret the measures of association? Explain.

2. Tables 13.29 through 13.34 are from a printout examining data on people who volunteer for direct services activities.

a. Write a sentence describing the findings of each table.

TABLE 13.29 VOLUNTEERING BY RESPONDENT AGE

	Age			
Volunteers	18–29 (331)	30–49 (529)	50–64 (301)	>65 (181)
Yes	25%	35%	20%	18%
No	75%	65%	80%	82%

Note: Lambda = 0.00; Cramer's V = .16; gamma = .14.

TABLE 13.30 VOLUNTEERING BY RESPONDENT EDUCATION

	Years of Education				
Volunteers	<8 (203)	9–11 (238)	12 (504)	13–15 (206)	16 (178)
Yes	8%	19%	28%	34%	48%
No	92%	81%	72%	66%	52%

Note: Lambda = 0.00; Cramer's V = .26; gamma = −.41.

TABLE 13.31 VOLUNTEERING BY EDUCATION FOR RESPONDENTS AGED 18–29

	Years of Education				
Volunteers	<8 (11)	9–11 (56)	12 (162)	13–15 (67)	16 (33)
Yes	18%	14%	25%	27%	42%
No	82%	86%	75%	73%	58%

Note: Lambda = 0.00; Cramer's V = .17; gamma = −.26.

TABLE 13.32 VOLUNTEERING BY EDUCATION FOR RESPONDENTS AGED 30–49

	Years of Education				
Volunteers	<8 (31)	9–11 (98)	12 (212)	13–15 (95)	16 (91)
Yes	6%	18%	34%	41%	60%
No	94%	82%	66%	59%	40%

Note: Lambda = 0.04; Cramer's V = .31; gamma = −.46.

TABLE 13.33   VOLUNTEERING BY EDUCATION FOR RESPONDENTS AGED 50–64

Volunteers	Years of Education				
	<8 *(89)*	*9–11* *(56)*	*12* *(89)*	*13–15* *(31)*	*16* *(30)*
Yes	6%	23%	23%	23%	37%
No	94%	77%	78%	77%	63%

Note: Lambda = 0.06; Cramer's V = .25; gamma = −.39.

TABLE 13.34   VOLUNTEERING BY EDUCATION FOR RESPONDENTS OVER AGE 64

Volunteers	Years of Education				
	<8 *(72)*	*9–11* *(28)*	*12* *(41)*	*13–15* *(13)*	*16* *(24)*
Yes	10%	25%	20%	38%	21%
No	90%	75%	80%	62%	79%

Note: Lambda = 0.08; Cramer's V = .21; gamma = .29.

b. Does education or age seem to play a greater role in whether a person decides to volunteer? Justify your answer.

c. Interpret the gammas for those tables. If you were reporting the findings, would you keep the signs for gamma the same as on the printout, or would you reverse them? Justify your answer.

d. Briefly discuss how you would use the above information to recruit volunteers.

DISK WORK

1. Analyze the Belle County data to see if there is a relationship between city residency (reside within city limits or outside city limits) and use of county services.

   a. Use computer software to create a contingency table, similar to Table 13.1 or Table 13.2, to examine the relationship between city residency and use of county services. When you analyze the data keep the five values of USESERV.

   b. Combine the values of USESERV to create three categories measuring use of county services. Repeat exercise 1a using the three category version of USESERV as the dependent variable.

   c. Which of the above two tables would you include in a report of your findings? Justify your choice.

   d. Write a very brief report identifying the relationship you studied, producing a contingency table to report the findings, and summarizing what you found.

2. As the number of cells in a contingency table increases, the difficulty of interpreting the table also increases. This exercise is meant to improve your table reading skills and to demonstrate the role of measures of association. The exercise asks you to analyze the relationship between use of county services and the opinion that county services are a good value (VALSERV).

   a. Analyze the relationship between use of county services (USESERV, the independent variable) and perceived value of county services (VALSERV, the dependent variable). When you analyze the data do not change the values for USESERV or

VALSERV. If available on the statistical software request lambda, Cramer's V, and gamma.

   i. Why are the values of lambda, Cramer's V, and gamma different?

   ii. What additional information does gamma give you that neither lambda nor Cramer's V gives you?

   iii. Specifically what does gamma tell you about the relationship?

   iv. Write a sentence summarizing the relationship.

b. Combine the values of USESERV and VALSERV to create three values for each variable. Using these variables analyze the relationship between use of county services and the perceived value of county services. If available on the statistical software request lambda, Cramer's V, and gamma.

   i. Which analysis (2a or 2b) would you include in a report? Justify your choice.

   ii. Write a very brief report of your findings: identify the relationship you studied and your operational definitions (including recodes); produce a contingency table to report the findings; and summarize what you found.

3. While gamma is a valuable measure of association for ordinal data, it can be misinterpreted. The following two questions present you with two common problems.

a. Use the Belle County database to analyze the relationship between use of county services (USESERV) and perceived quality of county services (JOBSERV). You may combine values of USESERV to create three values, and combine the "fair" and "poor" categories of JOBSERV. Request Cramer's V and gamma. Write a sentence summarizing the relationship. What does the negative value of gamma tell you about the relationship? How would you handle the negative value of gamma?

b. Use the Belle County database to analyze the relationship between age and use of county services. Create three age groups (younger, middle aged, older). Request Cramer's V and gamma. Which measure of association provides a more accurate summary of these data? Why?

4. Belle County has experienced explosive growth over the past five years. County officials are interested if new residents (those who have lived in the county no more than five years) differ markedly from other residents in their knowledge, use, and evaluation of county services. Analyze the variables measuring knowledge and use of financial aid services, environmental services, and the public schools and the variables measuring the perceived quality and value of these services. Report your findings in a table similar to Table 13.8, except report gamma values rather than Cramer's V.

a. Why is it appropriate to use gamma as a measure of association to summarize these relationships?

   i. How would you interpret a positive gamma for these relationships?

   ii. How would you interpret a negative gamma for these relationships?

b. What observations can you make about the differences between newer residents and other residents in the knowledge, use, and perception of county services?

5. Nominal and ordinal measures of association are particularly helpful in assessing the impact of a control variable. Use the Bell County dataset and use three of the following as control variables: respondent length of residency in the community (see exercise 4), residency in or outside the city, gender, age, income, and education. Analyze the data to see how each selected control variable affects the relationship between use of county services and their perceived value. To facilitate your analysis use recoded versions of USESERV and VALSERV (see exercise 2b) also reduce the number values for the variables, age, education and income. Request Cramer's V and gamma. For each control variable write a sentence summarizing its affect on the hypothesis, e.g., did the hypothesized relationship disappear, stay the same, intensify (distinctly stronger for some values of the control variable than others) or change directions? Cite evidence to support your observation.

6. This exercise gives you some experience in applying analysis of variance. Use the Belle County data set. Create three income categories to learn if income, the independent

variable, is related to the perceived importance of financial aid services.

a. Create a graphic similar to Figure 13.1.
b. Generate an analysis of variance table similar to Figure 13.2.

c. Compute eta.
d. What does your analysis tell you about the relationship between income levels and perceived importance of financial aid services?

RECOMMENDED FOR FURTHER READING

H. M. Blalock, Jr., *Social Statistics,* 2d ed. (New York: McGraw Hill, 1972) is the standard source of statistical details on statistics commonly used by social scientists.

G. W. Bohrnstedt and D. Knoke, *Statistics for Social Data Analysis* (Itasca, IL: F. E. Peacock, 1988) includes a good detailed discussion of statistics. They discuss the calculation of measures of association for contingency tables and analysis of variance.

K. J. Meier and J. L. Brudney, *Applied Statistics for Public Administration,* 4th ed. (Fort Worth: Harcourt, Brace, and Company, 1997) presents excellent examples and problems suggesting how administrators can use statistics in decision making. Calculations for statistics are worked out in detail and are easily followed.

M. Rosenburg, *The Logic of Survey Analysis* (New York: Basic Books, 1968). Rosenburg thoroughly discusses the use of control variables in the analysis of survey data. He covers virtually all possible situations in a very readable fashion. Readers should note that the only measures of association he uses are percentages.

A useful appendix on how to read contingency tables is included.

L. Meyers and N. Grossen, *Behavioral Research: Theory, Procedure, and Design* (San Francisco: W. H. Freeman, 1974), and F. Kerlinger, *Foundations of Behavioral Research,* 2d ed. (New York: Holt, Rinehart, and Winston, 1973) have excellent, nonstatistical discussions of analysis of variance. The reader seeking a conceptual understanding should find both of these helpful. D. B. Wright, *Understanding Statistics: An Introduction for the Social Sciences* (London: Sage Publications, 1997) Chapter 6 contains an excellent introductory discussion of analysis of variance models and statistics.

G. Keppel, *Design and Analysis: A Researcher's Handbook,* 2d ed. (Englewood Cliffs, NJ: Prentice-Hall, 1979) provides a thorough discussion of the experimental design, analysis of variance, and related topics, including details on statistical calculation and interpretation. His discussion is more accessible than that available in other excellent but more technical works.

Appendix 13.1

Some Measures of Association for Nominal and Ordinal Data

This appendix presents the equations and shows the calculations for a few common measures of association for variables measured at the nominal and ordinal levels. To illustrate the calculations, we use a Chapter 12 table, repeated here as Table 13.35, relating citizens' rating of the police department to their ages. If we were actually selecting a measure of association for this table, we would use an ordinal statistic because both variables are ordinal and the relationship is linear.

TABLE 13.35 RATINGS OF POLICE DEPARTMENT BY RESPONDENT'S AGE

Rating of Police Department	Age		
	<18 yrs.	18–59	>59
Poor (D to F)	2	33	6
Satisfactory (C)	10	137	27
Good (A or B)	12	453	150

Nominal Measures

Nominal measures of association are required if the independent and dependent variables are nominal. If only one of these variables is nominal and not dichotomous, the analyst would need to use a nominal measure or a measure specifically intended for nominal-ordinal combinations.

The chapter discusses lambda, also known as Goodman's lambda, at length, and nothing needs to be added here.

Cramer's V, a chi-square-based measure, also is used with nominal measure of association. The equation for Cramer's V is

$$V = \sqrt{\frac{\chi^2}{n \cdot \min(\text{row} - 1, \text{column} - 1)}}$$

For the data in Table 13.35: $\chi^2 = 13.9$, $n = 830$, $\min(\text{row} - 1, \text{column} - 1) = 2$. The value of $\min(\text{row} - 1, \text{column} - 1)$ is either the row minus 1 or the column minus 1, whichever yields the lower figure. If Table 13.35 had four rows and three columns, the $\min(\text{row} - 1, \text{column} - 1)$ would still equal 2.

$$V = \sqrt{\frac{13.9}{830 \cdot 2}} = 0.0915$$

The measure of association, phi (ϕ), is used for 2×2 tables. It has essentially the same equation as Cramer's V. Since the $\min(\text{row} - 1, \text{column} - 1) = 1$, the equation reduces to

$$\phi = \sqrt{\frac{\chi^2}{n}}$$

Ordinal Measures

This section includes three common ordinal measures of association for data in contingency tables: gamma, Somers' d, and Kendall's tau_b and tau_c. This chapter considers measures of association in two roles: (1) to filter out trivial relationships and (2) to show the effects of control variables. All three measures have the same numerator, so we will start by explaining how to calculate its components. First, the values of the variables must be in rank order; that is, they must be ordered along a continuum. The analyst begins the calculations by identifying the number of cases that are in agreement (A) or disagreement (D) with the rank ordering of both variables. The rank order suggested by Table 13.35 is: "The older the respondent, the higher the rating." Note the placement of the values of the variables, particularly those of the dependent variable.

To calculate A, we start with 2 in the upper, left-hand corner and count how many respondents are older than 17 who rate the police as better than "poor"; that is, 137 + 453 + 27 + 150 = 767. We then go to 10 and count the 603 (453 + 150) cases where people are older than 59 and rate the police as better than "poor." We repeat the procedures in the remaining columns. The value of A is based on the calculation:

$$A = 2 \cdot (137 + 453 + 27 + 150) + 10 \cdot (453 \\ + 150) + 33 \cdot (27 + 150) + 137 \cdot 150$$
$$= 1,534 + 6,030 + 5,841 + 20,550$$
$$= 33,955$$

To calculate D we go through a similar procedure, but we begin with the top, right-hand cell. Starting with 6 we count the number of people who are younger than 60 and rate the police as better than "poor"; that is, 137 + 453 + 10 + 12 = 612. The value of D is based on the calculation:

$$D = 6 \cdot (137 + 453 + 10 + 12) + 27 \\ \cdot (453 + 12) + 33 \cdot (10 + 12) + 137 \cdot 12$$
$$= 3,672 + 12,555 + 726 + 1,644$$
$$= 18,597$$

Gamma is an ordinal measure of association. It is a PRE measure and symmetric; that is, it makes no difference which variable is identified as the independent variable and which is the dependent variable. To calculate gamma (γ) the equation is

$$\gamma = \frac{A - D}{A + D}$$
$$= \frac{33,955 - 18,597}{33,955 + 18,597}$$
$$= .29$$

Somers' d (d_{yx}) is an asymmetric measure that builds on the gamma calculation. To calculate

Somers' d, the independent variable must be identified. The analyst calculates the number of ties, that is, the number of cases with the same value of the dependent variable as the cases being observed. Starting with 2 we count the number of people older than 17 who also rated the police department as "poor"; that is, 33 + 6 = 39. The value of T_r is based on the calculation:

$$T_r = 2 \cdot (33 + 6) + 33 \cdot (6) + 10 \cdot (137 + 27) \\ + 137 \cdot 27 + 12 \cdot (453 + 150) + 453 \cdot 150$$
$$= 78 + 198 + 1,640 + 3,699 + 7,236 \\ + 67,950$$
$$= 80,801$$

To calculate Somers' d, the equation is

$$d_{yx} = \frac{A - D}{A + D + T}$$
$$= \frac{33,955 - 18,597}{33,955 + 18,597 + 80,801}$$
$$= .12$$

The calculations for T_r assume that the independent variable heads the columns of Table 13.35. (The subscript r refers to rows. Note that we counted ties in the rows. In the next paragraph we show how to count ties in the column.) A table can be organized so that the dependent variable heads the columns and T_c, column ties, can be substituted for T_r.

Tau$_b$ is another ordinal measure of association. It considers both ties on the dependent variable and the independent variable; hence, it is a symmetric measure. The discussion of gamma and Somers' d has covered all but one component of the equation to calculate tau$_b$. We have shown you how to calculate agreements, disagreements, and ties on the dependent variable, leaving only ties on the independent variable to be covered. To calculate the ties on the independent variable (T_c), we start again with 2 and note how many people younger than 17 rated police as better than "poor"; that is, 10 + 12. The value of T_c was based on the calculation:

$$T_c = 2 \cdot (10 + 12) + 10 \cdot 12 + 33 \cdot (137 + 453) \\ + 137 \cdot 453 + 6 \cdot (27 + 150) + 27 \cdot 150$$
$$= 44 + 120 + 19,470 + 62,061 + 1,062 \\ + 4,050$$
$$= 86,807$$

To calculate tau$_b$, the equation is

$$Tau_b = \frac{A - D}{\sqrt{A + D + T_c}\sqrt{A + D + T_r}}$$

$$= \frac{33,955 - 18,597}{\sqrt{33,955 + 18,597 + 86,807}\sqrt{33,955 + 18,597 + 80,801}}$$

$$= \frac{15,358}{373.3 \cdot 365.2}$$

$$= .113$$

For nonsquare tables tau$_c$, a symmetric ordinal measure, should be used. Tau$_c$ is not a PRE measure. The equation for tau$_c$ is:

$$Tau_c = \frac{2(min(row, column))(A - D)}{N^2(min(row - 1, column - 1))}$$

Similar to Cramer's V, "min(row, column)" is replaced with the number of rows or the number of columns, whichever is lower. For the sake of simplicity, we will calculate tau$_c$ for Table 13.35:

$$Tau_c = \frac{2 \cdot 3 \cdot (33,955 - 18,597)}{830^2 \cdot (3 - 1)}$$

$$= \frac{6 \cdot 15,358}{1,377,800}$$

$$= .067$$

For further discussion of these measures, the text by Bohrnstedt and Knoke, *Statistics for Social Data Analysis,* listed in "Recommended for Further Reading," is especially recommended. Also see Blalock, *Social Statistics.*

Chapter 14

Regression Analysis and Correlation

In this chapter you will learn

1. how to interpret a linear regression equation with one or more independent variables.
2. about tests to determine how well a linear regression model fits a dataset.
3. common mistakes in interpreting a linear regression equation.
4. how to interpret logistic regression statistics.
5. use of regression to analyze time-series data.

Once administrators go beyond studying a single variable, their interest lies in studying the relationships among variables. Examining bivariate relationships is typically only a first step in studying complex relationships. With a little practice, administrators can accurately interpret contingency tables. Nevertheless, these tables quickly become cumbersome as more variables are added to the analysis. None of the contingency tables in our Chapter 13 examples had more than three variables, and the control variables only had two values. Try to visualize what the tables would look like if you wanted to control for several variables at the same time or if you were studying a control variable that had eight or nine values. Interpretation becomes elusive. Furthermore, contingency tables may not be the best way to analyze interval-level data.

Administrators who study multivariate relationships desire simplicity while maintaining statistical accuracy. Statistics for interval-level data offer an attractive alternative to contingency-table analysis. The major advantage of these statistics is their ability to make full use of the information contained in interval variables and to come up with more precise descriptions of the relationships in a model. These statistics greatly facilitate complex analysis and allow research findings to be reported in relatively direct, easily understood formats. Furthermore, statistics to measure associations among interval variables are versatile. They can be used to summarize or describe the distribution of interval variables.

infer population characteristics based on a sample.

argue, by statistically manipulating variables, that variables are causally linked.

forecast outcomes.

In this chapter we limit our presentation of interval statistics to linear regression and correlation. Both are widely used. Furthermore, they are fundamental to understanding analogous statistical models and more sophisticated linear models that have been developed to analyze complex and specialized problems.

An administrator can use regression profitably and appropriately with an understanding of a few basic principles. The chapter endnotes present a few analytic details. The references and our recommendations for further reading direct you to some excellent texts appropriate for the administrative analyst.

ANALYZING TWO INTERVAL VARIABLES

Although administrators and analysts typically want to learn about the relationships among several interval variables, we will begin with the two-variable model. The principles of bivariate regression analysis and correlation apply to multiple regression models, that is, models containing more than one independent variable. The major benefit of starting with a two-variable example is that we can illustrate the logic of linear regression with graphs. We cannot produce similar graphs for more than two variables. Similarly, some of the statistics are easier to explain and understand in the two-variable case.

To examine the relationship between two interval variables, an analyst produces a *regression equation* and a *correlation coefficient.* The regression equation describes the relationship between two interval variables. The correlation coefficient, a measure of association, indicates the amount of variation in the dependent variable associated with the independent variable.

The Regression Equation

The regression equation is the equation for the straight line that best describes a set of data points. The equation is asymmetric; therefore, the independent and dependent variables must be designated before calculating the equation. Deriving a regression equation involves four steps:

1. Obtaining data on two interval variables
2. Plotting the data on a graph:
   a. The dependent variable, Y, is graphed on the vertical axis
   b. The independent variable, X, is graphed on the horizontal axis
3. Determining whether the plotted data can be appropriately summarized by a straight line
4. Calculating the regression equation

TABLE 14.1   DATA ON CAR MILEAGE AND REPAIR COSTS

	Total Miles on Odometer (X) January 1	Repair Costs (Y) from January–December
Car 1	80,000	1,200
Car 2	29,000	150
Car 3	42,000	600
Car 4	53,000	650
Car 5	73,000	1,000
Car 6	80,000	1,500
Car 7	60,000	600
Car 8	13,000	200
Car 9	14,500	0
Car 10	45,000	325

To see how these steps are carried out, let's consider a simple study, reported in Table 14.1, to learn how cumulative car mileage is related to annual repair costs. We randomly selected 10 cars from a motor pool and we collected data on each car's mileage on the first of January and its repair costs over the following 12 months.

Next, we plotted the data on the graph. The dependent variable, the Y of the regression equation, was placed on the vertical axis. The independent variable, the X of the regression equation, was placed along the horizontal axis. The graph of plotted points is called a *scatterplot* (Figure 14.1). Examining the scatterplot is necessary so that the analyst can decide if he should use a linear model to summarize the relationship between the two variables. A linear model assumes that the relationship between the variables can be appropriately described by a straight line.

Figure 14.1   Scatterplot of Car Repair Costs and Miles Driven

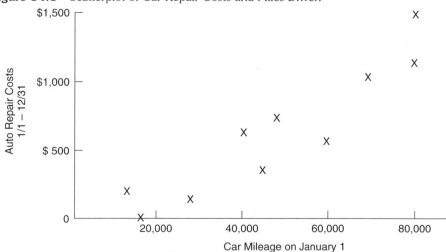

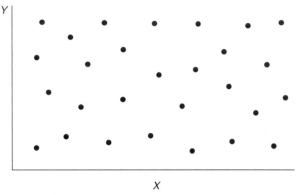

Figure 14.2   Scatterplot of a Random Relationship

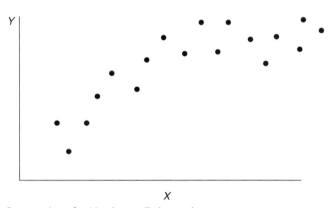

Figure 14.3   Scatterplot of a Nonlinear Relationship

The two scatterplots in Figures 14.2 and 14.3 illustrate cases where a straight line or linear model is inappropriate. Figure 14.2 shows no discernible pattern; the relationship between the two variables appears random. Figure 14.3 illustrates a nonlinear pattern. Use of linear regression to analyze the scatterplots in Figures 14.2 and 14.3 is a mistake because the analyst forces a linear model onto nonlinear data.

If a linear model is deemed appropriate, then the regression equation is calculated. (See the appendix to this chapter for equations and calculations.) In practice, analysts rely on computer programs or calculators to carry out the actual calculations.

The regression equation has the general format

$$Y = a + bX$$

where:

a = the constant or Y intercept
b = the regression coefficient or slope
Y = predicted value of Y, the dependent variable
X = the independent variable

For our example the equation of the regression line is

$$Y = -267 + .018X$$

where:

Y = repair costs from 1/1 through 12/31

X = car mileage in thousands of miles on 1/1

From the *regression coefficient,* we learn how a unit change in X, miles driven, affects Y, repair costs. For example, for every 100 miles driven, we expect the next year's repair costs to increase by $1.80. We obtained the figure $1.80 by multiplying .018 by 100. For every 1,000 miles driven, we expect repair costs to increase by $18.

Figure 14.4 shows the relationship between the regression line and the plotted points.

On the graph you can locate the point with an X value of 60,000 and a Y value of 600. The 600 is the cost of auto repairs for a car in the dataset that has been driven 60,000 miles. The Y equal to 600 is referred to as an *actual value of Y.*

Now, recall your algebra. For a given value of X, you can substitute its value in the equation and calculate the value of Y. For a car driven 60,000 miles, you would perform the following calculation:

$$Y = -267 + .018\,(60{,}000)$$
$$= 813$$

The 813 is the predicted value of the cost of a year's car repairs, Y, for a car that has been driven 60,000 miles. The *predicted value of Y* is the Y value on the regression line at the point where it intersects with X equal to 60,000.

The actual value of Y is often designated by Y_i, and the predicted value of Y by $\hat{Y}$. Specifically, Y_i means the actual value of Y when X equals X_i, and $\hat{Y}$ means the predicted value of Y when X equals X_i. The difference between Y_i and $\hat{Y}$ is

Figure 14.4 Scatterplot and Regression Line of Car Repair Costs and Miles

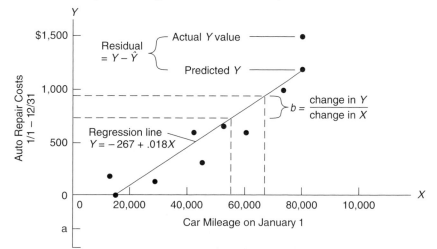

referred to as the *residual.* In the example, the residual is −213 (600 − 813). The "−" indicates that Y_i falls below the regression line; in other words, the regression equation overestimated the repair costs for the specific car. For any case you may calculate the residual with the equation

$$\text{Residual} = Y_i - \hat{Y}$$

A major use of the regression equation is to estimate population characteristics.[1] It is said to be the best estimator of the linear model because on the whole it yields the smallest residuals. If any other straight line were placed on the scatterplot, the sum of the squared residuals, the distance between the Y_is and $\hat{Y}$s would be larger.

Values of the dependent variable are estimated from the regression line. The predicted $\hat{Y}$ represents the expected value of Y for a specific value of X. Values can be predicted for values of X that do not appear in the dataset; however, predictions should not be made for values that are higher or lower than values of X in the dataset. To predict the repair costs for the entire motor pool, an investigator calculates the values of $\hat{Y}$ for each car in the pool and then adds all the $\hat{Y}$s together.

Tests of *goodness of fit* let an analyst decide how well the linear regression equation fits the data. A poor fit implies that the equation does a poor job of describing the data. One goodness of fit test is the visual evidence provided by a scatterplot. An analyst should routinely examine the scatterplot and satisfy himself that a linear model is reasonable.[2]

The Correlation Coefficient

A second test of goodness of fit is the correlation coefficient. The correlation coefficient is a measure of association for interval level data. Common terms used to identify the correlation coefficient include *Pearson's r, r*, and the *zero order correlation coefficient.* We shall refer to it as "*r*." An *r* of 1.00 or −1.00 indicates that every point on the scatterplot falls on a straight line, the regression line. An *r* equal to 1.00 indicates a direct relationship; an *r* equal to −1.00 indicates an inverse relationship. Similar to other measures of association, *r* equal to 0.00 designates a null linear relationship. The closer the value of *r* is to 1 or −1, the stronger the relationship. (The equation for *r* and a worked-out example are given in the appendix to this chapter.)

A valuable and intuitively attractive interpretation of *r* is given by r^2, called the coefficient of determination. The r^2 value indicates the proportion of the variance in the dependent variable associated with or explained by the independent variable. In the example, *r* equaled .93. The r^2 equaled .87, indicating that 87 percent of the variation in annual car repair costs was explained by knowing the car's cumulative mileage. The only value of reporting the *r*, instead of r^2, is that *r* gives direction.

The question of what size *r* is sufficiently large to merit attention does not have a definite answer. Instead, the value of a particular finding depends on the nature of the subject. An acquaintance, who is a geneticist, considers an *r* less than .95 to be worthless. Few, if any, social science studies approach that level of association. Values of *r* between .40 and .60 seem quite strong. In some studies a modest

r may be considerably larger than previous findings and therefore warrant attention. Nevertheless, remember that an r equal to .30 explains less than 10 percent of the variation in a dependent variable.

Other Factors in Interpreting a Linear Regression Equation

Four other factors affect the correct interpretation of a linear regression equation. They are: the size of the regression coefficient, the standard error of the regression coefficient, the range of X values used to calculate the regression equation, and the time interval between the measurement of X and Y.

The size of the regression coefficient does not necessarily imply the strength of a relationship. The size of the regression coefficient is partially a function of the measurement scale. In the motor pool example, if the X value was measured in thousands of miles, the regression equation would be $Y = -267 + 18X$. Remember, when X represented actual miles, the equation was $Y = -267 + 0.018X$. Eighteen is 1,000 times larger than .018; however, the two equations describe the same relationship and yield the same $\hat{Y}$ and the same r.

Not only does the measurement scale affect the size of the regression coefficient, but it also may cause estimation errors.

Users who ignore the specific measurement of a variable may substitute the wrong value for X in predicting Y. Students commonly puzzle over how to handle Xs that represent a percentage value. A percent should be treated as a whole number (10 percent, not 0.1). However, if the predicted values of Y do not make intuitive sense, you may investigate whether the calculations were based on proportions and not percents.

If the regression equation is calculated from a sample, some variation in the equations must be expected. The values of both the constant and the regression coefficient may vary from sample to sample. In Chapter 5 we used sample statistics to estimate population proportions and means. Similarly, we can estimate the relationship between two variables in a population. The *standard error of b* (se_b), also called the *standard error of the slope*, estimates the variability of the regression coefficient from sample to sample. The se_b has two uses. Analysts use it to estimate the true value of the regression coefficient. Se_b also determines whether the relationship is statistically significant, that is, the probability that b in the population equals 0.00.

In the motor pool example, the se_b equaled .0025. At the 95 percent confidence level, an investigator estimates that the actual regression coefficient for the entire motor pool falls between .013 and .023. (The equation for se_b and instructions on how to calculate the interval for the 95 percent confidence level are in the appendix at the end of this chapter.) From the original equation, we stated that car repair costs would increase by $1.80 for every 100 miles driven. We can refine this statement. For the motor pool as a whole, we can estimate at the 95 percent confidence level that the repair costs range between $1.30 and $2.30 for every 100 miles driven.

The se_b also is used to calculate the t-statistic and determine the statistical significance of the regression coefficient. The value of t, the t-ratio, equals the regression coefficient (b) divided by the se_b. One can use a t-table to determine the associated probability. The null hypothesis is that the actual regression coefficient is 0.00; that is, there is no relationship between car repair costs and the number of miles driven. In the motor pool example, the t-statistic equals 7.2 and the associated probability is less than .001. If the actual slope were 0.00, the probability of obtaining a slope as large as .018 is quite small. A convenient rule of thumb to remember is that if the t-ratio is greater than 2, the regression coefficient is significant at the .05 level.[3]

The regression equation is computed for a specific dataset from the data in it. One should not estimate a value of Y for values of X that are well below the minimum or well above the maximum X values in the dataset.

To illustrate the danger of estimating the value of Y for an X value outside the range of values used to compute the regression equation, let us return to the motor pool example. Consider a car that had been driven 160,000 miles by January 1. The predicted repair bill for the following year would be $2,613. In fact, the actual car repair bill was far less, only $100. Such "junkers" tend to stay in use as long as the costs of repairs do not get out of hand. In our dataset the most miles a car had been driven was 80,000, which was half as much as the junker. Clearly, the dataset did not reflect the repair record of superannuated cars!

In a small dataset the regression equation and correlation coefficient may show substantial changes with the addition or deletion of a single case. For example, the addition of just one car can have a marked impact on a regression equation. If the car with 160,000 miles and and repair costs of $100 had been included in the original dataset, the regression equation would have changed from $Y = -267 + .018X$ to $Y = 404 + .003X$. The r^2 would drop from .87 to .06. Such marked changes are most likely if the one case has an extreme value. One should be especially careful in drawing implications from a small dataset.

Extreme points well outside the range of the other data are called *outliers*. In addition to checking the scatterplot for random or nonlinear patterns, you also must look for outliers. An outlier will bias the statistics. The scatterplot in Figure 14.5 illustrates an outlier that may yield a regression equation and correlation coefficient that make the relationship appear stronger than it actually is.

Conversely, an outlier can draw the line away from the other points and make the relationship appear weaker than it actually is.

Figure 14.5   Scatterplot of a Relationship Where an Outlier Strengthens a Weak Relationship

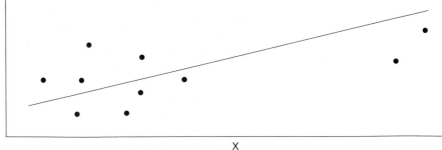

To handle outliers one may

1. limit the analysis to the appropriate values of X, and note that the model does not apply to other values of X.
2. consider if a non-linear model would better describe the data.[4]
3. look for reasons why the particular case is different from other cases. For example, data may have been collected at a different time.[5]

Another consideration is the time relationship between the independent and dependent variable. In many studies time order may be of little concern, but sometimes it is important. If a long time is expected to pass before the effect of the independent variable can be observed, an analyst may lag a variable. *Lagging a variable* means that X is measured at a time preceding Y, and that the time interval between X and Y is sufficient for X to have affected Y. In our example, we assumed that the cumulative mileage on a car affected its next year's repair costs. X was measured on January 1, and Y, representing repairs over the following 12 months, was measured on December 31, one year later. Similarly, one may assume a change in tax rate will affect spending three months later or that habits in one's youth will affect an aspect of his or her old age. In the case of tax rate, Y may measure spending three months after the tax rate change. In the case of tracing the effect of youthful habits, an interval of 40 or more years may be created.

REGRESSION ANALYSIS: THE MULTIVARIATE CASE

The Multiple-Regression Equation

Multiple regression has many advantages when compared to contingency tables. The analyst can present several variables in one equation. Furthermore, the regression equation gives the independent effect of each variable while controlling for the other variables in the equation. One format of the multiple regression equation for four independent variables is:

$$Y = a + b_{y1 \cdot 234} X_1 + b_{y2 \cdot 134} X_2 + b_{y3 \cdot 124} X_3 + b_{y4 \cdot 123} X_4$$

where:

Y = dependent variable

a = constant

$b_{y1.234}$ = regression coefficient for X_1 associated with Y, while controlling for X_2 through X_4

X_1 = independent variable X_1

$b_{y2.134}$ = regression coefficient for X_2 associated with Y, while controlling for X_1, X_3, and X_4

X_2 = independent variable X_2

$b_{y3.124}$ = regression coefficient for X_3 associated with Y, while controlling for X_1, X_2, and X_4

X_3 = independent variable X_3

$b_{y4.123}$ = regression coefficient for X_4 associated with Y, while controlling for X_1 through X_3

X_4 = independent variable X_4

The equation is normally written without the string of subscripts under each b, but viewing the subscripts may help you to understand the information in the equation. Each b, a *partial regression coefficient*, indicates the effect of the independent variable on the dependent variable while controlling for all other variables in the equation. The dot in the equation with subscripts separates the two variables being related from the variables being controlled. A more common format for the equation is:

$$Y = a + b_1X_1 + b_2X_2 + b_3X_3 + \cdots b_nX_n$$

We arbitrarily chose to include four independent variables in the equation. We could have included fewer or more variables. The basic equation remains the same. A given independent variable would be related to the dependent variable while controlling for the other independent variables.

The easiest way to explain the multiple-regression equation is to look at an example. A study published in 1986 illustrates several aspects of a multiple-regression model.[6] The author gathered data on selected employee characteristics from a sample of federal government personnel records to derive a regression equation to explain a person's grade level of entry into the federal career service. This equation is given in Table 14.2.

To interpret the equation, we first examine the variables. Several of the variables do not represent interval measures. Years of education, potential experience, and veteran's preference are the only variables measured at the interval level. The other variables represent dichotomies.

Dichotomous variables also are called *dummy variables*. A person either has the indicated characteristic or not. If the person has the characteristic, the variable is assigned value "1"; otherwise, the value "0" is assigned. In Table 14.2, field of study was broken into a series of dummy variables, including business and management, law, and the social sciences. For each variable, a person was assigned the value 0 or 1. Although regression requires interval-level data, use of dichotomous independent variables in regression equations is a common and acceptable practice.

Potential experience represents the author's attempt to measure previous working experience of a newly hired federal employee. Potential experience was the difference between the person's age when he or she completed school and age upon starting federal employment. Veteran's preference is a bonus added to certain applicants' scores; some applicants may be entitled to a 5- or 10-point veteran's preference.

The equation shows that female or minority status has a slight negative effect on a person's entry grade. Education has a positive effect, and degrees in either law or the physical and mathematical sciences markedly boost a person's entry grade. The coefficients for minority and female status control for years of education, veteran's preference, and specific degrees.[7]

TABLE 14.2   REGRESSION EQUATION TO PREDICT ENTRY GRADE INTO U.S. CIVIL SERVICE ($n = 2,146$)

Variable	Regression Coefficient
White female	−.08
Minority female	−.29
Minority male	−.17
Years of education beyond high school	.50
Major field of study	
Biology, agriculture, or health profession	.97
Business or management	.82
Engineering, mathematics, or physical sciences	1.59
Law	4.37
Social sciences	.36
Other	.06
Potential experience	.17
Veteran's preference	.10
Constant	2.42
$R^2 = .69$.	

SOURCE: G. B. Lewis, "Equal Employment Opportunity and the Early Career in Federal Employment," *Review of Public Personnel Administration*, Summer 1986, 1–18.

Example 14.1 shows how the equation can be used to find a predicted entry grade for specific cases. We use the word "predicted" advisedly. The predicted value represents the estimated mean Y value for persons with the given characteristics.

The regression equation predicts or estimates the average entry grade for people in the population, that is, persons with records in the sampled personnel files. The dataset used to calculate the equation did not include persons who applied for the federal civil service but either were never selected or turned down a federal position. Also excluded from the dataset were persons who never applied for the federal civil service. Furthermore, the dataset represented federal personnel policies during a specific time period. Over time, policies may change and estimates based on an old dataset may become less accurate. If you are familiar with current civil service entry-level grades, you may find that the estimate for your civil service grade level is too low.

We expect that the example helps you to appreciate the value of multiple regression. With the equation you could identify the factors affecting entry grades for people in the civil service. The equation is easy for most people to work with, it generates useful data, and it requires little mathematical ability to understand or to estimate values of Y.

You may have wondered why we kept the information on women and minorities in the equation since they seemed to make so little difference in predicting entry grade. By far the most important reason for keeping these variables in the equation was the purpose of the model. The model was to see what, if any,

EXAMPLE 14.1

Predicting Individual Entry Level Grade from a Multiple Regression Equation

Case 1: What entry level grade would you predict for a white male, law school graduate, who has no veteran's preference, was 26 when he finished school, and is now 28?

Recall that potential experience is the difference between entry-level age and school-finishing age.

The predicted grade level can be calculated by substituting the data from Case 1 into the equation given in Table 14.2. The equation may be fully written with the zero values or without them. Keeping the same order for the variables as given in Table 14.2, the equation is written:

Predicted Entry Grade = $2.42 - .08(0) - .29(0) - .17(0) + .50(7) + .97(0)$
$+ .82(0) + 1.59(0) + 4.37(1) + .36(0) + .06(0) + .17(2) + .1(0)$

The 0 values may be deleted in calculating the equation. The equation would then look like this:

Predicted Entry Grade = $2.42 + .50(7) + 4.37(1) + .17(2) = 10.63$

Case 2: What entry grade would you predict for an African American female with an M.S. degree in biology, who has no veteran's preference, was 24 when she finished school, and is now 25?

Predicted Entry Grade = $2.42 - .29(1) + .50(6) + .97(1) + .17(1) = 6.27$

Case 3: What entry grade would you predict for yourself?

Discussion: This example shows how to use the equation to calculate predicted values for the dependent variable. You actually predicted the average value of Y for people with a given set of characteristics. When you tried to apply the equation to yourself, you may have wanted to know more about how the variables were operationally defined. For example, if you studied engineering in school, graduated 10 years ago, and are now studying administration in an evening program, you may want more details on how the researcher defined potential experience and major field of study. The sample consisted of employees who had entered the federal civil service shortly after leaving school. Thus you may fall outside the range of Xs included in calculating the equation.

patterns of discrimination occurred in entry-level employment. Including the sex and race variables meant that the researcher could document how sex or race affected placement after eliminating the effects of education, previous experience, academic discipline, and veteran's preference. If the sex and race variables were deleted, the regression equation would be recalculated, since it no longer controls for sex or race. If sex and race were removed, the other regression coefficients should change only slightly since sex and race had a weak statistical association with entry-level grade.

Measure of Association for Multiple Regression

How good were the predictions from the equation? The $R^2 = .69$ means that the equation explains 69 percent of the variation in entry grade. R^2, called the *coefficient of multiple determination,* is a multivariate measure of association. R^2 indicates the degree of variation in the dependent variable explained by the model, that is, the independent variables included in the equation. By convention, r is used to indicate a bivariate relationship, while R indicates a multivariate one. Unlike r, R can only be positive. Thus only R^2 need be reported.

With the addition of variables, R may either stay the same or become larger. The addition of a variable will never make R smaller. This observation implies that with enough variables one can explain a large portion of the variation in a dependent variable. Trivial relationships may add .03, .02, or even smaller amounts to R.

With experience you will find that few variables, often five or less, will explain much of the variation in the dataset. For example, in the civil service study, the author found that when years of education was the only independent variable, R^2 equaled .60. When the dummy variables measuring field of study were added, the R^2 increased to .68. The remaining variables brought the value of R^2 up to .69. In other words, potential experience, gender, race, and veteran's preference explained an additional 1 percent of the variation in a person's entry-level grade.[8]

A serious mistake is to have more independent variables than cases or a large number of independent variables to analyze a relatively small dataset. The model then explains virtually all the variation in the dataset, but it is worthless because the equation is literally custom designed to fit the dataset.

To avoid being misled and misleading others, researchers may report the adjusted R^2. The adjusted R^2 equation "shrinks" the value of R^2 by "penalizing" for each additional independent variable (k = number of independent variables). The adjusted R^2 cannot be larger than R^2. It may be noticeably smaller if the model applies a relatively large number of independent variables to a small number of cases.[9]

$$\text{Adjusted } R^2 = 1 - (1 - R^2)(n - 1)/(n - k - 1)$$

You might wonder when to stop adding variables to a model. The best strategy is to follow the example of the researcher in the civil service study and include the variables that are theoretically important to the model.[10] As you may infer from the discussion above, simply seeking the highest value for R^2 is not recommended. Some investigators eliminate variables that are not statistically significant; however, with a large-enough sample, even the smallest regression coefficients may be "statistically significant."

The Importance of Each Independent Variable: Beta Weights

Note that with the information in Table 14.2, you cannot rank the independent variables in order of their contribution in explaining the dependent variable.

Remember that the regression coefficients are affected by how the independent variable is measured. Thus the .5 for years of education has a far greater impact on a person's entry grade than the .97 for a degree in a life science. Why? The independent variable, life science, has the value of either 0 or 1. Years of education after high school could easily range between 0 and 10, that is, from only high school to a Ph.D. So in the equation, a degree in biology raises a person's predicted entry grade by roughly one grade. Two years of school have the same effect.

Beta weights, the standardized regression coefficients, allow one to rapidly and precisely compare the relative importance of each variable. Beta weights are calculated by normalizing the variables, that is, rescaling a variable so that its mean equals 0 and its standard deviation equals 1. In other words, all the variables are in the same standard units.

The larger the Beta weight, the stronger that variable's relationship to the dependent variable. Beta weights are usually calculated as part of the regression statistics produced by computer software. You need not understand how the variables are normalized to correctly rank the strength of the association between the dependent variable and the various independent variables.

Example 14.2 illustrates the use of a regression equation in a study of student admissions. The researcher studied students admitted to a graduate business program to determine whether adding a scale quantifying personal achievements would improve admissions decisions.

In the example you can observe the role of Beta weights and compare the information they give to the information given by the unstandardized regression coefficients. Note particularly the unstandardized regression coefficient for the GMAT score. The coefficient is so small that one might erroneously conclude that GMAT scores had no relationship to GPA.

Some studies report both pieces of information. Beta weights alone tend to appear in studies where the meaning of the regression coefficient cannot be clearly interpreted. For example, neither the analyst nor the user will have a clear image of what a unit increase in an ordinal variable, such as satisfaction with a policy, means.

The standard errors of b also were reported in the example. Recall the rule of thumb that if the t-ratio, b divided by se_b, is larger than 2, the relationship is statistically significant at the .05 level. Five times out of 100, a regression coefficient as large as the one obtained may occur if the value of the slope in the population is zero. The regression coefficients for undergraduate average, GMAT scores, and admissions scales were the only ones that had a t-ratio greater than 2; these also were the variables with the largest Beta weights.

To refine the scale further, the authors checked how R^2 improved as different variables were entered into the admissions criteria. The findings are shown in Table 14.4.

The Beta weights, the t-ratio, and the changes in R^2 with each additional variable all supported the researchers' conclusion that only undergraduate grade point average, GMAT scores, and the score on the admissions scales should be considered in predicting success in graduate school.

EXAMPLE 14.2

Developing a Regression Equation to Quantify Admissions Criteria

Background: The analysts developed a 12-point scale to summarize personal qualities, such as previous work experience and evidence of undergraduate leadership. They calculated scale scores for admitted students and then computed a regression equation to see whether the scale would improve the quality of admissions decisions. Graduate school performance was the dependent variable. Two sets of equations were calculated. One equation examined performance throughout the graduate degree program; the other examined performance during the first semester.

The first semester equation is reported in Table 14.3.

TABLE 14.3 REGRESSION MODEL TO PREDICT STUDENT GRADE POINT AVERAGE

	Unstandardized Regression Coefficient (s.e.)		Beta Weight
Undergraduate average	.367	(.088)	.371
GMAT score	.00099	(.00045)	.188
Admissions scale	.036	(.016)	.188
Sex	−.019	(.080)	−.021
Years since college graduation	.014	(.012)	.104
Prior graduate work	−.055	(.054)	−.088
Constant	1.437	(.080)	
R^2	.188		

Note: GMAT = Graduate Management Admissions Test.

Discussion: To predict a student's first semester grade point average, the equation with the unstandardized regression coefficient would be used. To determine which admissions factors are most closely associated with first-semester grades, the standardized regression coefficients, Beta weights, would be examined. Probably most striking is the importance of Graduate Management Admissions Test (GMAT) score's tie with that of the admissions scale; the size of the unstandardized regression coefficient might lead one to conclude that GMATs had little to do with predicting a person's first-semester grades.

SOURCE: M. G. Sobol, "GPA, GMAT, and Scale: A Method for Quantification of Admissions Criteria," *Research in Higher Education* 20 (1984): 77–88.

The regression equation shows that the score assigned on the basis of undergraduate grade point average, GMAT scores, and the admission's scale explains only 18 percent of the variation in first-semester grades. In other words, 82 percent of the variation in first-semester grades is associated with some other factor(s) not present in the model.

TABLE 14.4   RELATIONSHIP BETWEEN FIRST-SEMESTER GRADES AND ADMISSIONS CRITERIA

Regression Equations	R^2
Undergraduate average (UA)	.104
UA + GMAT	.148
UA + GMAT + admissions scale (AS)	.181
UA + GMAT + AS + Sex	.184
UA + GMAT + AS + Sex + Previous graduate study	.188

SOURCE: M. G. Sobol, "GPA, GMAT, and Scale: A Method for Quantification of Admissions Criteria," *Research in Higher Education 20* (1984): 77–88.
Note: GMAT = Graduate Management Admissions Test.

STATISTICAL SIGNIFICANCE AND LINEAR REGRESSION

Two tests of statistical significance, the *t*-ratio and the *F*-ratio, are commonly reported along with regression findings. The *t*-ratio tests the hypothesis that the regression coefficient does not equal 0.00. A researcher may report *t*-ratio (b/se_b), its associated probability, or se_b. If se_b is reported, the *t*-value can be computed by dividing the regression coefficient by its standard error.

The *F*-ratio tests the equation as a whole. The *F*-ratio is the ratio between explained and unexplained variance. It indicates the probability that the regression equation could have occurred by chance. (See Chapter 13 to review the *F*-ratio and use of the table of *F*-values.) The null hypothesis is $b_1 = b_2 = b_3 = \cdots = b_k = 0.00$; *k* equals the number of independent variables. The hypothesis is that at least one of the independent variables is not equal to 0. The equation for the *F*-ratio is

$$F = R^2(n - k - 1) \div (1 - R^2)(k)$$

where:

R^2 = coefficient of multiple determination

n = number of subjects

k = number of independent variables

Example 14.3 shows several equations developed as part of an exploratory study to identify factors associated with the frequency with which management reports are used. Three equations are reported here to show how the regression coefficients and R^2 change as new variables enter the equation, the role of tests of statistical significance, and how the researcher decided on the relative value of the three equations.

MULTICOLLINEARITY

Sometimes in postulating a regression model, independent variables that are highly related will be incorporated into the model. The problem of having highly correlated independent variables in a regression model is termed *multicollinearity*. When two

EXAMPLE 14.3

Statistical Significance and Multiple Regression

Situation: An investigator wants to identify management report characteristics associated with their actual use. He measured several variables:

Y = average frequency that a manager discussed report information with others

X_1 = report frequency (e.g., 1 = annual, 12 = monthly, 52 = weekly)

X_2 = medium (0 = distributed printed report, 1 = accessible by terminal display)

X_3 = technical quality of the report

X_4 = accessibility of report information

X_5 = perceived value of the report

Strategy: Evaluate alternative exploratory models using multiple regression analysis (see Table 14.5).

TABLE 14.5   BETA WEIGHTS FOR THREE MULTIPLE-REGRESSION EQUATIONS

Independent Variables	Beta Weights		
	Equation 1	*Equation 2*	*Equation 3*
X_1	.41***	.39***	.39***
X_2	−.30***	.27***	−.28***
X_3		−.26	−.29
X_4			.11*
X_5		.31***	.27**
R_2	.10	.16	.16
F-Ratio	10.94***	9.02***	7.53***

Note: *$p < .05$.
**$p < .01$.
***$p < .001$.

Discussion: The first model, Equation 1, includes just two independent variables, X_1 and X_2; the model explains 10 percent of the variation in the frequency of report usage. In the second model, Equation 2, two additional independent variables are added to the model, X_3 and X_5. The addition of the new variables changes the Beta values for X_1 and X_2 slightly. With the addition of the two variables, the model now explains 16 percent of the variation in the frequency of report usage.

The researcher found that Equation 2 was the best model. It produced the highest R^2 value. Equation 3 did not improve upon Equation 2. Equations 2 and 3 each explained 16 percent of the variation. Thus the addition of variable X_4 to Equation 3 did not add to the explanation already provided by the other variables.

The Beta weights indicate that report frequency is the most strongly related to frequency of use and that the perceived value of the report also is strongly related.

Continued

EXAMPLE 14.3   *Continued*

The footnotes imply that a *t*-ratio was computed, and the researcher concluded that the relationships between frequency of use and report frequency, value, and medium were probably nonrandom (Beta not equal to zero). The lack of statistical significance suggests that the technical quality of the report may not be associated with the frequency of use.

The *F*-ratio corroborates the other information. There is a low probability that any of three equations happened by chance. The *F*-ratio and the *t*-test findings strongly imply that the regression coefficients for frequency of use, medium, and perceived quality were not equal to 0.00. All three equations are statistically significant at the .001 level.

SOURCE: E. B. Swanson, "Information Channel Distribution and Use," *Decision Sciences 18* (1987): 131–145.

---

independent variables are highly correlated, the regression equation cannot accurately estimate their independent effects on the dependent variable. A variable that actually is related to a dependent variable may appear to be unimportant. Multicollinearity can affect the decisions of policy makers. In his data analysis text, E. R. Tufte gives an example of trying to study the relationship of family income and air quality on health.[11] If the family income and neighborhood air quality of subjects are closely related, an analyst cannot determine how much the variation in health was associated with air quality and how much was due to socioeconomic factors. Yet, an administrator will want this information to decide whether investing in improving air quality is necessary.

The analyst will be particularly concerned with identifying multicollinearity. Symptoms of multicollinearity can be identified, and an investigator should review the analysis to make sure that it is free of these symptoms. Two symptoms of multicollinearity are: (1) the multiple regression equation is statistically significant, but none of the *t*-ratios is statistically significant, and (2) the addition of an independent variable radically changes the values of the Beta weights or the regression coefficients. If you review Table 14.5 in Example 14.3, you may note that neither of these conditions exist. Although all three equations are statistically significant, none of the equations has nonsignificant Beta weights. Similarly, the addition of new independent variables did not markedly change the value of Beta weights in the equations. Researchers commonly examine the data matrix that contains the correlation coefficient (*r*) for each pair of independent variables. If any *r* is $\geq.80$, the researcher may suspect multicollinearity. Nevertheless, this strategy is not perfect; multicollinearity may occur with lower correlation coefficients, and it is not necessarily present when *r* is as large as .80.[12]

Multicollinearity is considered a problem of sampling; that is, the type of cases does not allow estimates of each variable's independent effects.[13] Including cases that represent areas with wealthier families and poor air quality will reduce the association between these variables and may help a researcher to estimate each variable's effects on health. With more cases the problem may disappear, but gathering more data is normally infeasible. Sometimes, the researcher can do no better than note the problem of multicollinearity and her inability to solve it. Sometimes a researcher can modify the original model. She may decide two variables are measuring the same underlying concept and drop one of the variables. She may combine the variables into a single measure.[14] If a researcher includes city budget and number of full-time municipal employees as independent variables, she may find that the personnel costs constitute a sizable portion of the city budget and that the two variables are highly correlated. She may argue that the two variables represent the financial investment in city services and drop one of the variables. She may create a new variable, number of full-time employees for each $100,000 in the city budget.

Multicollinearity is not a problem if the purpose of the regression analysis is to forecast. When forecasting, the user is concerned with the accuracy of the prediction and not necessarily the accuracy of a specific regression coefficient. The accuracy of forecasting depends on past conditions interacting in the future the same way they did at the time the data were gathered.

REGRESSION AND NON-INTERVAL VARIABLES

One of the assumptions of regression is that the variables are measured at the interval level. In reading social science journals, you will often see ordinal variables in regression equations. If the values of an ordinal variable form a uniform scale the assumption may be relaxed. In their psychometric text, Jum Nunnally and Ira Bernstein argue that ordinal variables with 11 or more values can be treated as interval. Theirs is not a hard and fast rule. Education measures that may have only seven categories seem to work reasonably well.[15] If an ordinal variable has few values, the analyst should examine contingency tables or scatterplots to see that important dynamics of the relationship are not being missed.

As we pointed out earlier, interpreting dichotomous variables as interval measures is acceptable. Dichotomous variables may be included as independent variables in a regression equation. If the dependent variable is dichotomous, linear regression should not be used. Rather, an analyst may choose logistic regression or another statistical model analogous to linear regression. Logistic regression provides the advantages of the computational and interpretation ease of regression analysis without violating its assumptions.

Logistic Regression: An Application

The details of *logistic regression* are beyond the scope of this text.[16] Nevertheless, a review of how to interpret the *logistic regression coefficients* and a strategy for determining the goodness of fit of the model may be valuable. The review should enable you to identify situations where logistic regression could yield valuable information.

As an example we will use data from a pretrial release program.[17] Pretrial release involves releasing a defendant from jail until his or her trial is held. Program staff wanted to learn if their criteria for recommending pretrial release were effective. To make their recommendation, the staff weighed 24 factors including age, sex, marital status, employment history, nature of current charges, previous convictions, treatment for substance abuse, and ability to verify the defendant's information. They considered their program successful if released defendants appeared at scheduled hearings.

The dependent variable was "appeared in court" (1 = defendant appeared in court, and 0 = defendant did not appear in court). Table 14.6 reports the logistic regression coefficients.

To determine the probability (prob) of an event the following equation is used:

$$\text{Prob (event occurring)} = 1/(1 + e^{-Z})$$

where $Z = \text{Constant} + b_1 X_1 \ldots + b_i X_i$

e is the natural logarithm, a constant equal to approximately 2.71828.

Specifically, the equation predicts the probability that the event or outcome scored with a 1 will occur. To find the probability of the event not occurring, the probability of the event occurring, is subtracted from 1, that is:

$$\text{Prob (event not occurring)} = 1 - \text{Prob (event occurring)}.$$

Let's apply the equation to two individuals. First, we apply the equation to an individual who appears to be a poor risk for pretrial release. She is charged with driving while impaired, is being treated for substance abuse, has a prior conviction for a violent misdemeanor, has no current employment, has another pending charge, and information on her residency cannot be verified.

$$Z = -.318 + .853(0) - .624(1) - 1.125(1) + .908(1) + .008(0) - .843(1)$$
$$= -.318 - .624 - 1.125 + .908 - .843$$
$$= -2.002$$

TABLE 14.6 EFFECT OF DEFENDANT CHARACTERISTICS ON PROBABILITY OF MAKING COURT APPEARANCES

Variable	Logistic Regression Coefficient
Verified information (1 = yes)	0.853
Charged with driving while intoxicated (1 = yes)	−0.624
Treatment for substance abuse (1 = yes)	−1.125
Prior conviction for violent misdemeanor (1 = yes)	0.908
Time employed (in months)	0.008
Other pending charges (yes)	−0.843
Constant	−0.318

$$\text{Prob (appearing in court)} = 1/(1 + e^{-(-2.002)})$$
$$= 1/(1 + e^{2.002})$$
$$= 1/(1 + 7.404)$$
$$= 1/8.404$$
$$= .119$$

The probability that she will appear in court is less than 12 percent (.119 = 11.9%); she probably is not a good candidate for pretrial release.

Next, we apply the equation to an individual charged with something other than driving while intoxicated. He is not a substance abuser, has no previous arrests (thus no previous convictions nor pending charges), has worked for 24 months, and his residency and employment have been verified.

$$Z = -.318 + .853(1) - .624(0) - 1.125(0) + .908(0) + .008(24) - .843(0)$$
$$= -.318 + .853 + .192$$
$$= .727$$
$$\text{Prob (appearing in court)} = 1/(1 + e^{-.727})$$
$$= 1/(1 + .483)$$
$$= .674$$

The probability that he will appear in court is 67 percent. Clearly, he is a better candidate for pretrial release than our first example.

What about the other criteria the staff used? Their regression coefficients were not reported because they appeared to have a random (p < .10) relationship with whether or not a defendant appeared in court. The findings suggest that far fewer than 24 criteria were needed to select good candidates for pretrial release. Since verification has a large role in predicting success, the staff may continue collecting some information, such as residency, that does not appear in the final model. (The ability to verify information may actually measure a defendant's community ties, which are not directly captured by the other variables in the model.)

The next step is to evaluate how well the model works. Table 14.7 compares the outcomes predicted and the actual outcomes.

How good was the model? Note that 50 percent of the defendants failed to appear in court and 50 percent appeared in court. A coin toss could have just as well predicted 50 percent of the outcomes correctly. The logistic regression model yielded empirical evidence of how well the decision criteria were working. Although the model worked better than tossing a coin, the staff could expect to be wrong in 33 percent of the cases. The statistics confirmed that the staff was collecting data that were not helping them to predict correctly whether or not a defendant would appear in court. Based on the findings, the staff might identify and test other variables that may improve the accuracy of their predictions.

REGRESSION MODELS TO ANALYZE TIME-SERIES DATA

Time-series data may be collected to make forecasts, to identify patterns among variables over time, or to demonstrate a policy's impact. A researcher can use regression to analyze these data. Nevertheless, conducting forecasts, evaluating

TABLE 14.7   MODEL'S ABILITY TO CORRECTLY PREDICT COURT APPEARANCES

Actual	Predicted	
	Appeared in Court	*Failed to Appear*
Appeared in Court	84	46
Failed to Appear	39	91

Percent "Appeared in Court" Correctly Predicted

$$= \frac{84}{84 + 46} \cdot 100 = 65\%$$

Percent "Failed to Appear in Court" Correctly Predicted

$$= \frac{91}{39 + 91} \cdot 100 = 70\%$$

Percent of Cases Correctly Predicted

$$= \frac{84 + 91}{260} \cdot 100 = 67\%$$

relationships among variables, or determining a policy's impact requires knowledge of several models, including regression models. Selecting the appropriate model depends on the purpose of the study, the level of accuracy needed, and the cost of implementing a particular model. In this section we limit ourselves to the major considerations in applying regression to time-series data.

In Chapters 2 and 3, we suggested the value of time-series data and the use of graphs to study their variations. Time-series data are particularly valuable for making forecasts. Administrators commonly forecast future demands to make hiring, scheduling, and purchasing decisions. Economic decisions depend on forecasts; governments forecast tax revenues, while businesses forecast demand for their products. Forecast estimates have serious consequences in making economic decisions. Consequently, extensive research has been done on forecasting models to improve the quality of the estimates. In this section we examine a basic regression model used in forecasting; readers interested in forecasting should explore the forecasting literature. The forecasting literature includes other models that may be more appropriate for a given dataset. (For references, see the recommended readings.)

The linear regression model is appropriate for forecasting if over time the variable's values can be reasonably described by a straight line. Nevertheless, predictions based on linear regression may be inaccurate. First, *linear regression models* fail to react to changes in direction or in the rate of change. Second, short-term estimates, such as estimates of demand for tax forms in any given month, may be highly inaccurate because the model ignores seasonal and cyclical data.

Example 14.4 presents a model to illustrate this use of the linear regression; the model was built to forecast the size of the local government workforce in the

EXAMPLE 14.4

Forecasting the Value of a Variable with Linear Regression

Situation: A policy analyst wants to estimate the size of the local government workforce in the United States two years from now.

Strategy: He examines employment data for the previous nine years.

Number of Local Government Employees in 1,000s (Y)	Year
2,357	1
2,423	2
2,434	3
2,467	4
2,494	5
2,541	6
2,570	7
2,569	8
2,642	9

Scatterplot:

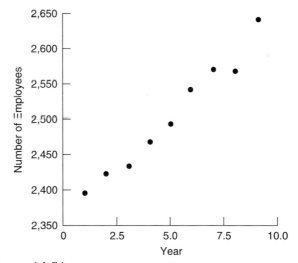

Figure 14.5A

Regression model:

$$Y = 2,357 + 29 \,(\text{Year})$$

To estimate the size of local government workforce in two years, that is, Year 11:

$$Y = 2,357 + 29(11) = 2,676 \text{ or } 2,676,000 \text{ employees}$$

SOURCE: U.S. Bureau of the Census, *City Employment, 1990,* Series GE-90-2. (Washington, DC: U.S. Government Printing Office), vi.

United States. Our example is rather elementary. It involves few years and ignores seasonal and cyclical fluctuations.

Before analyzing time-series data to determine the relationships among variables measured over time, a researcher needs to determine if autocorrelation is present. *Autocorrelation* refers to a nonrandom relationship among a variable's values at different time periods. In his monograph on time series, C. W. Ostrom uses the variable "U.S. defense budget" to illustrate autocorrelation. He posits two scenarios. In one scenario, the defense budget follows a consistent pattern of feast or famine. If the budget is quite large at Time 1, one may expect a decrease at Time 2. At Time 3 the defense budget again increases to offset the period of relative deprivation. In another scenario, if the defense budget is quite high, the forces in favor of keeping the spending high may thwart efforts to decrease spending; conversely, if spending is low, those favoring less defense spending may be able to successfully forestall efforts to increase spending. Either scenario is symptomatic of autocorrelation; that is, the defense spending at one time is associated with defense spending at a later time.[18]

Autocorrelation violates an assumption of the regression model that the residuals are independent of one another. If autocorrelation is present, the model will produce biased *t*-ratios, confidence limits, and hypotheses tests.[19] To check for autocorrelation, researchers begin their analysis by plotting the residuals.[20] If autocorrelation is present, a plot of the residuals will have a distinctive pattern. For example, if Ostrom's first scenario accurately describes the pattern of defense spending, every other residual will lie beneath the regression line. If his second scenario accurately describes the pattern of defense spending, the size of the residuals may increase for awhile, then decrease for a time, and then begin to increase again.

Autocorrelation may be eliminated if the researcher can identify and include an independent variable that explains some of the unexplained variance. One author notes that an apparently strong relationship between the number of suicides and the number of persons unemployed between 1900 and 1970 may have been due to population growth during the time period. If population size were included as a variable, the problem of autocorrelation might disappear.[21] If autocorrelation cannot be eliminated, a researcher should use a statistical model other than the ordinary least squares (OLS) regression model, the model described in this chapter.[22]

Regression has serious limitations when used to describe time-series data. One rule of thumb suggests at least 30 cases for a stable regression model. Working with 30 years' worth of data may introduce other problems. A complete set of data may not be available, or the operational definitions or the measurement intervals may have changed. To add cases, an analyst may divide the data into months or quarters, but this strategy may introduce seasonal variations. The OLS model is inappropriate if seasonal variations or autocorrelation occur. In addition, in working with social data, one may question how consistent the relationship between two or more variables is over a long time period.[23]

In reading this material, you may wonder how this discussion fits in with the interrupted time-series design. The difference lies in how the information is analyzed. In Chapter 3 we focused on graphical interpretations of time-series data to decide on the effect of a program or policy. In this chapter, we have applied linear regression, which is an inadequate model if autocorrelation or seasonal trends exist. Statistical methods exist that take into account autocorrelation and seasonal variations. An investigator with time and patience can work through practical examples, such as those found in L. J. McCain and R. M. McCleary's text, and develop the skills and understanding necessary to analyze time-series data.[24]

Conducting forecasts, evaluating the relationships among variables measured over time, and statistically analyzing interrupted time-series designs require knowledge of several models, including regression models. Selecting the appropriate model depends on the purpose of the study, the level of accuracy needed, and the cost of implementing a particular model.

REGRESSION AND CAUSALITY

In earlier chapters we discussed causality in the context of experimental and quasi-experimental designs. Experimental designs provide the best evidence that a treatment or other independent variable produces a particular outcome. The experimental design demonstrates the causal link between the variables and the specific nature of their linkage.

Nevertheless, many topics of interest to administrators and policy analysts cannot be studied experimentally. Multiple regression, including multiple regression of time-series data, and similar techniques have been employed to produce statistical evidence of causality.[25] The major value of these techniques may rest in their ability to eliminate alternative hypotheses by statistically controlling for possible causal variables.

The quality of the model affects the accurate estimate of a causal relationship. Control variables, which can demonstrate the spuriousness of the model, may not have been identified and included; thus a causal relationship may be erroneously assumed. Control variables, which interact with other variables, may have been left out, affecting the accuracy of the estimated relationships.

While the variables may be causally linked, their relationship may be nonlinear. Thus linear regression may not be the appropriate statistical model for analyzing the relationships among them.

In general, administrators are well advised to remember the shibboleth "Correlation does not equal causality." An assumption of causality seems defensible only after extensive model building, testing, and refinement.[26] Alternative models should have been tested and refined. Control variables believed to have an impact on the other variables should have been identified and tested. The surviving model should have been theoretically and statistically challenged. A thoroughly tested statistical model can improve the efficiency of experiments; it avoids wasting time and resources on poorly conceived models.

SUMMARY

Regression analysis makes available to administrators and other users a statistical technique that efficiently describes complex relationships. A regression equation allows the user to describe a dataset, to estimate population parameters, to infer causality, and to forecast.

The linear regression equation for the two-variable case is the equation for the straight line that is the best linear description of a dataset. An estimated value of the dependent variable for specific values of the independent variables can be calculated from the equation. The regression coefficients estimate the amount of impact of each independent variable.

To assess the adequacy of the linear-equation model, the analyst should examine the scatterplot to make sure that the bivariate relations are reasonably well described by a straight line. Furthermore, the analyst should look for outliers that may bias the resulting equation.

The correlation coefficient, r, measures the strength and direction of the association between variables. The r^2 value represents the percentage of variation in the dependent variable that is explained by the independent variable.

Multiple regression extends the two-variable regression model. Partial regression coefficients estimate the impact of an independent variable while controlling for the other independent variables in the equation. Beta weights, the standardized regression coefficients, indicate the relative strength of the association between each independent variable and the dependent variable. The user who assumes that the size of the unstandardized regression coefficient indicates an independent variable's importance in the model may be seriously misled.

The R^2, similar to r^2, reports the variation in the dependent variable that is explained by the variables included in the model. The R^2 may increase slightly with the addition of even trivial variables. Consequently, the analyst should be skeptical of the models with large values of R^2 and many variables. To determine what variables to include in a model, the analyst should consider the purpose of the model and each variable's contribution.

Whether a particular value of r^2 or R^2 merits attention depends on the nature of the study. Physical science researchers generally expect far higher values for these statistics than do social scientists. The differences reflect the disciplines' research questions and models. High R^2 values may occur if a dataset contains more variables than cases; the model is essentially hand-tailored. When examining a regression model, one should not assume that a low R^2 value is offset by statistical significance. If the model is based on a large sample, relationships may be nonrandom and very weak.

Although regression techniques have been used in forecasting and to infer causality, the administrator should be skeptical of such inferences. In forecasting, the length of the series, changes in the longer-term trends, and other fluctuations in the series may distort the estimate. A model that suggests a causal relationship based on time-series data may not be credible if the investigators did not test for autocorrelation and make appropriate adjustments. Multicollinearity precludes accurately estimating the effect of specific variables. The relationship among variables may be incorrectly described with a linear regression model.

Regression statistics assume that the variables are measured at the interval level. If ordinal variables can be assumed to form a uniform scale, the assumption is relaxed. Regression appears to work reasonably well if an ordinal variable has at least 11 values. Dichotomous independent variables may be used in multiple regression. Regression should not be used to analyze dichotomous dependent variables, rather logistic regression may be used. Logistic regression predicts the probability that an event will occur and indicate the statistical model's ability to correctly categorize the values of the dependent variable.

At this point we have surveyed the major approaches that administrators use to examine and analyze data. Chapter 15 discusses the last stage of the research process—how to report the findings. In addition, the chapter considers two serious issues—ethical considerations in reporting findings and requirements for keeping research records.

NOTES

1. For a further discussion on using regression to estimate parameters, see L. L. Giventer, *Statistical Analysis for Public Administration* (Belmont, CA: Wadsworth, 1996), chap. 13, which is organized around estimation. The Giventer chapter and K. J. Meier and J. L. Brudney, *Applied Statistics for Public Administration,* 4th ed. (Fort Worth, TX: Harcourt Brace College Publishers, 1997), chap. 17, cover the standard error of the estimate (used to calculate confidence limits around Y for a specific value of X), which we do not include in this chapter.

2. In addition to problems of randomness or a nonlinear relationship, the analyst should look for patterns suggesting that statistical assumptions have been violated. For a discussion on the statistical assumptions, illustrated with scatterplots, see Meier and Brudney, 324–332. Giventer has a similar discussion on pages 360 361. T. II. Poister, in *Public Program Analysis* (Baltimore: University Park Press, 1978), 523–525, has a clear discussion on how plots of the residuals can be evaluated to determine goodness of fit.

3. M. S. Lewis-Beck, *Applied Regression: An Introduction* (Newbury Park, CA: Sage University Paper, Quantitative Applications in the Social Sciences, no. 22, 1980), 32–33.

4. See Meier and Brudney, 331–333, for illustrations of non-linear scatterplots. A common strategy is to use logarithmic transformations. For a detailed discussion of logarithmic transformations, see E. R. Tufte, *Data Analysis for Politics and Policy* (Englewood Cliffs, NJ: Prentice-Hall, 1974), 108–131.

5. See Giventer, *Statistical Analysis,* 361 for an elaboration of this point.

6. G. B. Lewis, "Equal Employment Opportunity and the Early Career in Federal Employment," *Review of Public Personnel Administration* (Summer 1986): 1–18.

7. Ibid., 8. The regression coefficient for minority female status was statistically significant at the .01 level. In other words, if the actual coefficient was 0, there was a less than 1 percent chance of obtaining a regression coefficient as high as 2.29. The regression coefficients for white females and minority males were not significant at the .05 level.

8. Technically, the percentage of contribution of potential experience, gender, race, and veteran's preference depends on how the analyst built the model. If these had been entered before the education variables, the strength of their relationships might have been greater. This aspect of model-building strategies is beyond the scope of this text, but you should recognize that the analyst makes decisions that determine the specific values in a multiple regression equation.

9. This equation for adjusted R^2 is from J. Cohen and P. Cohen, *Applied Multiple Regression/Correlation Analysis for the Behavioral Sciences,* 2d ed. (Hillsdale, NJ: Erlbaum 1983), 105–106.

10. This issue is discussed as specification error, that is, omitting an important variable or including an irrelevant variable. See C. H. Achen, *Interpreting and Using Regression* (Newbury Park, CA: Sage University Paper, Quantitative Applications in the Social Sciences, no. 29, 1982), 51–56, or W. D. Berry and S. Feldman, *Multiple Regression in Practice* (Newbury Park, CA: Sage University Paper, Quantitative Applications in the Social Sciences, no. 50, 1985), 18–26.

11. E. R. Tufte, *Data Analysis for Politics and Policy* (Englewood Cliffs, NJ: 1974), 150.

12. Berry and Feldman, *Multiple Regression,* 43. Two common symptoms are high intercorrelations between independent variables or very large standard errors of b. For further discussion on symptoms of multicollinearity and possible solutions, see Tufte, *Data Analysis,* 148–155, Lewis-Beck, *Applied Regression,* 58–63, and Berry and Feldman, *Multiple Regression,* 42–50.

13. Tufte, *Data Analysis,* 150.

14. If multicollinearity is suspected, the analyst may increase the size of the sample, combine the involved variables to form a single variable or keep only one of the variables, or consider an experimental design. For

further discussion, see Tufte, *Data Analysis,* 148–155, and S. Welch and J. C. Comer, *Quantitative Methods in Public Administration* (Homewood, IL: The Dorsey Press, 1983), 215–216.

15. Jum C. Nunnally and Ira H. Bernstein, *Psychometric Theory,* 115–116. Observation about uniform scales is from Giventer, *Statistical Analysis,* 162.

16. The SPSS manual, *SPSS Advanced Statistics™ User's Guide* (Chicago: SPSS Inc., 1990), by Marija J. Norusiis has an accessible explanation of logistic regression. D. W. Hosmer and S. Lemeshow's *Applied Logistic Regression* (New York: John Wiley, 1989) is recommended as an introduction to the method.

17. The example is based on T. Benton et al., "A Comparison of Differences between Successful and Unsuccessful Participants in ReEntry's Pretrial Release Program" (Raleigh: Department of Political Science and Public Administration, North Carolina State University, Unpublished paper, 1986).

18. C. W. Ostrom, Jr., *Time Series Analysis: Regression Techniques,* 2d ed. (Newbury Park, CA: Sage University Paper, Quantitative Applications in the Social Sciences, no. 9, 1990), 11.

19. For discussions on detecting autocorrelation and its effects, see Ostrom, *Time Series Analysis,* 12–17, 25–35. S. Makridakis and S. G. Wheelwright, *Forecasting Methods for Management,* 5th ed. (New York: John Wiley, 1989), has a relatively clear discussion on autocorrelation, 126–130, 192–194.

20. Statistical tests, such as the Durbin-Watson, will test for autocorrelation.

21. M. M. Mark, "The Causal Analysis of Concomitances in Time Series." In *Quasi-Experimentation: Designs and Analysis Issues for Field Settings,* eds. T. D. Cook and D. T. Campbell (Boston: Houghton-Mifflin, 1979), 323.

22. For discussion of alternate models, see Mark, "The Causal Analysis," 321–339, or Ostrom, *Time Series Analysis.* The works of S. Makridakis and S. G. Wheelwright, Armstrong, and McCleary and Hays (cited in recommended readings section) provide more detailed information.

23. The 30 rule of thumb is from S. Makridakis and S. G. Wheelwright, *Forecasting Methods,* 208. For more elaboration on this discussion of the drawbacks of using linear regression, see Mark, "The Causal Analysis," 335–339.

24. L. J. McCain and R. M. McCleary, "The Statistical Analysis of the Simple Interrupted Time-Series Quasi-Experiment." In *Quasi-Experimentation: Designs and Analysis Issues for Field Settings,* eds. T. D. Cook and D. T. Campbell (Boston: Houghton-Mifflin, 1979), 292–293.

25. See J. Cohen and P. Cohen, *Applied Multiple Regression,* chap. 9; R. D. Cook and D. T. Campbell, *Quasi-Experimentation* (Boston: Houghton- Mifflin, 1979), chap. 7.

26. This argument is effectively made by Tufte, *Data Analysis,* 146–147.

TERMS FOR REVIEW

regression equation	outliers	multicollinearity
correlation coefficient	lagging a variable	linear regression model
scatterplot	partial regression coefficient	logistic regression
residual	dummy variables	logistic regression coefficient
goodness of fit	coefficient of determination	autocorrelation
regression coefficient	Beta weights	

QUESTIONS FOR REVIEW

The following questions should indicate whether you have a basic competency in this chapter's material.

1. Data are gathered on 40 countries to study variations in birth rate. Consider an equation derived in the study:

$$Y = 32 - .0018 X$$
$$r^2 = -.78$$
$$Se_b = .00024$$

where:

Y = birth rate per 1,000 population
X = per capita income

a. Identify the following:

the independent and dependent variables
the regression coefficient
the constant
the correlation coefficient
the coefficient of determination

the standard error of the slope (se_b)
the linear regression equation

b. What percent variation in birth rate is associated with per capita income?

c. What is the direction of the relationship between per capita income and birth rate? What evidence supports your answer?

d. What goodness of fit information is provided? How should you interpret this information?

e. Calculate the t-ratio. What can you infer about the relationship between per capita income and a nation's birth rate?

f. A country has a per capita income of $2,000. Estimate its birth rate.

g. Per capita income in the dataset ranges from $400 per year to $12,000. Can you estimate the birth rate for a country with a per capita income of $20,000 per year? Justify your answer.

h. If per capita income is measured as "per capita income in thousands of dollars," the regression equation is $Y = 32 - 1.8X$. Is this a better model of the relationship? Justify your answer.

i. Should you examine the scatterplot for this data? Why or why not? What pattern would you need to decide that the linear regression model is appropriate? What would you do if you found a curvilinear pattern or no pattern at all?

j. Should you examine a scatterplot of residuals for this data? Why or Why not? What would you hope to find?

2. The equation is recalculated to include information of the percentage of the population living on farms:

$$Y = 36 - .0018\,X_1 - .186\,X_2; R^2 = .67$$
$$\qquad\quad (.00023) \qquad (.066)$$

where:

   Y = birth rate per 1,000 population
   X_1 = per capita income
   X_2 = percentage of population living on farms
   se_b reported in parentheses

a. Interpret the information provided by "$-.0018$" and "$-.186$" in the equation.

b. What does the se_b indicate about the relationships between birth rate and per capita income and percentage of the population living on farms?

c. What variation in birth rate is explained by the multiple regression model? Do you consider this high, low, or in between? Explain.

d. What is the direction of the relationships between birth rate and per capita income and percentage of the population living on farms? What evidence supports your answer?

e. Predict the birth rate for countries with the following characteristics:

   (1) Per capita income of $10,100 and a farm population of 13%

   (2) Per capita income of $1,230 and a farm population of 35%

   (3) Per capita income of $4,100 and a farm population of 4%

f. What additional information would Beta weights provide that you do not currently have?

3. Use the equation below to predict values of Y for the following cases:

a. a department with an average grade point of 2.5 and no placement assistance

b. a department with an average grade point of 2.5 and formal placement assistance

c. a department with an average grade point of 2.7 and no formal placement assistance

$$Y = 5 + 20X_1 + 10X_2; R = .5$$

where:

   Y = percentage of department graduates placed within a month of graduation
   X_1 = mean grade point average of department graduates
   X_2 = formal placement assistance ($X_2 = 1$ if formal assistance; $X_2 = 0$ if no formal assistance)

d. What variation in placement success is explained by the multiple regression model?

4. What is meant when we note that the linear regression line is asymmetric?

5. Why should you learn the range of values of X that are used to calculate the regression equation?

PROBLEMS FOR HOMEWORK AND DISCUSSION

1. The following two problems refer to the multiple regression equation given in Review Question 3.
   a. If the data had been collected last year, how would they affect the ability of the university to forecast placement outcomes for this year's graduates?
   b. The original model included X_3, average aptitude test scores, for example, Scholastic Aptitude Tests (SATs) and Graduate Record Exams (GREs). The variable was dropped because of a problem with multicollinearity. Explain what is meant by multicollinearity in this context. How could it have been detected?
2. Table 14.8 appeared in a study of the income of planners. Note that planners' income is the dependent variable.

TABLE 14.8   PLANNERS' INCOME BETA COEFFICIENTS BY GENDER

	Men	Women
Age	.02	.08
Education**	.25*	.30*
Marital (married = 1)	.05*	.01
Race (white = 1)	.01	.02
Agency size	.19*	.17*
Centralization	.04	−.03
Job turnover	−.14	−.10
No. planner roles	.03	−.01
Yrs. professional experience	.53*	.37*
R^2	.600	.426

Note: *Significant at the .05 level.
**Education rescaled: (1) high school; (2) 1–2 years college; (3) 3 or more years college; (4) bachelor's degree; (5) 1 or more years graduate work; (6) master's degree; (7) 1 or more years graduate work after master's; (8) doctorate.
SOURCE: J. M. Mayo, Jr., "Job Attainment in Planning: Women Versus Men," *Work and Occupation* (May 1985): 152. (Copyright 1985 by Sage Publications, Inc. Reprinted with permission: Sage Publications, Inc.)

   a. Compare how well the model explains the variation of income among male and female planners.
   b. What factors have the greatest effect on the income of male planners? on female planners? What information did you use to reach this conclusion?
   c. Does the evidence suggest that job turnovers were associated with higher incomes? Briefly explain how you reached this conclusion.
   d. Does the evidence suggest planners' salaries were affected by racial considerations or marital status? Briefly explain how you reached this conclusion.
   e. What does the evidence suggest about the value of taking on many different planner roles?
   f. What is the difference between the starred (*) regression coefficients and the other coefficients?
3. To study factors associated with frequency of managers' use of report information, a researcher examined five linear models reported in Table 14.9. The independent variables consisted of:

TABLE 14.9   STANDARDIZED (BETA) REGRESSION EQUATIONS

	1	2	3	4	5
Independent Variables					
Frequency of report	.41	.42	.41	.39	.39
Medium	−.30	−.2	−.31	−.27	−.28
Technique		−.07	−.17	−.26	−.29
Accessibility			.19		.11
Value				.31	.27
R^2	.10	.10	.12	.16	.16

SOURCE: E. B. Swanson, "Information Channel Disposition and Use," *Decision Sciences 18* (1987): 131–145.

Frequency of report (annual = 1; monthly = 12; weekly = 52; daily = 260)
Medium (printed = 1; terminal screen = 0)
Technique (factor score representing objective information quality, for example, data reliability, precision, and timeliness)
Accessibility (factor score representing ability to obtain and interpret information)

Value (factor score representing value of information to specific user)

a. Based on the above information, which model best explains variations in managers' information use? Why did you choose this model?

b. Based on the above information, should an agency go to the extra expense of printing reports? Justify.

c. Based on the above information, should an agency concentrate on continually improving the quality of its information? Explain.

d. Which variable has the greatest association with the frequency of report use?

e. "Technique" has a Beta weight of $-.07$ in Equation 2 $(-.07X)$ and a markedly higher value in Equations 3 through 5 $(-.17X, -.26X,$ and $-.29X)$. Briefly explain why the coefficients in the four equations are different.

4. The following model was used to study variations in water consumption (measured as total sales) in communities:

$$Y = 600 + .019X_1 - 15X_2 - .02X_3 - 6X_4$$
$$- 682D_1 - 736D_2 - 626D_3 - 356D_4$$
$$+ 40D_6 + 244D_7 + 226D_8 + 2D_9$$
$$- 183D_{10} - 532D_{11} - 720D_{12}$$

where:
$\qquad Y$ = total water sales
$\qquad X_1$ = community population
$\qquad X_2$ = average yearly rainfall (in inches)
$\qquad X_3$ = public relations costs
$\qquad X_4$ = real price/acre
D_1–D_{12} = January–December

Adapted from L. J. Mercer and W. D. Morgan, "Impact of a Water Conservation Campaign," *Evaluation Review 4* (1980): 112.

a. What would be the predicted water consumption in January for a community of 50,000 with an annual rainfall of 10 inches, $1,000 in costs for public relations, and real price of $80/acre?

b. What is the effect on water consumption of every $100 spent on public relations?

c. What month is water consumption the highest? the lowest?

5. Table 14.10 reports data on verbal SAT scores and average daily attendance for 15 high schools.

TABLE 14.10   AVERAGE VERBAL SCHOLASTIC APTITUDE TEST (SAT) SCORES AND AVERAGE DAILY ATTENDANCE FOR COUNTY HIGH SCHOOL

School	Average Verbal SATs	Average Daily Attendance
Adams	281	77%
Bell	312	75%
Clark	439	96%
Day	282	91%
Edwards	294	81%
French	316	83%
Grant	365	84%
Hill	294	80%
James	308	79%
Key	257	85%
Lee	308	76%
Mann	387	95%
Nash	287	71%
Parr	394	91%
Rhodes	319	88%

The equation for the regression line is:

$$Y = -46 + 4.4X \qquad r = .66$$

where:
$\qquad Y$ = verbal SAT score
$\qquad X$ = average daily attendance

Note: Percents were entered as whole numbers; for example, the value entered for X was "20" for a school with 20 percent daily attendance.

a. Create a scatterplot for the data in Table 14.10.

b. Plot the regression line.

c. Calculate the residuals for Adams, Day, and Lee.

d. Do the data indicate that students who attend school regularly do better on their verbal SATs than students who do not? Justify your answer.

e. Interpret the relationship between school attendance and SAT verbal scores.

6. Researchers created an accounting test to replace a standardized test. They wanted to validate the test and to establish that the test did not discriminate against minority or female job applicants. To validate the test, the

researchers tested agency accountants and gathered data on two criteria:

Criterion 1 (C1): Behavioral scale demonstrating job knowledge

Criterion 2 (C2): Rating of overall job performance

Table 14.11 reports the correlation coefficients (r) between each test and validation criteria for various types of subjects. For instance, the .56 at the bottom of column 1 represents $r = .56$ for the relationship between the score on the behavioral scale demonstrating job knowledge (C1, a dependent variable) and the score on the created test for all nonminority subjects.

TABLE 14.11 CORRELATIONS BETWEEN PERFORMANCE ON TWO JOB TESTS AND TWO PERFORMANCE MEASURES BY SUBJECT CHARACTERISTICS

	Created Test		Standardized	
Test	C1	C2	C1	C2
All subjects	.44	.28	.12	−.18
Male subjects	.41	.20	−.03	−.14
Female subjects	.48	.56	.25	.11
Minorities	.37	.26	.18	−.21
Nonminorities	.56	.29	.20	−.10

SOURCE: G. A. Kesselman and F. E. Lopez, "The Impact of Job Analysis on Employment Test Validation for Minority and Nonminority Accounting Personnel," *Personnel Psychology* (1979): 99.

a. What type of validation did the researchers conduct?

b. Which test does the data suggest the agency should use to hire accountants? Why? Do you see any weaknesses in this test that should be rectified? What are they?

c. Based on the data, would you recommend using both criteria to validate future tests? Justify your answer.

7. Tables 14.12 and 14.13 were reproduced from a General Accounting Office report, "Infant Formula in the WIC program." The study estimated the effects of various factors on the cost of infant formula in the federal Women, Infant and Children's (WIC) program.

a. Estimate the cost of infant formula in a program in the West that uses sole source bidding, has an average WIC population of 5,000, serves approximately 60 percent of the eligible population, and does not have an infant formula manufacturing facility in the state.

b. What percent of the variance in the cost of infant formula is explained by the model?

c. Based on these data, would you recommend that a WIC program use sole-source competitive bidding or multisource? Justify your answer.

d. Do states that have an infant formula manufacturer in their state benefit? Justify your answer.

TABLE 14.12 DEFINITION OF VARIABLES USED IN REGRESSION ANALYSIS

Variable	Description
SOLE_BID	Equals 1 if WIC agency uses sole-source competitive bidding, 0 otherwise
MULTI_BID	Equals 1 if WIC agency uses multisource competitive bidding, 0 otherwise
WICPOP	Average monthly WIC infant population (June 1988 to May 1989) in thousands
MFGSTATE	Equals 1 if infant formula manufactured in the state, 0 otherwise
ELIG89	Proportion of the eligible population served by the WIC agency in fiscal year 1989
INDIAN	Equals 1 if the WIC agency represents an Indian tribe, 0 otherwise
MIDWEST	Equals 1 if the WIC agency is located in the Midwest, 0 otherwise
WEST	Equals 1 if the WIC agency is located in the West, 0 otherwise
SOUTH	Equals 1 if the WIC agency is located in the South, 0 otherwise
PRICE	Wholesale price minus rebate amount per 13-ounce can of formula as of June 1, 1989

TABLE 14.13   REGRESSION RESULTS

Variable	Parameter Estimate (B)	Standard Error	T-stat
INTERCEPT	0.53	0.10	5.39
SOLE_BID	−0.36	0.05	−7.91
MULTI_BID	−0.24	0.09	−2.85
WICPOP	0.0002	0.00082	−0.25
MFGSTATE	−0.01	0.07	−0.11
ELIG89	0.40	0.15	2.64
INDIAN	0.27	.06	4.45
MIDWEST	−0.04	0.06	−0.66
WEST	0.03	0.06	0.58
SOUTH	0.01	0.06	0.12

Notes: Number of observations, 56.
Adjusted R-square, 0.824.
F statistic, 29.67.
Probability of F statistic, 0.0001.
WIC = Women, Infants and Children.

DISK WORK

1. Load the Census Data Base and examine the relationship between poverty, measured by LOWINCPT, percent households with a money income of less than $15,000, and (1) education, measured by HGSCHDPT, percent adults with at least a high school degree; (2) traditional labor force, measured by WORKAGPT, percent of labor force employed in agriculture, forestry and fisheries; and (3) community growth, measured by POPCHGPT, percent change in population over 12 years.
   a. Write a hypothesis for each variable; remember to indicate an anticipated direction.
   b. Create a scatterplot for each relationship. Do the data fit a linear model? Explain why or why not.
   c. Use a statistical software program and obtain the following statistics for each relationship: constant, slope or regression coefficient, r, standard error of the slope.
      i. Write the regression equation for each relationship.
      ii. How well is each relationship described by the linear regression model? Cite evidence to support your observation.
      iii. For each relationship decide whether or not it supports the hypotheses you postulated in 1.a.
2. Load the Census Data Base and use a statistical software program to test a multiple regression model that links a county's crime rate to its unemployment level (NOWORKPT), education level (HGSCHDPT), labor force participation in traditional industries (WORKAGPT), and population change (POPCHGPT).
   a. Run a program to obtain R^2, b (unstandardized regression coefficient), B (standardized regression coefficient, standard error of b or value of t.
   b. Report your findings in a table similar to Table 14.3.
   c. Report your findings as an equation (for an example see problem 4 in the homework and discussion section)
   d. How much variation in crime rate is explained by the model?
   e. Would your model be better if WORKAGPT was dropped from the model? Justify your answer.
3. Load the Census Data Base. Use the variable Region (East, Central, and West) to create

dummy variables. Add these to the multiple regression model in exercise 2. Report your findings in a table similar to Table 14.3.

   a. Which variables have the strongest relationship to county crime rate? What criteria did you use to select these variables?

   b. Which variables have the weakest relationship to county crime rate? What criteria did you use to select these variables?

4. Load the Census Data Base. Use the regression model in exercise 2 and report separate equations for each region. Compare the models for the three regions.

5. Use the variables in the Census Data Base to create and test a multiple regression model.

   a. Write up a verbal model which includes four to five independent variables. Your write-up should suggest the value of studying the relationships, anticipate the direction of the relationships, and provide evidence supporting the hypothesized direction. (For this exercise the evidence may be modest and based on experience or "common wisdom.")

   b. Test your model and present your findings in a table or equation.

   c. Write a verbal summary of your findings. If your hypotheses were not supported suggest possible reasons for the lack of support.

RECOMMENDED FOR FURTHER READING

E. R. Tufte, *Data Analysis for Politics and Policy* (Englewood Cliffs, NJ: Prentice-Hall, 1974). This is a classic text with excellent examples and valuable observations about the interpretation of regression findings. Our discussion owes much to Tufte's presentation. He provides more detail and considers a variety of statistical models, such as logarithmic transformations.

For accessible explanations of regression statistics along with worked out examples, see L. L. Giventer, *Statistical Analysis for Public Administration* (Belmont, CA: Wadsworth, 1996), chaps. 12–14, and K. J. Meier and J. L. Brudney, *Applied Statistics for Public Administration* 4th ed. (Fort Worth, TX: Harcourt Brace College Publishers, 1997), chaps. 17–18, 20. Giventer's text includes computer printouts; Meier and Brudney also cover cubic and quadric transformations.

J. Cohen and P. Cohen's *Applied Multiple Regression/Correlation Analysis for the Behavioral Sciences*, 2d ed. (Hillsdale, NJ: L. Erlbaum, 1983), is a comprehensive guide to multiple regression, including causal modeling. The Sage Series, Quantitative Applications in the Social Sciences, has several monographs on regression.

W. F. Matlack, *Statistics for Public Managers* (Itasca, IL.: F. E. Peacock Publishers, 1993), chap. 12, reviews basic forecasting techniques. S. Makridakis and S. G. Wheelwright, *Forecasting Methods for Management*, 5th ed. (New York: John Wiley, 1989), is a comprehensive and relatively easy-to-follow presentation. J. S. Armstrong's *Long-Range Forecasting: From Crystal Ball to Computer*, 2d ed. (New York: John Wiley, 1985), is an extraordinary reference book. It literally overflows with valuable information and insights, including an appendix, "Rules for Cheaters," which tells one how to increase the value of R^2.

Other information on time series can be found in C. W. Ostrom, Jr., *Time Series Analysis: Regression Techniques,* 2d ed. (Newbury Park, CA: Sage University Paper, Quantitative Applications in the Social Sciences, no. 9, 1990); R. McCleary and R. A. Hay, Jr., *Applied Time Series Analysis for the Social Sciences* (Beverly Hills: Sage, 1980).

Appendix 14.1

Calculating Regression Statistics for Bivariate Relationships

This appendix reviews the equations for deriving a simple linear regression equation, the correlation coefficient (r), standard error of the estimate of the regression coefficient (se_b), and the t-ratio. (See Table 14.14.)

The calculations to obtain the regression equation involve two major steps. First, the value of the slope, or the regression coefficient, symbolized by b, is calculated. The equation to calculate the regression coefficient is:

$$b = \frac{\Sigma(X_i - \overline{X})(Y_i - \overline{Y})}{\Sigma(X_i - \overline{X})^2}$$

where:

X_i = the value of each X

$\overline{X}$ = the mean value of all the Xs

Y_i = the value of each Y

$\overline{Y}$ = the mean value of all the Ys

Second, the value of the Y intercept, or constant, symbolized by a, is calculated. The equation to calculate the intercept is:

$$a = \overline{Y} - b\overline{X}$$

TABLE 14.14   CALCULATIONS FOR b, a, AND THE LINEAR REGRESSION EQUATION

Car	Miles (1000s) (X)	Repair Costs (Y)	$X_i - \overline{X}$	$Y_i - \overline{Y}$	$(X_i - \overline{X})(Y_i - \overline{Y})$	$(X_i - \overline{X})^2$	$(Y_i - \overline{Y})^2$
1	80	1,200	31.05	577.5	17,931.38	964.10	333,506.3
2	29	150	−19.95	−472.5	9,426.38	398.00	223,256.3
3	42	600	−6.95	−22.5	156.38	48.30	506.25
4	53	650	4.05	27.5	111.37	16.40	756.25
5	73	1,000	24.05	377.5	9,078.88	578.40	142,506.3
6	80	1,500	31.05	877.5	27,246.38	964.10	770,006.3
7	60	600	11.05	−22.5	−248.62	122.10	506.25
8	13	200	−35.95	−422.5	15,188.88	1,292.40	178,506.3
9	14.5	0	−34.45	−622.5	21,445.13	1,186.80	387,506.3
10	45	325	−3.95	−297.5	1,175.13	15.60	88,506.25
Sum	489.5	6,225			101,511.29	5,586.20	2,125,562.8
Mean	48.95	622.5					

$b = (101511.3)/5586.225 = 18.17$

$a = 622.5 - 18.17(48.95) = 266.92$

$Y = -267 - 18X$

Using the same figures, we can calculate the correlation coefficient r with the equation:

$$r = \frac{\Sigma(X_i - \bar{X})(Y_i - \bar{Y})}{\sqrt{\Sigma(X_i - \bar{X})^2 \, \Sigma(Y_i - \bar{Y})^2}}$$

$$r = \frac{(101,511.3)}{(5,586.225)(2,125,563)}$$

$$r = .93$$

To calculate the se_b, the equation is

$$\sqrt{\frac{\Sigma(Y_i - \bar{Y})^2/(n - 2)}{\Sigma(X_i - \bar{X})^2}}$$

Table 14.15 uses the data from Table 14.10 to show the calculations for obtaining the value se_b for the car repair dataset.

$$se_b = \sqrt{(281,800/8)/5,586.225} = 6.31$$

The t-ratio $= b/se_b$; in our example the t-ratio is $18/2.5 = 7.2$. A table of the t distribution shows that the associated probability for $t = 7.2$, $df = n - 2 = 8$, is less than .01. In other words, a t-ratio as great as 7.2 would occur less than 1 time out of 100 if the regression coefficient in the population were 0.

TABLE 14.15   DATA AND CALCULATIONS FOR SE$_B$

Car	Miles (1000s) (X)	Repair Costs (Y)	$\hat{Y}$	Residual	Residual^2	$(X_i - \bar{X})^2$
1	80	1,200	1,173	27	729	964.1025
2	29	150	255	−105	11,025	398.0025
3	42	600	489	111	12,321	48.3025
4	53	650	687	−37	1,369	16.4025
5	73	1,000	1,047	−47	2,209	578.4025
6	80	1,500	1,173	327	106,929	964.1025
7	60	600	813	−213	45,369	122.1025
8	13	200	−33	233	54,289	1,292.403
9	14.5	0	−6	6	36	1,186.803
10	45	325	543	−218	47,524	15.6025
Mean	48.95	622.5				
Sum					281,800	5,586.225

Communicating Findings and Completing the Project

In this chapter you will learn

1. the information to include when presenting research findings.
2. how to include tables and graphs in a presentation.
3. elements of effective oral briefings and written reports.
4. ethical considerations in reporting research findings.
5. guidelines for storing data.

Most investigators find conducting quantitative research engaging and satisfying. From building the initial model through to the statistical analysis, they get caught up in the excitement of testing and refining their ideas. After they have received the last set of data and completed the analysis, the researchers prepare to report the findings. They report their findings in informal meetings, formal briefings, project reports, and academic papers. Their audiences rarely share the investigators' level of enthusiasm or interest in the research. If researchers want their efforts to influence policy decisions, they must tailor their presentations to engage audience interest.

This chapter examines the last stages of a research project. It focuses on the components of quantitative reports and how to present them. The chapter argues for clear, focused presentations tailored to the needs of a particular audience. The desire to be relevant and to enhance one's reputation can conflict with ethical practices. The last section of the chapter discusses ethical considerations in reporting research findings and in storing research data. Administrators should review the data storage section; failure to establish ownership of the data and determine where they will be kept and for how long wastes resources and prevents efforts to validate or refine findings.

VARIATIONS IN AUDIENCES AND THEIR NEEDS

In presenting a report and its findings, investigators focus on the presentation's purpose and the characteristics of its intended audience. Whether preparing a briefing or writing a report, researchers have expectations of an audience. Even the modest expectation of interest in a study is hard to satisfy in an age when professionals are bombarded by requests for their time and attention. Researchers have to contend with the ability of administrators and policy makers to protect their time and to ignore information that they do not want. Beyond getting an audience's attention, investigators want listeners and readers to identify correctly important findings and implied actions.

Technical communications texts consider audience analysis as preparatory to drafting oral or written presentations. One text points out that academic-paper writing gives students unrealistic expectations. The student writer can assume that instructors are knowledgeable, that they read each paper in its entirety, and that they try to understand unclear sections. "Real world" readers may not understand the paper, they may not care about the topic, they may ignore unclear discussions, or they may browse through a few sections. "Real world" listeners may let their minds wander, they may fall asleep, or they may slip out of the room. Of course, these behaviors may be witnessed in the classroom as well.

To counteract the freedom of audiences to ignore or misunderstand information, researchers identify their audiences and their audiences' characteristics and anticipated needs. The following five-step procedure for audience analysis seems well suited to administrative researchers.[1]

Step 1: Identify the uses of a communication and the route it will travel.

Step 2: Identify all possible audiences, including future audiences for a communication.

Step 3: Identify an audience's concerns and needs.

Step 4: Make communications clear and accessible.

Step 5: Identify arguments and approaches that will be effective with an audience.

Step one identifies probable audiences and suggests how they will use the information. Step two applies primarily to written communication. Once a report is written and released, its routing is uncertain. Administrators may give a report or handouts to their supervisors, staff, agency analysts, interest-group members, professional acquaintances, legislators, students, or the agency library. To satisfy diverse audiences, researchers need to write clear reports that fully document procedures and distinguish objective findings from opinions.

Step three is recommended so that researchers can learn if their perspective differs from that of an audience. To appreciate differences between themselves and their audiences, the researchers may wish to identify an audience's educational background and experience, knowledge of the subject, and expectations about the report presentation. Then the researchers should identify the same information about themselves.[2] This information will help them critique the clarity of a planned presentation and avoid making unwarranted assumptions about an audience's interests and values.

Step four recognizes the competition for an audience's attention. You may wonder if Steps one and two conflict with Step four. Providing full information can diminish a presentation's clarity or accessibility. Researchers resolve the dilemma by putting important information first and placing complicated or technical details in footnotes or appendices.

Step five builds on the information developed with the preceding steps and requires the investigators to consider how to tailor their presentation so that they communicate effectively to an audience. As part of this step, they may look for models for organizing a presentation. To learn agency preferences for organizing and presenting information, researchers may attend oral briefings or ask agency contacts to identify especially effective reports. The researchers use this information to infer what features of reports or briefings generate audience interest and involvement. As you read professional reports, save ones that seem particularly well done. You also may want to save an example of a poor report to remind yourself of features to avoid. When you attend oral presentations, note what seems to work and what does not.

COMPONENTS OF THE QUANTITATIVE REPORT

A quantitative research report includes: a summary of the report, a discussion of the study's background, a review of the literature, a description of the methodology, and the findings. Recommendations, references and a bibliography are included as appropriate. We assume that readers are familiar with standard documentation requirements, so we will not discuss them in this section.

Example 15.1 reproduces a table of contents for a report on citizen attitudes toward a local police department. It is typical of quantitative reports. Nevertheless, as is true of all reports, the specific sections and their content depend on the nature of the study. For example, since the study was conducted to meet accreditation requirements, the background section was brief and included in the discussion of purpose. The methodology was straightforward and could be communicated clearly in the body of the report. If the methodology is complex or a detailed discussion is needed, the investigators may place the technical details in an appendix. This study did not make recommendations to the police department; if it had, the recommendations would normally appear in the executive summary and at the end of the body of the report.

Executive Summaries and Abstracts

The *executive summary* highlights a report's content. The intended audience is the executive who has little time to read reports. Busy administrators and policy makers scan an executive summary to decide if and when to read the entire report or to refer it to an associate. Administrators with a limited interest in the topic skim a summary to keep themselves current. Policy actors may distribute

---

EXAMPLE 15.1

Sample Table of Contents for a Quantitative Report

Executive Summary   i
Purpose of Study and Accreditation Requirements   1
Sample Survey Design
   Survey instrument   1
   Sample design   2
   Instrument implementation   3
   Respondent characteristics   4
Findings
   Overall agency performance   5
   Overall competence of employees   8
   Citizen perceptions of officer behavior and attitudes   9
   Concerns about safety and security within the city   10
   Concerns about safety and security within neighborhood   13
   Citizen recommendations for improvement   14
Summary and conclusions   17
Appendix A: Survey instrument with frequencies   18
Appendix B: Approval from human subjects' committee   25
Appendix C: Selected indicators of citizen perceptions by district   26
Tables
   Table 1: Respondent characteristics   4
   Table 2: Reason for and date of most recent policy contact by district   6
   Table 3: Rating of police department by district   8

Comments: The report does not have some sections that commonly appear in quantitative reports. Specifically, it does not include a background discussion, recommendations, bibliography, or methodological appendices. The purpose of the study was to conduct and report on a citizen survey to meet accreditation requirements. This tended to focus the study and enable investigators to skip some of the detail that is found in other papers. The actual paper had more than three tables, but we wanted to give you an idea of what information was included.

SOURCE: J. Barlow et al., "An Analysis of Survey of Citizens' Opinions of City Police" (Raleigh: North Carolina State University, Unpublished paper, 1992).

---

summaries to communicate and endorse the report's findings. Investigators doing literature reviews can infer if a report is appropriate to their needs.

The executive summary is the last part of the report to be written. It includes only information in the report, but it can be read and understood independently of the report. The researchers condense the report. They decide what they want a reader, who will spend just a few minutes learning about the study, to know. They may visualize the impatient administrator who asks: "What's the headline?" The researchers go through the report and find sentences that concisely describe why the study was done, who the subjects were, how the data were collected, limitations in the methodology or its implementation, and what the major findings were. An executive summary may include recommendations.

EXAMPLE 15.2

An Executive Summary

Purpose: To meet accreditation standards, the police department must annually survey citizen attitudes and opinions. The department may combine survey findings with other information to aid departmental decision making. This report analyzes data gathered during the 1992 citizen survey.

Methodology: A telephone survey was conducted during October 1992 to gather opinion data from a sample of 898 city residents. The respondents were randomly selected from the city directory so that the same percentage of people came from each police beat.

Police department personnel took the lead in writing the survey questionnaire. The questions focused on how citizens felt about the department in the following areas: overall agency performance, competence of agency employees, officers' attitudes and behaviors toward citizens, concerns over safety and security.

Major findings:

In all districts among respondents who have contact with officers:

- More than 90 percent agree or strongly agree that police officers are competent.
- More than 80 percent agree or strongly agree that police officers have good attitudes.
- More than 85 percent agree or strongly agree that the overall performance of the officers present was good.
- City residents (91 percent) feel safe moving around the city, but 69 percent do not feel safe in downtown at night.
- Twenty-eight percent of respondents feel unsafe in Southern District.
- Over 50 percent of Southern District respondents expressed safety and security concerns. The most frequently mentioned concerns were related to drug problems.
- The most frequently mentioned concern in the rest of the city was break-ins.

SOURCE: J. Barlow et al., "An Analysis of Survey of Citizens' Opinions of City Police" (Raleigh: North Carolina State University, Unpublished paper, 1992).

Example 15.2 reproduces the executive summary for the report on citizen attitudes toward a city police department. The summary relies on clear direct sentences and visual cues to allow an individual to read it quickly. Its length and degree of detail are consistent with the length and complexity of the report, agency expectations, and the importance of the findings. In preparing an executive summary, the writer avoids compressing as many details as possible into the summary; otherwise, its benefits are defeated.

Journal articles have abstracts instead of executive summaries. Abstracts and executive summaries have a similar purpose and content. Abstracts are shorter, about 200 words, with highly condensed writing. They may liberally use technical jargon. In addition to prefacing articles, abstracts are reprinted in various compilations, such as *Sage Public Administration Abstracts.*

Background Information

Background information, which puts the study in context, may be included in the introduction as a separate background section or in a review of the literature. The report should include sufficient information for the audience to understand why the study was designed the way it was. The specific information needed depends on the report's audience and the study's purpose. A knowledgeable audience may need little background information.

We assume that public administration research studies start with a problem or a question to be answered. The background information includes a definitive statement of the study's purpose and a history of the problem or the source of the question. If the study involves a program or policy, the report may discuss its origins, implementation history, goals, relevant constituents or stakeholders, resources, and processes. If a formal research proposal was written, the investigators may include its background material in the final report instead of writing a new one.

To develop the background information, investigators rely on interviews, documents, and the research literature. In applied research reports, information from the literature may be woven into the background presentation, assigned to an appendix, or abbreviated in an annotated bibliography. In academic research the literature review may appear as a separate section.

The *literature review* establishes the value of the research and how it fits in with other research. It brings the reader up-to-date on previous research that applies to the given study. In academic publications, the literature review demonstrates that the research (1) addresses a question not investigated in previous studies, (2) fills in a gap in previous research, (3) tests a model under different conditions, (4) corrects for errors in previous research, or (5) resolves conflicting research findings.

Three literature review formats are common. The review may discuss previous research in chronological order. This strategy works best if there is a discrete body of studies that build upon each other. Or the literature review may organize the discussion around key variables or concepts. An article on citizen satisfaction with the police organized its literature review around three sets of independent variables. The authors first discussed studies that linked demographic variables (age, race, gender, and education) to attitudes about the police. Then, they considered studies that investigated the effect of individual political variables, such as political efficacy. Finally, they wrote about studies that examined the effect of objective delivery of services.[3] An analogous approach organizes the discussion around theoretical or methodological approaches instead of groups of variables. Organizing the discussion around variables, theories, or methodologies works best if there are diverse studies examining the same dependent variable.

The third format may be visualized as a set of concentric circles. The discussion begins by identifying studies relating to the general research topic; this is the outermost circle. In each subsequent section, the researcher moves closer and closer to the literature that generated the specific research question. In a study on incentives and response rates to mail surveys, the author first identified literature that confirmed the widespread use of mail surveys. He next cited a source documenting problems with response rates. He worked his way through research on the effectiveness of incentives in increasing response rates, on comparisons between the effectiveness of monetary versus nonmonetary incentives, and whether incentives should be mailed with a survey or sent after the response is received. At this point the stage was set for his study on the combined effects of timing and type of incentive on response rate.[4] This format seems to work best for research that is narrowly focused and fills in a research gap or applies a model under different conditions.

The amount of space devoted to any particular article depends on its relevance to the given project. At a minimum a researcher cites an article, establishes its relevance, and summarize its major finding. For articles that directly apply to the study, the researcher gives more details. These details allow a reader to compare and contrast the research findings with other research. Such details may include information on the model (what variables were included), the methodology (characteristics of the measures, sample, or research design), the method of analysis, and the findings.

Methodology Section

The methodology section describes a study's measures, sample, and research design. The amount of detail it contains varies widely depending on the audience. At a minimum it should have enough information so that audience members can decide if the findings are credible. The final project report should be comprehensive enough for others to verify the findings or replicate the research.

The measurement section implicitly or explicitly discusses the operational definitions, the scheme for assigning numerical values, how values were combined, how indicators were combined, and evidence supporting the reliability and operational validity of the measures. Customarily, researchers report only the findings from mathematical tests of reliability, strategies for establishing content validity, and evidence of criterion validity. Audience members can infer from an operational definition whether it meets the qualitative criteria for reliability or whether they consider it operationally valid.

The discussion of the sample identifies the target population, sampling frame, sampling design, response rate, and when the data were collected. There are different ways to compute the response rate. To avoid ambiguity, the investigator should report the sample size, how many members of the sample were contacted, how many of those contacted belonged to the target population, how many refused to provide data, and how many supplied incomplete data. Statistics comparing respondents and nonrespondents should be reported. Any other sources of nonsampling error should be mentioned. For example, if researchers suspect that their sampling frame was inadequate, they should explicitly note their suspicion.

Minimal discussion is needed to describe cross-sectional or time-series designs. For a cross-sectional design, the measurement and sampling discussions are usually enough. For a time-series design, the researcher notes the beginning and ending points of the time series and the frequency of intervals. Apparent sources of nonrandom fluctuations and problems with data comparability should be mentioned.

Laboratory or field experiments require more extensive discussion, distinct from the measurement and sampling sections. The narrative should imply or state how the design and its implementation controlled for various threats to internal validity. Researchers should describe the experimental environment so that subsequent investigators can determine what, if any, features of the research conditions constituted a threat to external validity. The final project report should contain enough detail so that another researcher could repeat the experiment.

An audience should remember that quantitative investigations are not flawless. A study's purpose and limited resources require researchers to settle for imperfect measures, samples, or research designs. Similarly, researchers should not hesitate to report the flaws and limitations in their methodology. They should be sure to note shortcomings that may lead audience members to misinterpret the findings.

The Findings

The findings section reports the research results. The authors include an explicit statement of what was found and the statistical or qualitative evidence to support it. This section may include interpretation of the findings and tentative explanations for unexpected findings. To communicate the findings effectively, researchers must (1) organize the findings into a coherent presentation, (2) focus on the important findings and avoid overwhelming the audience with unnecessary detail, and (3) decide on how to present the findings, including the use of tables or graphs.

Traditionally, a study's background, model, and methodology are presented before the research results. The audience is told what questions were asked, why they were asked, and how they were asked. This prepares the audience to listen to and remember the findings. The findings are organized around related themes, variables, or questions.

The logical structure of the presentation may help focus the audience's attention. For example, when we discussed how to present the literature review we cited a study of citizen satisfaction with the police. The authors discussed how each variable was measured using the same order presented in the review of the literature, e.g., (1) demographic variables, (2) political variables, and (3) objective indicators of police performance. They continued this strategy in presenting their findings; they first looked at the effects of the demographic variables, then the political variables, and finally the objective indicators.

Just as the executive summary acknowledges that administrators may only give a report a passing glance, a report presentation should facilitate a review by hurried and distracted audience members. Presented with an uninteresting analysis or an overwhelming amount of detail, audience members may stop listening or reading. Graphs and tables, which may complement the verbal presentation, underscore important points and exhibit data efficiently. The location and the amount of space devoted to words or graphics should signal the importance of the findings. Unimportant and trivial findings do not deserve major emphasis, and researchers should not waste space on graphics that illustrate unimportant points.

A detailed discussion of a large amount of data or many numbers is not very effective. It prevents comparisons within the data and is often difficult to follow. Attractive graphics and clear explanations allow readers to access the richness of the data. Tables show exact numerical values and work well when the data presentation requires many specific comparisons. For some data presentations, tables or graphs are conventional. Examples of conventional uses of tables include data arrays (Table 14.1), summary tables of regression statistics (Table 14.2 through Table 14.5), and contingency tables. Graphs are conventional for presenting time-series data and scatterplots. Graphs permit an audience to pick out long-term trends, cycles, and seasonal fluctuations; movements over time; and differences before and after an intervention.

Careful labeling of tables and graphs is important. Spell words out, avoid abbreviations, and do not use mysterious or elaborate codes. Try to place labels on the graphic rather than in a legend. Words on and around graphics are effective in telling viewers how to focus attention on the various parts of the display.[5]

The following summarizes several points and offers additional advice on presenting data:

1. Tables or graphs should have a precise, descriptive title. A title may list the dependent variable by independent variable by control variable (if any). Alternatively, a title may summarize a major finding supported by the graphic, for example, "City homicide rates have dropped over the past twenty years."

2. All variables and their corresponding categories should be clearly labeled, and appropriate units (e.g., years) should be indicated.

3. The independent variable should be listed along the column, or top, of the chart, and the dependent variable should be listed along the row.

4. If percents are used, a percent sign (%) should be entered at the top of the columns.

5. The number of cases on which the 100 percent is based should be indicated. The total number of cases used in analysis also should be indicated.

6. Statistical measures, if any, should be listed at the bottom of the table.

7. All terms open to interpretation should be defined in the footnote section below the chart.

8. The source of the data should be indicated in the footnote section.

9. Original tables should be dated. The date of preparation of tables using secondary data should be given.

10. A good table supplements, not duplicates, the text. The table and its data should be referred to in the text, but only the highlights should be discussed.

Recommendations

Program evaluations, policy analyses, and other studies done for a legislative or administrative client may include recommendations. Analysts may be reluctant to make recommendations. Analysts are trained to accurately describe a program or policy and what it is accomplishing. Recommendations are normative statements about changes that should be made in the program or policy. An analyst may be ill-equipped or uncomfortable in making normative statements or telling clients what they should do.

Research clients on the other hand may expect recommendations. Investigators may find that making recommendations improves the probability that their studies will be used. Recommendations should be carefully formulated; they may be developed and evaluated throughout the course of a study. They should naturally follow from the research findings, e.g., a reader should be able to figure out why the recommendations were made. In making recommendations the researcher should address changes that the client agency can make, for example, recommending a change in federal program requirements will not be of any value to a local social service agency. In some cases the costs and benefits of adopting a recommendation may be identified and included. Alternatively, the researcher may suggest several options for agencies to consider. [6]

Oral Presentations of Research Findings

Researchers who do studies for administrators need oral presentation skills. Administrators, depending on their learning styles and time demands, may prefer to listen to an oral presentation and ask questions rather than read a report. They may find that an oral presentation alerts them to what to look for in the report or, conversely, the oral presentation gives them an opportunity to ask follow-up questions. Oral presentations also have distinct advantages for researchers. They can better anticipate their audience and tailor their presentation to meet its needs and interests. Audience members may feel compelled to pay attention; analogous pressure to concentrate on a written report is virtually nonexistent. The social interactions among audience members may motivate the group or individuals to discuss and follow up on the findings.

The training of researchers stresses careful attention to detail and a willingness to examine findings from various perspectives. These skills can translate into tedious, unfocused presentations. In contrast, good oral presenters avoid covering too much; they concentrate on a few important points. A presenter may fill in the details or elaborate on alternative interpretations only if an opportunity opens up in a conversation or during a question-and-answer session.

Researchers should not discount the importance of one-on-one informal discussions of findings. Their informality can be deceptive. They offer an important opportunity to develop an administrator's interest in a project. A researcher should think about what she expects from informal communication. Does she want to alert an administrator to a problem? Does she want his insights about an unexpected finding? Does she want him to think about the value of the study and how its findings can be implemented? Her ability to communicate information clearly and to understand why she wants to communicate it to a particular administrator may improve her effectiveness.

Whether you are speaking to one person, a small group, or a large, formal audience, your ability to explain your work clearly will serve you well. Professionals feel continually pressed for time. Many people are "oral learners." Others value the chance to debate information and discuss it with researchers and other administrators. As teachers we have observed that many talented students avoid making oral presentations. These students lose opportunities to present their ideas clearly, to understand listeners' questions, and to provide effective answers (as well as to hone an important skill). If you are still in school as you read this chapter, consider the value of getting practice and feedback on your speaking skills. For additional materials on oral communications, see a technical communications text.

An effective presentation requires planning and practice. To plan a presentation, researchers select the points they want to emphasize, the evidence they will use to support these points, the order in which material will be presented, and visual aids. The researchers should have determined what the audience knows about their topic, what the audience wants to get from the presentation, and how long members will listen attentively.

The traditional order for a research presentation (background, methodology, and findings) usually works well. It develops the material logically. People with training in the sciences, including the social and behavioral sciences, have come to expect it. If audience members are informed about the program or policy, identifying the study's purpose and summarizing the methodology may be sufficient. Otherwise, a description of the program or policy is necessary to put the information in context and to help audience members to follow the presentation. Except for specialized audiences, technical details are not presented in the discussion of methodology. Presenters should encourage audience members to ask for the details which interest them especially those details that affect their willingness to accept the findings.

Visual aids may be used throughout a presentation. PowerPoint slides, tables or graphs focus the presenter and the audience. To select a visual aid, consider whether it distracts attention, slows down the presentation, requires special equipment, or communicates information effectively and clearly. Too many visuals can bore an audience. Technically sophisticated presentations can be fun to put together, but they are often distracting and draw attention away from the content of the presentation. Fumbling around with unfamiliar equipment creates a serious distraction. Poor lighting can also cause problems. Detailed images leave people in the back rows squinting or feeling left out; however, the problem can be solved if a handout contains the same information.

Selecting a visual aid without thinking about the audience can result in ludicrous situations. Employees of an agency for the blind were astonished that professionals, including ophthalmologists, consistently supplemented their presentations to agency staff with slides. Most of the staff had severe visual impairments and derived no benefit from the slide shows.

Inexperienced presenters may overlook the importance of practice. A researcher who has poured over a study may feel confident in her ability to ad lib the report. Unfortunately, this person may end up bogging down on the study's minutiae or moving erratically from point to point. One should practice with an audience of colleagues, team members, or friends. Practice session observers should make sure that the major points are clearly presented, the reiteration of key points does not become repetitious or condescending, the transitions are smooth, and the equipment operates correctly. The presenter should ask the observers to ask questions about the methodology or the interpretation of the findings. Preparing answers to "hard" questions avoids the embarrassment of stumbling around. If questions challenging the quality of the research go unanswered, the effectiveness of the entire report may be undermined.

ETHICAL ISSUES

In the 1980s the issue of professional research ethics began to receive systematic attention. Respected scientists were charged with scientific misconduct, including plagiarism and making up data.[7] To see what could be done to maintain the integrity of scientific research, a joint study committee of the National Academy of Sciences, the National Academy of Engineering, and the Institute of Medicine was convened in 1989. The committee was drawn from the biological and physical sciences, and its report focuses on practices of these sciences. The social sciences and administrative researchers have not received a similar degree of scrutiny. They still operate on an honor system, which assumes that researchers behave properly. Social scientists are probably no more ethical than biological and physical scientists. The stiff competition for basic research monies may make the latter professions more susceptible to misconduct and to having their misconduct discovered and disclosed.

Our discussion relies heavily on the committee's final report. The report categorized inappropriate scientific research behavior into three categories: research misconduct, questionable research practices, and other misconduct. Research misconduct consists of acts of fabrication, falsification, or plagiarism. Questionable practices concern data retention and sharing, record quality, authorship, supervision of research assistants, statistical analysis, and release of information. Other misconduct refers to acts that are unacceptable but not unique to researchers—for example, misuse of funds, vandalism, violations of government research regulations, and conflicts of interest.[8] Our discussion focuses on research misconduct, handling research errors, and record-keeping issues—issues that affect all researchers. For a more complete picture of the issues, a reader should consult the committee's report and background papers.[9]

Research Misconduct

The study committee defined *fabrication* as making up data or results, and *falsification* as changing data or results. We assume that every reader knows that fabrication is wrong and recognizes if he or she has made up data or findings. Falsification can be a bit more ambiguous.

An easy way to falsify results is to drop cases from a dataset. Dropping selected cases can rescue a weak statistical model. The researcher may rationalize his decision. For example, he may argue that the dropped cases were tainted by measurement error and therefore do not belong in the dataset. If he thinks that measurement error occurred, he should try to confirm the measurement error. If he does not have time to track down the source of error or he cannot confirm the error, he can remove the cases. If he removes cases, he must indicate in his reports what he did, why, and its effect on the results. The more marked the effect, the more diligent he must be in alerting an audience of his decision. A decision that markedly affects the finding does not get buried in the small print.

Plagiarism is falsely presenting another's ideas or words as one's own. Quoted material should be placed in quotation marks and references cited. Closely following another author's diction is wrong. The writer should either use her own words and sentence structure or quote directly from her sources.

Relying on the works of others is inevitable in research. No one knows this better than a textbook writer. We have referenced sources that we relied on to write segments of this manuscript or that provided a unique or valuable perspective on the material. We have not referenced sources for ideas and perspectives that we know are part of the common knowledge of social science researchers.

Younger researchers seem to cite sources for their ideas more frequently than experienced researchers. This probably does not occur because of different ethical standards. Younger researchers more often work on cutting-edge topics, and they read more original research. In our experience younger researchers are more likely to listen to panels at professional meetings and to read a wider range of journals. The experienced researcher is more familiar with the subject area. He can better distinguish between unique contributions to his thinking and ideas from the general body of knowledge about the subject.

Sometimes newer researchers may feel overwhelmed by the need to avoid charges of falsification or plagiarism. This need not be the case. To avoid charges of falsifying, a researcher documents her decisions and her reasons for them. The documentation makes her decisions accessible for peer review.

Avoiding charges of plagiarism should not be difficult. Diligent referencing and avoiding using another's wording should be adequate. If a report is to be published, the writer needs to pay attention to copyright laws. Researchers must get permission from the copyright holder to reproduce graphs, tables, long quotes, and other materials, including song lyrics, poetry, and cartoons. Government documents are not covered by copyright, and their contents can be reproduced without obtaining permission. Nevertheless, the researcher should use standard referencing procedures to cite a government document.

Handling Research Errors

Error is inevitable in research. Errors arise from constraints that force investigators to compromise the quality of their efforts. Errors also arise from any one person's or group's point of view, type of knowledge, and degree of ability. The potential for error occurs throughout the research process. The study committee identified four potential sources of error: the accuracy and precision of measurements, the generalizability of experiments, the quality of the experimental design, and the interpretation of the practical significance of the findings.[10] To reduce the persistence of incorrect knowledge, researchers fully disclose their research procedures, subject their work to peer review, and acknowledge and correct errors.

Full disclosure allows others to scrutinize the research. Errors may be found by examining the research documents or attempting to replicate the research. Concealing limitations is deceptive. Research reports should clearly identify and evaluate the limitations. The more troublesome a limitation, the more emphasis it should receive.

Complete information on research procedures can overwhelm readers with details and seriously diminish a report's effectiveness. The professional standards for program evaluation recognize the competing demands of providing useful information and full disclosure. To provide useful information, the standards advise evaluators to write clearly, present information that their audiences can understand, and indicate the relative importance of their findings and recommendations. To achieve full disclosure, the standards advise evaluators to state their assumptions, their constraints, and how readers may obtain full information on research procedures, including data analysis.[11] The standards relieve evaluators of the burden of providing complete research information in every report, but they must take reasonable actions to ensure the accessibility of the database and documentation.

Peer review helps detect errors prior to a report's publication. Peer reviewers are specialists who read and evaluate manuscripts and proposals submitted to academic journals or conferences. The specialists should be conversant with the research topic. The reviewers may recommend the research for publication or presentation. They may identify weaknesses that need to be addressed—for example, additional sources for the researcher to consult, sections of the papers requiring amplification, or alternative analytical procedures. A *blind review* means the reviewer does not know who conducted the research. Blind reviews diminish personal factors that may color a reviewer's judgment.

The peer-review process primarily interests academic researchers. Nevertheless, the public relies on peer review to "protect" it from flawed research. Whether we eat red meat, drink wine, or exercise regularly may be influenced by reports of research findings. Researchers may be tempted to go directly to the mass media with interesting results, but such behavior is viewed as inappropriate. Rather, researchers are expected to release their study first to their professional colleagues who are in a better position to detect its flaws.

Researchers should not assume that full disclosure or peer review absolves them from responsibility for ascertaining that data entry and analysis procedures were conducted correctly. Apparently innocuous errors, such as miscoding data, can seriously distort the findings. If research findings differ from what is expected, researchers pour over the data to discover what went wrong. They check the raw data and computer programs. Expected results rarely receive similar attention. Richard Feynman, a winner of the Nobel Prize for physics, reminded researchers that "the easiest person to fool is yourself." He suggests two strategies to avoid fooling oneself. First, before exploring unknown relationships, researchers should analyze the data to see if typically expected relationships between variables exist. Second, researchers should identify everything that could have caused the findings. Researchers should analyze the data to eliminate these alternative explanations.[12] Some plausible explanations cannot be empirically checked because the needed data were not collected. In publishing a final report, the researchers indicate what alternative explanations they examined, what they found, and what explanations they were unable to examine and their possible effects.

In 1993, an error in a study on a treatment for the human immunodeficiency virus (HIV) made headlines. An American research team reported an apparently successful drug therapy for treating HIV. The article appeared in the prestigious scientific journal *Nature.* Six months later the researchers announced their research was in error.[13] They had in fact fooled themselves. They had misread lab results. At the 10th cycle of two experiments the virus was undetectable, but by the 30th cycle it was flourishing. A columnist in the *New York Times* cited the error as a failure of the peer-review system. He suggested that the original research was flawed.

After the paper was published, researchers in the United Kingdom tried to replicate the experiment; their findings were contrary to the original findings. The Americans repeated their experiment and identified an error. The researchers sent a letter to *Nature,* correcting their findings. The researchers also publicly announced the flaw in the original research; their announcement was reported widely in national news media.

The example implies the dynamics of research on "hot" topics. The potential rewards for finding a successful drug therapy to treat HIV and AIDS are tantalizing. They may lead researchers to be less careful in their work and to push for acceptance of their theories. On the other hand, the research is more likely to receive scrutiny and criticism. Ultimately, researchers must be willing to listen and respond to challengers. Researchers are expected to acknowledge and take responsibility for any errors they subsequently detect. The *New York Times* columnist noted, "Many other scientists, who have made mistakes in far less visible and less important research, have not been as quick to publish corrections or retractions, if they reported them at all."[14]

Saving the Data

Data must be saved and be accessible to allow research audits, replication of results, refinement of the analysis, additional analyses, or incorporation of data into contemporary research designs. Research data include completed data collection instruments, procedures for collecting and entering data, experimental procedures, data files, computer printouts, field notes, videotapes, or audio tapes.[15] With this information an investigator can reconstruct or replicate the research. Audits may be a component of ensuring scientific integrity; they can substantiate charges of falsification or fabrication. Replication may be a part of a formal audit, or it may arise from an investigator's desire to confirm the findings. Researchers may work with "old" data to see if including different variables or changing the statistical analysis affects the original results. Existing data may be incorporated into a time-series design or a cross-sectional design.

Misunderstandings can be avoided if investigators and administrators agree on who will retain data, how long they will be kept, and the conditions governing data sharing. If such agreements are not made explicit, administrators may find that they cannot access the data for further analysis. The investigators may have discarded or misplaced data, information to retrieve data may not exist, or research documents may be scattered.

A review of professional scientific societies found that six had guidelines covering data retention.[16] The guidelines commonly held the principal investigator responsible for retaining the data. The American Psychological Association recommended that data be kept for at least five years after publication. This was the most specific recommendation on length of time.

Implicit in the question of storing data is deciding who can have access to the data. As mentioned in Chapter 8, issues affecting the confidentiality of respondents must be resolved prior to sharing data. Chapter 9 reviews the costs that primary researchers may incur in data sharing. These costs include competing interests, the openness of research versus proprietary rights of the researchers, promises of confidentiality, the competence of the secondary analyst, and costs of retrieving, duplicating, and transmitting the data.[17]

Administrative research ranges from exploratory studies to studies designed to answer specific one-time questions, to longitudinal studies conducted to evaluate programs and to guide policy making. A set of specific guidelines on storage may not adequately cover all types of studies. During any study, researchers should describe research processes and decisions and label all research documents. At the end of the study, researchers should organize and store the data and documents for a reasonable amount of time.

The exact amount of time may depend on the assumed "shelf life" of the data, agency custom, research agreements, or contracts. Completed questionnaires and records, needed primarily for research audits or to correct data-entry errors, may be kept the shortest time. Data files, data dictionaries, data collection instruments, and other research protocols may be saved indefinitely. Materials relating to a published work may be kept longer than those relating to an unpublished or in-house study. Alternatively, if an agency centralizes data collected on its behalf, it should develop a mechanism to exert quality control so that it does not get overwhelmed with useless data.

SUMMARY

Before presenting their findings, researchers identify the audiences for their information. The researchers identify each audience's characteristics: how to get its attention and how to motivate its members to follow through on the report's findings and recommendations. Perusal of agency reports or listening to oral presentations may suggest how to organize information effectively for an agency.

Presentations tend to include the same material, although the amount of time or detail will vary according to agency needs. These sections are an executive summary, a statement of the study's purpose, background information, the description of the methodology and results, along with supporting analyses. The methodology section describes the measures, sample, and research design. It explicitly identifies any limitations that may change the findings. The results section includes as appropriate the supporting statistical models, tables, or graphs. Researchers may include their own observations in a report; however, they should clearly separate observations based on data and observations based on judgment. Recommendations should be based on findings.

Reports are tailored for different audiences and different needs. Reports are organized so that important information is clearly distinguishable and receives major emphasis. Nevertheless, a researcher should remember that written reports may be passed around. He should not assume that every reader will know about a study's background or design. Consequently, he needs to include necessary elaboration and documentation in the report. The methodology and findings sections in particular should be sufficiently documented so that the careful reader can make her own judgment on the adequacy of the report.

Oral presentations involve a captive audience. Still, the presenters are not guaranteed its attention. They should practice the presentation so that it flows logically and listeners can easily follow it. Visual aids should be easily seen and interpreted. If visual aids require special equipment, the presenters should know how to operate the equipment with minimal effort.

Written reports include research proposals, final project reports, and academic papers. A research proposal's sections on the problem, related background information, the literature review, and the proposed methodology are later incorporated in the final project report. Final project reports and academic papers include similar material, but the project report may be organized to facilitate the needs of administrators, who vary in their degree of interest. Final project reports rely on clear chapter headings, subheadings, and highlighting to direct a reader's attention. Technical details are placed in an appendix.

The value of empirical research depends on ethical practice. Plagiarism, fabrication, and falsification clearly violate research ethics. Although human error is inevitable, researchers should take reasonable steps to minimize errors in their work. They should check entered data, computer programs, and data analyses to make sure that their findings are reported accurately. The descriptions of the study's methodology should disclose problems encountered, design limitations, and other information needed to facilitate critical review. Where possible, researchers should subject their work to peer review. After a research report has been reviewed by peers and published, researchers are expected to acknowledge any errors they subsequently discover.

When a study is initiated, investigators and administrators need to agree on who will retain data, how long data will be kept, and any conditions governing data sharing. During the study investigators should write up descriptions of research processes and decisions and label all research documents. At the end of the study, data and documents must be organized and saved. These steps ensure that data are available for audit, replication, or further analysis.

NOTES

1. L. A. Olsen and T. N. Huckin, *Technical Writing and Professional Communication,* 2d ed. (New York: McGraw-Hill, 1991), 66–69. For an alternative approach, see D. E. Zimmerman and D. G. Clark, *The Random House Guide to Technical and Scientific Communication* (New York: Random House, 1987), 90–100.

2. See Zimmerman and Clark, *Random House Guide,* 87–90.

3. K. Brown and P. B. Coulter, "Subjective and Objective Measures of Police Service Delivery," *Public Administration Review,* January–February 1963, 50–51.

4. A. H. Church, "Incentives in Mail Surveys: A Meta-Analysis," *Public Opinion Quarterly 57* (1993): 62–63.

5. Edward R. Tufte, *The Visual Display of Quantitative Information* (Cheshire, CT: Graphics Press, 1983), 182.

6. For further discussions of recommendations see R. C. Sonnichsen, "Evaluators as Change Agents," *Handbook of Practical Program Evaluation,* ed. by J. S. Wholey, H. P. Hatry, and K. E. Newcomer, (San Francisco: Jossey-Bass), 534–548, and M. Q. Patton, *Utilization-Focused Evaluation: The New Century Text.* (Thousand Oaks: Sage Publications, 1997), 324–329.

7. For statistical information on the recent history of scientific misconduct, see "Misconduct in Science—Incidence and Significance," *Responsible Science: Ensuring the Integrity of the Research Process,* Vol. 1, Report by U.S. Committee on Science, Engineering, and Public Policy, Panel on Scientific Responsibility and the Conduct of Research (Washington, D.C.: National Academy Press, 1992), 80–97. The chapter's bibliography identifies sources for information on specific cases.

8. *Responsible Science: Ensuring the Integrity of the Research Process,* Vol. 1, 5–7. The report referred to research misconduct as "misconduct in science." The same behaviors are labeled as "research misconduct" in

the Massachusetts Institute of Technology's "Report of the Committee on Academic Responsibility," *Responsible Science: Ensuring the Integrity of the Research Process,* Vol. 2, 171.

9. *Responsible Science,* Vols. 1 and 2.

10. *Responsible Science,* Vol. 1, 56–57.

11. The Joint Committee on Standards for Educational Evaluation, *The Program Evaluation Standards: How to Assess Evaluations of Educational Programs,* 2d ed. (Thousand Oaks, CA: Sage Publications, 1994). Seventeen standards address reporting issues. The standards' application is not limited to educational studies.

12. R. P. Feynman, "Cargo Cult Science," *Surely You're Joking Mr. Feynman!* (New York: Bantam Books, 1989), 308–317.

13. Information on this case is drawn from D. Brown, "Scientists Acknowledge Flaw in 3-Drug Attack on AIDS Virus," *Washington Post,* July 23, 1993, A–3m, and L. K. Altman, "The Doctor's World: Faith in Multiple-Drug AIDS Trial Shaken by Report of Error In Lab," *New York Times,* July 27, 1993, B6. The research paper and the follow-up letter were published in *Nature* by M. S. Hirsch and his colleagues, researchers at Massachusetts General Hospital.

14. Altman, "The Doctor's World," B6.

15. *Responsible Science,* Vol. 1, 47.

16. M. S. Frankel, "Professional Societies and Responsible Research Conduct," *Responsible Science: Ensuring the Integrity of the Research Process,* Vol. 2, 33–34. None of the societies included represented professional management associations or public administration; information was collected from societies representing historians, political scientists, sociologists, and psychologists.

17. *Responsible Science,* Vol. 2, 34.

TERMS FOR REVIEW

executive summary	falsification	blind review
literature review	plagiarism	
fabrication	peer review	

QUESTIONS FOR REVIEW

The following questions should indicate whether you have a basic competency in this chapter's material.

1. A study of citizen satisfaction with an urban police force found that residents living in the downtown area are markedly less satisfied with police performance. Based on the data, the researchers' recommend that the city increase police visibility in downtown neighborhoods.

a. Identify possible audiences for the report.

b. How might an oral briefing to police administrators differ from an oral briefing to the city council?

c. Contrast the information the researcher would include in the following three presentations: (1) an oral briefing to the city council, (2) the information in the final project report, and (3) the information in an article submitted to *Public Administration Review.*

2. Create a checklist for researchers to use to make sure that they have covered the necessary topics in a presentation.

3. Examine three different quantitative research articles. Compare and contrast (1) their content and organization and (2) the literature review as presented.

4. To study the benefits of educational programs in prisons, researchers surveyed inmates at five institutions. The surveys were administered by prison staff. The surveys from one institution show little variation, and the researchers feel certain that the data were fabricated. Should the researchers include the data in their analysis? What should they say about the data in their report?

5. Write a paragraph on plagiarism. Plagiarize this text without using a direct quotation.

6. A state agency plans to contract with a victims' advocacy group to collect and analyze data on victims' experiences with criminal-justice agencies. Make recommendations on who should keep the data, where, and for how long.

PROBLEMS FOR HOMEWORK AND DISCUSSION

1. Find an article of interest in a public administration journal such as the *Public Administration Review.*

a. Write an executive summary for the article.

b. Prepare a 10 minute oral briefing describing the research.

c. Participate in a debriefing session in which one person or a team presents the research and others ask questions. The questioners should take on appropriate roles—for example, policy analysts, political representatives, community activists.

2. Read an assigned article and see if and how the authors included the information on your checklist (Review Question in the previous section).

3. Write two memos, "Guidelines for Effective Oral Presentations of Research Results" and "Guidelines for Effective Written Presentations of Research Results." Work with your classmates to develop a class guide.

4. If you have worked on a quantitative study this semester, prepare an oral presentation which includes visual aids.

5. Find out what the practices are in your academic department or agency for data storage and retention.

6. Some organizations seem to keep data and data collection instruments for a long time, much longer than would be reasonably useful. Other organizations seem to discard data and records at the earliest possible moment. Why? In what ways are these organizations likely to differ? How and why are their goals and motives likely to differ?

RECOMMENDED FOR FURTHER READING

For information on effective oral and written research presentations, refer to technical-communications texts. Most university libraries have a large number of suitable texts.

W. Strunk, Jr., and E. B. White, *The Elements of Style,* 3d ed. (New York: Macmillan, 1979) is widely recommended to writers. Chapters 2 and 5 are especially valuable. Strunk and White's book also is available at http://www .columbia.edu/acis/bartleby/strun

R. T. Torres, H. S. Preskill, and M. E. Piontek, *Evaluation Strategies for Communicating and Reporting: Enhancing Learning in Organizations* (Thousand Oaks, CA: Sage, 1996) covers strategies for effectively communicating findings and common reporting formats.

Students interested in ethical practices in research should consult *Responsible Science: Ensuring the Integrity of the Research Process,* Vols. 1 and 2, Report by U.S. Committee on Science, Engineering, and Public Policy, Panel on Scientific Responsibility and the Conduct of Research (Washington, D.C.: National Academy Press, 1992).

Deni Elliott and Judy E. Stern, eds., *Research Ethics: A Reader* (Hanover, NH: University Press of New England, 1997) was designed for use by engineers and scientists in a graduate course on research ethics. It includes articles on scientific misconduct and reporting research issues. A similar text, Francis L. Macrina, *Scientific Integrity: An Introductory Text with Cases,* 2d ed (Washington, D.C.: American Society for Microbiology, 2000) has interesting, readable chapters on record keeping, data ownership, peer review, and relationships with mentors.

Glossary

100% count. The name of one of the Decennial Census forms that is no more than two facing pages of questions. This is one way the Census Bureau avoids overburdening respondents by limiting the number and content of questions so that respondents can complete the form within a reasonable amount of time.

Accuracy. A measure of the size of the sampling error. It is how close the sample statistic is to the population parameter.

Aggregate data. Data on groups or jurisdictions such as cities, counties, or organizations that are the result of a measure of smaller units within the larger group.

Alpha level. The probability that the investigator will reject as false a true null hypothesis. The probability of committing a Type I error.

American Statistical Index (ASI). An index providing reference to data made available by federal government sources.

Analytic mapping. Plotting the values of one or more variables on a map to analyze the relationships between variables and geographic location.

Anonymity. Collecting information so that researchers cannot link any piece of data to a specific, named individual.

ANOVA (analysis of variance). The primary statistical tool for analyzing experimental data and the differences between group means. Provides information on the statistical significance of a relationship.

Applications program. Software designed for a specific activity or set of activities other than operating the computer. Statistical packages, spreadsheets, and database managers are examples of application programs.

Arithmetic mean. A measure of central tendency determined by adding together the values of a variable for all cases in the distribution and dividing this sum by the total number of cases. The use of the arithmetic mean requires that data be measured at the interval or ratio level.

Array. A listing of the values for each variable for all cases.

Associated probability. The probability that a specific value of a test statistic will occur if the null hypothesis is true; usually combined with other evidence to make inferences about hypotheses.

Asymmetric measure. A measure of association between two variables which may have different values depending on the variable designated as the independent variable.

Autocorrelation. A nonrandom relationship among the values of a variable at different time periods; may be eliminated if the researcher can identify and include an appropriate independent variable.

Average deviation. Calculation obtained by adding the absolute value of the deviation of each case from the mean of the distribution and dividing by the number of cases.

Bar graph. A graph showing the variable and its values or categories along one side and a scale for the frequency or percentage of cases along the other. The length or height of a bar indicates the number or percentage of cases with each value of the variable. The width of a bar does not have meaning.

Beta weights. Standardized regression coefficients, calculated by first standardizing the measure of all variables so that they are in standard units. Beta weights indicate the relative influence of each of the independent variables on the dependent variable.

Between-group variances. Indications of how the mean and variances of each group differ from the other groups.

Bias. A systematic difference between a sample statistic and the population parameter it is to estimate. Because of a flaw in the sampling design, its implementation, or the data collection procedure, the sample either systematically under- or overestimates the population parameter. In survey research, it is inaccurate information resulting from an improperly worded question (see below).

Biased question. A survey question that elicits inaccurate information, because it is worded in such a way that respondents are encouraged to give one answer rather than another. (See Loaded question)

Bivariate analysis. The analysis of the association between two variables.

Bivariate distribution. The joint distribution of the values of two variables.

Blind review. Review of a report or study when the reviewer does not know who conducted the research; such reviews prevent bias against the researcher by the reviewer for personal factors.

Block numbering area. Smallest statistical area defined by the U.S. Census Bureau; a rural, well-defined piece of land bounded by a street, railroad, or similar physical feature.

Box plot. A graphic technique that illustrates the median of a variable, its minimum and maximum values, quartile locations, interquartile range, and in some cases outliers. It gives a quick view of both central tendency and spread.

Case. One unit of analysis.

Case study. A type of study in which a person, program, agency, or some other unit of analysis is examined in detail. Comparisons are not usually made with other units having different values of the variables of interest.

Categorical variables. Nominal and ordinal variables.

Census of Population and Housing. The census conducted every 10 years by the U.S. Census Bureau to count the population. Required by the Constitution of the United States.

Census tract. Statistical area encompassing a large neighborhood, averaging 4,000 in population and generally with a population between 1,500 and 6,000 within county lines; every metropolitan area is mapped with census tracts.

Census undercount. The underestimating of the total size of the U.S. population. Certain groups, particularly urban minorities are more likely to be undercounted.

Chi-square. A test of statistical significance intended for use with nominal measures. Often applied to data in contingency tables.

Circle graph. A graph or pie chart showing the proportion of a total made up by each component. The size of each wedge of the circle indicates what proportion of the whole it encompasses.

Classical experimental design. A design with at least one experimental group and one control group, with subjects randomly assigned to each by the investigator, with the independent variable under the control of the experimenter, and with a pretest and a posttest.

Closed-ended question. A type of survey question in which the respondent is given a list of possible answers and is requested to select an answer or answers from that list.

Cluster sampling. Probability sampling in which groups or jurisdictions comprising groups of units are randomly selected for a sample.

Coding. The process of converting information collected by surveys or other means into symbols, usually numbers, for storage, management, and analysis.

Coefficient of determination. The proportion of variation in the dependent variable that is accounted for, statistically, by one or more independent variables. Symbolized by r^2 or R^2.

Cohort. Cases experiencing the same significant event in a specific time period.

Comparison group pretest/posttest design. A quasi-experimental design similar to the classical experimental design. However, the subjects in each group are not randomly assigned by the researcher, and the occurrence of the independent variable may not be controlled by the researcher.

Computer-Assisted Telephone Interviewing (CATI). Administration of surveys in which the interviewer reads items from a computer terminal and keys in the responses. The computer paces the interview by branching for contingency questions and keeping track of the number of calls made and which numbers were called.

Concept. An abstract or general characteristic. Concepts are often broken down into their constituent variables.

Conceptual definition. A definition of a concept or variable in terms of other concepts. Essentially a dictionary definition of a concept or variable.

Concurrent validity. A type of operational validity established by collecting and comparing two different measures at the same time.

Confidence interval. An interval placed around the value of a sample statistic in which the investigator expects the value of the corresponding population parameter to be located.

Confidence level. The confidence that an investigator can have that a sample estimate is within a specified range of the population parameter.

Confidentiality. Protection of information, so that researchers cannot or will not disclose records with individual identifiers.

Confounding variable. A variable related to both the independent and dependent variables. The confounding variable may enhance or hide the relationship between the independent and dependent variables. (See Control variables)

Constants. Elements in a research model that do not vary.

Construct validity. Validity of the definition and existence of a concept as well as the means of measuring it.

Content validity. A type of validity in which the items included in a measuring instrument or test adequately represent the content of the property that the investigator wishes to measure.

Contingency question. A type of survey question applying only to some of the sample of subjects; respondents would be directed to answer or not to answer the contingency question depending on criteria set forth earlier. (See Filter question)

Contingency table. A table showing how the distribution of one variable may change depending on the values of one or more other variables.

Control group. The group that is not exposed to the independent variable.

Control variable. A variable included in an analysis to determine whether it affects the relationship between two other variables. The values of the control variable are "held constant," while the relationship between the other two variables is analyzed.

Convenience sampling. Nonprobability sampling in which units are chosen primarily on the basis of their availability.

Correlation coefficient. Usually meant to refer to the Pearson product-moment correlation coefficient, r, it is a measure of the strength and direction of association between quantitative variables. The correlation coefficient is also a test of the goodness of fit for a regression equation.

Covariation. The patterned relationship between an independent and dependent variable.

Cramer's V. A measure of the strength of association between two nominal variables. Typically used for contingency tables, it is based on the chi-square statistic.

Criterion validity. A type of validity in which statistical evidence is used to establish validity.

Cross-sectional design. A type of study used to collect data on all relevant variables simultaneously.

Current Population Survey. An extensive survey conducted monthly in person or by telephone by the U.S. Census Bureau to gather current population labor-force data.

Cyclical variations. Changes in a variable recurring over time at regular intervals, usually of one to five years.

Database. A set of related data records storing information shared by several users for multiple purposes.

Database manager. An application program to enter, store, organize, and retrieve data. Some database managers can relate data from separate files.

Data control log. A record listing users' names and when they entered, used, or accessed data.

Data dictionary. A component of a database manager that names and describes each element and its location in the database, how it can be obtained, and the code for each value.

Data snooping. Using a computer program to relate many variables in a set of data to every other one with no model or hypothesis to guide the effort.

Decennial Census of Population and Housing. The U.S. Census Bureau's major effort of counting the population every ten years.

Deductive disclosure. When information in a research project can be used to sort through the data to identify a specific person, or otherwise compromise the privacy of the subjects.

Degrees of freedom. A value needed for many statistical tests. This is the number of parameters that can vary independently of others.

Demographic questions. Survey questions that ask about a respondent's age, race, education, occupation, religion, and so forth.

Dependent variable. One of the variables in a hypothesis that represents or measures the characteristic or event being explained. It is sometimes referred to as an "outcome" or an "effect."

Dichotomous variable. A variable that has only two possible values.

Direct relationship. A distinct relationship between variables in which an increase in the value of one variable results in an increase in the value of the other variable.

Discriminant analysis. Also known as discriminant function analysis, this is a type of statistical analysis similar to regression in which the dependent variable is a dichotomous variable.

Disproportionate stratified sampling. A probability sampling procedure in which the sample comprises a larger percentage of the units in some strata than of others.

Dummy variable. A dichotomous variable, usually called a dummy variable when included in a regression equation.

Elements. The variables that are identified for inclusion in a model.

Elements in model. Characteristics or events in a research model.

Empirical validity. Empirical demonstration that an instrument measures what it has been designed to measure. Predictive validity is a type of empirical validity.

Enumeration. The process of ordering data by variable value and grouping and counting the number of cases with similar values.

Equivalence (of a measure). Different investigators using the same measurement procedure would produce the same results. Different versions of the same measuring procedure should produce the same results.

Eta. A measure of association between a nominal or ordinal and interval variable; used with analysis of variance.

Executive summary. A section located at the beginning or conclusion of the body of a report that highlights a report's contents and often makes recommendations for a department or organization. The intended audience is the executive who has little time to read reports; thus, this section is designed to be understood independently of the report.

Expected frequency. The number of cases expected to have a particular value or set of values if the null hypothesis is true.

Experiment. A type of study in which randomly assigned subjects are exposed to a deliberately manipulated treatment and compared to other subjects, also randomly assigned, who are not exposed to the same treatment.

Experimental design. A type of design in which the researcher can assign subjects to different research groups, control who is exposed to the independent variable, when they are exposed to it, and the conditions under which the experiment takes place.

Experimental group. The group that is exposed to the independent variable.

External validity. The extent to which a study design allows an investigator to apply the findings of that study to cases not in the study. It refers to the appropriateness of extending or generalizing research findings to a group or situation beyond those involved in the study.

Fabrication. Making up, or inventing, the data or results of a research effort.

Face validity. A measure that appears to be operationally valid. Methodologists do not define it as a validation technique, and at best if offers only superficial evidence of a measure's appropriateness.

Falsification. Changing the data or results of a report or research by a researcher; may be more ambiguous than fabrication because altering information may only result in dropping a study or group to tailor the report to the researcher's needs.

F-test. A statistical test of significance that evaluates the ratio between the total amount of variance in a variable and that explained by an independent variable or set of independent variables.

Factor analysis. A statistical procedure for identifying a small number of concepts underlying a large number of related measures and for reducing the larger number of measures to a few indices. Useful in identifying measures to include in indices and in creating indices.

Factor loading. A component of factor analysis that indicates how closely each individual item is associated with the underlying concept or factor.

Factor score. The value of a case or unit of analysis for an index developed by factor analysis.

Factor score coefficient. Weights for each item in factor analysis that are multiplied by a case's value on that item to arrive at a value on the index for each case.

Federal Register. A publication of the federal government listing regulations and proposed regulations of federal agencies. Used in this text in referring to regulations of the Department of Health and Human Services regarding research on human subjects.

Field. The columns occupied by the data for a variable.

File. A set of records.

Filter question. A type of survey question used to identify respondents who should answer other questions called contingency questions. (See Contingency question)

Fixed format. Data entered in such a way that the values for each variable are in the same location in the data record for each case.

Focus group. A research tool utilizing small group interviews to obtain qualitative data as well as items for questionnaires or surveys. Group interaction is an important component of a focus group.

Forced-choice question. A closed-ended question that requires the respondent to choose among available options with no provision for an "other" or "none of the above" response.

Forms manager. A computer program that takes data entered from a terminal and sets it up in a preset format in a record.

Frequency distribution. A table listing the variable values along with the number of cases with each value.

Frequency polygon. A line graph showing the frequency distribution of quantitative variables. A horizontal axis shows the values of the variable, and the vertical axis is a scale showing the frequency. The height of the polygon at any specific place indicates the number of cases with a particular value.

Gamma. A measure of the strength and direction of association between two ordinal variables.

Geographic Information System (GIS). A system of hardware and software that integrates computer graphics with a relational database to manage data about geographic locations. A GIS can display information on maps it generates to show the relationship between variable values and location.

Geometric mean. A measure used to calculate an average for rates of change measured over several successive time periods.

Goodness-of-fit test. A statistical test used to determine how well a statistical model, such as a regression equation, corresponds to the actual data that it is to describe.

Hardware. Computer hardware is the computer itself and peripheral equipment such as disk drives, printers, and other storage and input devices.

Histogram. A graph similar to a bar chart except that both the length and width of the bar have meaning. Bars in a histogram must be adjacent. Histograms can be used for quantitative (interval and ratio) variables.

Human subject. A living individual about whom an investigator obtains data through intervention or interaction with the individual or by obtaining identifiable private information.

Hypothesis. A tentative explanation for an observation, phenomenon, or problem that can be tested by further investigation.

Hypothesis testing. Also called significance testing, it is a procedure used to determine the probability that a statement, called a null hypothesis, about variables in a population is false given data from a sample of cases selected from that population.

In-person interviewing. Also known as face-to-face interviewing. A form of survey research in which the interviewer meets personally with the respondent and records the answers as the respondent provides them.

Incidence. Common measure of morbidity referring to the number of people who get a disease over a specified period of time, usually a year. Also applicable to other situations, for example, being a victim of a crime or having an accident.

Independent variable. One of the variables in a hypothesis that is used to explain the variation in the characteristics or event of interest. It is sometimes referred to as an "input" or "cause."

Index. A set of variables combined to measure a more abstract concept.

Index number. A number expressing the relationship between two figures, one of which is the base, that is used to describe changes over time in such things as prices, production, wages, and unemployment. The Consumer Price Index (CPI) is a well-known index number.

Inferential statistics. Statistics used to estimate the value of population characteristics from sample data.

Informed consent. The principle that subjects of research must be informed of the purpose of the research and of any risks and benefits that may be incurred by participating. Before being included in the research, subjects must give their explicit consent.

Institutional Review Board (IRB). An internal body created by an institution that receives federal money for research involving human subjects; the IRB reviews all institutional research involving human subjects to determine whether it conforms to ethical practices.

Intensive interviewing. An in-depth, lengthy, and extensive interview of respondents. It usually requires a skilled interviewer using an unstructured format. Typically a study using this technique involves relatively few respondents with information not possessed by others.

Internal consistency. The extent to which all items in a measuring procedure relate to the concept measured.

Internal validity. The extent to which a design provides evidence that a specific independent variable caused a change in a dependent variable.

Internet surveys. A type of research design where surveys are posted on the Web or sent as part of an email message.

Interquartile range. The range of values encompassing the middle one-half of the observations in an ordered distribution.

Interrater reliability. The extent to which two different observers using the same instrument to measure a concept obtain the same results.

Interrupted time-series design. A quasi-experimental design incorporating an independent variable other than time into the time-series design. Several measures of the dependent variable are taken before and after the occurrence of the independent variable.

Interrupted time-series design with comparison group. An interrupted time series is compared to another time series that is not interrupted or is interrupted at a different time.

Interval scales. A measurement scale that measures quantitative differences between values of a variable. Each unit of the variable has the same quantitative value as every other unit. Equal-distance intervals are measured between values of the variable.

Inverse relationship. A distinct relationship between variables in which an increase in the value of one variable results in a decrease in the value of the other variable.

Irregular fluctuations. Changes over time in a variable that cannot be attributed to long-term trends, or cyclical or seasonal variations.

Lagging. A process in which the value of the independent variable is measured at an earlier time than the value of the dependent variable.

Lambda. A measure of association between two nominal level variables.

Level of analysis. Either individual, in which case the data are from individuals, or aggregate, in which case the measures are of group characteristics.

Likert scaling. A method of index construction, also known as summated rating. A numerical value is given to the response to each of a number of items and the values are added or averaged to obtain a value for each case.

Linear model. A model that assumes that the relationship between the variables can be appropriately described by a straight line; if the linear model is appropriate, then a linear regression equation may be calculated.

Linear regression model. The relationship between variables when the regression equation is linear, $y = ax + b$.

Literature review. Section of a report that establishes the value of a research project and how it fits in with other research. It may illustrate that the research addressed a question not investigated in previous studies, filled a gap in previous research, tested a model under different conditions, corrected for errors in previous research, or resolved conflicting research findings.

Loaded question. A biased question worded in such a way that the respondent perceives that only one way of answering is acceptable. (See Biased question)

Logistic regression. Regression model in which the dependent variable is dichotomous. The regression equation calculates the probability that the dependent variable will have one of two values for given values of the independent variable or variables.

Logistic regression coefficient. Measures the predictive capability of the independent variables in a logistic regression.

Longitudinal design. A type of study utilized to collect information over time on each variable for two or more distinct time periods.

Long-term trend. General direction of movement in the value of a variable over a number of years, usually 5 to 20.

Macrodata. With reference to U.S. Census data, these are data aggregated by political jurisdiction or statistical geographical area. Data from individuals are not available.

Mailed questionnaires. A type of survey in which respondents are contacted by mail and are asked to fill out a questionnaire and return it by mail.

Mainframe computer. A very large computer capable of handling large amounts of data and performing extensive analysis. Most large agencies and universities have at least one mainframe computer.

Matrix. A listing of data in columns and rows. The rows constitute cases and the columns are fields containing the information for variables. The vertical dimension is related to the number of cases and the horizontal dimension to the number of fields.

Measurement. The process of assigning numerals to the values of variables according to a set of rules.

Measurement scales. Includes four scales of measuring data: nominal, ordinal, interval and ratio scales.

Measures of association. Statistics that measure the strength and nature of the relationship between variables. Common ones include lambda, gamma, and the Pearson product-moment correlation coefficient (Pearson's r).

Measures of central tendency. Measures indicating the value of a distribution that is representative, most typical, or central. These measures include the mode, median, and arithmetic mean.

Measures of dispersion. Measures that indicate the extent to which values in a distribution are different from each other. These include the range, interquartile range, percentiles, variance, and standard deviation.

Median. A measure of central tendency. It is the value of the case marking the midpoint of an ordered distribution of values. The median requires ordinal or quantitative level measurement.

Median absolute deviation. A measure of dispersion calculated by determining the average deviation of a set of cases from the median of the distribution.

Meta-analysis. A systematic technique utilized by researchers to analyze a set of existing studies. It is conducted to draw general conclusions from several empirical studies and to identify hypotheses that merit further testing.

Microdata. With reference to U.S. Census data, a sample of individual records with all identifying information removed.

MIS. Management Information System.

Mode. A measure of central tendency. It is that value of a variable that occurs most frequently.

Model. A representation of reality, it delineates certain aspects of the real world as being relevant to the problem under investigation and makes explicit the relationships among these aspects; it enables the formulation of empirically testable propositions regarding the nature of these relationships.

Model building. The process of constructing a research model, including stating the research question, and selecting elements, and postulating the nature of their relationship.

Multicollinearity. A condition existing when independent variables in a regression equation are closely related to each other.

Multiple regression. Regression analysis in which more than one independent variable is included in the regression equation and analyzed.

Multistage sampling. Probability sampling that proceeds in at least two stages. In each stage a grouping of units is selected as a sample and then a smaller grouping of units is selected as a sample from the first group.

Multivariate analysis. The statistical analysis of the relationships among two or more variables.

New error. Used in the calculation of Lamba, a measure of association. Equal to the non-modal responses for each category of the independent variable.

Nominal scales. Scales that categorize and label the values of a variable. The investigator can group cases by the variable categories but cannot order them.

Nonexperimental design. Designs that do not control for the threats to internal validity.

Nonlinear relationship. A distinct relationship between variables occurs, but the relationship cannot be described by a straight line.

Nonprobability sampling. Sampling done in such a way that the probability that any unit or set of units will be selected for the sample is unknown.

Nonrandom variations. Variations that are brought about by a condition or set of conditions that can be identified.

Non-response rate. The proportion of people who do not respond to a survey.

Nonsampling error (bias). Error resulting from a flaw in the sampling design itself or from faulty implementation.

Normal curve. A theoretical distribution with the following characteristics: it is bell-shaped and symmetrical; the mode, mean, and median have the same value; and a fixed proportion of the observations lies between the mean and any other value.

Null hypothesis. A hypothesis stating that two variables are not related in the population. It is the null hypothesis that is actually tested by tests of statistical significance.

Null relationship. Relationship that occurs if a change in the independent variable is as likely to coincide with an increase as with a decrease or no change in the dependent variable; a value of 0.00 for a measure of association designates a null relationship.

Numerical variables. Variables measured on an interval or ratio scale.

Observational design. A design for a study in which phenomena are observed and recorded as they occur; the investigator has no control over cases or the setting and does not manipulate any variables.

Open-ended question. A type of survey question in which respondents are required to provide their own answers without a listing of possibilities from the researcher.

Operational definition. Detail of the procedures for measuring a concept or variable and for assigning a value to a case for the variable.

Operational validity. The extent to which measuring procedures or instruments actually measure what they have been devised to measure.

Ordinal scale. A measuring scale that orders the values of a variable and allows an investigator to order cases based on their variable value. Ordinal scales do not, however, measure the quantitative difference between cases.

Original error. Indicates how much error there is in predicting the distribution of the dependent variable without knowing the values of an independent variable.

Outliers. In regression analysis these are data points well outside the range of the remainder of the data.

Panel design. A type of longitudinal design examining the same cases individually at each successive period; may reveal which individual cases change.

Parameter. A characteristic of a population. Analysts draw samples in order to estimate the values of population parameters.

Partial regression coefficient. Indicates the effect of the independent variable on the dependent variable while controlling for all other variables in the equation.

Pearson's r. A measure of the strength and direction of the association between two interval level variables.

Peer review. A process in which individuals well versed in a particular topic read and evaluate manuscripts and proposals submitted to academic journals, conferences, or funding agencies to detect errors or weaknesses prior to the publication of the materials or beginning of research.

Percentage. A relative frequency calculated by dividing the frequency of cases with a value of a variable by the total number of cases and then multiplying this result by 100.

Percentage change. A relative frequency that converts to a percentage the amount of change in the value of a variable from one time to another for the same case.

Percentage difference. The difference between the columns in the percent of cases in a row (category of the dependent variable). Calculated by subtracting across the columns of a contingency table; can be used to analyze a relationship between two variables.

Percentage distribution. A table showing the values of a variable and the percentage of all cases having each value.

Percentile. A value below which a certain percent of the ordered observations in a distribution are located.

Perfect relationship between two variables. Relationship in which a change in the independent variable is always associated with the same change in the dependent variable.

Pie chart. A visual chart represented by a complete circle, indicating a quantity that is sliced into a number of wedges. The graph conveys what proportion of the whole is accounted for by each component and facilitates visual comparisons among parts of the whole.

Pilot study. A small study designed to test the adequacy of a proposed data collection strategy.

Plagiarism. The presentation of another's ideas as one's own.

Population. A total set of units sharing at least one characteristic. It is from this set that the sample is selected.

Population variability. The extent to which members of a population differ from each other on the variables in which an investigator is interested.

Power. Refers to the probability that a test of significance results in the rejection of a false null hypothesis; it is related to the sample size and the strength of a relationship.

Practical significance. The extent to which a statistical finding is important.

PRE. Proportional Reduction in Error. A measure that indicates how much knowing the distribution of the independent variable reduces the error in predicting the distribution of the dependent variable.

Predicted value. In regression analysis it is the value of the dependent variable for a case computed by using the regression equation.

Predictive validity. A type of validity that requires that a measure correctly predicts a future outcome.

Pretest. An initial test of a proposed questionnaire given to a small group of subjects who represent common variations found in the target population.

Prevalence. Common measure of morbidity referring to the total number of people who have a disease at a given time.

Privacy. An individual's ability to control the access of other people to information about himself.

Probability sampling. A type of sampling in which each unit of the population has a known, nonzero chance of being in the sample.

Program file. A computer file containing instructions to the computer for running a program.

Proportion. A relative frequency determined by dividing the number of cases with a value of a variable by the total number of cases. A proportion is a decimal figure that is less than 1.

Proportionate stratified sampling. Probability sampling in which the same percentage of the units in each strata is selected for the sample.

Purposive sampling. Nonprobability sampling in which units are selected because the investigator judges that the units somehow are representative of the population. Also known as judgmental or expert-choice sampling.

Qualitative research. A general term referring to research involving detailed, verbal descriptions of characteristics, cases, and settings. Qualitative research usually involves fewer cases investigated in more depth than quantitative research.

Quality assurance. Assurance of proper delivery of services and completion of forms, case records, and applications. Important in the public sector.

Quality control. A set of procedures used by organizations to monitor the quality of goods produced or services delivered and to take corrective action if quality drops below a set standard. Probability sampling is important in quality-control programs.

Quantitative research. A general term referring to research in which values in which values of variables are characterized by numbers or symbols. Typically, many variables are measured for a large number of cases. Data are summarized and analyzed with statistical techniques.

Quantitative scales. A more inclusive term referring to both interval and ratio scales.

Quartile. Specification of a range of values in four parts; the first quartile is that value below which 25 percent of the cases are found. The second quartile is the median, the third quartile is the value below which 75 percent of the cases are found, and the fourth quartile is the maximum value in the distribution.

Quasi-experimental design. A design having some but not all of the characteristics of the experimental design. Often used in applied-research situations when the control necessary for a true experiment is not possible or practical.

Question sequencing. Arranging the questions in a survey in such a way as to obtain the most information and to encourage the maximum number of respondents to answer.

Questionnaire design. Question wording, sequencing, placement, and length of the physical layout of the questionnaire or survey.

Quota sampling. Nonprobability sampling in which the units are chosen for the sample in the same proportion as their characteristics are believed to exist in the population.

Random assignment. Subjects are assigned in such a way that there is no systematic difference between the groups. Each subject has the same chance as any other subject of being in either the experimental group or the control group.

Random digit dialing. A method of selecting a sample of respondents for telephone interviewing. A set of telephone numbers is selected in such a way as to result in a representative sample.

Random variations. Minor, unexplained variations which are not associated with long-term trends, cyclical variations, or seasonal variations.

Randomized posttest design. An experimental design with at least two groups and a posttest but no pretest.

Randomly related. Two variables are independent of each other and not related to each other.

Range. A measure of dispersion giving the quantitative distance between the lowest and the highest values in an ordered distribution.

Rate. A relative frequency used to standardize the occurrence of some event. Rates are calculated by dividing the frequency of occurrence of an event by a total frequency count, such as the population of a jurisdiction in which the events take place. The result is multiplied by a base number.

Ratio. A relative frequency found by comparing the number of cases with one value of a variable with the number of cases with another value of the variable.

Ratio scale. A measurement scale that allows researchers to rank objects on a scale and determine the exact difference between them, and also to use ratios to describe relationships between the values of the scaled objects. Ratio scales have an absolute zero point. In administrative work almost all scales that are interval are also ratio.

Reactive effects of experimental arrangements. The fact that study situations often are necessarily artificial, and this study setting itself may affect the outcome.

Record. The data from a case or unit of analysis. A line of data in a computer file.

Rectangular array. A method of organizing data in which each case or unit of observation is represented by a row, each variable by one or more columns, and each row is the same length.

Regression coefficient. The value in the regression equation (b or slope) that indicates how much the dependent variable changes with a unit increase in the independent variable.

Regression constant. Often symbolized by the letter a. It is a component of the regression equation and is added to the value of the slope times the value of the independent variable to obtain a predicted value for the dependent variable. It is also the Y intercept and is the value produced by the regression equation when the value of X is zero.

Regression equation. An equation computed from the data in a specific dataset for a straight line that best describes the set of data points. The equation gives a formula relating the values of the independent and dependent variables.

Relational database. A set of files in which two or more files have some variables in common allowing information from separate files to be linked for analysis and reports.

Relationship in model. The links between elements in a research model.

Relative frequency. The number of times that a value of a variable occurs divided by another frequency count such as the total number of cases, the frequency of another value of the same variable, or the frequency of a second variable. Percents, ratios, and rates are all relative frequencies.

Reliability. The degree of random error associated with a measurement. Reliable measures are those that produce consistent or dependable data.

Research design. General or specific plans that guide decisions as to what data to gather, from whom, when and how to collect the data, and how to analyze the information.

Research methodology. The steps needed to conduct a research model, including how to collect data describing each variable and how to analyze the relationships among the variables.

Research records. The data for the observations in a research project, individually or in aggregate.

Residual. The difference between a value of the dependent variable for a case predicted by the regression equation and the actual value of the variable for that case.

Respondent. Someone from whom we collect information, usually through survey research procedures.

Response rate. The percentage of survey respondents from a sample who respond to a questionnaire or who are interviewed.

Response set. The tendency of survey respondents from a sample who respond to a questionnaire or who are interviewed.

Sample. A subset of units selected from a larger set of the same units. The subset is used to tell the analyst something about the larger set, the population.

Sampling bias. A systematic misrepresentation of the population by the sample. It usually comes about because of a flaw in the design or implementation of a sampling procedure.

Sampling design. The set of procedures for selecting the units from the population to be in the sample.

Sampling error. The difference between a sample estimate and the population parameter that comes about because a probability sampling procedure has been used.

Sampling fraction. The percentage of the population units selected for the sample.

Sampling frame. A list of the specific set of units from which the sample is actually drawn.

Sampling unit. A unit or set of units considered for selection at a stage of sampling.

Scale. A measurement procedure that assigns a value to a case based on how that case fits into a pattern of indicators.

Scatterplot. A graph of plotted points where the dependent variable (Y) is placed on the vertical axis and the independent variable (X) is placed along the horizontal axis. Examining the scatterplot is useful in deciding whether a linear model should be used to summarize the relationship between the two variables.

Schematic model. A model that illustrates the important links and relationships between elements with lines and other drawings.

Seasonal variations. Changes in a variable over time occurring regularly during certain times of the year.

Secondary data. Existing data that investigators have collected for a purpose other than the given study.

Selection bias. The introduction of error due to systematic differences in the characteristics between those selected and those not selected for a given study.

Sensitivity (of measure of association). A criterion for selecting a measure of association. The ability of a statistic to detect small differences in the strength of a relationship by assigning different numerical values to relationships that may have slight, even subtle, differences in strength.

Simple random sampling. Probability sampling done in such a way that the following are true: (a) each unit of the population has the same, nonzero probability of being selected for the sample as every other unit; (b) the selection of one unit of the population does not affect the probability that some other unit will be selected.

Skew. A characteristic of a frequency distribution. If the mode or median have values different from the arithmetic mean, the distribution is skewed. A negatively skewed distribution is one in which the median is larger than the mean; in a positively skewed distribution the median is smaller than the mean.

Skewed distribution. Occurs when a distribution has a few extreme values, either high or low, affecting the arithmetic mean. A distribution will be skewed to the left, negatively, if the extreme values are low, and to the right, or positively, if the extreme values are high.

Skip interval. The number of units in a list to be skipped when drawing a systematic sample.

Snowball sampling (referral sampling). A type of nonprobability sampling where members of a population cannot be easily located by other methods and where the members of a population know or are aware of each other.

Software. Computer programs and instructions necessary for computers to operate and carry out various tasks.

Somers' d (dyx). An asymmetric measure of association for ordinal variables.

Specification (of a relationship). When someone wants to learn if the original relationship changes under different circumstances or if other variables are considered.

Sponsored research. Research financially supported by government agencies, foundations, or other organizations.

Spreadsheet. A rectangular matrix of rows and columns.

Spreadsheet program. An application program that displays a matrix on the computer screen and allows the user to enter labels, data, and mathematical formulas into the cells of the matrix. The user can manipulate data in the matrix and perform statistical and mathematical analysis.

SPSS. Statistical Package for the Social Sciences. A set of computer programs for the management and analysis of data. The programs are integrated, making it possible to conduct numerous types of analysis once the data have been entered and accessed.

Spurious relationship. An apparent relationship between two variables that exists because of the association of a third variable to each of the original two.

Stability.   The ability of a measure to yield the same results time after time, if and only if what is being measured has not changed.

Standard deviation.   A measure of dispersion. It is calculated by squaring the difference between the arithmetic mean of a distribution and the value of each case, summing these values, dividing by the number of cases, and taking the square root of the result. The standard deviation is the square root of the variance. It is used in numerous other statistical measures and tests.

Standard error.   A statistical measure of the size of the sampling error for a large number of probability samples of the same size. It is normally distributed.

Standard error of the slope.   An estimate of how much the regression coefficient, b, is likely to vary from sample to sample.

Standard score.   Also called a z-score, this expresses the values of a distribution in terms of units of the standard deviation of the distribution. It is calculated by subtracting the arithmetic mean from the value of a particular case and dividing the result by the standard deviation.

Statistic.   The value of a characteristic of a sample. Investigators use sample statistics to estimate population parameters.

Statistical package.   An application program containing several subprograms to perform statistical analysis of data.

Statistical Reference Index (SRI).   An index providing reference to data made available by sources other than the federal government.

Statistical significance.   The probability that the value of a statistic could have been found from a population in which the value of the corresponding parameter was much different.

Statistically significant relationship.   A relationship between variables in a sample that a statistical test suggests would also be found if the entire population from which the sample was selected could be studied.

Strata.   Subgroups within a larger population.

Stratified random sampling.   Probability sampling in which the population is divided into subgroups (strata) from each of which a probability sample is selected. Stratified sampling can be either proportionate or disproportionate.

Structured interviewing.   Surveys in which respondents are asked the same questions, in the same order, and in the same way. A set list of questions is provided either in questionnaire form or by an interviewer.

Subjects at risk.   A research design in which participants could experience negative consequences. Such consequences could range from permanently harmful effects to less significant reactions such as anger or humiliation.

Survey of Income and Program Participation (SIPP).   A survey conducted by the U.S. Census Bureau and the Social Services Administration to gather data on American people's income, employment, and receipt of government assistance.

Survey research.   A type of data collection procedure in which investigators question individual subjects in face-to-face interviews, over the telephone, or by sending a questionnaire to them through the mail.

Symbolic model.   A model using words, mathematical equations, or computer programs to illustrate the links and relationships among elements.

Symmetric measure.   A measure of association between two variables that has the same value no matter which variable is designated as the independent variable.

Systematic sampling.   Probability sampling using a list of population elements. The investigator selects units from the list after calculating a skip interval and randomly determining a starting place in the list.

***t*-test.**   A test of statistical significance requiring an interval dependent variable. It has wide application but is often used to test whether the difference between the arithmetic averages of two groups is significant.

Target population.   The set of units to which investigators wish to apply their results.

Test-retest.   A technique that requires that an instrument or test be administered to a subject at two points in time. This establishes the stability of a measure.

Text editor.   A computer program allowing the user to enter information, store, edit, and retrieve it for use.

Threats to external validity.   Factors that limit the ability to apply the findings of a study to cases not involved in the study.

Threats to internal validity.   A series of factors that could be the cause of a change in a dependent variable and represent alternatives to the independent variable of interest.

Time series.   A set of data obtained at regular intervals for a single case; a type of line graph with the units of time displayed along the horizontal axis and the values of a variable or frequency of an occurrence on the vertical axis.

Time-series design.   A design that collects data at several times at regular intervals on a quantitative measure.

True experiment.   A study in which the experimenter can assign subjects to either an experimental or control group and can manipulate the value and occurrence of the independent variable.

Type I error.   Rejecting a null hypothesis as false when, in fact, it is true.

Type II error.   Accepting a null hypothesis as true when, in fact, it is false.

Unit of analysis.   The object whose characteristics are measured and in which the analyst is interested.

Univariate analysis.   The statistical analysis of one variable at a time.

Univariate distribution.   The distribution of the values of a single variable.

Variable.   A measurable characteristic that can have more than one value. Researchers measure the values of the variables of the units of analysis.

Variance.   A measure of dispersion and variation. It is calculated by squaring the difference between the arithmetic mean of distribution and the value of each case, summing these values, and dividing the result by the number of cases. The variance is the square of the standard deviation. It is used in numerous other statistical measures and tests.

Vital records.   Records that include primarily vital statistics.

Vital statistics.   Information collected by federal, state, and local governments on births, deaths, marriages, divorces, abortions, communicable diseases, and hospitalizations.

Voluntary research participation.   When potential research subjects have clear and realistic information on the benefits and risks of participation, and have the ability to withdraw from a study at any time.

Weighting.   A process by which different items are weighted differently to have a different influence on the index.

Within-group variances.   The amount that the members within an experimental or control group differ from that group's mean.

Index

Accuracy, 149–156, 158, 161
Administrative issues, 243–244, 256–259
Alpha levels, 363–367, 372, 378
Alternative forms technique, 113
Analytic mapping, 319
Anonymity, 251–254
ANOVA, 410–416
Applications programs, 316–319
Archival information, 39
Area sampling, 143–144
Arithmetic mean, 337–338, 348
Associated probability, 368, 372, 378
Association, measures of, 389, 392–410, 415, 424–426. *See also* Relationships
   bivariate, 389–410, 414–416, 428
   logic of, 398–400
   for multiple regression, 439
   multivariate, 389–394
   nominal and ordinal, 415
   statistics and, 409–410
   symmetric and asymmetric, 403, 415
Asymmetric measure, 403, 415
Attitude questions, 210
Attitude scales, 292
Autocorrelation, 450–451
Average deviation, 343
Averages, 336–339

Bar graphs, 323–325, 348
Behavior questions, 210
Beta weights, 440–442, 452
Between-groups variance, 411–413
Biased questions, 225, 237
Bivariate analysis, 428
Bivariate distribution, 316
Blind review, 476

Block numbering area, 281
Box plot, 346, 348

Case control design, 88
Case studies, 25, 39–42, 48
Categorical variables, 106
Causality, 89–90
   obtaining evidence for, 66
   regression and, 451
CD Rom, 269, 270
Census Bureau, 265, 272–275, 286
Census data, 272–284
   comparability among, 280–284
   in current population survey, 280
   of population and housing, 276–279
   uses of, 280–284
Census tract, 281
Census undercount, 277
Central tendency measures, 334–339, 348
   guidelines for selection of, 338–339
Chi-square, 360, 367–369, 378, 403
   distribution, 385. Table 12.13
Circle graph, 325–326
Class intervals, 321
Closed-ended questions, 211, 215–217, 237
Cluster sampling, 137, 142–146, 161
   application of, 145
Coding, 316, 357–358
Coefficient of determination, 439
Cohort, 37, 88
Common Rule, 254–256
Comparison group design, 75–77
Computer-aided Telephone Interviewing (CATI), 180, 200
Computer data files, 316–319

Computer models, 12, 19
Computer programs, 316–319
Computers, 316 , 347
   in data management, 316–319, 347
   software for, 316–319, 347
Concept, 98, 127, 293
Conceptual definition, 98, 127, 293
Concurrent validity, 122–123, 128
   application of, 122–123
Confidence, 152–157, 161
   interval, 152
   level, 152
Confidentiality, 251–254
Confounding variable, 16
Constants, 13–14
Consumer Price Index (CPI), 32, 291, 307–308
Content validity, 118–122, 128, 293–294
Contingency questions, 217–218, 237
Contingency tables, 359, 374, 389–392, 401–402, 415
   comparison of, 392
   strength of association in, 397–398
Continuous variables, 106
Control group, 66–68, 75–76
Control variables, 16, 391–392, 404–409, 451
   effects of, 409, 415
Convenience sampling, 146–147
Correlation coefficient, 432–433
Covariation, 15
Cramer's V, 369, 398, 403, 407–408
Criterion validity, 122, 125, 126, 128
Cross-sectional design, 26–32, 48, 171, 265–266, 478
   application of, 31
Current Population Reports, 272, 280

Current Population Survey (CPS), 272–273, 280
Curvilinear relationships, 402–403
Cyclical variations, 33–34

Data. *See also* Census data; Information; Statistics; Vital statistics
accuracy of, 102
collection of, 196–199
computers and, 316–319, 347
displaying of, 319–328
management of, 316–319, 347
organization of, 347, 357–358
preparation of, 347, 357–358
secondary, 264. *See also* Census data; Vital statistics
access to, 267–270
evaluation of, 271–272
storage of, 264–265
Data arrays, 319–320
Data dictionary, 357–358
Data fields, 317
Data files, 317
Database
access to, 265, 267–270
evaluation of, 271–272
management of, 317–318
quality of, 272
Database management system (DBMS), 317–318
Datasets, 8
Decennial Census of Population & Housing, 28, 272, 276–279, 283
DECIDE technique, 212, 230, 232–234
Deductive disclosure, 253
Degrees of freedom (df), 374, 413
Demographic questions, 230
Dependability, 107–108
Descriptive designs, 24–48, 65
causality in, 55–56
external validity of, 57–58
Descriptive statistics, 315
Designs. *See also specific types of*
contamination of, 59, 61–62, 91
definition of, 24
for description, 24–48
for explanation, 55–92
to fill in details, 37–44
non-experimental, 25
for relationships and trends, 26–37
Direct observation, 39
Direct relationship, 15–16
Dispersion measures, 339–345, 348

Disproportionate stratified sampling, 141–142
application of, 142
Distributions, 320–322
describing characteristics of, 333–334
skewed, 339–340
Documents, 39
Dummy variables, 436

Elements, 3, 19
identification of, 6–10
Enumeration, 320
Equivalence, 108, 109
Errors
in measurement scale, 109–111
new, 399–400
nonsampling, 150, 159–160, 162
original, 399–400
proportional reduction in, 399, 403
sampling, 150, 159, 162
standard, 152
Types I and II, 359, 363–367, 369, 372, 378
Eta, 388, 413, 414
Ethical issues, 243–260
Executive summary, 465–467, 479
Experimental design, 57, 66–74, 90–92
classical, 66–74
Experimental group, 66–68
Experimental mortality, 58, 60, 62
Explanation, designs for, 55–92
Exploratory Data Analysis (EDA), 347–348
External validity, 57, 62–66

Fabrication, 474, 479
Face validity, 118, 125, 128
Factor analysis, 303–306, 307–308
Factor loading, 305
Factor score coefficient, 306
Factual questions, 210
Falsification, 474, 479
Filter questions, 217–218
Fluctuations, irregular, 33, 34–35
Focus group, 42–44, 48, 193–196, 201
Forced choice questions, 215
Fractions, 329–330
Frequency distributions, 320–322, 329, 338, 348
line graphs, 327–328
Frequency polygon, 327
F-test, 390, 412–413, 415–416, 418

Gallup Poll, 134
Gamma, 401, 403–404

Geographic Information System (GIS), 316, 318–319, 347
Geometric mean, 338
Goodness of fit test, 432
Graphical displays, 323–328, 348
Graphs, 315, 323–328, 348. *See also specific types of*

Histogram, 323–325, 348
Human subject, 255, 259
Humphreys study, 246
Hypothesis, 14–15, 20, 361–364, 369, 378

Incidence, 332–333
Index, 291–293, 295, 307
Index number, 307
Indicators, 291–308. *See also specific indicators*
Indices, 291–293. *See also types of*
construction of, 292–296, 307–308
content validity of, 293–295
examples of, 299–303
factor analysis and, 303–306, 308
selection of items for, 293–294
standardized indicators for, 296–299, 308
types of, 295–297
validity of, 293–295
weighting of items in, 295–297, 307–308
Inferential statistics, 315–316, 360,
Information. *See also* Data
interpreting and filling in of, 40–41
sources of, 39
Informed consent, 243–244, 247–249, 254, 259
Institutional review board (IRB), 254–256
Instrumentation, 58, 61, 62
Intensive interviewing, 189–193, 201
Internal consistency, 111–113
Internal validity, 57–58
Internet, 267, 269–270, 286
Internet surveys, 186–187, 200
Interquartile range (IQr), 341–342, 348
Interrater reliability, 113
Interrupted time series design, 78–84
application of, 83–84
with comparison group, 82–84
Interval scales, 104–106, 308
Interval statistics, 370

Interview,
    in-person, 187–195
intensive (unstructured), 189–193, 196
    practices of, 190–193
    structured, 188–189, 201
    telephone, 179–186
Interviewer training, 190–193
Inverse relationship, 15, 393–395
IQ scores, 105
Irregular fluctuations, 33–34

Job knowledge testing, 122
Job satisfaction index, 295–296
Job testing, 119–120
Judgement sampling, 147

Knowledge questions, 210

Lagging a variable, 436, 456
Lambda, 405, 406
Library information, 7–8, 19
Library research, objective of, 7
Likert scaling index, 299–303, 308
Line graphs, 327–328, 348
Linear model, 430–432, 448–450, 452
Linear regression equation, 428–435
    statistical significance and, 442
Literature review, 468–469, 479
Loaded questions, 225
Logistic regression, 445–447, 452
Longitudinal design, 32, 48
Long-term trends, 33–36
Lottery method, 137

Macrodata, 281
Maps, 5, 11
Market research, 201
Matching, 67–68
Mathematical models, 12, 20
Means, 337–338, 348
Measurement, 102
    operational validity of, 116–126
    reliability of, 107–116, 127–128
    scales for, 102–107, 127
    sensitivity of, 126–127
    transforming of, 295
    variables in, 106
Measures of association, 359–360,
    388–389, 392–398, 400–404,
    407–408, 409–410, 415, 439
Measures of dispersion, 339–345, 348
Median, 335–337, 348
Meta analysis, 44–47, 48
Microdata, 281
Milgram studies, 246–247
Mode, 334, 348

Models, 3–6, 19–20. *See also* Designs
    application of, 4
    building of, 6–10
    components of, 13–18
    elements in, 3
    limits, 12–13
    pretesting of, 8–10
    relationship in, 3
    sample, 4
    types of, 11–12
    use of, 3–6
Monotonically increasing or
    decreasing, 403
Motive questions, 210
Multicollinearity, 442–445
Multiple regression, 435
    equation, 435–438
    measure of association for, 439
    statistical significance and, 442
Multistage sampling, 142-144
    application of, 145
Multivariate analysis, 29, 316, 348, 414
Multivariate relationships, 427
Multivariate statistics, 316

Nominal association measures, 393,
    397, 403–404, 415
Nominal scales, 103, 367
Nonlinear relationship, 15, 402–403
Nonprobability sampling, 136,
    146–149
Nonrandom variation, 34–35
Nonsampling error, 150, 159–160, 162
Normal curve, 343–345
Null hypothesis, 16, 361–364, 369,
    370, 372, 378–379, 434, 442
    rejection of, 362–364, 378
Null relationship, 393–395, 397–398,
    409–410, 415
Numerical variables, 104–105
Nuremburg Code, 245

Observational design, 88–89, 92
One hundred percent count, 277
Open-ended questions, 175, 199,
    211–215, 237
Operational definitions, 98–102,
    127, 293
    formulation and evaluation of,
    98–102
    importance of, 100
Operational validity, 116–126, 272
Opinion questions, 210
Ordered categorical variables, 106
Ordinal association measures, 393,
    397, 400–403, 403–404,
    408–409, 415

Ordinal scales, 103–104, 340
Original error, 399–400
Outliers, 434–435, 452

Panel design, 32, 36–37, 48
Parameters, 135, 346, 360, 365
Partial regression coefficient, 436
Participant observation, 39
Pearson's r, 432
Peer interaction, 6–7
Peer review, 476, 479
Percentage change, 329–330, 337
Percentage difference, 390
Percentage distribution, 320–321, 329,
    390–392
Percentages, 321, 329, 347
Percentile, 341–342
Perfect relationship, 393–395,
    397–398, 401, 409–410
Periodicity, 139
Physical artifacts, 39
Physical models, 11
Pie charts, 325–326
Pilot study, 232–236, 238
Pilot test, 8–9, 19
Plagiarism, 475, 479
Planning, 1–2
Population, 135,136, 161
    estimates of, 280, 281
    size of, 154–155
    survey of, 276–280
    variability within, 150, 154
Potential experience, 436
Power, 158, 364
Practical significance, 361, 377–378
Predictive validity, 123–124, 128
    application of, 124
Pretest, 64, 66–67, 74–78
Pretest, sensitizing effect of, 70
Prevalence rate, 333
Privacy, 243, 251–254
Probability levels, 368
Probability sampling, 136–146
Proportion, 329, 347
Proportional reduction in error (PRE)
    measure, 399, 403
Proportional sampling, 154–156
Proportionate stratified sampling, 141,
    application of, 142
Prospective studies, 88
Purpose, statement of, 2
Purposive sampling, 147
    application of, 148

Qualitative information, 2
Qualitative research, 38

Quality assurance, 160–161
Quality control, 160–161
Quantification. See Measurement
Quantitative information, 2
   in decision making, 128
Quantitative research, requirement of,
   14–15, 37,
Quasi-experimental designs, 55, 57,
   74–84, 90–91
   definition of, 74
   validity of, 76
Quasi-random sampling, 140
Questionnaires, 207–211 *See also*
   Questions
   advantages of, 173
   content of, 208–211, 237
   design of, 227–231
   disadvantages of, 173–175
   factors affecting response rate of,
      173–178
   introduction of, 207–208
   mailed, 173–178
   postcards as follow-up reminders,
      178, 179
   postcards to monitor, 174
   pretesting of, 232–236
   question sequencing in, 227–230
   structure of, 211–218
Questions, 207–211. *See also* Questionnaires; specific types of
   biased, 225
   content of, 232–233
   contingency, 217–218
   filter, 217–218
   in-person interviewing, 172,
      187–188
   open- and closed-ended. See
      Closed-ended questions;
      Open-ended questions
   pretesting of, 232–236
   racial and ethnic, 277–279
   sequencing of, 227–230
   in telephone interviews, 180–181
   wording of, 218–227, 237
Quota sampling, 147–149

R values, 439, 452
Random assignment, 66–67, 91
   in quasi-experimental designs,
      75–76
Random digit dialing techniques, 173,
   181–183, 200
Random error, 107–108, 109–110
   degree of, 107
Random number table, 137
Random sampling, 137–138, 161

application of, 138
   principles of, 137
   stratified, 137, 140–141
Random variations, 33–35
Randomized posttest design, 70–72
   application of, 73–74
   efficiency of, 91
Randomly related, 360–361
Range, 340–341, 348
Rate, 330–333, 347
   selection denominator for,
      331–332
Ratio, 330, 347
Ratio scales, 104–106
Reactive effects of experimental
   arrangements, 63, 64–65
Reference librarians, 8, 267
Regression, 428, 445
   causality and, 451
   logistic, 445–447, 452
   ordinal data and, 445
Regression analysis, 428–429
   multivariate case, 435–441
Regression coefficient, 433–433
   partial, 436
   standardized, 440
Regression equation, 428–432,
   436–438, 451
   to quantify admissions criteria,
      440–442
Reinterviews, 279
Relationships, 2. *See also* Association,
   measure of
   casual, 55
   criterion for strength of, 397–398
   identification of, 30–31
   nature of, 13, 15–18
   null, 393–395, 397, 398,
      409–410, 415
   perfect, 393–395, 397, 398, 401,
      409–410, 415
   specifying of, 405–406
   spurious, 16, 405–406, 415
   statistical, 66–67
   strength of, 392–393
   study designs to find, 26–32
Relational database, 317
Relative frequency measures, 320–322
Reliability, 107–116
   criterion for, 107–108
   dimensions of, 108–109
   establishing of, 109–115
   interrater, 113
Research. *See also* specific types of
   administrator concerns about,
      256–258

deceptive, 246–247
   definition of, 1–2
   designs, 25
   ethical issues of, 243–252, 474–478
   preliminary steps in, 1–20
   purpose of, 1–2
   records, 7–8, 19
   release of results of, 472–474
Research literature, 19. *See also* Data,
   secondary
   locating of, 7–8
Research methodology, 24
Research question, 2–3
Residual, 432
Response rate, 172–173
   factors affecting, 173–178
Response set, 224
Retrospective designs, 88

Sample(s), 133–162. *See also* Sampling
   accuracy of, 152, 161
   assessing quality of, 160–161
   bias, 136, 150, 159–160
   design, 136–149. *See also* specific
      study designs
   means, 345–347
   probability, 136–137
   size of, 149–157
Sampling, 133–162. *See also* Sample(s)
   bias, 136, 150, 159–160
   designs for, 136–149. *See also* spe-
      cific sampling designs
   nonprobability designs for, 136,
      146–149
   parameters of, 135
   probability designs for, 136–146
   purposes for, 133–134
   sample size in, 149–157
   standard error in, 152
   terminology for, 134–136
   unit, 135
   units of analysis of, 135
Sampling error, 135, 150–151, 162
Sampling fraction, 136
Sampling frame, 134–135
Sampling unit, 135
   assumptions about, 140
SAS program, 316–317
Scale, 292
Scatterplot, 429–430, 434
   patterns in, 434–435
Schematic models, 11, 19–20, 90
Screening questions, 218
Seasonal variations, 33–34
Secondary data, 264–265, 271, 286
Security issues, 269, 286

Selection effects, 58, 60, 62, 148–149
Sensitivity, 107, 126–127
    of measure of association,
        397–398, 400, 401
Significance levels, 368–369, 374–375
Simple random sampling, 137, 161
    application of, 138
Skip interval, 139
Snowball sampling, 149
Social class index, 292
Somer's d, 403
Spreadsheet, 317
SPSS program, 316, 317, 318,
        372–373
Spurious relationship, 16, 405–406, 415
Stability, 108–109
Standard deviation, 342–343, 348
    calculation of, 342
Standard error, 152
    of b, 433–434
    calculation of, 167–168
    of slope, 433–434
Standardized indicators, 296–297
Statistic, 135
Statistical regression, 58, 59
Statistical relationship, 66–67
Statistical significance, 360–361, 364,
        367–368, 374–378
    testing of, 374–378, 409–410
Statistical software package, 316
Statistical techniques, 36
Statistics. *See also* Data
    accuracy of, 427–428
    bivariate case, 399–393, 414
    multivariate case, 404–407, 440
    univariate, 315–316
Stratified random sampling, 137,
        140–142
    proportionate, 141
    disproportionate, 141–142
Structured interviewing, 188–189, 201
Studies. *See also* Research
    designing, 6–10. *See also* Designs
    types of, 24, 55–56
Subjects at risk, 243
Subjects. *See also* Informed consent
    initial contact with, 171–173
    payment of, 250
    protection of, 251–254
    risk to, 248, 250
        versus benefits to, 249–250
    of, 66–74
        by matching, 67–68
    voluntary, 248–249
Survey research, 207–208

Surveys, 27. *See also* Questionnaires
    appropriateness of, 198–199
    internet, 186–187
    multiple participation, 198
    participation rates of, 198–199
    telephone, 171, 179–186
Symbolic models, 11, 20
Symmetric measure, 403, 415
Systematic random sampling, 139–140
Systematic sampling, 138–140, 161
    application of, 140

t-Distribution, 386. Table 12.14
Tables, 319–320, 323. *See also* Contin-
        gency tables
    labeling of, 320–322, 323
    proportion and scale of, 320
    showing data relationships,
        389–392
    size and dimensions of, 392
Target population, 134
Tau, 403
Telephone directory, 181
Telephone surveys, 171, 179–186
Test statistic, 367
Testing effects, 58, 60–61, 63, 64
Test-retest technique, 113
Threats to external validity, 63–65
Threats to internal validity, 58–62
Time series graphs, 327–328
Time series studies, 25, 32–36, 47
    applications of, 31
Transforming measures, 295
Trends, 26–37
    long-term, 32–35
Trimmed means, 346
t-Test, 359–360, 367, 369–371, 378
Tukey five-number summary, 346
Tuskegee Syphilis Study, 244–245

Undercount problem, 277
Unimodal distributions, 339
Units of analysis, 135
Univariate analysis, 315–348
Univariate distribution, 320
Univariate statistics, 315–316
Unordered categorical variables, 106
Unrestricted random sampling, 138

Validity
    concurrent, 122–123, 128
    content, 118–122, 128, 293–294
    criterion, 122, 125, 126, 128
    of experimental and quasi-experi-
        mental designs, 57–58, 91

external, 57–58, 62–63
    threats to, 63–66
    face, 118, 125, 128
    internal, 57
        threats to, 58–62
    in interrupted time-series design,
        79, 80–81, 83
    of measurement scales, 116–126,
        128
    operational, 116
    predictive, 122- 123, 126, 128
        application of, 124
Variables, 13–18, 20
    causally related, 55–57
    continuous, 106
    control, 16, 391–392, 404–409, 451
    dependent, 15, 20, 360
        causally related, 55–57
    dichotomous, 436
    discrete, 106
    distributions of, 320–322
    dummy, 436
    examples of, 13–14, 17
    independent, 15, 20, 25, 360
        casually related, 55–57
        importance of, 439–441
    interval, 427–435
    joint occurrence of, 389
    labeling of, 125
    measurement of, 98–128
    in measurement scales, 102–107
    nominal, 103
    number of, 30
    numerical, 104–105
    randomly related, 360
    relationships among, 348. *See also*
        Association, measures of;
        Relationships
    statistical relationship between, 67
    in time series studies, 33
Variance, 342–343, 348
Variation measures, 339–343
Verbal models, 11, 20
Vital statistics, 284–285, 286
Voluntary research participation,
        248–249, 259

Weighting, 295–296, 308
Within-groups variance, 413–414,
        416,

Zero order correlation coefficient, 432
z-Scores, 314, 344–345